FOOD IN CHINESE CULTURE

CONTRIBUTORS

Eugene N. Anderson, Associate Professor of Anthropology, University of California at Riverside

Marja L. Anderson, Riverside, California

Kwang-chih Chang, Professor of Anthropology, Harvard University

Michael Freeman, Assistant Professor of History, University of California at Santa Cruz

Francis L. K. Hsu, Professor of Anthropology, Northwestern University

Vera Y. N. Hsu, Evanston, Illinois

Frederick W. Mote, Professor of East Asian Studies, Princeton University

Edward H. Schafer, Professor of Oriental Languages, University of California at Berkeley

Jonathan D. Spence, Professor of History, Yale University

Ying-shih Yü, Professor of History, Yale University

FOOD IN CHINESE CULTURE

ANTHROPOLOGICAL AND HISTORICAL PERSPECTIVES

EDITED BY K. C. CHANG

NEW HAVEN AND LONDON
YALE UNIVERSITY PRESS

Designed by Sally Sullivan
and set in Times Roman type.
Printed in the United States of America by
The Vail-Ballou Press, Inc., Binghamton, N.Y.

Library of Congress Cataloging in Publication Data

Main entry under title:

Food in Chinese Culture.

　Bibliography:　p.
　Includes index.
　1. Food habits—China—History.　2. Dinners and
dining—China—History.　3. Cookery, Chinese—History.
I. Chang, Kwang-chih.
GT2853.C6F66　　　　394.1′2′0951　　　　75-43312
ISBN 0-300-01938-6; 0-300-02759-1 pbk.

13　　12　　11　　10　　9　　8　　7　　6　　5　　4

CONTENTS

ILLUSTRATIONS

CHINESE DYNASTIES

Hsia	21st–18th century B.C.
Shang	18th–12th century B.C.
Chou	12th century B.C.–221 B.C.
Ch'in	221–207 B.C.
Han	206 B.C.–A.D. 220
Three Kingdoms	220–265
Chin	265–420
Six Dynasties	420–589
Sui	581–618
T'ang	618–907
Five Dynasties	907–960
Sung	960–1279
Yüan	1271–1368
Ming	1368–1644
Ch'ing	1644–1911

INTRODUCTION

K. C. CHANG

To say that the consumption of food is a vital part of the chemical process of life is to state the obvious, but sometimes we fail to realize that food is more than just vital. The only other activity that we engage in that is of comparable importance to our lives and to the life of our species is sex. As Kao Tzu, a Warring States-period philosopher and keen observer of human nature, said, "Appetite for food and sex is nature" (trans. Lau 1970, p. 161). But these two activities are quite different. We are, I believe, much closer to our animal base in our sexual endeavors than we are in our eating habits. Too, the range of variations is infinitely wider in food than in sex. In fact, the importance of food in understanding human culture lies precisely in its infinite variability—variability that is not essential for species survival. For survival needs, all men everywhere could eat the same food, to be measured only in calories, fats, carbohydrates, proteins, and vitamins (Pike 1970, pp. 7–12). But no, people of different backgrounds eat very differently. The basic stuffs from which food is prepared; the ways in which it is preserved, cut up, cooked (if at all); the amount and variety at each meal; the tastes that are liked and disliked; the customs of serving food; the utensils; the beliefs about the food's properties—these all vary. The number of such "food variables" is great.

An anthropological approach to the study of food would be to isolate and identify the food variables, arrange these variables systemically, and explain why some of these variables go together or do not go together.

For convenience, we may use *culture* as a divider in relating food variables hierarchically. I am using the word *culture* here in a classificatory sense implying the pattern or style of behavior of a group of people who share it. Food habits may be used as an important, or even determining, criterion in this connection. People who have the same culture share the same food habits, that is, they share the same assemblage of food variables. Peoples of different cultures share different assemblages of food variables. We might say that different cultures have different food choices. (The word *choices* is used here not necessarily in an active sense, granting the possibility that some choices could be imposed rather than selected.) Why these choices? What determines them? These are among the first questions in any study of food habits.

Within the same culture, the food habits are not at all necessarily homogeneous. In fact, as a rule they are not. Within the same general food style, there are different manifestations of food variables of a smaller range, for different social situations. People of different social classes or occupations eat differently. People on festive occasions, in mourning, or on a daily routine eat again differently. Different religious sects have different eating codes. Men and women, in various stages of their lives, eat differently. Different

3

individuals have different tastes. Some of these differences are ones of preference, but others may be downright prescribed. Identifying these differences, explaining them, and relating them to other facets of social life are again among the tasks of a serious scholar of food.

Finally, systemically articulated food variables can be laid out in a time perspective, as in historical periods of varying lengths. We see how food habits change and seek to explore the reasons and consequences.

These observations provide some simple and practical clues for the beginning of a theoretical and methodological framework for the study of food as a cultural, rather than chemical, process. Strange as it may seem, considering the obvious importance of food in the life of every human being, every culture, every society, such a framework is not available in anthropological literature. Such a framework would comprise theoretically defensible borders of the field, commonly recognized, but not often resolved, problems, and accepted procedures for tackling issues within them. The studies of kinship, government, economy, and religion have such frameworks. The studies of food and a few other categories of daily life, such as clothing, do not have them. I believe the study of food has defensible borders, is centrally involved with problems of vital interest, and can be tackled by means of logical and generally practical procedures. To transform such beliefs into practice, and to explore the profitability of various approaches, we need a test case. What could be a better case than the Chinese?

Chinese food certainly has variety, and it also has a long documented history, probably longer than any other food tradition of comparable variety. Such, at least, are the assumptions that underlay my thoughts of using Chinese food as a test case in the development of "food-in-culture" studies.

My academic, aside from my gastronomic, interest in Chinese food came originally from a study of Shang and Chou bronzes. The use of the ritual vessels was related to the preparation and serving of food and drink, but without an understanding of the essential food variables I found it hard to understand the bronze vessels in their original context. My pertinent research (Chang 1973) convinced me that at least one of the best ways of getting to a culture's heart would be through its stomach. In the fall of 1972, two of my colleagues at Yale, professors Emily M. Ahern and Alison Richard, joined me in offering a graduate seminar on the anthropology of food and eating. Among my findings was that a rigorous methodology for the study of food and eating must still be developed. In late spring of 1973, I invited the collaborators of this volume to join with me in taking a first look at the facts and the significance of food making and food use throughout Chinese history. This would be a relatively detailed study of the food variables within a single culture, and our conclusions and observations could contribute to an understanding of the change and interrelationship of food variables and the rest of culture over a time span of several thousand years. Our efforts should, of course, be of interest to scholars of China, but they should also serve to demonstrate some fruitful approaches to the study of food in general.

I said a "first look" above, but that is not strictly correct. Shinoda Osamu has almost singlehandedly carved out the field of Chinese food studies through a series of learned articles, culminating in the collection of "Food Canons" (Shinoda and Tanaka 1970) and the monograph on the history of food in China (Shinoda 1974). But his emphasis and ours are quite different. Shinoda's studies are focused on descriptive history, ours on analysis and interpretation. The latter two are not possible without the former, but because of his works we have been spared the necessary task of compiling a lot of facts as a first step. Therefore, one may say that this volume has gone a step further.

It may be an indication of something profound and significant—though I don't know what—that my invitation was accepted by every one of my colleagues on my first approach. My request was a simple one: present the essential facts for your period, and discuss them with regard to topics that loom large in your data or in your mind. In methodology, the authors used no single preconceived framework, and their chapters demonstrate what seem to them to be the most fruitful approaches for their respective data. In terms of patterns of continuity and change of the food variables within the tradition of the Chinese culture, each author is responsible for his period, and the overall effect is plain as their chapters are read in the proper sequence. Since our efforts are exploratory, both in methodology and in regard to the history of Chinese food, there will not be a concluding chapter.

This book serves three purposes. It is a "case study," in which scholars of food-in-culture can see the ways in which ten of their colleagues have analyzed and interpreted their data. It is a descriptive history of food habits in China, where one should find facts both trivial (when *tou fu* began, when the Chinese first used chopsticks, and the like) and profound (the adoption of American food plants—sweet potato and maize, in particular—which had a large effect upon Chinese population). Finally, the book makes a significant contribution to Chinese cultural history, in which food and food habits played multifarious roles. Since this is a relatively new field, the multiple authorship better ensures exploratory breadth and creativity, but it makes it harder for the reader to detect common patterns and to draw generalizations.

My own generalizations pertain above all to the question, What charac-

terizes Chinese food? This question could, of course, be answered at several
levels. A patron at a restaurant in any Chinese city could point to a list of
specific dishes on the menu. A cookbook catering to the needs of contemporary families lists all the essential ingredients, utensils, and recipes. A
student of modern Chinese culture makes learned generalizations about the
common denominators and regional varieties. All of these characterizations
are evidently correct, but they serve very different purposes. The data and
studies in this book provide the basis for a characterization of a food style
over a period of thousands of years, during which time some variables
persisted, some died out, some were modified, and some new ones came to be
added. Accordingly, I see the following common themes that run through
the whole body of our data.

   1. The food style of a culture is certainly first of all determined by the
natural resources that are available for its use. Palaeolithic hunters the
world over relied heavily on animal flesh, which was cooked by a very
small number of techniques, among them broiling, drying, pickling, and
stone-boiling. The range of variations was probably limited, both for foodstuffs and for cooking methods, during substantial parts of the earliest
segments of hominid prehistory. But from an early time, gathering—of
fruits, nuts, berries, grubs, seeds, and other edible materials provided by
nature—had assumed an important role in supplying human diet. These
provisions varied from area to area depending on the natural distribution
patterns of the pertinent plants and animals. Therefore, Early Man's diet—
especially toward the Upper Palaeolithic period when a more diversified
use of the many local food resources became prevailing—was already a link
in the food chains of *local* ecosystems. When cultivated plants and domesticated animals began to provide the bulk of the foodstuff among many
peoples, the local pattern of food habits became increasingly pronounced
because the first plants and the first animals that were placed under domestic
use could only be those that were naturally grown in or readily adaptable to
specific regions.

   It is thus not surprising that Chinese food is above all characterized by
an assemblage of plants and animals that grew prosperously in the Chinese
land for a long time. A detailed list would be out of place here, and quantitative data are not available. The following enumeration is highly im-
pressionistic:

   Starch Staples: millet, rice, *kao-liang*, wheat, maize, buckwheat, yam,
      sweet potato.
   Legumes: soybean, broad bean, peanut, mung bean.
   Vegetables: malva, amaranth, Chinese cabbage, mustard green, turnip,
      radish, mushroom.

Fruits: peach, apricot, plum, apple, jujube date, pear, crab apple, mountain haw, longan, litchi, orange.

Meats: pork, dog, beef, mutton, venison, chicken, duck, goose, pheasant, many fishes.

Spices: red pepper, ginger, garlic, spring onion, cinnamon.

Chinese cooking is, in this sense, the manipulation of these foodstuffs as basic ingredients. Since ingredients are not the same everywhere, Chinese food begins to assume a local character simply by virtue of the ingredients it uses. Obviously ingredients are not sufficient for characterization, but they are a good beginning. Compare, for example, the above list with one in which dairy products occupy a prominent place, and one immediately comes upon a significant contrast between the two food traditions.

One important point about the distinctive assemblage of ingredients is its change through history. Concerning food, the Chinese are not nationalistic to the point of resisting imports. In fact, foreign foodstuffs have been readily adopted since the dawn of history. Wheat and sheep and goat were possibly introduced from western Asia in prehistoric times, many fruits and vegetables came in from central Asia during the Han and the T'ang periods, and peanuts and sweet potatoes from coastal traders during the Ming period. These all became integral ingredients of Chinese food. At the same time, despite the continuous introduction of dairy products and processes throughout the early historical periods, and despite the adoption of some dairy delicacies by the upper strata of society during the T'ang period, milk and dairy products, to this date, have not taken a prominant place in Chinese cuisine. This selectivity can be accounted for only in terms of the indigenous cultural base which absorbs or rejects foreign imports according to their structural or stylistic compatability. It also relates to the internal divisions of the Chinese food traditions, to be commented on later.

2. In the Chinese culture, the whole process of preparing food from raw ingredients to morsels ready for the mouth involves a complex of interrelated variables that is highly distinctive when compared with other food traditions of major magnitude. At the base of this complex is the division between *fan*, grains and other starch foods, and *ts'ai*, vegetable and meat dishes. To prepare a balanced meal, it must have an appropriate amount of both fan and ts'ai, and ingredients are readied along both tracks. Grains are cooked whole or as flour, making up the fan half of the meal in various forms: fan (in the narrow sense, "cooked rice"), steamed wheat-, millet-, or corn-flour bread, *ping* ("pancakes"), and noodles. Vegetables and meats are cut up and mixed in various ways into individual dishes to constitute the ts'ai half. Even in meals in which the staple starch portion and the meat-and-vegetable portion are apparently joined together, such as in

chiao-tzu ("Chinese ravioli" or "dumplings"), *pao-tzu* ("steamed bun with fillings"), *hun-t'un* ("wonton"), and *hsien-ping* ("pan-fried bun with fillings"), they are in fact put together but not mixed up, and each still retains its due proportion and own distinction (*p'i* ["skin"] = fan; *hsien* ["filling"] = ts'ai).

For the preparation of ts'ai, the use of multiple ingredients and the mixing of flavors are the rules, which above all means that ingredients are usually cut up and not done whole, and that they are variously combined into individual dishes of vastly differing flavors. Pork, for example, may be diced, sliced, shredded, or ground, and when combined with other meats and with various vegetable ingredients and spices produces dishes of utterly divergent shapes, flavors, colors, tastes, and aromas.

The parallelism of fan and ts'ai and the above-described principles of ts'ai preparation account for a number of other features of the Chinese food culture, especially in the area of utensils. To begin with, there are fan utensils and ts'ai utensils, both for cooking and for serving. In the modern kitchen, *fan kuo* ("rice cooker") and *ts'ai kuo* ("wok") are very different and as a rule not interchangeable utensils. The same contrast is seen in Shang bronze vessels between *kui* ("rice servers") and *tou* ("meat platters"). To prepare the kind of ts'ai that we have characterized, the chopping knife or cleaver and the chopping anvil are standard equipment in every Chinese kitchen, ancient and modern. To sweep the cooked grains into the mouth, and to serve the cut-up morsels of the meat-and-vegetable dishes, chopsticks have proved more serviceable than hands or other instruments (such as spoons and forks, the former being used in China alongside the chopsticks).

This complex of interrelated features of Chinese food may be described, for the purpose of shorthand reference, as the Chinese *fan-ts'ai* principle. Send a Chinese cook into an American kitchen, given Chinese or American ingredients, and he or she will (a) prepare an adequate amount of fan, (b) cut up the ingredients and mix them up in various combinations, and (c) cook the ingredients into several dishes and, perhaps, a soup. Given the right ingredients, the "Chineseness" of the meal would increase, but even with entirely native American ingredients and cooked in American utensils, it is still a Chinese meal.

3. The above example shows that the Chinese way of eating is characterized by a notable flexibility and adaptability. Since a ts'ai dish is made of a mixture of ingredients, its distinctive appearance, taste, and flavor do not depend on the exact number of ingredients, nor, in most cases, on any single item. The same is true for a meal, made up of a combination of dishes. In times of affluence, a few more expensive items may be added, but if the

times are hard they may be omitted without doing irreparable damage. If the season is not quite right, substitutes may be used. With the basic principles, a Chinese cook can prepare "Chinese" dishes for the poor as well as the rich, in times of scarcity as well as abundance, and even in a foreign country without many familiar ingredients. The Chinese way of cooking must have helped the Chinese people through some hard times throughout their history. And, of course, one may also say that the Chinese cook the way they do because of their need and desire for adaptability.

This adaptability is shown in at least two other features. The first is the amazing knowledge the Chinese have acquired about their wild plant resources. Thousands of plants are listed in the encyclopedic *Pen ts'ao kang mu* (S. C. Li 1930 ed.), and the notations about each plant include a statement concerning its edibility. The Chinese peasants apparently know every edible plant in their environment, and plants there are many. Most do not ordinarily belong on the dinner table, but they may be easily adapted for consumption in time of famine (*chiu huang*). Here again is this flexibility: A smaller number of familiar foodstuffs are used ordinarily, but, if needed, a greater variety of wild plants would be made use of. The knowledge of these "famine plants" was carefully handed down as a living culture—apparently this knowledge was not placed in dead storage too long or too often.

Another feature of Chinese food habits that contributed to their notable adaptability is the large number and great variety of preserved foods. Data are lacking for quantified comparison, but one has the distinct impression that the Chinese preserve their food in many more ways and in greater quantities than most other peoples. Food is preserved by smoking, salting, sugaring, steeping, pickling, drying, soaking in many kinds of soy sauces, and so forth, and the whole range of foodstuffs is involved— grains, meat, fruit, eggs, vegetables, and everything else. Again, with preserved food, the Chinese people were ever ready in the event of hardship or scarcity.

4. The Chinese way of eating is further characterized by the ideas and beliefs about food, which actively affect the ways and manners in which food is prepared and taken. The overriding idea about food in China—in all likelihood an idea with solid, but as yet unrevealed, scientific backing—is that the kind and the amount of food one takes is intimately relevant to one's health. Food not only affects health as a matter of general principle, the selection of the right food at any particular time must also be dependant upon one's health condition at that time. Food, therefore, is also medicine.

The regulation of diet as a disease preventive or cure is certainly as Western as it is Chinese. Common Western examples are the diet for arthritics and the recent organic food craze. But the Chinese case is distinctive for its underlying principles. The bodily functions, in the Chinese view, follow the basic *yin-yang* principles. Many foods are also classifiable into those that possess the *yin* quality and those of the *yang* quality. When yin and yang forces in the body are not balanced, problems result. Proper amounts of food of one kind or the other may then be administered (i.e., eaten) to counterbalance the yin and yang disequilibrium. If the body is normal, overeating of one kind of food would result in an excess of that force in the body, causing diseases. This belief is documented for the Chou period, several centuries before Christ, and it is still a dominant concept in Chinese culture. Eugene and Marja Anderson's chapter discusses this in detail for the southern Chinese. Emily Ahern (1973) has discussed similar concepts for the Taiwanese. In parts of North China, the same contrast of *liang* ("cool") food and *jê* ("hot") food occurs, sometimes taking the form of *pai huo* ("quelling the heat") and *shang huo* ("raising the heat"). In this latter pair, *huo*, or "heat," is regarded almost a priori as something undesirable, but in the "cold-hot" contrast neither is necessarily more beneficial or harmful in itself. Almost universally, within the Chinese tradition, oily and fried food, pepper hot flavoring, fatty meat and oily plant food (such as peanuts) are "hot," whereas most water plants, most crustaceans (especially crabs), and certain beans (such as mung beans) are "cold." A body sore, for example, or an inexplicable fever, could be due to overeating hot foods; and a man with a common cold could get into a lot worse shape by eating additional "cold" foods, such as crabs, and thus overloading the "cold" forces in his body.

But the yin-yang, cold-hot equilibrium is not the only guide to dietary health. At least two other concepts belong to the native Chinese food tradition. One is that, in consuming a meal, appropriate amounts of both fan and ts'ai should be taken. In fact, of the two, fan is the more fundamental and indispensable. In mess halls throughout the country, fan is called *chu shih*, the main or primary food, and ts'ai, *fu shih*, the supplementary or secondary food. Without fan one cannot be full, but without ts'ai the meal is merely less tasteful. The other concept is frugality. Overindulgence in food and drink is a sin of such proportions that dynasties could fall on its account. At the individual level, the ideal amount for every meal, as every Chinese parent would say, is only *ch'i fen pao* ("seventy percent full"). Related to this, is the almost sacred nature of grains in Chinese folk thought: grains are not something to play with or waste, and any child who does not finish the grains in his or her bowl is told that his or her future mate would be one with a pockmarked face (Liu 1974, pp. 146–48). These last facts make it clear that, although both the fan-ts'ai and the frugality con siderations are health based, at least in part they are related to China's traditional poverty in food resources.

5. Finally, perhaps the most important aspect of the Chinese food culture is the importance of food itself in Chinese culture. That Chinese cuisine is the greatest in the world is highly debatable and is essentially irrelevant. But few can take exception to the statement that few other cultures are as food oriented as the Chinese. And this orientation appears to be as ancient as Chinese culture itself. According to *Lun yü* (*Confucian Analects*, chap. "Wei Ling Kung"), when the duke Ling of Wei asked Confucius (551–479 B.C.) about military tactics, Confucius replied, "I have indeed heard about matters pertaining to *tsu* (meat stand) and *tou* (meat platter), but I have not learned military matters" (cf. trans. Legge 1893). Indeed, perhaps one of the most important qualifications of a Chinese gentleman was his knowledge and skill pertaining to food and drink. According to *Shih chi* and *Mo Tzu*, I Yin, the prime minister of King T'ang of Shang, the dynasty's founder, was originally a cook. In fact, some sources say it was I Yin's cooking skills that first brought him into T'ang's favor.

The importance of the kitchen in the king's palace is amply shown in the personnel roster recorded in *Chou li*. Out of the almost four thousand persons who had the responsibility of running the king's residential quarters, 2,271, or almost 60 percent, of them handled food and wine. These included 162 master "dieticians" in charge of the daily menus of the king, his queen, and the crown prince; 70 meat specialists; 128 chefs for "internal" (family) consumption; 128 chefs for "external" (guest) consumption; 62 assistant chefs; 335 specialists in grains, vegetables, and fruits; 62 specialists of game; 342 fish specialists; 24 turtle and shellfish specialists; 28 meat dryers; 110 wine officers; 340 wine servers; 170 specialists in the "six drinks"; 94 ice men; 31 bamboo-tray servers; 61 meat-platter servers; 62 pickle and sauce specialists; and 62 salt men.

What these specialists tended to were not just the king's palate pleasures: eating was also very serious business. In *I li*, the book that describes various ceremonies, food cannot be separated from ritual (see Steele 1917). *Li chi*, the book that has been called "the most exact and complete monography which the Chinese nation has been able to give of itself to the rest of the human race" (Legge 1885, p. 12), is full of references to the right kinds of food for various occasions and the right table manners, and it contains some of the earliest recipes of Chinese dishes. In *Tso chuan* and *Mo Tzu*, authentic Chou texts, references were made of the use of the *ting* cauldron, a cooking vessel, as the prime symbol of the state. I cannot feel more confident to say that the ancient Chinese were among the peoples of the world who have been particularly preoccupied with food and eating.

Furthermore, as Jacques Gernet (1962, p. 135) has stated, "there is no doubt that in this sphere China has shown a greater inventiveness than any other civilization."

Objective criteria may be used to measure the relative inventiveness in, and the degree of preoccupation with, food and eating among the peoples of different cultures and civilizations. What peoples are more so preoccupied? Were the Chinese among them? How do we measure their degree of preoccupation against other peoples'? Perhaps the following criteria may be used: quantitative, structural, symbolic, and psychological.

1. Quantitatively, the most direct measure may be taken of the food itself. How elaborately is it prepared? The absolute number of dishes that a people is capable of cooking is probably a direct indication of the elaborateness of their cuisine. Too, the percentage of income spent on food may be used as another quantitative standard of measurement. Between the contemporary Americans and the contemporary Chinese, for example, it is known that the Chinese spend more of their income on food than do the Americans, and in this sense the former is more preoccupied with eating than the latter. Surely this has a lot to do with a people's wealth. But it does mean that poor peoples require a greater percentage of their total time and energy to obtain and consume food than rich peoples, and this difference must make a significant difference in their relative cultural makeups. Furthermore, although there is an absolute maximum one *needs* to spend on food, there is no limit of how much one actually *wants* to. Two peoples may be coequals in terms of wealth, but they may differ vastly in regard to the percentage of their income devoted actually to eating as a matter of choice.

2. Structurally, what different kinds of foods do different cultures use on various occasions or in distinctive social or ritual contexts? One people may use a very small variety of foods and drinks for many different contexts, while another may require distinct varieties for each context. Also significant are the utensils, beliefs, taboos, and etiquettes associated with specific kinds of foods and drinks. All of this may be approached by a study of the people's terminological system for their foods and for behavior and other things related to food. The greater the number of terms used to designate foods and related matters, and the more hierarchically this terminological system is arranged, the more a people may be said to be preoccupied with food.

3. A third criterion is a symbolic one. Since foods and drinks are often used as media of communication, one could also attempt to ascertain the extent to which they are so used among the various peoples. The extent and the elaborateness of the use of food in rituals should give an excellent indication. The terminological system is again relevant here in accordance with Charles Frake's folk taxonomy hypothesis: "The greater the number

of distinct social contexts in which information about a particular phenomenon must be communicated, the greater the number of different levels of contrast into which that phenomenon is categorized" (Frake 1961, p. 121).

4. The fourth criterion is psychological. How much do the people think about eating in their daily life, or, stated differently, how much is the anticipation of eating a factor in regulating an individual's behavior in the short run, in the same way that the anticipation of death, for example, serves as a powerful factor in regulating his behavior in the long run? As Firth (1939, p. 38) says of the Tikopia, "To get a meal is the principal work on most days, and the meal itself is not merely an interval in work but an aim in itself." Another example of psychological preoccupation may be seen in this passage of Lin Yutang (1935, p. 338): "No food is really enjoyed unless it is keenly anticipated, discussed, eaten and then commented upon. . . . Long before we have any special food, we think about it, rotate it in our minds, anticipate it as a secret pleasure to be shared with some of our closest friends, and write notes about it in our invitation letters." Lin Yutang's favorite Chinese gourmet is a gentleman who lived about two hundred fifty years ago, by the name of Li Yü (or Li Li-weng). Li was fond of crabs, and he wrote in one of his literary works (Li 1730, vol. 15, sec. "Crabs") that "as far as crabs are concerned, my mind is addicted to them, my mouth enjoys the taste of them, and not a single day in my life have I ever forgotten about them."

This brings us back to the observation that the Chinese are probably among the peoples of the world most preoccupied with eating. In a number of recent publications, Lévi-Strauss (1964, 1965, 1966, 1968) seeks to establish some universal expressions of humanity through foods, cooking, table manners, and people's concepts about them. But these are all among the sharpest symbols of cultures, and to understand them one must first of all understand their uniqueness and the way in which they uniquely symbolize their cultures. In this sense, the Chinese preoccupation with food and eating provides its own explanation. There has been much attempt to see Chinese poverty as a culinary virtue. Gernet (1962, p. 135) explains the inventiveness of Chinese cooking in terms of "undernourishment, drought and famines," which compelled the Chinese people to "make judicious use of every possible kind of edible vegetable and insect, as well as of offal." This is certainly a useful explanation for some aspects of the Chinese food habits, as discussed above, but poverty and the consequent exhaustive search for resources provide only a favorable environment for culinary inventiveness and cannot be said to be its cause. If so, there would have been as many culinary giants as there are poor peoples. Besides, the Chinese may be poor, but, as Mote points out, by and large they have been well fed. The Chinese have shown inventiveness in this area perhaps for the simple reason that food and eating are among things central to the Chinese way of life and part of the Chinese ethos.

As characterized above, the Chinese food tradition is one with a distinctive assemblage of ingredients, prepared and served in accordance with the fan-ts'ai principle, typified by several features of adaptability, and associated with a cluster of beliefs concerning the health properties of various foods. Further, it is a tradition that occupies a special place in the total realm of culture. This tradition can be documented for at least three thousand years, during which changes surely occurred but without altering its fundamental character. This, at least, is the conclusion that I see emerge from the various chapters of this volume.

Within this tradition, countless food variables are articulated in countless ways by subsegments of the Chinese culture and in various social situations. By the differential manifestations of food in kind, quantity, and manner of service, the Chinese use or view food as symbols for the subsegment or for the situation.

The most obvious subsegments are the regional styles of cooking. There are various ways of regionally subdividing the Chinese cooking style, but they are all based on the major schools of restaurants in major cosmopolitan centers like Peking, Shanghai, Hong Kong, and Taipei. We hear about Ching ts'ai ("Peking dishes"), Shansi ts'ai, Shantung ts'ai, Honan ts'ai, Hupei ts'ai, Ning-p'o ts'ai, Ch'uan (Szechwan) ts'ai, Fu-chou ts'ai, Ch'ao-chou ts'ai, Kuang-chou ts'ai, and so forth—each ts'ai style being characterized by the province or city in which it is represented. But this is more a classification of restaurants than regional styles. For example, any Pekinese can tell you there is no such thing as Peking ts'ai in Peking itself; Peking ts'ai as served in restaurants outside Peking is really a ts'ai style combining many local specialities throughout North China. A thorough investigation of the regional cooking styles—and there certainly are major differences among them—can only be undertaken by means of China-wide field research, perhaps supplemented by studies of recipes collected from all over China, from villages as well as big cities.

Another set of subsegments concerns the food styles of different economic classes. Food is traditionally regarded as an economic index, as, for example, in the official dynastic annals where the volume on economy is often titled *shih huo*, "Food and Money." In the Peking dialect, to have a job is to have *chiao ku* ("the grains to chew"), and to have lost one is to have *ta p'o le fan wan* ("broken the rice bowl"). It is small wonder that the Chinese way of contrasting economic classes is to contrast their food styles. A common complaint is *chu men chiu jou ch'ou lu yu tung ssu ku,* or "while the wine and the meat have spoiled behind the red doors [of rich households], on the road there are skeletons of those who died of exposure." Similar contrasts were made by Mencius (fourth century B.C.): "There is fat meat in your kitchen and there are well-fed horses in your stables, yet the people look hungry and in the outskirts of cities men drop dead from starvation" (Lau 1970, p. 52). No wonder that John Barrow, as quoted by Jonathan Spence in his chapter on the Ch'ing period, made the observation that "in the assortments of food there was a wider disparity in China between rich and poor than in any other country of the world."

The belief in the desirability of frugality concerning food must be reviewed in the light of economic strata. For the peasants, frugality is a necessity, but for the elite it is a pronounced virtue that could be observed or disregarded at will. In revolutionary ideology, food style is often chosen as one of the symbols marking off the exploited from the exploiter. In their Hunan base in the 1920s, the Communist-led Peasants Association made the following rules about banquets:

> Sumptuous feasts are generally forbidden. In Shao-shan, Hsiang-t'an county, it has been decided that guests are to be served with only three kinds of animal food, namely, chicken, fish and pork. It is also forbidden to serve bamboo shoots, kelp and lentil noodles. In Hengshan county it has been resolved that eight dishes and no more may be served at a banquet. Only five dishes are allowed in the East Three District in Li-ling county, and only meat and three vegetable dishes in the North Second District, while in the West Third District New Year feasts are forbidden entirely. In Hsiang-hsiang county, there is a ban on all "egg-cake feasts," which are by no means sumptuous. . . . In the town of Chia-mo, Hsiang-hsiang county, people have refrained from eating expensive foods and use only fruit when offering ancestral sacrifices [Mao 1927, p. 50].

In addition to the amount and the degree of luxury permitted, the different systems of meals are also characterizable in ideological terms (e.g., H. Kao 1974). Other subsegments associated with distinctive food variables include the various religious orders, each with its taboos and preferences, the various ethnic groups within the area of China, and the various occupational groups with their respective eating styles appropriate to the convenience of each.

I have pointed out earlier that the Chinese people are especially preoccupied with food, and that food is at the center of, or at least it accompanies or symbolizes, many social interactions. The Chinese recognize, in their social interactions, minute and precise distinctions, and nuances of distinctions, in regard to the relative statuses of the interacting parties and the nature of the interaction. Consequently, they inevitably use food—of which there are countless variations, many more subtle and more expressive than the tongue can convey—to help speak the language that constitutes a part of every social interaction. Within each subsegment of the Chinese food culture, food is used again differentially to express the precise social distinctions involved in the interaction.

The role of food as social language is determined by an interplay of the status of the interacting parties and the occasion of the act. Some examples will show the principal types of the situation. A meal is a common occasion for getting together with family, relatives, and friends, but the food that is served can define the precise distance between the participants. Francis and Vera Hsu, in their chapter, describe the use of *chiao tzu* for New Year festivities. There are many reasons why chiao tzu is suitable for New Year consumption, but one of the reasons is that chiao tzu is something that family members and close relatives, who may not see and talk to each other often in their busy lives, can cook and consume together without having too much of their attention diverted by complicated cooking steps.

However, chiao tzu, intimate but simple, would not usually be suitable for entertaining friends. If the host has a family cook and a maid, they could easily prepare and serve a sumptuous meal. But if then the host himself, or the hostess herself, goes to the kitchen to cook up some specialty of the house, and if the hostess serves the dishes (that is, brings them from the kitchen to the table) in person, then these must be very special guests indeed—the cooking skills and the flavor of the food, be they better or worse than the cook's fare, becoming more or less beside the point. When a mother cooks the favorite dishes of a home-coming child, or a maiden prepares her specialties for a suitor, or a husband makes wined-chicken for his wife who has just given birth, words of affection are being delivered and consumed along with the food. In this regard the Chinese are no different from any other people, but it is the specific words that are used (food variables) that distinctively characterize the Chinese food language.

If the occasions are formal and the statuses socially prescribed, appropriate food must be served since the parties involved know exactly what is being said—be it correct, showing extraordinary effort, or insulting—from the kinds and the amount of food that is served. Spence's examples illustrate this well: Nagasaki's Chinese merchants' first-class meal of sixteen dishes, second-class meal of ten dishes, and third-class meal of eight dishes, and the Imperial Courts' six basic grades of Manchu banquets and five of Chinese. In Republican China we see that grades of restaurant banquets are rated according to purchase price: 500 *k'uai* banquets, 1,000 *k'uai* banquets, 10,000 *k'uai* banquets, and the like. The grade must be geared to the occasion and to the importance of the guests being entertained. Too high for the occasion or for the status of the party, and it is branded a vulgar overkill engaged in only by the uncultured new rich; too low, you become a tightwad and get contemptuously laughed at. It is extremely important to know what is exactly appropriate because the range of variation is so very large, and the language of food takes many years to learn.

The range of variation differs with economic class. The expectation varies with economic capability and with the presumed knowledge—linguistic code—that goes with it. The awkward situation Pao-Yü encountered in *Hung-lou meng*, as Jonathan Spence so aptly relates, is an eloquent testimonial to the class barriers of food: During a rare visit by Pao-yü to the home of one of his maid-servants, "after surveying the carefully arrayed dishes of cakes, dried fruits, and nuts, the best that [she and her family] could offer to their young master, Pao-yü's maid realized sadly 'that there was nothing there which Pao-yü could possibly be expected to eat.'" Master and maid do not interact at meals, and food language appropriate for the occasion is hard to find.

Food linguistics suggests to us that the economic barrier is harder to cross than that between life and death, or that between the secular and the divine. The Chinese have clear mourning food prescriptions and elaborate customs for the ritual use of food. The various ways in which food may be used in a ritual context are again directly related to the status of the interacting parties (who on ritual occasions include both living and dead, and both human and divine). Emily Ahern's studies of the varying uses of food for hall worship and grave worship in a Taiwan Chinese village are particularly illuminating and are quoted below at some length:

Grave worship on the whole differs radically from hall worship. The most obvious difference is the sort of food that is offered at the grave as opposed to that presented in the hall. The food offered for ordinary death-day sacrifices before the tablets in the lineage hall or on a domestic altar is essentially the same as the common fare of the villagers though it may be richer in meat and other delicacies.... Chopsticks and bowls are always provided. After these offerings are made, the food is eaten without further cooking by the members of the family and their guests.

In stark contrast, foods presented at the graves, though potentially edible, are not soaked, seasoned, or cooked; most of them are dry and unpalatable. These offerings, consisting basically of 12 small bowls of foodstuffs, commonly include dried mushrooms of various sorts, dried fish and meat, dried noodles, and dried bean curd.

The difference between these offerings, taken together with other data about the kinds of food offered to the gods, leads me to suggest that the kind of food offered to a supernatural being is an index of the difference between that being and the living beings making the offerings. The scale along which the offerings differ is one of transformation from potential food in its natural state to edible food. . . .

Supernatural beings are offered food that is less transformed, and therefore less like human food, according to their difference from the humans making the offerings. For example, of all the supernaturals, the ancestors are probably the most like those who offer them food. As ancestors in halls or domestic shrines, they are well-known kinsmen with distinctive, individual identities; they can be spoken to, apologized to, thanked, and so on. They are generally accessible and familiar beings. Consequently, they are offered food that is precisely like the food consumed by those who offer it. . . .

The gods, on a more distant level, receive different offerings according to their rank. The lowest god in the supernatural hierarchy, Tho-te-kong, the earth god, receives food like the fare of humans except that it is unseasoned and uncut. . . . Tho-te-kong is only somewhat different from humans. . . .

Moving to the top of the hierarchy, the highest god, Thi-kong, receives the most untransformed food on the occasion of elaborate *pai-pais*: raw fowl with a few tail feathers left unplucked and the entrails hanging about their necks; a live fish; a whole raw pig with its entrails hanging about its neck; and sometimes two stalks of sugarcane, uprooted whole from the ground with roots and leaves still intact, constituting the vegetable equivalent of the whole, raw animal offerings. . . . I suggest Thi-kong is offered food that differs markedly from human food because he himself is so different from human beings and human-like beings such as the hall and domestic ancestors. . . .

Looking at the difference between the offerings to the ancestors in the hall and the offerings to them at the grave in the light of the scaling of the offerings to the gods, . . . we are led to investigate the nature of the difference between the ancestors in those two locations. The raw, live or dry food offered to Thi-kong marks distance in power and accessibility from human beings; the dry food offered at the grave may mark an equally great distance between the ancestor as resident of the hall and the ancestor as resident of the grave. . . .

In sum, the grave, located outside of the settlement, is very different from the hall in that access to it cannot be controlled; it is freely haunted by the souls of the dead. These dead persons, like the ancestor buried there, are living but are no longer part of the familiar, observable *iong* world. When someone visits the grave he is exposing himself to one of the gates of the *im* world and must deal with dangerous ghosts on their terms. In contrast, when the souls of the ancestors visit the hall they rejoin the *iong* world; living people can relate to them as known, familiar ascendants. This difference ... begins to make the contrast between edible food offered in the hall and inedible substances offered at the grave intelligible. [Ahern 1973, pp. 166–74]

In the above discussion, the spectrum of variability consists of different degrees of "cookedness." As such, it is a relatively simple and stark example among many variables in an area where the supernatural interacting partners are numerous, the distinctions complex, and the nuances of the food language particularly refined. From the earliest ritual records of China, the oracle bone inscriptions of the Shang, one finds that kings planning ancestral sacrificial rituals would, by divination, consult with the receiver of the offerings about the kind and number of sacrificial animals desired: cattle? sheep? kid? humans? how many—one? five? forty? In later times and at present such questions are no longer asked, presumably because both the variety and the quantity have been conventionalized, that is, clearly understood between giver and particular receiver. Consequently, from the ritual food that is being offered, the ethnographer can determine the social distance to the receiver and also his or her placement in the social hierarchy in the sacred world.

From the above it becomes obvious that food semantics offers a potentially fruitful area of inquiry into the Chinese social system, or any social system in which food plays a significant part in social interactions. By food semantics I refer to the terminological systems (i.e., hierarchical classifications), and the functional relevance of such systems, of food, drinks, preserving and cooking processes, cooking utensils, serving utensils, food personnel, and the behaviors and beliefs associated with all of the above.

I have discussed, here, the following issues concerning the study of Chinese food from an anthropological perspective: the characterization of a Chinese food culture tradition, the segmentation of this food culture within the Chinese tradition, and the minute study of food variables that could eventually lead to food semantics as an approach to Chinese systems of social interaction.

One advantage offered studies like these by a long historical civilization such as the Chinese, is the opportunity to make such studies in a historical perspective. To be sure, a descriptive history of food in China, such as Shinoda's work, is of interest in itself and is a requisite for analytic history. But we are interested in food in Chinese history for two other, interrelated reasons. The first is to see to what extent historical dimension is significant for an analytic framework for food-in-culture studies. The second is to find out if food history can be used—and if so, to what extent—as an approach to add a new dimension to Chinese cultural and social histories.

This book can only be said to mark a beginning in such efforts. What are my own immediate thoughts after reading the various chapters in the book? I have two such thoughts. First, continuity vastly outweighs change in this aspect of Chinese history. Second, there are enough changes to warrant some preliminary efforts to give the periodization of Chinese history a new perspective. The former is self-explanatory, is another proof of the change-within-tradition pattern of Chinese cultural history, and requires no further comment. As far as the changes are concerned, the various chapters of this volume trace the changing history of the Chinese food culture from the beginning to the present day, and I will let my authors speak for themselves in regard to the major events in each of the periods. Allow me, however, to point out just one thing: Most changes involved the geographic movements of peoples with their particular food habits, but truly important changes having to do with the total alignment of the society are very rare.

In the food history of China I recognize at least two and probably three first-order thresholds, which mark changes in certain food variables that significantly affected the alignment, or realignment, of most if not all other variables. The first such threshold is the beginning of farming—that of millets and other cereals in the north and of rice and other plants in the south—which alone could possibly have established the fan-ts'ai principle of Chinese cooking. Undoubtedly, the preagricultural knowledge of wild plants and animals was carried over, contributing to the characteristic Chinese inventory of foodstuffs. Also, in cooking and preserving methods and in ideas about food and health, the transformation to agriculture was presumably cumulative and gradual. But the Chinese food style is simply unimaginable without Chinese agriculture.

The second threshold that I recognize is the beginning of a highly stratified society, possibly in the Hsia dynastic period and certainly by the Shang period of the eighteenth century B.C. The new societal realignment was essentially one based on the distribution of food resources. On one side were the food-producers who tilled the land but had to submit much of what they produced to the state, and on the other stood the food-consumers who administered instead of toiled, which gave them the leisure and the incentive to build up an elaborate cuisine style. Small wonder that such a stratified, exploiter-exploited society is in China considered, in traditional popular phraseology, a "man-eats-man" society. It was this event—the split of the Chinese population along food lines—that created the economic subsegmentation of the Chinese food culture. The great Chinese cuisine was based upon the wisdoms of vast ages and vast areas but was made possible in large part through the efforts of the leisurely gourmets of means, and by the complicated and exacting food etiquette befitting a complex and multistratified pattern of social relationships.

The historical segment initiated by this second threshold comprises practically the entire span of Chinese history, from Hsia and Shang through the last decades. What we know to be the traditional Chinese food culture is the food culture of this segment.

The third threshold is—if the information proves to be correct—happening right in our own time. In the People's Republic of China, the food-based social polarization has apparently given way to a truly national distribution of the food resources. I don't know very much about the events associated with this, nor do I have data on how other aspects of the Chinese food culture—such as the health aspect, the status of gourmets, and the socially differential use of food—are changing, or have changed, with this fundamental alteration in food distribution. But the potentials are clearly present.

1: ANCIENT CHINA

K. C. CHANG

Our study of food in ancient China begins with the Yangshao culture, approximately 5000–3200 B.C., and ends with the Chou dynasty, just before 200 B.C. This is the period of Chinese civilization in which much of its later styles, including its style of cooking and eating, were formed and crystallized. We could go back quite a bit further and begin with the dietary habits of Peking Man, but there are only extremely meager data on food for the entire Pleistocene period in China. Peking Man lived on game meat, mostly that of a deer with thick antlers (*Sinomegaceros pachyosteus*), and wild plants such as hackberry (*Celtis barbouri*). Fire was used to cook the meat, presumably to broil it, but of their culinary details we know nothing (Chaney 1935; Movius 1949, p. 392). At other Palaeolithic sites, one can again presume the use of game meat (at times broiled) and wild plants, but scientific investigations necessary for the recovery of the dietary habits of the ancient hunters (e.g., Brothwell and Brothwell 1969) have not yet begun in China. Thus, we have real knowledge about the food, drink, and cooking of the Chinese only after they began to farm, settle down, and leave behind eating and cooking utensils and garbage heaps. But even then, we still had to wait until the coming of the written texts for a reasonably complete picture to emerge (Lin 1957; Shinoda 1959).

Before describing the food habits of the various cultures of ancient China, we should outline these cultures. In north China we begin with the Yangshao culture, characterized by farming villages and painted pottery, and dated from the fourth to the fifth millennia B.C. In the third and early second millennia B.C., the Lungshan culture, known by its black and gray pottery, filled the northern Chinese area. The Shang civilization followed, beginning around 1850 B.C. From about 1100 to about 200 B.C. was the period of the Chou civilization. For central and south China, the cultural sequence is slightly different. Parallel to the Yangshao was an early culture characterized by cord-marked pottery and known in Indochina as the Hoabinhian. In the fourth millennium B.C., several advanced rice-farming cultures were formed in the coastal areas from the Huai to the Pearl River valleys, known archaeologically as the Lungshanoid cultures. The north China Lungshan culture may, in fact, be regarded as a northern Lungshanoid culture. The Lungshanoid cultures continued in south China, but the Shang and Chou civilizations made increasing inroads into the south. The Ch'in and Han empires finally united most of China during the last two centuries before Christ (see K. C. Chang 1968).

Our studies for the Shang and Chou civilizations are based primarily on textual data, but archaeology provides the main source of information for the prehistoric cultures. Except for the first section, this chapter has largely been taken from a previously published paper (K. C. Chang 1973).

Foodstuffs

Grains

The principal grains in the north, throughout the ancient period, were millets of various kinds (fig. 1). The Yangshao culture site at Pan-p'o, near Sian, yielded many remains of the foxtail millet (*Setaria italica* Beauv.) (Shih et.al. 1963, p. 223), which is also reported from other sites and appears to be the staple food of the Neolithic Chinese (K. C. Chang 1968, p. 89). The Shang word for cereals, *ho*, is said by some scholars to designate this plant (H. W. Yü 1957, p. 105), which is also identified with another character, *chi*. Chi is known to be a leading staple during the western Chou period; in fact, the founding ancestor of the Chou clan is called Hou Chi, or Lord Chi. In *Shih ching*, the character *chi* is one of the grain names that appear most often (Ch'i 1949, pp. 268–69). From the Spring-Autumn period on, however, the word *chi* came to be seen increasingly less, and a new word, *liang*, seems to have replaced it in importance (Ch'ien 1956, pp. 16–17). Some botanists believe that both chi and liang should be identified with *italica*, but that they were of different varieties—chi being the smaller-eared, lower-yield *italica* var. *germanica* Trin., and liang being the higher-quality *italica* Beauv. var. *maxima* Al. (C. J. Yü 1956, p. 120).

Of apparently equal importance in ancient north China is another millet —shu (*Panicum miliaceum* L.). Archaeological remains of this plant have been reported from a single Yangshao site, in Ching-ts'un, Shansi (Bishop 1933, p. 395), but in the written texts of both Shang and Chou it is clearly of great importance. The word *shu*—the identification of which with *P. miliaceum* is unquestioned—appears frequently in the oracle bone inscriptions (H. W. Yü 1957; P. C. Chang 1970) and in *Shih ching* (Ch'i 1949) and other Chou texts (cf. C. Y. Hsü 1971).

The *Setaria* and *Panicum* millets provided the starch staples of the ancient Chinese; when in texts they mentioned "grains" or "cereals," they referred mostly to these millets. Botanists have not given us a universally accepted place of origin for either millet. North China is given such a role by many, but other areas of the Old World are also thought possible (Renfrew 1973; Whyte 1973). In view of their utmost importance in north China, these millets may be characterized as being distinctively Chinese, although their botanical histories still require and deserve much future research. At least, wild species of the *Setaria* millets (*S. lutescens* Beauv.; *S. viridis* Beauv.) grew natively in north China (Keng 1959, p. 710–13) and were utilized by the Chinese from the Neolithic period (Bishop 1933, p. 395) to the Chou (W. Y. Lu 1957, p. 60).

Other cereals (fig. 2) planted in the north during the period in question included wheat (*mai, Triticum aestivum* L.), hemp (*ma, Cannabis sativa* L.), barley (*mou, Hordeum vulgare* L.), and rice (*tao, Oryza sativa* L.). These assumed varying importance in Shang and Chou texts, but their archaeological history is weak. No remains of barley have been reported, and one or two instances of each of the others are known in a Yangshao context (K. C. Chang 1968, p. 89). Wheat is known from the northern Huai valley, but the dating of its remains there has been variously put from the Neolithic to the western Chou periods (Chin 1962; Yang 1963). Also reported from a Yangshao site are purported remains of *kaoliang* (*Andropogan sorghum* var. *vulgaris*), but their identification has been questioned (Ho 1969a, b), and no indisputable textual evidence can be given for its cultivation in ancient China.

By late Chou times, the northern Chinese had come to regard the shu and old foxtail millets as commonplace grains, and the new foxtail millet (*maxima*) and rice as superior or expensive grains (Ch'ien 1956, p. 22). Rice was favored probably because it could not be extensively planted in the north, even though in the ancient period north China was warmer and more humid than at the present. In central and south China, however, rice had had a long history, possibly as ancient as the northern millets. Carbonized grains and straws and their impressions in clay have been found widely in sites of the Ch'ing-lien-kang, Ch'ü-chia-ling, Liang-chu, and related cultures of central and southeastern coastal China. These cultures have been grouped under the common banner of Lungshanoid and dated to the third and fourth millennia b. c. (K. C. Chang 1968, pp. 144–45; 1973). The word for rice, *tao,* is tentatively identified in Shang inscriptions (Hu 1945, p. 87), but Chou texts leave no doubt that it is the leading crop of the south.[1]

Other Plant Foods

Among the most important legumes grown in China today are the soybean (*Glycine max* L.) and the peanut (*Arachis hypogaea* L.). The peanut is generally considered of lowland South American origin (Krapovickas 1969; Leppik 1971) and is not believed to have come to China until the sixteenth century, about the same time that the sweet potato was introduced (Ho 1955, p. 192). But remains of peanuts have been reported from Lungshanoid sites in Chekiang (Chechiang Sheng 1960) and Kiangsi (Ch'in et al. 1962), from layers dated by radiocarbon to the third millennium b. c. (K. C. Chang 1973). Some scholars are skeptical of the claim that peanuts were found from such an early date; they point out that sesames and broad beans were also reported from the same layer, and these again are plants thought not to have been introduced to China until later (Ho 1969a, pp. 205–09; An 1972, pp. 40–41;

Harlan and de Wet 1973, p. 54). It should also be noted that after their reported Lungshanoid occurrence peanuts disappeared from known Chinese texts until the sixteenth century.

Soybeans (fig. 3-C), known as *shu* in Chou texts, are generally considered to have been first cultivated somewhere in China (Hymowitz 1970; Leppik 1971). However, their history cannot yet be traced farther back than the western Chou period, on the basis of palaeography (T. C. Hu 1963), and the first known archaeological finds date only from the Spring-Autumn period (S. C. Chang 1960, p. 11).

Many other beans are regarded by botanists as having had long cultivation histories in China—the velvet bean (*Stizolobium hasjoo*) and the red bean (*Phaseolus angularis*) (fig. 3-D) among them—but as yet they have not been identified in the ancient period. The broad bean (*Vicia faba*), usually regarded as of Mediterranean origin, is represented by an archaeological find at the Lungshanoid site at Ch'ien-shan-yang (Chechiang Sheng 1960). In any event, from Warring States texts (Hsu 1970, p. 6) we have learned that beans of one kind or another were common, sometimes cheap, food items in parts of north China.

The importance of taro (*Colocasia antiguorum*), yam (*Dioscorea esculenta*), greater yam (*D. alata*), and the Chinese yam (*D. batatas*) (figs. 3-A, 3-B) in South China and tropical Southeast Asia is commonly recognized. So far, however, there have been no archaeological remains found of any of these plants in the area of China from antiquity, although some or most of them may antedate rice as important staples in south China.

The *Shih ching* mentions no fewer than forty-six plant names that may be called vegetables, most of which probably grew wild (Lu 1957). The ones that appear frequently, or are known from other sources to be important, include malva (*k'ui, Malva verticillata*, and *shou, M. sylvestris*), melon (*kua, Cucumis melo*), gourd (*hu, Lagenaria leucantha*), turnip (*feng* or *man-ch'ing, Brassica rapa*), Chinese leek (*chiu, Allium odorum*), lettuce (*ch'i, Lactuca denticulata*), field sowthistle (*t'u, Sonchus arvensis*), common cat-tail (*p'u, Typha latifolia*), smartweeds (*liao, Polygonum hydropiper*, and *ling, P. reynoutria*), various kinds of wormwood grasses (*lou, Artemisia vulgaris; fan, A. sieversiana; ai, A. argyi; kao, A. apiacea; wei, A. japonica*), ferns (*chüeh, Pteridium aquilinum*), wild beans (*wei, Vicia angustifolia*), a kind of white grass (*pai-mao, Imperata cylindrica*), and lotus roots (*ho, Nelumbo nucifera*). In addition, Chinese cabbage (*Brassica chinensis*), mustard greens (*Brassica alba, B. cernua*), garlic (*Allium sativum*), spring onion (*A. fistulo-sum*), amaranth (*Amaranthus mangostanus*), Chinese waterchestnuts (*Trapa natans, T. bispinosa*), bamboo shoots (*Polygonum aviculare, Phyllostachys edulis*), and so forth, are also significant (H. L. Li 1969, 1970) (fig. 4). Very few of these, however, are archaeologically substantiated. At the Pan-p'o site, remains of seeds have been identified with the genus *Brassica*, but several different species of vegetables are possible (Shih, et. al. 1963, p. 223). Melon seeds have been recovered from the Lungshanoid site at Ch'ien-shan-yang (Chechiang Sheng 1960) and the Spring-and-Autumn city of Hou-ma in Shansi (S. C. Chang 1960, p. 11).

Animal Food

Animals provided the ancient Chinese with meat and fat, as well as bones, antlers, skins, and feathers, but milk and milk products were apparently not used. A few mammals were domesticated, but others, together with most birds and fish, were caught. Of the domesticated animals, dogs (*Canis familiaris*) and pigs (*Sus domestica*) had the longest histories in China, as they were found in large quantities at the neolithic Yangshao and Lungshan sites and at all Shang and Chou sites. Undoubtedly, they were principal sources of meat.

Cattle, sheep, and goats have occurred at some Yangshao sites, but they were probably not fully domesticated until the Lungshan period. The Shang site at An-yang has yielded numerous bones of sheep (*Ovis shangi*), cattle (*Bos exiguus*), and water buffalo (*Bubalus mephistopheles*) (Teilhard de Chardin and C. C. Young 1936; C. C. Young et. al. 1949), but C. J. Shih (1953) pointed out that their bones were found mostly in sacrificial burials rather than among living debris. From oracle bone inscriptions and from ancient texts it is clear that beef and mutton were used for rituals. Undoubtedly, they were also consumed outside the ritual context, but perhaps not as commonly as pork.

Of the wild animals, deer and rabbit were apparently the most frequently eaten throughout the period in question. The most commonly used deer were probably the elaphure (*Elaphurus menziesianus*, *E. davidianus*)—which Teilhard and Young thought were kept by the Shang for their antlers—the sika deer (*Pseudaxis hortulorum*), and the water deer (*Hydropites inermis*). In addition, many other wild animals were hunted, including wild dog, wild boar, wild horse, bear, badger, tiger, panther, common rat, bamboo rat, monkey, fox, and antelope, but the quantity of any of them caught was unlikely to be other than occasionally significant. Bones of whale, elephant, tapir, and Ussuri bear were found at An-yang, prompting Teilhard and Young to speculate about imported delicacies.

Fowls that were mentioned in Chou texts with frequency include chicken, pullet, goose, quail, partridge (or finch), pheasant, sparrow, and curlew. Chicken was mentioned frequently in Shang oracle bone writings, and its bones are common finds at An-yang (C. J. Shih 1953). An-yang has also yielded bones of the cinereous vulture (*Aegypius monachus*), the silver pheasant (*Cennaeus* cf. *nycthermerus*), and the peacock (*Pavo* cf. *muticus*) (Paynter 1960, personal communication). Both vulture (*Aquila* sp.) and chicken (*Gallus* sp.) bones were identified at Pan-p'o, although the domestic nature of this chicken is questionable.

Archaeological remains of several kinds leave no doubt that fish was a major diet source at the Pan-p'o village in Yangshao times, although the only fish that has been archaeologically identified there is a kind of carp. Carps of several kinds (common carp, *Cyprinus carpio*; blue carp, *Mylopharyngodon aethiops*; grass carp, *Ctenopharyngodon idellus*; and *Squaliobarbus curriculus*) were identified at An-yang (Wu 1949), and yellow "gigi" (*Pelteobagrus fulvidraco*) at both An-yang and the Lungshan site at Miao-ti-kou, western Honan (An, Cheng, and Hsieh 1959). An-yang has also yielded gray mullets (*Mugil* sp.), a marine fish.

Other water produce include turtles and various kinds of shellfish. Bees, cicadas, snails, moths, and frogs were among the other animal foodstuffs that have been mentioned.

Beverages, Condiments, and Seasonings

Chou texts mention four kinds of alcoholic beverages (*chiu*): *li, lo, lao*, and *ch'ang* (S. S. Ling 1958, p. 887). Ling (1958) believes that they were all fermented and that, with the possible exception of lo which may be made from fruits and berries, they were all made from grains, primarily millets (see also 1961). That millet-fermented beverages of one kind or another were used by the Shang Chinese requires no elaboration. Textual accounts and archaeological remains of bronze and pottery drinking-utensils point to the indulgence of Shang noblemen in this vice, and archaeologists have even found a possible factory site where alcoholic beverages were manufactured (Honan Sheng Wen-hua-chü Wen-wu Kung-tso-tui 1959, p. 29). Some of the Shang drinking utensil forms occur in the Neolithic Lungshan culture, and alcoholic beverages were, without doubt, at least that old in China. Whether or not they could be pushed back to the Yangshao culture is controversial (Y. S. Li 1962; Y. Fang 1964).

Alcoholic beverages were an indispensable part of every feast, many meals, and important ritual occasions of both Shang and Chou periods. Such uses are too numerous and well known to be described here, but they were also used for cooking (see below, footnote 3, the "Steeped Delicacy," for one example).

Chou texts (e.g., *Tso chuan*, 20th Year of Chao Kung) mention *liu* as a seasoning; it is usually interpreted as "vinegar," but of its manufacture and ingredients we know nothing. A sour taste was known to be provided in food by plums. Plums were often mentioned with salt (*yen mei*) as the chief seasoning agents. In addition, meat sauce (*hai*) was also so used, and in all likelihood soy sauce was known toward the end of the Chou period (see *Shih chi*, "Huo Ch'ih Lieh Chuan"). Other known spices were fagara (*chiao*) and cinnamon (*kui*).

Cooking Methods, Dishes, and Utensils

Methods and Dishes

One Chinese cookbook (Chao 1972, p. 39) lists twenty methods of cooking: boiling, steaming, roasting, red-cooking, clear-simmering, pot-stewing, stir-frying, deep-frying, shallow-frying, meeting, splashing, plunging, rinsing, cold-mixing, sizzling, salting, pickling, steeping, drying, smoking. For studies in this area, textual data are essential, and there are adequate data only from the Chou period. We will discuss the Chou data first and then attempt to push some of these back in time.

In Chou texts, many of these methods are encountered, although in some cases precise identification is difficult. A notable exception is stir-frying, a very important cooking method today, but one that does not seem to have been used by the Chou Chinese. Their most important methods appear to have been boiling, steaming, roasting, simmering-stewing, pickling, and drying.

It has been said that what makes Chinese food Chinese lies, essentially, not so much in the methods of cooking as in the way in which foodstuffs are prepared before cooking, and the manner in which they are then put together into distinctive dishes. As Lin Yutang (1935, p. 340) said, "the whole culinary art of China depends on the art of mixture" (see also Lin and Lin 1969, p. 12). Dishes are designed on the basis of combinations of flavors and ingredients. This does not mean that Chinese dishes are never made of single flavors, but, from the point of view of the whole range of Chinese dishes, minced ingredients and the mixing of flavors are characteristic. In this crucial sense, the Chou cooking is definitely "Chinese." The culinary art in Chou texts is often referred to as *ko p'eng*, namely, "to cut and cook." (This word is still used in Japan.) There were many words meaning "to cut" or "to mince," and the most common kind of dishes was *keng*, a kind of meat soup or stew which is characteristically an art of mixing flavors.[2] But the Chinese way of cooking only begins with flavor mixing. The proportions of ingredients, the amount and length of heat applied to each, and the proper seasonings applied at each stage, are also important. As *Lü shih ch'un ch'iu* pointed out, "the variations within the cooking pot are so delicate that they cannot be described" ("Hsiao Hsing Lan," sec "Pei Wei," C. J. Yin 1958, p. 14; my translation).

Such cooking efforts in Chou China, as in modern China, must have resulted in hundreds or even thousands of individual food dishes ranging from simple to complex. Because of the nature of the evidence, most of the dishes that we know something about were those used in rituals and feasts enjoyed by upper-class people. Very few recipes for simple vegetable dishes, for example, are known. But, whatever the complexity, many dishes were elaborately prepared, and they ranked among the best-treasured enjoyments of life. Nowhere is this more vividly and convincingly illustrated than in the two poems in *Ch'u ts'e* that "summoned the soul," asking it to return home to the good life, a life in which such good dishes satisfy the palate. In "Chao Hun" ("The Summons of the Soul"), we read:

> O soul, come back! Why should you go far away?
> All your household have come to do you honour; all kinds of good
>   food are ready:
> Rice, broom-corn, early wheat, mixed all with yellow millet;
> Bitter, salt, sour, hot and sweet: there are dishes of all flavours.
> Ribs of the fatted ox cooked tender and succulent;
> Sour and bitter blended in the soup of Wu;
> Stewed turtle and roast kid, served up with yam sauce;
> Geese cooked in sour sauce, casseroled duck, fried flesh of the great
>   crane;
> Braised chicken, seethed tortoise, high-seasoned, but not to spoil the
>   taste;
> Fried honey-cakes of rice flour and malt-sugar sweetmeats;
> Jadelike wine, honey-flavoured, fills the winged cups;
> Ice-cooled liquor, strained of impurities, clear wine, cool and refresh-
>   ing;
> Here are laid out the patterned ladles, and here is sparkling wine.
>
> [trans. Hawkes 1959, p. 107.]

In the other poem, "Ta Chao" ("The Great Summons"), these were the delicious dishes, viands, and drinks that were offered as bribes to lure back the lost soul:

> The five grains are heaped up six ells high, and corn of zizania set out;
> The cauldrons seethe to their brims; their blended savours yield fra-
>   grance;

Plump orioles, pigeons, and geese, flavoured with broth of jackal's
  meat:
O soul, come back! Indulge your appetite!
Fresh turtle, succulent chicken, dressed with a sauce of Ch'u;
Pickled pork, dog cooked in bitter herbs, and zingiber-flavoured
  mince,
And sour Wu salad of artemisia, not too wet or tasteless.
O soul, come back! Indulge in your own choice!
Roast crane is served up, and steamed duck and boiled quails,
Fried bream, stewed magpies, and green goose, broiled.
O soul, come back! Choice things are spread before you.
The four kinds of wine are all matured, not rasping to the throat:
Clear, fragrant, ice-cooled liquor, not for base men to drink;
And white yeast is mixed with must of Wu to make the clear Ch'u
  wine.
O soul, come back and do not be afraid!

[trans. Hawkes 1959, p. 111.]

Ch'u's style of cooking was probably somewhat different from that in north
China, but the dishes that are described in such mouth-watering vividness
in these poems are, without doubt, basically identical with those we find in
the contemporary, but much more sedate, works in the north, such as *Li chi*.
In the north, animal or fish flesh was the main ingredient of all the important
dishes that are described for ritual and feast occasions, Once in a while, raw
meat (*hsing*) was used, and whole animals, hair and all, may be roasted (*p'ao*),
but more often the meat was dried, cooked, or pickled. If dried, it was cut
into squares (*p'u*) or oblong strips (*hsiu*), seasoned with ginger, cinnamon,
and the like, and then dried. If cooked, the meat was cut in one of three ways:
pieces and chunks with bones (*hsiao*), slices (*tzu*), or mince (*hui*). It was then
boiled (*chu*), stewed (*ju*), steamed (*cheng*), or roasted (*chiu, fan, shao*). In the
process, other ingredients were added. If the amount of the other ingredients
was small and the purpose wholly to supplement, the result was a meaty dish.
If there were important parallel ingredients to achieve "harmony" of flavors,
and if the method of cooking was boiling or stewing, then there would be a
meat soup, keng. Some examples of the meaty dishes are: "a suckling-pig
[that] was stewed, wrapped up in sonchus leaves and stuffed with smartweed;
a fowl, with the same stuffing, and along with pickle sauce; a fish, with the
same stuffing and egg sauce; a tortoise, with the same stuffing and pickle
sauce" ("Nei Tse," *Li chi*, trans. Legge 1885, p. 460). Examples of the meat
soups are: "snail juice and a condiment of the broad-leaved water-squash
were used with pheasant soup; a condiment of wheat with soups of dried

slices and of fowl; broken glutinous rice with dog soup and hare soup; the riceballs mixed with these soups had no smartweed in them" (ibid.).

Finally, meat was often pickled or made into a sauce. It appears that for this one could use either raw meat or cooked meat, but Cheng Hsüan (d. 200 A. D.), the authoritative commentator of *Li chi*, gave only one recipe: "To prepare *hai* (boneless meat sauce) and *ni* (meat sauce with bones), it is necessary first to dry the meat and then cut it up, blend it with moldy millet, salt, and good wine, and place it in a jar. The sauce is ready in a hundred days" (*Li chi*, 1:1). The meat sauce or pickle was often used as an ingredient of a hot dish or soup. Pickling, aside from boiling and drying, also seems to be a favorite method for anthropophagy; famous historical personages that ended up in a sauce jar include the marquis of Chiu (of Shang) ("Yin Pen Chi," *Shih chi*) and Tzu Lu (a disciple of Confucius) ("T'an Kung," *Li chi*).

The only elaborate recipes for Chou dishes are those of the so-called Eight Delicacies, described in *Li chi* ("Nei Tse"), to be specifically prepared for the aged. They are the Rich Fry, the Similar Fry, the Bake, the Pounded Delicacy, the Steeped Delicacy, the Grill, the Soup Balls, and the Liver and Fat.[3]

For cooking and serving the characteristic food dishes of the Chou period, the Chou Chinese employed a characteristic assemblage of utensils and vessels. In addition, they had an elaborate set of wine vessels. An account of both the current classifications of bronze vessels and the textual lexicons for food and drink utensils results in the major categories which follow (cf. Hayashi 1964).

Food Utensils

Cooking vessels. Included in this group are *ting, li, hsien, tseng, fu, hu,* and *tsao.* All of these were made of pottery and bronze, except for tsao, the stove, which is known only in pottery. Ting, li, and hu were probably for boiling and simmering-stewing; hsien, tseng, and fu, for steaming.

Preserving and storage vessels. This is a category presumed on the basis of the archaeological remains of grain-containing jars and the record of meat and vegetable sauces and pickles. No bronze vessels are regarded as being so used, although some of the wine containers (see below) could certainly have been used for these purposes. But perhaps pottery jars and urns were used most often.

Serving utensils and vessels. In this category, I place five principal kinds of things—chopsticks, spatulas, ladles, vessels for grain food, and serving utensils for meat and vegetable dishes. Of the first three, little need be said except that they were used during the Shang and Chou periods, although hands were probably used more often than chopsticks. Vessels for grain and vessels for dishes, however, are complex in form and material. Grain vessels, including such types as *kui, hsü, fu,* and *tui,* were bronze, pottery, or basketry, while those for dishes, such as *tou, pien,* and *tsu,* were mostly pottery, wooden, or basketry. Tou, for example, the most important serving vessel for meat dishes, was never made of bronze during the Shang period (C. J. Shih 1969). Another way of stating this is to say that bronze serving vessels were primarily for grain food and seldom for dishes. This is an important distinction—one that we will come back to below.

Drink Vessels

Water and wine containers.   Bronze, pottery, wood and so forth.
Wine drinking cups.   Bronze, bottle-gourd, lacquered wood, pottery.
Ladles.   Bronze, wood, and bottle gourd.

The close connection between this assemblage of utensils and the characteristic Chou cooking methods is obvious. The Chou Chinese ate their grains more often whole than floured, and they used steamers to cook them and wide bowls, spatulas, and chopsticks to serve them. Meat and vegetables were served in morsels. Ting, li, and other cooking vessels were used to cook them, and chopsticks helped serve them.

The characteristic assemblage of food utensils of the Chou provides a useful basis for the study of cooking methods of the Shang and the Neolithic Chinese, whose methods are not recorded in texts as the Chou's are. Here one has only to make a sweeping generalization: that the cooking and serving utensils of ancient China, from the Neolithic Yangshao culture to the Shang and the Chou, were essentially identical. We do not have any prehistoric chopsticks, and many Shang and Chou bronze vessels can only be pushed back in time in the medium of another material—clay. But otherwise, the continuity is almost total. One can only conclude that many, or even most, of the cooking methods described for the Chou must have a Shang, or even a prehistoric, origin.

Meals, Feasts, and Ritual Use of Food

From a nutritional point of view, once foodstuffs are prepared into dishes, they can be served with whatever utensils there are, be simply consumed, and, once in the stomach, the whole affair of eating ends. From the point of view of one whose major interests in life include food, eating alone is of little consequence other than the satisfaction of hunger and anticipation, but

eating with others, while observing special patterns of behavior, is the cli-
mactic phase. Food is taken to sustain life, but food is not so much taken as
given and shared. This sentiment was expressed in the Chou poem "Kui
Pen":

> A cap so tall,
> What is it for?
> Your wine is good,
> Your viands, blessed.
> Why give them to other men?
> Let it be brothers and no one else.
> [Sec. "Hsiao Ya," *Shih ching*, trans. Waley 1960]

In another poem, "Fa mu," we see feelings such as this:

> They are cutting wood on the bank.
> Of strained wine I have good store;
> The dishes and trays are all in rows,
> Elder brothers and younger brothers, do not stray afar!
> If people lose the virtue that is in them,
> It is a dry throat that has led them astray.
>
> [Ibid.]

Other poems describe the atmosphere and the provisions of feasts, and, from
this, one must agree with Creel that eating was an "enjoyment of life"
(Creel 1937, pp. 323ff.). But eating was also a serious social business,
governed by strict rules. As a Chou poet said of an ancestral sacrifice-feast,
"every custom and rite is observed, every smile, every word is in place"
(poem "Ch'u Ts'e," trans. Waley, loc. cit.).

Let us first take a look at the physical setup of a meal. The arrangement of
table and chairs is a rather modern feature in China, not earlier than the
Northern Sung period (A.D. 960–1126) (Shang 1938, p. 119–20). In the Shang
and Chou periods, the gentleman class ate kneeling on individual mats;
a stool was sometimes placed alongside to provide support. The poem
"Hsing Wei," in the *Shih ching* (sec. "*Ta Ya*"), describes a meal setting thus:

> Tender to one another should brothers be,
> None absenting himself, all cleaving together.
> Spread out the mats for them,
> Offer them stools.
> Spread the mats and the over-mats,
> Offer the stools with shuffling step.
> Let the host present the cup, the guest return it;

> Wash the beaker, set down the goblet.
> Sauces and pickles
> For the roast meat, for the broiled.
> And blessed viands, tripe and cheek;
> There is singing and beating of drums.
>
> [Trans. Waley, loc. cit.]

Again, in the poem "Kung Liu":

> Stalwart was Liu the Duke
> In his citadel so safe.
> Walking deftly and in due order
> The people supplied mats, supplied stools;
> He went up to the dais and leant upon a stool.
>
> [Ibid.]

Placed before or beside each person was a set of vessels, containing the food and drink of a meal. The definition of a meal is significant: it consists of grain food, meat and vegetable dishes, and either water or wine or both. (More will be said about this later.) Each person was said to need four large bowls of grain to fill his stomach (poem "Ch'üan yü," in the *Shih ching*), but the number of dishes varied according to an individual's rank and age. According to *Li chi*, a minister of the upper rank was entitled to eight tou-dishes, and one of the lower rank, six ("Li Ch'i"). A man sixty years of age may have three tou-dishes; a man of seventy, four; one of eighty, five; and one of ninety, six ("Hsiang Yin Chiu").

The utensils and dishes were placed in front of and beside the person in this arrangement:

> The meat cooked on the bones is set on the left, and the sliced meat on the right; the [grain] is placed on the left of the [person], and the soup on [his] right; the minced and roasted meat are put outside (the chops and sliced meat) and the pickles and sauces inside; the onions and steamed onions succeed to these, and the drink and syrups are on the right. When slices of dried and spiced meat are put down, where they are folded is turned to the left, and the ends of them to the right. ["Ch'ü Li," *Li chi*, trans. Legge 1885, p. 79].

> The cup with which the guest was pledged was placed on the left; those which had been drunk (by the others) on the right. Those of the guest's attendant, of the host himself, and of the host's assistant;—these all were placed on the right. In putting down a boiled fish to be eaten, the tail was laid in front. In winter it was placed with the fat belly on the

right; in summer with the back. . . . All condiments were taken up with the right (hand), and were therefore placed on the left. . . . When the head was presented among the viands, the snout was put forward, to be used as the offering. He who sets forth the jugs, considered the left of the cup-bearer to be the place for the topmost one. The jugs and jars were placed with their spouts towards the arranger. ["Shao I," ibid., pp. 78–79; see also *Kuan Tzu*, "Ti Tzu Chih"]

It should be mentioned in passing that children were trained at an early age to eat with their right hand ("Nei Tse," *Li chi*).

Finally, strict rules at the dining mat were prescribed. According to *Li chi* (secs. "Ch'ü Li" and "Shao I," trans. Legge 1885), the following rules were among the most prominent:

1. "If a guest be of lower rank (than his entertainer), he should take up the [grain], rise and decline (the honor he is receiving). The host then rises and refuses to allow the guest to retire. After this the guest will resume his seat."

2. "When the host leads on the guests to present an offering (to the father of cookery), they will begin with the dishes which were first brought in. Going on from the meat cooked on the bones they will offer of all (the other dishes)."

3. "After they have eaten three times, the host will lead on the guests to take of the sliced meat, from which they will go on to all the other dishes."

4. "A guest should not rinse his mouth with spirits till the host has gone over all the dishes."

5. "When (a youth) is in attendance on an elder at a meal, if the host give anything to him with his own hand, he should bow to him and eat it. If he do not so give him anything, he should eat without bowing."

6. "When feasting with a man of superior rank and character, the guest first tasted the dishes and then stopt. He should not bolt the food, nor swill down the liquor. He should take small and frequent mouthfuls. While chewing quickly, he did not make faces with his mouth."

7. "When eating with others from the same dishes, one should not try to eat (hastily) to satiety. When eating with them from the same dish of [grain], one should not have to wash his hands."

8. "Do not roll the [grain] into a ball; do not bolt down the various dishes; do not swill down (the soup)."

9. "Do not make a noise in eating; do not crunch the bones with the teeth; do not put back fish you have been eating; do not throw the bones to the dogs; do not snatch (at what you want)."

10. "Do not spread out the [grain] (to cool); do not use chopsticks in eating millet."

11. "Do not (try to) gulp down soup with vegetables in it, nor add condiments to it; do not keep picking the teeth, nor swill down the sauces. If a guest add condiments, the host will apologize for not having had the soup prepared better. If he swill down the sauces the host will apologize for his poverty."

12. "Meat that is wet (and soft) may be divided with the teeth, but dried flesh cannot be so dealt with. Do not bolt roast meat in large pieces."

13. "When they have done eating, the guests will kneel in front (of the mat), and (begin to) remove the (dishes) of [grain] and sauces to give them to the attendants. The host will then rise and decline this service from the guests, who will resume their seats."

It should be remembered that all the above rules of table arrangement and table manners were purported to represent the norm of late Chou upper-class gentlemen. We do not know how strictly they were adhered to, whether or not they represent any norms wider than north China and the upper class, or if the Chinese of the Shang and early Chou periods had identical or similar rules. From the descriptions given in many poems in the *Shih ching*, it appears that meals and feasts in these earlier periods were partaken of with a lot more spirit and gusto and less formality than those recorded in *Li chi* (fig. 16). When Confucius expansively proclaimed that "with coarse [grain] to eat, with water to drink, and my bended arm for a pillow;—I have still joy in the midst of these things" (*Confucian Analects*, trans. Legge 1893, p. 200), he was obviously thinking of a rather minimum level of a meal —without all those rules and manners—which would still, of course, constitute a meal. But was not the Master merely philosophizing? (Remember, in matters of the palate Confucius was in real life rather particular and a very difficult person to accommodate, according to another section of the *Analects*.)[4] Did poor people necessarily eat like lone boors? Did they not also have their own rules in their own company? They must have, but, alas, their rules are not preserved in the available records.

Food Semantics

Is there a code, in the linguistic sense of the word as Mary Douglas used it (1971), in the meal system or food habits of the ancient Chinese? Was the essence of the ancient Chinese civilization codified in the grain and dishes its people served themselves and their guests? The following hierarchy, though not necessarily a code, appears to be pertinent:

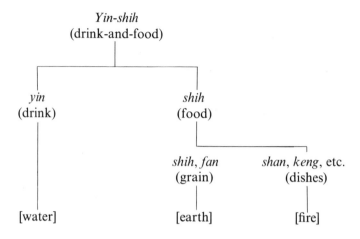

Unlike English, there is a word in Chinese (both ancient and modern) for food and drink combined—*yin-shih*. This, of course, is a compound word, made up of *yin* (drink) and *shih* (food); and that bifurcation is clearly shown in the texts, as we will describe later. Within shih itself, there is a clear and strong dichotomy between *shih* in the narrow sense meaning fan or grain food, and dishes of meat and vegetables (*ts'ai* in modern parlance). This arrangement of food classes, and the beliefs and rules associated with them, is in my opinion the structural essence of the Chinese way of eating, and it has not changed from at least the Chou period to this day.

In ancient texts, wherever enumerations of things to eat and drink appear, the same hierarchy of food-drink contrasts is shown. The following are some outstanding examples (italics added):

Admirable indeed was the virtue of Huei! With *a single bamboo dish of shih (grains), a single gourd dish of yin (drink)*, and living in his mean narrow lane, ... he did not allow his joy to be affected by it. ["Yüng Yeh", *Lun yü*, trans. Legge 1893, p. 188]

[Ch'ien Ao], *carrying with his left hand some shih (grain), and holding some yin (drink) with the other*, said to him, 'Poor man! Come and eat'. ["T'an Kung," *Li chi*, trans. Legge, 1885, p. 195]

With coarse shih (grain) to eat, with shui (water) to drink, and my bended arm for a pillow:—I have still joy in the midst of these things. ["Shu Erh," *Lun yü*, trans. Legge 1893, p. 200]

The people brought baskets of shih (grain) and jars of chiang (water), to meet your Majesty's host. ["Liang Hui Wang," *Meng Tzu*, trans. Legge 1895, p. 170]

These passages make it clear that a minimum meal consisted of some grain (usually millet) and some water. But when we follow up the scale of elaborateness of meals, we find that a third item is added, namely, the dishes. In *Li chi*, chapter "Nei Tse" ("Internal [Family] Regulations"), the category of *shan* is added between fan (i.e., shih) and yin. Under it are listed twenty tou-dishes of various preparations of meat. In *Chou li*, the officer Shan Fu is stated to be in charge of the king's shih, yin, and *shan-hsiu*. The last refers to various kinds of dishes. Since the dishes often contained meat, the contrast within the category *shih* (food) was often made between shih ("grain") and keng ("meat soup"): "[Keng] soup and *shih* boiled grain were used by all, from the princes down to the common people, without distinction of degree" ("Nei Tse," *Li chi*, trans. Legge 1885, p. 464). "A small basket of *shih* (grain) and a platter of *keng* (soup)" ("Kao Tzu" and "Chin Hsin," *Meng Tzu*). "*Fan* (grain food) of beans and *keng* (meat soup) of weeds" (*Chan Kuo ts'e*).

The contrast between grain and dishes within a Chinese meal is a living institution of major importance. As Buwei Yang Chao pointed out in her cookbook (1972, p. 3):

A very important idea everywhere is the contrast between *fan* (in a narrow sense), "rice," and *ts'ai*, "dishes." Most people who are poor eat much rice (if that) or other grain food as the main food and only a little *ts'ai* or dishes. The dishes only accompany the rice. . . . Whenever they can, Chinese children like to eat little rice and much of the dishes, . . . but even children in well-to-do families are called good when they are willing to eat much rice. All this to make clear the opposition between rice and dishes in a Chinese meal. If there are noodles or steamed bread, they are considered "rice," that is, grain food.

Compare this with the following statement about Confucius more than two thousand years ago: "Though there might be a large quantity of meat, he would not allow what he took to exceed the due proportion for the *shih* (grain)" ("Hsiang Tang," *Lun yü*, trans. Legge 1893). One must assume that there is some very strong reason for both Confucius and Mrs. Chao's Chinese children (or their parents) to make a clear distinction between the grain food (the staple, basic, absolutely important food) and the dishes (used to *p'ei*—"match," "supplement," or "complement"—the grain and make it easier and more enjoyable to eat), and for them to refrain from overindulgence in the dishes.

The contrast between grain and dishes may be seen as a significant difference between food that is of grain, and food (primarily meat) that is cooked with fire. In *Li chi*, chapter "Wang Chih," we find the following classification of "barbarian" peoples on the four sides of the Chinese people:

The people of those five regions—the Middle states, and the Jung, Yi, (and other wild tribes round them)—had all their several natures, which they could not be made to alter. The tribes on the east were called Yi. They had their hair unbound, and tattooed their bodies. *Some of them ate their food without its being cooked with fire.* Those on the south were called Man. They tattooed their foreheads, and had their feet turned in toward each other. *Some of them ate their food without its being cooked with fire.* Those on the west were called Jung. They had their hair unbound, and wore skins. *Some of them did not eat grain-food.* Those on the north were called Ti. They wore skins of animals and birds, and dwelt in caves. *Some of them did not eat grain-food.* [Trans. Legge 1885; p. 229; italics added]

Clearly both eating food (meat) without its being cooked with fire and not eating grain food were regarded as being non-Chinese, but these two things are not equated. One could eat grain but also eat raw meat or one could eat his meat cooked but eat no grain. Neither was fully Chinese. A Chinese by definition ate grain and cooked his meat. Clearly grain and cooked meat (main ingredient of dishes) were contrasting items in the Chinese regime of eating.

The secondary nature of dishes relative to grain food is not only shown in the use of the same word, *shih,* for food or meal in general and for grain food in particular; it is also shown in the mortuary taboo of the Chou Chinese: "After the burial," according to *Li chi,* "the presiding mourner had only coarse grain and water to drink;—he did not eat vegetables or fruits.... After the change of mourning, towards the end of the year, they ate vegetables and fruit; and after the subsequent sacrifices they ate flesh" ("Sang Ta Chi," trans. Legge, loc. cit., pp. 183–84). This means that grain and water were the basics, and when one went beyond the basics, vegetables and fruits would come before meat. When one resumed eating meat, one would first eat dried meat and then fresh meat ("Sang Ta Chi" and "Hsien Chuan," *Li chi*). In sum, the following two points may be said to be quite firmly established: first, within the food category there was a grain–dishes contrast, and second, of the two, grain was superior to or more basic than the dishes.

In the Chou texts we find two separate accounts for the origin of rituals—one revolving around grain, and the other around the use of fire for the cooking of meat. First, the theme of grain and the origin of ritual appears in a legend of the Chou people as related in the poem "Sheng Min":

> She who in the beginning gave birth to the people,
> This was Chiang Yüan.
> How did she give birth to the people?
> Well she sacrificed and prayed

That she might no longer be childless.
She trod on the big toe of God's footprint,
Was accepted and got what she desired.
Then in reverence, then in awe
She gave birth, she nurtured;
And this was Hou Chi ["Lord Millet"].
Indeed, she had fulfilled her months,
And her first-born came like a lamb
With no bursting or rending,
With no hurt or harm.
To make manifest His magic power
God on high gave her ease.
So blessed were her sacrifice and prayer
That easily she bore her child.
Indeed, they put it in a narrow lane;
But oxen and sheep tenderly cherished it.
Indeed, they put it in a far-off wood;
But it chanced that woodcutters came to this wood.
Indeed, they put it on the cold ice;
But the birds covered it with their wings.
The birds at last went away,
And Hou Chi began to wail.
Truly far and wide
His voice was very loud.
Then sure enough he began to crawl;
Well he straddled, well he reared,
To reach food for his mouth.
He planted large beans;
His beans grew fat and tall.
His paddy-lines were close set,
His hemp and wheat grew thick,
His young gourds teemed.
Truly Hou Chi's husbandry
Followed the way that had been shown.
He cleared away the thick grass,
He planted the yellow crop.
It failed nowhere, it grew thick,
It was heavy, it was tall,
It sprouted, it eared,
It was firm and good,
It nodded, it hung—
He made house and home in T'ai.

> Indeed, the lucky grains were sent down to us,
> The black millet, the double-kernelled,
> Millet pink-sprouted and white.
> Far and wide the black and the double-kernelled
> He reaped and acred;
> Far and wide the millet pink and white
> He carried in his arms, he bore on his back,
> Brought them home, and created the sacrifice.
> Indeed, what are they, our sacrifices?
> We pound the grain, we bale it out,
> We sift, we tread,
> We wash it—soak, soak;
> We boil it all steamy.
> Then with due care, due thought
> We gather southernwood, make offering of fat,
> Take lambs for the rite of expiation,
> We roast, we broil,
> To give a start to the coming year.
> High we load the stand,
> The stands of wood and of earthenware.
> As soon as the smell rises
> God on high is very pleased:
> "What smell is this, so strong and good?"
> Hou Chi founded the sacrifices,
> And without blemish or flaw
> They have gone on till now.
> ["Ta Ya," *Shih ching*, trans. Waley 1960, pp. 241–43]

Here meat is mentioned, but Hou Chi was above all the "Lord Millet," and the ritual one in which grains played a central role.

The other story is about the relation of rituals and cooked meat, and is related in the "Li Yün" section of *Li chi*. This section contains many ideas and concepts that scholars have long suspected of being Taoist (Kao 1963, pp. 38–41), and perhaps the following account was closer to the folk-peasant tradition than the previous poem, which was in the tradition of the Chou rulers:

> At the first use of ceremonies, they began with [food] and drink. They roasted millet and pieces of pork; they excavated the ground in the form of a jar, and scooped the water from it with their two hands; they fashioned a handle of clay, and struck with it an earthen drum. (Simple

as these arrangements were), they yet seemed to be able to express by them their reverence for [ghosts and gods].

(By and by), when one died, they went upon the housetop, and called out his name in a prolonged note, saying, "Come back, So and So." After this they filled the mouth (of the dead) with uncooked rice, and (set forth as offerings to him) packets of [cooked] flesh. Thus they looked up to heaven (whither the spirit was gone), and buried (the body) in the earth. The body and the animal soul go downwards; and the intelligent spirit is on high. Thus (also) the dead are placed with their heads to the north, while the living look toward the south. In all these matters the earliest practice is followed.

Formerly the ancient kings had no houses. In winter they lived in caves which they had excavated, and in summer in nests which they had framed. They knew not yet the transforming power of fire, but ate the fruits of plants and trees, and the flesh of birds and beasts, drinking their blood, and swallowing (also) the hair and feathers. They knew not yet the use of flax and silk, but clothed themselves with feathers and skins.

The later sages then arose, and men (learned) to take advantage of the benefits of fire. They moulded the metals and fashioned clay, so as to rear towers with structures on them, and houses with windows and doors. They toasted, grilled, boiled, and roasted. They produced must and sauces. They dealt with the flax and silk so as to form linen and silken fabrics. They were thus able to nourish the living, and to make offerings to the dead; to serve the spirits of the departed and God. In all these things we follow the example of that early time.

Thus it is that the dark-coloured liquor is in the apartment (where the representative of the dead is entertained); that the vessel of must is near its (entrance) door; that the reddish liquor is in the hall; and the clear, in the (court) below. The victims (also) are displayed, and the tripods and stands are prepared. The lutes and citherns are put in their places, with the flutes, sonorous stones, bells, and drums. The prayers (of the principal in the sacrifice to the spirits) and the benedictions (of the representatives of the departed) are carefully framed. The object of all the ceremonies is to bring down the spirits from above, even their ancestors; serving (also) to rectify the relations between ruler and ministers; to maintain the generous feeling between father and son, and the harmony between elder and younger brother; to adjust the relations between high and low; and to give their proper places to husband and wife. The whole may be said to secure the blessing of Heaven.

They proceed to their invocations, using in each the appropriate terms. The dark-coloured liquor is employed in (every) sacrifice. The blood with the hair and feathers (of the victim) is presented. The flesh, uncooked, is set forth on the stands. The bones with the flesh on them are sodden; and rush mats and coarse cloth are placed underneath and over the vases and cups. The robes of dyed silk are put on. The must and clarified liquor are presented. The flesh, roasted and grilled, is brought forward. The ruler and his wife take alternate parts in presenting these offerings, all being done to please the souls of the departed, and constituting a union (of the living) with the disembodied and unseen.

These services having been completed, they retire, and cook again all that was insufficiently done. The dogs, pigs, bullocks, and sheep are dismembered. The shorter dishes (round and square), the taller ones of bamboo and wood, and the soup vessels are all filled. There are the prayers which express the filial piety (of the worshipper), and the benediction announcing the favour (of his ancestors). This may be called the greatest omen of prosperity; and in this the ceremony obtains its grand completion. [trans. Legge, loc. cit., pp. 368–72]

Each of the two accounts above, "Sheng Min" and "Li Yün," relates mainly to one side of the grain-dishes contrast. Why this contrast? Why are they differentially emphasized in separate accounts? One is tempted to explain this basic concept of the Chinese meal system in terms of a mixture of two class, or ethnic, traditions. Interestingly, the food that is considered the major partner of the pair (i.e., the grain) is the much more recent invention, and it is also the invention that is identified with the Chinese as opposed to the barbarian. But all this, plus a detailed analysis of the two accounts of ritual origins, must be the object of further studies. In the present connection, I rather think that the dichotomy in meals is a part of the dualism that permeated the whole Chinese civilization, and that the *yin* and the *yang* concepts are playing a role here also. Complete or even satisfactory demonstration of all this is not in sight, but I would like for now to return to food vessels and to archaeology, for it is in these areas that I see a flicker of light.

Ideas about Food

I maintained above that Shang and Chou bronze and pottery vessels may be studied in the context of the Chinese food habits of those periods. Now that we have provided a beginning of such a context, what, if any, new insights have we gained insofar as the archaeology of food vessels is concerned?

The most important insight for me is that the study of vessels as food vessels must not be confined to those of a single material. In archaeology we are used to studying bronzes, pottery, lacquerware, and so forth, as categories discrete from one another. In the actual use of the vessels for meals and for rituals, there is invariably a mixture of them made of different materials: bronze, pottery, bottle gourd, wood, lacquerware, ivory, bone, and so forth. There was a presumable, though not always apparent or provable, correlation of use and material depending on the physical properties of the various materials. An intriguing question is whether there were rules that governed the mixture of vessels of different materials.

One evident rule is that bronze was for the most part confined to vessels for grain food and for drinks made from grain. Pien and tou, the two most important vessels for serving meat dishes, were wooden, basketry, or pottery. They are not known to be made of bronze during the Shang and early Chou periods. Tou appeared in the latter half of Chou in bronze, but presumably there were many more pottery and wooden tou than bronze ones even during this brief interval, and from the beginning of Han onward tou was again an almost exclusively wooden utensil (Shih 1950, p. 10). Shih Chang-ju tried to explain the failure of the Shang to make bronze tou by appealing to the physical properties of that metal: "Most bronze vessels of the Yin period were objects that were suitable for liquids but unsuitable for solids. *Tou* appears to be a utensil for solid objects. Wooden *tou* vessels, when engraved and painted in red, were the most glamorous-looking. The reason that the Yin period lacked bronze *tou* was possibly because the bronze was not suitable for casting *tou*, or because bronze *tou* could not achieve the desired appearance due to the low level of metallurgical skills" (Shih 1969, p. 79).

An alternative interpretation is that the Shang grouped the food and drink vessels into those whose contents were made of or from grain (cooked grain or fermented grain or wine) and those whose contents included meat. Clay, wood, and basketry may make vessels of both kinds, but bronze could be cast for vessels of the grain kind but not the meat kind. That is, bronzes were not for serving dishes.

We can only speculate as to why this was so. Perhaps food and drinks were cognitively classified by the Shang and Chou into different categories similar to the five elements, and different vessel materials could only come into contact with certain kinds of food and drinks according to specific rules. We don't know how far back we can trace the idea of the *five elements*— metal, wood, water, fire, earth. According to Liu Pin-hsiung (1965, p. 108), the five elements existed in the Shang period not only as a pervasive, basic cosmological conceptual system, they were even related to the social divisions of the royal house. But, according to others (e.g., H. S. Li 1967, p. 47), both the yin-yang theory and the five elements theory had a much later origin. In any event, in texts of the Warring States (*Mo Tzu*) and early Han (*Huai Nan Tzu*, and *Shih chi*) periods, the element fire and the element metal were regarded as conflicting and antagonistic, and when and if they did come into contact with each other fire usually prevailed over metal. Earlier we have shown that grain food was in the Chou concept associated with earth, and that dishes, in which cooked meat was a major ingredient, were associated with fire. Earth and metal were harmonious elements, whereas fire and metal were disharmonious elements. If this idea has an earlier origin, perhaps it would help explain why dishes should not be served in bronze containers. To be sure, meat was not a necessary element of every dish, and some dishes could be of vegetables only. But meat was invariably a part of ritual dishes cooked for and by the rich, and bronze vessels were used by the rich also. When the ritualists avoided using bronze for certain categories of vessels, there must have been a reason. In *Li chi* (chap. "Chiao T'o Sheng"), we find various references to the nature of food and the appropriate vessels:

> In feasting and at the vernal sacrifice in the ancestral temple they had music; but in feeding (the aged) and at the autumnal sacrifice they had no music: these were based in the *yin* and *yang*. All drinking serves to nourish the *yang*; all eating to nourish the *yin*. . . . The number of *ting* and *tsu* was odd [yang], and that of *pien* and *tou* was even [yin]; this also was based in the numbers belonging to the *yin* and *yang*. The *pien* and *tou* were filled with the products of water and the land. . . .
>
> At the (Great) border sacrifice, . . . the vessels used were of earthen ware and of gourds; they emblem the natural (productive power of) heaven and earth. [Trans. Legge 1885, pp. 418–19]
>
> The pickled contents of the ordinary *tou* were water-plants produced by the harmonious powers (of nature); the sauce used with them was from productions of the land. The additional *tou* contained productions of the land with the sauce from productions of the water. The things in the *pien* and *tou* were from both the water and the land. [Ibid. p. 434]

Thus, drinking is yang, and eating is yin. But within eating itself, some food was yang and some yin. Meat dishes cooked by fire were probably yang, and food and drink from grain (from the earth) were probably yin. There may be rules of what food may be served by vessels of what materials, and the overall rule may be that *yang* combines with *yin* and vice versa. We do not know any of the rules, but here in food and food vessels we probably encounter once again the dualistic principles that we had encountered in the area of social organization (K. C. Chang 1964). Just how this yin-yang dualism worked together with the five elements is a most interesting question.

Some related questions involve the possible correlation between the decoration of the vessels and their roles in the food system of the Shang and Chou Chinese. Was there any attempt to decorate the vessels with the images of some of the animals whose meat was to fill them? On the surface the answer may be an easy no, for mythological animals are obviously not foodstuffs, and the animals that decorate the Shang and Chou bronzes were certainly mythological. But mythological animals were almost always based on actual animals, the most commonly represented being cattle, sheep, and tigers. They were probably all food animals, and so were probably the other less frequently represented animals such as deer, elephants, rhinoceroses, and goats. Birds were among the prominent decorative motifs. Although their species are difficult to determine, there is no question that birds of many kinds were a major food item. Thus, the question is not one easy to dispose of without much additional research.

Interestingly, many of the mythological animals have been referred to, since the Sung scholars, as *t'ao-t'ieh*. We do not know for certain whether or not *t'ao-t'ieh* is among the bronze decorative motifs of Chou (*Lü shih ch'un ch'iu*: "Chou *ting* are decorated with *t'ao-t'ieh*"). However, t'ao-t'ieh, according to *Tso chuan* (Eighteeth Year of Wen Kung), is the name of an ancient villain known for his gluttonous greed—one who ate and indulged too much for his own good. In *Mo Tzu* (chapter "Chieh Yüng," or "Moderation of Expenditures," part 2), we find that the ancient sage-kings are said to have authorized the code of laws regarding food and drink, saying:

> Stop when hunger is satiated, breathing becomes strong, limbs are strengthened and ears and eyes become sharp. There is no need of combining the five tastes extremely well or harmonizing the different sweet odours. And efforts should not be made to procure rare delicacies from far countries.

How do we know such were the laws?

> In ancient times, when Yao was governing the empire he consolidated Chiao Tse on the south, reached Yu Tu on the north, expanded from where the sun rises to where the sun sets on the east and west, and none was unsubmissive or disrespectful. Yet, even when he was served with what he much liked, he did not take a double cereal or both soup and meat. He ate out of an earthen liu and drank out of an earthen hsing, and took wine out of a spoon. With the ceremonies of bowing and stretching and courtesies and decorum the sage-king had nothing to do. [Mei 1929, pp. 120–21]

This is, of course, Mo Tzu's own philosophy, but overindulgence in food and drink was probably cautioned against in ancient times as well as today. Confucius, we recall, "did not eat much." It is possible that t'ao-t'ieh was used on food vessels as a reminder for restraint and frugality. However if what is recorded about the eating and drinking of the Shang is true, such reminders obviously went unheeded (fig. 15).

Overindulgence was something only the upper class—the users of the bronzes—could afford. For most people, pottery was probably the most basic material for vessels. And of all materials, at least those that are durable and archaeologically important, pottery seems to be acceptable for all essential uses: cooking, preserving, storing, drinking, serving both grain and dishes. Archaeological remains do indicate that in pottery vessels one finds the whole range of food needs served. In the two archaeological burial sites of the Chou period, one near Sian (Chung-kuo 1962) and the other near Loyang (Chung-kuo 1959), a large number of graves contained pottery vessels. In the overwhelming majority of graves, vessels that served the whole range of food uses were found in sets in individual burials, including vessels for cooking and serving grain (li and kui), vessels for serving meat dishes (tou), and vessels for drinking (hu and kuan). This serves to show that the hierarchical taxonomy that we have worked out of the Chou texts is archaeologically significant. It also goes to show that in the archaeological study of ancient China, including the study of bronze and pottery vessels, the textual materials, and the kind of information only textual materials provide, are indispensable.

NOTES

1. In *Chou li* ("Chih Fang"), the major crops of the Nine Provinces (Chiu Chou) of late Chou and Han China are listed as follows:

Yang Chou (lower Yangtze): rice

Ching Chou (middle Yangtze): rice

Yü Chou (Honan and the Huai valley): Five Crops (*Panicum* millet, *Setaria* millet of the *germanica* variety, soybean, wheat, and rice, according to Cheng K'ang-ch'eng's annotation)

Ch'ing Chou (E. Shantung): rice and wheat

Yen Chou (northern Honan, northwestern Shantung, and southern Hopei): Four Crops (*Panicum* millet, *Setaria* millet, rice, and wheat, according to the Cheng annotation)

Yüng Chou (north-central Shensi): *Panicum* and *Setaria* millets

Yu Chou (northern Hopei): Three Crops (*Panicum* millet, *Setaria* millet, and rice, according to the Cheng annotation)

Chi Chou (central Hopei and northeastern Shansi): *Panicum* and *Setaria* millets
Pien Chou (central-south Shansi): Five Crops [same as in Yü Chou]

2. The *keng* soup formed the basis of a metaphoric discourse by a Chou philosopher-politician, supposed to have taken place in 521 B.C., as recorded in *Tso chuan*:

When the marquis of Ch'i returned from his hunt, Yen Tzu was in attendance on the platform of Ch'uan, and Tzu Yu (also known as Chü) drove up to it at full speed. The marquis said, "It is only Chü who is in harmony with me!" Yen Tzu replied, "Chü is an assenter; how can he be considered in harmony with you?" "Are they different," asked the marquis,—"harmony and assent?" Yen Tzu said, "They are different.

"Harmony may be illustrated by soup. You have the water and fire, vinegar, pickle, salt, and plums, with which to cook fish and meat. It is made to boil by the firewood, and then the cook mixes the ingredients, harmoniously equalizing the several flavours, so as to supply whatever is deficient and carry off whatever is in excess. Then the master eats it, and his mind is made equable.

"So it is in the relations of ruler and minister. When there is in what the ruler approves of anything that is not proper, the minister calls attention to that impropriety, so as to make the approval entirely correct. When there is in what the ruler disapproves of anything that is proper, the minister brings forward that propriety so as to remove occasion for the disapproval. In this way the government is made equal, with no infringement of what is right, and there is no quarrelling with it in the minds of the people. Hence it is said in the ode (*Shih* IV, iii, od. II),

> "There are also the well-tempered soups,
> Prepared beforehand, the ingredients rightly proportioned.
> By these offerings we invite his presence without a word;
> Nor is there now any contention in the service.

"As the ancient kings established the doctrine of the five flavours, so they made the harmony of the five notes, to make their minds equable and to perfect their government." [Trans. Legge 1872, p. 684]

Yen Tzu was not the only Chou philosopher who used cooking as a metaphor to convey deep thoughts. Chuang Tzu was another. He used the cutting skills of a cook to illuminate some fine points of the Tao (Lin and Lin 1969, p. 23).

3. The recipes are as follows in *Li chi*:

For the Rich Fry, they put the pickled meat fried over rice that had been grown on a dry soil, and then enriched it with melted fat. This was called the Rich Fry.

For the Similar Fry, they put the pickled meat fried over the millet grains, and enriched it with melted fat. This was called the Similar Fry.

For the Bake, they took a suckling-pig or a (young) ram, and having cut it open and removed the entrails, filled the belly with dates. They then wrapped it round with straw and reeds, which they plastered with clay, and baked it. When the clay was all dry, they broke it off. Having washed their hands for the manipulation, they removed the crackling and macerated it along with rice-flour, so as to form a kind of gruel which they added to the pig. They then fried the whole in such a quantity of melted fat as to cover it. Having prepared a large pan of hot water, they placed in it a small tripod, which was filled with fragrant herbs, and the slices of the creature which was being prepared. They took care that the hot water did not cover this tripod, but kept up the fire without intermission for three days and nights. After this, the whole was served up with the addition of pickled meat and vinegar.

For the Pounded Delicacy, they took the flesh of ox, sheep, elk, deer and muntjac, a part of that which lay along the spine, the same in quantity of each, and beat it now as it lay flat, and then turning it on its side; after that they extracted all the nerves. (Next), when it was sufficiently cooked, they·brought it (from the pan), took away the outside crust, and softened the meat (by the addition of pickle and vinegar).

For the Steeped Delicacy, they took the beef, which was required to be that of a newly killed animal, and cut it into small pieces, taking care to obliterate all the lines in it. It was then steeped from one morning to the next in good wine, when it was eaten with pickle, vinegar, or the juice of prunes.

To make the Grill, they beat the beef and removed the skinny parts. They then laid it on a frame of reeds, sprinkled on it pieces of cinnamon and ginger, and added salt. It could be eaten thus when dried. Mutton was treated in the same way as beef, and also the flesh of elk, deer, and muntjac. It they wished it dry, they ate it as eaten (at first).

For the (Soup) Balls, they took equal quantities of beef, mutton and pork, and cut them small. Then they took grains of rice, which they mixed with the finely cut meat, two parts of rice to one of meat, and formed cakes or balls, which they fried.

For the Liver and Fat, they took a dog's liver, and wrapped it round with its own fat. They wet it and roasted it, and took it in this condition and scorched it. No smartweed was mixed with the fat. [Trans. Legge 1885, pp. 468–70]

4. "He did not dislike to have his rice finely cleaned, nor to have his minced meat cut quite small. He did not eat rice which had been injured by heat or damp and turned sour, nor fish or flesh which was gone. He did not eat what was discoloured, or what was of a bad flavour, nor anything which was ill-cooked, or was not in season. He did not eat meat which was not cut properly, nor what was served without its proper sauce. . . . He did not partake of wine and dried meat bought in the market. He was never without ginger when he ate. He did not eat much." [Chap. "Hsiang Tang," *Lun yü*, trans. Legge 1893, pp. 468–70]

2: HAN

YING-SHIH YÜ

In 558 B.C. a nobleman of the Jung people told a Chinese statesman, "Our drink, our food, and our clothes are all different from those of the Chinese states" (*Tso chuan*, fourteenth year of Duke Hsiang). Thus, in one simple sentence this Jung nobleman of the Spring-Autumn period aptly distinguished the Chinese from the non-Chinese. Culture may sometimes be defined as a way of life. If so, can we think of anything more fundamental to a culture than eating and drinking? It is on this assumption that I shall attempt, in what follows, to understand the Han culture through a study of food and eating in Han China.[1]

Recently, some very distinguished anthropologists have embarked on the ambitious undertaking of finding universal food meanings common to all mankind. Being a historian by training I am far from qualified to play this new anthropologist's game. The central task I set for myself in this study is therefore confined primarily to finding out what sorts of food and drink were available to the Han Chinese and how they ate and drank them. Fortunately, in the last three or four years, Chinese archaeology has shed tremendous light on the Han culinary history. Important and interesting as they are, however, archaeological finds are not easy to use fruitfully. For one thing, they are extremely scattered. For another, they require a historical context to make them meaningful to us, who are some twenty centuries too late to eat and drink together with the Han Chinese. I shall not consider it a complete failure if my efforts in the pages that follow can provide no more than the beginnings of such a historical context. I reserve the intriguing and fascinating question of why the Han Chinese ate and drank in the way they did for those who are wiser and more learned.

Food and Foodstuffs Found in "Han Tomb No. 1 at Ma-wang-tui"

In 1972 China made a spectacular archaeological discovery on the eastern outskirts of Ch'ang-sha, Hunan, uncovering what is now known as "Han Tomb No. 1 at Ma-wang-tui." The worldwide renown of this discovery was earned initially on the basis of the owner of the tomb, whose body had been so remarkably preserved that her skin, muscles, and internal organs still retained a certain elasticity when the coffin was opened. Originally, this tomb was dated from between 175 and 145 B.C. Thanks to the excavation of Tombs No. 2 and No. 3 in 1973, however, the identity of the lady in this tomb can be more positively determined. She was most likely the wife of Li-ts'ang, the first Marquis of Tai (reigned 193–186 B.C.) and died a few years after 168 B.C. at about the age of fifty (Hunan Sheng 1974, 46–48). It has been rightly claimed that the preservation of the corpse in such an excellent condition over the long span of some twenty-one centuries must be regarded as a miracle in medical history. But what particularly interests us here is the extreme importance of the entire discovery for our knowledge of food and eating in Han China.

In the lady's esophagus, stomach, and intestines 138½ yellowish-brown musk melon seeds have been found, clearly indicating that she had eaten musk melons not too long before she joined her husband, who was buried in Tomb No. 2, which borders hers on the west side. Musk melon turned out to be only one of the many foodstuffs that she had enjoyed in life. Among the rich burial remains unearthed from Tomb No. 1 are forty-eight bamboo cases and fifty-one pottery vessels of various types. Most of them contained foodstuffs (figs. 17, 18). In addition, several hemp bags of agricultural products were also uncovered from the side compartments of the tomb chamber. All of these food remains have been identified and the whole list is as follows (Hunan Sheng 1973, 1:35–36):

Grains:	rice (*Oryza sativa* L.), wheat (*Triticum turgidum* L.), barley (*Hordeum vulgare* L.), glutinous millet (*Panicum miliaceum* Linn.), millet (*Setaria italica* [L.] Beauv.), soybean (*Glycine max* [L.] Merr.), red lentil (*Phaseolus angularis* Wight)
Seeds:	hemp (*Cannabis sativa* L.), malva (*Malva verticillata* L.) mustard (*Brassica cernua* Hemsl.)
Fruits:	pear (*Pyrus pyrifolia* Nakai), jujube (*Zizyphus jujuba* Mill. var. *inermis* [Bunge] Rehd.), plum (*Prunus mume* [Sieb.] Sieb. et Zucc.), strawberry (*Myrica rubra* Sieb. et Zucc.)
Roots:	ginger (*Zingiber officinale* Roscoe), lotus root
Animal Meats:	hare (*Lepus sinensis* Gray), dog (*Canis familiaris* Linn.), pig (*Sus scrofa domestica* Brisson), deer (*Cervus nippon* Temminck), ox (*Bos taurus domesticus* Gmelin), sheep (*Ovis aries* Linn.) (See also Y. T. Kao 1973, 76–78.)
Bird Meats:	wild goose (*Anser* sp.), mandarin duck (*Aix galericulata* L.), duck (Anatidae), bamboo chicken (*Bambusicola thoracica* Temminck), chicken (*Gallus gallus domesticus* Brisson), pheasant (*Phasianus colchicus* L.), crane (*Grus* sp.), pigeon (*Streptopelia* sp.), turtledove (*Oenopopelia tranquebarica* Temminck), owl (Strigidae), magpie (*Pica pica* L.), sparrow (*Passer montanus* L.)
Fish:	carp (*Cyprinus carpio* L.), crucian carp (*Carassius auratus* L.), bream (*Acanthobrama simoni* Bleeker), two other kinds of carp (*Xenocypris argeuteus* Günther and

Elopichthys bamausa Richardson), perch (*Spiniperca* sp.)

Spices: cinnamon bark (*Cinnamomum chekiangense* Nakai), *hua-chiao* ["fagara"] (*Zanthoxylum armatum* D.C. and *Z. planispinum* Sieb. et Zucc.), *hsing-i* (buds of the *Magnolia denudata* Desr.), galangal (*Alpinia officinal-rum* Hance)

Apart from food remains, there are also 312 inscribed bamboo slips which give additional information not only on food but on cooking as well. The slips itemize a number of foodstuffs which are not found among the remains. For instance, melon, bamboo shoots, taro, wild ginger, and goosefoot in the vegetable category, together with quail, wild duck, and eggs within the bird group. Altogether, these make a good supplementary list. More importantly, the slips tell us a lot about seasonings and methods used in Han-period cooking. The seasonings included salt, sugar, honey, soy sauce (*chiang*), *shih* ("salted darkened beans"), and leaven (*ch'ü*). Cooking and preserving methods consisted of roasting, scalding, shallow-frying, steaming, deep-frying, stewing, salting, sun-drying, and pickling.

A variety of dishes mentioned in these bamboo slips also merit attention. The first kind of dish to be noted is *keng* ("stew"), a thick liquid dish with chunks of meat or vegetables or both. The list of dishes begins with nine *ting* ("tripod cauldrons") of "Grand [meat] Stew" (Yü-keng or Ta-keng)[2] (fig. 19). Keng, it may be pointed out, was the most common kind of Chinese main dish from antiquity through the Han period. As will be shown below, while keng was characteristically made of mixed ingredients, the Ta-keng, or Grand Stew, alone was not. Han Confucianists, like the author of *Li chi* and Cheng Chung (first century A.D.), were all in agreement that the Ta-keng, whether as a sacrificial offering or as a dish for guests, should always be unseasoned in order to honor its simplicity (*Li chi*, 8:8a; cf. Legge 1967, 1:435. *Chou li Cheng chu*, 4:35). Wang Ch'ung (A.D. 27–100?) also said, "The Grand Stew must of necessity be flavorless" (C. Wang 1974 ed., p. 452, my translation). The nine Ta-keng listed on the bamboo slips are respectively made of ox, sheep, deer, pig, suckling pig, dog, wild duck, pheasant, and chicken.

The mixed keng was normally a seasoned combination of meat with grain or vegetables. Bamboo slip number 11 names *niu-pai-keng*, which has been correctly identified as "beef-rice stew" (Hunan Sheng 1973, pp. 131–32). It is important to note that meat-grain stew was a very common type of keng in Han times. Other keng mixtures recorded on the bamboo slips include the following: deer meat–salted fish–bamboo shoots, deer meat–taro, deer meat–small beans, chicken–gourd, crucian carp–rice, fresh sturgeon–salted fish–lotus root, dog meat–celery, crucian carp–lotus root, beef–turnip, lamb–turnip, pork–turnip, beef–sonchus (a wild grass), and dog meat–sonchus.

The bamboo slips also reveal how discriminating the Chinese taste had become in terms of the use of the various parts of different animals by the Han Chinese. The slips mentioned, among other things, deer flank, beef flank, dog flank, lamb flank, beef chuck, deer chuck, pork shoulder, beef stomach, lamb stomach, beef lips, beef tongue, beef lungs, and dog liver. Slip number 98 lists a pottery vessel of horse-meat sauce. No remains of horse have been found however (Y. T. Kao 1973, p. 78), although it is well known from literary sources that horse meat was a favorite dish in Han China. The only part of the horse that was inedible in Han times was the liver. Emperor Ching (reigned 156–141 B.C.), a contemporary of the owner of "Han Tomb No. 1 at Ma-wang-tui," once said, "No one accuses a man of lacking good taste in food because he eats other meats but refrains from eating horse liver" (*Shih chi* 1, p. 3123). Emperor Wu (reigned 140–87 B.C.) also told the court necromancer Luan Ta that Shao-weng, Luan's predecessor, had died, not because he was executed on an imperial order, but because "he happened to eat some horse liver" (*Shih chi* 1, p. 1390; trans. 1961, 2:46). True or false, in Han times it was generally believed that horse liver was deadly poisonous. The absence of horse liver in the extensive food lists from the tombs helps confirm that this was a popular belief.

According to a preliminary report on the two other Han tombs at Ma-wang-tui, similar food remains and food lists have also been found in Tomb No. 3. Grains and meats are essentially the same as those of Tomb No. 1. However, some additional fruits have been identified, such as orange, persimmon, and water caltrops (Hunan Sheng 1974, p. 45). It must be emphasized that to date the excavation of these Han tombs at Ma-wang-tui is the single most important archaeological contribution to the study of food and eating in Han China.

What makes the Ma-wang-tui discovery doubly interesting is the amazing degree to which the food list from Tomb No. 1 agrees with the list given in the "Nei tse" ("Internal [Family] Regulations") chapter of *Li chi*. Virtually all the foodstuffs and prepared dishes listed above can be found in that chapter (*Li chi*, 8:19a–21b; Legge 1967, 1:459–63). But for well over twenty centuries, the food list in the "Nei tse" chapter had remained a regulation on paper, which, like a drawing of a cake, as the Chinese proverb goes, can hardly satisfy our hunger. It was the archaeological finds at Ma-wang-tui that finally transformed the regulation into a reality.

Kitchen Scenes in Han Mural Paintings and Stone Reliefs

Recent archaeology adds still another important dimension to the study of food and eating in Han China. By this I refer particularly to the discovery of many kitchen and feast scenes in mural paintings and stone reliefs in Han tombs. Han literature, especially poetry and *fu* ("prose-poetry"), often contains descriptions of kitchen and feast scenes, but none of them can compare in vividness and vitality with the scenes shown in the murals and reliefs. In this section and the next, I shall discuss such scenes in paintings and stone reliefs from several Han tombs, while, at the same time, introducing additional archaeological and literary evidence to supplement my discussion.

A very elaborate kitchen scene (fig. 9) has been found among the mural stone reliefs of a Han tomb at Ta-hu-t'ing in Mi-hsien, Honan, excavated from 1960–61 (C. H. An and Y. K. Wang 1972, p. 61). The scene shows ten people working in the kitchen. In the upper middle of the picture, one man is stirring meat which is cooking in a huge ting (cauldron). On the other side of the ting, a man is carrying firewood toward the stove in the upper right-hand corner. Another man to the side of the stove seems to be cooking something over the stove. Left of the center of the picture, two persons appear to be walking out of the kitchen, the one in front holding a dish of fish, the other carrying a round tray with drinking cups and other food-serving vessels on it. In the lower left-hand corner stands a large-sized *fu* ("pot") in which it looks as if keng is being made since the man to the side of the fu is using a long-handled ladle, possibly to spoon the keng out of the fu. Facing him, toward the lower center of the picture, is another man in a squatting position washing or mixing something in a basin with his left hand while he gestures with his right hand. It looks as if the squatting man is showing the man with the ladle where to put the keng. Behind the squatting man and to the right, a man is working with both hands in a big container. Finally, to the lower right there is a well with a wooden frame over it, from which suspends a well bucket. Between the well and a large jar to the right stands a man who is drawing water from the well, and on the other side of the jar, a man holding a basin is coming to fill it with water.

In addition to the activities described above, this lively tableau also reveals other things about a Han kitchen. For instance, it gives us a picture of the various types of Han food vessels and utensils, which are scattered throughout the picture, and their uses. What is even more interesting are the two meat racks, from which different kinds of meat are hanging, in the upper left corner. Although the meats are not readily identifiable, they definitely range from birds to animals. Right beneath the two racks, however, we can clearly see an ox head and an ox leg lying on the ground.

Another important kitchen scene comes from a mural-painted tomb of late Later Han date, situated in Pang-t'ai-tzu in the northwestern suburb of the city Liao-yang (in southern Manchuria). This tomb was first discovered by the villagers in the autumn of 1944, but no detailed account of it was given until 1955 (W. H. Li 1955). In the summer of 1945, the tomb and its mural paintings became known to a group of Japanese, skilled copiers in Liao-yang who, however, named it the Tung-wa-yao-tzu tomb. The Japanese group had made copies of the paintings, but unfortunately they were not able to make the fruits of their long months of labor known to the scholarly world as they left Manchuria empty-handed after the end of World War II (W. Fairbank 1972, pp. 146–47, 174–78). Thus far, no copy of the kitchen scene from the Pang-t'ai-tzu tomb has been produced. The following discussion is based entirely on Li Wen-hsin's report and line drawings.

The cooking operation in this kitchen scene (fig. 10) is on a scale even larger than that of the Ta-hu-t'ing tomb described just above. Altogether, twenty-two people are shown working in the kitchen. Unlike the scene from the Ta-hu-t'ing tomb in which the cooks and helpers are all men, the present scene includes at least four women. The women's jobs look less strenuous, however, compared to the activities of the eighteen men in the kitchen. For instance, one woman is about to take a vessel from the stove while another takes one from a cabinet. The other two are sitting on the ground apparently doing some kind of light work. By contrast, the men's jobs, such as meat roasting, food mixing, or pounding some sort of food into pulp, require either skill or greater physical strength. The range of different tasks here is also much wider than in the scene from Ta-hu-t'ing. The chores vary from butchering an ox or a pig to removing duck's feathers.

Like the Ta-hu-t'ing scene, meats are also shown hanging from a wooden rack in the kitchen. But in this case, the various meats are so well painted that most of them are recognizable. According to Li Wen-hsin, they are, from left to right, turtle, animal head, goose, pheasants, birds (of unknown kind), monkey, animal heart and lungs, suckling pig, dried fish, and fresh fish. Each is hung on an iron hook which seems firmly nailed to the rack. This kind of meat rack, it may be noted, must have been very common in the Han kitchen since at least five iron meat hooks have recently been found in a Han tomb in Honan (Honan Sheng 1973, pp. 47–48).

There is another kind of meat holder in this kitchen scene from the Pang-t'ai-tzu tomb which has not yet been found in other Han mural paintings. It is a high pole with two horizontal rods near the top. On these rods are hung meat strips, intestines (possibly sausages), stomachs, and so on. The rods are up so high that a man is shown using a long-handled hook to reach the food. Meats were placed this high, understandably, in order to prevent land creatures, such as dogs, from getting them. To illustrate this point, right below the pole we find a dog, undoubtedly with watering mouth, depicted gazing up at the meats on the rods.

Similar kitchen scenes have been discovered in other mural-painted Han tombs, especially in Liao-yang, such as San-tao-hao clay pits No. 2 and No. 4 (fig. 11), and San-tao-hao Tomb No. 1 (W. H. Li 1955; Tung-pei 1955, pp. 52–54). In the famous Han stone reliefs of Wu Liang Tz'u and the I-nan tomb (both in Shantung) kitchen scenes are also present (Shinoda 1974, p. 49; Hua-tung 1954, p. 41; Tseng *et al.* 1956, pp. 20–21, pl. 48). Particularly worth mentioning are two such scenes found in Inner Mongolia. In May 1956 a Han tomb rich with mural paintings was excavated in T'o-k'e-t'o *hsien* (county), Inner Mongolia, the first of its kind ever found in that region. A kitchen scene is painted on the rear, left, and front walls of the left chamber. Illustrated in the scene are containers, a stove, a black pig, a yellow dog, two chickens, and a meat rack, on which are hung a pair of pheasants, a piece of meat, a pair of fish, a pair of chickens, and a piece of beef (F. I. Lo 1956, p. 43). Recently, in 1972, another important mural-painted Han tomb was found in Ho-lin-ko-erh (Suiyuan). The kitchen scene there (fig. 13) shows people cooking and drawing water, as well as a meat rack on which hang such foodstuffs as an animal head, intestines, fish, meat, pheasant, and hare (Nei Meng-Ku 1974, p. 11; Museum of Fine Arts, North Kyūshū 1974, pl. 19; Anonymous 1974, pl. 26). The two scenes described here are almost identical with those found in Liao-yang, Honan, and Shantung. One is very tempted to say that in Han China the upper-class kitchen setup was more or less standardized, whether in inland China, such as Honan and Shantung, or in the frontier region, such as Manchuria and Inner Mongolia.

Hanging meats on a wooden rack or beam, for instance, was a universal practice in Han times. A painted brick from Szechuan (fig. 12) (H. T. Ho 1958, p. 96) and a newly discovered mural painting from Chia-yü Kuan, Kansu (fig. 14) (Chia-yü Kuan Shih 1972, p. 40, fig. 34), both show cooking scenes in which a meat rack is in a dominant position. It was the sight of meats hanging from a rack that gave rise to the descriptive term "meat forest" (*jou lin*) (*Han shu*, 61:76). But this practice apparently had a pre-Han origin, for Ssu-ma Ch'ien already spoke of Chou, the last king of Shang, as having "hung meats to make a forest" (*hsüan-jou wei lin*) (*Shih chi* 2, 3:11a). On the whole, from Han mural paintings discovered in various places, one can hardly detect any regional differences in terms of foodstuffs and cooking utensils. It is particularly interesting to note that animal meats of the three major categories (land, air, and water) which are shown hung on the racks basically tally with the list of meats found in the Ma-wang-tui Tomb No. 1.

There is, however, one interesting feature of the Han kitchen that has not yet been found in kitchen scenes in mural paintings, namely, an ice chamber, which had been in use since antiquity (N. H. Lin 1957, pp. 136–37). According to Wang Ch'ung, Han Chinese broke ice in winter to make an "ice chamber" (*ping shih*) for food storage. How to keep food, especially meat, cold so that it would not spoil must have been a problem that bothered Han Chinese constantly. Wang Ch'ung further reports that some imaginative scholars even dreamed up a kind of "meat fan" in the kitchen which would automatically make wind to keep food cool (C. Wang 1974 ed., p. 268).

Han Feasts in Painting and in Reality

Feast scenes are even more numerous in Han mural paintings than kitchen scenes (figs. 20–25). For convenience, we again begin our discussion with a scene from the Ta-hu-t'ing tomb and then will bring in other archaeological and historical evidence to amplify it.

The scene (fig. 20) unfolds from the middle with a man sitting on a very low, rectangular, presumably wooden couch (*t'a*), which has screens both to the back and to the sitter's right.[3] In all likelihood, the man on the couch is the host. To his right, we see a seated guest looking in the direction of the host; on the host's left-hand side, two guests sit together and are apparently engaged in polite conversation. The guests are sitting on mats instead of couches. At the right end of the scene behind the host, a servant is ushering in two more guests. In addition, four manservants are represented serving drinks and food.

In front of the host's couch, there is a low, rectangular serving table, known as *an* in Han times. On the table are placed wine cups and dishes. This kind of long table seems to have been specially made to match the size of the wooden couch. Two identical screened couches with tables of matching size can be found in mural paintings from San-tao-hao Tomb No. 4. Very interestingly, a writing brush is clearly shown to be sticking into one of the San-tao-hao tables (W. H. Li 1955, p. 30, figs. 18–20). It seems safe to conclude that a table matching a screened couch was not made exclusively for serving food and drink. It was also used as a sort of writing desk. Ordinary food-serving tables are much smaller in size, such as the ones placed before the guests in this feast scene. This explains why the virtuous lady Meng Kuang was able "to raise the table as high as her eyebrows" each time she served a meal to her husband, Liang Hung (*Hou Han shu*, 83 : 14a). Generally speaking, Han food-serving tables are of two shapes, round and rectangular (sometimes square). When not being used, they are piled up in the kitchen, as shown in the kitchen scene from Pang-t'ai-tzu and by earthware tables found stacked in this manner at Shao-kou, Lo-yang (W. H. Li 1955, p. 27, fig. 14; Lo-yang Ch'ü 1959, pp. 137–39, fig. 64, pl. 35). If the table was round, it was called *ch'iung* (S. Hsü 1969 ed., p. 122; H. Y. Ch'ü 1937, p. 131).

We do not know what the occasion was for this feast in the Ta-hu-t'ing scene. The owner of the tomb has been tentatively identified as Chang Po-ya, governor of Hung-nung in Honan during the Later Han dynasty. Possibly the scene shows one of the feasts he gave to his subordinates in the governor's mansion. At any rate, the host in this scene occupies a central position, perhaps the seat of honor. Such a seating arrangement was quite logical for a governor and his subordinates in Han China. A similar seating arrangement is also discernible in feast scenes in stone reliefs from the famous Han shrine at Hsiao-t'ang Shan, Shantung (K. Lao 1939, p. 100).

The Ta-hu-t'ing scene shows only the beginning of a feast. Thus, in the painting, only drinks are being served and no food is visible. We must therefore turn to some of the recorded historical feasts for more concrete knowledge as to what constituted a "feast" in Han times. The best-known feast during this period is "The Banquet at Hung-men" which took place in 206 B.C. Before coming to that great historical event, however, let us first introduce a Han mural painting which has been identified by Kuo Mo-jo as the artistic representation of the Banquet at Hung-men. The painting, which is done in vermilion, green, blue, yellow, and brown, comes from an Earlier Han tomb excavated at Lo-yang in 1957. The tomb has been dated from between 48 and 7 B.C. Since all the mural-painted Han tombs we know are of Later Han date, this one can surely claim to be the oldest tomb with mural paintings ever found in China (Honan Sheng 1964, pp. 107–25, pl. 2; Anonymous 1974, pls. 2, 3).

A synopsis of Kuo Mo-jo's explanation of the painting is as follows: The back wall of the chamber is decorated with scenes depicting the story of the Banquet at Hung-men. On the right side of the design, a man is shown broiling a joint of beef over a stove, while another man with a staff stands by watching. The wall behind the people is hung with joints of beef and an ox head. To the left of the stove, two men are shown seated on the floor and drinking. The one holding a drinking horn probably represents Hsiang Yü, while the other, who is more elegant in appearance, represents Liu Pang. The man standing by the side of Liu Pang represents Hsiang Po. A huge seated tiger to the left of Liu Pang is actually a design painted on a door. Two men standing with folded hands to the left of the tiger design represent Chang Liang and Fan Tseng. A fierce-looking man with a sword in his hand who is about to stab Liu Pang represents Hsiang Chuang (M. J. Kuo 1964, p. 6).

There can be no doubt that the scene depicts a feast held in a military camp. However, that it is a description of the Banquet at Hung-men is debatable. A full and lively account of the Banquet is given by the Grand Historian in the *Shih chi*, as follows:

Hsiang Yu invited Liu Pang to stay for a banquet. He and Hsiang Po sat facing east, the patriarch Fan Tseng faced south, Liu Pang faced north, and Chang Liang, who was in attendance upon him, faced west. Several times Fan Tseng shot Hsiang Yu meaningful glances and three times, as a hint, raised his jade *chueh*. But Hsiang Yu did not respond. Finally Fan Tseng rose and went out. Summoning Hsiang Chuang, he said:

"Our lord is too kindhearted. Go in, drink a toast, and offer to perform a sword dance. Then strike the lord of Pei [Liu Pang] down where he sits. If you don't do this, we will all end up his captives."

Hsiang Chuang went in to offer a toast, after which he said, "Our prince is drinking with the lord of Pei, but we have no entertainers in the army. May I perform a sword dance ?"

"Very well," said Hsiang Yu.

Hsiang Chuang drew his sword and began the dance, and Hsiang Po followed suit, shielding Liu Pang with his body so that Hsiang Chuang could not strike him.

Chang Liang went out to the gate of the camp to see Fan Kuai, who asked, "How are things in there?"

"Touch and go," replied Chang Liang. "Hsiang Chuang has drawn his sword to dance. He means to kill the lord of Pei."

"This is serious?" said Fan Kuai. "Let me go in and have it out with him."

Sword and shield in hand he entered the gate. Guards with crossed halberds tried to bar the way, but he charged and knocked them down with his tilted shield. Bursting into the tent, he lifted the curtain and stood facing west, glaring at Hsiang Yu. His hair bristled, his eyes nearly started from his head. Hsiang Yu raised himself on one knee and reached for his sword.

"Who is this stranger?" he asked.

"This is the lord of Pei's bodyguard, Fan Kuai," answered Chang Liang.

"Stout fellow!" said Hsiang Yu. "Give him a stoup of wine."

Wine was poured and presented to Fan Kuai, who bowed his thanks and straightened up to drink it standing.

"Give him a leg of pork," directed Hsiang Yu.

A raw leg of pork was given to Fan Kuai, who set his shield upside down on the ground, placed the pork on it, carved it with his sword and began to eat.

"Stout fellow!" cried Hsiang Yu. "Can you drink any more?"

"I am not afraid of death; why should I refuse a drink?" retorted Fan Kuai. . . .

Hsiang Yu could not answer.

"Sit down," he said.

Fan Kuai took a seat next to Chang Liang. Presently Liu Pang got up and went out to the privy, beckoning Fan Kuai to go with him [*Shih chi*, trans. Yang and Yang 1974, pp. 218–19]

Checking this account against the mural painting, we immediately find that there are more discrepancies than correspondences between the two pieces. The seating arrangement and the absence of Fan Kuai in the painting are very difficult to explain if the story is about the Banquet at Hung-men. The fierce man at the left end whom Kuo takes to be Hsiang Chuang looks more like Fan Kuai in the Grand Historian's description. But then, Hsiang Chuang would be missing from the scene. Moreover, both Hsiang Chuang and Hsiang Po are supposed to be performing a sword dance together in the banquet.

Identification of the feast scene in the Lo-yang mural painting is not our main concern here, however. What particularly interests us is the light the Banquet at Hung-men throws on our understanding of a Han feast. The first thing to be noted is the seating arrangement of the banquet, which is recorded in the *Shih chi* but not in the *Han shu*. As we have seen above, in this banquet Hsiang Yü and his uncle Hsiang Po sat facing east. Hsiang Yü thus shared the seat of honor with his uncle. Evidence reveals beyond a doubt that the seat facing east was the place of honor at a Han feast. Take the following case of T'ien Fen, prime minister under Emperor Wu's reign, as an example: One day T'ien Fen invited guests to a drinking party and made his elder brother, the marquis of Kai, sit facing south while he took the place of honor facing east. He explained that family etiquette must not be allowed to detract from the prime minister's dignity (ibid., p. 361).[4] Moreover, in 32 B.C., the prime minister K'uang Heng was also accused of having violated the rules of propriety by assigning the east-facing seat of honor to one of his subordinates during an official banquet (*Han shu* 76:25a). It must be pointed out that this particular rule was not a Han invention but traceable to at least the late Chou period (P. H. Shang 1938, pp. 283–84). The seating arrangement at the Banquet at Hung-men was therefore definitely a meaningful one. It conveys the important message that Liu Pang had actually accepted Hsiang Yü as his superior. This perhaps explains why Hsiang Yü no longer had the heart to do away with Liu Pang after everyone had taken his seat at the banquet. Indeed, the way of eating could also become a subtle political art.

Another observation I wish to make about this historical banquet concerns the cooking of meat. The feast scene from the Lo-yang mural-painted tomb shows a man broiling (or roasting) a joint of beef on a stove. The rectangular-shaped four-legged stove was possibly painted after the model of an iron one as was found in the immediately neighboring Han cemetery at Shao-kou (Lo-yang Ch'ü 1959, pl. 58, figs. 3, 4). Interestingly enough, the whole operation in the painting strikes the modern eye very much as a scene of an outdoor open-fire barbecue. But perhaps it would not be too farfetched if we take this portion of the mural painting to be suggestive of the way meat was cooked for the Banquet at Hung-men. It may be recalled that Fan Kuai had been given a raw, uncut, leg of pork to eat. It is not inconceivable that the "raw" pork leg was but a half-way or even less than half-way broiled piece of meat not ready for serving. Hsiang Yü's order was given so suddenly that the cook simply had no time to finish the broiling. A careful reader of the textual account would agree that the chain of events, from Hsiang Yü's giving the order to Fan Kuai's eating the leg of pork, makes much better sense if the food was prepared right in the feasting place, as shown in the afore-mentioned painting. After all, we must remember, the banquet took place in a wartime military camp. Furthermore, broiled or roasted meat was a prized dish for the Han Chinese. Chia I (d. 169 B.C.), for instance, included it in his proposed menu for Han restaurants on the border in order to attract the Hsiung-nu to China's side. In his optimistic estimation, "When the Hsiung-nu have developed a craving for our cooked rice, keng stew, roasted meats, and wine, this will have become their fatal weakness" (I. Chia 1937 ed., 4:41). Roasted or broiled meat also has been found in a mural-painted tomb of late Later Han date at Chia-yü Kuan, Kansu. In this case, however, the meat is cut into small pieces skewered on a three-pronged fork, ready for serving (Chia-yü Kuan Shih, p. 25, pl. 7, fig. 1, and fig. 34 on p. 40).

Finally, in the Banquet of Hung-men, Hsiang Chuang made the excuse to perform a sword dance by saying "We have no entertainment in the army." Thus he introduces us to another component of a Han feast: entertainment. A formal Han feast was often, though not always, accompanied by amusements of various kinds, including music, dance, and acrobatics.

As a matter of fact, in many of the Han mural paintings and stone reliefs the feast scene includes diversions of some sort as an integral part. Archaeologically, this point can be vividly illustrated by the recent discovery of a whole set of figurines in an earlier Han tomb at Wu-ying Shan, Tsinan. The figurines may be conveniently divided into four different groups: two girls dancing face to face, four men performing acrobatics, two girls and five men playing music, and three gentlemen drinking together while enjoying the show (Chinan Shih 1972, pp. 19–24). Ordinarily, however, it was music and dance that went together with a feast in Han times. In literature, both Fu I's and Chang Heng's fu entitled "Dance" clearly indicate that a formal banquet is usually accompanied by music and dance (K. C. Yen 1958 ed., pp. 705–06, 769). Chang Heng provides us with even more specific information about the order of such performances in a feast. According to him, when music begins, wine will be served, and when the drinkers become intoxicated, beautiful girls will then rise to perform dances. Even at an informal dinner party, musical entertainment was sometimes present. Chang Yü (d. 5 B.C.) often brought his favorite student, Tai Ch'ung, to the inner hall for drink and food in the company of a band (*Han shu*, 81:14a).

Feast scenes in Han mural paintings can only provide us with a skeleton of a Han feast in real life. Historical records are also, as a rule, silent about the sorts of food and drink that were offered and how. Therefore, for the flesh and blood, so to speak, of a Han feast, we must turn to the descriptive literary pieces. But here we run into difficulties of another nature: many of the foods mentioned in such literary pieces are only names to us today. This is the case with names from about a dozen or so fu by Han writers from Mei Ch'eng (second century B.C.) to Hsü Kan (early third century A.D.).

I have found that, among the recognizable items, the following are often mentioned as foodstuffs or prepared dishes in a Han feast:[5]

Meats:	beef flank, fatted dog, bear's paw, panther's breast, suckling pig, deer meat, lamb shoulder.
Birds:	baked owl, wild duck stew, sparrow broth, roasted wild goose, chicken, snow goose, crane.
Fish:	finely minced fresh carp, perch (from Lake Tung-t'ing), turtle stew, boiled turtle.
Vegetables:	bamboo shoots, edible rush shoots, leeks, turnips.
Spices:	ginger, cinnamon, fagara.
Fruits:	litchi, pear, hazelnuts, melon, orange, apricot.
Seasonings:	peony sauce, salt, plum sauce, meat sauce, sugar, honey, vinegar.

Needless to say, the above list is by no means an exhaustive one, but it does give us some idea of the sorts of foods the Han Chinese usually enjoyed in a feast.

A few supplementary remarks are necessary to make the list more meaningful, however. First, cooking methods mentioned include stewing, boiling, frying, roasting, baking, steaming and pickling. The mixture of the "five flavors" (bitter, sour, hot, salty, sweet) to achieve "harmony" was also considered to be fundamental to the art of cooking. In this respect, cooking in Han China was more traditional than innovative. However, the art of cutting seems to have been stressed more emphatically than previously. Several Later Han writers speak of mincing and slicing fish and meat to the thinnest degree as a built-in feature of fine food. In fact, as we shall see later, there were also significant new developments in the history of food and cooking during the Han period. It would be wrong to assume that Han Chinese simply followed the eating tradition of classical antiquity.

Second, as always, grain food is ever present in the Han literary descriptions of a feast. Rice (both ordinary and glutinous) and millet (especially *liang, Setaria italica* Beauv. var. *maxima* Al.) are particularly praised as being delicious. We can therefore assume that they were preferred to other kinds of grain available.

Third, wine is by definition an indispensable part of the feast. A second century B.C. writer, Tsou Yang, in his fu on wine distinguishes between the two alcoholic beverages *li* and *chiu* and, further, says that wines are manufactured from rice and wheat (H. Ko 1937 ed., 4:4a–5b). The li and chiu contrast is also found in Chang Heng's "Ch'i pien," where we are told that chiu is dark in color whereas li is white (K. C. Yen 1958 ed., p. 775). In the early Earlier Han dynasty, a Confucian scholar named Mu, at the court of Prince Yüan of Ch'u, did not like chiu, so the prince always prepared li for him at a feast. According to the T'ang commentator Yen Shih-ku, li tastes sweet. It is manufactured with less "starter" (*chü*) and more rice than are required for the preparation of chiu (*Han shu*, 36:26). Since antiquity, both li and chiu were put in two separate *tsun* beakers during a feast (*I li*, "Hsiang-yin-chiu li"). This practice was still followed in the Han period. As a Later Han song says, "[For] entertaining guests in the north hall . . . there are two tsun containers, one for clear (*chiu*), and the other for white (*li*) (M. C. Kuo 1955 ed., vol. 2, chüan 37, p.2). On the other hand, chiu (or *ch'ing-chiu*, "clear wine") seems to have been a more popular beverage. Conceivably, chiu is much stronger than li. The Later Han dictionary *Shih-ming* tells us that li could be made overnight (Liu Hsi 1939 ed., p. 66), while according to Chia Ssu-hsieh of the sixth century, the fermentation of clear wine is a very complicated process and therefore takes a much longer time (S. H. Shih 1958, 3:460–62).

In the two Man-ch'eng tombs (in Hopei) of Earlier Han date, altogether thirty-three pottery wine jars were found in 1968. Several of the jars bear inscriptions describing such wines as "*Shu* [glutinous panicled millet] wine", "Sweet *lao*", "Rice wine", and "Shu wine of *shang-tsun* quality" (Chung-Kuo 1972:14). Li wine made from wheat is also mentioned in Ts'ai Yung's letter to Yüan Shao in the early third century A.D. (K. C. Yen 1958 ed., p. 872). Thus we know that wines in Han times were made from virtually all kinds of grain, including rice, millet, and wheat (see also S. H. Shih 1962, p. 81).

The term *shang-tsun* needs a word of explanation. According to a Han law quoted by Ju-shun, wine made from rice is classified as *shang-tsun* (upper grade), wine made from *chi* (*Setaria italica* Beauv. var. *maxima* Al.) is *chung-tsun* (middle grade), and wine made from *su* (*P. miliaceum*) is *hsia-tsun* (lower grade). But Yen Shih-ku believes that the grade of wine had nothing to do with the kind of cereal from which it was made. Rather, the grade of wine in Han times was determined by the degree of its thickness: the thicker the wine, the better its quality (*Han shu*, 71:12b). Now, with the discovery of the inscription "Shu wine of shang-tsun quality" from tombs of none other than Prince [Liu] Sheng of Chung-shan and his wife, it seems that Yen Shih-ku's theory is correct after all.

We have found out, above, what sorts of food and drink were commonly available at a Han feast. It is now time that we try to reconstruct the relative order in which food and drink were served to the guests. First, wine would be offered to the guests. This is not only indicated in the above-quoted song of the Later Han period, it also is shown in the Banquet at Hung-men. It may be recalled that Fan Kuai was first given a cup of wine and then a leg of pork. After this initial wine serving, keng (stew) would be the opening dish of the feast. The *I li* says that "When keng is ready, then the host asks the guests to take their seats" (*I li,* p. 89; my translation). Ying Shao of the second century A.D. also reports that, in his day, shu-meat stew was always the first dish presented to the guests in a feast (K. C. Yen 1958 ed., p. 680). After keng, other dishes, if any, would follow. We are reasonably sure that grain food was the last to be served. The Later Han song quoted above further reveals that toward the end of the feast the host would hurry the kitchen to prepare grain food (lit. "rice") so that guests might not be detained too long (M. C. Kuo 1955 ed., chüan 37, 1b). Han Chinese, like their descendants today, considered a meal incomplete if grain food of some kind were not offered. Thus, Ko Kung of the early second century A.D. found it necessary to write apologetically to a friend about the fact that when the latter visited him some evening before he had only shrimp to offer and no grain food (K. C. Yen 1958 ed., p. 780).

Finally, at the end of the meal, fruit would be presented to the guests, perhaps not as a part of the meal, but in the sense of the Western dessert. Wang Ch'ung, for instance, considers it the correct order of eating when he comments on the story that Confucius had eaten millet first and peach later (C. Wang 1974 ed., p. 451). Fu I (early second century A.D.) also makes it very clear in his "Ch'i Chi" when he describes that pears from Yung Chou are offered after the meal (K. C. Yen 1958 ed., p. 706). But the end of a feast may not have been necessarily the end of eating and drinking. According to Ying Shao, sometimes it happened that when the feast was finished the host still wanted to continue drinking with his guests. In such cases, it was already too late for the kitchen to prepare any fresh food, so dried meat and fish seasoned with fagara, ginger, salt, and *shih* ("salted darkened beans") were served instead (K. C. Yen 1958 ed., p. 676). This story seems to indicate that as early as the Later Han period Chinese had already developed the habit of always having some kind of food when drinking wine.

To conclude our discussion of the Han feast, let us quote a passage from the famous "Contract for a slave" ("T'ung-yüeh") by Wang Pao of the first century B.C. The "Contract," dated 59 B.C., is a semi-humorous account of Wang Pao's purchase of a bearded slave named Pien-liao at Ch'eng-tu, Szechwan. Among the numerous household tasks Wang Pao assigned to the slave was to prepare feasts for guests. The "Contract" says:

> When there are guests in the house he [the slave] shall carry a kettle and go after wine; draw water and prepare the evening meal; wash bowls and arrange food trays; pluck garlic from the garden; chop vegetables and mince meat; pound meat and make stew of tubers; slice fish and roast turtle; boil tea and fill the utensils. [Trans. Wilbur 1943, p. 385, with minor alterations]

The passage speaks for itself. The only point to be briefly noted is whether or not tea was already in use in China this early (Wilbur 1943, p. 391, n. 19). However, based on various pieces of literary evidence including the "Contract," Ku Yen-wu came to the conclusion that tea drinking had begun in the Szechwan region even before the Han dynasty (Y. W. Ku 1929 ed., 3: 55–57). The spread of tea drinking as a habit to the rest of China, especially the north, probably came much later (S. M. Lü 1948, 2:1136–37).

Food and Eating in Everyday Life

Because of the nature of the evidence at my disposal, I have thus far confined my discussion of food and eating in Han China to the upper classes. Food remains and food lists from Ma-wang-tui, kitchen and feast scenes from various mural-painted tombs, the historic Banquet at Hung-men, the numerous delicacies described in a mouth-watering fashion by men of letters—all these belonged exclusively to the rich and the powerful who constituted but a small fraction of the sixty million Han Chinese. Now I must try to find out what sorts of foods were generally available to the great majority of people in their everyday life during the Han period. This is easier said than done since historical records and archaeological finds normally reflect the life of people of at least some means. Moreover, it is also desirable at times to bring the well-to-do into the discussion which follows both for contrast and comparison.

Grain was the main food for the Han Chinese, as it still is for Chinese today. What then were the major categories of grain that were cultivated in Han China? The Han Chinese, following the ancients, often talked about "five grains," "six grains," "eight grains," or "nine grains." But scholars from Han times down to the present have never come to a complete agreement as to the identification of these grains (S. H. Ch'i 1949, pp. 266–69). Thanks to recent archaeological discoveries, however, we are now on a much more solid ground to determine the staple grains on which the Han Chinese lived, philological confusion notwithstanding.

As listed at the beginning of this study, the following grain remains were uncovered in the Han Tomb No. 1 at Ma-wang-tui: rice, wheat, barley, two kinds of millet, soybean, and red lentil. With the exception of red lentil, all have long been included, one way or another, in the identification lists of traditional exegetes and philologists. Grain remains have also been found elsewhere. At Shao-kou (northwestern outskirts of Lo-yang), a total of 983 earthenware grain containers were unearthed in 1953 from 145 tombs datable from middle Earlier Han to late Later Han. Found in many of the containers are grain remains of the following: millets of various kinds (*P. miliaceum* Linn., *Setaria italica* Beauv. var. *maxima* Al., spiked millet, etc.), hemp, soybean, rice, and Job's tears (*Coix lacryma-jobi*). Moreover, most of the containers bear inscribed labels indicating the food content of each. In addition to the grains just given above, we also find the following names: wheat, barley, bean, lesser bean, hulled white rice, and others (Lo-yang Ch'ü 1959, pp. 112–13, table 26). The rice remains from Shao-kou, it is interesting to note, were analyzed by a Japanese expert and turned out to be closer to the Indian rice, *Oryza sativa* var. *indica* (Nakao 1957). In 1957 more such inscribed grain containers with remains were discovered at another Lo-yang site, at Chin-ku-yüan village (S. P. Huang 1958). Based on these archaeological finds, we can now say with confidence that the major categories of grain generally accessible to the Chinese in Han times included millets of various kinds, rice, wheat, barley, soybeans, lesser beans, and hemp. It is particularly noteworthy that this archaeological list matches very closely the "nine grains" recorded in the agriculturist book by Fan Sheng-chih of the first century B.C. (S. H. Shih 1959a, pp. 8–11). Unlike Han exegetes such as Cheng Hsing and Cheng Hsüan, whose knowledge of agriculture was mainly bookish, Fan was a professional agriculturist and had actually taught people in the vicinity of Ch'ang-an the art of farming (S. H. Shih 1959a, pp. 42–44).

It is almost superfluous to say that not all these grain foods were equally available in all parts of Han China. Since antiquity, various kinds of millet had been the grain staple in north China, whereas rice had been the main starch food for southern Chinese. This situtation seems to have continued well into the Han period. Moreover, we have reasons to believe that, on the whole, Han China produced much more millet than rice (S. H. Ch'i 1949, pp. 304–05). According to the *Huai-nan Tzu,* only water from the Yangtze River was suitable for rice cultivation (W. T. Liu 1974, 4:10a). Pan Ku, in the geographical section of his book *Han shu,* also singles out Szechwan and the Ch'u region (mainly Hunan and Hupei) as the two major rice-producing areas (*Han shu,* 28b:20a, 33b–34a). This point has been borne out recently by archaeological excavations. In 1973 a group of nine tombs of early Earlier Han date was excavated at Feng-huang-shan, in Chiang-ling, Hupei. From tombs 8, 9, and 10, food remains of various kinds and over 400 inscribed bamboo slips were found. The remains include rice, melon seeds, kernels of fruits, eggs, millet, chestnuts, and vegetable seeds. Many of the bamboo slips also yield information on grain (Ch'ang-chiang 1974, pp. 41–54). The slips record rice, glutinous rice, millet, wheat, beans, and hemp. Judging by the number of slips and quantity of the remains, it seems safe to conclude that rice and millet, but especially the former, were the grain staples of this area during the Han (S. C. Huang 1974, pp. 76–77). By contrast, it is interesting to note that millet of various kinds comes in much greater quantities than rice from the Shao-kou tombs in Lo-yang (Lo-yang Ch'ü 1959, pp. 112–13). Allowing for this geographical difference between the north and the south, it still may not be too farfetched to say that millet by and large was more common than rice as the main grain food in Han China. In antiquity, rice had been regarded as an expensive and delicious grain food even by nobility. There is no evidence to suggest that the situation had undergone a drastic change under the Han dynasty.

Next to rice and millet in popularity were wheat, barley, soybeans, and hemp. A word about hemp first. It is common knowledge that hemp fiber provided the basic material for manufacturing cloth in traditional China. But hemp seed proved to be edible also, and for that reason it was often classified by the ancients as a "grain." The *Yen-t'ieh lun* reports that the early Han Confucian scholar Pao-ch'iu Tzu had hempseed for his grain food

(K. Huan 1974 ed., p. 41; for Pao-ch'iu Tzu, see P. C. Wang 1958, p. 65). However hempseed as food did not appear to assume an importance comparable to that of other grains.

To the existence of the very poor, soybeans and wheat could be even more vital than millet. Although Han China undoubtedly produced more millet (of various kinds) than other grains, the consumption of millet was probably even greater. There was therefore always a pressing demand for soybeans and wheat as substitutes. As Pan Ku points out, the poor only had soybeans to chew and water to drink (*Han shu*, 91:3a; Swann 1950, p. 419). The *Yen-t'ieh lun* also mentions "bean stew" as the simplest kind of meal (K. Huan 1974 ed., p. 41). Fan Sheng-chih has given us a good explanation as to why this was the case. He says:

> From soybeans a good crop can be easily secured even in adverse years, therefore it is quite natural for the ancient people to grow soy as a provision against famine. Calculate the acreage to be covered by soybeans for members of the whole family according to the rate of 5 mou *per capita*. This should be looked at as "the basic" for farming [S. H. Shih 1959a, pp. 19–21].

Wheat was regarded as a coarse grain food together with beans. There is a famous story about bean conjee (gruel) and wheat food being prepared as a hurried meal by Feng I for Emperor Kuang-wu and his soldiers during a period of military campaigns. Many years later the Emperor wrote to Feng I apologizing that he had not yet returned the latter's favor of bean conjee and wheat food (*Hou Han shu*, 17:3a and 12a). Wang Ch'ung also says, "Although bean and wheat are coarse, they can nevertheless satisfy our hunger" (1974 ed., p. 131). In A.D. 194, when there was a great famine in the vicinity of the capital, prices for grains went up sky-high: 500,000 coins for only one *hu* of unhusked grain (millet) and 200,000 coins for one hu of beans or wheat (*Hou Han shu*, 9:8a).[6] This shows conclusively that beans and wheat were considered much inferior to millet as grain food. An official would be highly praised for having led a simple life if after his death it was found out that he had left behind only a few bushels (hu) of wheat or barley (*Hou Han shu*, 31:22b, 77:4b).

But even the same grain varied considerably from fineness to coarseness. In Han times, one hu of unhusked grain (*ku* or *su*) would normally yield six parts to every ten of the same grain husked (*mi*) (L. S. Yang 1961, p. 154). The husked grain was considered coarse (*li*) if its ratio to the unhusked grain was seven to ten (See Chang Yen's commentary to the *Shih chi* 1, 130:5a). Sometimes grain food for the poor was even coarser. *Tsao* ("distilled grain") and *k'ang* ("husks") are also mentioned as grain food (*Hou Han shu*,

41:18b–19a). The "So-yin" in the *Shih chi* even defines *tsao-k'ang* as food for the poor (*Shih chi* 1, 61:8b). But this could be just a literary exaggeration. According to Meng K'ang (ca. A.D. 180–260), the so-called k'ang was but leftover unhusked wheat (*Han shu*, 40:11b). In any case, tsao-k'ang was an expression for grain food of the coarsest kind.

What sorts of dishes, if any, went along with grain food for the Han Chinese in their everyday life? Keng is the usual answer. The *Li chi* says, "*Keng* was eaten by all, from the princes down to the common people, irrespective of status." Cheng Hsüan comments that keng was the main food in a meal (*Li chi*, 8:22a). Here the Han commentator was obviously speaking from his own daily experience. Keng could be cooked with or without meat. The following is the only clear description known to me of meat keng in reality under the Han. During Emperor Ming's reign (A.D. 58–75), Lu Hsü of Kui-chi (in modern Chekiang) was imprisoned in the capital, Lo-yang. One day when he was given a bowl of meat keng to eat, he immediately knew that his mother had come to Lo-yang to see him. He told the people around that the kind of keng he had just received could have been cooked by none other than his mother. As he described it, "When my mother cuts the meat, the chunks always come in perfect squares, and when she chops the scallions, the pieces always come in sections exactly one inch long" (*Hou Han shu*, 81:21a-b). From this story we know that meat stewed with scallions was a common type of keng. But meat keng was more a luxury than a daily necessity in Han China. During Wang Mang's reign, a eunuch bought fine millet food and meat keng from the market place to deceive Wang Mang about what the residents in Ch'ang-an ordinarily had for meals (*Han shu*, 99c:21b–22a). This act of deception on the part of the eunuch proves that meat keng was beyond the reach of people of ordinary means. A first-century scholar, Min Chung-shu of T'ai-yüan (in Shansi), being impoverished, of ill-health, and advanced in age, could not afford meat which he badly needed. Instead, he daily bought a piece of pork liver from the meat shop, without perhaps knowing that it was rich in vitamins (*Hou Han shu*, 53:2a). In Min's case, the meat he wished to have was probably pork, although beef and mutton seem to have been more in demand in the Han market (C. Wang 1974 ed., p. 221). Beef was especially prized because the ox was such a useful animal that the government occasionally prohibited its slaughter (*Hou Han shu*, 41:3a-b; S. Ying 1937 ed., 9:5a–6a; K. C. Yen 1958 ed., pp. 543–44). In theory, meat was exclusively reserved for the aged and nobility (S. M. Lü 1947, pp. 571–72). In an imperial decree of 179 B.C., Emperor Wen ordered the government to provide the aged (eighty or older) in the empire with monthly provisions of grain food, meat, and wine (*Han shu*, 4:6b–7a). Throughout the Han dynasty, similar decrees had been issued from time to time. Evidence shows, however, that officials in charge rarely took such orders seriously.

Of all animal meats, chicken was probably more within the reach of the common people than other kinds. Local officials also made special efforts to encourage people to raise pigs and chickens as a supplementary household occupation (*Han shu*, 89:5a–b, 13a). Pottery chickens, pigs, and pig houses have been found in many Han tombs, especially those of Later Han date (Lo-yang Ch'ü 1959, pp. 140–42; Kuangchou Shih 1957, p. 74; Kueichou Sheng 1972, p. 44). This may well be taken as a faithful reflection of an ordinary Han household. Pig butchering was, however, a rather large operation for an individual family. According to Ts'ui Shih, it took place only once a year in the family a few days before the New Year—a practice which had generally been followed by the rural Chinese until the present century (S. Ts'ui 1965 ed., pp. 74–76). When one or two guests came for dinner, therefore, the Han Chinese, like their ancestors in the time of Confucius, usually had only chicken to offer. In fact, chicken paired with glutinous millet (shu) was regarded as a very presentable food for guests both in pre-Han and in Han times (P. H. Shang 1967, p. 105). But to the very poor, even the pleasure of chicken meat was denied. Mao Jung of the second century A.D. had only one chicken for his aged mother and none for his honorable guest Kuo Lin-tsung (*Hou Han shu*, 68:4b). Also under the Later Han, it is said that an old lady had to steal her neighbor's chicken which she cooked for herself and her daughter-in-law (*Hou Han shu*, 84:14a–b).

We have shown that both meat and poultry were not as readily available to the common people as they were to the rich and the powerful. The only other category of dishes that occupied an important place in everyday meals of the great majority of Han China was, therefore, vegetable dishes of various kinds. As mentioned above, keng was by no means necessarily associated with meat, though the list of keng from Ma-wang-tui does seem to create such an impression. In fact, it was perfectly legitimate to speak of vegetable keng in Han as well as pre-Han times. Han Fei, for example, already mentioned *li-huo chih keng* with coarse grain food (C. Y. Ch'en 1974, 2:1041). *Huo* was bean leaves, which, according to Fan Sheng-chih, "can be sold as greens" (S. H. Shih 1959a, pp. 38–39). We are not sure what *li* was, but it has been described as a scallion-like plant (Yen Shih-ku's commentary in *Han shu*, 62:4a; N. S. Wang 1939 ed., 7:1170). The *li-huo* expression later became so stereotyped that it came to mean collectively any kind of coarse vegetable eaten by the poor.

In history we find only a few dietary details concerning the poor. The aforementioned Min Chung-shu was, on another occasion, given some garlic by a friend, to go with beans and water (*Hou Han shu*, 53:1b). Also, in the first century A.D., Ching Tan was once offered wheat grain and scallions for a meal which he nevertheless refused to eat (*Hou Han shu*, 83:10b–11a). Thus we know that garlic and scallions were most likely to be on the food list of the impoverished. But I must hasten to add that scallions could sometimes be very expensive during the Han depending on who ate them. In 33 B.C., Shao Hsin-ch'en obtained the approval of Emperor Yüan to close down an imperial "greenhouse" for the cultivation of out-of-season vegetables, among which were scallions and leeks. As a result, the court saved several tens of millions (of coins) a year (*Han shu*, 89:15a; on this greenhouse, see M. C. Chiang 1956, p. 14). Generally speaking, however, scallions, garlic, and leeks appeared to be quite common in Han times. Their cultivation has been reported in various sources (*Han shu*, 89:13a; *Hou Han shu*, 51:7b; S. Ts'ui 1965 ed., pp. 13–15).

Another kind of vegetable easily within the means of the common people was taro or yam. Under the reign of Emperor Ch'eng (32 to 7 B.C.) the prime minister Chai Fang-chin (whose courtesy name was Tzu-wei) had caused the breakdown of a major irrigation dam in Ju-nan commandery (in Honan). Agriculture in the whole region was therefore seriously affected. To register their complaint against Chai, the people of Ju-nan created a song which reads, "It was Chai Tzu-wei who destroyed our dam,/Now all we have for food is soybeans and yam." As the commentary by Yen Shih-ku makes clear, the second line means that the people cooked soybeans as grain food (*fan*) and yam as keng (*Han shu*, 84:22a). That yam or taro was a staple vegetable in Han China is fully testified to by Fan Sheng-chih's agriculturist book in which detailed instructions of planting and cultivating it are given (S. H. Shih 1959a, pp. 24–27, 40–41).

In the everyday life of the Han Chinese there is yet another category of food to mention, namely, dried grain food known as *pei, hou,* or *ch'iu*. It is difficult to distinguish clearly the three kinds of dried provisions from one another except that both pei and hou are said to be dried boiled grain (*kan-fan*) while ch'iu is sometimes described as being made from pulverized grain. Moreover, ch'iu is also believed to be dried by fire such as by baking or roasting. Rice, wheat, barley, millet, and beans could all be transformed into dried grain food (N. S. Wang 1939 ed., 6:935–36). Dried grain food had probably already been extensively used by soldiers and travelers as early as the Chou period (S. H. Ch'i 1949, p. 293). However, it was under the Han that this kind of food came to play a role of vital importance in the daily lives of millions of Chinese.

First, it was the main food for all Han travelers irrespective of status. Wang Mang, for example, ordered his imperial attendant to prepare dried grain food and dried meat for his tour of inspection in A.D. 14 (*Han shu*, 99B:26b). Empress Teng, wife of Emperor Ho (A.D. 89–105), also had large quantities of dried grain food stored in her royal residence (*Hou Han shu*, 10A:28b). In fact there was an official in the court whose duty was to select grain for making dried provisions for imperial use (*Hou Han shu*, "Chih" section, 26:2b). Second, repeated large-scale military campaigns against the Hsiung-nu in the north made Han warriors rely entirely on dried grain food for survival. According to Yen Yu (first century A.D.), the Chinese soldiers, once sent to fight the Hsiung-nu in the desert, lived on dried provisions and water in all seasons. In Yen's estimation, for an expedition of 300 days each soldier would need eighteen hu of pei. This put a man's consumption of pei at exactly 0.6 *sheng* a day (*Han shu*, 94B:24a, 25a). In 99 B.C., when Li Ling's army was surrounded by the Hsiung-nu in the neighborhood of Tun-huang, he gave each of his fighting men two sheng of pei and a piece of ice to get out of the encircled area one by one and later reassemble in a Han fort (*Han shu*, 54:12b). Obviously, the fort must have been within a three-day journey from the battlefield. Third, the Han government always kept large quantities of dried grain food in store for uses in addition to those military. Thus in 51 B.C., some 34,000 hu of pei were sent to the Hsiung-nu by the Han court as a reward for their recent submission: this was the largest single amount of dried provisions ever recorded in Han history (*Han shu*, 94:4b). Last, but not least, dried grain food was also consumed by men working in the field. As Ying Shao pointed out, both warriors and farmers carried hou with them (S. Ying, 1962 ed., 1:35b). The *Ssu-min yüeh-ling* advises that people make as much pei as possible out of the newly harvested wheat (S. Ts'ui 1965 ed., p. 43). Indeed we can surely say that in Han China hardly a day passed without some people eating dried grain food.

Before I bring this section to a close, I wish to say a word about food vessels in Han China. But the subject of food vessels is so important and complicated that an extensive treatment would definitely involve at least another chapter. In the following, therefore, I will merely point out a few salient features of Han food vessels, with special reference to the distinction between vessels shown in kitchen scenes in mural paintings and those actually used by the common people in their everyday life.

One safe generalization scholars have been making from time to time is that in Han times the upper classes used mainly lacquerware while the common people relied entirely on earthenware for cooking, eating, and drinking (Chung-kuo 1958, p. 133; C. S. Wang 1956, p. 71). Previously, in speaking of Han lacquerware, people always turned to the two important archaeological discoveries in Lo-lang and Noin-Ula for illustration (Y. S. Yü 1967, p. 24). Now Lo-lang and Noin-Ula have both been dwarfed in this respect by Ma-wang-tui Tombs No. 1 and No. 3 (*K'ao Ku* 1972, p. 41). It is certainly no exaggeration to say that the Ma-wang-tui finds "represent the largest and best preserved group of Western [Earlier] Han lacquerware, as well as the most diversified in vessel types, ever unearthed in China" (Hunan Sheng 1973, English abstract, p. 5). Lacquerware found in Ma-wang-tui Tombs No. 1 and No. 3 consists mostly of food and drink vessels.

In ancient China there had been a fundamental contrast between eating and drinking (K. C. Chang 1973, pp. 509–10). That the same contrast persisted in the Han period is fully attested to by many of the examples given above. Lacquerware from the two Ma-wang-tui tombs reveals that the contrast is also reflected in the vessels. It is very interesting to note that food vessels and drink vessels are clearly distinguished from each other by the two contrasting inscriptions *Chün hsin shih* ("Please eat food, sir") and *Chün hsin chiu* ("Please drink wine, sir"). Another interesting point to observe is that vessels for food and those for drink seem to have come in separate sets.

On the basis of the two contrasting inscriptions, then, we can easily distinguish the set of drink vessels from that of food vessels. The former includes *fang* vases, *chung* vases, *i* pitchers, *chih* cups, *shao* ladles, and winged wine cups; the latter includes *ting* tripods, cake boxes, *lien* food boxes, plates, and winged food cups. Some of the food and drink vessels still contained remains at the time of their excavation, and their actual functions were therefore unmistakably indicated. Moreover, cups and plates came in different sizes. For instance, wine cups have a capacity of 4 sheng, 2 sheng, 1.5 sheng, or 1 sheng (Hunan Sheng 1973, pp. 76–96; 1974, pp. 44–45). Scholars who actually examined the finds already have indicated that some of the vessels can be better understood if taken in sets rather than in individual pieces (*Wen Wu* 1972, p. 67). It may be additionally noted that among the lacquerware pieces, the chih cups, winged cups, and i pitchers were the most common types of vessels for drink used by the Han Chinese, and the food cup *pei* was a vessel for keng. None of them was the monopoly of the upper classes (C. T. Wang 1964, pp. 1–12). Needless to say, although the common people used the same types of vessels, the materials from which theirs were made—earth or wood—were much inferior in quality. Archaeological finds show, however, that pottery vessels in Han China sometimes were also made in sets, perhaps in imitation of lacquerware (C. T. Wang 1963, pp. 13–15; Lo-yang Ch'ü 1959, p. 149). As we know, the price of lacquerware in Han times was much higher than not only earthenware or woodenware but bronze as well. Lao Kan is certainly right in saying that, under the Han, lacquer food vessels basically replaced ancient bronze ones (1939, p. 99).

The Han Chinese were status conscious as far as the material of their vessels for food and drink was concerned. Toward the end of the Earlier Han dynasty, a ranking official, T'ang Tsun, was accused of hypocrisy because he used earthenware vessels (*Han shu*, 72:30a). Under Emperor Kuang-wu's reign, Huan T'an, in a memorial essay for the monarch, attacked some of the hypocritical court officials of ministerial position who sought to achieve reputations of frugality by using plain wooden cups for eating and drinking (K. C. Yen 1958 ed., p. 536). Interestingly, Liu Hsiang also has a disciple of Confucius making comments which clearly imply that earthen food vessels and boiled food (*chu-shih*) befit only the poor (H. Liu, 1967 ed., chüan 20, p. 13a). Boiled food was considered inferior presumably because the poor always cooked their wheat, beans, and bean leaves by boiling.

Finally, what were the most essential cooking utensils for the Han Chinese? The answer can be given without the slightest hesitation: *fu* and *tseng*. These two utensils were basic to every Han Chinese kitchen, rich and poor alike. The fu (cauldron) was used mainly for cooking keng and the tseng ("steamer") primarily for steaming or boiling grain food. In actual cooking, the tseng was always placed on top of the fu. Archaeologically, therefore, the two are always found together as if they were an inseparable pair. Most of the fu and tseng were made of clay, such as those found at Ma-wang-tui (Hunan Sheng 1973, pp. 124–25), Yü-ch'eng in Shantung (Shantung Sheng 1955, p. 86), Canton (Y. H. Mai 1958, p. 64), and Shao-kou (Loyang Ch'ü 1959, p. 135). But metal fu were also made. An iron fu was found at Shao-kou (ibid., p. 196), and seven bronze ones with a lot of fish bones in them were discovered in tombs in Canton (Y. H. Mai 1958, p. 68). From Han tombs at Li-chu, Shao-hsing (in Chekiang) a number of fu of all three materials— pottery, bronze, and iron —were unearthed in 1955. But the number of iron fu was greater than the other two kinds (Chekiang Sheng 1957, p. 137). In historical writings we also often find mention of the fu accompanied by the tseng (*Shih chi* 2, 7:10a; *Han shu*, 31:14a; *Hou Han shu*, 81:28b). It is probably safe to conclude that since keng (stew) and fan (grain food) were the two most basic kinds of food for the Han Chinese, the pairing of fu with tseng simply reflects this fundamental dietary reality in Han China.

Toward a Culinary Revolution

Thus far in this study, no special reference has been made to what was significantly new in the Han culinary history. Now, by way of conclusion, I wish to point out emphatically that Han Chinese were as innovative as they were traditional in matters pertaining to food and eating. In the following, I shall first list a few important exotic edibles that were brought to China for the first time, and then proceed to discuss two major Han contributions to the art of cooking which, in my biased view, produced far-reaching revolutionary consequences in Chinese culinary history.

The Han dynasty is marked, among other things, by expansion, and expansion inevitably opened China to things non-Chinese, including foods. Post-Han literary works credit Chang Ch'ien, the greatest traveler of early Han times, with the introduction of almost all the exotic edibles from the western regions. The list includes, for instance, grape, alfalfa, pomegranate, walnut, sesame, onion, caraway seeds, peas, coriander from Bactria, and cucumber. In fact, however, as Kuwabara Jitsuzo has convincingly shown, none of these plants was introduced to China by Chang Ch'ien himself (Kuwabara 1935, pp. 47–52, 117–27). But there can be little doubt that some of the foreign foods listed above were brought to the Han soon after Chang Ch'ien. Grape and alfalfa seeds were brought back to China by Han envoys from Ferghana around 100 B.C. (*Shih chi* 2, 2:280). Grape is further mentioned in a Later Han literary piece (K. C. Yen 1958 ed., p. 784). Grape wine imported from the western regions was greatly prized as late as the end of the second century A.D. (Y. S. Yü 1967, p. 196). K'ung Jung wrote a thank-you note to a friend for a gift of walnuts (K. C. Yen 1958 ed., p. 922). In the *Ssu-min yüeh-ling* we find alfalfa, sesame, peas, and onion (S. Ts'ui 1965 ed., pp. 13, 20, 26, 41, 46, 56). Sesame seems to have been particularly important, for it alone appears three times in the text. The kind of "barbarian grain food" (*hu-fan*) enjoyed by Emperor Ling (A.D. 168–188) was in all likelihood grain food cooked with the flavorful sesame (*Hou Han shu*, chih 13:8b).

Mention may also be made of the renowned *long-an* and *litchi*, which, though coming from the tropical southern border of the Han, were still considered more or less new and exotic throughout this period. Both fruits were sent to the court by special fast horses from Kwangtung (*Hou Han shu*, 4:25a–b). During Emperor Shun's reign (A.D. 126–144), Wang I, in his fu on litchi, praised it as the leading tributary fruit (K. C. Yen 1958 ed., p. 784). At the end of the Han, Chung-ch'ang T'ung still criticized his contemporaries for having overindulged in the taste of litchi (K. C. Yen 1958 ed., p. 956).

Earlier we have seen that both soybeans and wheat were primarily foods for the common people. But it was due to soybeans and wheat that a quiet culinary revolution began in Han China. By this I refer particularly to the manufacturing of shih (salted, darkened beans) and the making of wheat flour. As Shih Sheng-han pointed out:

Shih is very popular in a vast area of China; especially among the rustic population leading a very simple life. . . . It was almost the only relish they can afford to enjoy. The date of shih is not yet well-traced, but Ssu-ma Ch'ien mentioned it in Shih Chi as one of the merchandise in cities, so it must already have been produced in large quantities in his time. The *Ch'i Min Yao Shu* gives the first known instructions for its preparation. [S. H. Shih 1962, p. 86]

In the learned opinions of K'ung Ying-ta of the T'ang and Chou Mi of the Sung, however, shih was invented sometime around 200 B.C. (*Tso chuan*, 49:542; Chou 1959 ed., 2:115). It had already become a basic condiment in the early Han, and it was on a very short list of food supplies that Prince Liu Ch'ang received from the government after his plot of revolution had been discovered (*Shih chi* 1, 2:364). The name *shih* even found its way into an elementary Han textbook, the *Chi-chiu p'ien*—a clear indication of its great popularity (K. W. Wang 1929 ed., 10b; Y. Shen 1962, p. 66). Now, with the excavation of Ma-wang-tui Tomb No. 1, shih remains become a concrete archaeological fact for the first time (Hunan Sheng 1973, pp. 127, 138). The earliest bean curd is also reported to have been made in the Han, but the textual evidence is too weak to support such a claim (C. P. Li 1955, p. 200).

However, what we today call *mien* ("noodles") was clearly a unique contribution by the Han to Chinese culinary art. In Han times, "noodle food," in a broad sense, was known as *ping* ("cakes"), while the character for mien was defined as wheat flour in the standard dictionary *Shuo-wen* (Y. T. Tuan 1955 ed., p. 234). That noodle foods came into existence in the Han period but not earlier may be explained by the simple fact that the techniques required for large-scale flour grinding were not available to the Chinese until the Han. Such techniques were probably introduced to China from the West in the latter part of the Earlier Han dynasty as a result of the Han expansion (Shinoda 1974, p. 54). For instance, the flour mill is suspected to have been a borrowing from another culture rather than an indigenous Chinese invention (Laufer 1909, pp. 15–35). Three stone mills have been found in Shao-kou tombs datable to the end of the Earlier Han and beginning of the Later Yan (Lo-yang Ch'ü 1959, p. 206, pl. 62). We can therefore assume that the Han Chinese made wheat flour around the second half of the first century B.C. at the latest. The word *ts'o* was specifically coined for wheat grinding (Y. T. Tuan 1955 ed., p. 234).

Under the Later Han, a great variety of noodle foods were cooked, including boiled noodles, steamed buns (modern *man-t'ou*), and baked cakes with sesame seeds (S. H. Ch'i 1949, pp. 294–95). According to the *Shih-ming*, noodle food was called *ping* because the word indicates the idea of blending (*ping*) flour with water (H. Liu 1939 ed., p. 62). In connection with this, a flour-kneading scene has been found in Han and Wei-Chin tombs such as I-nan (C. Y. Tseng et al. 1956) and Chia-yü Kuan (Chia-yü Kuan Shih 1972, p. 40, fig. 31). Boiled noodles and swung noodles are also mentioned in the *Ssu-min yüeh-ling* (S. Ts'ui 1965 ed., pp. 44–45). Boiled noodles were so popular in the second century A.D. that even the emperor ate them (*Hou Han shu*, 63:14b–15a). It was probably no accident that from Wang Mang's time on selling noodle food became a noticeable business (*Han shu*, 99B:18b; *Hou Han shu*, 64:23b, 82B:12a; P. H. Shang 1967, p. 105).

The Western Chin writer Shu Hsi (late third and early fourth centuries) composed a fu on noodle food ("Ping fu"). According to him, people in Chou times knew wheat grain food but not noodles, which had developed only in his very recent past. He made a special reference to the art of flour kneading by describing vividly how the cook's skillful hands and fingers moved in molding the flour dough into a variety of shapes. He also mentioned how noodle food could be delicately cooked with meats (especially mutton and pork) and seasonings (including ginger, scallions, fagara, and above all, shih). But from the historical point of view, the following observation which he made on the origins of noodle food interests us even more: "The various kinds of noodles and cakes were mainly the invention of the common people, while some of the cooking methods came from foreign lands" (K. C. Yen 1958 ed., pp. 1962–63; my translation). In other words, it was the ingenuity of the Han Chinese in experimenting with the most common of eating materials, coupled with a willingness to learn from other cultures, that eventually led to the opening of an entirely new chapter in Chinese culinary history.

NOTES

1. As this book was going to press, Hayashi Minao's detailed study of food and drink in Han times (in Japanese) came to my attention. Like my chapter, Hayashi's is also based on both archaeological and textual evidence, although our approaches are different. The reader is therefore referred to Hayashi's valuable work for additional information on the subject. See Hayashi 1975.

I wish to take this opportunity to thank the Institute of Chinese Studies, the Chinese University of Hong Kong, for providing me with research assistance in the fall term, 1974–75, which facilitated the preparation of this chapter. I am indebted to Miss Susan Converse for her research and editorial help.

2. However, in the light of bamboo slips found in "Han Tomb No. 3 at Mawangtui," the identification of Yü-keng with Ta-keng may still be an open question. See Chung-kuo k'o-hsüeh yüan k'ao-ku yen-chiu so, and Hunan Sheng po-wu-kuan 1975, 1:55.

3. We know that this kind of couch was not uncommon in the Han period because

we find it not only in the P'ang-t'ai-tzu mural painting (W. H. Li 1955, pp. 17–18) but in a painted brick from Szechwan, though in the latter case the couch has no screens on the sides (Ch'ung-ch'ing shih 1957, p. 20). Moreover, the *Kao-shih chuan* also reports that Kuan Ning of the third century often sat on a wooden couch (quoted in *San-kuo-chih*, "Wei-chih," 11:27b).

4. According to *Han shu*, however, the marquis of Kai faced north (*Han shu*, 52:4b).

5. These are based on many literary pieces collected in K. C. Yen 1958 ed., pp. 238, 403, 623, 624, 644, 706, 713, 714, 768, 775, 827, 963, 975, 976.

6. Normally the price of one hu of unhusked grain was around 100 coins only (K. Lao 1960, pp. 58–59).

3: T'ANG

EDWARD H. SCHAFER

If one inspects the contemporary sources which might reasonably be drawn on for a study of T'ang dynasty food and cooking there is an initial impression of riches. The bibliographic section of the official T'ang history lists a considerable number of books called *Shih ching,* "Food Canons" (definitive texts on food), and also incorporates that phrase in longer titles (*Hsin T'ang shu,* chap. 59). Unfortunately, many of these books, both those compiled during the T'ang period (618–907) and those which had survived until then from earlier ages, have since disappeared, wholly or in part, and we are fortunate if we can find a few quotations from one or another of them in later compilations. In any case, it would be a mistake to regard these ancient books as cookbooks in the modern sense. They were dietary guides whose paramount purpose was to instruct members of the elite class about the correct preparation of balanced dishes which would not disturb somatic equipoise and might improve the internal climate of the body and so contribute to longevity.

The recommendations of learned pharmacologists must have had an immense effect on the practices of cooks, whose recipes thus modified came in time to be regarded as authoritative designs for gourmet dishes. Venison with ginger and vinegar was first recommended for its tonic properties but was ultimately appreciated as an ambrosial delight. So it comes as no surprise that, in a study of the cuisine of the T'ang period, one is inevitably led to the surviving writings of, for example, the eminent seventh-century pharmacologist Meng Shen. These now exist only as fragments and quotations, most notable among which are portions of his food canon, preserved in a somewhat later Japanese compendium, the *I shin hō* (Tamba 1935).[1] On inspection, however, these particular citations prove to be of little interest to the student of the history of food. Almost every recipe is a recommendation to physicians, and they are not even restricted to internal medicine. For instance, there is a prescription for a paste of ground walnut meats mixed with white lead as a cure for baldness (Tamba 1935, 4:6a). Still, for the men of T'ang, this came properly under the rubric of *food*—that is, substances used to improve the condition of the human body. Even we enlightened moderns speak of "skin food" and the like.

In the end, although the fact of the intimate connection between diet and medicine must never be forgotten, the best, and the most interesting, information about T'ang eating habits comes, not from official sources on the virtues of edible materials, but from literary sources—above all from poetry. It is in the verses (happily preserved in abundance) of the educated men of T'ang that we learn what was truly relished and what was served to favored guests or eaten with pleasure in the quiet of one's own garden.[2]

Foodstuffs

The old reliable foodstuffs retained their popularity in T'ang. A quick survey confirms the continued importance of millet, rice, pork, beans, chicken, plums, spring onions, and bamboo shoots. But wheat had certainly increased vastly in importance since Han times. It is hard to guess the relative importance of such local staples as yams and taro (Schafer 1963, p. 140). Some of the dietary changes which were taking place were related to the conflict between the Chinese and ethnic minorities. For instance, in the south, as the original cultivators of the valley bottoms were gradually displaced by the Chinese, more and more of the indigenes found it necessary to abandon their wet rice fields and to push up into the mountains where, perforce, they had to resort to the primitive slash-and-burn technique. This antique mode of cultivation was, I suspect, on the increase for a time, to the detriment of the soil and forests (Schafer 1967, p. 52; Hutchinson 1973). While these and other changes in the nature and quantity of production were taking place, the Chinese were overcoming their ancient prejudices and, among upper-class persons at least, experimentation with novelties was becoming increasingly prevalent. But in the main, the millet cake or bowl of rice remained central to the Chinese diet.

"True" millet (*chi*; *Panicum miliaceum*)*, the most classical of all the Chinese cultivated grasses, remained an important food source in T'ang times despite the inroads made by wheat and the continual expansion of the paddy fields in the south. It was particularly characteristic of the northernmost part of China and was most abundant of all "north of the frontier defenses" (*sai pei*) (T. C. Ch'en in S. C. Li 1965 ed., 23:70). A glutinous variety (*shu*) was traditionally used for making wine in regions north of the zone where glutinous rice was grown (K. Su in S. C. Li 1965 ed., 23:78). Foxtail millet —also called spiked millet or Italian millet (*su*; *Setaria italica*)—was grown both in the north and in the south. In the north it had to be hoed to prevent it from being killed by weeds. It flourished easily in the south, where it was grown in the ashes of the slash-and-burn fields (S. Meng in S. C. Li 1965 ed., 23:76). A superior variety was sent to the palace annually as local tribute from western Shantung. Other local varieties were the purple straw millet (*tzu kan su*) of southern Shensi and the yellow millet (*huang su*) grown around the mouth of the Yangtze.

Shensi, the region of the T'ang capital, appears to have been the center for

---

*The reader will note that Schafer identifies the word *chi* as *Panicum miliaceum*, whereas Chang equates it with *Setaria italica*.—Ed.

production of wheat (*hsiao mo; Triticum vulgare*) (K. Su in S. C. Li 1965 ed., 22:58).

Barley (*ta mo*), evidently more ancient in China than wheat, was an autumn-planted, summer-harvested crop used in making broths. It was grown widely in the Yellow River plain. The pharmacologists recommended that it be used unhulled to obtain the best balance between heating effects (from the meal) and cooling effects (from the bran) (K. Su and T. C. Ch'en in S. C. Li 1965 ed., 22:54). A variety named white barley, grown in the Ordos region north and west of the capital, was planted in the spring (T. C. Ch'en in S. C. Li 1965 ed., 22:54).

Although rice had been known to the Chinese since prehistoric times, it was only with their centuries-long expansion into the south that it was gradually allowed an increasingly greater role in their diet. But even though rice was grown in the north in T'ang times, it could not rival wheat and millet there. There were both wet and dry varieties of rice, and glutinous and non-glutinous varieties. The ethnic minorities in the far south found it profitable to plant dry rice ("fire rice") in their burned-over fields (S. Meng in S. C. Li 1965 ed., 22:66). But paddy-grown rice in the wet southern valleys was the prime favorite. The non-glutinous variety (*keng*) was produced in the greatest abundance in the Huai-Ssu area—around the Grand Canal, from Honan southeastward into Kiangsu and Anhwei (ibid.). There was also a subvariety called *hsien,* which ripened early and could be harvested in the sixth and seventh months of the lunar year. This included Champa rice (*chan tao*), which was introduced from Champa by way of Fukien in the tenth century but was not well established in the Yangtze valley until the beginning of the eleventh century. Much admired "aromatic" non-glutinous rice (*hsiang keng*) was sent to the imperial court from Chekiang and Kiangsu. Glutinous rice (*no*), valued most for wine making, was widely grown in the south.

An occasional substitute for the standard cultivated cereals was a grass whose pearly white seeds we call Job's tears (*i-i; Coix lacryma-jobi*). There is a southern variety sometimes called adlay. Although not much noticed in conventional accounts of Chinese food, this plant has a long and respectable history in China. Before the dawn of history, the mother of the Great Yü became pregnant when she swallowed the seeds of the divine plant. The heroic Wave Conqueror, Ma Yüan, of the Later Han period, kept himself in good health by eating this grain—perhaps the adlay variety—while subduing the peoples of the malarial tropics (*Hou Han shu* 1, 54:0748a). In the T'ang period both wild and cultivated varieties continued to be a standard supplement to the important cereal crops, bearing the same relation to them as sago did to the flours made from them. As Wei Chuang noted in the ninth century:

"Grains are shamed—lacking Job's tears; Flours rejoice—having sagwire [sago palm]" (*Ch'üan T'ang shih*, 3:12b).

Legumes (*tou*) constituted an important part of the Chinese diet. A few examples follow chosen from many kinds that were significant in T'ang times. Soybeans (*ta tou*; *Glycine max*) had a variety of uses and received considerable attention from the T'ang pharmacologists, who claimed to have discovered different somatic effects of the beans according to the way they were prepared. For instance, stir-roasted they were excessively heating, boiled they were too chilling, made into a relish (*shih*) they were very cool, but pickled (*chiang*) they were balanced. Stir-roasted, however, and taken in wine, they were said to be curative of certain kinds of paralysis (T. C. Ch'en in S. C. Li 1965 ed., 24:89–90). The young shoots of a variety of soybean called white legume (*po tou*) were much admired for their flavor, either cooked or raw and were reputed to be good for the kidneys (Meng and S. M. Sun in S. C. Li 1965 ed., 24:101). Garden peas (*Pisum sativum*) of European origin were an early introduction into China. In T'ang times they were known under a variety of names, including *hu tou* ("foreign legumes"), *wan tou*, and *pi tou* (T. C. Ch'en in S. C. Li 1965 ed., 24:102).

Leaf vegetables, root vegetables, and seeds (other than grains and legumes) in bewildering variety had their greater or lesser roles in the diets of the people of T'ang. We can only discuss a sampling of them here. Many were old or recent introductions from foreign countries—for example, spinach and kohlrabi from the West. It appears that there must have been a certain amount of official experimentation to produce superior varieties in the imperial parks and orchards, where every interesting kind of fruit and vegetable was grown—the exotic with the best of the native—to grace the imperial table (*Hsin T'ang shu*, 47:11b). There are interesting anecdotes—some incapable of verification—that tend to support the belief that the superintendent of parks (*ssu yüan*) did more than propagate accepted varieties. A believable example is the successful fruiting of "sweetpeel" tangerines (*kan*) in the gardens of the imperial palace in A.D. 751 during the reign of Hsüan Tsung—an occasion for formal congratulations to the monarch on his divine charisma (C. S. Tuan 1937 ed., 18:146; *Ch'uan T'ang wen*, 962:15b–16b). This means that there must have been some sort of hothouse arrangement to allow the simulation of subtropical conditions in the northern capital.

Let us make a quick survey of some characteristic edible leaves, stems, and roots of the T'ang period. One was so important as to deserve a special department on the palace grounds called the *ssu chu chien*. This department was in charge of the imperial bamboo gardens which provided tender shoots for the sovereign's kitchen (*Ta T'ang liu tien*, 19:22b). An excellent variety of bamboo shoot was sent to the court from the Yangtze estuary, and there was a winter variety of fine quality grown in southern Shensi. Ordinary varieties became available in spring, however, as attested by Po Chü-i in the ninth century, and were extremely abundant in some places. Most tasty of all were the sprouts of the spotted bamboos of Hunan, whose mature growth was reputed to show the tear stains of the wives of Shun.

Then there was rhubarb (*ta huang; Rheum officinale*), of great medicinal value, a plant that favored the northwest. Water shield, or water mallow (*ch'un; Brasenia purpurea*), a water plant used to make delicious soups, and the soft, mucilaginous shoots and leaves of several varieties of the true mallow (*k'ui; Malva verticillata*), described as "the most important leafy vegetable in ancient China" (H. L. Li 1969, p. 256), were still an important element in the T'ang diet. Later their prestige declined, and they were gradually replaced by the "cabbage" *pak-choi* (also called *sung; Brassica sinensis*). In recent times the venerable mallow has come to be regarded as a weed (H. L. Li 1969, p. 256; K. Su in S. C. Li 1965 ed., 16:89).

One could have expected to be served cooked bracken in a remote mountain monastery (Wang Yü-ch'eng 1922 ed., 7:11b);[3] the water drop-wort (*ch'in; Oenanthe stolonifera*), sometimes misleadingly called celery, which grew wild and was cultivated in paddies, was a familiar vegetable (H. L. Li 1969, p. 258; K. Su in S. C. Li 1965 ed., 26:82); the smartweed (*liao; Polygonum hydropiper*) provided pungent edible leaves (H. L. Li 1969 p. 258; C. Chen in S. C. Li 1965 ed., 16:131); a nasturtium (*t'ing-li; Nasturtium indicum*) was a minor vegetable which, like the mallow, later came to be regarded only as a weed (H. L. Li 1969, p. 257; C. Chen in S. C. Li 1965 ed., 16:112); shiny asparagus (*t'ien men tung; Asparagus lucidus*), hemlock parsley (*ch'iung-ch'iung; Conioselinum univittatum*), paper mulberry leaves (K. Su in S. C. Li 1965 ed., 36:78), a violet (*chin*, possibly *Viola verucunda*) (H. L. Li 1969, p. 259; K. Su in S. C. Li 1965 ed., 26:83), and even that common forage plant alfalfa (H. L. Li 1969, p. 259), all provided green leaves for the T'ang table. The algae of coastal waters also had a significant place in the diet. The purple-leaved laver (*tzu ts'ai; Porphyra* sp.), gathered from coastal Kiangsu to Kwangtung, was particularly familiar (S. Meng and T. C. Ch'en in S. C. Li 1965 ed., 28:17), but there were also green laver, or "sea lettuce" (*shih ch'un; Ulva* sp.), rich in iodine (T. C. Ch'en in S. C. Li 1965 ed., 28:18), and the sugary sweet tangle (*k'un-pu*), a brownish kelp (ibid., 19:111).

The odorous leaves and bulbs of the members of the genus *Allium* were generously used in T'ang cookery and highly recommended for their warming, tonic properties. Garlic (*suan; Allium sativum*), apparently an early introduction from the West, was regularly eaten in cooked dishes; an especially esteemed variety was the summer garlic of southern Shensi (H. L. Li 1969, p. 257; S. C. Li 1965 ed., 26:53). On the other hand, the shallot (*hsieh*; *Allium bakeri*) was a Chinese native; there were red and white varieties, of which the latter was preferred and the bulb regularly pickled (H. L. Li 1969, p. 257; K. Su in S. C. Li 1965 ed., 26:50). The spring onion (*ts'ung*; *Allium fistulosum*) was also ancient in China in several varieties. It was used as a seasoning, and its warming properties were strongly recommended to counteract the winter cold (H. L. Li 1969, p. 258; K. Su and S. Meng in S. C. Li 1965 ed., 26:44–45). Also native was the leek (*chiu*; *Allium ramosum*)—a different species from the familiar leek of the West. Meng Shen warns his contemporaries that it should not be eaten at the same time as beef or honey (H. L. Li 1969, p. 258; T. C. Ch'en and S. Meng in S. C. Li 1965 ed., 26:40).

Root vegetables played an important role in Chinese eating habits, but generally they were not respected as much as the cereals, and some were regarded as famine foods at best. Domestic yams (*shu-yü*; *Dioscorea* sp.) had been known in central and south China since antiquity. A white variety, sun-dried and powdered, was considered to have an excellent flavor; a blue-black variety was less valued. The court demanded the yams of the region just south of the Yangtze as tribute (K. Su in S. C. Li 1965 ed., 27:119). Taro (*yü*; *Colocasia esculenta*) is of tropical origin but is one of the oldest cultivated plants in China. In immediately pre-T'ang times, at any rate, it was considered the most important tuber crop (H. L. Li 1969, p. 256). There were blue, white, and purple varieties, and some lesser ones, grown mostly in the warmer parts of the country. The blue variety is poisonous and had to be leached before cooking. The wild taro was thought to be even more poisonous and was not to be eaten under any circumstances. Otherwise, taro made an excellent broth with meat (K. Su in S. C. Li 1965 ed., 27:117). The court obtained a root of superior quality from northern Hupei. Both the roots and the tender shoots of the radish (*lai-fu*; *Raphanus sativus*)[4] were apparently not as important in T'ang times as now; the radish has gradually replaced the turnip (H. L. Li 1969, p. 257). The turnip (*wu-ching*; *Brassica rapa*) was a northern plant like the radish; its root was commonly toasted (T. C. Ch'en in S. C. Li 1965 ed., 26:66). The roots of the lotus and licorice plants were believed to have remarkable tonic properties and, like ginseng, were probably more important in medicine than in cookery.

A source of meal that, in the vicinity of Canton, rivaled milled grain in making cakes was sago—although it always remained second to rice. This substance was yielded by several native palms and cycads, of which the most important was a sugar palm (*kuang-lang*; *Arenga saccharifera*), sometimes called gomuti or sagwire (from Portuguese *sagueira*, "sago tree"). It was commonly taken with water buffalo milk (C. S. Tuan 1937 ed., hsü, 10:249; Liu Hsün 1913 ed., B:3; T. C. Ch'en in S. C. Li 1965 ed., 31:19). The same tree yielded a sugar called jaggery and was the source of a wine called toddy. But the classical source of sago in Southeast Asia, and the one admired most for the light, delicate flavor of its yellow white meal, was the sago palm (*sha mu*; *Metroxylon* sp.) (T. C. Ch'en in S. C. Li 1965 ed., 31:20).

One should include the Far Eastern eggplant or brinjal (*ch'ieh*; *Solanum melongena*) under fruits, and indeed it is the only fruit, properly speaking, that I am including here under vegetables although this may perplex the Western reader. In any event, the plant was of tropical origin (hence Sui Yang Ti called it *K'un-lun tzu kua*, "Malayan purple melon"), and evidently several varieties were known in China. It was eaten both cooked and raw (H. L. Li 1969, p. 256; T. C. Ch'en in S. C. Li 1965 ed., 28:2).

It is difficult to assess the importance of mushrooms in the T'ang cuisine. A poem by Wang Chen-po praising an honored Buddhist sage for preparing mushrooms in an ancient cauldron does little more than testify to his old-fashioned virtues. It tells us nothing about the realities of everyday life. One pharmacologist called the black kind that grows on cow dung "particularly excellent" (T. C. Ch'en in S. C. Li 1965 ed., 28:29), while others praise the bracket fungi that grow on the trunks of mulberry, paper mulberry, elm, willow, and many other trees (K. Su and C. Chen in S. C. Li 1965 ed., 28:22).

Fruits, nuts, and seeds are essentially the same thing and are best treated collectively as fruits in the strict botanical sense, ignoring the question of their attractiveness to the palate. In T'ang times it was clear to everyone that there were classical fruits—that is, those familiar to the ancient Chinese—whose virtues were embalmed in the honored books inherited from the remote past. They were familiar on everyone's table and were distinguished from the newer, exotic fruits, although these were becoming known to the aristocracy and were even desired as prestige dishes on otherwise conservative boards. It was important, however, that the eternal verities should be maintained in official documents, and so it is not surprising that at the T'ang court the fruits and flowers of central Honan, the ancient center of Chinese civilization, were regarded as the nation's finest. Here was situated the garden city of Lo-yang, supposedly a paradise of beautiful and tasty plants. Accordingly, the palace, in its published evaluation of fruits, ignored the delicious new products of the Yangtze basin, to say nothing of the even newer and more delicious products obtainable in the Canton region.

Any list of the classical fruits of China should begin with the peach, which figures prominently in folklore, traditional religion, literature, and popular affection. New, exotic varieties were introduced from Central Asia in T'ang times. For example, the golden yellow peaches of Samarkand, the size of goose eggs, were successfully transplanted in the imperial orchards at Changan, although there is no evidence that they spread beyond these sacred precincts (Laufer 1919, p. 379). The Chinese cherry (*Prunus pseudo-cerasus*) has been noticed in literature more for its spring blossoms than for its delicious fruit (H. L. Li 1959, p. 157). The plum (*li*; *Prunus salicina*) was equally familiar. Meng Shen notes that it should not be eaten with the flesh of small songbirds or with honey (S. C. Li 1965 ed., 29:34). Even more conspicuous in literature was the "Japanese" apricot (*mei*; *Prunus mume*), often miscalled a plum (H. L. Li 1959, p. 48). A buckthorn fruit sometimes called "rat plum" (*pi*; *Rhamnus japonicus*) was so well thought of in high circles that it was ceremoniously brought to court from southern Hupei. The pear, including a fancy variety styled "Phoenix perch" pear (*feng ch'i li*), was a northern fruit, the best of which came from Shansi (S. C. Li 1965 ed., 30:62–63). Closely related to the pear was the flowering crabapple (*hai t'ang*; *Malus spectabilis* and other species), a beautiful tree—the variety called Overseas Red (*hai hung*) was imported from Korea—but evidently the fruit was not important in the T'ang cuisine (ibid., 30:65). Closely related was the sweet crabapple, considered a pear by some taxonomists (*kan t'ang*; *Pyrus betulaefolia*) (ibid., 30:74). The crabapple, steeped in honey and cinnabar, was eaten in south China after dinner with wine as a stimulating elixir (Schafer 1967, p. 183). The apricot (*hsing*; *Prunus armeniaca*), however, was commonly dried for eating and was considered good for heart disorders (S. M. Sun in S. C. Li 1965 ed., 29:36). The muster roll of delicious fruit was almost endless. There were the small, sour Chinese crabapple (*lin-ch'in*; *Malus asiatica*) (S. C. Li 1965 ed., 30:74), the thorn apple—the fruit of the hawthorn (*cha tzu*; *Crataegus* sp.)—which was eaten south of the Yangtze (T. C. Ch'en in S. C. Li 1965 ed., 30:69), and its also edible cousin the wild thornapple (*shan cha*; *Crataegus pinnatifolia*), of a distinctly red color (K. Su and T. C. Ch'en in S. C. Li 1965 ed., 30:71). The quince (*mu kua*; *Cydonia sinensis*) was also eaten then (S. C. Li 1965 ed., 30:66–67). The persimmon (*shih*; *Diospyros kaki*) was supposed to relieve drunkenness (ibid., 30:75). The "poplar apricot," or "strawberry tree" (*yang mei*; *Myrica rubra*), of the far south was especially found in the malarial foothills of Lingnan (T. C. Ch'en in S. C. Li 1965 ed., 30:93). There was also the familiar loquat (*p'i-p'a*; *Eriobotrya japonica*) (S. C. Li 1965 ed., 30:91). Melons were extremely important on the medieval table (H. L. Li 1969, p. 254). Among the available species were the pickling melon of the south (*Yüeh kua*; *Cucumis conomon*), the cucumber (*hu kua*; *Cucumis sativus*), the white gourd, or winter melon (*tung kua*; *Benincasa hispida*), and the bottle gourd (*hu*; *Lagenaria siceraria*)

(T. C. Ch'en in S. C. Li 1965 ed., 28:12; S. Meng in S. C. Li 1965 ed., 28:9; H. L. Li 1969, pp. 254, 256).[5] The leaves as well as the fruits of some of these were eaten.

Many other fruits, little known to Westerners, figured in some degree in the T'ang diet. Rather than enumerate them, let us turn to some plants of foreign origin that played a significant role. Examples from the West, introduced by way of Central Asia, include the table grape, which was cultivated in Shansi. It was thought to be "so delicate that it became worthless when transported to the capital" (Schafer 1963, p. 143). But grapes were imported from Qočo (Kao-ch'ang) in Central Asia in many forms: as wine, dried, "crinkled," "parched," and as a syrup. Evidently several varieties of raisin were involved here (*Hsin T'ang shu*, 40:10b). The jujube (*tsao*; *Zizyphus vulgaris*), resembling the date, was an ancient and honorable product of China. There were several edible varieties grown in the northern provinces, including the sour jujube (S. M. Sun in S. C. Li 1965 ed., 29:57), but the aromatic jujube was imported from Turkestan. Iranian lands contributed the fig, among many other vegetable products. The Arab merchant Sulayman states that it was cultivated in China in the middle of the ninth century (Laufer 1919, pp. 412–13).

Almost but not quite exotic were the tropical fruits of Lingnan, a region long claimed by the Chinese as their own but in T'ang times still plagued by insurrections of the native inhabitants. Most celebrated of its products, and justly so, were its many delicious citrus fruits, some of which ultimately made their way around the world. Against these glories of the south, the old northern homeland could offer only the thorny lime (*chih*; *Citrus trifoliata*), sometimes called trifoliate orange. Its fruits were sent for the delectation of the Chinese court from southern Shensi and northern Honan. Among southern rivals of this fruit, the most widely known was the so-called coolie orange, or Canton orange (*ch'eng*; *Citrus aurantium*). This excellent orange throve as far north as Szechwan and southern Hupei in T'ang times. Its sour variety was introduced into the Mediterranean region in the ninth or tenth century during the Arab domination of western Asia, and ultimately it became the familiar Seville orange, which makes superior marmalade. Its sweeter variety came to Europe in the fourteenth century with the crusaders and generated both the Valencia and navel oranges. Much more prized in China itself were the delicious southern tangerines—the "bitterpeel" tangerine (*chü*; *Citrus deliciosa*), and the "sweetpeel" tangerine (*kan*; *Citrus nobilis*)—varieties of which also grew in many parts of the central Yangtze basin. The bitterpeel, which was much used in medicine, existed in many varieties, among them the vermilion bitterpeel, the teat bitterpeel, the mountain bitterpeel, and above all, the winter-ripening golden bitterpeel of the deep south, which we know as the kumquat (*Fortunella* sp.) (T. C. Ch'en in S. C. Li 1965 ed., 30:80–84, 87, 90). The amber-colored rind of the golden kumquat, steeped in honey, was highly prized in Lingnan. The range of the sweetpeel was, if anything, more extensive than that of its tarter cousin since it was found all the way from Kwangtung to southeastern Kansu. It, too, occurred in many varieties: vermilion sweetpeel, yellow sweetpeel, teat sweetpeel, stone sweetpeel, and others. Of these the teat sweetpeel was reckoned the best (ibid., 30:87). Finally, there were two early introductions from Indochina, the pomelo (*yu*; *Citrus grandis*), with its thick sweet rind and bitter or sweet flesh (K. Su in S. C. Li 1965 ed., 30:89), and the bitter citron (*chü-yüan*; *Citrus medica*), including the grotesque variety called "Buddha's hand" (K. C. Ch'en 1965 ed., 30:90).

However, the true pride of the Canton region was the wonderful litchi (*li-chih*; *Nephelium litchi*). This fruit was grown in Fukien and Szechwan, but it was widely agreed that the best varieties came from coastal Lingnan. Among them was a large seedless variety and a yellowish "wax" litchi. Cantonese litchis were demanded by the court as local tribute, and it is reported that Yang Kui-fei was so inordinately fond of them that a special "pony express" was established to get them to her in Changan while they were still relatively fresh (Liu Hsün 1913 ed., 4b–5a). This tale may be a myth, however, since a T'ang pharmacologist reports that the odor of the fruit alters in one day and the flavor in two (H. Li in S. C. Li 1965 ed., 31:2). Happily, it was believed that eating this incomparable fruit tended to nullify the effects of drinking too much wine (see Wang Chien's poem in *Ch'üan T'ang shih*, 3:7b). This virtue must have been especially important in Canton in the ninth and tenth months of the lunar year, when great festivals were held to celebrate the ripening of the fruit and the trees were splendid with their crimson shells. Closely related to the litchi are the pleasantly subacid rambutan (*shao tzu*; *Nephelium lappaceum*) and the longan, which is smaller than the litchi and not quite so tasty.[6] Indeed, the great eighth-century minister and poet Chang Chiu-ling wrote in *Li-chih Fu* (in *Ch'üan T'ang wen*) that although he had heard the litchi compared with the longan and even with table grapes, there was really no comparison. He believed it worth offering in ancestral temples—virtually a heresy, since it was not a classical food—and worth serving to kings and nobles (Schafer 1967, p. 190; Liu Hsün 1913 ed., 2:5a; S. C. Li 1965 ed., 31:4).

Unavoidable in any listing of the tropical fruits employed by the Chinese of T'ang are the three myrobalans—the emblic (*an-mo-le* = *āmalakī*; *Phyllanthus emblica*), the belleric (*p'i-li-le* = *vibhītakī*; *Terminalia bellerica*), and the chebulic (*ho-li-le* = *harītakī*; *Terminalia chebula*). The fame of these three astringent fruits was widespread through southern Asia and Southeast

Asia, and even their wild relatives were substituted for them in trade and medicine. Some grew, either wild or as garden plants introduced from the south, in the vicinity of Canton. Their reputation as tonics and rejuvenators was sky-high: they were, in effect, magical drugs in the same class as ginseng and accordingly figured more in medicine than in cookery (K. Su and T. C. Ch'en in S. C. Li 1965 ed., 31:7–8).

Several kinds of bananas ornamented the gardens and pleased the stomachs of the people of T'ang. The basic form was *Musa basjoo* (*pa-chiao*), whose leaves yielded valuable fibers for making textiles and papers, but which was chiefly an ornamental in gardens. *Musa paradisiaca* (*kan chiao*) had similar practical uses but was primarily a food plant. *Musa coccinea* (*mei jen chiao*) had edible fruit also but was most admired in south China for its splendid red flowers (K. Su in S. C. Li 1965 ed., 15:61–62).

Many kinds of useful palms were familiar to the southern Chinese. We have already noted two which yielded sago flour. There were also the coir palm (*tsung-lü*; *Trachycarpus excelsa*) and the fan palm (*p'u-kui*; *Livistona chinensis*), which had significant technological uses. More to our purpose here, however, are the coconut palm, the areca palm, and the date palm. Li Hsün notes the virtue of the fluid in the coconut (*yeh tzu*; *Cocos nucifera*) in that, though it resembles wine, it does not intoxicate (H. Li in S. C. Li 1965 ed., 31:16–17). The feather palm, *Areca catechu*, produced a nut— sometimes styled betel nut—which is still used as a masticatory throughout Southeast Asia. The flesh was grated and served with burned lime (often derived from sea shells), and sometimes with Borneo camphor, on a leaf. This was considered a correct gift for a guest. In T'ang times the dainty stimulant was well known in the Canton region and was submitted to the imperial court annually—doubtless because of its medicinal value. The Indonesian name of the areca nut, *pinang*, passed into Chinese as *pin-lang* (K. Su in S. C. Li 1965 ed., 31:13–14). Persian dates were imported to Canton, where they were named Persian jujubes for their resemblance to the native fruit, and by the ninth century the date palm (*Phoenix dactylifera*) was being cultivated in the same region (Liu Hsün 1913 ed., B:4a–b).

Another small fruit, comparable to the jujube in size, was the so-called Chinese olive, perhaps better styled kanari (*kan-lan*; *Canarium album*). The tropical tree on which it grew also yielded an elemi which was used in making varnish for ships' hulls. The fruits themselves were highly prized in the north as well as in the south. Eaten fresh they were sour, but steeped in honey they became remarkably sweet. They were said to be superior to cloves for sweetening the breath (S. Meng in S. C. Li 1965 ed., 31:5).

Nuts of many sorts, both native and exotic, were consumed in abundance. The best hazelnuts (*chen shih*; *Corylus* sp.) came from western Shensi. The seeds of the arborvitae (*po shih*; *Thuja orientalis*) were also valued: they were produced in Honan and northern Shansi. Pine nuts (*sung shih* or *sung tzu*; *Pinus* sp.) were also obtained in mountainous Shansi but the most delicious were imported from Korea. The latter were the large, aromatic, and nutritious seeds of the Korean pine (*Pinus koraiensis*) (H. Li in S. C. Li 1965 ed., 31:11–12). Chestnuts (*li*; *Castanea vulgaris*) were old favorites: the best were thought to grow in northern Hopei. They were either sun-dried or roasted before eating and were sometimes ground into a flour. It was thought that they benefited the kidneys (S. Meng, S. M. Sun, and K. Su in S. C. Li 1965 ed., 29:54–55; T'ang Yen-ch'ien in *Ch'üan Tang shih*). The delicious nuts of the Chinese torreya (*fei shih*; *Torreya grandis*) were taken as a peptic (T. C. Ch'en and S. Meng in S. C. Li 1965 ed., 31:10). An ever-green oak south of the Yangtze yielded edible nuts (*chu tzu*; *Quercus myrsinae-folia*) (T. C. Ch'en in S. C. Li 1965 ed., 30:102). *Aralia papyrifera* (*t'ung ts'ao*) is best known for its pith, which is used to make the miscalled rice paper, but its seeds were regarded as a delicacy by the people of T'ang (K. Su and T. C. Ch'en in S. C. Li 1965 ed., 18:63).

Some valuable nuts and seeds were imported from the West: among them a number were also grown by T'ang horticulturists. Of these, the walnut (*hu t'ao*) was reputed, probably wrongly, to have been an ancient introduction from the West by the famous explorer Chang Ch'ien. By T'ang times it was being cultivated in northern orchards, but the pharmacologists warned that eating too many was bad for the heart and might cause vomiting (Laufer 1919, pp. 264–65; S. M. Sun in S. C. Li 1965 ed., 30:97). Pistachio nuts (*a-yüeh-hun tzu* or *hu chen tzu*) were imported from Iranian lands and were thought to increase sexual vigor and to improve the health generally. By the ninth century the pistachio tree was being grown in Lingnan (T. C. Ch'en and H. Li in S. C. Li 1965 ed., 30:101). Our familiar almond (*p'ien t'ao jen*; *Prunus amygdalus*) was imported from Turkestan and, according to the merchant Sulayman, was being cultivated in China by late T'ang times (Schafer and Wallacker 1958, p. 219; Laufer 1919, p. 407). Sesame seeds (*hu ma*, "foreign hemp") are probably of Iranian origin but were familiar to Mediterranean peoples very early. It is not clear when they became known to the Chinese—probably in pre-T'ang times. Sometimes sesame was confused with flax in the Far East. It was chiefly of interest as a source of oil, but the seeds were also dry-fried and eaten (Laufer 1919, p. 288–96; also see poem by Wang Chien in *Ch'üan T'ang shih*).

It does not appear that the common people of T'ang ate much flesh. For one thing, domestic animals were more valuable for other purposes. But more important was a long-standing preference for cereal preparations, perhaps ultimately related to the ancient notion that domestic animals were intended as food for the gods rather than for men. It is true that in antiquity dried meat and pickled meat had been standard fare, among the upper classes at any rate, and to a certain extent this was still true in T'ang times. But lists of T'ang delicacies give little place to meat preparations, and the pharmacologists rate them poorly, especially beef. Meng Shen, for example, states that eating the flesh of the common yellow ox was conducive to illness, and that the flesh of the black ox should be avoided at all costs. The proper use of such bovines, he writes, is to assist in the cultivation of crops (figs. 5–8) (S. Meng in S. C. Li 1965 ed., 50:64–65). Still, they were eaten to some extent, as was the carabao (water buffalo) of the south (T. C. Ch'en in S. C. Li 1965 ed., 50:64–65). Indeed, the flesh of this patient beast was highly regarded in Lingnan. The animal was baked whole or barbecued.

The great exception to this general rule was the diet of the wealthy and noble classes—the royal court in particular. The poet Wei Ying-wu refers to the casual acceptance of boiled veal and baked lamb as a sign of the extravagant wastefulness of palace banquets. Mutton was more a food of the northern nomads than of the Chinese. Both Meng Shen and the eminent Taoist doctor Sun Ssu-mo warned against the evil effects of overindulgence in pork—presumably a dish more likely to be encountered on the ordinary table than beef (S. C. Li 1965 ed., 50:26–27). The flesh of dogs, on the other hand, was believed to be beneficial, especially to the kidneys (S. Meng and S. M. Sun in S. C. Li 1965 ed., 50:44). In the north, the Bactrian camel, a dependable and indispensable pack animal known both wild and domesticated, could occasionally lend itself to a feast. The hump in particular was a much-appreciated ingredient in a rich stew, as the poets Tu Fu and Ts'en Shen have recorded. Still, this could not have been everyday T'ang fare.

Blood preparations were not unknown, but it is hard to estimate the degree of their popularity. An example is a dish called *je* Lo Ho ("Hot Lo and Ho [Rivers]"), served at the eighth-century court of Hsüan Tsung. There was also a concoction of goat's blood with relishes and wine, and a kind of haggis using both blood and flesh—but these may have been rarities (*T'ai p'ing yü lan,* vol. 858).

However, domestic prudence appears to have made the flesh of wild animals more acceptable than that of good barnyard cattle. Indeed it appears that both lord and peasant relied heavily on wild game to supplement their diets. (The lord probably acquired his game by organized hunts or from hired trappers, while the peasant obtained his with a bow and arrow, a clever snare, or a trained hawk.) Venison was long a significant part of the northern Chinese diet. This was probably more true of ancient China than of medieval China, since the great increase in human population and the simultaneous deforestation of the north had inevitably brought about the decline of all wild populations. Among the dwindling species was the elaphure (*mi lu*; *Elaphurus davidianus*), a large deer of the swamps and water margins. It had been a major quarry of noble hunters in pre-Han times but is now extinct in its native land, although it has been preserved in some Western zoos. There were still herds to be found in T'ang times, so the beast still found its way into many pots. However, Meng Shen advised against overindulgence in its flesh, and indeed it seems to have been regarded as rather mediocre fare— a great fall from its ancient eminence as a prime meat (S. Meng in S. C. Li 1965 ed., 51:34; see poem by Kuan-hsiu in *Ch'üan Tang shih*).

Besides the bulky elaphure, there were many other Chinese deer to provide protein: large ones such as the sambar in the south, middling ones such as the sika deer (almost everywhere), and little ones such as the musk deer (more valued as a source of medicine and perfume), the water deer, the tufted deer, and the muntjac. The latter, at least, was considered a tasty and tonic dish if prepared with ginger and vinegar (S. Meng and T. C. Ch'en in S. C. Li 1965 ed., 51:37, 41).

Among other wild animals, the unique goat-antelopes of China—the serow, the goral, and the takin—were also hunted for food, and their flesh was much appreciated (S. Meng in S. C. Li 1965 ed., 51:23). The wild boar was spit-roasted, allowing the feasters to avoid the moral qualms that attended the destruction of a domestic pig (K. T'ao 1920 ed., 2:44a–b). The wild rabbit was an ancient object of the commoner's hunt—a perpetual inhabitant of the stew pot. It was snared or hunted with grained goshawks and sparrowhawks. A symbol of food readily available in the wild, its only rival was the pheasant. Despite its popularity, Ch'en Ts'ang-ch'i warns against overindulgence in rabbit flesh except during the autumn. Doubtless this admonition had some basis in ancient prohibitions against eating animals during the mating and breeding season, while autumn was the recognized season of death and slaughter (T. C. Ch'en in S. C. Li 1965 ed., 51:54). Another small animal destined for the pot was the so-called raccoon-dog (*li*; *Nyctereutes procyonoides*), a fox-like creature which is neither raccoon nor dog. Sun Ssu-mo regarded its flesh as a highly beneficial tonic, but Meng Shen warned against eating it in the first month of the year (S. C. Li 1965 ed., 51:45). In the western highlands of Kansu, Szechwan, and Tibet, the native people—apparently Chinese and non-Chinese alike—dug marmots out of their burrows for food (their furs also made warm garments). These were the so-called Szechwan marmots whose Mongolian name *tarbagha* passed into Chinese as *t'o-pa* (*Marmota himalayana robusta*) (T. C. Ch'en in S. C. Li 1965 ed., 51:69).

Even lowlier mammals were not disdained. Bamboo rats (*chu liu*; *Rhyzomys sinensis*) were submitted to the imperial kitchens by the local magistrates of Hopei. In Lingnan, newborn rats, stuffed with honey, crawled about the banquet table peeping feebly, to be picked up with chopsticks and eaten alive. Apparently this was an aboriginal custom adopted by Chinese settlers. Even the playful sea otter, whose range extended from the waters off north China across the Bering Strait and south to California, found its way into the cauldrons of T'ang (T. C. Ch'en in S. C. Li 1965 ed., 51:60).

Among well-established specialties for the southern table, the elephant was the greatest. In T'ang times the pachyderms were still abundant in the far south, and for that matter herds of them were not uncommon in remote parts of central China. The natives of Lingnan killed the monsters— especially a black variety with tusks of pink ivory—and feasted on their barbecued trunks. The flavor of this delicacy was compared to that of pork, but it was thought to be more digestible (K. L. Tuan 1968 ed., p. 306). The magnificent python was also a favorite food, especially when finely sliced in vinegar (K. Su and T. C. Ch'en in S. C. Li 1965 ed., 43:69).

Since antiquity the flesh of the lesser soft-shelled turtle (*pieh*; *Amyda* [= *Trionyx*] *sinensis*) and of the giant soft-shelled turtle (*yüan*; *Pelochelys bibroni*) was an essential ingredient in gourmet soups, and the eggs of these reptiles were also valued. Ch'en Ts'ang-ch'i approved boiling turtle flesh with the "five flavors," but Sun Ssu-mo warned strongly against eating it at the same time as pork, rabbit, or duck, and especially with mustard seeds (T. C. Ch'en and S. M. Sun in S. C. Li 1965 ed., 45:13). But these pleasant concoctions were coarse when compared with the delights provided by the famous green turtle (*kou-pi*; *Chelonia mydas*), familiar throughout the tropics of the world. The gelatinous essence extracted from the plastron of this resident of the South China Sea was as much admired in the richest soups served at court banquets in Changan as it was at Buckingham Palace in England.

But now on to fowl. Here it will not be necessary to discuss the domestic separate from the wild. Many varieties had long ago evolved from the primitive jungle fowl of Southeast Asia, and the T'ang experts were eager to point out the different effects on the human body made by the consumption of these variously shaped and colored races. Meng Shen, for instance, found the flesh of the black hen excellent for the digestion but warned against eating dark ones with white heads (S. Meng in S. C. Li 1965 ed., 48:70). The white domestic duck was highly approved of, but Meng Shen looked askance at the black ones as poisonous. Sun Ssu-mo regarded duck soup as so beneficial that it could reconcile estranged wife and husband (S. C. Li 1965 ed., 47:59). Geese, both wild and domestic, were also considered excellent fare, especially spit-roasted (Han Hung in *Ch'üan T'ang shih*). The ingestion of songbirds was not interdicted by law or by custom—they were eaten all year round—but Ch'en Ts'ang-ch'i, at least, thought them best during the winter months, when they increased male potency (S. Meng and T. C. Ch'en in S. C. Li 1965 ed., 48:97; 49:6).

China is a land of many pheasants—common food since earliest times. This was especially the case with the ring-necked pheasant (*yeh chi* or *chih*; *Phasianus colchicus*), but other species were also consumed, such as the bold Manchurian snow pheasant (*ho chi*; *Crossoptilon mantchuricum*). Like other food animals, pheasants were subject to taboos: for instance, they should not be eaten with walnuts (S. Meng in S. C. Li 1965 ed., 48:88). Perhaps it is worth noting that pheasants were commonly taken with trained goshawks, while sakers were favored for catching herons and other large game birds, and peregrines were set after ducks and other waterfowl. A lucky yeoman might own a sparrowhawk for hunting such smaller woodland birds as quail.

In any case, wild birds formed a distinctly prominent part of the T'ang cuisine, with partridge and quail being only a little less important than pheasant. The small speckled eastern quail (*yen*; *Coturnix coturnix*) was eaten in abundance, even though Meng Shen advised against taking it at the same time as pork (T. C. Ch'en in S. C. Li 1965 ed., 48:94; Shinoda 1963b, p. 317). There was a comparable taboo on the ingestion of the flesh of the popular chukar (*che-ku*; *Alectoris* sp.)—said to be tastier than either chicken or pheasant—together with bamboo shoots (S. Meng in S. C. Li 1965 ed., 48:91). The most beautiful of southern birds, which we would reserve to decorate formal gardens and aviaries, suffered the indignity of passage through the human stomach: the handsome green Far Eastern peacock was stewed—its flavor was said to resemble that of duck—and its flesh was sometimes dried and stored for later consumption. Even the colorful little parakeets of Lingnan were not spared a similar fate.

Fish formed a very significant part of the T'ang diet. They were harvested from the sea, from rivers, and from lakes and ponds, in every conceivable variety. Catching them in nets and weirs was profitable. Angling with rods and lines was pleasurable. Edible fish could also have secondary uses: the roe of certain species, notably the orphe, sometimes called ide, or grass carp (*huan*; *Ctenopharyngodon idellus*), was planted in paddy fields where, after gorging themselves on weeds, the plump adults could be sold at a profit in the marketplace. Indeed, many other useful and edible creatures, such as mollusks and crustaceans, were kept in paddy fields and lily ponds.

Above all, the ornamental carp (*li*; *Cyprinus* sp.) was a favorite not only for its flesh but for its golden scales and placid domesticity. Of many species, one of the most prized was the golden carp (*chi*; *Cyprinus auratus*), particularly common in southern lakes. Sometimes it grew eight feet long, although there were much smaller varieties. In any event it was delicious (C. S. Tuan

1937 ed., hsü, 8:243). The so-called white fish (*po yü*) was another carp (*Cyprinus carpio*), while the blue fish (*ch'ing yü*; *Mylopharyngodon aethiops*) is also known as the black carp. Fresh white carp was mixed with a bean relish to make a soup (S. Meng in S. C. Li 1965 ed., 44:93), and, marinated in wine lees, it was sent as local tribute to the court from Anhwei. Snowflake-thin slices of the flesh of the black carp were thought to go very well with oranges (Wang Ch'ang-ling in *Chüan T'ang shih*). The snakehead mullet (*li*; *Ophicephalus* sp.) was highly recommended stuffed with pepper and garlic, or cooked with beans, radishes, and onions (S. Meng in S. C. Li 1965 ed., 44:107–08). The flat, round silver pomfret (*ch'ang*; *Stromateoides* sp.) of Lingnan was delicious broiled (T. C. Ch'en in S. C. Li 1965 ed., 44:97). The same southern coast produced whitebait (*yü*; *Leucopsarion* sp.), relished when salted in slivers as fine as goose feathers (K. L. Tuan in S. C. Li 1965 ed., 44:106). The name *lu* was applied to the prickly sculpin (*Trachydermus* sp.) but also to other similar fish (e.g., *Lateolabrax* sp.); it was highly regarded in snowy flakes simmered with tender vegetables (*Ch'üan T'ang shih*, Lu Kui-meng 1:5a, and Yüan Chen 11:7b). The char, a kind of trout (*chia yü*; *Salvelinus* sp.) which lives in caves and crevices along rocky shores, was regarded as a delicacy (S. Meng and T. C. Ch'en in S. C. Li 1965 ed., 44:97). A tiny inhabitant of southern streams, the barilius (*shih pi yü*; *Barilius* sp.) made a wonderful fish sauce (T. C. Ch'en in S. C. Li 1965 ed., 44:104).

Seacoasts and estuaries were the homes of the esteemed striped mullet (*tzu*; *Mugil cephalus*), which was even sent as a royal gift from Manchuria. Equally appreciated was the scaly mullet (*ch'iu*; *Lepidotrigla* sp.), the mud-burrowing loach (*ts'a*; *Cobitis* or *Miscurgus* sp.), and the flatfish—possibly sole or halibut. The sturgeon (*Acipenser mikadoi*) of the great rivers was commonly called yellow fish, but Ch'en Ts'ang-ch'i describes it as "pure ashy" colored, adding that it had the power to transform itself into a dragon (S. C. Li 1965 ed., 44:112). It was also called *chan*. Similar was the so-called beaked sturgeon, or paddle fish (*hsün*; *Psephurus* sp.), a ganoid fish unique to China. It too had affinities with the dragon but was eaten with dried bamboo shoots or made into a pungent relish. Its roe was said to give a person the glow of health (T. C. Ch'en and S. Meng in S. C. Li 1965 ed., 44:113). Sharks (*chiao* or *sha yü*) were abundant off the southern coast and were sliced or made into a relish (K. Su, T. C. Ch'en, and S. Meng in S. C. Li 1965 ed., 44:130). Freshwater eels (*man-li yü*) were eaten, but greater emphasis was put on their medicinal value in T'ang times (S. C. Li 1965 ed., 44:109). Mud eels (*shan*; *Fluta* sp., *Monopterus* sp., and others) were boiled down into a thick nutritious broth (T. C. Ch'en in S. C. Li 1965 ed., 44:110). Even the whimsical seahorse (*shui ma*; *Hippocampus kelloggi*) could not avoid the gullets of the people of T'ang.

The technical term *kuai*, although sometimes applied to the cutting up of pork and other mammalian flesh, is very common in accounts of the preparation of fish. I have used it above a number of times, vaguely translated as "finely sliced," or "minced." This translation understates the case. The word was used for a refined technique achieved by chefs of the highest order. Fish—especially those with pure white flesh—were sliced into wispy slivers. These were regularly compared to heaps of snow and frost. The poems of Tu Fu, who relished fine food, refer repeatedly to the delicious "snowflakes" flying under the expert hand of the cook. For example, he matches the image of "silver threads of golden carp" with the "frosty" glitter of a chopping knife (various poems in *Ch'üan T'ang shih,* box 4, vols. 1–4). One of the precious gifts presented to An Lu-shan, when he still enjoyed the favor of his sovereign, was a fine knife for slicing fish (C. S. Tuan 1937 ed., 1:3). We may read of a specialist who could chop so thinly that the slivers would blow up into a current of air. On one occasion, it is said, a pile of them formed during a storm, turned into butterflies, and flew away (ibid., 4:40). Ch'en Ts'ang-ch'i, however, warning against overindulgences of various sorts, advises his readers to avoid fish slivers in the evening, with cold water, with milk products, or with melons (S. C. Li 1965 ed., 44:131).

Crustaceans, mollusks, and cephalopods were almost as important as fish in the T'ang diet, although not necessarily in that order. They were collectively called sea savories (*hai wei*), and the best of them were sent to the imperial court from coastal Chekiang. Crabs of various sorts were prepared in many ways. For instance, they were much enjoyed preserved in vinegar, while their rich yellow fat, enhanced with the five savory substances, was a treat of the far south (H. Liu 1913 ed., 3:6a; S. Meng in S. C. Li 1965 ed., 45:18). Shrimps and their cousins were eaten, but T'ang pharmacologists looked askance at them. They could be deadly when made into fermented sauces (S. Meng and T. C. Ch'en in S. C. Li 1965 ed., 44:126–27). Possibly this belief was related to the contamination by the feces used as fertilizer in the irrigation ditches and flooded fields in which these little animals throve. Superficially similar to the crustaceans was the horseshoe crab (*hou*; *Limulus* sp.), which is not a crab at all but a relative of the spiders—an odd survival from the remote history of life on earth. It is better named xiphosuran. Han Yü noted it as a specialty of the south, where its flesh was much used in the manufacture of pickles and sauces (H. Liu 1913 ed., 3:1b; C. S. Tuan 1937 ed., 17:139; Han Yü in *Ch'üan T'ang shih*, 6:6b).

Among the mollusks, we hear more of bivalves than of the snaillike gastropods. Certainly every sort was sought along the extensive seacoasts of the T'ang empire. Most prominent were the figured bivalves (*wen ko*), a loose category that included members of the *Lucinidae* and especially the venus clams of *Veneridae*. These were harvested for the northern elite along rocky shores from Shantung to Fukien. Several varieties of oysters (*Ostrea* sp.) were available, both to the pearl divers of coastal Kwangtung and to gourmets who liked to eat them with wine. Our popular notion that they increase sexual potency seems not to have been familiar to the Chinese. On the contrary, Meng Shen announces that they inhibit nocturnal emissions— literally "copulation with ghosts and emission of sperm" (S. Meng in S. C. Li 1965 ed., 46:22). A Korean bivalve called *tamna* (*tan-lo*) was prized as an ingredient in a healthy soup to which was added the edible laver *kompo* (*k'un-pu*) (T. C. Ch'en in S. C. Li 1965 ed., 46:34). Mussels shaped more or less like knives, including the genera *Tellina* and *Mytilus*, were a favorite food among coastal dwellers. Of these the type species was *Mytilus edulis* (*tan ts'ai*). The pharmacologists warned against eating them simply broiled but found them beneficial when cooked with radishes, melons, and other vegetables (S. Meng and T. C. Ch'en in S. C. Li 1965 ed., 46:25, 40). Among the more intelligent cephalopods, the squid was most important in T'ang cuisine. It was preserved by salting and drying but also fried with ginger and vinegar (H. Liu 1913 ed., 3:2a).

We are accustomed to the idea that there is a line which divides eastern Asia into two cultural groups—one which depends on milk and milk products (Indians, Tibetans, and many Central Asian nomads), and one which rejects them with loathing. In the latter group we place the Chinese. Indeed, some evidence for this classification can be found at every period of Chinese history, even though warm milk was regarded as a highly nutritious food from very ancient times (Cooper and Sivin 1973, p. 227). It seems, however, that after Han times, when the intermingling of Chinese and Altaic customs became pronounced to a new degree, the barrier of prejudice broke down, and by T'ang times milk products formed a significant part of the diet of the upper classes. This change must have been due both to the close relations between the aristocracy of north China and the noble families of the frontier nomads, established in the Han-T'ang interval, and to a simple, gradual intermingling of peoples whose tastes had formerly been believed to be irreconcilable.

In north China during the T'ang period, goat's milk was widely regarded as a salubrious beverage, of especial value to the kidneys (K. Su in S. C. Li 1965 ed., 50:54). Po Chü-i stated plainly that nothing could please him more on a cool spring morning than rehmannia (*ti huang*) taken with milk (in *Ch'üan T'ang shih*, 30:4b). I Tsung, who reigned over a disorganized domain in the middle of the ninth century, honored his scholarly advisers with gifts of "silver cakes," in which milk was an important ingredient (T. P. Wang 1968 ed.). In the south as well, milk was used in the preparation of many popular foods. This seems mostly to have been the milk of the carabao. Sago extracted from the arenga palm taken with milk was a staple that gave the southerners great pleasure (C. S. Tuan 1937 ed., hsü, 9:249). A sweet named "stone honey" (*shih mi*), made in Szechwan and Chekiang but also imported from the Iranian lands of the West, was made of milk—especially that of the water buffalo—and sugar (K. Su and S. Meng in S. C. Li 1965 ed., 33:60).

Milk was modified in many ways. It was curdled to make, for instance, *ju fu*, analogous to bean curd (S. Meng in S. C. Li 1965 ed., 50:92). Indeed, much more popular than unaltered milk were a number of fermented or soured derivatives. Three of these in particular, conventionally classified in a hierarchy representing the level at which each was derived from another, were highly valued. This triad appears in literature metaphorically, representing the stages of the development of the soul—especially in Buddhist belief. The most common of them, and therefore the lowest member of the triad, was kumiss (*lo*), usually prepared by heating animal milk in a pan, where it would ferment by the action of lactobacillus.[7] (It is noteworthy that one of a long list of expensive gifts given by Hsüan Tsung to An Lu-shan was *ma lo*, that is, kumiss made from mare's milk [C. S. Tuan 1937 ed., 1:3]). One step higher was *su*, corresponding to kaymak, or, in our own culture, to clotted, or Devonshire, cream. It was removed, even rolled, from the top of the kumiss preparation after the latter had cooled. It was much used in dishes of high quality (Tannahill 1973, p. 134). The third, final, and most highly regarded member of the triad was *t'i-hu*, which strongly resembled our clarified butter. It was a sweet oil made by reducing kaymak over heat, storing it until it coagulated, and then skimming small quantities of the butter-oil from the top.[8] In religious imagery, accordingly, it represented the ultimate development of the Buddha spirit.

It appears that in early antiquity beverages given the name *lo* were also prepared from grain and even from fruit products (S. S. Ling 1958, p. 888). Throughout historic times, however, the word was applied almost exclusively to milk products, particularly the milk of horses, although that of the water buffalo was considered particularly rich (K. Su in S. C. Li 1965 ed., 50:90). There was also a dried, possibly powdered, variety of kumiss (T. C. Ch'en in S. C. Li 1965 ed., 50:90). The liquid was an ingredient in many complex dishes. Mixed with sago it made palatable cakes (ibid., 31:19). Prepared with flour and camphor and then refrigerated it made a delicious hot weather food, comparable to our ice cream. Its clotted derivative, which I have compared to kaymak, or Devonshire cream, was a much admired delicacy, especially in the north: the court exacted quantities of it annually from the herdsmen of Anhwei, Shensi, Szechwan, and Tsinghai. (There was some dissension among the pharmacologists as to the relative superiority of cow kaymak and goat kaymak—Su Kung preferring the former, Meng Shen favoring the latter [S. C. Li 1965 ed., 50:90–91]). The delicate flavor of kaymak was attested to by the poet P'i Jih-hsiu, who described a lavish, and apparently imaginary, feast in the company of a Taoist hermit set out in a "shaded palace" (that is, a mountain cave), where he was served "the flesh of swallows" (the Chinese equivalent of peacock tongues at a Neronian orgy). P'i Jih-hsiu flattered this elegant dish by rating it easily as flavorsome as kaymak (P'i Jih-hsiu in *Ch'üan T'ang shih*, 7:9a). Kaymak was also used in the finest pastries. Several of these are named in a menu for the celebrated banquet of Wei Chü-yüan. Among them is one in which the kaymak was mixed with honey, another named "jade dew balls," and still another with the fascinating name "[Yang] Kui-fei pink" (K. T'ao 1920 ed., 46a–48b). T'i-hu, similar to the ghee of India, was symbolically more refined than kaymak as the *Nirvana-sutra* was more refined than the *Prajñaparamita-sutra* from which it was derived. It was used in the preparation of the most exquisite dishes, and Sun Ssu-mo regarded it as a powerful tonic for bones and marrow and conducive to a long life (K. Su and S. M. Sun in S. C. Li 1965 ed., 50:91). Not unnaturally, poets found this excellent oil congenial in descriptions of Buddhist monasteries, as when Shen Ch'üan-ch'i, describing a magnificent monastery in a mountain forest, adds to the images of sandalwood and gaudy parrots the equally appropriate one of clarified butter mixed into a fine wine (in *Ch'üan T'ang shih*).

After a crop failure, or the depletion of food resources for other reasons, the people of T'ang were compelled to look for substitutes for their normal articles of diet. To an upper-class man this might mean eating what he would regard as "poverty food," that is, the normal diet of a poor peasant, such as simple cereal gruels and bean dishes (*Hsin T'ang shu 1*, 169:5a; *T'ai p'ing yü lan*, vol. 858). A poor man was much worse off: he might be compelled to turn to such things as the sediment left from the fermentation of wine (*T'ai p'ing yü lan*, vol. 854). It was also sometimes necessary to give up domestic plants altogether in favor of wild plants. Among those recommended in T'ang sources are "China root" (*t'u fu ling*; *Heterosmilax japonica*) (T. C. Ch'en in S. C. Li 1965 ed., 18: 47) and the roots of water chestnuts (*p'ing p'eng ts'ao*) (ibid., 19:105). Or again, the seeds of the fleabane (*p'eng*; *Erigeron kamschaticum*) were made into a flour, while the leaves of the sophora (*huai*) were the basis of a kind of sauerkraut (*Hsin T'ang shu 1*, 52:7a).

Some of the worst famines occurred in cities under prolonged siege. Then the citizenry had to turn to anything that could be swallowed, however repugnant normally. When, in 759, Kuo Tzu-i besieged An Ch'ing-hsü in Yeh-ch'eng, the price of a single rat rose to 4,000 cash (*Tzu chih t'ung chien*,

221:1b). During the prolonged siege of Kuang-ling by Yang Hsing-mi, in 887, the unlucky populace was compelled to eat cakes of mud, flavored with whatever weeds they could find (ibid., 257:9b). There were even more unpleasant necessities: during the siege of Hao-chou by rebels in 869, the inhabitants turned to slaughtering each other to obtain meat (*ibid.,* 251:17a). Cannibalism was also resorted to during famines unconnected with war. An example is the great famine in the Huai and Yangtze areas late in 761, when men were obliged to eat other men (ibid., 222:7a).

Sweeteners

Probably the oldest and certainly one of the most respected sweeteners was honey. Despite formidable rivals, it remained so in T'ang times. The bees of most of north China provided it for the tables of the great, and the "white" honey of the region around Changan was considered by far the finest—certainly preferable to that produced south of the Yangtze (K. Su in S. C. Li 1965 ed., 39:57). A superior variety of honey was also imported from Tibet. The ambiguous term *stone honey* (*shih mi*) was sometimes applied literally to honey taken from the rock homes of cliff-dwelling bees. More often the expression referred to little honey or sugar cakes—but we shall come to them presently. In any event honeyed preparations of many sorts were much appreciated, such as honeyed bamboo shoots and honeyed ginger.

Another ancient sweetener was maltose—a kind of malt sugar (*i*) derived from germinating grains (especially of barley). Its production was closely related to the manufacture of wine. The sugar beet (*Beta saccharifera*) was probably introduced from the West in T'ang times. It is reported that it was steamed and eaten in the south in that period, but whether it was treated as anything but a sweeter variety of the common beet (*t'ien ts'ai*) is not clear (Laufer 1919 ed., 399–400; K. Su in S. C. Li 1965 ed., 27:93).

Manna did not come to the people of T'ang from heaven, but from the arid lands near the Mountains of Heaven in Central Asia, especially in the vicinity of Qočo (Kao-ch'ang). This was the honeylike exudate of a leafless desert plant usually called *tz'u mi* ("thorn honey") but sometimes *yang tz'u* ("sheep thorn"). We Westerners call it camel thorn (*Alhagi camelorum* or *Alhagi maurorum*). It was well known to the Persians and Arabs and not unnaturally connected by the Chinese with the auspicious "sweet dew" that was said to fall, at exceedingly rare intervals, from heaven to signify the inauguration of a season of blessed peace among men (Laufer 1919 ed., 343–45; T. C. Ch'en in S. C. Li 1965 ed., 33:61).

A common substitute for bee honey was the sweet extract of the seeds, boughs, and young leaves of the so-called Japanese raisin tree (*chih-ch'i*; *Hovenia dulcis*), a southern plant sometimes styled "tree honey" in Chinese (K. Su and T. C. Ch'en in S. C. Li 1965 ed., 31:26). Another semi-exotic, although perhaps not so extensively used, sweetener was the sugar yielded by the sap of the sagwire, or arenga palm, whose other virtues we have already observed.

Now we return to stone honey, mentioned above. Most commonly, the term referred to cakelets made from honey and milk. These tasty morsels were produced along the Yangtze basin from Szechwan to Hangchow Bay. The kind most fit for the imperial table, however, came from southern Shansi, Hunan, and Szechwan. But, delightful as they were, these honey cakes disintegrated readily and were therefore soon replaced by sugar cakes in the affections of those who could afford an expensive substitute. These were imported from abroad and were made from the refined cane sugar of Magadha (*T'ai p'ing yü lan*, 857:2a; *Ts'e fu yüan kui*, 970:12a–b; Wang P'u 1935 ed., 100:1796; Schafer 1963, p. 153). Indeed, not only the product but the technique of refining the juice of sugarcane was imported. The method consisted of boiling down the juice of the cane to make a granular substance called "sand" sugar (*sha t'ang*), doubtless comparable to what we call raw sugar. The knowledge of this technique came from eastern India to China in the seventh century. Yang-chou, where the Grand Canal joins the Yangtze, a great city both for industry and pleasure, soon became the acknowledged center of sugar manufacture. The new product was much superior to the old, but an even better one was soon to appear. It is virtually a certainty that a refined white sugar called *t'ang shuang* ("sugar frost")—a kind that we might recognize at our own tables—was being made in Szechwan in late T'ang times (Laufer 1919, pp. 376–77; S. Meng and K. Su in S. C. Li 1965 ed., 33:58–59). Sugar seems to have been used as a pleasant additive to dishes in which we would deem it inappropriate, such as the "sugar crabs" (*t'ang hsieh*) produced on the central coast in T'ang times.

Condiments and Spices

The pharmacologists of T'ang studied all potential foodstuffs hoping to ascertain their virtues and the complex effects they had on the human body, especially in conjunction with, or in reaction against, other edibles. They were particularly concerned with the prolongation of youth, the lengthening of life, the blackening of hair, the restoration of waning sexual powers, and other such blessings. Pungent and spicy materials seemed especially likely to have these desirable properties in more concentrated form than did ordinary materials, proportional to the greater effects they had on the olfactory and gustatory cells. Therefore, small quantities of these potent substances were much in demand as additives to prepared dishes. For us, however, it is not always easy to discover the evidence for the degree of their exploitation in T'ang cookery, since the arts of pharmacology and perfumery were not sharply distinguished from the kitchen arts. Cloves and nutmeg are examples of vegetable substances whose roles are hard to evaluate for this reason.

For centuries the part played by pepper in our own cuisine was played in China by the peppery seeds of a group of plants called fagara (*chiao*; *Zanthoxylum = Xanthoxylum* sp.). Common varieties were given local names, such as fagara of Ch'in (Ch'in *chiao*) or fagara of Shu (Shu *chiao*). Very similar was the evodia (*shih chu-yü* or Wu *chu-yü*; *Evodia officinalis*),[9] whose pungent seeds were familiar to the residents of Chekiang and Fukien (K. Su and T. C. Ch'en in S. C. Li 1965 ed., 21:28–29, 41). Fagara was sometimes taken in tea with clotted cream. There were, however, eccentric opponents of this overstimulating kind of cookery: the mysterious monk Han-shan—who, in some of the verses attributed to him, appears as an outraged puritan—wrote with loathing of "roast duck tinctured with fagara and salt."

With the gradual development of trade between China and the nations of southern Asia, such traditional condiments as fagara and evodia fell out of favor, to be replaced at the tables of gourmets by "foreign" fagara (*hu chiao*), which we know as black pepper. This more pungent substance from Magadha and other tropical countries was admired to the extent that meat dishes of foreign origin without it came to be inconceivable to most persons, much as chutney seems to us indispensible with our "Indian" curries (K. Su in S. C. Li 1965 ed., 32:35; C. S. Tuan 1937 ed., 18:152). Other kinds of pepper were also imported from southern India in the so-called Persian trade, and they, like black pepper, were used for giving a more acrid tinge to some foods. Important among these was "long" pepper, which also grew in Magadha. It was considered even more fiery than black pepper. The men of T'ang knew it under a corrupted version of its native name, *pippali* (*pi-po*, **pyit-bat*) (K. Su in S. C. Li 1965 ed., 14:32; C. S. Tuan 1937 ed., 18:152). Similarly, the cubeb, a pepper imported from the Indies, was known in T'ang by a word (**pyit-dyĕng-gya*) derived from some cognate to the Sanskrit *viḍaṅga*. It was highly regarded as an appetizer (T. C. Ch'en and H. Li in S. C. Li 1965 ed., 32:36). Finally, the leaf of the betel pepper (*chü chiang*) was widely grown in Lingnan, where, like other peppers, it was well-thought-of as a digestive and was taken in a variety of foods and beverages.

Here must be included the several kinds of cardamom that grew in southernmost China or were imported from Indonesia. The word *tou-k'ou* referred primarily to the species *Amomum globosum* but was also applied loosely to the seeds of other members of the genus. The black, or bitter, cardamom (*i chih tzu*; *Amomum amarum*), chiefly an Indonesian plant, was occasionally found in Lingnan. Its bitter seeds were thought to be an excellent tonic when crushed and dry-fried with salt. They were also cooked with honey in a kind of dumpling (T. C. Ch'en in S. C. Li 1965 ed., 14:31). Red cardamom was rejected as deleterious to the appetite (C. Chen in S. C. Li 1965 ed., 14:26). Finally, the nutmeg, so well-known to cooks of our own day, was regarded as a kind of cardamom. The people of T'ang called it fleshy cardamom (*jou tou-k'ou*) and imported it from the South Seas. It was being planted in Lingnan by early Sung times at the latest (T. C. Ch'en and K. Su in S. C. Li 1965 ed., 14:34). A seed, or flower, of Indonesia that later formed the basis of a worldwide trade was just becoming familiar to the Chinese. This was the clove, a good breath sweetener and well-thought-of by the pharmacologists, but not, it seems, very important in cooking at this time. Its T'ang name was "chicken tongue aromatic" (*chi she hsiang*), apparently from its shape. Later it became known as "nail" aromatic (*ting hsiang*), also from its shape.[10] The name is comparable to the English term *clove*, which is related to Old French *clou*, "nail" (T. C. Ch'en in S. C. Li 1965 ed., 34:100–01).

Ginger root (*chiang*; *Zingiber officinale*), both fresh and dried, had been admired since antiquity both as a medicine and as an additive to food. It was essentially of southern origin, and in T'ang times it grew best in the south. The court culled the finest varieties from Chekiang and Hupei. The effects of ginger on the human body were not uniform, and if its healing powers were to be most beneficially exploited, the root had to be used with care. If, for instance, fresh ginger was used with the intent of counteracting the effects of other components of a meal or of a medicinal compound, especially with its supposed cooling property, it should be left with its skin intact. If, however, the opposite effect was looked for, and warming was the objective, the root should be peeled (ibid., 26:73). A closely related root called Mioga ginger (*jang-ho*; *Zingiber mioga*), which grew in shady places and was sometimes cultivated, also provided edible flower stalks and young shoots (H. L. Li 1969, p. 258). By name, at least, the Chinese put another root in the ginger class. This was the so-called ginger of Kao-liang (Kao-liang *chiang*; *Alpinia kumatake*), a product of southern Kwangtung and Hainan Island, from where it was sent to the imperial court with the annual tribute allotment.

Close to ginger in form and significance was the celebrated ginseng root (*jen-shen*; *Panax ginseng*), widely regarded as a panacea. Chen Ch'üan, for instance, notes that it brings every sort of hurt and injury under control and is a general tonic for all of the viscera. Some of the virtues ascribed to it must have been magical, like those ascribed to the mandrake root by our own ancestors. Indeed, Li Hsün reports that the best Korean ginseng has (like mandrake) a human shape and is provided with hands and feet. Most of the T'ang ginseng was imported from Korea, although the tribute lists also make it a product of eastern Shansi, Hopei, and Manchuria (C. Chen, H. Li, and K. Su in S. C. Li 1965 ed., 12:89). Doubtless it was an expensive drug, and its use was restricted to the kitchens of the rich, much like the employment of truffles in our own times.

A more economical spice was provided by mustard seeds. The leaves of mustard plants were also used in some preparations. A variety with large, white seeds, named white mustard (*po chieh*), or sometimes mustard of Shu (Shu *chieh*; *Brassica alba*), was grown in north China by T'ang times but was originally of Western origin. It was considered both more acrid and more tasty than the native varieties (K. Su and T. C. Ch'en in S. C. Li 1965 ed., 26:62–63; Laufer 1919, p. 380; H. L. Li 1969, p. 257). One of the more popular native species was called *yün-t'ai* (*Brassica chinensis* v. *oleifera*) (H. L. Li 1969, p. 257).

Some plant products which added both flavor and medicinal value to prepared dishes but were not really significant articles of diet might best be considered here. Among these were small parts of the Chinese cinnamon tree (*kui*; *Cinnamomum cassia*), which grew abundantly in the south and indeed formed dense forests in southern Hunan and in Lingnan—forests which are no longer to be seen. The best cinnamon was the bark scraped from young branches. This was usually designated heart of cinnamon (*kui hsin*) (S. C. Li 1965 ed., 34:88). But the dried, immature fruits, or seeds, of the tree (*kui tzu*) were also greatly valued. Licorice (*kan ts'ao*) was another highly rated additive: it was believed to counteract every sort of poisonous ingredient in vegetable and mineral preparations (C. Chen in S. C. Li 1965 ed., 12:81). Flavorsome, but not as potent as these, was the sweet basil of southern Hunan, named for an important town there (*Ling-ling hsiang*); it seems, however, to have sometimes been confused with sweet clover (*Melilotus* sp.). Among the condiments of alien origin was coriander (*hu sui*; *Coriandrum sativum*), originally from a Mediterranean land but introduced into China in very early times (T. C. Ch'en in S. C. Li 1965 ed., 26:79; H. L. Li 1969, p. 258). As familiar to us as to the peoples of the Far East is dill. It was imported to T'ang from Sumatra in the "Persian" trade, as was saffron, brought from Kashmir and other parts of India (Laufer 1919, pp. 317–18).

In our world, salt and pepper go together naturally, but this was not always the case, either in the West or in the East. Although salt was needed by everyone in T'ang China, only a few were familiar with pepper or could afford it. Consequently, salt was controlled by a government monopoly, and its production and sale were strictly supervised—although this did not always prevent the enrichment of an occasional imperial salt agent. The pharmacologists had nothing but good to say about the mineral. Ch'en Ts'ang-ch'i, for instance, claimed that it banished every sort of evil vapor and other undesirable invaders of the human body, that it harmonized the interactions of the visceral organs, and that it was generally conducive to robust health (S. C. Li 1965 ed., 11:37–38). The chief salt inspectorates—that is, the imperial agencies for the management of the monopoly—were at four places in coastal Chekiang and on Hangchow Bay.[11] These places were comfortably close to the control center of the monopoly at Yang-chou, at the southern terminus of the Grand Canal.

Li Po expressed his admiration for "the salt of Wu—like flowers—shining white as snow" (*Ch'üan T'ang shih*, 6:5a)—a salt that was produced in places other than seacoasts and by mining as well as evaporation. A coarsely crystalline kind was produced by the evaporation of brine in northern Shensi, but this was probably a highly concentrated brine from shallow desert lakes. This form was styled "sigilliform" salt (*yin yen*) (K. Su in S. C. Li 1965 ed., 11:37). Rock salt was brought from the "salt hills" of eastern Kansu. But salt and salt substitutes were also extracted from plants, for instance by burning bamboo (T. C. Ch'en in S. C. Li 1965 ed., 11:37). The seeds of a species of sumac (*yen fu tzu*; *Rhus semialata*) of central China were covered with a salty coating, which was used in the preparation of soups (ibid., 32:42).

Pickles and Preservatives

The use of vinegar as a preservative of edibles is very ancient in China and was still common in T'ang times. Vinegar was concocted from a variety of substances, among them rice, wheat, peaches, and grape juice (K. Su in S. C. Li 1965 ed., 25:24; Laufer 1919, p. 233). Sometimes its flavor was enhanced by the addition of such substances as the acidic leaves of the kumquat of south China (H. Liu 1913 ed., 2:1a), and even peach blossoms were made to serve a similar purpose (C. Feng 1939 ed., 4:31). There were a number of substitutes for vinegar, among them a juice extracted from the bark of a southern Chinese tree, said to resemble the chestnut. This was combined with brine to make the preservative. (The identity of the tree remains uncertain; its name was *yüan*.) It was used in T'ang and Sung times for preserving duck eggs, which it turned a dark brown color (M. Sun 1935 ed.).

But the most characteristic and traditional Chinese methods of preserving both vegetables and meats involved pickling by such processes as fermentation, hydrolysis, and induced decomposition—that is, reducing proteins into their component amino acids and amides by the action of enzymes, ferments, and molds. A very typical species of pickle was called *chiang*, which has been aptly translated "bean-pickle." The word *chiang* appears in altered form as the first syllable of the Americanized Japanese expression for shoyu—soya.[12] However, in pre-modern times, chiang was not necessarily a soybean product. Indeed, the word was sometimes applied to pickles based on meats and seafoods (S. H. Shih 1959a, 84–85). There were also forms of chiang based on such vegetables as the gourd (C. Feng 1939 ed., 4:31). There was still another prepared from the eggs of the xiphosuran, which was popular in the south (C. S. Tuan 1937 ed., 17:138), and a greatly admired one prepared from ant eggs. I shall use the term *bean-relish* to represent the Chinese word *shih*, the name of a popular relish of decomposed soybeans that assumes a dark color by interruption of the hydrolytic process or by drying at a high temperature (S. H. Shih 1959a, p. 87). The name was given to a number of similar concoctions, some prepared with wine, some with vinegar, some with brine, and so on. The differences were frequently local. One authority mentions a variety peculiar to a region in Honan that was made from steamed soybeans, with salt and fagara added. It matured in two or three days of warm weather (S. Meng in S. C. Li 1965 ed., 25:1–2). It was said that this salty pickle could be kept for ten years without spoiling (T. C. Ch'en in S. C. Li 1965 ed., 25:1–2).

Pickled vegetables, fermented by microorganisms that thrive on the lactic acid in plant juices, were called *tsu*. Salt or wine could help their production and preservation (S. H. Shih 1959a, p. 88; S. Meng in S. C. Li 1965 ed., 26:82). Varieties appear to have been diverse and numerous, as suggested by Tu Fu when he wrote of "winter vegetable pickle of Changan, both sour and green" (*Ch'üan T'ang shih*, 2:12b; my translation). A survey of such varieties would be prolix, but a few examples are noteworthy: the popular kind made from the water dropwort (K. Su in S. C. Li 1965 ed., 26:82); a species employing the slightly narcotic root of the "sleep vegetable" (*shui ts'ai*), which we call bogbean or marsh trefoil, and which was grown in flooded fields like the lotus; and one based on a white-flowered aquatic relative of the sweet potato (*yung ts'ai*; *Ipomoea aquatica*), native to Lingnan. Melon pickled in rice mash was sent as local tribute to the palace from southern Shensi and northern Hupei. Dill (*shih-lo*) had already been introduced from Sumatra and was used in pickling by the Chinese, although they were warned not to combine it with asafetida lest it lose its desirable flavor (H. Li in S. C. Li 1965 ed., 26:87).

The milky bean curd—also known to Westerners by its Japanese name, tofu (Chinese *tou-fu*)—was a ferment made from many kinds of beans and peas. It was an ancient and familiar product (S. C. Li 1965 ed., 25:5).

The word *hai* was used in T'ang times for a very important class of pickled products, which I shall call meat-pickle, in whose preparation vinegars, acid, and amino acids were normally employed. The *Hsin T'ang shu*, for instance, gives prominence to deer meat-pickle, rabbit meat-pickle, goat (or sheep) meat-pickle, and fish meat-pickle in the court cuisine (48:7a). The antiquity and respectability of such preparations as these are so distinguished as to inhibit further comment on them here.

An important subclass of this notable group was fish-pickle, which had its own special name, *cha*. There were many varieties of this southern specialty, which was plainly akin to the evil-smelling fish sauces of modern Indochina, to say nothing of the *liquamen* of the ancient Romans (Tannahill 1973, p. 97). Normally, the Chinese made them of fish flesh fermented in milk products (that is, butyric acid), although we also read of cha preserved in fermented rice or in salt (S. H. Shih 1959a, p. 89; S. C. Li 1965 ed., 44:131–32). Many kinds of fish were used in these pastes, or relishes, among them the paddlefish (*hsün*; *Psephurus* sp.), a ganoid fish known best from the mouth of the Yangtze, the striped mullet, and very commonly the carp (Shinoda 1963c, pp. 351–52).[13] Some varieties of cha went far beyond the everyday kind of fish paste in their delicacy and rare artistry. An example was a kind produced in the Wu-Yüeh region named, in the tenth century, "translucent peony" fish sauce. It was composed of the thinnest possible slices of pink flesh, arranged like the leaves of an opening peony, on a serving dish (T'ao Ku 1920 ed., 2:45a). The image of *sashimi* is inevitable but this is probably misleading, since we are here dealing with a specially treated and preserved fish. There are occasional anomalies in the use of the word *cha*: it was used not only for fish preparations but also for some other pickles—so we may read about cha of wild pig (C. S. Tuan 1937 ed., 1:3). There must have been an affinity in the mode of preparation.

There were still other and in some cases simpler ways to keep food products from spoiling. We have already taken note of the use of salt in conjunction with vinegar and the like in making preserves, and also of the employment of salt as a seasoning or condiment—that is, as what we would call table salt. But salt was also used as a simple packing to keep some fresh products edible as long as possible. An example is oranges stored in salt: kept this way they were reputed to have the added virtue of relieving the results of drinking too much wine (S. Meng in S. C. Li 1965 ed., 30:88).

Drying was also a simple but ancient and honorable method of preservation. Perhaps it was not as important in T'ang times as in early antiquity, but we observe that dried strips of deer flesh were required from the region of Anhwei in T'ang times as local tribute. Some vegetable products were especially well suited to this kind of preservation. From the Chinese dominions in Turkestan came not only grape juice (perhaps some kind of syrup) and grape wine but also what appear to have been three distinct kinds of raisin: parched (*chien*) grapes, crinkled (*chou*) grapes, and dried (*kan*) grapes. Even Shansi, the chief grape-growing region of T'ang China, sent parched grapes to the court, and by the ninth century at the latest, raisins were abundant in Yünnan—although this could only facetiously be regarded as Chinese territory at that time (Laufer 1919, p. 231). Closely allied to drying was the art of smoking, an example being the black smoked apricots of Hupei.

To keep foods through the hot months of summer, ice had to be brought from the high mountains in winter or early spring. It was kept in pits, and these ice pits were important places of refrigeration for fruits and vegetables—for melons in particular. The imperial palace was, as might be expected, very well furnished with such units (*Hsin T'ang shu 1*, 48:12a). Indeed, the ice-gathering industry was as important to the well-to-do aristocracy as it was to royalty. All who could afford it used chunks of ice not only for preventing the spoilage of vegatables and fruits but also for cooling their houses during the summer. T'ang texts also refer frequently to ice pots and ice urns, but many of these passages are metaphorical allusions to the supposed purity of heart of a true Confucian gentleman, symbolized as a fine, jade container packed with ice—much as we might represent a noble, southern senator in the guise of a silver julep cup or a champagne bucket.

Cooking

I have already alluded many times to the cooked dishes of T'ang and will have occasion to refer to others in later sections of this chapter. Accordingly, only an outline of the common modes of cooking is necessary here. The most common of the special words for cooking that I have encountered in T'ang literature are these: *chien* ("parch," "dry-fry," "reduce liquid content by heating"); *ch'ao* ("stir-roast" in a pan); *chu* ("decoct"); *ao* ("dry-fry"); *chih* ("spit-roast," "barbecue," "broil"); *p'eng* ("cook," especially by boiling); *p'ao* ("roast," "bake," especially in a wrapping). (There are some differences between T'ang and modern usages of certain words and, presumably, between the techniques they refer to: some that are common now were rare then, for example, *cha*, "fry in oil.") Many, but not all, of these words were used primarily with reference to cooking meat dishes. Parching, for instance, was appropriate equally to wheat, to "shiny" asparagus (*t'ien men tung*), to litchis, and to apricots (*T'ai p'ing yü lan*, vol. 858). Steaming (*cheng*) was as good for pears as it was for suckling pigs (C. S. Tuan 1937 ed., 1:3). Beef could be boiled (see Li Po in *Ch'üan T'ang shih*, 8:8a).

Camel humps might be spit-roasted (C. S. Tuan 1937 ed., 7:56) as readily as the conventional chunks of beef (Li Hsien-yung in *Ch'üan T'ang shih*, 1:2a). Dried meat, wheat flour, and bamboo shoots were all equally suited for making soups (K. T'ao 1920 ed., N:49a). A curious cooking method was to heat pork, mutton, or eggs in natural sulphur hot springs. The finished dish was thought to be very beneficial to the health, especially in the case of invalids (T. C. Ch'en in S. C. Li 1965 ed., 5:48). But these variations and refinements could be pursued indefinitely. Let us leave them to take note of a few examples of cooked dishes whose preparation does not fall under any of the customary rubrics listed above.

I have in mind such commonplace preparations—generally regarded as poor and meager fare—as simple porridges, gruels, and other plain foods based mainly on cereals and water, although sometimes enriched with bits of meat and, occasionally, with even more savory substances. Ordinarily, these composed the unavoidable meals of the poor or the infirm, and sometimes they were the chosen austerities of otherworldly recluses and ostentatious clerics. However, the degree to which, for example, such traditional dishes as *san* (a rice soup with meat balls) and *kao mi* (a larded rice soup) were eaten, and whether they were universally or only locally consumed in T'ang times is difficult to ascertain (*T'ai p'ing yü lan*, vol. 858). Certainly *mi* ("gruel") and *chou* (the latter regarded as a thinner sort of mi) were common enough generic terms in T'ang literature—sometimes in the context of a hermit's cell, sometimes in soldiers' barracks, or even as a last-resort meal picked up along the road or as something digestible for a trembling old man. These unattractive but necessary dishes were sometimes eaten cold (examples in *Ch'üan T'ang wen*, 494:15a; *Chiu T'ang shu 2*, 19A:2b; Hsü Hun in *Ch'üan T'ang shih*).

But T'ang texts give the greatest attention to cakes (*ping*). Clearly, the many kinds and shapes of doughy objects represented by this term were highly popular. Indeed, the ubiquity of the word, often much qualified by modifying terms, suggests that cakes were the gold of the T'ang dinner table. They were cooked in many ways, the sole constant being, it seems, a milled cereal as the chief ingredient. In short, the word *ping* appears to have been as variable and comprehensive in its applications as the Italian word *pasta*. Certain cereals were favored over others in the cooking of cakes in T'ang times. Although, for instance, we read of a kind of barley cake named "yellow steam" (*huang cheng*)—it was wrapped in hemp leaves, hence the name—it is clear that barley did not enjoy much prestige. The most popular cakes and cakelets were made of wheat or rice (K. Su in S. C. Li 1965 ed., 25:15).

Frying seems to have been the most popular manner of preparation. A host of references to rich, fried delicacies survives—unfortunately without clear indications of the details of their preparation. For instance, we can be fascinated by the exotic image of a sweet, ring-shaped cake fried in oil (*san*)—we can only call it a doughnut—without being quite sure what the proportions of its constituents were, or precisely how it was cooked, or even what its flavor was (see *T'ai p'ing yü lan*, vol. 853). Fortunately, archaeologists have found actual examples of T'ang dynasty cakes. A roll of wheaten bread fried in oil has been preserved from the eighth or ninth century. Also a pair of *chiao-tzu* (Chinese ravioli), still much appreciated, survive from that age (Anonymous 1973, illus. 259–61, p. 133). The word *chiao-tzu* was not current in T'ang times, and the fossil "raviolis" are probably what was then called *hun-t'un*. This word had interesting linguistic associations with, for instance, an expression used by astronomers to describe the sky as a spherical envelope around us all (not the traditional hemispheric umbrella)—like the dough that completely encases the meat in hun-t'un. Hun-t'un were typically based on rice and were a specialty of the far south that had acquired a recent vogue in the north (C. S. Tuan 1937 ed., 7:56; Schafer 1967 p. 249). Often classed with them were *man-t'ou*, a kind of steamed cake, whose name is cognate to that of the familiar gift cake of modern Japan, the *manju*, but whose essence was different: the Japanese version contains bean paste. In T'ang times the man-t'ou was a rice cake which, like the hun-t'un, had attracted the attention of the northern elite (Chang Shih-cheng n.d.). In any event, the rice cake, in its several forms, was thought of as a special delicacy of Cantonese origin (K. L. Tuan 1968 ed., p. 306).

Also extremely popular in T'ang times were the "foreign" (*hu*) cakes, apparently varieties of fried or steamed breads introduced from the West. Particularly well liked was a steamed variety containing sesame seeds (Hsiang 1957, pp. 45–46).[14] In the capital city, these were sold by foreign vendors— seemingly Iranians for the most part—on street corners. An interesting variety, said to have the special virtue of curing hemorrhoids, was a rice cake cooked with camel fat (Hsiao in S. C. Li 1965 ed.). We also discover a number of references to a kind of pastry called *pi-lo*. There were a number of varieties of this confection, such as a cherry pi-lo and an aromatic "heavenly flower" pi-lo (C. S. Tuan 1937 ed., 7:56; C. Y. Wei 1920 ed., 10:69b; Shinoda 1963b, pp. 314–15). Some of these fancy pastries that enriched the T'ang cuisine, many of them newly introduced from abroad, were distinguished by their incorporation of foreign ingredients, especially spices and other aromatic substances, while others were based on foreign recipes, although the ingredients might be readily available in China. An example of the latter is the "Brahman cake" of steamed wheat paste. Needless to say, some of these dumplings, cakes, and assorted pastas were combined with other materials (like the hun-t'un mentioned above). There were, for example, dumplings wrapped in the leaves of wild rice (*tsung*; *Zizania latifolia*) (*T'ai p'ing yü lan*, vol. 851).

Beverages

Since the earliest times, drinking *chiu* ("wine") was a basic part of Chinese living, whether in the highest rituals, where aromatic beverages were proffered on state altars to the gods, or in any casual moment of relaxation from work or worry by the lowliest member of society. In translating the word *chiu* by the term *wine*, however, we usually do wrong. That is, we are misapplying the word if we accept the technical definition now current in the West that wines are fermented from fruits while beers are brewed from cereals.[15] *Chiu* (although ultimately the name came to be extended to all kinds of alcoholic drinks) was originally applied to millet and wheat products and sometimes to those based on other cereals, often with the addition of medicinal or flavoring ingredients. These additives played the same role as the mysterious ingredients of Benedictine and Chartreuse, which, however they may be treated now, were once considered potions and elixirs whose herbal components were intended to maintain somatic harmony and physical health. Some were added for ritual purposes, since the rich vapors escaping from sacrificial liquors carried their essences upward to the greedy gods.

But ignoring these fine preparations for the moment, the basic brew of which they were derivatives came from a cereal mash altered by the vigorous working of ferment cakes, which provided molds and yeasts for the mixture. They in turn created the essential alcohol for the final product. (For details see, especially, Huang and Chao 1945, pp. 28–29.) In antiquity millet was the chief source of what I shall from now on call wine, but by T'ang times millet-based wine was regarded as a peculiarity of the far north. This was at a time when rice-based wines were being imported from the south in considerable quantity, so that most T'ang wines can fairly be said to have been the products either of glutinous millet or of glutinous rice[16] (T. C. Ch'en and K. Su in S. C. Li 1965 ed., 23:70, 78; Shinoda 1963a, pp. 323–24). It is thought that the building of the Grand Canal from Yang-chou to the Yellow River basin, in the Sui-T'ang era, led to the transfer of advanced wine-making technology—including some things learned from the imported art of making grape wine—into the heart of the rice-growing area, to the great advantage of drinking men in the south (Shinoda 1963a, p. 322).

The moldy ferments were traditionally bred in the sixth or seventh lunar month (T. C. Ch'en in S. C. Li 1965 ed., 25:16; Shinoda 1963a, p. 329). The wine itself was started in the ninth month and was called "winter" wine when ready. But in T'ang times a more popular wine, celebrated in poetry, was "spring" wine, which was fully mature and most palatable when the first flowers of the cherry and peach trees were appearing. This wine played an important part in the many festivities—some solemn, some casual—that signalized the beginning of the life cycle in the new year—that is, usually late in January or early in February. Wine, love, and flowers were all superficial tokens of a sincere devotion to the meaning of a serious cosmic event (Shinoda 1963a, p. 329). Universally admired, spring wine was produced in many places, and the best vintages were eagerly sought out by connoisseurs. The best in T'ang times, to judge from the tribute records, was brewed in central Szechwan.

Wine-making techniques were not exclusively concerned with the manipulation of materials. Not only did the herbs added to Chinese wines sometimes have a magical purpose (hardly to be distinguished from a medical one), but the process of preparing the ferment—a delicate and critical matter—was accompanied by the recitation of spells and the employment of other modes of obtaining supernatural aid (Huang and Chao 1945, pp. 23–29; Shinoda 1963a, p. 322).

Wines could be distinguished according to the cereal on which they were based or by the particular technique employed in their brewing. In addition, there were some peculiar subvarieties. An example was the amber-colored unfiltered wine (*p'ei*), frequently identifiable by the bits of husk floating in it.[17] These enjoyed the popular name of "floating ants" (*fou i*). They are frequently alluded to in the poetry of the whole period from Han to T'ang (Shinoda 1963a, p. 327. For an example see Li Ho's poem in *Ch'üan T'ang shih*, 4:3a). This debris was also known by other names (K. T'ao 1920 ed., 2:38a–b).

But however colored or contaminated with unassimilated matter, wine derived from cereals was always important, either for good or for evil. On the latter point, even the learned pharmacologists disagreed. Meng Shen, for instance, warns against the prolonged drinking of rice wine, which "injures the spirit and impairs longevity." He also deplores bathing in cold water when intoxicated and warns alchemists on special cinnabar diets to abstain from alcohol altogether. On the other hand, the emphasis of Ch'en Ts'ang-ch'i is on the benefit done to the blood stream by wine. Also, he tells us, it gives a glossy luster to the skin. Best of all—and probably few of his contemporaries would have disagreed with him—it dispels anxiety (S. C. Li 1965 ed., 25:26).[18]

Although millet and rice were standard, the T'ang bon vivant had many other types of wine to choose from. There were wines flavored with pepper or fagara, chrysanthemum wine, pomegranate flower wine, ginger wine,

"Persian" myrobalan wine (available in the taverns of Changan), and bamboo leaf wine (so named for its color) (W. Hung 1952, pp. 22–23). Some of these were preferred for particular annual festivals. There was also saffron-flavored wine and honey-sweetened wine—evidently not actual mead (Schafer 1963, p. 141; Shinoda 1963a, p. 332; Stuart 1911, p. 419). One authority observes that some T'ang tipplers developed a taste for "ashy" additives—that is, alkaline ingredients—to counteract the acidity of wines. There was even a highly favored wine brewed in a liquid taken from limestone caves. This grotto water would certainly have a high alkaline content and, in addition, would offer the magical advantages that accrued from long association with these mysterious places—the underground residences of supernatural beings (T. C. Ch'en in S. C. Li 1965 ed., 5:48). *Sang-lo* wine, a specialty of Su-chou, was made of glutinous rice. It is said to have been named for the autumn season when mulberry (*sang*) leaves fell (*lo*). This was a particular favorite of the nobility (Shinoda 1963a, p. 335). The court kept brewers who were familiar with its preparation (*Hsin T'ang shu 1*, 48:7a), and it is listed among the precious gifts that Hsüan Tsung bestowed on An Lu-shan (C. S. Tuan 1937 ed., 1:3). Wisteria seeds were put in another variety of wine to keep it from spoiling (T. C. Ch'en in S. C. Li 1965 ed., 18:85). Other kinds of wine were named after famous wine-making places. The names added undeserved prestige to the beverages. Thus "fine wine of Hsin-li" was brewed far from the Han village of Hsin-li (Shinoda 1963a, p. 335).

The exotic wines from the far south formed a class in themselves. They were the product of a land famous for toddies and fruit extracts. Not that there were no fruit wines in the north, which had grape wine, pear wine, and jujube wine (Marugame 1957, pp. 313–14), but the southern novelties were more varied, more strange, and in some cases probably more richly flavored.[19] On occasion, lacking imports, the connoisseur doubtless had to wend his way south of the Tropic of Cancer to savor the delights of the palm wines—notably the liquor fermented from the flowers of the coconut palm and the toddies derived from the areca and other palms (*Chiu T'ang shu 2*, 197:1b, 2b–3a).

Grape wine constitutes a special and important case. Grapes—by which I mean grapes of Western origin, not the wild, indigenous grapes of China—had become known to the Chinese early in the Han period, both as table fruit and as a reputed source of wine, after the adventurous mission of Chang Ch'ien through the Iranian nations of Central Asia. It is not certain, however, that the hero was personally responsible for their introduction. It is even less certain when the Chinese began to make wine from them. In any case, grape wine was being imported in some quantity from Central Asia (especially from Chāch, modern Tashkent) at the beginning of the T'ang period, even though the technology of its manufacture was already known in China. Apparently the industry was still little developed there (Laufer 1919, p. 232; *Ts'e fu yüan kui*, 971:7b). It was claimed that the grape wine of Serindia remained drinkable up to ten years—a claim that will surprise no consumer of Bordeaux wines. We hear of the importation of several varieties of foreign grapes in early T'ang times. A spherical grape called "dragon pearl" was one. Cuttings of the elongated, purple "mare teat" variety were successfully planted in the imperial park after the Chinese conquest of Qočo (modern Turfan) in 640, and gifts of this famous grape came to the court from the Turkish Yabghu in 647. As was often the case with introduced plants, the imperial horticulturists mastered the art of vine cultivation, and their knowledge was disseminated in the Chinese countryside. In T'ang times the chief centers of grape production were in Kansu and, especially, Shansi. Travelers in those provinces could indulge themselves with a goblet of the grape served by the "charmers of Yen. " Although much imported grape wine was drunk in the seventh century, it seems that, with the decline of relations between China and the states of Serindia, after the middle of the eighth century, the grape wine of Shansi continued to be popular. This implies that it was no longer regarded as an exotic fad, dependent on external factors for its continuance. There were other Chinese sources. The grape wine of Liang-chou, a fine oasis town on the silk route in the far northwest, was esteemed by the people of T'ang, and it is reported that Yang Kui-fei drank it from a jeweled cup. The art of making grape wine was soon transferred to a small native grape which grows wild in Shantung (*ying-yü*; *Vitis thunbergii*). Apparently, the possibility that the juice of this purple black fruit might be susceptible to the foreign technique had not occurred to anyone during the Han-T'ang interval.

Finally, we come to the problem of distilled spirits. In the sixteenth century Li Shih-chen wrote that the art of their manufacture had been an introduction of the Yüan period, in the thirteenth to fourteenth centuries (S. C. Li, 1965 ed., pp. 34–35). He equated "burnt" wine (*shao chiu*) and "fire" wine (*huo chiu*) with the familiar word *arrack*,[20] which he represents in the form *a-la-chi* (**alaki*). Shinoda confirms this belief (1963a, pp. 325–26). However, it is hard to brush away the evidence of at least two T'ang poems which tell of the famous shao chiu of ninth-century Szechwan.[21] (This Chinese expression should be compared with our word *brandy*, cognate to the German *Branntwein*—that is, "burnt wine.")

The southern plant which produces tea leaves is botanically close to the camellia. An infusion of the leaves appears to have been drunk already in Han times, but its real popularity among the Chinese of the north did not come until the T'ang period. Then it became as routine as it is in England today. We can be even more specific about the date: Lu Yü, the author of the famous *Ch'a ching*,[22] a definitive handbook on tea, lived in the middle and late eighth century, and the T'ang history states plainly that the vogue for tea-drinking reached its climax in the second half of the eighth century. The fad even affected the Uighur tribesmen, then at the height of their power and influence in the Middle Kingdom: when any of them visited the capital they made sure to hasten to the tea market immediately to lay in a good supply of the novel, exciting, and (to them) exotic beverage (*Hsin T'ang shu 1*, 196:10a; Schafer 1963, p. 20).

Already there were various ways of preparing the leaves for decoction. They were sometimes marketed as "cake" tea (*ping ch'a*) and sometimes as "powdered" tea (*mo ch'a*). There were varieties flavored with such substances as ginger and tangerine peels—fancy mixtures comparable to our jasmine tea. [23] Even kaymak was taken with tea, just as the English favor milk with theirs (Nunome 1962, passim. For a specific example see poem by Po Chü-i in *Ch'üan T'ang shih*, 28:9a). "Bamboo" tea had bamboo-shaped leaves and was much admired. Also esteemed was the "silver flower" fine tea from western Chekiang—fit for a royal table.[24] Although tea was grown in many provinces, particularly in the south, it appears that the products of Chekiang and Szechwan were rated most highly. (Curiously, the *Ch'a ching* mentions the fine teas of Fukien and Lingnan only in the most perfunctory way [Lu Yü 1968 ed., p. 428].) Accordingly, the barges pressed up the Grand Canal from Chekiang to the capital, heavily laden with the fanciest leaves, bringing wealth to the commercial and pleasure city of Yang-chou, which was already being enriched by its crucial position in the transport of salt (*Tzu chih t'ung chien*, 234:7b).[25]

At any rate, this mid-T'ang passion for tea drinking led to the establishment of a tea-drinking ritual, or rather several refined rituals. The best known of these cults is attributed to Lu Yü and his *Ch'a ching* (Nunome 1962, passim).[26] Refinement went so far as to specify, in a precise hierarchy, the relative quality of different waters that might be used for brewing tea. At least one source asserts that the best water was to be found at a spot near the mouth of the Yangtze. Even the waters of the second class were very highly esteemed: they came from specified regions in Chekiang and Anhwei. There also seems to have been a preference for springs and sources close to important Buddhist monasteries in this region (see Chang Yu-hsin in *Ch'üan T'ang wen*). The numinous quality added to the water by the near presence of powerful spiritual forces must have been an important factor in their evaluation.

The effects of tea drinking on the body and spirit were disputed but were on the whole taken to be favorable. The common idea appears to have been

that it was a good stimulant (K. T'ao 1920 ed., 2:45a). Thus, at times it was
taken independently of meals, especially as a kind of pick-me-up after a doze
(Po Chü-i's poem in *Ch'üan T'ang shih*, 7:12a). The other side of the coin
was that it could cause insomnia (T. C. Ch'en in S. C. Li 1965 ed., 32:44).

Utensils

In pre-T'ang times, pots and other containers used in the kitchen were
made of ceramic materials, or sometimes of stone, and the use of these
materials continued into T'ang times. But during the T'ang, these came to be
replaced more and more by metal utensils, especially in well-to-do households
(Okazaki 1955, p. 117). Copper was common enough—except when the use
of copper utensils was prohibited because of a shortage of metal available
for making official currency—but also iron and, possibly, other metals were
used. The traditional Chinese stove (*tsao*), equipped with fire hole and
chimney, was still being used (Okazaki 1955, p. 113). It was normally made
of a ceramic material, or even of dried clay (*ni tsao*) (Wang Chien in *Ch'üan
T'ang shih*, 3:4a–b). Ordinarily, a pot (*fu*), which might support a steamer
(*tseng*), sat on the stove. This arrangement was well suited to the old-style
cooking of whole grain, but by T'ang times, when flour was the usual form
in which cereals were marketed and metal was beginning to triumph over
ceramics in the kitchen, the pot-steamer combination came gradually to be
replaced by a wide pan (*kuo*) suitable for the preparation of the wheaten
cakes so characteristic of that period (Okazaki 1955, p. 118). [27] Occasionally
one encounters the word *ting*, the ancient term for a tripod cauldron (e.g.,
Tu Fu's poem in *Ch'üan T'ang shih*, 10:4a–b). It is hard to ascertain whether
this usage is to be taken literally. I suspect that it is a conscious poetic
archaism, with *ting* replacing *fu*.

In the writings of the poets at least, the most commonly used word for a
secondary heating device is *lu*. This was a kind of charcoal brazier used to
warm wine and other beverages. It was often a ceramic artifact but was
sometimes made of stone (e.g., P'i Jih-hsiu in *Ch'üan T'ang shih*, 10:5a).
We also read of *tang*, made of metal, used for warming tea or wine. It is not
clear whether or not in T'ang times this was simply a metallic form of the lu.

Vessels designed to hold food and drink on the upper-class table after
their preparation in the kitchen were made of a number of valuable substances. We are much better informed about these fine utensils than we are
about containers made of humbler substances, such as wood—the only ones
available to the greater part of the population of T'ang. Accordingly, it will
be necessary to give our attention almost entirely to the former.

Metals, especially precious metals, were important in a way they had never been before T'ang times. By then the metalworkers had learned the Iranian technique of beating gold and silver into thin-walled utensils, which became to the people of T'ang what the heavy, thick-walled, mold-cast metal vessels had been to the men of classical antiquity. Gold utensils, sent as local tribute to the court, came chiefly from Yang-chou and from southern Kwangsi. Silver utensils were manufactured in the same regions and also in southern Anhwei and northern Kwangsi. The manufacture of copper utensils had a similar distribution. Tableware, including cups, dishes, bowls, and jars, was also cut out of such precious stones as agate, carnelian, and jade, although some of these—as were some utensils of precious metal—were imported. Of these, jade had the highest reputation and was different from the others in that it was required for important utensils employed in state religious ceremonies.

Some vegetable materials were also used in the manufacture of useful objects. The gourd is an outstanding example (K. Su in S. C. Li 1965 ed., 28:5), but gourd containers were probably uncommon in the most noble households. Pitchers and jars were made of the beautifully polished and decorated inner shells of coconuts.

Porcelain was just coming into its own as a prized manufacture, particularly desirable for cups. Tribute porcelain was sent from Hang-chou and southern Hopei. Lacquerware had been used continuously since early antiquity. In Han times at least, lacquered wood was the most widely used material for containers. It was not forgotten in T'ang, when the best work was reputed to come from northern Hupei.

The use of blown glass was relatively new. Fine glass utensils were made in a multitude of shapes and decorated in a variety of ways, many of them showing pronounced Western influence. This was also true of bowls, dishes, cups, and the like, made of silver and gold, and ornamented by chasing, repoussé, inlay, or parcel gilding. (The best Chinese ware in chased precious metals came from Szechwan.) The decorations and forms of these show strong Iranian (more particularly Sasanian) influence, as do the forms of many T'ang glass vessels. Elaborate representations of flowers, animals, and mythological scenes are characteristic. Some, however, have designs— animal figures, for instance—in the archaic manner of Han, just as objects of utility were sometimes cut from brownish jade in the old style of the late Chou period (Trubner 1957, nos. 326–54). Another point about form: T'ang dishes were often in the shape of a leaf or a cluster of leaves, and many stood on a short pedestal.

A number of special decorative techniques make T'ang utensils noteworthy. "Purple gold" is one. An example is the "wine vessel of purple gold" sent by Chao Tsung to Chu Ch'üan-chung in 903. This may have been fashioned in the same way as the purple gold found in Tutankhamen's tomb: the color effect was achieved by adding a trace of iron to the gold melt. Ceramic utensils could be very colorful: three-color glazes, for instance, might be used to brighten ordinary pottery, while porcelain bowls might, for instance, be ornamented with applied medallions (examples in Anonymous 1973, pl. 289, color pl. 305). Laquerware might be modified by carving or by underpainting in oil. (The best lacquerware was attributed to northern Hupei.) An opulent technique called *p'ing-t'o* consisted of designs in cut foil of gold or silver embedded in the lacquer: among the many rich articles given by Hsüan Tsung to An Lu-shan were a number ornamented in this way, including a spoon, chopsticks, and a bowl for *hun-t'un* (ravioli) (C. S. Tuan 1937 ed, 1:3). Oil painting on wood was a standard technique of T'ang times: among the lavish gifts to An Lu-shan just mentioned was an "oil painted food cabinet" (*yu hua shih tsang*) (ibid.).[28] Color was an important quality in blown glass vessels: among those preserved in the Shōsōin are a dark blue beaker, a green cup, and a brownish dish.

Other materials used at this time for certain utensils include rattan, agate, and jade. Some more unusual substances, however, were fashioned into wine cups and beakers: sulfur,[29] camphor, red gastropod shells, "tiger" crab shells striped red and yellow, xiphosuran shells, red prawn shells, mother-of-pearl, the casque of a hornbill, chestnut shells, and lotus leaves. Teacups seem invariably to have been made of porcelain. I do not know what purpose the beautiful ostrich egg cups from Bukhara and Samarkand were put to, but the tiny cups of rhinoceros horn may have been intended to counteract poisons in food. Chopsticks might be made of jade, ivory, rhinoceros horn, bamboo, or with gold p'ing-t'o insets.

Visual Aspects

Food was commonly served in a manner intended to please the eye as well as the palate, especially on festive occasions. Sometimes fancy decorative arrangements, comparable to flower arrangements, were constructed, sheerly for display. These offerings to the visual sense might take the form of delicately carved or engraved fruits, often tinted with pleasant colors and designs. Most of these seem to have originated in the culture of south China. Lingnan, for example, specialized in dried and salted apricots dyed pink in an effusion of hibiscus flowers and shaped into little vases and pots (K. L. Tuan 1968 ed., p. 308). Sometimes these confections were very elaborate: we read of a Buddhist nun who made spectacular displays in many colors out of vegetables, meat slices, and pickles of every sort (K. T'ao 1920 ed., 2:45b). Women of the south carved the images of birds and flowers on golden citrons soaked with honey and tinted with rouge. These were sent north for exhibition in the aristocratic homes of the capital. Similar embellishments were added to quinces in Hunan (Liu Hsün 1913 ed., 2:5b).

The color of wine was also a matter of importance but tended to follow personal taste. Green wine was esteemed by most and is frequently mentioned in T'ang poetry. But yellow wine also had its partisans. There were also white wine, red wine, and dark blue green (*pi*) wine. An allusion to a color like that of bamboo leaves is particularly common, suggesting that the preferred shade of green was a rather pale one. The color of green wines was thought to make a pleasing contrast to the red or purple color of a carefully chosen cup. Red wine—dripping in red pearls from the cask (poem by Li Ho in *Ch'üan T'ang shih*, 4:10b)—might sound like a red Burgundy or Bordeaux but does not refer to grape wine. It was a cereal wine colored by an easily grown red mold (*Monascus* sp.) and is still made on Taiwan (Shinoda 1963a, pp. 329–32). (There are many references to T'ang wines of various colors collected in Juan Yüeh 1922 ed.)

The *Ch'a ching*—in its extant form at least—exalts purple tea leaves above green ones. Presumably we should infer that the purple leaves tasted better. However, the color itself was a factor too: the reddish tinge imparted to the infusion by the leaves of best quality was compensated by the use of porcelain cups of suitable hue. The best cups were made in Yüeh-chou and had an icy blue color (Lu Yü 1968 ed., p. 421).

Geographical Differences

We have already noted many local food preferences and eating habits in China, along with the continuous introduction of foreign foodstuffs and their position, whether transient or permanent, in the T'ang cuisine. These themes need some elaboration. To us it is curious that the widely traveled monk I-ching, a good observer, found Chinese cooking bland and simple when compared with that of the Buddhist nations he visited in south Asia. His account of the matter states that ". . . in China, people of the present time eat fish and vegetables mostly uncooked; no Indians do this. All vegetables are to be well cooked and to be eaten after mixing with asafetida, clarified butter, oil or any spice" (Takakusu 1896). This observation makes sense only if it is taken to refer to the food of the common people of T'ang. At any rate, during the reign of Hsüan Tsung, in the eighth century, the situation was much different in aristocratic households, where foreign food (to say nothing of foreign clothes, foreign music, and foreign dances) was rigorously required at tastefully prepared banquets, and this necessarily included dishes cooked in the Indian style. Among these, steamed or fried breads and cakes ranked most highly. But there is a certain ambiguity here: cakes and breads cooked in oil were everyday fare in T'ang times. Still, they were considered a little quaint and outlandish, and doubtless this exotic quality added to their attractiveness. Such preparations must have had something of the charm with which Greek olives and Hawaiian maitai are invested in our own hybrid culture—though familiar, they are indicative of our broadmindedness (C. S. Tuan 1937 ed., 18:152). In short, Chinese table fare was undergoing a revolution during a period when the climate of taste tended to be highly permissive, and this liberal attitude towards foreign manners and customs ultimately led to the richness and variety of modern Chinese cookery (Hsiang 1957, pp. 42–45).

Imported foodstuffs were hardly to be distinguished from imported drugs. Their importation was subject to strict controls, and assurance of their physiological value had to be certified. The magistrate at the customs barrier where they entered the country was responsible for verifying their identity and purity and for fixing their value before they could be passed on to the imperial capital, their normal destination (*Ta T'ang liu tien*, 18:17a; Schafer 1963, p. 141). But in fact, foreign dishes of the more popular sort did not require imported ingredients, In many cases, it was a matter of cooking, not of components. A good example is the "light and high" Brahman steamed cakes that graced the tables of the elite during the T'ang (C. Y. Wei 1920 ed.; Hsiang 1957). Indeed, the difference between a T'ang food and a foreign food was often hard to detect. For instance, the official T'ang history makes a special point of the fact that mutton was regularly offered to the gods in distant Nepal, adding, rather haughtily, that it was partaken of with the fingers, "without spoons or chopsticks" (*Hsin T'ang shu 1*, 146a:1a). We hear also that "sheep steamed whole" was a specialty of Khotan (K. T'ao 1920 ed., 2:54a). But mutton was a familiar Chinese dish too, and although perhaps usually reserved for special feasts, it could hardly be regarded as an exotic viand (see poem by Li Po in *Ch'üan T'ang shih*, 21:4a). Of course, it was possible to be self-consciously exotic, even about mutton. Ch'eng-ch'ien, the son of T'ang T'ai Tsung, who liked to speak Turkish and to live in a Turkish tent, made a point of slicing pieces of flesh from a boiled sheep with his sword. It was not so much a matter of the food itself as a matter of manner and attitude. All in all, the men of T'ang seem to have been highly adaptable and flexible about such things, despite the proud xenophobic airs of some purists and the strictures of Buddhism. As to the latter, the seventh-century monk Huai-su, a disciple of Hsüan-tsang, did not disdain to write, for instance, that "an old monk eats fish in Ch'ang-sha, but when he comes to the walled city of Changan—he eats meat in abundance" (Huai-su, "Shih yü t'ieh," in *Ch'üan T'ang wen*; my translation).

Local diversity was an established fact of the T'ang cuisine. But although some men were tempted by out-of-town specialities, others were repelled by them. Generally speaking, the special fruits and vegetables, for instance, of the region we now call central China, such as persimmons, pears, apricots, peaches, tea, and the like, were well thought of by the northern gentry. They were, after all, products of the moderate, pleasingly warm south. There was less certainty about, and acceptance of, the products of the distant, dangerous south, whence came bananas, litchis, longans, and many citrus fruits, although some gourmets took great pains to procure these and other semi-exotics for their tables.

But we do not yet know a great deal about local eating habits in T'ang times. It is possible to state that sago cakes were much liked in the Kwangtung region (Liu Hsün 1913 ed., 2:11), as were dried oysters with wine. We can take note that deer tongues were a specialty of Kansu, Venus clams of Shantung, dried pit viper flesh of Hupei, and we can record many other local specialties, some of which were regarded as tasty contributions to elegant palace banquets. But the list is endless, and it does not tell us what we really want to know—local eating customs and preferences. We have learned only what has been chosen from among local products by northern aristocrats, according to whim or to fashion. There were men in Changan and Lo-yang, and possibly in Yang-chou as well, who deserved the title of *arbiter elegantiarum,* but it is probable that conservative northerners with traditional tastes were not quite ready for the rich spices, fruits, and strange sea creatures that the southern provinces could easily supply. In general, cooking must have been a more temperate art in the north than in the south simply because traditional concepts hung more heavily over it.

What evidence I have seen suggests that cooking was more likely to be a female art in the south than in the north. The superior position of the male in the north, determined by ancient tradition, gave that sex a monopoly of all the arts, both practical and imaginative. We do not read about female cooks in the traditional literature of China at all, except with reference to the south. In the north, women could shine as the ornaments of elite households or as the stars of the world of professional entertainment, but their talents for cooking got little recognition. Perhaps they were never encouraged: we do not notice cooking among the classical enumerations of proper female accomplishments, such as raising silk worms, embroidery, and, on a more popular level, playing the lute and the harp. In the far south, however, the prejudices of the old Chinese homeland were not much honored. There a woman was honored for her skill in the kitchen. It was not a question of proficiency as such, rather it was a difference of cultural geography. In Lingnan you could make a good marriage if you could make good pickles;

and if you were a perfectionist in the preservation of snakes and yellow eels, you were destined for wedded bliss (C. L. Fang 1846 ed., 483:5b).

In any case, southern cooking was a matter of great interest and concern to the men of T'ang and was frequently a subject of controversy. It was observed that, because of the absence of a true winter in the south, there was no concern about the withering and disappearance of food-bearing plants. The cycle of seasons as exemplified in the life and death of plants and animals was basic to northern ideas about nature. These changes took on an ethical and moral significance. That they were relatively invisible in the south was a matter of wonder and even anxiety to all "native-born" Chinese.

For every southern specialty that was accepted in the north as a delicacy, there necessarily remained hundreds of oddities which did not attract the attention of northern gourmets or resisted the transfer to a new habitat. Notable exceptions were such fruits as tangerines and litchis, which had the advantage of thriving in such intermediate zones as Szechwan, where northern palates could readily adapt to them. But let us take a specific example of a southern food plant that was not accepted in the north. It is galangal (a modern trade name), whose properties and appearance are much like those of ginger, and which was valued as much for its supposed medicinal properties as for its tastiness. *Galangal* is actually a collective name for members of the distinct genera *Alpinia* and *Kaempferia* and is as imprecisely applied as were its corresponding Chinese names, *shan chiang* ("mountain ginger") and Lien *chiang* ("Lien ginger"). The root stock of these plants was a favorite substitute for real ginger in the far south (T. C. Ch'en in S. C. Li 1965 ed., 14:22; C. Chen in S. C. Li 1965 ed., 14:24), but galangal remained strange and alien to northerners. The poets of T'ang seem to have been rather more aware of the qualities of such southern oddities than were most men. Here is an example. Yüan Chen warned his friend Po Chü-i, bound for the southeast, that he must look forward to a diet of water shield (*ch'un*; *Brasenia* sp.), eels, wild rice, taro soup, baked turtle, and much else that was not normal on respectable northern tables (*Ch'üan T'ang shih*, 12:3b). But although Yüan Chen was well enough informed, his choices are conventional: "Dear friend, this is what you must look forward to," he is saying. "But even if it is not your regular fare, there is nothing there that lacks some classical precedent." (Even the flesh of the soft-shelled turtle had been an accepted item in the cuisine of the north since antiquity.) This tone is very different from that adopted by Han Yü in his well-known poem on southern food. There he is writing about the far south and tells of strange mixtures of saline and sour, and of fagara and oranges—combinations that would surprise no one who eats Cantonese food today (Schafer 1963, p. 150).

But there were edibles that were even more incredible, especially the dishes that were peculiar to the southern aborigines. An example is the contents of the stomach of the water buffalo. It can hardly be expected that even the most tolerant Chinese would find this delicacy eatable even when flavored with salt, ginger, cinnamon, and milk, although the animal's flesh baked in a wrapper or roasted might be acceptable to him (Liu Hsün 1892 ed., 855:2b).[30] Another southern dish, probably as repellent to the T'ang Chinese as it is to us, though for different reasons, was a soup containing small taro roots or bamboo shoots: live frogs were added to the cauldron—they clutched the vegetables and were served in this agonized posture.

The wonders of southern cooking, acceptable or not, were endless: small shrimp served up with green vegetables and rich sauces (Liu Hsün 1913 ed., 3:4b); the fruit of the kanari (*kan-lan*; *Canarium* sp.), thought to be an antidote to poisons in wine and prized as a superior breath sweetener (ibid., 2:5a); a rich soup made of the flesh and bones of goats, deer, chicken, and pigs, enriched with herbs and spices, onions and vinegar (ibid., 1:8b). But among these exotic preparations, the ones that seem to have given the most trouble to the northern palate were those, as above, in which frogs were the chief constituent. Frogs were eaten in many parts of the far south but were an especial favorite of the residents of the Kuei-yang region (C. Feng 1939 ed., 6:44; 7:49). To almost all northerners, however, they were detestable. An example of this adverse attitude is provided by Po Chü-i in his poem entitled Frogs. In it he writes about water creatures that might suitably be used as offerings in ancestral temples: "But what is *un*usable is the frog—filthy in form, rank of skin and flesh" (in *Ch'üan T'ang shih*, 1:19a; my translation). Han Yü, however, who had become familiar with the south under rather unfortunate conditions, was able to exhibit a shade more tolerance. In a poem addressed to Liu Tsung-yüan dated 819, he wrote: "At first I could not get them down my gullet—lately, though, I can manage just a little" (ibid., 6:7a–b; my translation). Further along in the same poem, however, he expresses his fear that his habits might be showing the contamination of "foreign" ways.

Taboos and Prejudices

The frog was not the only animal to be regarded in this prejudicial manner. Indeed, the learned pharmacologists thought that some animal flesh was not merely disgusting but actively poisonous. Meng Shen, for instance, warned against the ingestion of the harmful flesh of the dhole, or wild dog (*ch'ai*; *Cuon* sp.) (in S. C. Li 1965 ed., 51:52). Ch'en Ts'ang-ch'i included among tabooed meats the flesh of a black ox or goat with a white head, a single-horned goat, domestic animals that had died facing north, deer spotted like leopards, horse liver, and meat that a dog had refused to eat (ibid., 50: 102–03). Many of these taboos doubtless had their origin in ancient magical beliefs—a different thing from unpalatability as such—but certainly many persons found them unpalatable simply because they had been forbidden as toxic. These taboos were comparable, but opposite, to the prescriptions which advocated, for instance, the ingestion of the flesh of the goshawk reduced to ashes, as a defense against wild foxes and goblins (S. C. Li 1965 ed., 419:17). It was believed that the power and ferocity of the hawk were transferred to the man who ate its flesh.

In short, a considerable number of dietary regulations are best described as fossilized magical taboos, even though their avowed purpose was the promotion of physiological harmony. For instance, a balance between "heating" and "cooling" elements required, among other things, that wine be served warm in the late autumn and winter, but cool in the spring and summer, even though it was generally felt that there was something a little improper about serving cool wine (Shinoda 1963a, p. 337). But the attempt to achieve balance through opposites could be carried too far. Accordingly, Ch'en Ts'ang-ch'i had to warn against the eating of ice during the summer— a potential cause of illness (in S. C. Li 1965 ed., 5:42).

Some dietary taboos were of religious origin. These were particularly prominent in Buddhist belief. Traditionally, the most generally recognized group of forbidden foods was called the "five strong-odored foods" (*wu hun*). Ordinarily this class included members of the *Allium* genus, such as garlic, onion, and scallion, but there were many variant lists. Sometimes the flesh of animals was included in them. The Taoists had several comparable lists (Stuart 1911, p. 28).

In a category by themselves were transient taboos, especially those on drinking wine. An example is an imperial order of 18 March 833 which forbade the drinking of wine on days of national mourning (*kuo chi jih*). But this was just one of many prohibitions against demonstrations of merriment on such ill-omened days (*Chiu T'ang shu 1*, 17b:8b).

Finally, there were dietary taboos prescribed for individual persons, the outstanding example being the regulations that determined the food of the Son of Heaven, the king himself, conforming to the passage of the seasons. But this ordinance rested on cosmic foundations and could be added to the class of taboos whose origin was religious.

Food in Ceremonies and on Special Occasions

J. Huizinga has pointed out the unique character of feasts and festivals, which combine aspects of frivolity and play with aspects of mystery and consecration (Huizinga 1949, p. 21). This dictum is as applicable to T'ang China as it is to any other culture, and its significance was particularly marked at the imperial table. Indeed, all imperial meals possessed a ceremonial quality. We have already taken note of the cosmic and seasonal elements in designing the sovereign's cuisine, which necessarily reflected his semi-divine nature and position, constantly attuned to cosmic changes. To assist in making the proper selections, the court maintained a host of functionaries under a special office called *shang shih chü*, the "Office of the Provost of Foods," among whose important personnel—aside from preparers of meat, pastry cooks, picklers, brewers, and other technicians, and a corps of sixteen butlers (*chu shih*) to supervise the service—were eight dieticians (*shih i*), who were required not only to make sure that the sovereign's meals were correctly planned but also to prescribe the proper viands for feasts and great ceremonies (*Ta T'ang liu tien*, 11:95; *Hsin T'ang shu 1*, 47:11a–b; 48:6b).

A special situation, somewhat different from ordinary feasts and ceremonial meals, was the feeding of visiting foreigners—tributary rulers and their suites, and ambassadors. Elaborate rules governed the choice of the wine and food to be served them (*Hsin T'ang shu 1*, 16:1a ff.). But the Son of Heaven could not eat, drink, or listen to music in their company (ibid., 215A:2a). In short, ancient tradition forbade him to share the ritualized part of his life with mere foreigners.

There was a strong tendency towards conservatism in all such matters. Although we know from other sources that novel and exotic viands were relished in the palace, official sources indicate that the table of the sovereign was supposed to be set in accordance with classical precedents and was to favor classical foods, however plain—for example, many varieties of pickle (ibid., 47:11a–b; 48:6b).

Both inside and outside the palace, it was customary before any ceremony of significance for the chief celebrant to purify himself in various ways, of which the most important was fasting. An exalted example is the ritual gesture made towards the traditional female role of household caretaker of the silkworms and the mulberries on which they fed. The empress was a kind of high priestess of the minor cult based on this custom. She prepared for her annual rite by periods of fasting in various buildings of the palace (ibid., 15:1a).

The old, traditional foods and beverages were emphasized in the important state ceremonies addressed to the great nature deities and to the spirits of departed sovereigns. Outstanding among the offerings on these occasions were the many sorts of aromatic, perfumed wines, most containing fagara, in accordance with such ancient books as the *Li chi*. The ritual foods were served on the altars of the gods in bamboo panniers or on wooden platters, as well as in other containers thought to resemble those used in antiquity. The quantities were strictly regulated in proportion to the status and power of the spirit concerned. For instance, in the seventh century, celestial and terrestrial deities received four containers of each viand, the imperial ancestors merited twelve each, but the rain and wind gods were deemed worthy of only two each (Wang P'u 1935 ed., 17:349).

Customarily, offerings to the gods consisted, in part, of meat products, including the stewed flesh of one of the five sorts of sacrificial animals—the kind depending on the dignity of the spirit being honored. There were also more conservative platters of fish and dried strips of meat (*Hsin T'ang shu 1*, 48:7a). It is a little surprising to find the flesh of wild animals among the meat dishes prescribed in T'ang times as offerings to Heaven. Seemingly these replaced, to some extent, the traditional meats of domestic origin. Among them were dried venison and pickled deer flesh, to say nothing of pickled rabbit, along with a host of other edibles (*Hsin T'ang shu 1*, 12:6b–7a).

Vegetable products also had important roles to play on these grand occasions. Most of them appear to have been pickled or salted—water caltrops, chestnuts, jujubes, hazelnuts, bamboo shoots, and much else (*Hsin T'ang shu 1*, 12:6b–7a; 48:7a; Li Po in *Ch'üan T'ang wen*).

We have already referred to the aromatic wines usual in important sacrifices. (It should be noted that wine drinking by the chief functionaries was a regular feature of court rituals [*Hsin T'ang shu 1*, chaps. 11–22].) It is remarkable to note, however, a T'ang reference to the offering of milk and milk products to stellar deities, although it seems that this was not a matter of official ritual, but a Buddhist custom. For example, kumiss was offered to the spirit of the lunar station *mao*, the Pleiades (Tao-shih 1922 ed., 5:18a–20b).[31]

Wine also had a role on such occasions as weddings, births, funerals, and the like (Shinoda 1963a, pp. 337–38). On the simpler levels of society, some of these rites might feature shamanistic performances of antiquity: a poem of the eighth century tells of a new bride offering wine to the spirits while a man plays the lute, and a woman—doubtless a shaman—dances (Wang Chien in *Ch'üan T'ang shih*, 2:4a). This sounds remarkably as if there was a degree of identification of the bride with the shaman or, possibly, with a presiding goddess invoked during the ceremony.

There were also seasonal occasions for wine drinking. In the middle of the eighth century, for example, all local officials were required to supervise a formal party, at which music was played and wine was served, in honor of the worthiest of the elderly persons under their jurisdiction (*Tzu chih t'ung chien*, 212:2a; cf. Shinoda 1963a, p. 338). Or again, at the time of the *ch'ung yang* ("double nine") festival it was the custom to drink "chrysanthemum" wine (Shinoda 1963a, p. 338).

A very special kind of ritual food was human flesh. It was by no means an uncommon occurrence for outraged T'ang citizenry to chop up the body of a corrupt or tyrannical official and eat him. A few examples of ceremonial cannibalism follow. In 739 an officer of the court, who enjoyed the monarch's favor, accepted a bribe to cover up the crime of a colleague; the affair came to light, and the ruler had the offender beaten severely, after which the official supervising the punishment cut out the culprit's heart and ate a piece of his flesh (*Tzu chih t'ung chien*, 214:7a). Again, in 767 a man murdered his rival, who had accused him of misdeeds, and having sliced his body into gobbets, he partook of them (ibid., 224:5a). In 803 a military officer led a mutiny against his commander, killed him, and devoured him, presumably with the help of his associates (ibid., 226:5b).

Closely allied to the ritualized kinds of eating and drinking discussed above were more secular kinds of feasts, on every level of formality. Perhaps the most ceremonious among them—in the sense that it was proclaimed by the sovereign himself, though shared in by all the people—was a species of drinking festival, a public debauch at government expense. This was accompanied by such entertainment as processions of floats which displayed historical and mythical scenes, simultaneously edifying and enjoyable.[32] These official bacchanals were proclaimed for fixed periods, usually three to five days. Their avowed purpose was to allow the free expression of national rejoicing. T'ang examples of such feasts include one in 630, which celebrated two great victories over the Turks; another in 682, in honor of the birth of a son to the heir designate; one in 732, following an imperial sacrifice to the earth god; and one in 754, following the bestowal of an honorific title upon Hsüan Tsung.

On a somewhat smaller scale were the celebrations that honored local scholars who had qualified for participation in the great examinations in the capital city, success in which might lead to a distinguished place in the official hierarchy. At the lowest level, these feasts were drinking parties held in the separate counties after the selection of the worthiest young men (*chü jen*). They were accompanied by musical performances on the reed organ and the display of the poetic accomplishments of the ambitious candidates themselves (Hou T'ang Ming Tsung).[33] Similarly, at the higher level of achievement, when the list of new *chin shih* ("advanced gentlemen") was posted at the pagoda in the great Buddhist monastery Tz'u En Ssu in Changan, a great banquet was held for the fortunate nominees at the Ch'ü Chiang lake garden, in the southeast corner of the city (T. P. Wang 1968 ed., p. 248). In mid-

T'ang times, and perhaps in other periods, when a high minister was newly appointed to office, a fantastic feast was held in his honor. This had the name "tail burning" (*shao wei*) (*Hsin T'ang shu 1*, 125:1b).

Every example cited above illustrates Huizinga's belief in the semi-ceremonial character of all feasts: they occurred at special times, were devoted to special purposes, and were in part detached and set aside from everyday affairs.

Similar to these, but more personal—indeed, sometimes limited to two participants—were parties given for men about to leave for a new post, or for a period of disgraceful exile, in the provinces. Such seeing-off feasts were usually held near the city gate which faced in the direction of the traveler's destination. On these occasions, often tinged with melancholy, there was much improvisation of suitable poetry. For instance, if the departing official was being sent into exile in the far south for a political offense, the farewell poems would often be laden with unpleasant allusions to the horrors ultimately to be faced by the unhappy wayfarer—malarial mists, forest demons, head-hunting savages, and poisonous snakes.

A final note on serving guests: it is customary all over the world to offer food or drink or both to a guest. A T'ang example tells of the unusual condescension of Hsüan Tsung: when Li Po was introduced to that monarch, he was offered food, and the soup was flavored by the imperial hand itself (*Hsin T'ang shu 1*, 202:8b). With the rising importance of tea drinking during the T'ang period, it became customary to offer tea to a visitor—as is done in modern England, for instance (e.g., Chang Chi in *Ch'üan T'ang shih*). It was usual to offer wine to a guest after a meal, and each person present drank his cup in turn. This contrasts with the Sung custom of drinking wine with each course served (M. Ishida 1948, pp. 93–94).

Inns and Taverns

The theme of farewell parties and guests leads naturally to the subject of wine shops and hostelries where food and drink might be available to the public. The evidence for places where food was served is very slim indeed, but T'ang literature is full of references to places where wine was available. Only a few examples need be cited.

The weary traveler in T'ang China could follow the old custom of stopping off for rest and refreshment at a Buddhist or Taoist monastery. An edict of Te Tsung declared that such institutions throughout his realm should be kept in good condition for receiving secular visitors, since, he pointed out, an important goal of both religions was the welfare of all living beings (Te Tsung in *Ch'üan T'ang wen*). Otherwise, there were hostels called *kuan* throughout the realm, especially along well-traveled roads. The form of the character that represents this word shows its relationship to the word for "official," *kuan*. In short, etymologically the name signifies a "lodging place for officials traveling on state business." By T'ang times hostels designated by this word may have offered their hospitality to other travelers as well, but it appears, from the abundant references to them in T'ang poems written by members of the bureaucracy, that the old sense of the term still prevailed, and I have noticed two prose references that make it plain that the official character of these places persisted (Wang Po in *Ch'üan T'ang wen*; *Hsin T'ang shu 1*, 124:3a–b).[34]

There were lowlier places, both in towns and in the country, which specialized chiefly in the service of wine, and sometimes in the provision of entertainment, evidently for any customer who might choose to enter. These were called *chiu tien*, "wine shops," (sometimes *chiu ssu* or *chiu lou*), but we occasionally find a reference to a roadside *lü tien*, "traveler's shop," which may have accommodated overnight guests. During the most prosperous part of the eighth century, when commodities were abundant, food cheap, and travel safe, there were restaurants (*ssu*) all along the public roads "to wait upon wayfarers with food and wine" (*Hsin T'ang shu 1*, 51:4a). Hostels tended to be situated in much frequented places, such as the great markets, upper-class mansions, and boat moorages (Marugame 1957, pp. 309–13). Purveyors of wine were easily recognized by the special flag (*chiu ch'i*) that they displayed; these are frequently referred to in poetry (e.g., Lo Yin in *Ch'üan T'ang shih*).

A special kind of wine shop offered the extra allurement of service by pretty girls, more often than not, it seems, women of exotic origin. When Li Po writes of a "courtesan of Wu" (Wu *chi*) offering him a drink, he may be merely allusive and complimentary—although he was in fact in the Wu area when he wrote the poem (Li Po in *Ch'üan T'ang shih*, 14:6b). But here we have to do only with the classically near-exotic. What romantic thoughts crossed the minds of passersby in Lingnan, where the women who tended the wine shops solicited their patronage by offering a sample of the house wine, we shall perhaps never know (Liu Hsün 1892 ed., 845:7a). But service by truly exotic waitresses—a common Chinese designation for them was *tang lu*, "she who attends the [wine-] warmer"—was easily found in the major cities, especially Changan. Doubtless many of these foreign Hebes were of Tocharian or Sogdian extraction, and it appears that many had light-colored hair and blue eyes (Schafer 1963, p. 21. See also Ho Chao in *Ch'üan T'ang shih*; Li Po, ibid., 2:7b). These handsome young women, commonly called *hu chi*, "western courtesans," brought to their customers rare wines, sometimes in goblets carved from precious stones, while the sound of flutes and strings, along with singing and dancing, helped the patrons attain a state of euphoria.

NOTES

1. Other quotations from early medieval books on Chinese dietetics are preserved in tenth-century Japanese glossaries of names of foods and drugs drawn largely from the Chinese materia medica, but their character is essentially the same as that of Tamba's sourcebook (Shinoda 1963b, pp. 317–19).

2. Much of the following discussion has appeared in the author's previous writings (Schafer 1950, 1954, 1956, 1959a, 1959b, 1962, 1963, 1965, 1967, 1970; Schafer and Wallacker 1958). Specific reference to these earlier writings will be made only in exceptional cases. Most literary materials that are quoted or referred to below may be found in *Ch'üan T'ang shih* and *Ch'üan T'ang wen*.

3. Wang Yü-ch'eng lived in the tenth century, but I assume that his testimony applies to the T'ang. The poem is named "Tseng Hu-chou Chang tsung shih."

4. This word, in various graphic guises, appears to be cognate to *rape, rapa, raphanus*.

5. Infusions of gourd were found useful in treating beri-beri, the vitamin B^1 deficiency disease, in the predominantly rice-eating south, as was observed by Han Yü among others. Areca nut was also considered valuable in treating the disease (Lu and Needham 1951, pp. 13–15, 19; Schafer 1967, p. 175; T. C. Ch'en in S. C. Li 1965 ed., 22: 63). A common symptom of beri-beri is dropsy, hence the Chinese name for it, *chüeh ch'i*.

6. Taxonomists are not in agreement about the closeness of the relationships among these fruits. Some, instead of classifying them all in the genus *Nephelium*, make them *Litchi sinensis, Euphoria longan,* and *Nephelium lappaceum*.

7. Shinoda (1963a, p. 334), in the course of discussing such exotic beverages as pomegranate wine and coconut wine, displays some bafflement over the "milk wine" (*ju chiu*) of Tibet and the Mongolian steppes. This is plainly another name for kumiss.

8. These equivalents are my own, but I have some faith in them, although they do not correspond entirely to modern Chinese usage. A rather different set of translations appears in Pulleyblank 1963, pp. 248–56—viz., *lo* is "boiled or soured milk," *su* is "butter," and *t'i-hu* is "clarified butter." Obviously, I disagree with him mostly in respect to the T'ang meaning of *su*.

9. The evodia is classified by some taxonomists as a species of *Xanthoxylum*.

10. In T'ang poetry, *ting hsiang* refers regularly to the flowerlets of the lilac, for the same reason. This ambiguity has led to many ludicrous errors of translation.

11. The four locations of the salt inspectorates were Yung-chia, Lin-p'ing, Hsin-t'ing, and Lan-t'ing. For information on the administrative control of salt "ponds," see *Hsin T'ang shu 1*, 48:13a.

12. Modern shoyu is made of fermented boiled beans immersed in brine.

13. Shinoda discusses some interesting varieties of cha here, including one that suggests some kind of medieval Japanese *sushi* (cold pickled rice). He notes however that a word used in the description is not necessarily to be taken for its meaning but

is apparently a phonetic transcription: *p'u* leaves are unsuitable for such a preparation, and he thinks the syllable *p'u* represents the beginning of some expression like the *pura-hā* of modern Thai, which stands for a kind of sushi.

14. In some cases, *hu ping* is an abbreviation of *hu ma ping* ("sesame cakes"). But in the end the two are identical. See, for instance, Po Chü-i in *Ch'üan T'ang shih*, 18:4a, in which the *hu ping* of the title becomes *hu ma ping* in the poem itself. The poet writes, "the flour is light, the' oil is fragrant," clearly referring to a fried cake. I am not sure how common the fried cake called *pou-t'ou* and the sweet steamed cake called *tui* were in T'ang times.

15. We might hope to find an analogue for beer in *li*, in which barley-derived malt was an important ingredient, and which might therefore be compared to a fine English ale—but we would probably be deceived. (See S. S. Ling 1958, pp. 890–92, for li based on barley sprouts.) Ling compares the resultant brew with wines based on chewed grains, in which the enzyme ptyalin helps the conversion.

16. *Shu* was the common word for glutinous millet, and *no* was that for glutinous rice. The millet belonged to the class of true millets (*Panicum* sp.), or witchgrasses. The typical Chinese leavens used in ferment cakes by Chinese brewers (called *ch'ü*, or "mother of wine," *chiu mu*) generated black molds. There were other molds, of the type commonly found on bread (Shinoda 1963a, p. 328).

17. A distinction was also made between turbid wine (*cho chiu*), somewhat contaminated by residue, and clear wine (*ch'ing chiu*), that is, filtered, or clarified, wine. Ch'ing chiu was a favorite metaphor for the superior man, but despite this literary favoritism, cho chiu was by no means a despised drink (Shinoda 1963a).

18. During T'ang, wine came sporadically under government control. Sometimes this amounted only to a tax on private brews, but sometimes there was a true government monopoly of the sale of ferments and wines. (For details, see Marugame 1957, pp. 292–93, 303–06).

19. One T'ang authority notes that in "the southern quarter" (from the context, he refers to Lingnan) they do not use yeasts and leavens of the familiar sort but start the fermentation process with extracts from native plants (C. L. Fang 1846 ed., 233: 3b–4a).

20. The term *arrack* is apparently of Arabic origin and was filtered through various Indo-Iranian dialects.

21. The poems are by Yung T'ao and Po Chü-i. For details, see Schafer 1967, p. 190, and also Shinoda 1963a, p. 337, with its references to "burnt spring" (*shao ch'un*), i.e., "burnt" (presumably distilled) spring wine.

22. There is reason to believe that the existing version of this classic, which was so influential in establishing the tea cult in Japan, is not entirely the original work of its putative author. The place names in it, for instance, do not agree with those of the known tea and porcelain producing centers of T'ang. Possibly they were "corrected" in Sung editions of the text.

23. For instance, we find Wang Chien writing of the invigorating properties of "ginger tea" taken with a meal (Wang Chien in *Ch'üan T'ang shih*, 3:3a).

24. The tea of the highest quality was made from young leaf buds, called *ch'a ya* (Schafer and Wallacker 1958, p. 222).

25. The tea tax was first imposed in A.D. 793, although contrary testimony holds that the appointment of Wang Yai as tax commissioner marked the inauguration of a tea tax. This was during the reign of Wen Tsung, in the ninth century.

26. Nunome detects Taoist elements—like the search for an elixir of life—in this cult.

27. A modern dictionary, the *Tz'u hai*, takes *kuo* to be a vernacular synonym of *fu*. An example is the expression *ch'a kuo* in a poem by Li Tung (*Ch'üan T'ang shih*). But I am inclined to agree with Okazaki that this was a matter of cultural history. I observe also that P'i Jih-hsiu wrote a poem entitled "Ch'a tsao" (*Ch'üan T'ang shih*, 4:10b). I take the title to refer to a small stove designed to heat water for tea.

28. Specimens decorated with oil paintings from about the same period survive in Japan.

29. Sulfur, which had "heating" properties, was to be used in making cups for serving cold beverages, while warm drinks could be given balance by serving them in porcelain vessels floating in water (Feng Chih 1939 ed.).

30. The Eskimos of the twentieth century have comparable tastes. We find in Tannahill (1973, p. 28) that in cud-chewing animals, which have complex systems of stomachs, a partial fermentation of the herbal contents takes place, which evidently helps to make them palatable.

31. It may be relevant that milk products are normally ingested in India and many other places which, as it happened, fell under the influence of Buddhism. So the association between Buddhism and milk drinking is only an accident of history. It is curious that the same source (Tao-shih) states that the flesh of birds should be offered to the lunar station *nü* ("woman"), in our Aquarius.

32. The origin of this custom goes back to Chou times, and its T'ang version survives today in Japan as the Gion festival of Kyoto.

33. This information comes from an edict of the Later T'ang, restoring a custom which had apparently fallen into disuse.

34. Some, perhaps all, of these inns bore elegant, and even fantastic, names. An example is the Hostel of the Divine Woman (Shen nü kuan), alluded to by Tu Fu. It was located, appropriately, on the Yangtze in a haunt of the goddess (Tu Fu in *Ch'üan T'ang shih*, 15:17b).

4: SUNG

MICHAEL FREEMAN

Sometime in the generation of the fall of north China to the Jurchen invaders from the north, an obscure court artist named Chang Tse-tuan painted his only known masterpiece, a long scroll called *Spring Festival on the River* (*Ch'ing-ming Shang-ho t'u*). [1] It describes for us with incomparable freshness and detail the life of the old city, taking us by stages and with mounting excitement from a countryside newly green and stirring after the long winter through busy suburbs to our ultimate destination, the capital itself, with its great thoroughfares crowded with travelers of all nationalities, its myriad shops, its great private mansions and public wine houses. Today we call Chang's city Kaifeng, and we know that in our time and in his it was hot and dusty in summer, cold and dank in winter, subject to floods, militarily indefensible, and an altogether unsalubrious place for the seat of a major dynasty. Chang Tse-tuan knew none of these things. His name for the city was Pien-ching, Capital at the Pien, and for him it combined the bustle and excitement of a great commercial city with the majesty which attended the residence of the Son of Heaven. When we look at *Spring Festival*, we see a vision of life not only as it was but as it ought to have been, the product of a memory of prodigal richness and equally rich feelings about the city.

The focus of this vision is not really the emperor and the government, with all they imply in Chinese history for the display of military grandeur—the painting ends long before we enter the Inner Quarters. Rather, it centers on the life of the city and its people and, particularly, on the food that they ate. Food, from production to distribution to consumption, is a central narrative theme of the painting. We begin as we pass through fields in the countryside, ready for the new planting. Our path joins the river, crowded with great squat boats bulging with grain for the capital. The inns and tea shops, at the beginning simple and rude, grow numerous and more elaborate. Then we pass into the city itself, and the full measure of its richness and splendor are reflected in the wine restaurants elaborately decorated with scaffolding and flowers and flying their official flags. The streets are crowded with simple food stalls and vendors hawking every delicacy known in the empire. Everywhere is suggested culinary richness and variety; not far from the center of the painter's loving memories were thoughts of the old capital's food.

Thoughts of food much occupied the minds of many men of Sung. Poets celebrate it, writers of memoirs list it, even philosophers thought it worth their consideration. Happily, they were moved not by obsession but by delight, by fascination with culinary riches beyond any their ancestors had imagined. Sung cooks were the beneficiaries of twin revolutions, in agriculture and in commerce, and enjoyed, especially in the two capitals, an unprecedented abundance that probably made city dwellers the best-fed mass population in world history to that time. Foods which had been luxuries became necessities for not only many of the officials and bureaucrats who crowd Chang Tse-tuan's streets but also for the vast numbers of merchants, shopkeepers, and artisans.

The history of food in any society so signally successful in feeding its own members surely merits our study. But material abundance also led to the development and refinement of conscious and rational attitudes about food, in all its aspects, within that substantial portion of Sung society that could afford to eat well. In Sung times, particularly in Southern Sung (1127–1279), emerged the first of the world's cuisines, and it is this sophisticated and self-conscious tradition, revised and enriched by new ingredients and new techniques, which has come down to the present day.

The question of what differentiates a cuisine from ordinary traditions of cooking has been frequently assayed, though mostly in relation to Western cookery. It is usually agreed that Americans are without a cuisine, but that the French, whose word it is, have one. A cuisine is surely more than the "manner or style of cooking" of the dictionary definition; we can hardly speak of "short-order cuisine." Our definition is historical: the appearance of a cuisine, a self-conscious tradition of cooking and eating, implies the confluence of certain material factors—the availability and abundance of ingredients—with a set of attitudes about food and its place in the life of man.

The development of a cuisine implies, first of all, the use of many ingredients. Such multiplicity might derive in part from cooks' and consumers' willingness, inspired perhaps by necessity, to prepare and ingest seemingly unlikely substances. Such was China's tradition of famine food, a store of folk knowledge to be drawn upon in time of dearth. But to sustain the extensive experimentation that leads to a real cuisine, many ingredients, including some which are not naturally produced in a given locale, are necessary. In the Sung period, great and varied eating was to be had, not in the countryside, where people were close to folk traditions, but in the cities and especially in the capitals: Kaifeng before the fall of the north and Hangchow afterwards. Here the products of the whole empire and beyond were gathered, here the cooks had the greatest scope for experimentation. Moreover, a cuisine does not develop out of the cooking traditions of a single region. Ingredients are apt to be too limited, cooks and eaters too conservative. A cuisine historically has derived from no single tradition but, rather, amalgamates, selects, and organizes the best of several traditions.

A cuisine requires a sizable corps of critical, adventuresome eaters, not bound by the tastes of their native region and willing to try unfamiliar food. This elite audience for good cooking must be a large one. The existence of a cuisine implies standards broader and more permissive than that of traditional cooking but still genuine, and such standards can be maintained only when the group of consumers is large enough to transcend the tastes of a single individual. An individual ruler or a tiny elite may command superlative cooking, but cannot create a cuisine. The eaters must also be sophisticated enough to encourage culinary adventures, and this implies a degree of rational reflection. As long as a native of Szechwan, like the Sung poet Su Shih, thought of the food of his native province simply as sustenance, he could not support the development of a cuisine; when he identified it as "food in the Szechwan style" and began to combine it with dishes of other traditions, he was participating in the creation of a Chinese cuisine.

Finally, a cuisine is the product of attitudes which give first place to the real pleasure of consuming food rather than to its purely ritualistic signifi- cance. Many historians of French cuisine date its inception from the arrival of Catherine de Medici in Paris with her Italian chefs, but the real beginning was, not in the grandiose meals of the subsequent French court, but in the extension of a version of that style of cooking to a much broader part of society after the French Revolution. The trend in French cuisine has con- sistently been away from elaboration toward a style of cooking which, though immensely sophisticated, is simpler and truer to its ingredients. Food meant primarily for ritual, while perhaps wonderfully rich and sophisticated, is imprisoned by concerns other than gustatory, too much obliged to conform to the ways of the past.

The appearance of a cuisine, then, involves the availability of ingredients, many sophisticated consumers, and cooks and diners free from conventions of region or ritual. A happy coincidence of developments in agriculture and commerce, related to political events and attended by shifts in attitudes about food, occurred in China during the reign of the house of Chao (960– 1279) and led to a cuisine we still recognize today as Chinese.

Changes in Supply and Distribution

An important element, perhaps the decisive one, in the development of Chinese cooking during the Sung period was the changes in agriculture which took place then. Such changes were important, first of all, because they increased the overall food supply. China's was not an agriculture of scarcity during the Sung; famines were rare, and those that occurred were usually local and related to a breakdown in the system of distribution. The popula- tion increased to around one hundred million, a peak that was not again reached for some centuries after the Sung, but production outraced it. What is more, the farmer was able to produce foods in greater variety, so that once all but unobtainable items became common in the markets, and others, for example tea, that had been common to only small segments of the population came into general use. Many scholars, Chinese, Japanese, and Western, have contributed to our understanding of agricultural and commercial change during the Sung.[2] In summarizing their findings only insofar as they form a background to our understanding of food supply, two changes appear particularly significant. First, the appearance of new strains of rice greatly increased production of that cereal and, along with the loss to the Jurchen of areas which relied on wheat and millet, it encouraged the continuing shift toward reliance on rice. Second, the concomitant commercialization of agriculture in many of the most productive regions led not only to greatly increased production but also to the variety of ingredients that characterized Sung cooking.

In 1027, in response to famine brought on by drought in Fukien, in the southeast, the Emperor Chen-tsung ordered the distribution of a new kind of rice seed imported from Champa, modern Vietnam. The imperial government was not moved solely by solicitude for the suffering masses; the capital and the imperial armies depended on tax grain from the southeast. Thus it was in the government's interest, as it had been since T'ang times, to carefully monitor and encourage grain production in the southeast. The new seed had two advantages and came to be widely used. It matured early so that in some areas double-cropping became feasible. Equally important, the Champa variety was highly resistant to drought and, therefore, could be planted with reasonable expectation of success in areas of higher elevation where no rice could be grown before. The Champa rice potentially doubled the yield from some cropland and opened new areas to farming (See P. T. Ho 1956, pp. 200–18; and Perkins 1969, chaps. 2,3).

In a sense, Chen-tsung's act was symbolic of a broader change. Farmers in the Yangtze delta region had for some time been seeking early-ripening varieties of rice, and they tended to adopt the variety most profitably cultivated in a given area. In the most productive areas of the delta, farmers preferred the slower-maturing "rice of moderate gluten content," *keng-mi*, to the Champa varieties, as it was more productive and produced a grain preferred by the tax collector, both for its superior taste and its keeping qualities. Shu Lin, a Southern Sung observer, wrote that "from keng-mi, only a little hulled rice is obtained. It is expensive and, other than being used to pay taxes, is only eaten by upper-class families. From lesser [Champa] rice, much hulled rice can be obtained. It is cheap and eaten by everyone, from those owning a moderate amount of property downwards" (quoted in Shiba 1968, p. 151; my translation). Champa rice was the main variety in private rice trade and the one most eaten in the cities.

These two by no means exhaust the list of rice varieties grown and consumed during the Sung. Champa rice itself had varieties which matured in eighty, one hundred, or one hundred and twenty days. Special rice of extremely high gluten content, used in the production of wine, was grown as a cash crop. Contemporaries refer to numerous kinds of rice available in the markets, including red rice, red lotus-seed rice, yellow keng-mi, fragrant rice, and "old rice," rice sold off at a discount by the official granaries (T. M. Wu 1957 ed., p. 281).

In northern China, where the rainfall is not adequate for the cultivation of rice, the staple crops were then, as they are now, wheat and various kinds of millet. Evidently, improvements in cultivation of rice did not extend to other grains; production did not increase, and the economic importance of the north continued its decline throughout the Sung. Sorghum, or *kaoliang*, useful as food, fodder, and the raw material for the potent liquor of the same name, was first cultivated in China during the Southern Sung, probably in Szechwan and probably in no great quantity, since almost all the wine consumed when Marco Polo passed through China just after the Sung had fallen to the Mongols was made of rice mixed with spices (Hagerty 1940).

The production of several food items was dominated by commercial considerations. And while these items were far less important than rice for the general good, they nevertheless illustrate the great expansion of available foodstuffs which took place. During the Sung, sugarcane came to be an important cash crop in parts of Szechwan and Fukien. Sugarcane had been known since ancient times, but it was only in the T'ang that techniques of refining became widely disseminated. The Northern Sung author of a treatise on sugar, the *T'ang-shuang p'u*, asserts that in Sui-ning in Szechwan more than 40 percent of the peasants were employed in its production (S. Wang 1936 ed., p. 2). Fang Ta-tsung, in the Southern Sung, noted disapprovingly that "the fields of Hsien-yu [in modern Fukien] are consumed by sugarcane, and I don't know how many tens of thousands of jars are transported to Huai-nan and Liang-che each year (quoted in Shiba 1968, p. 148; my translation). One writer claims that sweet things are preferred by "barbarians and country folk," but references to sweet confections, pastries, and candied fruits indicate that city dwellers could not have ranked far behind.

Of all the foodstuffs which came into common use, tea was perhaps the most important. Tea drinking was not new, but its practice on all levels of society represents a change both in patterns of mass consumption and in the manner in which tea was produced. Sung commentators agree that the consumption of tea was no longer a luxury but a daily necessity, which even the humblest household could not be expected to forego. The government carefully supervised the production and distribution of tea and profited immensely by its control of the trade.

Rice, tea, and sugar represent, on a large scale, the changing patterns of production which typified a host of lesser products. Their distribution is also emblematic of the commercialization which pervaded the Sung economy. Major items of consumption often reached the market by extremely complicated routes. Wu Tzu-mu says that "as to the rice that is sold daily in the markets—leaving out palaces and government offices, the mansions of the wealthy, and the employees in the official departments who get salaries [partly in rice]—the ordinary people in the city and suburbs consume no less than one to two thousand piculs daily, all of which they must get from rice shops. . . . The brokers of the rice guild receive the merchants who have brought the rice for sale. . . .The rice shop proprietors, within and without the city walls, arrange the price at the market solely in consultation with the head of the guild, after which the rice is taken directly to the shops for sale. The rice shop owners agree on a day on which they will pay for the rice; small brokers from the market come in person to each shop to supervise the selling (1957 ed., p. 269; my translation). Officials constantly complained of rice merchants in their great boats who bought up the whole production of an area, leaving it without sufficient supplies.

The production of some lesser commodities was probably even more commercialized than that of staple crops. Ts'ai Hsiang in his *Li-chih p'u* (Treatise on Litchis) explains that "when the branches first blossom, the merchants estimate the crop grove by grove and draw up contracts on the basis of their estimates. They can tell if the harvest will be good or bad." Ts'ai notes that merchants make large profits in the litchi trade, but that the peasant producer does not have a chance to eat his own fruit (1927 ed., p. 2; my translation). Merchants found the means to deliver all manner of food products to the lucrative urban markets, even live baby fish, which were carried in bamboo and paper baskets by couriers who had constantly to replenish and agitate the water (Shiba 1968, p. 101).

While we may assume that the greatest merchants traded in the capital or in large cities, there existed in Sung times a whole network of local periodic markets, most often held one day in ten, but often one in three or six. Much of the trade in these markets was in kind and on a small scale, though the larger ones had shops and inns for traveling merchants. Such markets evidently occurred in even the most remote and backward areas, allowing the peasants to enjoy at least a few of the pleasures of urbanites brought by the merchants and peddlers who frequented these markets. Most commodities delivered to the capital were sold for consumption or resale at great urban markets. The markets, open from dawn until, in one case, late at night, were the wonder of contemporary observers. Marco Polo writes that in Hangchow "there are ten principal open spaces, besides infinite others—a Chinese description says 414—for the districts which are square, that is half a mile for a side. And on each of the said squares three days a week there is a con-course of from forty to fifty thousand persons who come to market and bring everything you can desire for food, because there is always a great supply of victuals; that is to say of roebuck, francolins, quails, fowls, capons, and so many ducks and geese that more could not be told; for they rear so many of them that [West] Lake, (which borders the city), that for one Venetian silver groat may be had a pair of geese and two pair of ducks" (trans. Moule and Pelliot 1938, p. 328). Polo describes the many kinds of vegetables and fruits, especially the giant white pears, "which weigh ten pounds a piece," and the enormous quantity of fresh fish, of which he observes, "whoever saw the quantity of said fish would never think that it could be sold, and yet in a few hours it has all been taken away, so great is the multitude of inhabitants who are used to live delicately; for they eat both fish and flesh at the same meal" (ibid.).

Most of the great markets, both in Kaifeng and Hangchow, specialized in a single product. In Hangchow the grain market was outside the north gate at the head of Black Bridge. There were two markets for pork, the south-ern outside the Gate for Awaiting the Tide, the northern on Strike Swine Alley. There were markets for vegetables, for medicinal herbs, for meat other than pork, for fish fresh and preserved, for crabs, for fruits. Oranges were sold in a special area "behind the market street." (Chou 1957 ed., pp. 440–41). "The people of Hangchow," observes a Southern Sung writer, "are merchants and sellers of food and drink" (T. M. Wu 1957 ed., p. 281; my translation). His lists of ingredients available for purchase in the city bear him out; he mentions foods in such bewildering variety that they escape us; our language does not properly distinguish his more than thirty varieties of vegetable or seventeen kinds of beans. Vegetables and fruits were sold mostly in the many neighborhood markets, and numerous butcher shops throughout the city prepared meat. In Kaifeng, butcher shops were "a meat table, where three to five men are lined up wielding knives, and the meat is broadly cut, sliced, finely slivered, or pounded with the blade, according to the desires of the customer" (Y. L. Meng 1957 ed., p. 27; my translation). In Southern Sung Hangchow, such butcher shops abounded, and "each day each shop hangs sides of pork—not less than ten sides. In the two holidays of winter-time, [around New Year's] each shop sells several tens of sides daily" (T. M. Wu 1957 ed., p. 270; my translation). Other kinds of meat readily available to the urban cook included beef, horse, donkey, venison, rabbit, a variety of fowl, and fish and seafood of all kinds.

Commodity prices are, in Sung times as in every other, difficult to deter-mine exactly, especially since they fluctuated considerably over the course of three hundred years. The very volume of the trade in vegetables—a whole island of some two hundred *li* in breadth was given over to their production to serve the urban market at Nanking—indicates that a large segment of the population could afford them (Shiba 1968, p. 83).

Specific figures on income are rare and unreliable, in the sense that it is difficult to be certain whether the figures given are typical. An ordinary sailor on a hired government boat was paid a daily wage of one hundred cash and two-and-one-half pints of rice and received a bonus of five strings of a thousand cash each on the day of hiring. In 1156, 1167, and 1173 the government paid, respectively, 1.5, 1.3, and 1.5 strings of cash for one *shih* (roughly one hundred and thirty pounds) of hulled rice. In other words, the sailor could have purchased far more rice in a day than he could eat (Perkins 1968, p. 117). But even this simple and rough comparison has many difficulties of interpretation.

Meng Yuan-lao recalls fondly after the fall of the north that in Kaifeng in the old days a dish in a restaurant could be purchased for only fifteen cash. He reports further that "in the winter months, when all the fish from distant parts come up the Yellow River, they are called cart fish, and cost less than one hundred cash per catty. As for jujubes, when ordinary people bought them, one cost ten cash." A small lotus leaf was used for wrapping. (Y. L. Meng 1957 ed., pp. 17, 50; my translation). Even if available figures are atypical, it is evident that, at least in normal times, an ordinary working man could occasionally afford to vary his diet with some sort of fresh or prepared food. And a very great many people could do a good deal better than that. Historians have long recognized the burgeoning of the civil bureaucracy, the social shift from an elite composed of a relatively small number of great aristocratic landholders to a much broader group of middling holders. The usual estimate of the number of officeholders in Southern Sung is about twelve thousand; not a very large number, but when the number of students, families, and other dependents of officeholders are considered, the total is very much greater. And, of course, by no means all potential bureaucrats won or even sought office. Moreover, much to the chagrin of Confucian moralists, the number of merchants, shopkeepers, brokers, and others whose occupations seemed all too dubious, was enormous. Ch'en Shun-yü's lament is typical: "Long ago there used to be only four classes of commoners, of whom the farmers were one, but now there are eight in all, namely scholars, farmers, artisans, merchants, Taoists, Buddhists, soldiers, and vagrants, and of these the farmers are but one; . . . more artisans and merchants practice extortion upon the peasants and never grow tired of cheating them" (quoted in Shiba 1968, p. 483; my translation). Such persons could afford an elaborate diet, just as they could afford luxurious clothing and housing. The government found it so often necessary to issue sumptuary laws to control unseemly displays of luxury that we may assume the regulations could not be enforced.

China's systems of agriculture and distribution had reached a level of efficiency that permitted fairly widespread consumption of food and drink far beyond that needed for subsistence. All the possibilities inherent in traditional cooking, once almost the sole preserve of the emperor and a very few great aristocrats, if not accessible to the masses, were still enjoyed by a segment of the population large enough to support a well-developed food-service industry, with fine restaurants, caterers, and professional chefs.

Patterns of Consumption

In Sung, one's eating habits mirrored one's social position. The well placed and the rich had access to food in greater richness and variety, if not necessarily in greater quantity, than did the poor. There was not, however, a complete disjunction between the cooking styles and ingredients of the rich and the poor. The poor man's staple was millet or perhaps Champa rice; the rich could afford the more desirable rice strain known as "official" rice, so called because it alone was accepted by the government in tax payments. But generally speaking, the difference in diet was one of degree rather than kind; the poor ate the lesser *fan* and had less and poorer *ts'ai*, but their methods of cooking were largely the same.

Wu Tzu-mu reported in the late Southern Sung that "the things that people cannot do without every day are firewood, rice, oil, salt, soybean sauce, vinegar, and tea. Those who are just slightly better off cannot do without *hsia-fan* ["food to help get the rice down"] and soup [both presumably of vegetables]. Though they be the poorest people, this must always be so" (T. M. Wu 1957 ed., p. 270, my translation). While this minimum diet hardly sounds appetizing, it is fairly nourishing, as it includes the carbohydrates and bulk of the rice, the protein of the soybean, and the various vitamins contained in vinegar.

Having laid out what came to be called the "Seven Necessities," Wu and his contemporaries go on to indicate, often indirectly, the ways in which this diet was supplemented. Large amounts of preserved fish were imported into Hangchow and sold in special shops. In inland cities like Kaifeng, fish was probably less important than entrails, especially of pork. Marco Polo refers to "the shambles, where they slaughter the large animals like calves, oxen, kids and lambs, the which flesh the rich men and great lords eat. But the rest who are of low position do not abstain from all the other kinds of unclean flesh, without any respect" (trans. Moule and Pelliot 1938, p. 328). All of the main sources of information on food in the Sung capitals refer to particular wine shops or restaurants frequented by working men, and the lists of dishes served in them both confirm Marco Polo's observation and demonstrate that every scrap of animals was used. In Kaifeng heavy soups or potages were common: blood soup, flour soup, and dishes made of heart, kidneys, lungs. Many of the same dishes were served in Hangchow, as were various kinds of buns, steamed or deep-fried and often filled.

We can surmise what methods of cooking were used by lower-class families by references to utensils and by the cooking methods used in restaurants with a lower-class clientele. We read, for example, of a section of Hangchow where woks and *t'iao* (long-handled pans) were repaired and where such items as braziers, spoons and chopsticks, bowls, cups, vegetable pots, and baskets for steaming were sold. These items are all familiar in the modern-day Chinese kitchen; references to deep-fried foods sold at restaurants or by vendors suggest that this too was a common method of cooking.

Both people in Northern Sung and those in the south a century-and-a-half later took three meals a day. Wu Tzu-mu says that, in the morning, vendors sold twice-seasoned soup, fried puff-pastry shreds, and little steamed cakes. At noon they offered sweet conjee (rice gruel), *shao-ping*, toasted *man-t'ou*, steamed cakes, peppery vegetable cakes, spring cakes, and the like. The evening meal was the most substantial and presumably included several courses. These meals were frequently supplemented by snacks, *tien-hsin*. Restaurants were open and vendors at work late, for "men of the capital, in managing public and private affairs, stay abroad until late at night ..." (T. M. Wu 1957 ed., p. 243; my translation). Meng Yuan-lao, describing Northern Sung Kaifeng, found the "night market" most extraordinary. He reports that it ran straight through to the third watch (3:00–5:00 A.M.) and recommenced at the fifth (7:00–9:00 A.M.), and again "right up to the third watch there were those who brought forward their jars and sold tea." Even "in the winter months, though there were great winds, snow, and rain, still they held the night market" (Y. L. Meng 1957 ed., p. 21; my translation).

Wealthy merchants and shopkeepers, as well as the families of bureaucrats, enjoyed a standard of consumption much more generous than that available to the poor. But cooking techniques, the basic organization of the meal, and, indeed, many dishes were shared by rich and poor. One such common dish is "blood soup," referred to in both Kaifeng and Hangchow and eaten in cheap restaurants and at an imperial banquet.

It is possible that class distinctions in eating were more sharply drawn in the Southern Sung than earlier. Phrases such as "respectable people do not go to such places" or "these places are not very high-class" are frequent Southern Sung commentaries (Kuan P'u Nai Te Weng 1957 ed., p. 94; T. M. Wu 1957 ed., p. 262). In contrast, Meng Yuan-lao never uses such class-conscious expressions, although he does point out that some Kaifeng restaurants had a clientele of working men. Far from excluding the unwashed, Meng refers to a remarkable willingness among Northern Sung restaurateurs to serve them and even to allow them to use their costly silver cups and chopsticks. Whether Meng exaggerates the harmony in which his former townsmen once lived, as he sometimes exaggerates the old capital's charms, or if he really observed a social situation that had changed in his lifetime is hard to determine; however, that considerable social flexibility existed in eating habits, there is little doubt.

Surviving Sung genre paintings reveal that the rich and influential dined in comfortable and elegant surroundings (fig. 26). Of some really noteworthy extravagances we shall have more to say later, but even the ordinary well-off household was not wanting in any of the creature comforts. During the Sung, the transition from sitting on the floor to the use of tables and chairs was completed. In one painting from the Five Dynasties or early Northern Sung, *The Night Revels of Han Hsi-ts'ai*, we find the "revellers" in various vignettes enjoying food and music. They are seated on raised platforms, the backs of which are decorated with paintings, and consume food which has been placed on small, low, light tables which appear to be lacquered and rather resemble TV trays. Other paintings show what are supposed to be T'ang court ladies seated on chairs around a table; this may be an anachronism or, quite possibly, an indication that in the Five Dynasties and in early Sung both styles of seating were used interchangeably. The *Sung shih* biography of Chao P'u, the Sung founder's prime minister, says that T'ai-tsung, the son of the founder, once visited Chao's house and that they had wine together on the floor.[3] Certainly the style of small tables continued into Southern Sung, for they are depicted in several paintings.

Restaurants and inns must have found small tables inconvenient, for in the *Spring Festival on the River*, we find diners and drinkers seated on benches before large rectangular tables, both in wayside tea houses and at the most elaborate restaurants (fig. 30). It is probably impossible to give any exact date for the complete abandonment of floor seating, and both large table and small table seating continued through the Sung.

The rich ate from porcelain dishes, several of them for each diner, since meals included several courses. Both chopsticks and spoons were used. Chopsticks, spoons, and wine cups, as well as bowls and other serving dishes, were sometimes made of metal, and among the very wealthy and in the highest class of restaurants they were of silver.

Lists of dishes served by wealthy households do not survive, but since all such households would have had at least one cook, it seems likely in a food-conscious society that people would eat well at home. The food of the wealthy differed from that of the poor, primarily in its use of rare and costly ingredients and a relative de-emphasis of staple foods. Yang Fang, in the Southern Sung, complains that the sons and grandsons of officials "will be unwilling to eat vegetables and will look on greens and broth as coarse fare, finding beans, wheat, and millet meager and tasteless, and insisting on the best polished rice and the finest roasts to satisfy their greedy appetites, with the products of the water and the land and the confections of human artifice set out before them neatly in ornamentally carved dishes and trays" (F. Yang 1935 ed., 9:1–1b).

Both rich and poor ate pork, lamb, and kid; the rich had the better cuts. In addition, they ate horse meat, beef, rabbit, and various kinds of game, including venison, pheasants, and other kinds of wild birds, large and small. Game figures prominently in many lists of Sung dishes, probably because wealthy urbanites appreciated the novelty of such unusual ingredients as owls, magpies, or wildcats. As might be expected, these rarer meats were sometimes faked; the purchaser of venison might well be eating donkey. Some especially great delicacies, like camel's hump, were reserved for the imperial table.

Lamb, or kid, or mutton (Chinese has one word for all three) is unexpectedly prominent among Sung ingredients. Although not as common as pork, which frequently occurs in sources simply as "meat," it was nevertheless widely consumed. There seems little reason, moreover, to suppose that the liking for lamb or kid is linked to the influence of the northern steppe people. The Chinese were well aware that their northern neighbors ate a great deal of mutton, but they seem neither to have accepted nor rejected it for that reason. We find, too, that references to sheep and flocks crop up occasionally in poetry, even that written in the south, suggesting that the animals were a familiar sight in the countryside. Beyond this we must simply say that these meats were a part of the Sung diet not considered repulsive, and that some of the greatest delicacies, such as "lamb's head," used meat from sheep and goats.

All levels of society ate fish, which was especially abundant in the great cities of the southeast coast. Describing Hangchow, Marco Polo says that "there comes every day, brought from the Ocean sea up the river for the space of 25 miles, great quantity of fish, and there is also a supply from that lake (for there are always fishermen who do nothing else), which is of different sorts according to the seasons of the year, and because of the impurities which come from the city it is fat and savoury" (trans. Moule and Pelliot 1938, p. 328). Freshwater fish of many varieties were probably preferred to ocean fish, since if the description of a dish is more specific than simply "fish," it more often refers to freshwater species. However, that great delicacy of the modern cuisine, shark fin, appears to have become popular at this time. From the sea came shelled creatures of many kinds: scallops, sea snails, mussels, clams, and conches. Shrimp and especially crabs were highly prized.[4]

Vegetables, both leafy and root, were available to the well-to-do in prodigious variety. In the south, fresh greens were available almost year round, but Meng Yuan-lao says that in Kaifeng "in the tenth month, five days before the Beginning of Winter, the Western Imperial Garden submits winter vegetables. The capital area grows cold, and in the winter months there are no fresh vegetables . . . " (Y. L. Meng, 1957 ed., p. 55; my tranlation). Since, however, he refers a few pages later to "onion bulbs and fresh greens" in the twelfth month, we should probably take him to mean only that in the winter months the supply and the variety of vegetables were limited. Rich households had a passion for obtaining the very first eggplants of the season as well as for various kinds of cabbage and mustard, several members of the onion family, spinach, turnips, cucumbers, and some less familiar vegetables, various mountain herbs, for instance, and asparaginous grasses. The growing tips of melons and other kinds of plants were picked, usually floured, and then fried.

Of all the fresh foods eaten by the wealthy of Sung China, their most enviable riches were surely their fruits. Evidently, fruit was a much more common element in the diet than it is today and was eaten not only as dessert but also before and at intervals during meals. Marco Polo refers specifically to a great pear, soft, white, and fragrant inside, that can probably be identified with the present-day snow pear, and Chinese sources refer to several other varieties, sand pears and "Phoenix roost pear," for example. Both white and yellow peaches of several kinds, plums, haw apples, arbutus, apricots, prunes, and pomegranates were eaten. Sung fruit was more varied than our own in all but one respect: they seem to have had only one variety of apple.

Although fresh fruit "in season" is most frequently mentioned, fruit was preserved several ways. Sugared or honeyed fruit sold by street vendors or, in Kaifeng, in pots was especially popular. Most fruits were also available dried, most notably the banana, which could not withstand even the mild winters of the southern capital. Some perishable fruits were brought to the capital from very great distances—apricots from Szechwan, the "face fruit," which is said to have markings resembling a human face, from Vietnam. Oranges and mandarin oranges and grapes, which in earlier times would have been a novelty, especially in northern China, were commonly available (Y. C. Han 1936). Dried orange peel was produced in large amounts and figures in many dishes served in better restaurants. Shiba Yoshinobu quotes estimates of from seventy-five to ninety thousand pounds per year in a single orange-growing area (1968, p. 213).

Despite the widespread adoption of tea drinking, it remained, in Sung times, the most prestigious beverage and, as in the T'ang, it was the object of much connoisseurship (H. Ts'ai 1936a ed.). That most learned and pretentious Northern Sung scholar Ou-yang Hsiu, for example, examines in great detail the question of where the best water for the preparation of tea was to be found (1967 ed., 8:15). One of the tea's attractions for the literati was probably that so very many varieties, grown principally in Szechwan and Fukien but also to a lesser extent in many regions of the country, were known and seemed to invite sampling and comparison. Presumably, tea was also more respectable than wine. Marco Polo informs us that in Hangchow rice wine, which was mixed with various spices, was preferred to that derived from grapes, which was uncommon but not unavailable (Moule and Pelliot 1938, p. 328). The technology for distilled liquors was developed during the Sung; the first technical manual dates from about 1117, but the paucity of references to them indicates that they were not widely known.[5]

The most unexpected beverage on the list of those commonly consumed during the Sung is kumiss, fermented mare's milk, which in later times was regarded as a barbarian drink. There is no question that it was a well-established item in the Sung diet: the emperor had a special office for its production, some restaurants specialized in serving it, and it occurs many times in the lists of banquet foods. In the Sung it was not particularly identi-fied with the northern nomads, although everyone knew that they had a great love for it. A Northern Sung encyclopedia of origins of things says simply that kumiss had been known since antiquity and in no way regards it as foreign or barbarian. (C. Kao 1969 ed., pp. 616–17). Kumiss, like wine or tea, had many different grades of quality and graduated prices to reflect the difference.

The rich man's larder was thus well stocked, and the list above is by no means exhaustive. There is absolutely no question that the means were at hand for superlatively varied cookery. But who did the cooking? And was cooking in private homes better than that available in the best restaurants? Here we must surely distinguish between the enormous kitchen staffs of the few immensely wealthy families, like that of the late Northern Sung prime minister Ts'ai Ching, which was said to have numbered in the hundreds, and those of the more moderately well off. The very wealthy could compete with the restaurants in quality and variety—in fact, some restaurants billed themselves as serving "official-style" food; the moderately wealthy probably could not. Fine as the cooking in the houses of the rich was, restaurants were, in fact, the places where much of the finest cooking was done. Even the Inner Palace, with resources that infinitely exceeded that of even the richest commoner, sometimes "sent out for" some restaurant's specialty. The Emperor Hsiao-tsung of Southern Sung is said to have made visits to the market districts and enjoyed the food available there. Moreover, very great events and elaborate banquets were frequently not held at home but, in Hangchow, were catered and took place in such pleasant surroundings as the palaces on the two small islands of West Lake.

Wu Tzu-mu says that cooking, like singing, dancing, and sewing, was regarded by his townsmen as a fit occupation for women. We hear of some officials' wives cooking for their husbands, and there was apparently a Hangchow tradition of female chefs, very few in number, who worked in the grandest households. Nonetheless, although some of the restaurants were, judging from their names, owned by women, the terms of address used for cooks in Kaifeng and Hangchow indicate that most or all of them were male. With notable exceptions, cooking tended to be a profession of the lower classes, as gentlemen continued to heed Confucius's counsel to stay clear of the kitchen.

The greatest of the great houses was, of course, the imperial family. In the Sung, preparation of food for this establishment was so sizable and complex a business that it should be regarded as a unique enterprise. The Imperial Household had its own channels of supply and required for its victualling the services of several different offices of government. In early times, a good deal of the emperor's food came directly from taxes in kind; this was no longer true in the Sung. Both capital cities had markets outside one gate of the Inner Palace that catered especially to the Imperial Household. As might be expected, "all the food in these markets is of wonderful flavor, the condiments at the peak of the season, the vegetables extraordinarily fine, with nothing lacking" (Wu Tzu-mu 1957, p. 193; my translation). Various establishments within the Inner Palace sent their orders to a catering office which obtained what was required in the market. These supplies were, in Southern Sung, taken to the Imperial Kitchens, in the Chia-ming Hall. Of these kitchens, Wu Tzu-mu says "everything is closely guarded, and there is a balustrade over which one is not allowed to pass" (ibid., p. 193). He describes in great detail the men charged with accounting for the foodstuffs as they entered the kitchens (ibid., p. 193). Had Wu been allowed to go into the kitchens themselves, he presumably would have seen a total of 1,069 cooks and assistants at work producing meals whose dishes were so numerous that forty boxes were required to carry them to the dining hall (Hsü Sung 1957 ed., pp. 7371–75). Besides their kitchens, Sung emperors had various granaries and storehouses to supply their needs. In Northern Sung we read of wine stores, the Office for Sheep and Cattle, an agency for making kumiss, and an oil and vinegar storehouse.

Obviously, much of the cooking done for the emperor was not intended for his consumption and tells us very little of his own preferences in food. Such a plethora of dishes was meant purely for display, an extravagant and ritualistic demonstration that the emperor could command all things and was materially the master of all under heaven. Such conspicuous consumption was by no means unknown among commoners in the Sung, though of course on no such grand scale, and is perhaps a nearly universal use of food. One supposes that such riches so remorselessly reduplicated were more burden than pleasure for most emperors, and we can sympathize with their occasional hankering for marketplace food.

Commercially Prepared Food

Prepared food purchased either in one of many kinds of restaurants or from a vendor was, for people of Sung times, part of an activity both casual and deeply felt that brought them very close to what it meant to be a citizen of the greatest city of the world. Experience and, for Meng Yuan-lao, memory were suffused with food: "double-cooked purple Su-chou fish," "quail eggs fried in oil," "fried Lo-yang snow pears." Scarcely a section in any of the well-known memoirs of life in the capitals fails to mention some popular restaurants, some eating custom, some favorite food. Meng observes in his preface that "the precious and rare of the four seas were all brought to be traded in the market of Kaifeng; gathered together were all the flavors of the realm, each of them in the kitchens. The radiance of flowers fills the way; what household back from spring gambols? The clamor of pipes and drums; how many houses holding nighttime banquets?" (Y. L. Meng 1957 ed., p. 1; my translation).

Eating at restaurants was an inseparable part of being a city dweller. Restaurants created a demimonde with its own delights, hazards, bywords, and peculiar flavor. "If there is a green, inexperienced customer, they set down the chopsticks before him indifferently, and he is the object of much laughter" (Kuan P'u Nai Te Weng 1957 ed., p. 92; my translation). The writers thus guide us through a teeming world of courtesans and common whores, dives where "rough food" was served, and elegant restaurants where the serving pieces weighed a hundred ounces of silver. Vendors swarmed the streets from dawn to late at night, hawking all manner of food and drink. We are told where to eat the food of every region of China and how to feast while afloat on the West Lake or throw a catered banquet in a rented palace. This world repelled conventional Confucian moralists at the same time that it fascinated ordinary Confucians. Sung food centered in the world of restaurants, and there it acquired its special characteristics.

Restaurant life in the Sung was entwined with the world of the prostitutes, so great in number, says Marco Polo, "that I dare not say it" (trans. Moule and Pelliot 1938, p. 329). With very few exceptions, restaurants did not exclude prostitutes. Rather, the grander ones had prostitutes' quarters adjacent; we read of a lane where "both the restaurants and the brothels were extremely numerous" (Y. L. Meng 1957 ed., p. 20), while a Southern Sung writer describes places called "convent wine shops," where one could dine alone, but which were provided with "small couches" for the convenience of the guests (Kuan P'u Nai Te Weng 1957 ed., p. 92). Restaurants were also associated with drinking. Most of the great restaurants, the seventy-two *cheng-tien* ("first-class shops") of Kaifeng, the tea houses and wine shops of Hangchow, were actually places where one went drinking, so that eating was intimately connected with the pleasure of drink as well as of sex. To visit such a place was to give rein to sensual indulgence, to leave behind the call of duty and ritual for an hour, or sometimes for two days.

This world of restaurants and of pleasure centered on the *cheng-tien* in Kaifeng and on the tea houses along the Imperial Way through the center of Hangchow. Physically they conformed to the pattern of all large city houses; they had an entry, a forecourt, and a main hall behind. These were substantial buildings, tile-roofed in Kaifeng, and having as many as 110 private rooms for the accommodation of customers. One source reports that some restaurants advertised themselves as serving food like that consumed by officials, and some of the restaurants were in fact former officials' dwellings which had been made over. To enter a building like the Shop of Humane Harmony outside the Sung Gate in Kaifeng meant that "wind and rain, cold and heat do not occur, and day mingles with night . . . " (Y. L. Meng 1957 ed., p. 16; my translation).

"In all of [Kaifeng's] wine shops, they tie bright festoons in the doorway, but in the best establishments, after entering the gate, one went straight through the main corridor for about one hundred paces. To both sides of the courtyard were two passageways, both of which had little side doors, and towards evening lamps and candles twinkled and glittered, upper and lower reflecting each other, and the elaborately adorned sing-song girls—several hundred of them—would crowd along the corridor and, holding out wine, would call to the guests, so that gazing at them was like seeing fairies" (ibid., p. 15). The entryways were decorated with an elaborate lattice-work construction with lamps, flags, and festoons of red and green. The two passageways often had a second story, and the prostitutes were in chambers behind them, concealed by screens which rolled down (Y. L. Meng 1957 ed.,

p. 15 and passim). Another writer says that in Hangchow the wine halls
sometimes were two or even three stories high. These establishments were
referred to as "mountains;" "one mountain, two mountain." But if "the
signboard has 'mountain' written on it, that does not mean that it has more
than one story but indicates that the wine there is potent" (Kuan P'u Nai
Te Weng 1957 ed., p. 93).

Wine and tea houses in both Kaifeng and Hangchow lured customers
with such luxuries as paintings by famous artists, flowers, miniature trees,
cups and utensils of silver or of porcelain, and of course, with fine food.
Most of our sources do not describe the wine or tea served at various shops
nearly so elaborately as they do the food, and they generally rank them on
the quality of their food rather than their drink. A Southern Sung source
gives a "casual list" of two hundred and thirty-four famous dishes that
such places served, a list from the Northern Sung has fifty-one. Dinners
probably started with a soup or broth like "hundred-flavors" soup, which
heads both lists. They could then choose from dishes made from almost any
variety of flesh, fowl, or seafood—milk-steamed lamb, onion-strewn hare,
fried clams or crabs. Several kinds of "variety meats," lungs, heart, kidneys,
or caul were cooked in various manners. Some kinds of buns and cakes were
also available, though other kinds of restaurants specialized in such things.
"Imitation" dishes comprised a relatively large part of the menu—"imitation
river globefish," for example, and "imitation barbecued river-deer" (Y. L.
Meng 1957 ed., pp. 15–17; T. M. Wu 1957 ed., pp. 264–66).

The foods prepared to order by the kitchen of the wine house were by no
means the only ones available to diners. Vendors brought in such items as
barbecued chicken or sheep shanks and various dried fruits carried on
trays (fig. 31). The food carried in tended to be prepared food, not cooked
to order, but included some of the items on the restaurant menu. In addition
to vendors, practitioners of various other trades frequented the restaurants.
Small boys, whom one addressed as "Elder Brother," served the pederast.
Ladies with lofty hairdos who pressed food and drink on the guests were
referred to as "Hot Dregs." Other people took advantage of the inebriation
of inexperienced youths by persuading them to pay for drinks or prostitutes.
Lower-class prostitutes gathered in front of the hall, sang songs, and left
only when given a few cash. Sellers of fruits and herbs who did not ask the
guests if they wanted anything, "scattered their wares among the seated
guests" and then tried to collect from them (Y. L. Meng 1957 ed., p. 17).
Evidently, this uproarious scene was confined to the lower floor, and
customers who went upstairs avoided some of the commotion. However,
"when you go into a shop, you cannot casually go up to the upper stories,
because they are afraid that you will order too little. If you do not buy much

wine, you have to sit about on the bottom floor, which they call the 'gate-bed horse track'" (Kuan P'u Nai Te Weng 1957 ed., p. 93; my translation).

Ordering was done in approximately the same way in Kaifeng and in Hangchow, where all restaurants had menus. "The men of Kaifeng were extravagant and indulgent. They would shout their orders by the hundreds: some wanted items cooked and some chilled, some heated and some prepared, some iced or delicate or fat; each person ordered differently. The waiter then went to get the orders, which he repeated and carried in his head, so that when he got into the kitchen he repeated them. These men were called 'gong heads' or 'callers.' In an instant, the waiter would be back carrying three dishes forked in his left hand, while on his right arm from hand to shoulder he carried about twenty bowls doubled up, and he distributed them precisely as everyone had ordered without an omission or mistake. If there were, the customers would tell the 'head man' who would scold and abuse the waiter and sometimes dock his salary, so severe was the punishment" (Y. L. Meng 1957 ed., p. 27; my translation).

In Kaifeng, but especially in Hangchow, restaurants came into and went out of fashion regularly. In the north we hear of a set number of great establishments, the best of which was White Kitchen on An-chou Alley in the Western Precinct of the city, followed by the House of Li's Blessing at Chick's Alley, and several others. However, "after the Cheng-ho period [1111–17], the Pavilion of Lengthy Blessings, under the east wall of the Ching-ying Palace, flourished exceptionally" (ibid., p. 16; my translation). The citizens of Hangchow were even more fickle and given to following fashion, although there is some indication that there, and probably in Kaifeng too, people became regulars at a particular restaurant.[6]

A step down from the wine restaurants were those which specialized in a particular food, a particular style of cooking, or, as with the noodle shops, a category of food. Restaurants which specialized in one particular food, more characteristic of Hangchow, served iced foods, or food with kumiss or fish, or "temple food," vegetarian food cooked in the style of the Buddhist temples.

The noodle shops, a good deal humbler than the wine restaurants, fall into Meng Yuan-lao's category of "laborers' shops." They served no wine but offered various kinds of noodle dishes, specializing in either noodles with meat or noodles with vegetables. Another kind of inexpensive restaurant which had mostly soups advertised their specialty by a calabash hung over the door. These shops did not really serve full meals but were convenient for a lunch or snack for the customer in a hurry. Nor were they always physically permanent or substantial. Some evidently squatted on unoccupied city land and were often little more than latticework covered by thatch.

Two common kinds of prepared food shops sold *ping* ("cakes" or "pastries"). There were two main kinds of ping—oil ping and hu-ping, the latter deriving its name from the Hu people, northern nomads from whom the Chinese had borrowed the recipe. The shops specialized in one of the two kinds of ping: oil ping shops offered steamed ping, sugared ping, and stuffed pastries; hu-ping shops sold deep-fried puff pastries in various forms, similar to present-day *yu-t'iao*. Like all eating places, the *hu-ping* shops were lively and noisy; Meng Yuan-lao recalls that "each place had three to five men to prepare and mix the dough and man the braziers. From the fifth watch [7:00–9:00 A.M.], their voices could be heard far and wide." The two most successful shops in Kaifeng, Chang's of Hai-chou and Ch'eng's, "both had upwards of fifty ovens" (Y. L. Meng 1957 ed., p. 27; my translation). Other prepared food shops sold man-t'ou (steamed buns with a filling), tien-hsin (snacks), cooked pork, preserved meat and fish. Some shops specialized in goodies for children, such as sweetened fruits, "shrimp beards," or thick sweetmeats (Kuan P'u Nai Te Weng 1957 ed., p. 94). Thus, there was a broad range of prepared foods, and according to all accounts, the number of places selling them was very large. The production of at least some of these items was further professionalized, at least in Southern Sung, by the practice of manufacturing them in large workshops, which among other items made man-t'ou, dumplings, roasted goose, duck, pork, and lamb, sugared or honeyed jujubes, stuffed lungs, and pulse-bean soup (Chou 1957 ed., p. 444).

These workshops supplied at least some of the vendors who filled the streets of the large cities, starting at dawn and persevering until past midnight. In the morning, vendors hawked breakfast items and, also, tea and water for washing one's face; by late evening they were selling warming broiled and gingery items. Evidently, one had only to step from one's front gate to be subjected to the attentions of sellers of both prepared and raw food, cakes, pastries, and fruits. Even at night, "people who carry dishes on a frame slung on a shoulder pole [offer various foods, mostly ping]. They sing out along the side of the road. People in the capital consider this perfectly commonplace, but if a rustic from some distant place should be confronted with it, he would think it extraordinary" (Kuan P'u Nai Te Weng 1957 ed., p. 94; my translation). Although the food that the vendors sold was neither as elaborate nor as expensive as that available in restaurants, it was regarded as tasty, and no one hesitated to eat it.

For anyone wealthy enough, Hangchow afforded an unusual service; "tea and wine kitchens" furnished everything necessary for a banquet: they reserved the hall, arranged for the food, conveyances, dishes, and napery, and, if necessary, guided the customer in the appropriate etiquette for his party. Some businesses even rented appropriate hempen garments for mourners at funerals (Chou 1957 ed., p. 443; see also T. M. Wu 1957 ed., pp. 302–03). When one rented a boat for a party on West Lake, everything necessary for dining was provided by the owner of the boat. On holidays these excursions were extremely popular, and it was difficult to find a boat to rent; the very wealthy maintained private boats.

Marco Polo writes unequivocally that Hangchow "is the greatest city which may be found in the world, where so many pleasures may be found that one fancies himself to be in Paradise" (trans. Moule and Pelliot 1938, p. 326). For the people of the city who could afford its delights, one of the greatest was obviously the food. And the restaurants, above all, made of dining both a sensual pleasure and an adventure.

Attitudes about Food

While our need for sustenance is imperative and easily expressed, the attitudes of most peoples about food have been complex. In Sung society, in which most ate adequately and a fair number splendidly, food was far more than sustenance, eating far more than fueling the body. To dine was a highly expressive act, for it revealed the diner's origins, his social and economic position, his attitude towards his fellow diners, and probably his religious and intellectual leanings. In a sense, we might almost say that what and how a man ate could be conceived of as an act of self-identification, of defining oneself in relation to others.

Scarcely an event or a situation marking a person's life failed to involve eating of some kind. Worship was ritual feeding of the dead or of the gods. Birth, marriage, and death were accompanied by food. To travel was to experience different kinds of food, to stay at home meant the observance of the seasonal food cycle. One might pass beyond the pale of civilization; if that happened, one could tell by the food. Food affirmed the ritual order and the political order. Properly understood, eating attuned one to that greater order of which ritual and politics were a part and insured good health and a long life. Purely physical pleasure could be had from eating, as could the perhaps even more exquisite pleasure of being known as someone who knows his way around town. One could study nature in the pursuit of food, or delve into the classics for learned allusions to dishes whose recipes were half-forgotten. Eating moved the whole man from purely physical satisfaction to the highest flights of speculative philosophy. To describe what was eaten, how, and by whom is only the basis for the study of Sung food, for it seldom existed for people of those times in such simple terms. Food was understood in complex ways, ways which want at least the beginnings of definition. Here we shall consider food and eating as ritual, as definer of time and space, as intellectual pursuit, and as self-expression.

To fully describe the ritual and religious uses of food is an impossibly broad task, if for no other reason than the immense variety of religious practice and ritualistic expression that existed from region to region. All we can do here is point out how food was used in several contexts and in some different systems of belief and ritual practice. The importance of food as ritual object varied greatly, of course, within Sung society. City dwellers were, as Jacques Gernet observes, more pious in practice than in conviction and were therefore less interested in the ritual uses of food (1962, p. 203). Other segments of society—the peasants, perhaps, and certainly the ruling house—were more punctilious and fervent in ritual practice than the urban population. Predictably, the emperor's ritual activities are best recorded by the sources, both because, in the minds of contemporaries, the exercise of political power was closely bound up with its ritual practice and because the great sacrifices and ceremonies were grand spectacles, the greatest shows of all in two cities that delighted in show.

If we have suggested that, generally speaking, the Sung period was characterized by attitudes rational and empirical, it must be added that both Buddhism and Taoism, each with its own dietary practices, had some influence. It was not a pious age, but Buddhism in particular played a role in everyone's life, if only because so many Buddhist customs and holidays were almost universally observed. The great temples continued prosperous and influential, their markets very often playing the central role in the new commercial age. Abbots lived in great luxury; temples gave rich and elaborate maigre feasts on Buddhist holidays (Y. L. Meng 1957 ed., p. 19). Taoist dietary practices were less pervasive than those of the Buddhists, not so much because Taoism had lost favor as because the Taoist dietary regimen of abstinence from grains was more costly to practice than vegetarianism.

Buddhism's most important influence on the Sung diet was the relative unpopularity of beef. Shiba Yoshinobu has shown how cattle were brought to market, but beef is not mentioned explicitly in the lists of dishes made for banquets or by restaurants, which suggests that it was held in some disfavor and was eaten only for its novelty (1968, pp. 233–37). Sung beef would not have been very tasty in any case; in south China oxen and water buffalo were used as draft animals. Purely aside from religious feeling, their flesh must have been tough, stringy, and dry after a career of pulling a plow.

A number of dishes and pastries were eaten in association with Buddhist holidays, including the special cakes eaten on the ninth day of the ninth moon and the "seven-treasure five-taste" conjee eaten on the eighth day of the twelfth moon. (See Y. L. Meng 1957 ed., p. 61). Such food was not unique to the Sung and is characteristic of the period only to the degree to which the food and the holidays themselves had lost some of their religious importance and had become simply secular, seasonal customs.

People offered food to their ancestors, a most ancient custom and one sanctioned by Buddhism in the belief in "hungry ghosts." Various references hint that this ritual food for the deities or the deceased was for the most part prepared in the same way as that intended to be consumed, and in all probability, it was eaten by the worshipers after the ceremony. We find, for example, that the agency charged with obtaining the emperor's meat, the Office of Cattle, Sheep, and Goats, was responsible for animals used in sacrifices (T. M. Wu 1957 ed., p. 207). Ritual food was in some cases anachronistic. A certain kind of millet, for example, although no longer eaten, was grown by farmers only for use in the sacrifices. That there existed at least some gap between ritual and regular food is easily understandable; the contemporary diet, dominated by foods from the south, differed considerably from that of the northern Chinese culture of a millennium before the Sung, when ritual practice was codified.

Food was central to rituals involving the living as well as the dead. Events such as marriage and birth were accompanied not only by banquets but also with the preparation and consumption of special foods that often had symbolic or punning significance. As part of the protracted marriage ceremonies described by Meng Yuan-lao, the groom's family received a gift of steamed cakes called "honey-harmonizing-with-oil" cakes, symbolizing the union of two differing elements (Y. L. Meng 1957 ed., p. 32). Confinement and childbirth were attended by numerous special foods and dishes. Friends sent stalks of ripe grain and special man-t'ou called "share the pain." At the ceremonial first bathing of the infant, various foods, including fruits and garlic, were put in the bath water. "As soon as the jujubes [*tsao-tzu*] are put in the tub, the women compete to get them, thus seeking for a son [*tsao-tzu*, "early son"]" (ibid.).

In Sung times, the greatest rituals were performed by the emperor. Even more, perhaps, than collecting taxes or making war, the first responsibility and most important activity of the ruler was his performance of ritual. His sacrifices, his worship of his ancestors, his imperial progresses were great and splendid occasions. If his capitals, primarily commercial rather than administrative, were less well suited for their performance than those of earlier ages, these cities still lived in rhythm with his yearly cycle of rituals. Just as Kaifeng and Hangchow were stages for the playing out of a ritual drama, the emperor himself was, in much of his daily existence, a player obliged by custom and for reasons of state to perform his leading role.

In the China of the tenth through thirteenth centuries, imperial ritual still

had powerful political overtones. Describing the feast given for foreign
envoys by the emperor before the fall of the north, Meng Yuan-lao reports
that unlike the other diplomats, only the envoy of the Liao, the great northern
enemies of Sung during most of the Northern Sung period, had special
dishes of pork and mutton and a saucer of leek-garlic vinegar (1957 ed., p.
52). This deviation from the regular menu could not be taken lightly. The
emperor's doings were intended to assert and express his position as center of
the world and arbiter of human culture. That there should be deviation from
ritual order, which reflected the larger political and ultimately cosmic order,
revealed either imperial weakness or moral depravity and probably both.
Thus, even in less formal occasions than the entertainment of ambassadors,
we find that imperial dining adhered to ritual practices reflecting the em-
perior's position in the whole order of things. "In the tenth moon of the
twenty-first year of the Shao-hsing reign period [1151–52], Kao-tsung [the
first emperor of Southern Sung] made a progress to the house of the Prince
of Ch'ing-ho" (Chou 1957 ed., p. 491). There, a great banquet was held
consisting of more than thirty courses and some hundreds of dishes, presented
and removed with clockwork regularity. Fresh and preserved fruit courses
gave way to courses of foods deep-fried with honey, of preserved things, and
of preserved meat. Food on skewers, dishes to encourage wine bibbing, and
many other courses followed; "finishing food" alone consisted of fifty
individual portions. And all the while, musical performances were presented
between courses.

This Lucullan meal was served with the finest dishes and utensils. Chou
Mi reports that articles of jade, silver, and pearl were used. Among the
vessels were a "dragon-designed *ting*, three vessels from the Shang Dynasty
[1766–1122 B.C.], and four from the Chou [1122–221 B.C.]" (Chou 1957
ed., p. 504). Especially fine pictures and calligraphies were hung for the feast,
including works by Wu Tao-tzu, Chü-jan, and Tung Yuan, to name only
the most familiar. Numerous rolls of fine silk were distributed to the assembled company. All this the emperor could command—fabulous quantities
of the finest food, the best to be had in the world, served in a manner that
revealed his inexhaustible resources. The antiques and the works of art
symbolized the imperial role as carrier of Chinese tradition, the emperor's
appreciation and mastery of the best of China's past.

The form of the banquet itself reflected the gradations of political power
as it extended from the emperor. High officials who served in the palace
itself enjoyed eleven courses. Officials of the third rank had seven dishes, one
box of sweet deep-fried food, and five pitchers of wine. Those of the fourth
rank had five dishes, a box of fruit, and two pitchers of wine, while those of
the fifth rank got but three dishes and one pitcher, thus perfectly reflecting

in culinary terms the formal structure of government (Chou 1957 ed., pp. 491–95). The frequent accounts of such affairs in contemporary literature suggest that they were much enjoyed, not as dining, despite the splendid food, but as wonderful spectacles with singing, dancing, flag waving, and displaying of martial skills. That no emperor could possibly have savored all that was offered is beside the point; he could command abundance, and in doing so affirmed his own place.

Kao-tsung's meal is an extreme example of intentions symbolic rather than epicurean. Yet almost any public dinner surely had both an element of ritual, as the diner sought to identify himself with certain social values and place himself in the company of a particular group, and an element of pure enjoyment of the food. Contemporaries who describe imperial banquets have in mind ritual affirmation, pleasure in the ability to command pleasure for the senses rather than the pleasure itself. Wealthy city dwellers, in this case, were more fortunate than their ruler, for they could satisfy the demands of social etiquette without losing the joys of eating. Restaurant dining had its rituals and customs, but attitudes were free and easy; ritual was designed to enhance the food. Sung diners were probably less bound by the constraints of custom than are moderns. Restaurants were noisy places where customers shouted out their orders. The diners were fickle and demanding, "their calculations quite casual"; if two men encountered each other in a wine shop, they would fall to eating and drinking and spend large sums of money. Even a single person "would still drink from a silver bowl." (Y. L. Meng 1957 ed., p. 26). This was a new kind of ritual, a style of self-definition not bound by class but open to anyone of sophistication and money.

Our sources on city life during the Sung contain much material about great festivals, some of which were Buddhist holidays and others of which were associated with the changing seasons. We read about the characteristic customs of each festival, and the lengthiest and most exhaustive descriptions are of the foods of the season. For country folk, the seasonal markers were, of course, changing tasks: plowing, seeding, transplanting, harvesting, and so on, through the year. But for the city dweller, work was not seasonal, or at least far less so, so that time was marked by the cycle of fruits and vegetables available in the markets and by the special foods consumed at festivals.

At the time of the Ch'ing-ming festival, fifteen days after the spring equinox, the people of Kaifeng made jujube swallows with dough and strung them on willow branches above their doors. Then on the day of the Festival of the Dead, everyone left town to sweep the graves, taking jujube cakes, steamed ping, and duck eggs. On this day too, sweetmeats, wheat cakes, cheese made with milk, and milk ping were sold. As summer approached, apricots and cherries appeared in the market. On the inauspicious fifth day of the fifth month, people ate fragrant candied fruit and a special dish made by wrapping glutinous rice or millet in a three-cornered package of bamboo leaves. Thereafter peaches were available. By the sixth month, one could buy melons, all kinds of peaches, and pears. At the time of the mid-autumn festival, people began to eat crab claws, chestnuts, grape sprouts, and oranges, while on the ninth of the ninth moon, pomegranates, pine nuts, and a special steamed wheaten cake topped with figures of lions made of flour were eaten. Autumn was also the best time for jujubes, and a certain place within the Liang Gate had the best, so that "even the Inner Palace sent out for them" (ibid., p. 50). As winter arrived, the people of Kaifeng began to eat preserved ginger, goose pears, quince, and crabs and clams.

Time and, thus, memory were suffused with impressions of food. For the nature poet, the flow of the seasons could become the hackneyed images of the prunus in spring or the chrysanthemum of autumn; the memoirist, struggling to recapture the rhythms of life in his city, is more immediate and particular in his writing. When he seeks to describe a time rather than a place, he resorts very often to references to the seasonal foods which shaped time in the city dweller's life and were evidently often uppermost in his mind. Food was considered natural, in the forceful sense that it was linked to the grander flow of time and nature and, like nature, was constantly renewed.

The merchant, plying his trade in many regions, and the bureaucrat, often on the road and obliged by the rules of avoidance to serve outside his home region, came into contact willy-nilly with many local varieties of cookery. Sometimes, as in the capital, natives of a particular area could enjoy their own dishes and ingredients, for some restaurants specialized in regional cooking, but more often the traveler must have been obliged to make do with unfamiliar food despite his prejudices. Some of these men developed a liking for the foods of different regions, so that, for example, restaurants which had been established in Kaifeng to indulge the preferences of officials from the southeast came to have a wider clientele. Sung city dwellers loved novelty and were great followers of fashion, even in their eating habits. Especially in Hangchow, restaurants responded to the temper of the times not only by serving up dishes made with unusual ingredients but also by specializing in the cooking of various regions.

Contemporaries recognized three primary regional styles: northern, southern, and Szechwanese. We have since added a fourth, Cantonese, but the Kwangtung area was backward in Sung times, and its style of cooking had evidently not yet coalesced. The qualities of the three styles were generally similar to those of their modern equivalents. Northern food tended to be bland, included much lamb and many preserved foods—one writer says northerners like "sour" foods (Y. Chu 1939 ed., p. 73)—and was based on wheat or millet, which were converted into noodles, buns, dumplings, and cakes, often with a filling. The preface to *Liang-fang* (Good Recipes), a Sung work attributed to Shen Kua and Su Shih, declares that "southerners eat pork and fish and are healthy; northerners eat pork and fish and get sick . . . " (Su Shih and K. Shen 1939 ed., p. 2; my translation). Southern cooking referred to the food of the Yangtze delta region rather than to the far south and was based on rice. Contemporaries held that it was more highly seasoned than northern food and observed also that fish was widely used as an ingredient, as was pork, in one area said to be "cheap as dirt." Szechwanese food is not identified by commentators as particularly hot, but references to peppers and a fiery kind of garden pea suggest that it was. Szechwan cooking was based on rice. Actually, Szechwanese food is discussed most often in relation to tea and medicinal herbs, as it was the great center for the production of those items during the Sung period. The *Liang-fang* says that "in Shu [Szechwan] there is a vegetable that resembles the pea. It is excellent. . . . By nature it's very hot. If you eat it, it will cause gasping and gaping. But if you dry it with a little wine and then steam it, it is very good and causes no harm" (ibid., p. 81; my translation).

Naturally, some people could not tolerate the food of other regions, and many others enjoyed poking fun at what were supposed to be the outrageous eating habits of others. "People from Fukien and Chekiang eat frogs. People from the Hu and Hsiang regions [the central Yangtze valley] eat *ho-chieh*, which are large frogs. People from north China all laugh about people from the southeast who eat frogs. There was a relative of the imperial house who was stationed in Che[kiang]. He got the thighs of a frog and dried them. Then he tricked his clansmen by telling them it was preserved quail meat. After they ate it, he told them the truth. After that, their slanders of the southeast abated a little" (Y. Chu 1939 ed., p. 21; my translation). Whether their slanders abated because they found frogs tasty or because they were dumbfounded by their relative's trickery, the author does not tell us.

This sort of mild byplay concerning the eating habits of China's various regions was not very serious; most literate people would have tried food from other regions. This is not to say that such a person would try foreign, non-Chinese food, which could be expected to be repulsive or even harmful. In the extreme south, for example, "they eat snakes. When Su Shih's wife Ch'ao-yün was with him in exile in Hui-chou, she bought and ate food from a retired soldier. Thinking it was fresh sea fish, she asked its name. When he replied 'snake,' she vomited. She was ill for several months and in the end she died." The uncivilized wretches of Hainan "eat creatures like flies, gnats, and earthworms. They catch them and stuff them into sections of bamboo and steam them. Then they break open the bamboo and eat them." The Fan people of the south ate rancid fish and honeyed musk-deer brains. Nor was the food of the northern nomads any more suitable for a civilized person. Chu writes of his father's inability, while serving as ambassador to Liao, to drink his kumiss with fat floating in it (ibid., pp. 21–23; my translation).

The sophisticated gentleman, then, had catholic tastes, but he distinguished the foods which fell within and without the pale of Chinese civilization. Food from another province might not be foreign to him, but that eaten by other cultures appeared alien, repulsive, and probably poisonous.

Food and Thought

Sung intellectual life was typified by an urge to order, a desire to classify and organize both nature, in cosmology and in natural history, and man, in ethics and in history. The great works of the intellect in Sung times, in whatever branch of learning, were intended to organize experience into a comprehensible whole. This may be said of Shen Kua, the greatest scientist of the age, of Ssu-ma Kuang, its greatest historian, or of the great moral philosopher, Chu Hsi. Attitudes about food were marked by a similar concern: to integrate this facet of human experience into a comprehensible whole.

Within the general flow of Sung thought, we can distinguish two streams, sometimes complementary but often at crosscurrents. On the one hand, the Sung intellectual elite was often practical, empirical, and willing to experiment. Men like Shen or Su Shih had, above all, an intense curiosity about all manner of experience. Writers took pleasure in finding the unique and the unusual; travel literature was common, as were collected odd bits of information about politics, local customs, the lives of famous men, and the like gathered together in great untidy works whose organizing principle, often enough, existed only in the author's mind. All of them are storehouses of information on life in Sung times. In the hands of the best writers, such works as *Tung-ching meng-hua lu* or *Wu-lin chiu-shih* achieve the status of portraits of a time. Men of this temper were great collectors, and we find that the Sung was the first great era of antique collecting and of connoisseurship in painting, as well as a time when the making of etymological dictionaries was a minor rage among scholars. Clearly, the acquisition of knowledge, whether by empirical, historical, or classical studies, took precedence over its organization.

On the other side, a facet of the Sung mind was intensely logical and rationalist, concerned far more with the ethical implications of experience than with experience itself, and sometimes puritanical in tenor. On this side were the great neo-Confucian philosophers, who put all aspects of human life and experience into ethical order. Far from seeking knowledge through indiscriminate experience, these men thought such experience very often stood in the way of true knowledge.

The relationship between these two facets of Sung thinking is by no means simple. Sometimes it is possible to identify a person or a school of thought with one side or the other, but just as often the two tendencies coexist in the mind of one thinker. Thus, Ssu-ma Kuang, the latitudinarian in historiographical practice, the voracious collector of all sorts of knowledge, was also the stern and puritanical moralist who held that the way to true knowledge was not to seek but to ward off experience. Indeed, this polar tension is common to most Sung thought and is very much present in thinking about food.

It is not at all difficult to make out where the authors of works on Kaifeng and Hangchow stood in their attitudes toward experience of all kinds, including sensual. City dwellers loved pleasure, as Marco Polo observed; the cities were the founts of novelty and variety in all kinds of experience. To love the city was to take a well-defined intellectual and moral stance. In eating, it meant enthusiasm for new tastes, new ingredients, new dishes. It implied a degree of self-indulgence and hedonism. To love the city—its restaurants and its markets—was to assent to the luxurious commercial culture which a part of the Sung mind found abhorrent.

At the other pole stood those thinkers, influenced by Taoism and rather dogmatic Confucian ethics, who detested the city and all its ways. Most of the Confucians would count themselves in this group which enthusiastically championed the virtues of the simple rural life but very rarely lived it. Nevertheless, attitudes adopted by such men had a distinct influence on Sung eating and ideas about it, especially those connected with medicine.

Diet and the study of medicine were virtually indistinguishable (Nakayama and Sivin 1973; Needham 1970). The *Liang-fang*, which I have translated as "Good Recipes," might equally well be read "Good Prescriptions," for it makes no verbal distinction between healthful food and medicine and, in fact, lumps them in the same category. Alchemical experimentation, through most of imperial history, was common among the members of the literate elite, and numerous substances were ingested—from compounds of mercury which would have led to the demise of the experimenter, to various organic materials whose medical efficacy has been documented. What is important for our study of food is the degree to which such concoctions as the "secret-of-yang pill," "the four divine pills for regulating the humors," or "powder of cinnabar" formed a continuum with common, everyday food.

What constituted a healthy diet? Physicians were by no means able to agree, and indeed it seemed that one man's meat was another's poison. Northerners could not stomach pork and fish, southerners thrived on them. All sorts of considerations—astrological, geographical, and personal—had to be taken into account in arriving at each individual's healthiest diet. Among all the rules, cautions, and systems of diet, a few basic principles can be discerned, the most general being the rule that nothing should be consumed to excess. Many common foods were considered "poisonous," but if over-indulgence were avoided, they could be eaten with perfect safety. There was some value placed on naturalness in eating. That is, one should avoid food out of its proper season. A dish with a salutary cooling effect in summer might well prove fatal in cold weather. Moreover, simple foods, herbs, and vegetables grown and prepared by oneself were valuable. Su Shih held that one did not necessarily need rare or exotic ingredients to achieve a healthy diet. "For medicine that is both cheap and useful," he wrote, "there is nothing like burweed. Some medicines, though cheap, are not produced in some areas. But burweed is everywhere; anywhere there is soil it is produced. Its flowers, leaves, roots, and fruit are edible. You eat it like a vegetable, and it controls illness without poisoning. Fresh or prepared in pellet or powder, any form is fine. Taken for a long time, it causes the bones and marrow to be well filled out" (Su Shih and K. Shen 1939 ed., pp. 97–98; my translation).

There was some suspicion among Sung commentators that the rich food and rich life which attended an official career was unhealthful and that the simple meals of mountain villagers were to be preferred. But appreciative descriptions of diet in the villages and discussions of common people's food were not merely theoretic idealism. The lowest bureaucrats, starting their careers in some obscure subprefecture, and losers in factional struggles in the capital who retired or were exiled to the provinces sometimes found themselves obliged to be satisfied with little better than peasant fare. In a sense, then, some of those who praised plain cooking were making a virtue of their necessity. Su Shih explains this in his little essay "Tung-p'o keng tsan" (In Praise of Tung-po's Soup). "Tung-po's soup is a vegetable soup that he cooked when he was living in retirement [actually in political exile]. It did not contain fish or meat or the five flavorings, but it had a natural sweetness. His recipe was this: he took *sung* cabbage, rape-turnip, wild daikon, and shepherd's purse and scrubbed them thoroughly to get rid of the bitter sap. First he took a bit of oil to coat the pot, then he put in the vegetables with water, along with a bit of rice and fresh ginger . . . " (Su Shih 1970 ed., hsü-chi 1:1 b).[7] In the preface to a prose-poem on the same dish, Su recalls that he invented it when he was extremely poor and that "the recipe doesn't use condiments but has a natural taste" (ibid., hsü-chi 3:21).

A key term in understanding Sung conceptions of a healthy diet is *tzu-jan* ("natural"), which is used twice in describing Su's soup. On one level, there is nothing of itself natural about highly sophisticated members of the elite gathering up herbs and cooking up stews, nothing unnatural about their dining luxuriously in restaurants at the capital. If one is natural and the other is not, then the diner has made them so; he must have self-conscious attitudes about eating and diet. For Su Shih and for many others of the intellectual elite, naturalness was itself a value, and their interest in mountain herbs and peasant dishes reflected a broader concern for health, society, and self-definition. The praise of simple food, held up in opposition to the elaborate cookery and costly ingredients of the city, was attuned to common intellectual concerns. First, it was commendable from the point of view of Confucian ethics: it centered on farms and villagers, it eschewed luxury and took sober pleasure in the humble. Second, it allowed the learned to travel about the country, poking into this and that, tasting the other, and collecting the lot. Interest in this kind of food combined opportunities for experience and experimentation with opportunities for displays of erudition. The *Pen-hsin chai shu-shih p'u* (Treatise on Rough Food from the Studio of Original Mind) reflects this linkage; it consists of twenty recipes or, rather, descriptions of dishes, all of which are "rough and coarse" (Anonymous 1936 ed.). The first five are dishes drawn from classical literature, the other are for herbs and vegetables as prepared by the author, who lived in retirement and studied Taoism.

The Sung conception of natural food is most complex. It includes, first of all, edible plants, roots, mushrooms, and the like gathered in the mountains and forest. It was further expanded to encompass ingredients natural in the sense of being common or readily available, so that foods natural in the north might not be so in the south. Finally, it implied a style of cooking without artifice—"plain and thus elegant! Showing its clarity"—which refused to deny the basic nature of its ingredients by masking their flavor or appearance. Thus golden utensils should not be used, for "they completely cut off the astringent taste and entirely lose the food's basic nature" (Su Shih and K. Shen 1939 ed., p. 85). This ideology of cooking meshed nicely with the predilections of formal philosophers whose aim was intergrative, not in a strictly mechanistic sense, but in the sense that they sought harmony and order within and between the human and the natural worlds. They agreed that the *chün-tzu* (the "accomplished man") or the sage would never go to extremes, either in indulgence or in self-denial, but would maintain a dynamic balance appropriate to the individual and his station.

Some people, however, went to excess, and their gluttonies entered the historiographic tradition as demonstrations of their imperfect characters. We read, for example, that Wang Fu had three larders of pickled orioles, and that the "bad last" prime minister of Southern Sung, Chia Ssu-tao, had stored away several hundred jars of sugar and eight hundred piculs of pepper (Shiba 1968, p. 468; quoting Chou Mi, *Ch'i-tung yeh-yü*, Chap. 16). Curiously, it would seem that inattention to one's food was almost as bad as gluttony. A story about the great reforming minister Wang An-shih that appears in several memoirs by his enemies recalls that as a prominent young official he had taken part in a party given by the emperor Jen-tsung. One of the entertainments was the feeding of fish, but Wang absentmindedly ate his fish food, which, so we are told, made a very poor impression on the emperor, who never gave Wang a high position on the grounds that only someone seeking to draw attention to himself would eat fish food.

The strong appeal of simple country food for the intellectual elite helps to explain why, although we have the names of hundreds of dishes served at banquets or in restaurants, the recipes that survive are for dishes like Su Shih's soup or steeped *yü-yen*, a kind of mountain vegetable. The formal study of food and cooking was centered, not in restaurants or the kitchens of great households, but in the quasi-philosophical-medical meditations of intellectuals, and the most elaborate cooking was in the hands of cooks who, for the most part, lacked the ability to set down their secrets in writing. We must imagine that many Sung writers on food composed their praises to rough food while enjoying the sophisticated creations of their anonymous cooks.

Sung Food and Chinese Cuisine

Sung emperors, like their fellow monarchs throughout historic times, commanded a rich and varied diet. Indeed, the emperor's diet in Sung times was impossibly so; his banquets became very nearly pure spectacle. Disregarding the addition of a few new ingredients and, because communications improved, the more frequent availability of others, there is no reason to suppose that during Sung times imperial cooking saw any more than a gradual evolution and elaboration of well-established patterns. It was the elite bureaucratic class, vastly larger than that of earlier times, and the merchants, beneficiaries of a commercial revolution, who profited most from the changes in structure of Chinese society which took place before and during the Sung. And these two groups took the lead in changing dietary habits. Furnished with an abundance and variety of materials beyond anything their ancestors could have imagined, mobile, experimental, and egalitarian in temper, little influenced by dietary taboos, they brought about the creation of a Chinese cuisine.

Wu Tzu-mu makes a somewhat disapproving comment on the state of cookery in Southern Sung: "Formerly, in Pien-ching (Kaifeng), southern-style noodle shops and Szechwanese tea houses were made for gentlemen from Chiang-nan, who said they didn't care for northern food. In the two hundred or so years since the move south, the people have become habituated to the climate, the cooking has become mixed up, and there's no division of north and south" (T. M. Wu 1957 ed, p. 267; my translation). Like the emperor and his court, like many of the great bureaucratic families, the restaurateurs had made their way to Hangchow from the old capital after its fall; they had reestablished their restaurants and had continued to serve their wealthy clientele. As one commentator emphasizes, however, the name was maintained but the reality lost. No longer could one order a meal in a "southern" restaurant and expect down-home cooking. Cooking carried from its native region, thrown in contact with all the other kinds of cooking in the empire, could not remain unaffected. It adopted the ingredients from one region, the nuance of seasoning from another, until cooking was indeed "mixed up." More important, perhaps, a particular regional cooking was no longer the unconscious expression of the eating habits of a population defined by locally available ingredients. To cook northern food in Hangchow implied a conscious choice among possible ingredients and possible styles of cooking; it became, in other words, a style of cooking set loose from its local moorings and the product of a consciously maintained tradition.

If this confusion of styles and eating habits was evident among restaurants, it was far more so among those who patronized them. A well-traveled and sophisticated eating public enjoyed a dish, or even a meal, of the specialties of one region, but most would prefer to enjoy at one time or another many more of the dining possibilities available. Customers were fickle and demanding; if a particular dish was not available, the restaurant would send out for it. To order a meal, to weigh and balance off the almost infinite possibilities of flavor, texture, and color, was an act that implied a degree of reflection and of knowledge. While the codification of systems by which a balanced and elegant meal was created by diner and cook was not completed until later dynasties, the Sung saw the changes in eating which made such systems both possible and necessary.

Although it shared many of the dishes and all of the cooking techniques of imperial cookery, the hybrid style of cooking that prevailed in Hangchow was not to develop in the same directions as imperial food had done. The enthusiasm of intellectuals for simpler eating, for commonplace ingredients, for a carefully balanced diet made itself felt in the Sung. Such rather abstract concerns were not influential in the great city restaurants, but they set the pattern for the dynamic tension between richness and simplicity, suaveness and asperity that typifies Chinese cuisine.

NOTES

1. Many thanks are due to Professor James Cahill of the University of California, Berkeley, whose excellent photographic reproductions of the scroll I used for this study.

2. I have relied heavily on the pioneering work of Shinoda Osamu, the great specialist on early Chinese food, and on Shiba Yoshinobu's *Sodai shogyo-shi kenkyu* (1968), partially and helpfully translated by Mark Elvin as *Commerce and Society in Sung China*, (Michigan Abstracts of Chinese and Japanese Works on Chinese History, no. 2, 1970).

3. In twenty-three characters describing a meal, the biographer of Chao P'u nicely defines Chao's place as a valued, intimate advisor to the throne. "They roasted meat over charcoal. P'u's wife came in with wine. The Emperor addressed her as *sao* ("elder sister-in-law")" (*Sung-shih*, 256:1).

4. The Sung writer Kao Ssu-sun wrote an essay called "Hsieh-lüeh" (Crabs).

5. Shinoda gives an excellent account of this work, the *Pei-shan chiu-ching*, by Chu I-chung. See Shinoda 1974, pp. 151–52.

6. Wu Tzu-mu (1957 ed., p. 268) says that "market food is always available; you order as you please and you don't have to worry about regularly patronizing any one seller" (my translation). This was presumably in contrast to the usual practice in restaurants.

7. The five flavors—sweet, sour, bitter, pungent, and salty—were linked in cosmological theories based on the five elements to earth, wood, fire, metal, and water.

ILLUSTRATIONS

1. Millets (A, *su, Setaria italica germanica;* B, *liang, S. italica maxima;* C, *shu, Panicum miliaceum*) (from Wu Ch'i-chün, *Chih Wu Ming Shih T'u K'ao,* 1848)

2. Other major cereals (A, *kaoliang, Andropogen sorghum;* B, *mai, Triticum aestivum;* C, *ma, Cannabis sativa;* D, *tao, Oryza sativa;* E, *p'i, Echinochloa crusgalli;* F, *i-i, Coix lacryma-jobi*) (A, E, F, from Keng I-li, comp., *Chung-kuo Chu-yao Chih-wu T'u Shuo—Ho Pen K'o,* Peking, Science Press, 1959; B, C, D, from Wu Ch'i-chün, *Chih Wu Ming Shih T'u K'ao,* 1848)

A

B

C

A

B

C

D

E

F

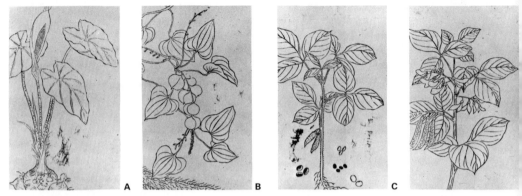

3. Additional crops and beans (A, taro; B, yam; C, soybean; D, red bean) (from Wu Ch'i-chün, *Chih Wu Ming Shih T'u K'ao,* 1848)

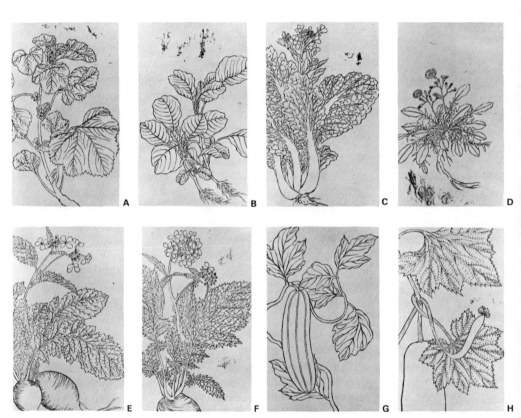

4. Some Chinese vegetables (A, malva; B, amaranth; C, Chinese cabbage; D, sonchus; E, radish; F, turnip; G, melon; H, gourd) (from Wu Ch'i-chün, *Chih Wu Ming Shih T'u K'ao,* 1848)

5. Mural scene of cattle plowing in the field, from an Eastern Han tomb at Holingor, Inner Mongolia (from *Han T'ang Pi Hua*, Peking, Foreign Language Press, 1974)

6. Brick painting of cattle plowing in the field, from a tomb of the Wei-Chin period (ca. 220–316), at Chia-yü-kuan, Kansu (from *Han T'ang Pi Hua*, Peking, Foreign Language Press, 1974)

7. Brick painting of cattle plowing in the field, from the Chia-yü-kuan tomb (from *Wen Wu*, no. 12, 1972)

8. T'ang mural of cattle plowing, from Li Shou's tomb at San Yüan, near Sian, Shensi (from *Han T'ang Pi Hua*, Peking, Foreign Language Press, 1974)

9. Mural of kitchen scene, from late Eastern Han tomb at Ta-hu-t'ing, Mi Hsien, Honan (*Wen Wu,* no. 10, 1972)

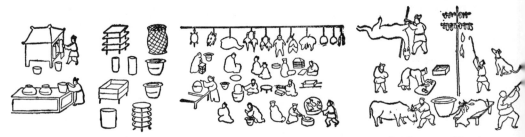

10. Han murals of kitchen scenes from a late Eastern Han tomb at Pang-t'ai-tzu-t'un in Liao-yang, Liaoning (from *Wen Wu Ts'an K'ao Tzu Liao,* no. 5, 1955)

11. Mural of kitchen scene from a late Han dynasty tomb at San-tao-hao, Liao-yang, Liaoning (from *Wen Wu Ts'an K'ao Tzu Liao,* no. 5, 1955)

12. Han brick rubbing of kitchen scene, Ch'eng-tu, Szechwan (from Ho Hao-t'ien, *Han Hua yü Han Tai Shê Hui Sheng Huo,* Taipei, Chung Hua Ts'ung Shu Editorial Commission, 1969)

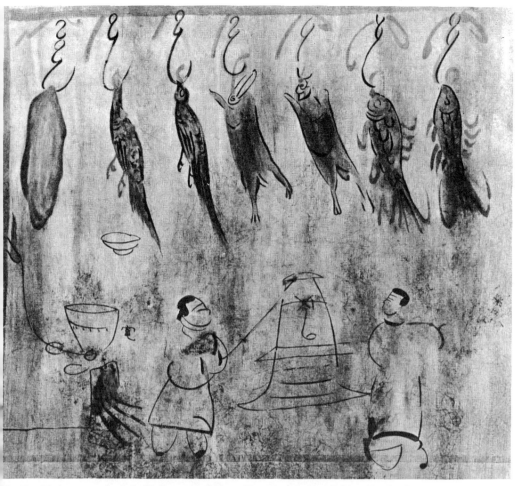

13. Han kitchen scene from the Holingor tomb (from *Han T'ang Pi Hua*, Peking, Foreign Language Press, 1974)

14. Brick paintings of kitchen scenes at the Chia-yü-kuan tomb (*Wen Wu*, no. 12, 1972)

15. A Shang feast, painting by Alton S. Tobey (*Life*, 29 September 1961)

16. Ritual scenes on a bronze bowl of Warring-States period, in the collections of the Shanghai Museum (from Charles Weber, *Chinese Pictorial Bronze Vessels of the Late Chou Period,* Ascona, Switzerland, Artibus Asiae, 1968)

17. Food dishes in a tray, found in the Western Han tomb at Ma-wang-tui, Ch'ang-sha, Hunan (from *Ch'ang-sha Ma-wang-tui I Hao Han Mu,* vol. 2, Peking, Wen Wu Press, 1973)

18. Four food dishes found at Ma-wang-tui (from *Ch'ang-sha Ma-wang-tui I Hao Han Mu,* vol. 2, Peking, Wen Wu Press, 1973)

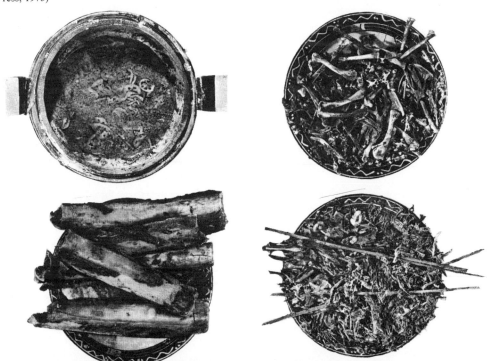

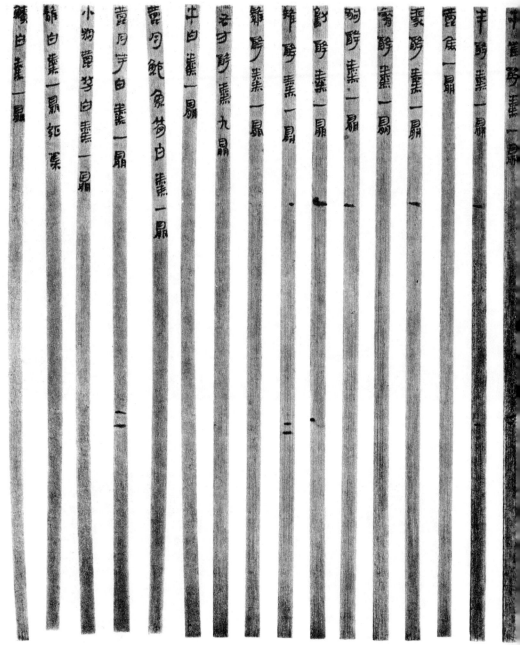

19. Bamboo slips from the Han tomb at Ma-wang-tui, listing names of food dishes furnished in the tomb (from *Ch'ang-sha Ma-wang-tui I Hao Han Mu*, vol. 2, Peking, Wen Wu Press, 1973)

20. Han feast scene, from the Ta-hu-t'ing tomb (*Wen Wu,* no. 10, 1972)

21. Han feast scene in the Chu Wei shrine in Ching-hsiang, Shantung (from Wilma Fairbank, *Adventures in Retrieval,* Cambridge, Mass., Harvard-Yenching Institute, 1972)

22. Han mural of an ancestral offering, in a tomb at Ying-ch'eng-tzu near Lü-ta, Liaoning (from Wilma Fairbank, *Adventures in Retrieval*, Cambridge, Mass., Harvard-Yenching Institute, 1972)

23. Rubbing of a Han tile, depicting a food and drink scene, Ch'eng-tu, Szechwan (from Wilma Fairbank, *Adventures in Retrieval*, Cambridge, Mass., Harvard-Yenching Institute, 1972)

24. Brick painting of feast scene from the Chia-yü-kuan tomb (*Wen Wu*, no. 12, 1972)

25. Brick paintings of food serving (left) and feasting-and-music scene (right), from the Chia-yü-kuan tomb (from *Wen Wu*, no. 12, 1972)

26. Banquet for scholars, a painting attributed to Emperor Hui Tsung of Sung dynasty (from B. Smith and W. G. Weng, *China, A History in Art,* New York, Harper and Row, 1973)

27. A banquet scene in the imperial palace of the Ch'ing dynasty for visitors from tributary states and tribe (from *Tōdo Meishō Zue*, 1806)

除日保
外和殿宴
古外藩蒙

29. K'ung Ming making offerings to the river Lu, from a seventeenth-century woodcut (from *Ying Hsiung P'u T'u Tsan*, reprinted, Shanghai, Hua Hsia Publishing Co., 1949)

28. Making offerings to the agricultural god, from a seventeenth-century woodcut (from *The Cooking of China,* Time-Life Books, 1968)

30. Restaurants in the Sung dynasty capital at Pien Ching (from Chang Tse-tuan, *Ch'ing Ming Shang Ho T'u,* Peking, Wen Wu Press, 1958)

31. Food shops in the Sung dynasty capital at Pien Ching (from Chang Tse-tuan, *Ch'ing Ming Shang Ho T'u,* Peking, Wen Wu Press, 1958)

32. Peking street scene in 1717, showing food shops and restaurants (from Wang Yuan-ch'i, ed., *Wan Shou Sheng Tien*, Peking, 1717)

5: YÜAN AND MING

FREDERICK W. MOTE

The two dynastic eras making up the period under consideration here constitute a span of four hundred years in what many historians look upon as China's early modern history. To remind the reader of some comparisons, in European history those centuries witnessed the flowering and the waning of the Middle Ages, followed by the Renaissance, the Reformation, the Counter Reformation, and the emergence of the modern nation-states of Europe. The Crusades, the fall of Constantinople to the Turks, the discovery of America and the circumnavigation of the globe, the age of mercantilism and the beginnings of the European colonial empires in Africa, Asia, and the Americas—all of those events belong to that chain of developments by which separate histories were transcended and mankind increasingly found itself involved in one integrated world history.[1] At the beginning of the period which concerns us here, China can be regarded, in significant senses, as an appendage of Inner Asian history; a series of steppe conquerors had imposed their rule on parts of north China from the tenth century onward, and in the thirteenth century, the Mongols created the first great empire briefly linking the far reaches of the Eurasian landmass. By the end of our period, in the seventeenth century, Europeans were bringing New World exotica as well as Old World religions, techniques, and ideas to China, in exchange for the riches of the Orient. By 1644, the year when the Ming dynasty fell to the bandit Li Tzu-ch'eng to be quickly superseded by the Manchu invaders from the north, the Portuguese forerunners, among other invaders from the West, had already held Macao for a century. From still another direction, the Manila Galleon sailed regularly from Acapulco to the Philippines, linking many nations around the globe in a trade which turned crucially on the exchange of New World silver for Chinese luxuries. By 1644 China was part of world history, deeply affected by the movement of silver in the world's trade, by the dissemination of crops and foodstuffs which would transform its agriculture, by weapons and warfare, and by plagues and products which bore on the daily life of the Chinese people. In the consciousness of peoples, whether Chinese, Europeans, or others, the national entities of Eurasia were worlds apart and would remain so until very recent times. Yet in many ways which influenced strongly such things as their food—products, production technology, distribution—the civilizations and national entities of Eurasia were becoming mutually responsive.

Food Supply and Demography

Demographic change is not exclusively a response to food supply and nutrition, yet population growth must demonstrate either the increase of food supplies or the decrease of per capita consumption, and in pre-industrial societies there has been very limited flexibility in the latter. China has been, throughout its history, essentially a self-sustaining food economy; not until the present century has it imported or exported significant amounts of food or of products such as fertilizers, machinery, and fuels that might be relevant to food supply. Basically an agricultural people, the Chinese have enlarged the use of their land, both by extending the area under cultivation and by using that more intensively, and have improved their agriculture, particularly during the last millennium of the imperial era in which our period falls—that is, the period roughly 1250–1650 in the millennium 900–1900.

It has recently been calculated that the population of China (including both Southern Sung China and Chin China) stood at about 150 millions early in the thirteenth century, that it was less than 100 millions by the end of the fourteenth century, and that it was again approaching the 150 million mark at the end of the Ming dynasty in the mid seventeenth century (P. T. Ho 1959, esp. pp. 22, 264; Perkins 1969, pp. 192–209). If those estimates are correct, they show considerable increase during the eleventh and twelfth centuries, before which the population of the Chinese nation probably had never passed 100 millions. Then the population declined by 40 percent or more during the Mongol period and only again reached the thirteenth-century high mark of 150 millions in the mid seventeenth century. Since all these calculations are for essentially the same geographic area, they represent a series of sharp demographic reverses, notably, two gradual upward curves separated by a sharply downward plunge. What is their explanation?

The two upward curves reflect improvements in the production and distribution of food; in particular, they display demographic growth in two areas where the margin in agriculture was higher—the Szechwan basin and the mid- and lower-Yangtze drainages. The downward plunge reflects the warfare and destruction of the Mongol era—both that which extended Mongol rule over the whole Chinese region, in the period 1215–1280, and that which accompanied the breakdown of Mongol authority and the emergence of the Ming dynasty, in the decades 1330–1380. In themselves, those bare population estimates reveal merely a population recovery by the end of the Ming period; they fail to reveal the large changes in society that accompanied this demographic development.

In the food life of the Chinese we can discern two phases of what has been called an agricultural revolution. The widespread consequences of the first phase are evident in the centuries just before 1250 A.D. and account in large measure for the increase in the population to the early thirteenth-century peak of about 150 millions. During this phase of the agricultural revolution, early-ripening rice was introduced from Champa in the beginning of the eleventh century; it was widely adopted throughout China's rice-growing regions and was greatly improved through selective breeding on the part of Chinese farmers.[2] This led to some increase in the double-cropping of the cereals and also encouraged terracing, the drainage of lowlands, and small-scale water controls. More important, no doubt, the possibility of producing a rice crop in the second half of a growing season after the first crop had been destroyed by flood, drought, or insects provided a much-improved defense against famine. Because the introduction of the rice strains accompanied, and encouraged, the shift of China's demographic center to the central regions where rice was grown, the improved agricultural conditions were extended to an ever increasing portion of the Chinese nation. Other new crops, particularly the sorghums (*kaoliang*), also appear for the first time in the annals of Chinese agriculture in the twelfth century. China was at a peak of prosperity and growth in all sectors of life in the Southern Sung state that fell before the Mongol onslaught in the 1260s and 1270s.

The Yüan period introduced devastation in the northern half of the country, depletion of the inhabitants in some regions, dislocation in domestic economic relations, and internal movement of population. The Mongols' conquest of the Chin and then of Sung China required long decades of warfare, and half a century later the decline of the Mongol Yüan dynasty was accompanied by more long decades of civil war. The period was not without some interesting, and perhaps effective, official attention to agricultural rehabilitation.[3] Moreover, the general standard of living in the richer regions of central China did not decline as sharply as in the north. Yet, on the whole, the period was one of stringent hardships for millions of people, and this is reflected in the reduction of the population.

The Ming dynasty brought into power a government genuinely and effectively concerned about rural conditions; moreover, it was able to maintain peace and order for well over two centuries. From the first century of the dynastic period to the middle of the fifteenth century was a period of gradual recovery. There was continued intensification of land use in the richest areas of central China, made possible by continued improvements in agricultural technology and by investment in hydraulic engineering. Lake and marsh areas were drained and planted, continuing the pattern of Southern Sung times. A seawall was built to protect the Chekiang-Kiangsu coast between Hangchow and Shanghai from storm tides that previously had periodically caused inundation of delta lowlands. A counterpart to marsh reclamation was the improvement of canals for both drainage and transport; the latter enhanced the growth of distribution networks for foods and all commercial products.

The last century and a half of the Ming period, from roughly 1500 to 1650, was a period of renewed growth. Moreover, at the very end of that period, new food products from the Americas began to be disseminated in the provinces of China via three important routes: Chinese and other shipping into the ports of the southeast coast; the land routes through Southeast Asia into Yunnan; and the long silk route from Persia and Turkey. The most important of these new crops were maize, sweet potatoes, peanuts, and tobacco. These provided the materials for a second phase of the continuing agricultural revolution. These foods, probably beginning to arrive in the 1550s and 1560s, occasionally are noted in the Late Ming literature. Although new and strange materials, they probably can be said to have been adopted more quickly and more widely in China than in any other part of the world to which they were spread in that time, even though that is not claiming very much. It is especially curious that the other American food product that became important to the world's diet—the white, or Irish, potato—became very important as human food in Europe from the eighteenth century onward, but it is the poorest of these New World foods in nutritional value and is one which held the least attraction for the Chinese. The significance of the late Ming period for the history of food supply is that, no matter what role we assign the new agricultural products (a much debated problem), the continuing improvements in land use and technology created conditions aiding rapid explosion in the Chinese population after 1650.

Staple Foods and the Common Diet

It has been calculated that the Chinese were among the best fed populations of Asia, perhaps of the world, throughout the later imperial centuries. Their daily caloric intake averaged in excess of two thousand calories and probably was increasing throughout the centuries under consideration here and on into the centuries of rapid population growth that followed, at least well into the nineteenth century. This appears to be as good a performance as any traditional economy has achieved, and far better than most (Perkins 1969; see especially chaps. 1, 2, and appendixes F, G). In one view, it testifies to the capacity of Chinese agriculture to keep pace with the demands placed upon it; in another, it created the conditions generating those demands. The achievement is a fact, regardless of what causality we seek. It is also true however that, compared with peasants in many traditional societies, the Chinese peasants were relatively lightly taxed by their government. The organizational capacities of the society and certain features of the civilization—such as the preference for hot foods and the insistence on drinking tea or boiled water—have also contributed to the health, and hence the productivity, of the population. While regional and local famines could afflict China at any time, history records in the Yüan and Ming periods few, if any, great national famines, no national disasters, and no national epidemics such as the Black Death of western European medieval history. The masses of the Chinese people were basically well fed, well clothed, and well housed throughout most of their history. It is essential to our understanding of food and eating in Chinese civilization to realize that most Chinese people ate well enough and had enough of a sense of security about survival to think beyond that primary problem. Thus, food could be used both seriously and playfully—as an adjunct of ritual, as a means to health and long life, or as an arena of aesthetic involvement and sensory delight.

Even though the stratification of Chinese society is clearly evident in the varied uses of food and the extent to which gourmet tastes could be cultivated, the attitudes underlying all the uses of food appear to be congruent throughout all levels of society. Skills in the preparation of varied and excellent foods were not confined to an elite. All of the Chinese people, particularly as we encounter them in the informal literary materials of the Yüan and Ming periods, appear to have been highly attuned to elaborate and intricate uses of food. The best proofs of that assertion are to be found in the great variety of foods regularly available throughout the year, in all parts of China and to all levels of society, and in the elaborate focus on food in ritual and social contexts, and also in the evidence of a preoccupation with variety and quality in food.

Rice—whose cultivation was limited to central and southern China by the availability of water rather than by restrictions of temperature, growing season, or soil conditions—was the standard daily fare of the majority of people in the Yüan and Ming dynasties. The Japanese writer Shinoda Osamu was surprised to find this so, for in Japan rice became a standard daily food of the masses only in the seventeenth century or later. He notes that, in what corresponds to late Ming times, the Japanese elite still consumed wheat or other flours in the form of noodles—rice being too rare or expensive (Shinoda 1955, pp. 75–76). In China, by contrast, not only was rice generally eaten on all levels of society throughout the rice-growing regions, which held the bulk of the population, but even in north China rice was commonly eaten by the elite. About two million kilograms (four million piculs) of rice—surplus taken in taxes from the Yangtze delta—were sent annually to the capital at Peking in Yüan times, and more during the Ming.

Additionally, already by Sung times rice had become a major item in commerce, with national markets and widespread distribution networks (H. S. Ch'üan 1948; Shiba 1968, pp. 142–83). The late Ming writer on natural and technological matters, Sung Ying-hsing, surveyed the production of basic grains in all parts of the country and stated in his work *T'ien-kung k'ai-wu*: "Nowadays seventy percent of the people's staple food is rice, while wheat and various kinds of millet constitute thirty percent" (1966 ed., p. 4, trans. by Sun and Sun; see also pp. 3–33).

The Chinese of Yüan and Ming times, as before and since, consumed cereal grains as the main item of each meal. That means rice, whether boiled or steamed or cooked into gruel, in central and south China. In the north, it means that they ate wheat or other flours made into steamed or baked breads, or into noodles, or ate whole-grain millet cooked into a paste or a gruel. (The very poor at all times, and the general population in times of scarcity, ate coarse grains, chaff, oilseed hulls after the oil had been pressed out, and beans of many varieties.) Is the consumption of grains in such quantities the basis either for a balanced diet or for a tradition of gourmet excellence? Since the historical evidence is that the Chinese were remarkably successful in achieving both, the answer must take the form of explanations and descriptions of how they used those grains and what they added to them in the preparation of daily foods. Luxury foods and gourmet delights will be discussed in another section of this essay.

The best scholarly opinion is that the Chinese in the last six or seven centuries have been producing grain in sufficient quantities to supply each person with about three hundred kilograms (or six piculs) per year, and that they have used very small amounts of that for fodder, alcohol, or purposes other than human food. That is reckoned a high per capita production for a society that did not consume meat fattened on grain. In fact, it was near the maximum amount that people can consume; their consumption of meat was very low, and seems to have remained stable at low levels for many centuries. (All of the above statements draw on Perkins 1969, particularly on appendix F, pp. 297–307.) Because the Chinese also used virtually no dairy products, to maintain nutrition they had to supply protein, calcium, fats, and vitamins in ways quite different from those our society employs. Vegetables, in one way or another, supplied all of those things. The soybean undoubtedly was the most important diet adjunct, being richer in protein than equivalent weights of red meat, richer in digestible calcium than equivalent amounts of milk, and also being an important source of oil and certain vitamins. Excellent cooking oils also were made from sesame, turnip seed, rape seed, and other plant materials (*T'ien-kung k'ai-wu*, trans.

by Sun and Sun 1966, pp. 215–21). The other varieties of beans and peas of which the Chinese regularly produced a great profusion also supplied important nutritional elements. Unlike Westerners, the Chinese regularly demanded a large variety of fresh vegetables for their daily diet. The northern Europeans, before the age of refrigeration, salted down vats of cabbage, stored a few apples and pears and tubers (after the eighteenth century, potatoes also) in root cellars, and kept some extremely hardy plants, such as kale, leeks, and brussels sprouts, growing long after the frosts ended the normal growing season. Then, with their salted and preserved meats, they settled down to winters of dreary eating. The north Chinese long ago perfected methods for growing a great variety of vegetables through the winter, in order to have fresh things regularly. They found varieties that resisted the cold, and they found ways of protecting the intensive truck gardens from frost, by covering them with straw mats that could be rolled back on warm, sunny winter days, by planting over beds of manure, and by other such means. Such fresh produce was not a luxury item, for the tables of the elite only; the poor of China ate better in this respect than did the rich of Europe and, later, of America.

As in the past, meats were consumed more often as flavoring for vegetables and as the basis of a sauce than as the principal component of a dish. But the range of meats used was very great. Pork was the basic meat, and fowl the next most important. Many persons, probably under Buddhist influence, avoided beef, and many found both beef and mutton too malodorous to eat. Of the many varieties of common fish and shellfish, freshwater fish were considered vastly preferable to saltwater fish, for that same reason. Fish were commonly farmed in the ponds, regularly harvested, and sold live in the markets. Fowl, the most common being chicken, duck, and goose, was also normally purchased live, the emphasis on freshness in food products being extremely strong. (Fresh meats and vegetables declined sharply in price if more than one day old.) Range and variety in meats resulted in part from butchering methods; almost all parts of animals were eaten, and the carcass was very carefully butchered in order to present each part at its best. Variety was also achieved by consuming many animals we do not normally think of as food; beyond such relatively ordinary items (in the West) as hares, quails, squabs, and pheasants, a Ming dynasty source also mentions as standard foods: cormorants, owls, storks and cranes, peacocks, swallows, magpies, ravens, swans, dogs, horses, donkeys, mules, tigers, deer of several varieties, wild boars, camels, bears, wild goats, foxes and wolves, several kinds of rodents, and mollusks and shellfish of many kinds (Chia Ming 1968 ed.). One difficulty in enumerating these, as with the even more numerous varieties of fresh vegetables and fruits, is that we lack convenient English names for the great numbers of foods that the Chinese identified and differentiated in ordinary table speech.

Clearly at hand were the means with which to expand upon the basic cereal diet to achieve nutrition and variety. The search for variety displays an attitude toward food that is also expressed in the preoccupation with the art of cooking. Food in ritual, in hygiene, and in its sensual and aesthetic dimensions will be examined in what follows, on the evidence supplied by Yüan and Ming sources. Before proceeding to that, however, it may be useful to consider whether new patterns in the basic diet or in the eating habits of the Chinese may have appeared during the Yüan and Ming dynasties.

The answer is a cautious negative. Although Yüan and Ming sources have been used for specific detail in the foregoing paragraphs, much of the description of the basic diet is not distinctive for the Yüan and Ming periods; it could also apply with accuracy to earlier and later periods. The history of food in the later millennium of Chinese imperial history is one of limited change within stable patterns. That is not to overlook some notable additions to the diet: tea drinking among the Chinese dates no earlier than the Han period, and customs associated with the use of tea have changed considerably as its use increased through time; the use of sugar cane for sugars increased as manufacturing processes were improved in T'ang times (but note H. T. Liu 1957 ed., p. 104), and as commerce distributed the sugar supply more widely in the Sung and later times; sorghums (kaoliang) were introduced as an important new cereal crop in the twelfth century and spread from Szechwan throughout the empire during the Yüan dynasty; the technology for the distillation of alcoholic beverages (in China distilled principally from sorghums) became known only in the twelfth or thirteenth centuries. If these are among the most important additions to the arena of food, there were other less important ones also, and the incremental effect of these through time has been great. Yet, they did not radically alter the long established pattern. The period of alien incursions and rule over parts of North China, commencing in the tenth century and culminating in the Yüan dynasty, which brought Mongol overlords to all parts of China, exposed the Chinese to some exotic foods and eating customs; some Jurchen recipes, for example, from the Chin dynasty, have recently been translated from a standard household encyclopedia, the *Shih-lin kuang-chi*, which was first produced in late Sung times but was republished with the addition of new material during the Yüan and Ming periods (H. Franke 1975). But again, these recipes, appearing in books intended for wide circulation in China, demonstrate attitudes of interest and curiosity about all matters gustatorial more than they reflect transformation of food habits.

The one occasion in imperial Chinese history when a number of new agricultural products, introduced in a short span of time, could have worked a transforming effect on Chinese agriculture—and thereby on the Chinese diet—was in the sixteenth century when the four or five most important New World plants were brought to eastern Asia (as they were being disseminated throughout the globe) from the Spanish colonial empire in the Americas (Perkins 1969, p. 50). Eventually they did work a transformation of the Chinese agricultural economy; P. T. Ho refers to it as the second phase of an agricultural revolution (1959, p. 183 and elsewhere). But the assessment of that is not generally agreed upon by the specialists in the field, and even the description of the process by which those products became agents of change presents many difficulties (See Perkins 1969). Yet, in any event, all of the materials under present purview suggest that Yüan and Ming society, although undoubtedly becoming increasingly conservative in many matters of social and intellectual relevance, was quite open minded and progressive in agriculture and in matters of diet. On those social levels where tastes, rather than necessities, governed choices, a people preoccupied with excellence and variety in food was eager for gustatorial titillation. Simultaneously, on all social levels, economic pressures and inducements encouraged innovation where that could increase production. This combination of factors should have assured rapid and widespread use of the New World crops. However, having merely suggestive fragments of information and lacking fuller evidence, one can only surmise about the early history of their adoption in China.

Food in Ritual and Ceremonial Contexts—The Period of Mongol Rule

In Yüan and Ming times, as throughout history, China's society can be described as highly ritualized; and formalized ceremonial behavior extended from specifically religious activities to many aspects of secular life. Here the words *ritual* and *ceremony* are used in the broadest sense, to include the full range of social behavior for which generally acknowledged formal proprieties existed. To distinguish between the religious and the secular in Chinese life in terms of the uses of those words in Western societies is somewhat misleading, both because Chinese religion was essentially "secular" (that is, "of this world" and "independent of any church"), and because, given the character of Chinese religion implicit in that statement, it would be difficult to prove that some religious element or point of origin did not underlie all the ceremonial proprieties. In any event, the ceremonial uses of food were numerous and pervaded all levels of society. Moreover, the details of ritual and of ceremonial behavior had models in books that were given the authority of antiquity. By the second

century B. C. the three classics of the rites, the *Chou li* or *Chou kuan*, the
I li, and *Li chi*, all existed substantially in the form in which the men of
Yüan and Ming times knew them, and all three were, and are, taken as
records of still earlier traditions (K. C. Chang 1973). Those classical writings
concern the forms, the proprieties, the underlying principles and the physical
accouterments for the full range of ritual acts and ceremonial behavior.
The rites described in them conventionally have been categorized under
five headings: *Chi-li*, or the auspicious rites, meaning sacrifices (of the state
and the imperial shrines, of family ancestral shrines, to local deities
patronized by the state, etc.); *Hsiung-li*, or the rites for inauspicious events
(funerals, national disasters, etc.); *Pin-li*, or the rites for ceremonial visits
(of the state and in high royal and official circles, both public and private);
Chün-li, or the rites for martial occasions (in conjunction with wars, field
exercises, and to standardize relations within the military); and *Chia-li*, or
the rites for festive occasions (especially weddings, but also betrothals,
births, capping ceremonies, feastings and rejoicings, congratulations and
celebrations, etc.). The *Chou li* further subdivides those into 36 subcate-
gories and suggests hundreds of specific situations in which the varieties of
ceremonial behavior apply. It is suggested by some scholars that the ideal
underlying the application of these norms to the whole society was expanded,
virtually invented, in Han times, and that the Confucianized ideal of a
ritualized daily life did not pervade Chinese society until the neo-Confucian
era.

Even should that view be correct, by Yüan times the rites and proprieties
were universally accepted and profoundly influential in society, and their
value was, if anything, enhanced for important segments of the population by
the fact that their alien rulers lacked them. Moreover, the ritual classics were
heavily encrusted with scholarly commentary and tradition long before
Yüan times. During the Yüan and Ming dynasties, there were further
accumulations of such scholarship, yet qualitatively new developments in
the traditions and the practices of ceremonial behavior seem not to have
been significant. If the Yüan was a dynastic era during which the Mongol
rulers of China remained more or less ignorant, even contemptuous, of
Chinese ritualized behavior, the Ming court was first of all concerned with
recovering the old norms and, thereafter, was punctilious in maintaining
them. The many uses of food in ceremonial life of Yüan and Ming China
reveal facets of those truths.

Even as rulers of China for a century or more, the Mongols retained
a deep attachment to their own civilization while adapting superficially
to the Chinese political forms necessary for governing the Chinese state.
It is not surprising then that the Chinese found them to have remained

more or less apart from Chinese ritual except in the area of the sacrifices. Those were of considerable political significance; the great sacrifices of the state in particular were necessary to display legitimacy in possession of the mandate and to embellish their rulership in the eyes of the Chinese and, no doubt, in their own as well. In the prefatory comment to the section Treatise on the Rites, the *Yüan shih* (Yüan History), written within the first years of the Ming dynasty by Chinese literati who had lived under Mongol rule, states:

> The Yüan dynasty's emergence as a state occurred in the far northern desert wastes. In their proprieties for the meetings of their court and for banquets and feastings, [the Mongols] mostly followed their original customs. . . . Only in the year 1271 did the Emperor Shih-tsu [Kublai Khan] get around to having [high Chinese advisors] Liu Ping-chung and Hsü Heng devise ritual forms for the conduct of the court. . . . But in their Great Banquets [*Ta-hsiang*] for imperial clansmen and in feasts tendered their chief officials, they continued to follow mostly the usages of their own people.[4]

Thus the Mongols, whose cuisine has never evoked much admiration from any observers, appear to have been particularly conservative in retaining their steppe eating formalities and, presumably, the steppe food itself, even in the presence of the Chinese alternative. That must be counted a display of grim, outlandish determination, unmatched again in history until, in the nineteenth century, the Western colonial servants, merchants, and missionaries set up their embassies at Peking and their various establishments in the treaty ports. In those enclaves, they too clung to ways as un-Chinese as they could make them (Kates 1967, pp. 76–81).

The Mongols' ritual and dietary conservatism is alluded to in the *Yüan shih* under the heading "Kuo su chiu li" (Old Rites Observing Mongol Custom) (1370, chap. 77). There it is noted that when the Mongols engaged in their traditional sacrifices to their clan ancestors, employing their own shamans as masters of ritual and using the Mongol tongue, they stressed such typical steppe cultural elements as sprinkling the sacrificial ground with mare's milk, making offerings of mare's milk or koumiss, and of meat dried in the steppe fashion, and the sacrificing of horses. Mare's milk, whether fresh or in the form of koumiss (*ma ju*; *ma tung*), figures heavily in the accounts of their ritual sacrifices, ritual oaths, and other religious acts; the alcoholic drink koumiss was the essential beverage of their great feasts (K. F. Yüan 1967). Mare's milk, butterfat made from mare's or cow's milk, and mutton have been looked upon by Chinese and non-Chinese writers as three items differentiating the Mongol cuisine and the Mongol way of life. This is understandable, although the implication that the Mongols introduced them to China is inaccurate.

A building for preparing koumiss and a pen for live sheep are mentioned as parts of the palace complex, near the kitchens, in a late Yüan description of the Peking palaces (T. I. T'ao 1939 ed., chap. 21). Antiquarians know that an alcoholic beverage used for ritual purposes, made from fermented mare's milk, and called *ma tung* (written with a different *tung* character than that commonly used for koumiss in Yüan period sources) was known to the Chinese as early as the Han period (K. F. Yüan 1967). Yet for all intents and purposes, the Mongols made mare's milk and koumiss a new element in the life of China during the Yüan dynasty, and the existence of a special building in the palace complex to house the extensive preparation of the drink must be counted an innovation of the times. However, gardens to supply the imperial table, and pens for the livestock needed by the imperial kitchens have existed as part of the palace in all dynasties. The Mongols surely did use a larger proportion of mutton to other meats than did the Chinese, yet the figures (cited below) for the Ming court's requisitions show that 17,500 sheep per year, or about 48 head per day, were required for the immense Peking palace and court complex. One figure available for pre-Yüan times also indicates large Chinese consumption of mutton, at least on that official level,[5] and all the ritual texts show that oxen, sheep, and swine have been the standard sacrifical animal since antiquity. The use of butterfat (*lo su, su yu*) made from cow's milk (to a lesser extent from the milk of sheep and horses, also that from camels) has been known to the Chinese from much earlier times and has always been a peripheral element of the Chinese diet, standard for making pastries and sweets for luxury consumption, though never widely used among the Han Chinese.[6] With the exception of koumiss, which seemed distinctive and new to the Chinese of the time, the strangeness of Mongol food and drink probably was more a matter of balance among basic items, of the ways of preparing them, and of the manner of eating or of offering them in sacrificial contexts, than of genuinely exotic food products themselves.

Koumiss deserves special comment. That of the best quality, made from "the milk of young mares which have not conceived" and specially manufactured for the imperial table, has been described by thirteenth century travelers from Europe (Rubruck and Polo) as similar in color and quality to good white grape wine.[7] The Mongols' ceremonial drinking at the great banquets offered by the rulers to their court officials and clansmen appears always to have demanded koumiss. The banquets of the highest dignity were familiarly called "koumiss feasts," and more formally *jisun*, or "one-color," banquets, because at those all the guests wore garments of the same color. These usually went on for three or more days, the color being changed with each day. Such banquets started with parades, races, and feats of horsemanship, and normally seem to have ended in a drunken rout. In the eyes of both Chinese and Western observers, the Mongols drank to excess, and several of the Mongol rulers of China died of alcoholism. An early thirteenth-century work describes the effects of drinking at a Mongol feast thus: "[The host,] on seeing his guests in their drunkenness becoming noisy and indecorous, vomiting and lying prostrate, will say happily: 'By their drunkenness my guests show that in their hearts they are one with me!'" (*Meng-ta pei-lu* 1221, quoted in K. F. Yüan 1967, p. 143; my translation).

Beyond the consumption of koumiss which was both their standard drink and the drink of ceremonial significance, the Mongols and the Chinese of the Mongol era also drank grape wine, "honey wine" (mead?), rice wine, and distilled liquor. The latter, new in China about the time of the alien incursions against the Sung in the twelfth or thirteenth century, is referred to in certain Chinese texts of the time as *ha-la-chi* (from the Arabic *'araq*; "arrack") (T. C. Yeh 1959 ed., p. 68). Whether this differed from *shao-chiu*, the standard name at that time for the distilled liquor made in China from sorghum (kaoliang), is not clear. William of Rubruck, who was in China in the middle of the thirteenth century, also names the above alcoholic beverages as the ones used at the Mongol courts he had visited (Rockhill 1900, pp. 12, 83, 112; also Odoric of Pordenone 1913 ed., pp. 199–200; Pelliot 1920, p. 170).

The evidence from Chinese sources strongly suggests that the Mongols in China ate steppe food served in the steppe manner most of the time, not only in their feasts and on the ceremonial occasions described above. Thirteenth and fourteenth century travelers to the various parts of the Mongol world agree in describing meals consisting primarily of mutton cooked by boiling the sheep whole and cut up in the presence of the guests, so that meat with the bone was served to each person (e.g., Ibn Batutta, ca. 1350, quoted in Spuler 1972, p. 194). A fourteenth century Chinese in central China, who had associated with Mongols socially, wrote: "The Northerners [Mongols] at their ordinary meals pay great attention to carving and cutting [their food]. The small daggers which they wear at their waists are made of the finest steel [*pin-t'ieh*, *ting-t'ieh*] and are worth more than gold; they are indeed extremely sharp. Princes and nobles and persons of status all wear them" (T. C. Yeh 1959 ed., p. 68; my translation). Nothing could have been more remote from Chinese cuisine and table custom than the sight of the eaters carving their meat with their own daggers!

To the Chinese scholar T'ao Tsung-i, whose learned notes and sketches date from the last decade of Mongol rule in China, praise was due the last

Mongol ruler of the dynasty for practicing economy in the number of sheep used each day in the emperor's own kitchens: "In this dynasty, in the preparation of food for the imperial table it has been the regular practice to use five sheep each day; since the present emperor ascended the throne that number has been reduced by one each day. Calculated over the span of a year that is a considerable saving" (T. I. T'ao 1939 ed., chap. 2; my translation). The regulation that required the slaughter of five sheep each day for the emperor's table has something of the quality of a ceremonial usage, and the imperial order to reduce that number to four sheep each day in the interests of economy is purely a ceremonial act. The ritual quality of this austerity is heightened by what we know otherwise of the excesses at that Yüan court in its last decades. Yet it indicates that mutton was looked upon as the staple food of the Mongol rulers in their palaces at Peking, just as it was on the steppe, and that view probably is correct. Ch'üan Heng, a contemporary of T'ao's, also reflects the widely held Chinese view that the kitchens of the Mongol palaces were equipped for boiling whole sheep as the standard daily fare. Among the lurid, and factually unreliable, anecdotes is one set forth under the events of the year 1339. In that year high officials of the court informed the then nineteen-year-old last Mongol ruler in China that the empress dowager was not his real mother. She had been murdered by a jealous sister-in-law, who pushed her into a convenient kitchen vat in which whole sheep were being boiled. Whether she was then served at table is not stated (Ch'üan Heng 1963 ed.).

There is a mountain of evidence that the Mongols continued to eat simple and coarse fare, principally boiled mutton, resisting both Persian and Chinese delicacies. However, whether the Chinese also ate mutton in larger quantities because of that nomad influence in their midst is much more difficult to determine. The Yüan dramas frequently mention mutton in meals whose menus are specified, but so do earlier and later writings, particularly the works of Ming fiction. In neither the dramas nor the later works of fiction, however, are Chinese ever seen consuming sheep cooked whole in the Mongol style.[8] *Shuan-yang-jou*, paper-thin slices of mutton cooked quickly by the eater in a boiling pot (called "Genghis Khan firepot" in Japanese restaurants today), and *k'ao-yang-jou*, thin slices of mutton cooked by the eater (or in his presence) on an iron grill over an open fire, are ways of eating mutton that are associated with Moslem restaurants in twentieth century China, especially in Peking and the north. (In northwest China, k'ao-yang-jou refers to pieces of mutton brazed on skewers, or shish kebab.) Although there is a tendency to associate these dishes with the Mongols or with the steppe, references to them are lacking in Yüan and Ming sources. Indeed, they may well attest to the influence of Inner Mongolian cookery, but it may be surmised that they are a later, perhaps nineteenth century, addition to Chinese restaurant fare and not at all evidence of a Mongol influence on Chinese eating habits dating from Yüan times.

The Chinese appear to have been little attracted to Mongol cuisine or to Inner and Western Asian elements present in China during the Mongol period. Still less were they won over to the Mongol banqueting style. Nevertheless, they recognized that the Mongols practiced elaborate hospitality in which ritual feasting played an important part. The Chinese records constitute the principal documentation for Mongol history in China. While these records generally display an open-minded attitude toward the Mongols as fellow human beings (especially those dating from before the mid fifteenth century), they reveal the Chinese as distinctly disdainful of the Mongol primitive way of life, differing, as it did, so sharply from mankind's universal civilization, of which the Chinese were the formulators and the guardians. The Chinese proprieties, systematized in ritual behavior, embodied mankind's one great Way. Although the Chinese recognized some crude analogies to their own formalized etiquette in aspects of Mongol behavior, they could not accept Mongol ritual and ceremonial as more than curiosities from the steppe way of life. The great Mongol ceremonial banquets were displays of barbaric splendor in their eyes. The Chinese writers of the thirteenth and fourteenth centuries recognized in them a highly ordered use of symbol, with religious and political meaning, yet often they were not impelled to investigate that meaning or to preserve full records of the Mongol ways. T'ao Tsung-i, a meticulous learned observer of fourteenth-century Chinese life, also reports on Mongol ways in some detail. Yet he, for example, leaves us a description of Mongol drinking customs, noting that toasts were formally delivered over the wine, surmising that in this the Mongols had retained a Jurchen custom from the Chin dynasty, which they had conquered in the period 1210–34. He quotes several key terms in Chinese transliteration of Mongol words but explains that he "has not had the chance to find out what they mean" (T. I. T'ao 1366, chap. 21, "Ho chan"; my translation). In short, he reports curiosities about the ruling dynasty and the nation of aliens which it represented without in any sense identifying their values and customs. The exotic glitter of Mongol high life is a common feature in the Chinese reports, as it is in Marco Polo. The Chinese recognized that there was a ritualized pattern of procedures at a state feast, yet even the learned Chinese associates of the Mongol rulers appear to have remained apart from and somewhat ignorant of those Mongol rituals (Yanai 1925; K. F. Yüan 1967).

In England, Anglo-Saxon ways were deeply altered during the first century of Norman rule, and in India a century of British rule transformed elite Indian ways. A century of Mongol rule simply did not have comparable impact on Chinese civilization. More specifically, there seem to be no reasons to believe that significant numbers of new foods or new ways of preparing foods for ordinary use, much less for the ritually prescribed ones, resulted from the century-long contact with the Mongols, during the Yüan dynasty. In contrast, there is evidence from subsequent social history that the Mongols living closer to China, along the Great Wall boundary between the two distinct worlds of China and the steppe, tended eventually to be deeply affected by Chinese life-styles, in later Ming and Ch'ing times, especially in matters of food and dress.

Food in Ritual and Ceremonial Contexts—The Ming Dynasty

Upon proclaiming the founding of the Ming dynasty, to commence with the Chinese New Year, January 20, in 1368, the founding emperor, Chu Yüan-chang (r. 1368–98) sought vigorously to restore the ideals and forms of Chinese life which he felt the long period of alien rule had undermined. The Ming Founder was a ruffian from the lowest stratum of Chinese peasant society, reared in an impoverished and brutalized region. A man who acquired literacy only as an adult and who never acquired polish, let alone erudition concerning China's Great Tradition, his manner of governing displays many influences from the Mongol era incongruous with that venerated past. Yet he was punctilious about restoring the purity of Chinese ritual norms. Such are the anomalies of early Ming social history.

The strong-minded emperor set commissions of scholars to work drawing up compendiums of ceremonial usage for his new government. More than a dozen works on aspects of ritual were produced during the thirty years of his reign (*Ming shih*, chap. 47, prefatory comments to the Treatise on the Rites; Li Chin-hua 1932). In many of the ritual regulations established at the Ming court during the last quarter of the fourteenth century, one can perceive some details of the close relationship that existed between the imperial table, the offerings regularly prescribed for ancestral and state shrines, and the ceremonial state banqueting that was resumed on traditional Chinese models. Some of the Ming sources are worth noting, for although they reveal little that was historically new, they occasionally provide details that are not available for earlier periods. An overview of Ming ritual regulations is given in chapters 43 through 117 of the official *Ta Ming hui-tien* (Collected Statutes of the Ming Dynasty). A convenient summary is found in the Treatise on the Rites, comprising chapters 47 through 60 of the *Ming shih* (1736). There, as in many of the dynastic histories, the arrangement follows the five-fold categorization of the rites described above. The regulations for procuring and preparing and serving food in the imperial household and at court are included under these ritual statutes.

The Ming Court was housed in a city within the capital city, first at Nanking, and after 1420 at Peking. It came to have tens of thousands of residents, all members of the imperial household or staff serving that household. Its kitchens operated a vast culinary enterprise. Foods for all imperial purposes and needs—including the emperor's daily fare and that of his vast household and court, as well as his ritual sacrifices and his great banquets of state—were procured, prepared, and served by three groups of palace workers. The first group were the *ch'u-i*, or "kitchen servants." The second group were those eunuchs specially detailed to the management of foods and wines and the procurement of materials. The third group were "palace women" (*kung-nü*) to whom were assigned specific duties in connection with food. The relationship between these three groups is not entirely clear, but one trend is apparent: the eunuchs appear to have encroached upon, and somewhat superseded, the roles of the other two groups, particularly the kung-nü, by mid and late Ming times, without entirely eliminating them in the functions relevant to our concerns here.

The Treatise on the Rites gives the impression that the ch'u-i were the principal group, designated to manage all food matters. These were common subjects of the empire, recruited in all parts of the country for their qualifications as culinary experts and for their sound physical health. They were to have no physical deformities, no record of serious illnesses, and no criminal record, and in theory they were assigned to hereditary service. In early Ming times, under the influence of Yüan period models introduced from steppe society, a number of hereditary occupation groups were established in Chinese society, including the military and most artisan households. Hereditary status did not fit the realities of Chinese society, and such status was widely abandoned in fact, though not always in name, by the mid fifteenth century. The regulations governing kitchen servants provide elaborately for failure of the posts to be filled on a hereditary basis and specify relatively mild punishments for flight from the service. Therefore, we can assume that the kitchen servant quotas were filled largely by recruitment and that persons recruited for their special skills in fact filled such posts. The *Ta Ming hui-tien* states: "Those kitchen servants [ch'u-i] who are under the administration of the Court of Imperial Entertainments [*Kuang-lu Ssu*] provide the foods and delicacies for the imperial table; those under the Court of Imperial Sacrifices [*T'ai-ch'ang Ssu*] prepare the sacrificial offerings. Their numbers have been increased through successive reigns, and quotas have become quite excessive. Here we have thoroughly examined the matter and record the properly stipulated quotas" (chap.

116; my translation). Figures for the beginning of the dynasty are not given. An edict of 1435 provided for 5,000 kitchen servants to be employed under the Court of Imperial Entertainments, to supply the imperial table and prepare the emperor's state banquets. That number reached 7,874 at some point in the sixteenth century, but later regulations limited the number to the range from 3,000 to something over 5,000. Kitchen servants assigned to the Court of Imperial Sacrifice were fewer but, if anything, were selected even more carefully. The Ministry of Rites, under which both of the Courts here involved were administered, was required to investigate the cause of death of parents and to issue approval before new kitchen staff members could be hired to work in the Court of Imperial Sacrifice. In particular, it was required to assure that no person who had committed a crime would enter the shrines where sacrificial foods were offered. The statutes provided for 400 at the beginning of the dynasty and increased that number to 600 in the early fifteenth century, after two capitals had been established and two sets of shrines were in existence. From the mid sixteenth century onward, the regulations allowed more than 1,000, the largest number being 1,750 provided for by a revision of the statutes issued in 1583. One set of regulations governed most of the management of both sets of kitchen staff, and their duties clearly were conceived of as being analogous, whether they were cooking for the living or the dead.

The growth of the palace eunuch staff is an important feature of early Ming government, and one wrapped in legend that obscures the facts (Huang Chang-chien, 1961). The *Huang Ming tsu-hsün-lu* (Ancestral Admonitions), issued first in 1381 during the reign of the Ming founder, stipulated that separate bureaus within the palace eunuch staff be designated for maintaining the several palace and state shrines, and that other bureaus be designated to manage the various aspects of attendance upon the emperor and his household. Those bureaus included the following, which bore upon the problems of food and drink: the palace pharmacy; the imperial wine bureau (to oversee the production of wines and of soybean meal, bean curd, etc.); the imperial flour mill (to supervise the milling of flour for the palace and to prepare gluten); the imperial vinegar works; the bureau of herds and flocks (specifying the care of sheep, geese, chickens, and ducks); the bureau of vegetable gardening. The structure of eunuch services was under continuous revision throughout the Founder's reign. By 1384 a *Shang-shan Chien* ("Directorate of Imperial Foodstuffs") had been created as one of twelve Directorates within the eunuch staff (Hucker 1958, pp. 24–25). The duties of this Directorate as specified in a revision of 1396 were: "To provide the offerings of food for the Temple for Offerings to the Imperial Forebears [Feng Hsien Tien, within the palace precincts] as well as the food for the imperial table and all foodstuffs used within the palaces, and to supervise the Court of Imperial Entertainments in all matters pertaining to the provision of food and drink for all imperial banquets held within the palaces" (quoted in Huang Chang-chien 1961, p. 85; my translation). The eunuch staff grew steadily from the fifteenth century onward; Hucker quotes one estimate that eunuchs serving in the twelve Directorates, four Offices, and eight Bureaus numbered seventy thousand at the end of the dynasty, the majority of whom were employed at the capital (Hucker 1961, p. 11). Probably no more than a small fraction of that number was concerned with food. The Directorate of Imperial Foodstuffs continued to exist throughout the dynasty, aided by other eunuch offices and bureaus responsible for manufacturing special products, supervising agricultural and horticultural production, and procuring goods from without. Although it is not entirely clear, eunuchs probably supervised the preparation of foods by the ch'u-i away from the inner palace quarters, brought them into the inner precincts of the palace, and served them to the imperial family.

Finally, there was the third staff of palace workers, the palace women. The Founder apparently intended that palace women should provide most of the services in attendance upon the ruler, including preparing and managing his food and clothing. One of the six bureaus of women officials in the palace established in 1372 was that responsible for the emperor's food (C. T. Sun 1881 ed., p. 178). Hucker believes that eunuchs had superseded women in these duties by the early fifteenth century; however, he also quotes a Ch'ing source in the estimate that there were nine thousand women in the palace at the end of the dynasty (Hucker 1961, p. 11). The inner palace in Ming times was a large city populated entirely by women and eunuchs, except for the emperor and his minor children. The various roles of the women in relation to those of the eunuchs are not well understood. In any event, between the kitchen servants on the outside but attached directly to the palace, and the women and eunuchs within the inner palaces, there were thousands of hands available to work on foods, for all the purposes foods served in that world.

The procurement of all things needed in the palaces of the Forbidden City was in the hands of eunuchs; in the name of the emperor, they controlled foreign trade, the management of imperial estates, the management of imperial factories, the warehouses and stories, the gardens and herd grounds, and the purchase of materials in the markets. To cite one example, in 1393 it was stipulated that the Court of Imperial Entertainments should requisition from the Ministry of Works, through the Ministry of Rites, an annual order of 10,000 pieces of porcelain for palace use; later the number was increased to 12,000 pieces per year, but this was still found insufficient to meet the needs of the Forbidden City (*Ta Ming hui-tien*, chap. 116). In its section on procurement in the Treatise on Food and Money, the *Ming shih* states that the imperial household had a stock of more than 307,000 pieces of porcelain, manufactured under the supervision of the Southern (i.e., Nanking) Ministry of Works, at the imperial porcelain kilns in Kiangsi and elsewhere. The same source notes that in 1468 the Court of Imperial Entertainments required more than 1,268,000 catties of fruits and nuts, a 25 percent increase over the amounts originally stipulated (*Ming shih*, chap. 82; Wada 1957, pp. 925–62; K. C. Chu 1959 ed., p. 42). These random items indicate the scope of the culinary operation of the Ming imperial household.

The procurement of animals, fish, fowls, ice, cooking pots, dishes, vegetables and fruits, grains and condiments, oil, wines—in short, all the elements of an elaborate cuisine—was done more or less uniformly, whether the ultimate use was to be food for the living or a sacrificial offering to the dead. The principal difference was that sacrificial animals were required to be free of blemish and must be of one color, unmarked by spots or patches. For many of these animals, quotas to be sent to the Forbidden City were levied on the administrative subdivisions of the empire; others came from imperial estates. Those levied under local quotas were delivered in kind until 1468, when the more distant provinces were allowed to remit in silver, to pay for equivalent items purchased by the imperial household from places closer to the point of delivery. The *Ta Ming hui-tien* states that approximately one hundred thousand live animals and fowls were obtained each year under the levies.[9] The figures given there include the following: 160 sacrificial swine; 250 sacrificial sheep; 40 young bullocks of one color; 18,900 fat swine; 17,500 fat sheep; 32,040 geese; 37,900 chickens. The sacrificial animals are a small proportion of the total, but they were selected according to rigorous standards and were meticulously cared for on the palace grounds, in preparation for being sacrificed on the appropriate occasions. Normally that meant ritual slaughter by a civil official (or in his presence, by a military aide), followed by cooking the animal whole in a bronze or iron cauldron according to ancient regulations (C. T. Sun 1968 ed., p. 63). The other animals and fowls had to meet high standards of quality, but without the same attention to appearance; they were used both for the dining table and for making the many prepared foods that were offered at shrines.

To deliver the delicacies of the Yangtze region and further south to the palace in Peking, the Grand Canal fleet of barges was used. A late Ming writer gives an interesting sidelight on the procurement system managed by the eunuch staff of the imperial household. Although the Directorate of Ceremonials (*Ssu-li Chien*), the chief division within the eunuch bureaucracy, commanded the highest priority on canal facilities, the Directorate of Foodstuffs had the next highest priority for its shipping. The account states, in part:

> The second category was for the Grand Commandant[10] and the Directorate of Foodstuffs, to transport: fresh plums, loquats, the fruit of the strawberry tree [*yang-mei*; *Arbutus myrica rubra*], fresh bamboo shoots, and shad [under refrigeration]. The third category, assigned to the Grand Commandant, was for things not requiring ice, namely: *kan-lan* [*Burseracea carnarium album*], new tea, cassia [flowers for seasoning], pomegranates, persimmons, and tangerines. The fourth category was for the Directorate of Foodstuffs, [also] for items not requiring ice, namely: swans, pickled vegetables, bamboo shoots, cherries preserved in honey [*mi-ying*], Su *kao* ["Su-chou cakes"?], cormorants. The fifth category was assigned to the Bureau of Gardens [of the eunuch bureaucracy] and was for: water chesnuts, taro, ginger, lotus root, and fruits. The sixth category was for supplies sent to the palace warehouses, such as fragrant rice and ginger roots. Other categories of procurement of the imperial palace all had lower priorities for shipping facilities than the foodstuffs listed above. [Ku Ch'i-yuan, 1618, 6:12b–13a; my translation]

References to refrigerated storage are of course found throughout the imperial era and are not limited to imperial usage. Here we see that refrigerated shipping also appears to have been taken for granted in Ming times; even though the account speaks only of procurement for the imperial palace, we can be sure that others also benefited from the ability to ship perishables under refrigeration. In pre-imperial times, the prerogative of storing ice to keep sacrificial objects fresh was in theory limited to the feudal nobility. In late imperial times, the supplying of ice—by cutting blocks of ice from frozen rivers and ponds during the winter, packing it in clean straw, and storing it in caves or trenches—was itself an activity supervised by eunuchs, in conjunction with the Embroidered Uniform Guard, for the Court of Imperial Sacrifices of the Ministry of Rites (*Ta Ming hui-tien*, chap. 116; see also K. C. Chu 1959 ed., p. 325, and T. Liu 1957 ed., p. 29). Here again we see the continued overlapping of the ritual and the secular aspects of food, in this instance in the ritual and the practical uses of ice.

We are fortunate that some important items of information going beyond official materials and concerning the foods prepared in the imperial kitchens still exist. One such item, which reveals important aspects of food in early Ming life and which has been somewhat fortuitously preserved in several versions, merits translation and some discussion here. On assuming imperial dignity, the Ming Founder conformed to tradition in building a *t'ai miao*, or shrine to the imperial ancestors, in which were placed the spirit tablets of his paternal ancestors for four generations. Offerings of prepared foods and fresh produce appropriate to the season were made there on the first of each lunar month (*Ming shih*, chap. 51). That was the authentic traditional convention, as determined by a gathering of Confucian scholars expert in the history of the rites. In the third year of his reign, however, the Ming Founder decided that the conventional sacrifices to his ancestors, maintained by officials of the state at a shrine outside the palace precincts, were "inadequate to reveal filial consciousness." Therefore, he ordered that a second temple to his ancestors be built inside the palace precincts, calling it the Feng Hsien Tien, or Temple for Offerings to the Imperial Forebears. He said that "the T'ai Miao symbolized the Outer Court; the Feng Hsien Tien symbolized the Inner Court" (*Ming T'ai-tsu shih lu*, 59:1151–52).[11] At the inner temple, the emperor or males of his line performed ritual observances morning and evening, while the empress led the imperial consorts in making daily offerings of prepared foods (*Ming shih* chap. 52). On special festivals, anniversaries, and the first of each moon, fresh products of the season were offered. The *Ta Ming hui-tien* (chaps. 86, 89) records lists of the conventionally prescribed sacrificial offerings at both the T'ai Miao and the Feng Hsien Tien. Those adhere to the prescriptions found in the ritual classics and their commentaries. Fortunately, a late Ming scholar writing in the 1590s has preserved a more detailed list of the prepared foods which the empress and the imperial consorts offered in person each day during the reign of the Founder in Nanking in the 1370s. Because these offerings were expected to convey the spirit of the offerings made to ancestors in ordinary family life, we can assume that they reveal the tastes and food ideals of the former poor peasant family which now found itself the imperial family, and that the foods offered were also those actually eaten in the imperial household:

The regular offerings are changed each day. On the first day [of each moon], rolled fried cakes; on the second day, finely granulated sugar; on the third day, tea from Pa [eastern Szechwan]; on the fourth day, sugared butter cookies; on the fifth day, twice-cooked fish; on the sixth day, steamed rolls with steamed mutton; on the seventh day, clover honey biscuits; on the eighth day, sugared steamed biscuits; on the ninth day, pork fryings; on the tenth day, sugared jujube cakes;

on the eleventh day, open-oven baked breads [*shao-ping*]; on the twelfth day, sugar-filled steamed breads; on the thirteenth day, mutton-filled steamed breads; on the fourteenth day, rice-flour cakes; on the fifteenth day, fat-filled pastries; on the sixteenth day, honey cakes; on the seventeenth day, puff-paste baked breads; on the eighteenth day, "elephant eye" [i.c., rhomboid shaped] cakes; on the nineteenth day, flaky filled pastries; on the twentieth day, marrow cakes; on the twenty-first day, rolled cookies; on the twenty-second day, crisp honey biscuits; on the twenty-third day, scalded-dough baked breads; on the twenty-fourth day, sesame-oil noodles; on the twenty-fifth day, Chinese pepper-and-salt breads; on the twenty-sixth day, water-reed shoots [*chiao-pai*; *Zizania latifolia*]; on the twenty-seventh day, sesame-sugar-filled baked breads; on the twenty-eighth day, smartweed flowers; on the twenty-ninth day, sour cream [*lo*]; on the thirtieth day, thousand-layer baked breads. If the month has twenty-nine days, the offering for the thirtieth is offered on the first, along with the offering for that day.

The fresh offerings of the season (*chien hsin*) are changed each moon. In the First Moon they are: fragrant leeks [*Allium odorum*], fresh greens, shepherd's purse [*Bursa bursa-pastorum*], clams, perch, chicken and duck eggs. In the Second Moon they are: new tea, rapeseed greens, celery, southernwood leaves, goslings. In the Third Moon they are: new bamboo shoots, amaranth greens [*hsien ts'ai*; *Amaranthus mangostanus*], cabbage, carp, chicken and duck eggs. In the Fourth Moon they are: turnips, cherries, loquats, plums, apricots, cucumbers, piglets, pheasants. In the Fifth Moon they are: pumpkins, gourds, wild lettuce [*k'u-mai ts'ai*; *Lactuca denticulata*], eggplant, haw apples, peaches and plums, pullets, wheat grains, barley grains, wheat noodles, shad. In the Sixth Moon they are: fresh lotus seedpods, watermelons, muskmelons, winter melons, dried shad, shredded shad cured with red wine dregs, herring. In the Seventh Moon they are: snow-white pears, fresh horned nuts [*Trapa bicornis*], water-lily seeds [*ch'ien-shih*; *Euryale ferox*], fresh jujubes, grapes. In the Eighth Moon they are: small-panicled millet [*Setaria*], large-panicled millet [*Panicum miliaceum*], rice, lotus root, taro, water reeds, new ginger shoots, mandarin perch, crabs. In the Ninth Moon they are: chestnuts, oranges, bream, small red beans. In the Tenth Moon they are: yams [*shan-yao*; *Dioscorea sativa*], chrysanthemums, tangerines, hares. In the Eleventh Moon they are: buckwheat noodles, sugarcane, venison, roebuck venison, wild geese, swans, cormorants, storks, quails, partridge, sunfish. In the Twelfth Moon they are: spinach, mustard greens,

silver pomfret, bream. [Yao Shih-lin, 1937 ed., 2:3a–4b; my trans-
lation][12]

Instructions appended to the lists give details of placement on the shrine's
altars in relation to the wine beakers, the rice and tea, and other items
offered. They advise certain changes in the supporting food items—for
example, glutinous rice dumplings (*tsung tzu*), steamed wheat-flour rolls
(*man-t'ou*) and other special cereals, breads, noodles, and cakes should be
substituted for rice on certain anniversaries and festivals. The writer
comments that the emperor, who practiced austerity at his own table,
offered the profusion of sacrificial foods to his ancestors in the spirit of the
legendary ruler of antiquity the Great Yü, and refers to Confucius's
comment on Yü in the *Analects*: "I can find no flaw in the character of Yü.
He used himself coarse food and drink, but displayed the utmost filial
piety toward the spirits" (*Lun yü*, 8:21; trans. Legge 1893, p. 215). The
Ming Founder's insistence on a special shrine inside the palace, at which
he and other members of the imperial family could make daily offerings
in person, appears to have been an eccentricity from which various advisors
failed to dissuade him; the later historian has no choice but to explain
it as an exceptional virtue.

Quite similarly, offerings of ordinary daily foods were made in the households of officials and commoners, in front of the spirit tablets of the ancestors,
usually on the first and the fifteenth of the lunar month as well as on special
festivals and on anniversary occasions. Food so offered was not wasted;
after being placed before the spirit tablets of the deceased family members
for an appropriate time, it was taken away and used by the living family
(figs. 28–29).

Feasting the living at the Ming palaces, according to the rites for ceremonial visits or the rites for festive occasions, was also intricate in ritual
arrangements and meaning, the more so because it was conducted on the
highest official level. Institutionally, the feasts for the spirits of the dead and
the great banquets for the living were both the responsibility of the Ministry
of Rites. Philologically, two characters with the transliteration *hsiang*, both
of which mean "to accept offerings" and "to make offering," were used
interchangeably in Ming writings, although philologists traditionally have
noted that the one refers to "the way of the spirits" and the other to "the
ways of men." The underlying parallels between sacrifice and hospitality
should not be overlooked, yet neither should they be overinterpreted.
Banqueting belonged to the world of men, the world of government. The
great banquets of state affirmed the legitimacy of the imperial mandate and
of the hierarchical order in society.

The early Ming regulations for official court banqueting, not surprisingly, are intricately complex. To begin with, they distinguish imperial banquets on four levels: the Great Banquet, the Medial Banquet, the Normal Banquet, and the Minor Banquet. All included music to which choruses intoned ritual texts extolling the imperial ancestors, proclaiming the cosmic legitimacy of the dynasty's mandate, and making many references to the ideological foundations of dynastic power. They also powerfully reaffirmed the correctness and the value of human civilization which we, less magnanimously, call Chinese civilization. At the feasts for envoys from the states beyond the empire, precedence was given to those states which had achieved the closest and most honored status in the history of their relationship to China. At all feasts, the individual achievement of the Chinese participants was also recognized; they filed in and out according to the rank they held on merit, as at the convening of the court, and sat at tables whose proximity to the imperial dais reflected the occupants' official seniority or honorific noble rank. The proper order of human society, as well as the cosmic relationships, were symbolized in all the regulations and alluded to in all the words spoken at these occasions.

Thus it must have held great meaning for the scholar-officialdom of China when on the fourth day of the New Year (or January 23, 1368), only the third day after proclaiming the new dynasty, the Ming Founder gathered all the officials of his new government at the great palace Hall of Heaven's Trust (Feng-t'ien Tien) to tender them a *Ta-yen-hsiang*, or Great Banquet (*Ming T'ai-tsu shih-lu*, 29:486). The Yüan dynasty's alien emperors had not done that according to traditional Chinese ritual proprieties, so a century had elapsed since so auspicious an event had last been held. The regulations for the ordering of actions and the arrangement of the banquet had been newly compiled by a team of experts. New texts for the ritual music had been written, to be sung by choruses from the Office of Music (*Chiao-fang Ssu*), which also supplied the orchestra of thirty musicians and the teams of dancers. Banners had been hung, guard units in somber uniforms were posted at the gates, a throne with its dining table was on the dais, which in turn was surrounded by service pavilions from which the wine and food were distributed. Dancers were ranked below the dais, and orchestras were both within and outside the great hall. All officials of fourth rank or above were accommodated within the hall on this occasion (later revisions in the regulations allowed officials of third rank and above to enter the main hall); the rest sat at tables on the terraces just outside. The guests filed in and stood in ranks, music played, the emperor entered, and as a master of ceremonies presided, the guests took their seats. According to an intricate scenario, music started, music stopped, people stood, people sat, verses were sung, flowers were scattered, dancers performed, food was served, and the guests kowtowed each of the nine times the emperor proffered wine to them. Finally the feasting ended, the emperor departed, the officials all stood facing north toward his throne, bowed, kowtowed, formed ranks, and filed out.

Such formal banqueting, whether at the court or in private homes, usually commenced at midday. At least on that first imperial banquet of the Ming era in 1368, after the feast the emperor called the court into session to deliver a lecture on the meaning of the dynastic founding and to charge the officials with their new responsibilities. Thus the banquet must have ended well before evening. Feasting in the evening hours by candlelight and lamplight is also known, both at court and in private homes, but evening feasting assumed a mood of festive informality for which there were no ritual prescriptions.

Unfortunately, the food actually to be served at this or other great state banquets is not prescribed in detail and is not so described in any memoir known to this writer. Feasts of the Great Banquet category were only given four to six times a year, once always at the New Year festival, when foreign emissaries were at the court and were therefore specially included. Feasts of the lesser three ranks differed principally in the number of times the emperor proffered wine, whether that be seven times or five or three instead of the nine times required at the Great Banquets. The ritual regulations governing the feasts were revised slightly throughout the dynasty (*Ta Ming hui-tien*, chap. 72). The texts sung to *yu-shih-yueh* ("music to encourage eating") (found in chap. 73, and in *Ming shih*, chap. 63) accumulated throughout the dynasty as special events demanded new songs. In the use of music to accompany banqueting (or to accompany the emperor's daily private meals), the parallels with ritual sacrifices may again be seen.

On all such ceremonial occasions, when the emperor was feasting the court, the empress with the imperial consorts of all ranks, the dowagers, the wives of imperial sons, and the imperial daughters were hostesses of a feast in the Palace of Female Tranquility (K'un-ning Kung) in the Inner Quarters, at which the wives of chief ministers and high officials were the guests. They too had music, but from female musicians, and the other formal arrangements paralleled those for the emperor's banquets. However, the empress at her feasts proffered wine only seven times, and the food was served in five courses (*Ming shih*, chap. 53). The separation of men and women at formal banquets of state, as in the formalities of offering foods to the spirits at shrines, was a model for the most formal private banqueting in elite homes. However, just as the Ming Founder ate his private meals at the table with his empress and family members, in most elite homes and, we must assume all homes of commoners, unless formally invited guests were present, men and women usually ate together.[13] This norm, and the pattern of the exceptions to it, become obvious from analysis of the inadvertant references to meal situations in Yüan drama and Ming fiction and other informal writings.

Formal feasting also went on at provincial and local levels of government; Ming works on rituals and institutions provide regulations for some of the standard banqueting on those levels. Celebrations to congratulate winners in the annual and triennial civil service examinations, at the various levels of government, were one standard occasion for such feasts; another, for which rather elaborate regulations are provided, is the rural wine-drinking ceremony, at which local officials feasted village elders and impressed upon the community their obligation to maintain order and morality (*Ta Ming hui-tien*, chap. 79). It is much more difficult to construct a picture of the official feasting on lower levels of government, and still more difficult to learn about actual meals served, their quantity and quality, and the proportion of local government expenditures which they absorbed.[14]

For evidence about ceremonial banqueting in private life in Ming times, we must turn to the Ming period fiction and informal literature. The most food-conscious work of Ming fiction is the famous novel of sensuality, the *Chin-p'ing-mei*, known in Egerton's translation as *The Golden Lotus*. In the following section it is drawn upon for descriptions of food in various contexts, since the daily enjoyment of food and drink is among the sensual pleasures to which the book is so wholeheartedly devoted. Here, we are provided with some descriptions of private households' uses of foods and of banqueting in ritual contexts. In their ritual offerings of foods and in their ceremonial feasting, the elite of Yüan and Ming times (and to some extent also the commoners of sufficient means) took seriously the Confucian norms and forms specified for the "auspicious rites" and for the "rites for festive occasions." Yet the ceremonial uses of food and the ceremonial situations centering on eating extended throughout the entire society in ways not possible to reconstruct from ritual regulations, and into far more contexts than those which have been regularized in the Confucian writings.

The protagonist of this novel is Hsi-men Ch'ing, a middling-rich merchant in a small Shantung *hsien* city (county-seat) at the end of the sixteenth century.[15] In Confucian terms, he is a corrupt member of society; also, he does not display seriousness about the values of Taoism or Buddhism. Yet he participates in the ritual activities formally associated with all three. Food in the ritual life of the ordinary people, in this case focusing on a household rather wealthier than ordinary, but with many scenes of commoner life, is illustrated throughout the long novel. In chapter thirty-nine,

"The Temple of the Jade King," there is an excellent description of Taoist prayer ceremonies, which would have been incomplete, indeed, which could not have taken place, had there not been an elaborate exchange of foods and gifts, and which culminated in a lavish feast and a night of drinking, held on the temple premises. The chapter should be read as an integral unit and in Chinese, since the Egerton translation, although fuller and more accurate than the others, is based on the shorter, Ch'ung-chen era (1628–44) edition instead of on the fuller text published in the Wan-li period (1573–1619). Specific details of food are among the elements that have been eliminated in that later version. Here some passages specifying foods are singled out, paraphrased from the Wan-li text or, when indicated, taken from the Egerton translation.

It is the Twelfth Moon for the year, and Hsi-men Ch'ing is busy sending and receiving gifts for the New Year season that is at hand. Most of these are gifts of food and drink. The servant announces that a young novice from the Temple of the Jade King has brought a gift from its abbot, consisting of four boxes—one containing pork, one containing ice-fish (*Salanx cuvieri*, a great delicacy of the season in north China), and two boxes of steamed shortbreads with various fruit and vegetable fillings. Sent with these were some Taoist charms and ritual texts. This is an unexpectedly lavish gift, considering Hsi-men Ch'ing's slight relationship with the temple and its chief priest. As he remarks on this, his wife reminds him that he had made an offhand vow to contribute a sacrifice should he have a son. The child is now some months old, and he is urged to fulfil his vow. He also decides to ask the priest to "enroll the son's name" at the temple, in that act bestowing a religious name on the infant. He discusses this with the young novice, sets the date of the ninth day of the First Moon for the ceremony, drinks tea, and sends "fifteen taels of silver for the expenses of the sacrifice, and one tael in return for the Abbot's gift." On the eighth day of the First Moon, Hsi-men's servant "was sent to the Temple with a measure of fine rice, a supply of paper money, and ten catties of official candles. He also took with him five catties of incense, and sixteen rolls of unbleached material for other things needed by the priests. In addition, Hsi-men Ch'ing sent two rolls of brocade, two jars of Southern wine, four live geese, four live chickens, a set of pig's trotters, a leg of mutton and ten taels of silver. All this was for the enrollment of the baby's name" (trans. Egerton 1939, pp. 168–69).

According to the Wan-li text of the novel, Hsi-men Ch'ing had never previously visited the Taoist temple, even though it is only five *li*, or less than two miles, from his residence within the walls of Ch'ing-ho Hsien city. The sacrifice of prayers and enrollment of his son's name becomes an appropriate occasion for offerings of food to the temple, and for a grand banquet in the main hall of the temple for the men of his household, and for four intimate friends and males of their households.

On the day of the ceremony, after having abstained from meat and wine on the previous day, Hsi-men Ch'ing rides to the temple early in the morning. He is received there by the abbot and priests, exchanges compliments and drinks tea:

> Hsi-men Ch'ing went up to the shrine. Before the table of incense stood a boy, with a ewer, in which Hsi-men Ch'ing washed his hands. Then an acolyte knelt down and invited him to burn incense. Hsi-men Ch'ing prostrated himself before the alter. Abbot Wu was wearing a hat of the Nine Yang Thunder, with rings of jade and a sky-blue vestment, broad-sleeved and embroidered with the crane and the twenty-eight stars. A silken girdle was about his waist. He came down from the lectern and made a priestly reverence to Hsi-men Ch'ing.
>
> "Unworthy priest that I am," he said, "your misdirected kindness has often made me its object, and I have frequently received precious gifts from you. Consequently I feel that if I refuse them, I shall not be truly sincere; and if I do accept them, I must be ashamed. It is my duty to pray that your son may have length of days. Why should you send me such valuable presents? I am truly embarrassed. Besides, your gifts for the purposes of the sacrifice have been far too generous."
>
> "But it is I who feel grateful for the trouble you have taken," Hsi-men Ch'ing said. "I have done nothing to repay you. These things are a very slight token of my appreciation, and nothing more."
>
> After these polite exchanges, the priests who stood on either hand came to greet Hsi-men Ch'ing, and he was invited to go to the Abbot's cell. This was a large hall, three rooms wide, called the Hall of Pine Trees and of Cranes. There tea was served.

Fairly lengthy ceremonies ensue, including the reading of long prayers, with responses, incense lighting, prostrations, and the beating of drums. The guests invited for the feast begin to arrive, each bringing gifts of food to be eaten with tea, or money "in lieu of tea." A vegetarian meal follows, as a kind of prelude to the feast proper. The menu is not reported in detail, but we are informed that, in addition to a great variety of vegetarian dishes, there are forty plates and bowls containing the principal courses. A large jar of Chin-hua wine is opened. At one point, women of Hsi-men Ch'ing's household send an unexpected gift, delivered by two servant boys:

> The two boys came, carrying boxes which they presented on their knees. When the boxes were opened, it was seen that they contained

all kinds of delightful cakes, and tea with rose-petals. Hsi-men Ch'ing asked Abbot Wu to accept them. Hsi-men Ch'ing said that the two boys must have food, and the Abbot sent them to a room aside. Even the porters who had come with them were given a meal.

In the afternoon there were further devotions. The Abbot had prepared a large table of food, a jar of Chin-hua wine [and elaborate gifts of clothing for the baby, including priest's gowns, caps, and shoes]. ... The parcels were tied with yellow string and set upon a square tray. Plates of fruit were on the table.

Later some other men of the Hsi-men household return home and report that Hsi-men Ch'ing and his principal guests are still at the temple and probably will not return that night, because the priests are keeping them to drink and feast into the night. Hsi-men's son-in-law reports to his wife:

> "Father saw that the service would not be finished for some time," Ching-chi said, "and as he knew there was no man in the house, he told me to come back, and Tai An to stay and wait upon him. The Abbot would not let me go. He pulled me and dragged me about, and gave me two or three great cups of wine. Then, at last, I got away." [Trans. Egerton 1939, p. 178]

This scene of ritual turned into sensual excess and indecorous behavior is starkly contrasted with the scene among the women at Hsi-men Ch'ing's home on the same evening. There his principal wife and some of his concubines are ceremoniously entertaining a group of Buddhist nuns, who tell them pious fables and eat with them a meal designed with elegant restraint, strictly observing dietary prohibitions while nonetheless enjoying delicacies fashioned to resemble the forbidden meat dishes. One of the pious old women cannot see well and has to be convinced that the foods can be eaten:

> When she finished these stories, Nun Wang chanted a psalm. Then the Moon Lady said: "Teachers, you must be hungry, we had better have something to eat." She bade Tiny Jade bring four plates of vegetarian food and another four plates of pies and cakes, and asked Aunt Wu, Aunt Yang, and old woman P'an to join the two nuns.
>
> "I have just had something to eat," Aunt Wang said. "Ask Aunt Yang. She has been fasting."
>
> The Moon Lady put the cakes on small gilded plates and offered them first to Aunt Yang and then to the two nuns. "Take some more, old lady," she said to Aunt Yang, but the old lady protested that she had had enough.

"There are some bones on the plate," Aunt Yang said. "Please, sister, take them away. I might put them in my mouth by mistake."

This made everyone roar with laughter.

"Old Lady," said the Moon Lady, "this is vegetarian food made to look like meat. It has come from the temple, and there can't possibly be any harm in eating it." [trans. Egerton 1939, pp. 179–80]

This scene continues as the old nuns preach their homilies far into the night. It is a somber and passionless setting, yet even here we are reminded of the drunken party at the Taoist temple by the intrusions of the returning son-in-law into the household of women, and more subtly, by the contrast between the women in the household who respond with deepened faith to the nun's foolish teachings and those who mock them with suggestions of lasciviousness.

In the construction of this entire chapter in *Chin-p'ing-mei*, contrasting the restraint, elegance, and piety (if foolish) of the overall tone in the Buddhist meal with the excess, vulgarity, and secular cynicism in the Taoist temple scenes, the author exploits food and drink as keys to the character and values of each individual. Above all, the uses of food are instrumental to the action and are, simultaneously, indicators of the sham in all the ritual involvements. The Buddhist nuns eat "meat" which is by great artifice made to have all the physical and connotative qualities of meat but one—it is not in fact flesh of animals. The Taoist feast with its roisterous aftermath, in which both priests and guests share, nullifies whatever serious hopes or spiritual strivings the forms of the rituals might have suggested. The skillful contrasts between these two scenes turn very much on the roles assumed by food. The ritual contexts remind us of norms of meaning and value that the civilization lived by; the individual acts are set against those by an author of genius, intent upon revealing to us all of their human particularity.

Food and Hygiene

The intellectual bases of traditional Chinese views on the properties of foods in relation to health—or, "iatro-dietetics"—are closely related to the conceptions underlying the ritual uses of food. That is, the purposes of ritual and the legitimacy of its forms draw upon the same organismic cosmology that underlies Chinese views about the properties of foods. The harmony which animates the cosmos and its microcosm, the human body, manifests a balance between the complementary dynamic forces, and among their manifestations in the five agents. That harmony can be maintained by counteracting imbalance. When the properties of foods are known, and when they are consumed with an eye to maintaining a balance among all the interacting properties and conditions, health results, for health is the normal state of the body, expressing the functional harmony that should prevail in all things. Some early Confucian thinkers, notably Hsün Tzu (third century B.C.), kept the ideological foundations of ritual philosophically abstract, abjuring mechanical or manipulative interpretations of it. However, they did not find it incumbent on themselves to insist that all men be philosophers and recognized that lesser men might make magic of ritual. Early Chinese medical thought appears to have emerged from non-Confucian (although not necessarily anti-Confucian) practitioners of the yin-yang and "five agents" (*wu hsing*) theories, and from the congenial counterparts to those in magical and alchemical Taoism. Thus, medical theory shared the grand cosmological conceptions of the Confucian world but, at the same time, sought immediate causes and cures in the alchemical properties of physical things and attempted to manipulate those in a semi-magical, semi-rational manner according to the five agents theory. For over two thousand years the growth and systematization of knowledge has been an activity dominated by Confucians, and the best physicians were expected to be *ju-i*, or scholarly Confucian medical specialists.[16]

It is perhaps not surprising that a civilization preoccupied with food, and confronted with the greatest range of food products and ways of preparing them known to history, should seek to define the medical properties of foods. All material things were considered part of an organismic cosmos in which all the parts belonged, interacted, and responded to the same dynamism. As the Chinese sought to determine the properties of foods and to relate those to the health of the human body, they have with ingenuity maintained a relationship between empirical discoveries (the knowledge of which accumulated and was refined and disseminated by a scholar elite that included medicine among its proper fields of learning) and the theoretical or systematizing efforts of thinkers. Our modern consternation over the resulting juxtaposition of often excellent empirical knowledge and usually flimsy, if not irrelevant, theory is not ours alone. Occasionally, thoughtful critics of much earlier times anticipated us in skepticism toward the theories; and we must assume that a realistic concern for results remained primary in the development of Chinese medicine.[17]

From one point of view, then, all foods are medicines, for all have their basic properties which, interacting with other foods and with conditions of the eater and the circumstances under which he consumes them, may have curative properties. Contrarily, all things ingested may work damaging effects under certain conditions. Most medicines were ordinary plant and animal matter, and early Chinese physicians recognized the practicality of combining therapy with food. Needham paraphrases an eleventh-century writer: "... old people are generally averse to taking medicine but are fond of food. It is therefore far better to treat their complaint with proper food than with drugs. Nutritional therapy should be resorted to first and drugs prescribed only after proper feeding has failed" (Needham 1970, p. 358). Although Needham and Lu see remarkable beginnings of iatro-chemistry in Taoist alchemy and note "proto-endocrinology" in very early Chinese treatment of thyroid deficiency, diabetes, and other diseases (ibid., pp. 284–87; 297 ff.), they find perhaps the most important medical advance recorded in the Yüan dynasty to be that in the field of dietary medicine. The work which attracted Needham's attention is the *Yin-shan cheng-yao* (Principles of Correct Diet) of 1330, by Hu Ssu-hui, or Hoshoi, whom Needham describes as "the Imperial Dietician" between 1315 and 1330, late in the Yüan dynasty. The guiding principle in this work is summarized in the aphorism: "Many diseases can be cured by diet alone." Here the emphasis is on positive steps toward cure by supplementing deficiencies through diet.[18]

The *Yin-shan cheng-yao* is undoubtedly important in the history of Chinese science, but it may be less typical of Chinese attitudes toward food and eating in relation to hygiene than some other works that have less importance in the history of science. Another fascinating work from the fourteenth century is Chia Ming's *Yin-shih hsü-chih* (Essential Knowledge for Eating and Drinking; 1368), which stresses prevention rather than treatment. Chia Ming was from a wealthy family in Hai-yen in northern Chekiang. If not an original scholar of any importance, he had nonetheless acquired a broad Confucian education and had held a minor government post at the end of the Yüan dynasty. He was in his hundredth year of age in 1368 when the Ming dynasty was founded, and the Ming Founder summoned him to the court to honor him for his longevity. In the polite conversation that ensued, the emperor of course asked him the secret of his long life, to which Chia replied: "The essential is to be most cautious about what one drinks and eats." When the emperor asked further about that, Chia replied that he had written a book on the subject, which he would be happy to submit to the throne. He did so; it is the book named above, which has been widely printed in the centuries that followed. Chia returned to his home after this encounter and died there at the age of 106, not (of course!) of any apparent ill health, but in response to an auspicious dream.[19]

Chia Ming's book is divided into eight chapters, devoted to (1) forty-three kinds of water and fires; (2) fifty kinds of grains, including legumes and some seeds used for food; (3) eighty-seven kinds of vegetables; (4) sixty-three kinds of fruits and nuts; (5) thirty-three kinds of "flavorings," including condiments, seasonings such as wines and vinegar, oils, and preserved seasonings such as fish sauces; (6) sixty-eight kinds of fish and shellfish; (7) thirty-four kinds of fowl; and (8) forty-two kinds of meats. Each of these four hundred and sixty items is a principal entry, under which related varieties and similar species are discussed, so the total number of food items considered is substantially larger. The discussion under each entry ranges from a few sentences to a long paragraph. The formula for discussing each food is, first, to indicate to which of the five flavors it belongs. Those are: sweet, sour, bitter, pungent, and salty; related respectively to the five agents (or five elements), earth, wood, fire, metal, and water. Although not made explicit in this work, one medical theory holds that the flavors relate to the five viscera, through their corresponding agent: the stomach (earth), the liver (wood), the heart (fire), the lungs (metal) and the kidneys (water). In the numerology of Chinese civilization, the system of fives also relates the flavors and the viscera, through their corresponding agents, to the seasons, the directions, the processes of generation and destruction, and to many other things. Following the identification by flavor category, the "character" of the item is then specified by a degree of hotness or coolness, from very hot to very cold. This is a spectrum indicating affinities for yang properties (hot) or for yin properties (cold). Armed with this basic information, the home physician-theorist can make his own further judgments about the consequences of eating each item and about all possible combinations of items under all possible sets of circumstances. But Chia Ming does not rest there; he also gives specific information on things to be avoided in connection with each food item, his emphasis being preventive medicine. Almost nothing is said about the positive properties of most foods, about how they supplement deficiencies, or about their restorative powers. Occasionally, however, the author reveals his gourmet interests, pronouncing certain items to be particularly delicious, or sympathizing with persons who are addicted to some of the tasty but harmful foods. His brief preface states:

> Drink and food are relied upon to nourish life, yet if one does not know that the natures of substances may be opposed to each other and even incompatible with each other, and [one] consumes them all together indiscriminately, at the least, the five viscera will be thrown out of harmony, and at the most, disastrous consequences will immediately arise. Thus it is that persons nourishing [successfully] their lives have always avoided doing such damage to life. I have examined

all the commentaries and subcommentaries in all the various authorities' herbals and have found that, for each substance discussed, both good and bad properties are noted, so that the reader is left not knowing what to do. I have made a point of selecting those facts relating to opposition and incompatibility, in compiling the present work, as a contribution to those who in practicing reverence for life will find it convenient to investigate matters here. [M. Chia 1968 ed.; my translation]

Some examples for several of the eight chapters will illustrate the character of the Chia Ming's *Yin-shih hsü-chih*. From chapter one, Waters and Fires:

Natural rainwater: its flavor is sweet though mild; its character is cold. Rainwater from violent storms should not be used. Constant rains and pouring rains produce flood water; its flavor is sweet but thin.

Rainwater that falls on the beginning of spring: its character possesses the force of "spring rising and life beginning." For a married woman without children, husband and wife should each drink a cup of this water on this day, in order more easily to conceive. This draws on the idea [represented by that season in the annual cycle] of all things being generated.

Winter frost: its flavor is sweet, its character is cold. To collect it, use chicken feathers to sweep it into a bottle. Seal it tightly and store it in a dark place. It can be kept a long time without spoiling.

Water from a stalactite cavern: its flavor is sweet, its character warm. When weighed, if it is found to be heavier than other water and, when heated, if things like salt crystals appear, this then is the true stalactite cavern fluid. When one drinks this, it produces the same beneficial effects as does stalactite stone. The mountains [where stalactite caverns are found] will have jade, and the plants and trees will be luxuriant. Among the people living near such a mountain, many will attain longevity. Thus do the beneficial consequences of the jade stones' moisture [literally, "saliva"] become evident. [Ibid.]

Unlike the general character of Chia Ming's book, here—in discussing these beneficial waters—the positive note is strong. Jade, the most auspicious of earth's materials, is credited with remarkably beneficent properties. His other comments on waters include very sensible observations on well waters—how they are fouled when people live too close together in a city or when floods overflow them, and how to purify water by boiling and precipitating; interesting observations on the nature of water from hail;

and quite fanciful explanations of why mountain spring water may become poisonous. Discussions of the distinctive qualities of the water from particular springs, streams, and the like, probably because of the importance of suitable water for making tea, abound in Yüan and Ming writings (e.g., Hsieh 1959 ed., pp. 76–79; K. C. Chu 1959 ed., pp. 335–40). For one of the varieties of fire, we find:

Mulberry fuel fire: it is suitable for cooking all kinds of restorative medicines. One must not use it to cook pork or mud loaches or eels, and one cannot use it for burning moxa, for it will injure the skin. [M. Chia 1968 ed.; my translation]

From chapter two, Grains:

Glutinous rice: its flavor is sweet; its character is warm. Eaten in excess it causes fevers, and it impedes the action of the pulse. It makes the body weak and the muscles slow to respond. Eaten over a long time, it induces heart palpitations and causes pain in any sores or scabs. If eaten along with drinking wine, it induces drunkenness and retards the return to sobriety. Glutinous rice is sticky and digests slowly, so children and sick persons should all the more avoid it. If pregnant women eat it along with meat, it will be bad for the child, causing it to have sores, scabies, and tapeworms. Horses on eating it develop stumble-feet. If young cats and dogs eat it, their legs will become bent so that they cannot walk. When people eat it to excess it "arouses the *pneumata*" [*fa feng tung ch'i*; see Lu and Needham 1951, p. 267], causing one to become dazed and sleepy. If eaten together with chicken or eggs, it will cause one to have intestinal worms. If a person has become ill from eating too much duck, drinking the hot water from cooking glutinous rice will dispel that.

Soybeans: their flavor is sweet; raw, their character is warm, and when fried [or cooked] it becomes hot. They are slightly poisonous. Eaten in excess they block the lungs, produce phlegm and arouse coughing, induce ulcerated sores, and cause a person to become yellow of face and heavy of body. They must not be eaten together with pork. Small greenish black beans, also red and white beans, are similar to soybeans in flavor and character. None should be eaten with fish or mutton. [M. Chia 1968 ed.; my translation]

From chapter three, Vegetables:

Fragrant leeks [*chiu ts'ai; Allium odorum*]: their flavor is pungent and slightly acid; their character is warm. Eaten in the spring season, they are fragrant and quite beneficial. Eaten in the summer, they are malodorous. Eaten in the winter, they cause a person to arise during the night to get a drink. Eaten during the Fifth Moon, they cause a person to become dizzy and weak. In the winter, before the shoots have emerged from the soil, they are called blanched leeks [*chiu huang*]; those forced in cellars are called yellow-sprout leeks [*huang ya chiu*]. Eating these impedes the *pneuma*, apparently because they retain in them some of the suppressed force of latent growth. Eating fragrant leeks after the frost has fallen on them causes vomiting; eaten to excess, they dull the senses and dim the eyes. One must especially avoid them after drinking wine. If one suffers from a chronic chill of the chest and abdomen and eats them, it will worsen that condition. If eaten ten days following a fever, they may induce drowsiness. They must never be eaten along with honey or beef, for that will cause intestinal blockage. Eating fragrant leeks causes bad breath; that can be dispelled by sucking candy. [Ibid.]

This marvelous vegetable, eaten in China in so many forms throughout the year, thanks to the ingenuity of the Chinese gardener, is one of the very numerous vegetables common in China for which no satisfactory English name exists. Needless to say, many positive iatro-dietetic attributes as well as its palate-pleasing qualities could also be listed. For example, the great Ming dynasty herbal by Li Shih-chen, the *Pen-ts'ao kang-mu* (1590), lists it first among vegetable items important as medicine (chap. 26) and finds that it possesses the following general virtues: "It restores the spirit and calms the five viscera, eliminates fever in the stomach, and benefits a sick person. It can be eaten over a long period of time." A long list of specific medical benefits follows. This more learned medical work reports none of the baleful consequences of eating *Allium odorum*, yet Chia Ming's warnings are not his inventions; they also are based on an aspect of the accumulated Chinese knowledge about food. Some of his sentences can be traced to known Sung-dynasty works, and all can be fitted into a speculative system based on the properties of things as known within the theories of yin-yang and the five agents.

Also discussed in the chapter on vegetables:

Spinach: its flavor is sweet, and its character is cold and slippery. Eaten to excess it may cause a weakening of the feet and will bring about pains in the waist and arouse chills. If a person who previously has been afflicted by stomach chills should eat spinach, it certainly will rupture his stomach. It must not be eaten together with eels, for that can induce cholera. If northerners, after eating meat and noodles cooked over a coal fire, should then eat spinach, that will neutralize the [bad] effects. If southerners eat moist fish with rice and then eat spinach, that will gain a cooling effect. Spinach makes the small and large intestines cold and slippery. [Ibid.]

From chapter four, Fruits:

Persimmons: their flavor is sweet, their character cold. Eaten to excess, they arouse phlegm. Eaten when drinking wine, they cause one easily to become drunk or cause heart pains that make one think he is near death. Eaten along with crabs, they cause stomach pains and diarrhea, or vomiting and dizziness; then only thistle roots ground into a paste and forced down can bring relief. "Deer-heart" persimmons should especially be avoided, for they can cause stomach chills and intestinal pains. Dried persimmons must not be eaten with turtle, for that becomes indigestible and causes blockage. Red-colored persimmons which are not yet ripe can be immersed in cold salt water and stored that way for a year or more, but persimmons stored in salt water become slightly poisonous. [Ibid.]

From chapter five, Flavorings:

Vinegar: its flavor is acidly sweet and bitter; its character is slightly warm. It counteracts the poison in the flesh of fish, melons [cucumbers?] and vegetables. Rice-wine vinegar is excellent, but used to excess it damages the flesh and bones and harms the stomach. It is not beneficial to males; it damages their teeth and makes the visage pale. It can also activate poisons and must never be taken with any medicines. Persons taking medicines, including pine-root fungus [*fu ling*], red ginseng, or whitlow grass [*Draba nemorosa*], should especially avoid it. Persons suffering from colds and coughs, diarrhea or malaria should not use it.

Distilled spirits [*shao chiu*]: its flavor is sweet and pungent; its character is very hot. It is poisonous. Drunk to excess it damages the stomach and injures the spleen, disintegrates the marrow and weakens the muscles. It injures the spirit and shortens life. Persons who have *huo cheng* [tendency to have local fevers?] should avoid it. If one consumes it together with ginger, garlic, or dog meat, it will induce hemorrhoids and will activate any chronic illnesses. If a pregnant woman drinks it, it can cause the child to have convulsions. Should one drink it to excess and develop a fever, he can be restored to clarity by being placed in cold water newly drawn from a well, or by having his hair soaked in that. Persons who have been poisoned by it can be somewhat restored by drinking cold salt water with green-pea flour. Or, take a pint of large black beans and boil them to make one to two pints of soup. This, drunk in large quantities to induce vomiting will dispel the poison.

Milk [*ju lo*]: its flavor is sweet and acid; its character is cold. Persons suffering from diarrhea must not consume it. Sheep [goat] milk taken together with preserved fish [seasoning] will cause intestinal blockage. It does not go with vinegar. It should never be consumed along with perch. [Ibid.]

The items translated above from among the four hundred and sixty such items comprising the book include none of the longer and more detailed discussions, but they may suffice to illustrate the author's concerns. The compilers of the Ch'ing dynasty imperial library catalog (*Ssu-k'u ch'üan-shu tsung-mu t'i-yao*, chap. 22) condemned Chia Ming's book as mere cribbing from various herbals, with no new material. Yet the book has its importance as a reflection of Chinese beliefs about foods as active agents in the cosmic processes of generation and decay. It seems probable that most Chinese, learned or not, were in some degree aware of the concepts on which the book is based, and that there was much commonsense knowledge in society about such qualities of foods. However, we must also assume that most persons relished food and relegated its medical properties to a distinctly secondary level of significance. Indeed, to observe fully and literally all the warnings and taboos cited in Chia Ming's eight chapters would make eating virtually impossible. Therefore, in this as in so many things, we can imagine the ordinary Chinese pragmatically and non-dogmatically applying this kind of information where it seemed reasonable, heeding it more fully when he was ill, enjoying its symbolic implications even as he ignored its instructions, and savoring it as an additional dimension of the all-absorbing subject of food and eating. Such a general social attitude may not have advanced the cause of scientific eating, but neither did it allow so important a subject as food to become ruled by a sterile fanaticism that might have become codified into the kinds of dogmatism imposed on the eating habits of some other civilizations—although religious dietary laws have often had a basis in empirical knowledge in those cases also. The difference lies, not in the ability to perceive the real qualities of foods, but in the ways in which authority is extended to such daily life activities as eating and drinking. Chia Ming's pursuit of food knowledge is avid, and his urge to classify and utilize that knowledge is intense, even though his learning is poor by the Chinese standards of that time. In his book, the enterprise of learning, advising, and instructing remains humane, subject to reasonable human purposes and values; he is far more absorbed in the compiling, even amused by the details, than he is anxiety ridden. To encounter such attitudes, even at less than the highest levels of the great tradition, informs us very usefully. In examining what Chia Ming takes to be the philosophical underpinnings of the concepts surrounding foods as active agents in the cosmic process (as also in examining the uses of foods in ritual and ceremonial), we have come face to face with the sources of authority on which all the Chinese drew in ordering and maintaining all the constituents of their civilization. The attitude toward authority which is revealed in this case, as in general, is humanly reasonable.

The Enjoyment of Food

Those attitudes toward food which account for the Chinese achievement in the arts and skills of cooking and eating are part and parcel of their view of life in general: Life is good, and its meaning is to be found here and now, yet the cosmic whole of life and death, past and present, affects all our present involvement. That is why the spirits were treated as living people would want to be treated: they were feasted with the best things man could reasonably be expected to provide. At the same time, the bodies of living persons were nourished as part of the organismic process; those living bodies, too, would respond to the same dynamics.

A most important fact about food and eating, however—perhaps the most important thing about it—is that food and drink should be good, not just functionally adequate to all the cosmic interactions, or simply adequate to maintain health. All the ritual and hygiene functions of food might have been supplied by symbolic offerings of bizarre items or by grim diets. Aztec gods demanded hearts plucked from living human victims, and Kali demanded the warm blood of sacrificial goats. Chinese spirits had no need of such sacrifices. Medieval Christian hermits survived on such things as cold stale bread, and saints in other civilizations have denied themselves all the eating pleasures, in one regimen or another. The Chinese seldom denied the value of good food in those extreme ways. Foods for all purposes, ritual or daily consumption, were from one kitchen and of one cuisine and reflected the same attitudes and values. In all contexts, as far as people could achieve it, food was varied, elaborate, and excellent.

Simply stated, food was pleasure, and pleasure, within quite flexible limits, was good. The cultivation of that pleasure reveals marvelous ingenuity; it drew upon accumulated wisdom and high technical skills. A lore of food was richly developed before Yüan and Ming times, as the foregoing essays in this book have demonstrated. The abundance of the Yüan and Ming period materials permits us to expose aspects of that rich development in considerable detail, reflecting, if not a complete cross section of Chinese life, a broader spectrum than is exposed to us in the documents from earlier times. In what follows, several facets of food as pleasure will be touched upon. The information is gleaned from the entertainment literature characteristic of the period, such as the Yüan and Ming dramas, the Ming novels and short stories, and the informal writings often referred to as collections of notes and sketches.[20]

The Rare and the Delicious

In the Yüan drama *Pai-hua t'ing*, dating from about 1250, an actor dressed as a fruit vendor comes on the stage and delivers the following patter:

Fruits on sticks for sale, fruits on sticks for sale! I've just left the tile districts [pleasure quarters], departed the tea houses to swiftly pass the pleasureland of kingfisher green and worldly red to enter the district of orioles and flowers. . . . This fruit is homegrown, just picked. There are juicy-juicy-sweet, full-full-fragrant, sweet-smelling, red and watery fresh-peeled round-eye lichees from Fu-chou; from P'ing-chiang [Su-chou] some sour-sour-tart, shady-cool, sweet-sweet-luscious, yellow oranges and green tangerines with the leaves still on; there're some supple-supple-soft, quite-quite-white, crystal-sweet, crushed-flat candied persimmons from Sung-yang; from Wu-chou I have snappy-snappy-crisp, juicy-juicy-fresh, glitter-glitter-bright dragon-twined jujubes kneaded in sugar; there are ginger threads from Hsin-chien split fine and dipped in honey sugar as well as Kao-yu water caltrops wrinkled by the sun, dried by the wind and skinned; I have the blackest of black, reddest of red fingertip-size large melon seeds gathered in Wei; from Hsüan-ch'eng some half-sour, half-sweet, half-sweet, half-sour soft peaches skewered just right. I can't exhaust the list, so I'll lay out several kinds before your eyes. Oh, you sweet elegant ladies, beautiful women from fragrant chambers and embroidered kiosks; great and noble gentlemen from high halls and great buildings—I'm not just bragging to make false claims, but try mine and you'll forsake all others. You'll be sure to buy them once you try them. Oh! Sticks of fruit for sale! [West 1972, pp. 158–59]

In that passage (colorfully translated by Stephen West), full of inadvertent information offered as the dramatist creates a credible street scene, we are told that the ordinary buyer in the streets of a thirteenth-century city was

offered the most delectable fruits representing the specialized production of
four or five provinces, a region half the size of western Europe. Those are
attractively advertised as the most rare and delicious, by all the standards
of color, fragrance, and flavor; those sold by competitors cannot compare.
It seems unlikely that the ordinary buyers in the world's cities beyond China
at that time, and for a long time thereafter, were half so well served by
interregional trade in their taste for fragile, perishable foods. The local
speciality, frequently a food product, has been for centuries a major component of Chinese commerce. The poets tell about fresh litchis going from
Szechwan to the court at Changan by pony-express, to please a harem
favorite in the eighth century; by the fourteenth century we have full descriptions of regular, large-scale refrigerated transport of perishable foodstuffs
going the whole eleven-hundred miles of the Grand Canal. No doubt only
the rich shared those most costly items with the court, but ordinary buyers
had access to an extraordinary variety of delicacies. Even though some
undoubtedly were imitations bearing the name of the nationally famous
pacesetter (*mao-t'ai* liquor in China today has become just a general name
for the rare product formerly made by one small distillery in Kweichow;
and for decades, perhaps centuries, chestnuts labeled "Liang-hsiang" for
the Hopei source and pears called "Tang-shan" after the northern Kiangsu
county have been harvested all across China) that nonetheless is testimony
to an awareness of quality, a demand for the best. Innumerable references
to such famous food products are found as part of the inadvertent information (which thereby assumes high credibility) in the Yüan and Ming
period entertainment and informal literature.

A Nanking writer of about 1600 offers a variation on this theme—a
catalog of lovingly described "best items" in each category of good food for
which that great city was famous. A short essay called "Chen-wu" (Precious
Things) begins as follows:

> Among the finest of fruits are jujubes [*tsao*] from the Yao-fang Gate;
> they sometimes exceed two and one-half inches in length and have a
> skin as red as blood, or sometimes a red splashed with yellow and green,
> most enticing in their mottled appearance. Their flesh is whiter than
> gleaming snow, their flavor sweeter than honey. The fruit is crisp yet
> soft; if one falls from the tree it splatters on impact. Only those produced
> on one tract, on only a bit over ten *mou* in size [about two acres], on the
> Lü Family Hill are truly like that. Even stock moved from that place to
> be planted elsewhere will produce fruit that is distinctly different.

> The lotus root of [Nanking's] lakes and ponds is as big as a strong
> man's arm, yet it is sweet and crisp, totally without any pulpy residue.

All the other lotus root of the entire Chiang-nan region is inferior to it.

The red horned nuts [*ling-chiao*; *Trapa bicornis*] of Ta-pan [Bridge] are like frosty snow in the mouth. They dissolve without being chewed.

The cherries of Ling-ku Temple are especially large. They are as red as garnets, their flavor sweet and rich, and their seeds small. They have the shape of pointed-tip peaches. In my view, they are what is really meant by the word *cherries*. [Ku Ch'i-yuan 1618, 1:15a–16b; my translation]

This essay goes on and on, describing the ginko nuts, the shad, the *ho-t'un* fish [*Spheroides vermicularis*]—famous as the most delicious of all fish but deadly poisonous if not prepared with exquisite care—the small carp [*chi yü*] of the Hsüan-wu Lake, just outside the north city wall, and also the best of the daily fare vegetables and fruits, such as turnips, onions, celery, cabbage, and pears, which at their gourmet best are also great delicacies. This tradition of cataloging the best foods of a place, informing true connoisseurs where and when to get the best, was a minor branch of learning which continued. About 1930 a Nanking antiquarian and gourmet, Chang T'ung-chih, produced an account of the city's most delectable foodstuffs (*Pai-men shih-p'u*), based on Yüan Mei's eighteenth-century model, which allows interesting comparisons with the above late Ming work as well as that of Yüan Mei (cf. Shinoda in Yabuuchi and Yoshida 1970, pp. 386–87).[21]

The centrality of gourmet interests to the broad elite and sub-elite stratum of Ming society (not meaning to suggest that the appreciation of food was limited to such an upper stratum) is well illustrated by the following entry in an early seventeenth-century collection of miscellaneous notes and sketches:

Yuan-ts'ai [an unidentified contemporary] has said that the five things in his whole life that he most resents are: one, that shad has so many bones; two, that kumquats are often sour; three, that the nature of spinach is cold [see Chia Ming's discussion of spinach, p. 231 above]; four, that flowering crabapple blossoms are not fragrant; and five, that [the Sung dynasty essayist] Tseng Kung was not a good poet. I also have five resentments: one, that the *ho-t'un* fish is poisonous; two, that *chien-lan* plants [*Cymbidium ensifolium*] are so difficult to grow; three, that the nature of cherries is hot; four, that the scent of jasmine is so heavy; and five, that the Three Hsiehs, Li Po, and Tu Fu [pre-eminent poets of the fourth to fifth centuries and the eighth century] were not skilled essayists. [*Yung-ch'uang*, p. 218; my translation]

Each of those lists of "most hated things" is limited to cultivated aesthetic concerns. If we take the reference to jasmine to be to its common use in flavoring teas and foods, the gustatory focus accounts for three of the five items on each list.

Is it not possible in the great profusion of such writings, of which the two examples above are representative, to discern a romanticized mystique of gourmet excellence? We see that ideal supported by learning and by literary art, as a well-developed adjunct of the elite life, no doubt pervasively imitated, if less fully experienced, on many sub-elite levels of Chinese life as well (see Hsieh 1959 ed., p. 315–19). We have also noted its caricature in the vulgarity of the marketplace, where the common folk shared its appeal in their own way. Yüan and Ming literature also depicts the humorously entertaining, as well as the thoughtfully serious, rejections of all such ostentation and excesses of refinement, but even the renunciation is characteristically sensitive to gourmet ideals. One late thirteenth-century rural rhapsody inserted by the great dramatist Kuan Han-ch'ing into one of his dramas includes the lines: "The fall harvest is gathered in. Let's set a feast out under the gourd trellis, drink wine from earthen bowls and porcelain pots, swallow the tender eggplants with their skins, gulp down the little melons, seeds and all. The turnips are sliced in a salty sauce; the country wine goes down by the bowlful ... " (*Ku-pen*, no. 5, p. 8a; my translation. Numbers refer to abstracts of dramas in vol. 1.).[22]

At all these levels, and in all these modes, a full spectrum of attitudes toward food—except an attitude of unconcern or disdain—is evident. The preoccupation of the civilization with good food is displayed in the sharp detail with which its infinite variety is savored secondhand, in literature.

Cooking Skills

How were cooking skills developed and transmitted in Chinese society? The characteristics of the social structure are reflected in some obvious elements of the answer. It was a society without castes, without hereditary professions, with few closed social groups. Superior cooking skills may well have been transmitted from parent to child in particular families, whether or not cooking was their profession. A woman of the common people, who made a famous soup, might have a son who would become the cook in a great household, but she might also have a son who would become governor of the province, although statistically the former case is a greater probability. The openness of the society and the fact that clan structures cut across the lines of social stratification allowed for ready diffusion of special skills throughout the society. The famous family recipe could be widely disseminated and probably was. If a woman developed superior cooking skills learned from relatives, employers, servants, or others, she had an inducement to utilize and display those, no matter what her social level. That a man would develop superior cooking skills was more apt to occur within the profession of cook, yet men, other than professionals, who knew how to cook well probably also appeared at most social levels. And, of course, those experts who wrote about cooking were always learned men! We again encounter the usual if misleading situation—that it is the male professionals and the female amateurs who are recorded in the annals of cooking, as in some other arts, such as tailoring, singing, and playing musical instruments. Cooking skills clearly were not sex specific in Yüan and Ming China, and the interest in food throughout the society was so great that no skilled practitioner was likely to remain undiscovered. Thus, although no references to a Yüan or Ming governor who cooked a famous dish of this or that has been noted, in the entertainment literature we find much evidence that women of any status might practice the art and be honored for it.

A famous Ming story that probably has Sung dynasty antecedents tells of the "more than one hundred" wine houses, or restaurants, on the shore of the West Lake at Hangchow in the twelfth century. At one of those, there was a woman who had learned to make a fish soup at one of the most famous restaurants of the Northern Sung capital, and who had fled to Hangchow when the Jurchen invasions forced the government to move to Hangchow, after 1126. The emperor, remembering the old days, ate her soup and pronounced it delicious, bringing fame and fortune to her. The Ming dynasty author has inserted a poem in the story:

> A bowl of fish soup isn't worth more than a few cents;
> Yet, made as in the days of former capital, it brings smiles to the
> imperial face.
> So people come in droves to buy it at twice the price;
> In part, they are buying the imperial gesture, and in part they buy
> the soup.
>
> [M. L. Feng 1947 ed., chap. 39; my translation]

No one need doubt that it was a superb soup; the same, or its imitation, has been sold at the West Lake from that day to this.

The transmitter of that famous recipe from K'ai-feng to Hangchow is said to have been from the family of restaurant proprietors. Other early seventeenth-century stories show officials' wives who were renowned for a particular dish. In a story conventionally set in an earlier period, but probably reflecting Ming society, a county magistrate invites the county director of Confucian Studies to dine. Freshwater turtle is served. The guest tastes it and weeps: "The flavor of this is remarkably similar to that which my deceased wife used to cook; that is why I am so overcome with sadness," he explains (M. C. Ling 1967 ed., chap. 27; my translation). Of course, it turns out that his wife had not died; she is now in the magistrate's household and has in fact cooked the very dish that brought the tears. That is a long and irrelevant story; what is relevant is that it was not a servant but an official's wife who did the cooking. A Nanking antiquarian has written: "In early times wives supervised the kitchen; most of the wives and daughters in Nanking's great households were highly skilled in the art of cooking" (Chang T'ung-chih 1947, p. 5; my translation).[23]

In addition to high amateur standards and informal recruitment of talent, however, there must also have existed in Yüan and Ming times a system of recruitment and training for the highly skilled profession of the chef. Was there a guild of master chefs? Did the system of apprenticeship vary from one city to the next? The information at hand does not permit precise answers.

The professional cook often appears in Yüan and Ming dramas, invariably as a white-nosed rascal, often one who amusingly victimizes the villain of the piece and therefore is a comical agent of unintended good deeds. In a typical scene, the master of the household or the head of the government office in whose kitchen the cook is employed calls in the head cook and orders him to prepare a banquet: "Now, come and prepare the shopping list. First, buy a fat sheep." "Oh, yes, a sheep, a sheep. These days a big fat sheep is easy to find. For seven dollars you can buy one weighing a hundred and twenty catties. Those big-tailed woolly sheep [i.e., not a goat] are dirt cheap." Later the cook is given the money and realizes that he has the opportunity to do the shopping and the accounting unsupervised. He quickly adds: "Sir, just in the last couple of days the price of mutton has really gone up" (Ku-pen, no. 36, p. 6a–b).[24] This is a stock scene; it appears almost in the same words in other plays (cf. Ku-pen, no. 70, p. 2b). When the rascally cook is required to propose a menu, the naming of the dishes becomes a scene of sly humor when the dishes named are all elaborate puns. Such a cook will be clever enough to steal the master blind. In another instance, the naming of the dishes planned for a feast becomes a farcical scene when the food choices display both the cook's and the master's incompetence to plan a banquet; the audience knows that incompetence in the kitchen is in itself a revelation of the ridiculous. Thus, food and eating on the stage were complementary to the enjoyment of food in real life.

Special ingredients

The Japanese specialist in the history of Chinese food and eating, Shinoda

Osamu, has noted that the masses of the Chinese farming population in the past existed mainly on cereal grains, their proteins coming mostly from beans. To this extent, he finds their diet quite similar to that of pre-modernized Japan's common people and that of farming populations elsewhere in Asia. Traditional China's diet was strikingly different from the Japanese in two respects: the consumption of oils and fats was four or five times higher in China, and everyday cooking demanded more basic materials. The things required to keep an ordinary kitchen going day by day in Yüan and Ming times are sometimes enumerated in the entertainment literature, encapsulated in the formula of "the seven things." Shinoda refers to "Yüan drama" for one enumeration of those, probably having in mind the line spoken by a busy housewife: "From the moment I get up in the morning, I'm busy about the seven things—fuel, rice, oil, salt, soy sauce, vinegar, and tea" (*San-shih chung*, p. 261). He notes that other such lists often include or add, as indispensable to the daily fare, wine, sugar, spices, and other common ingredients. He concludes from all this that the Yüan and Ming ordinary Chinese had a diet both richer and tastier than that of the Japanese and other pre-modern people. (Shinoda, in Yabuuchi 1955, pp. 74–92).[25] If a relatively wide range of ingredients was regularly necessary and available for the daily fare of the common people, an immensely rich stock of cooking ingredients was handy to those same people for the important feasts, and to the upper strata for their daily fare.

It would be impossible to list all the foodstuffs and ingredients of cooking that appear, in the contemporary references to food, as ordinary facts of Yüan and Ming life. The many foods itemized as offerings at shrines or discussed in the works on hygiene, some of which are described above, give additional force to the idea that a very rich range of foods was widely present. Ming period local gazetteers often list the products of a region; from the several hundred such gazetteers still extant, one could compile a comprehensive catalog containing thousands of items known as ingredients of food in Ming China. Merely to come again to the subject of the variety and quality of food, from yet another point of view, becomes in itself repetitious, but only in that way do we begin to apprehend its import. To the Chinese themselves, the full exploitation of that vast grocery list was an ever-present challenge. Perhaps the Chinese were spurred by the consciousness of all the gustatory possibilities to seek still further variety. This led occasionally to bizarre foods and often to food fantasizing.

Fantasies about food encountered in the entertainment literature often took the form of genies' banquets, with ineffably delicate and beautiful foods served in (literally) entrancing circumstances. There were also devils' feasts, where the ingredients of the principal dishes might be rare and strange sea creatures, somewhat repulsive sounding, or centipedes, toads, and other unpleasant objects (*Ku-pen*, no. 27, p. 8b; *Ming-jen*, p. 720).[26] Those seemingly unpalatable things usually were mysteriously beneficial to physical or spiritual health. A Ming short story tells of a Taoistic old gentleman who accepts an invitation to dine at a hidden mountain retreat with a group of alchemists. After the old man has drunk some wine with his hosts and has sampled the canapes, the two main dishes arrive. The lids are removed from the tureens. In one he sees floating in a broth the body of a white hairless dog, and in the other that of a human infant, both served whole. He recoils in horror, refusing to eat, but not wishing to create a scene. He stammers out an explanation: "I've been a strict vegetarian all my life, even in the face of ordinary meats; I'd rather die than touch my chopsticks to those things." The hosts politely urge him to taste these "special vegetables," as they call the two main dishes. The old man still refuses but remains politely seated, as a guest should, while they munch away. Later they inform him that the repellent objects, now consumed, were in fact the curiously shaped roots of medicinal plants, thousands of years old and capable of imparting immortality to the eater. Regretfully, he philosophizes that his state of enlightenment is not advanced enough to permit him recognition of the true nature of the food, so he does not yet merit immortality (M. C. Ling 1957 ed., chap. 18).

The flesh of the dog, which repelled the old man in that story, appears not to have been repellent to many Chinese. Whenever it is specified, however, it carries a special significance. It is, for example, a favorite food of the irascible counterfeit monk Lu Chih-shen, one of the great heroes of the fourteenth-century picaresque novel *The Water Margin*.[27] In other Yüan and Ming period literature, persons who prefer dog meat appear to share the quality of hot-blooded animal energy, of which Lu Chih-shen is the symbol. In a Ming drama, barbarians from the Inner Asian steppe, coming to the Chinese court, compare the food of the Chinese capital with their steppe fare; a fierce Mongol general says that in the steppe: "Every day, at all three meals, we eat dog meat" (*Ku-pen*, no. 141, p. 7a).[28] The association with fierce and wild behavior is clear. Other bizarre eating habits beyond the pale of Chinese civilization are also occasionally noted. One Ming writer from the lower Yangtze region seems to have felt it odd that "south of the mountain ranges" (in Kwangtung), people ate snake (K. C. Chu 1959 ed., p. 749). Many kinds of game, however, were highly prized, and hunters who supplied the market with venison, pheasant, rabbits, fresh or dried and salted, were a special profession. A famous late Ming story describes a woman in Shantung who practiced this profession, in the absence of a long-departed husband, and who thus supported herself and her mother-in-law quite adequately. She occasionally added a fresh tiger to her catch of wild game, and the story turns on a would-be male hero who is overawed and frightened away by this appealing amazon. No doubt the tiger meat in her diet contributed to her forceful personality (M. C. Ling 1957 ed., chap. 3, prologue story). Most bizarre of all the ingredients in Yüan and Ming food is human flesh. Several references to steamed dumplings filled with minced humans appear in *The Water Margin*. They are sold only at "black deeds inns," where evil and violent persons gather to plot crimes, and they become a cliché, a symbol of heinous crime.[29] Whether gourmet cannibalism was really practiced in Yüan and Ming times remains doubtful, although the cannibalism of desperation accompanying times of famine and disaster is sometimes reported, again somewhat symbolically, as the measure of calamity.

Regional and Other Variations

In recent times, China is sometimes said to have had four or five great regional cuisines, and cities have had restaurants identified as representative of the Peking (i.e., Shantung) cuisine, the Yangchow (or Yangchow-Chenkiang-Shanghai) cuisine, the Szechwan (or Hunan-Szechwan) cuisine, or the Cantonese cuisine, or others. In Yüan and Ming writings, that awareness is not manifested. Instead, there is a general awareness that food was apt to be plainer in the north than in the rich Yangtze drainage area of central China. Beyond the Great Wall, in the northern provinces, a southerner would find the food poor. For example, a traveler in a later Ming short story recalls: "At the inns in Shantung one doesn't get any special dishes to accompany the rice or to eat with the wine. Instead there will be nothing more than a couple of small plates of garlic and a few steamed breads. In this inn . . . they had the famous, most ferocious, yellow distilled liquor" (M. C. Ling 1967 ed., 14: 267; my translation). In contrast with that spartan scene, the same author describes a pleasure boat on the West Lake at Hangchow, a floating restaurant which a rich man can rent for his exclusive use while enjoying the lake and its famous cuisine with his family: lanterns and singing and lavish foods served in silver and gold vessels, course after course of delicacies, complete the scene without giving the culinary details (ibid., 18: 324–25). The novel *Chin-p'ing-mei*, from the end of the sixteenth century, also has a Shantung setting. In its detailed descriptions of food and drink, some sense of the northern locale is apparent, but the richness of the cuisine in the private households of wealth matches anything found in descriptions of southern food of the time. Nonetheless, when the novel's protagonists are forced to take meals in ordinary temples or inns, they too complain about the simple and crude fare (chaps. 71, 96). Petty merchants eating at a common travelers' inn in Su-chou, however, are brought, along with their few cents worth of wine, a leg of mutton and several plates of chicken, fish, pork, and vegetables, offered as a matter of course and eliciting no comment (M. C. Ling 1967 ed., 8: 145).[30] Thus, it seems that the very rich could enjoy luxury at any place in China, but for the ordinary people, the north-south distinction was somewhat sharper.

Hsieh Chao-che, who received his *chin-shih* degree at Peking in 1592, compared the north with his native Fukien when he first went to the capital as a youth and noted changes that had occurred by the time he made further visits there later in his life: "When I was a youth and would go to the markets in Peking, it was difficult to find most anything. There was chicken, goose, mutton, and pork, but to get a fish was considered a rarity. Now, twenty years later, fish and crabs are cheaper there than in the Yangtze, while clams, ice fish, razor clams, mussels, and crabs are piled up in all the markets. This is proof that life-styles move from south to north" (Hsieh 1959 ed., 9: 265). Hsieh's point may not be proved, but the observation is not without meaning. This is considerable evidence that standards of living and levels of consumption increased significantly during the sixteenth century, and that the increases were earlier and greater in the richer Yangtze provinces. Hsieh may be observing the subsequent spread of that greater prosperity to the north of China, at the end of the century.

Restaurants; Prepared Foods for Sale

Merchants, government officials on assignment, and students away from home to take examinations have long appeared in Chinese fiction as the principal categories of travelers stopping at inns and eating in restaurants. Yüan and Ming drama and fiction provide no exception, but some new elements are to be seen in the restaurant business by Ming times. The increased volume of travel among the above three groups and the growing links between those categories of travelers led to the emergence of a new kind of establishment to serve their needs, the *hui-kuan*, or hostelry for travelers from the same province or prefecture.[31] Characteristically, the hui-kuan had a staff of employees from the home locality, including cooks. The Su-chou merchant or statesman residing temporarily at the Su-chou hui-kuan in Peking, at any of the important centers along the Grand Canal or the Yangtze, or at other important locations, could expect to hear his Su-chou speech and to eat his fine Su-chou soup noodles and pastries for breakfast. Although this is mere conjecture, one might assume that the great expansion of the hui-kuan institution from mid Ming times onward contributed much to establishing provincial cuisines in all the major cities.

Another development of the mid and late Ming period is the growth of tourism. Even though a famous site, such as the West Lake at Hangchow, drew travelers intent merely upon the enjoyment of the scenery as early as the Sung period, by the mid Ming such travel became a new form of ostentatious consumption. The late Ming short story cited above for its descriptions of pleasure boats, complete with food, music, and other entertainment, describes two travelers among those who have come to Hangchow to enjoy that entertainment: One of them is a rich gentleman named Mr. P'an, from Sung-chiang in southeast Kiangsu; he has been a student at the National University, probably by purchase of the title, but he is a man of learning nonetheless, and he is stopping at an inn by the lake just to enjoy the scenery. He sees another traveler arrive "from some distant place, accompanied by a wife—also to enjoy the pleasures of the lake; he brought a great quantity of baggage, and a full array of servants and household staff." He rented the largest boat on the lake for daily excursions, entertained lavishly, and spent vast sums. Such travelers and their less affluent counterparts appear to be a new feature of Ming life. Scenic places throughout the central provinces developed facilities to entertain them, and the tourist's guidebook became a new genre of writing.[32]

Persons eating in restaurants were not only travelers from afar; local persons also patronized the restaurants of their own towns, but more often, perhaps, invited the local restaurants to cater large dinner parties in their homes. The Chinese restaurants' "take home" food also appears often in Ming entertainment literature. Elaborate delicacies to accompany tea are often mentioned, but precooked meats and other dishes could also be bought.[33] Some restaurants specialized in mutton dishes only or in vegetarian meals or in beef cuisine or in other specialties demanded by religion, taste, or fad.

Eating Customs

Some late Ming writers see the middle of the sixteenth century, or the Chia-ching reign period, 1522–66, as a turning point in the expansion of commerce, in institutional changes affecting taxes and urban life-styles, and in the achievement of a general prosperity affecting all aspects of life. One of those writers is Ku Ch'i-yüan, 1565–1628, who illustrated that idea in many ways. In one short essay, he quotes his maternal uncle, who, like Ku himself, was a Nanking antiquarian and expert on local history, to show how changes in dining customs reflect changes in the society. What follows is part of that essay on "banqueting at the southern capital in days gone by":

In Nanking during the Cheng-t'ung reign period [1436–49], when

inviting guests to dinner, one merely sent a young servant boy early on
the day of the banquet to the home of each guest to say: "You are invited
to dine." By the hour *ssu* [9:00 to 11:00 A.M.], the guests would have
gathered. When there were six guests or eight, a large square table for
eight [*pa-hsien cho*; "eight immortals table"] would be used. The main
dishes would number only four, on large platters, with four minor
accessory dishes at the four corners of the table. There would be no
[preliminary] sweetmeats. The wine would be drunk from two large
wine cups, used in turn by the guests. At the center of the table there
would be a large bowl filled with water; one would rinse the wine cup,
refill it, and pass it on to the next person. That was called the "rinsing
bowl." The dinner party would disperse following the *wu* hour [after
1:00 P.M.].

By some ten or more years later, one informed guests of an invitation
on the day before, and on the next morning again sent a reminder. The
table and the dishes of food were as before, but four wine cups were now
used, and there were those who used eight cups. After some ten more
years or so, people first commenced to send an invitation card on the
previous day. The card was about 1.3 or 1.4 inches wide and perhaps
5 inches long. One did not write [conventionally polite] forms calling
oneself "such and such junior person" but just wrote "with respects
from," plus surname and given name. Above that would be written:
"Dinner at the noon hour on such and such a date." The table and the
dishes of food still remained as previously.

After another ten or more years had passed, they commenced using
the [accordion-] folded card, but one of not more than three folds, five
or six inches long and two inches wide. On this would be written [such
polite and formal expressions as] "your humble senior relative" or "your
humble junior attendant, so and so, offers respects." At this time was
initiated the practice of making separate table settings with two persons
for one [small] table and with sweetmeats and dishes to the number of
seven or eight for the preliminary servings. Then, also, they went on to
the main banquet during the ssu hour [by 11:00 A.M.] and would not
finish until the end of the *shen* hour [at five P.M.]. It was during the
Cheng-te and Chia-ching reign periods [1506–66] that there commenced
the practices of providing music and belaboring the kitchen help. [C. Y.
Ku 1618, 9:14b; my translation]

This appears to suggest that remarkably plain customs prevailed in
Nanking, the former capital of the Ming empire and still its secondary
capital, until the end of the fifteenth century. If correct, and if general for

China, it constitutes evidence that during the first half of the Ming period customs were much simpler than they had been in Sung and even in Yüan times. The idea that customs had become considerably more lavish after 1550 is a theme that runs through Ku Ch'i-yuan's book (ibid., 1:28b–29a and 31a–b, and passim).[34] It probably exaggerates but does not invent. The novel *Chin-p'ing-mei* dates from Ku's lifetime, and the collections of late Ming short stories were first published during the decade following his death. Throughout those, the banqueting customs of the elite reflect the more elaborate practices which Ku deplores as evidence for the recent decline of simpler, older ways.

Banquets beginning at the noon hour seem to have been the standard practice, yet evening and all-night feasts and parties were not unknown. Even Ku Ch'i-yuan, in the same work, notes that at betrothal feasts among the well-to-do the music and entertainment might go on all through the night (ibid., 9:14b). At the great wine halls (*chiu-lou*), combination brothels and restaurants as well as hostelries for government guests, built at Nanking at the beginning of the Ming dynasty, the lights burned all night long. In the *Chin-p'ing-mei* we frequently see a dinner at a private home coming to an end late in the afternoon, after which the male guests go on to a "sing-song" house for more wine and pleasure, sometimes not to return for a day or two. One may assume that most family banquets ended by dusk, but that eating and associated pleasures were not limited to that prime time.

Within officialdom, then as now, attending banquets was an inescapable duty. One late Ming scholar official quotes a contemporary from the same stratum of society who said:

> For long I declined all dinner parties of relatives and ordinary friends; it was only the parties offered by scholar-officials that one could not fail to attend. One feared that such persons would think you refused because of differences, and [they] might therefore resent you and speak ill of you. Later, thinking carefully about that, I decided that to neglect one's health and devote one's very life to accompanying others is, despite any comments, a bit ridiculous. Therefore, since gaining my chin-shih degree, I have declined all scholar-official gatherings, and I drink [i.e., feast] only with family and ordinary friends. Even if one wished to avoid giving rise to malicious talk, would he ever succeed? [K. C. Chu 1959 ed., "Yin-hui," p. 402; my translation]

A modern bureaucrat or corporation executive can no doubt feel the force of this complaint that official dinner parties are a perversion of the joys of eating and drinking. However, the more one learns about the food which those long-suffering late Ming bureaucrats encountered in their official banquets, the more one must conclude that our moderns have the more substantial complaint.

Food and Sensuality

That the enjoyment of food is a form of sensuality which if carried to excess becomes depravity was obvious to most Chinese observers of life and troublesome to some. China was a society that usually ate well, but which could know famine, and in which starvation was a standard cause of death. An austerely moralistic strain in Confucianism, particularly in the neo-Confucianism of the Yüan and Ming periods, while not characteristic of the Chinese mentality, was always close at hand. Perhaps more important than that as a restraining factor, however, all schools of thought in China deplored excess as something unreasonable. Society at large was pervaded by a restraining reasonableness. The restrictions on sensuality were typically of that derivation: nondogmatic, rational, yet clearly insistent.

Chinese entertainment literature has often found broad humor in gluttony and in heroic drinking leading to unrestrained behavior; nonetheless, a literature of gross hedonism seems not to have emerged. When, in the second half of the sixteenth century, the *Chin-p'ing-mei* appeared, a massive novel that wallows in sensuality, it became accepted as an important, even classic, work on the grounds that it attempts to dissect the souls of humans who have inflicted uninhibited sensuality on themselves and on others. Critics have seen the novel's achievement in its mastery of those psychological elements of human tragedy.

Whether or not that assessment of the book is valid, the *Chin-p'ing-mei* undoubtedly depicts the experience of sensuality in the fullest detail of any traditional Chinese work. It is important in the history of food for two reasons. First, it employs food explicitly as the counterpart to sex, conceiving of food as an element of experience. Food and sex are the essential stuff of the novel. Clothing, jewels, houses, gardens, flowers, and other creature comforts perceived sensually are also present, but somewhat farther from its focal plane. Food and sex are so intertwined in the telling of this story that it may not be unjustified to claim for it a "bi-sensual modality." The action occurs mainly in multi-phased events in which the experience of food leads to the experience of sex, leading again to food, and then back to sex. Sometimes these phases occupy successive moments or hours in the protagonists' lives; sometimes they are successive scenes in the story's telling. On one or two occasions, ingestion and copulation occur simultaneously. Although sex must be regarded as the major mode of the book, throughout it the involvement with food, the "other mode," occupies more importance than any third realms of action. Those third realms provide merely a setting and establish the credibility of the account. It is through food and sex that the characters are driven to their self-realization, or if that is too positive, to their fullest revelations of themselves.

For this reader, the novel is not a success. As a story it holds a certain fascination, and not merely that of prurience. Recollecting it, some of the minor characters are more memorable than its principals, and the inadvertencies of its telling—all the detail of the setting—hold more meaning than the plot does. One reads it, finally, for the careful depiction of the props rather than because of any identification with its people. If, then, it fails as a novel, it remains an inexhaustible storehouse of Ming social history. That is a sad fate for a work of art, but this work probably deserves that fate. In its bi-sensual modality, the opportunities for saying something new and perceptive about sex eventually run thin; the hero's flamboyant finale may be tragically compelling, but it is also ludicrously contrived.

On the other hand, the opportunities for new and meaningful detail about the humdrum events of daily life and about the continuously stirring experiences of food and drink allow the author to display an unending inventiveness. That is the second reason for the book's importance here. No writer of traditional Chinese entertainment literature was so food conscious. As this book develops its interlocked themes throughout one hundred long chapters, the experience of food and drink remains a vital propellant of its action and of the reader's interest. To the very end, the descriptions of foods and drink transcend formula and offer ever fresh detail. Moreover, although the sex is often engaged in without critical or aesthetic acumen, the food characteristically is offered and received with unfailingly sensitive judgment. Chinese gustatory virtuosity here triumphs over the obvious competitors.[35]

In this novel we perceive an eccentric but wholly Chinese delectation of food and drink as counterparts to the sensations of sexuality.[36]

To illustrate this aspect of the book's reliance on the details of eating and drinking, the scene chosen could be any of a large number. But it may as well be the infamous lovemaking scene in the grape arbor of Hsi-men Ch'ing's garden, in chapter twenty-seven, which the leading modern critic declares is the one the Chinese have traditionally considered to be most obscene (C. T. Hsia 1968, p. 191). Its other qualities, therefore, have often been overlooked. In fact, it is a scene of total sensual involvement, of all kinds, having little action other than a wide spectrum of responses to highly varied sensory stimuli. It begins with a description of intensely hot summer weather and the effects on the senses. A discussion—omitted from the version translated by Egerton—describes three kinds of persons who suffer the most from such heat. Those are peasants in the fields, merchants on the roads, and soldiers on the frontiers. They are graphically contrasted with the imperial household, the noble elite, and the idle rich, whose circumstances permit them such luxury and leisure that they need not fear the heat. Thus, the human body's capacity for varied sensations is brought to the reader's attention, as we turn to Hsi-men Ch'ing, the sensualist hero of this erotic novel. We find him in his garden, enduring the intense heat of midday, listlessly wandering about with his hair let loose, wearing the lightest dress. He watches the young servant boys watering the luxuriantly blooming flowers, whose full color and fragrance he admires. Two of his concubines enter, comparable to flowers in their summer dresses and adornment; the color of their flesh, their lips, their teeth is vividly described. Then begins a long hot afternoon of languid dalliance, commencing with tantalizing remarks, mock reprimand, emotional engagement. They reprove him for his still uncombed hair and offer to help him wash and to dress his hair, there in the garden. One of the women leaves temporarily, and he is greatly moved by the sight of the other's red underclothing, seen through her thin, white, flowing gown. He engages her in sex, in an impromptu fashion appropriate to their sense of freedom and languor, in the less than private corner of the garden; in the course of that, she askes him not to make her endure too long an encounter, as she is newly pregnant.

As they are so involved, Golden Lotus, the other concubine, returns, waits out the scene, then approaches to display her irritation and jealousy. "Why haven't you combed your hair yet?" "I was waiting for the maid to bring the jasmine-scented soap so I can wash my face first." "Must your face always be washed whiter than other people's bottoms?" And so on. The women in his attendance minister to him as he washes and combs; then they bring lutes and play and sing for him, using up the midday. Lotus, however, jealous of the attention granted her pregnant rival, refuses to perform. Wine is ordered. A serving maid immediately brings wine, a bowl of ice with plums, and slices of melon. In the cool garden house they relax, eat, rest, wait. Several pots of delicious wine are consumed, along with trays of exquisite food delicacies. The women, again with the exception of Lotus, play lutes and sing. Hsi-men Ch'ing hands the red ivory castanets to the other concubine and a maid servant. Another maid cools them with a fan. Hsi-men Ch'ing leans indolently in a reclining chair and watches their movement, savoring the sight. More wine is passed around. Golden Lotus, consumed by jealousy and passionate longing, leans over the bowl of chilled fruit and eats. Questioned about her appetite for cooled, raw fruit, she replies that she is not pregnant so need fear no ill consequences. Reprimanded, she parries with a metaphor about the old and plain ones who get only dried preserved meat to eat and must be satisfied with that.

A sudden summer storm blows up clouds and swirling mists. A heavy rain squall passes quickly, as they wait it out in the garden house. A pair of poetic lines inserted here describes the bright greens and reds of rain-washed bamboo and pomegranate blossoms. The cool air following the rain revives them, in the late afternoon, and the sparkling garden scene is described in sensuous language.

The women, after more singing, decide to return to the house, but Hsi-men Ch'ing restrains Golden Lotus. She now agrees to play the lute and sing, and she tantalizes him. Love play now begins in earnest as they dally, wander in the garden, amuse themselves with the flowers, then stop under the grape arbor. Servants now bring food and wine. Here the reader is forced to consider the details of the food which pleasantly distracts the lovers; perhaps the reader's impatience at such points has influenced the deletion of many details in the later editions of the work. In the earlier *Tz'u-hua* text, however, we find the details of the food lovingly set forth. One maid enters carrying a pot of wine, followed by another with a covered sweetmeat box atop which there is a bowl of chilled fruits. Hsi-men Ch'ing turns to this box and opens its lid. Within there are eight divisions containing eight foods: ducks' webs cured in rice-wine dregs; shreds of cured pork cut in a special way; flakes of icefish; sliced pullet wings in jellied sauce; green lotus seeds; fresh walnut meats; fresh pond horned-nuts; peeled raw water chestnuts. The foods evoke a wide range of colors, textures, and flavors, and the feeling of luxury. The center division of the box contains a small but elegant silver wine ewer, containing grape wine, two gold cups in the shape of lotus seedpods, and two pairs of ivory chopsticks. These items are placed on a porcelain table, and the two principals sit facing each other, continuing their games as they eat, their connoisseurship in both food and love depriving the scene of urgent haste. Yet the wine begins to take effect on Golden Lotus; they send the maid for sleeping mats and pillows and for a pitcher of a special medicinal wine. Without waiting for the latter to appear, the infamous love scene begins. It is interrupted by more wine drinking and by an amorous dalliance with the maid who brings the special wine. Lotus is immobilized, her feet tied to the posts of the grape arbor. The scene continues with all three and includes drinking bets between Hsi-men Ch'ing and the maid about whether he can win the game of "tossing golden pellets to bring down the silver swan." The "golden pellets" of the game are jade yellow plums from the bowl of chilled fruits; these are tossed at the nude, supine body of Lotus by the nude Hsi-men Ch'ing, seated with the maid; some of the plums, before or after serving their part in the game, are also eaten, and more wine is drunk. There follows more sex, more drinking, some napping to rest, and more of everything, until dusk and the evening chill remind them all to go off to their quarters in the house to eat and rest.

This is no frantic orgy; passions are aroused and physical action is occasionally vigorous, but there is a calculated, leisurely experiencing of all the sensations of taste, color, fragrance, temperature, form, and action.[37] Without the full range of these sensations, especially those in response to food and drink, the scene would lose its meaning. The particular qualities of very special, highly individualized foods give this scene the stamp of a unique event, even more so than the ingeniously inventive sex play. The specific details concerning the particular foods that appear here are less numerous than in many other scenes,[38] but the role of food in the spectrum of sensations is nowhere better in evidence. In a society in which most people were not idle rich dallying in a garden through the hot summer days, this is ostentatious consumption of an intricately refined sort. This novel of sensuality is by no means typical of the civilization, yet it is, particularly in its uses of food, unlikely to take place in any other civilization.

NOTES

1. This concept is taken from unpublished papers of Joseph Fletcher who proposes the idea of the integrative history of Eurasia and who sees the shift to the integration of the separate histories as having occurred in the sixteenth century.

Dr. William S. Atwell first called my attention to chapter 2, "Daily Bread," and chapter 3, "Superfluity and Sufficiency: Food and Drink," in Fernand Braudel, *Capitalism and Material Life, 1400–1800* (New York, 1973). Braudel's subject is Europe, and the time span of his coverage makes his work interesting for comparison with Yüan and Ming China. He is seriously uninformed and misinformed about China, and about Asia in general, where he attempts comparisons between Europe and "the rest of the world"; I assume that he is reliable in the interesting material he presents on Europe of those centuries.

2. P. T. Ho (1959) on pages 170–71 summarizes his own well-known studies on the history of early-ripening rice. Dwight Perkins (1969) on page 38 ff. questions the interpretation that the importation of superior strains from Champa or elsewhere was alone or principally responsible for the improvement of Chinese varieties of rice, noting the continuous improvement in strains effected by farmers quite on their own, using indigenous varieties.

3. The officially produced *Nung sang chi-yao* (Essentials of Agriculture and Sericulture) of 1270 is credited by Wu Han (1960, pp. 11–13) with having had beneficial impact in government efforts to bring about economic rehabilitation. Other officially sponsored works on agriculture, as well as important privately compiled ones, also date from the Yüan period. See also Amano 1965, and his brief discussion in Yabuuchi 1967, pp. 341–42.

4. Later Ming writers found the Mongol neglect of the ritual proprieties more shocking; *vide* the comments by the late Ming literatus Chang P'u (1602–41), appended

to chaps. 9 and 10 of Ch'en Pang-chan's (*c.s.* 1598) *Yuan-shih chi-shih pen mo*. On the one hand, Chang comments: "They came from the northern wastes, so one can scarcely blame them." But on the other, noting that the Mongol emperors were nonetheless Sons of Heaven, he comments: "How then could the mandate long be enjoyed by them?" The late Ch'ing scholar K'o Shao-min, in his preface to the Treatise on the Rites of his *Hsin Yüan shih* (New History of the Yüan Dynasty) is still more critical (chap. 81).

5. A Ch'ing work on political institutions, compiled under imperial auspices, the *Li-tai chih-kuan-piao* of 1780, cites Sung sources saying that during the *chia-yu* reign (1056–63), of Northern Sung times, the imperial kitchens slaughtered 280 sheep per day.

6. Wada Sei and associates, in annotating their Japanese translation of the Treatise on Food and Money of the *Ming shih*, have called attention to *su yu*, or butterfat, which in early Ming times was supplied to the Ming court by 3,000 cows from an imperial herd of 70,000 (later 30,000) cattle kept for this purpose but also to supply sacrificial cattle and table beef; early in the fifteenth century these herds were sharply reduced, yet imperial dairy herds still supplied butter for shortbreads and pastries at the end of the dynasty. Wada probably is wrong, however, in considering *su yu* to mean "butter" whenever the term is encountered in Ming texts. The same term has long been used to mean any animal fat, particularly mutton tallow and beef tallow (Wada 1957, pp. 929–30).

7. See also a brief comment by Shinoda Osamu in Yabuuchi et al. 1967, p. 325.

8. Shinoda Osamu states that a consequence of Mongol rule was the increased consumption of mutton in northern China. This appears to be merely a plausible notion; no evidence for it is cited (Yabuuchi et al. 1955, p. 79). *Yang chiu*, or "mutton and wine" (sometimes meaning "live sheep and wine") as the standard ceremonial gift for certain kinds of occasions had become a cliché by Han times; dictionaries cite the Biography of Lu Wan as a *locus classicus* for the term (*Shih chi*, chap. 93; Watson 1961, 1:238). The raising of sheep in China and the use of mutton (or of goat, an alternative meaning of *yang* loosely used) is probably underestimated in the minds of many, in part because sheep characteristically were not and are not herded in pastures but are confined, one or two per household, in small pens and thus have not been very visible in the Chinese landscape.

9. In addition to these special levies, the court received large quantities of unusual local products as annual tribute (*sui chin*). Many of these were food products. Regulations governing some of these are found in the *Ta Ming hui-tien*, chap. 113. A full listing of local products submitted to the throne in Ming times appears not to exist; such a list could be painstakingly compiled from gazetteer records, in so far as those exist for all prefectures. The *Ming shih* makes only sketchy references to the procurement activity, in chap. 82; the annotation of the Japanese translation (Wada 1957) usefully supplements that information at some points.

10. For the term *Grand Commandant* (*shou-pei*), see Hucker 1958, p. 61. The garrisons at Nanking, responsible for much of the Grand Canal shipping among other things, frequently were under eunuch command. Ku Ch'i-yuan's account, translated in part here, describes what Ku held up as the proper functioning of the system, in the first

half of the sixteenth century; he complains that it had become subject to much misuse by the early seventeenth century when he was writing.

11. The Ming Founder's sense of the distinction between the Outer and Inner courts, here perceived by him in a quite personal light, holds considerable import for the history of Ming government. No reference to this aspect of the issue is included in the *shih-lu* entry for the day *chia-tzu* (the ninth) of the Twelfth Moon of the Third Year of the Hung Wu reign (December 27, 1370). Nothing other than Sung dynasty precedents are advanced by T'ao K'ai, the Minister of Rites, whose recommendation for establishing the Temple included the statement: "Such sacrificial offerings should employ ordinary daily foods and be conducted as private household rites" (*Ming T'ai-tsu shih-lu*, 59:1151–52).

12. These lists of "ordinary prepared dishes," offered according to a daily schedule, and "fresh produce of the season," offered according to a monthly schedule, with two offerings of each made every day, are not found in the official statutes, although more routine lists of the latter category of items, to be offered each month at the various shrines, are found in many of the works on rites. A list of the daily offerings is also found in Sun Ch'eng-tse's *Ch'un-ming meng-yü lu*, chap. 18. Sun's work dates from shortly after the end of the Ming dynasty, probably from about 1660. It differs in detail from Yao's list somewhat, mainly in that different days are listed for certain foods in a number of cases. Sun's work has, appended to the list, a discussion of costs and of the history of these offerings in later Ming reigns. As far as possible, here and elsewhere in this essay, names of plants are translated according to Y. R. Chao, 1953, and names of fishes according to I. C. Liu et al., 1935, chap. 11, pp. 960–62.

13. It is one of the many peculiarities of the famous Cheng clan of P'u-chiang in Chekiang, in Yüan times, that, in their extreme form of family organization, they separated husbands from wives as well as boys over sixteen from their mothers and sisters at all meals and other family activities. Although honored for their rigorous maintenance of supposed antique forms, the Chengs were not emulated. See John D. Langlois, Jr., "Chin-hua Confucianism under the Mongols, 1279–1368," (Ph. D. diss., Princeton, 1973).

14. Shen Pang's *Wan-shu tsa-chi*, first published in 1593, contains incomparably rich details about arrangements, foods and food supplies, and expenses for official feasts at the *hsien* (county) level; see, for example, pages 136–142 (1961 ed.) for details on the feast for provincial examination winners. Wan-p'ing Hsien, the county government whose operations are described in this work, was one of two county governments attached to the capital at Peking, so its activities may not be typical of all counties in late Ming China. Shen's information may be compared with the much less detailed regulations for feasts to honor new *chin shih* after the triennial palace examinations, in *Ta Ming hui-tien*, chap. 114. Shen Pang's work is being studied by James Geiss of Princeton University, who called this information on county government feasts to my attention.

15. The novel uses the device of setting the action in a previous dynastic period, but all writers have taken it to be an authentic reflection of many aspects of late Ming society. See C. T. Hsia 1968, pp. 165–202; Hanan 1962, pp. 1–57; and Hanan 1963,

pp. 23–67. Specifically on the historical and social relevance of the novel is an article by Wu Han, 1957.

16. The important research on Chinese medical science of Joseph Needham and associates, particularly Dr. Lu Gwei-djen in the field of medicine, is to be presented in a forthcoming volume of Needham's *Science and Civilization in China.* Until that appears, the most important publication in the field relevant to food and hygiene are certain articles by Needham and Lu, particularly five articles (nos. 14–18) reprinted in Needham's *Clerks and Craftsmen in China and the West,* 1970. This is to acknowledge a very large debt to Needham and Lu, while reserving the right to interpret some things differently. Needham is concerned with the intrinsic importance of discoveries in the history of science; this writer is more concerned with the function of knowledge (or what was taken to be knowledge) in the life of the Chinese people.

17. For one example of such skepticism, note the highly rational tone of the prefatory remarks to the Treatise on the Five Agents, which in this context refers primarily to the reporting of prodigal phenomena of nature, in chap. 28 of the *Ming shih.*

18. The *Yin-shan cheng-yao* is the work of a non-Han author. L. C. Goodrich concluded that he was a Mongol (1940), and The Imperial Catalogue of the Ch'ing dynasty (*Ssu-k'u ch'üan-shu tsung-mu t'i-yao,* chap. 22) adopts a new transliteration, indicating that he was held to be of Mongol or other non-Han identity. His ethnic identity is not certain, although Needham writes his name, and writes of him, as if he were a Han Chinese. Lu and Needham (1951) have published a paper in which they claim for the author of the *Yin-shan cheng-yao,* or for the tradition of iatro-dietetics which it represents, "the empirical discovery of vitamins through the study of deficiency diseases." Shinoda Osamu (in Yabuuchi 1967, pp. 329–40) offers a useful survey of the book's contents. Important discussions of philological and other issues are found in Lao Yan-hsuan 1969, and Franke 1970.

19. For a biographical sketch of Chia Ming, see Tung Ku 1937 ed., 28:15b ff. If the interview with the Ming Founder is recorded in the *Ming T'ai-tsu shih-lu,* it has escaped my notice. Shinoda Osamu includes a brief note on the *Yin-shih hsü-chih* in Yabuuchi and Mitsukuni 1970, p. 353.

20. From the vast corpus of Yüan and Ming dramas, fictional works, and informal notes and sketches, I have surveyed for the purposes of this section of this essay the following items: *Ku-pen*; *San-shih chung*; Chu Kuo-chen 1959ed; Feng Meng-lung 1947ed, 1958, 1959; Hsieh Chao-che 1959ed; Ku Ch'i-yuan 1618; Lang Ying 1959ed; Liu T'ung 1957ed; T'ao Tsung-i 1939ed; Yeh Tzu-ch'i 1959. (For details see Bibliography). Also consulted were *Shui-hu Chuan* (14th century), *Chin-p'ing-mei* (late 16th century), and *Ming-jen Tsa-chü Hsüan* (30 dramas by Ming period writers).

I must record here my gratitude for help and guidance to Ch'en Hsiao-lan, whose knowledge of the Yüan and Ming entertainment literature is particularly broad.

21. For another listing of superior foods, from Fukien in late Ming times, see Hsieh 1959 ed., pp. 315–19.

22. Also in *Ku-pen Yüan-Ming tsa-chü,* see no. 12, the opening scene and, especially, no. 110, where rustic delights and rustic eating are the central theme. For Kuan Han-ch'ing's life and work, see Chung-wen Shih 1973, p. 2, and 1976.

23. Ling Meng-ch'u tells of a wife of a high official who herself cooks a feast for her husband's official guests (1967 ed., 30:633). It is not told as extraordinary for that reason. The story is conventionally laid in the T'ang dynasty but can be taken as a reflection of Ming social conditions.

24. Compare this with the rascally cook who cheats a scoundrelly master in *Ku-pen*, no. 16, p. 2a.

25. Shinoda's studies included in Yabuuchi et al. 1967, and in Yabuuchi and Mitsu-kuni 1970, are extremely useful; his *Chūgoku Shokkei Sōsho*, compiled in conjunction with Tanaka Seiichi (1972, 2 vols., Tokyo), has not been available to me.

26. For a genie's banquet, see M. L. Feng 1947 ed., 34:4b. Cf. names of foods served to the immortals, in Y. Ch'ü 1957 ed., pp. 90–91, and as discussed in Ch'ü, fnn. 63–65. The "celestial kitchen" there is the name of a constellation, near the "purple palace" constellation—the essential components of the astral spheres thus matching those of earth.

27. See the episode superbly translated by C. T. Hsia, 1968, pp. 89–92; cf. *Shui-hu chuan*, chaps. 3, 4.

28. See also *Ku-pen*, no. 12, p. 1a, and M. C. Ling 1957 ed., chap. 22. But note M. L. Feng 1958, chap. 15, prologue story, in which a Taoist priest who loves dog meat beomes gentle and benevolent on eating his fill of it.

29. Note also the human-flesh steamed dumplings mentioned in M. L. Feng 1947 ed., 36:10a.

30. Compare this with the humble K'ai-feng inn, which served very good food (M. C. Ling 1957 ed., 11:245).

31. P. T. Ho's work *Chung-kuo hui-kuan shih lun* is the first effort to write a history of the *hui-kuan*, for which he proposes the translation *Landsmannschaften*.

32. Mote calls attention to the emergence of tourists' guidebooks in the sixteenth century, and to some rare examples in the Gest Oriental Research Library of Princeton University (1974, pp. x–xi).

33. The evidence is too extensive to be cited in detail; *Shui-hu chuan* and *Chin-p'ing-mei* both have dozens of relevant passages. See also: M. C. Ling 1957 ed., 14:299, 303; M. L. Feng 1958, 5:3b and 28:9a.

34. The full evidence for the growing extravagance of upper-stratum life in the sixteenth century has not been assembled. Some items bearing on that include: K. C. Chu 1959 ed., p. 398, under the heading "Chiu chin"; Hsieh 1959 ed., pp. 310–15; Wu Han 1935. Robert van Gulik (1951, "Essay," p. 105) also has noted the abundance of the writings from the late sixteenth century devoted to the epicurean appreciation of all civilization's refinements, especially food.

35. The assessments of the novel offered here are not intended as evaluations of its literary merit or of its importance in literary history; for such evaluations see the expert opinions in C. T. Hsia 1968, and in Hanan 1961, 1962, and 1963.

36. In order to apprehend this first, essential aspect of the book, the reader should, preferably, study the novel in the earlier of the two extant Ming redactions (unfortunately, not the one well translated by Clement Egerton under the title *The Golden Lotus*).

37. Egerton, pp. 376–87, translates the corresponding pages of the later edition, which eliminates many of these details.

38. For full descriptions of food and etiquette at major feasts, see, for example, the description of the banquet offered by the women of Hsi-men's household to the women of another household on the important occasion of a betrothal (chap. 43); for detailed descriptions of fancy prepared foods see chap. 42 and passim. For a general discussion of *Chin-p'ing-mei* in relation to the history of food and eating, see Shinoda Osamu in Yabuuchi and Mitsukuni 1970, pp. 380–82.

6: CH'ING

JONATHAN SPENCE

In an odd and grim essay, written during the reign of Chia-ch'ing, Kuan T'ung wrote of "The Land of Hunger." In this land no grains grew and no animals lived, there were no fish, no fruit. It was a terrible journey to this land, but the brave-of-heart could reach it in ten days if they persevered. They would find "an open, bright country which looks as if it were a new universe, [where] management falls into disuse and thought comes to a stop" (T. A. Hsia 1968, pp. 18–19). It was the land of those who had died of starvation, and for Kuan T'ung there was a moral value in reaching this land if suicide was necessary to preserve one's integrity. But for many Chinese, in the Ch'ing period as before and after, the Land of Hunger was a terrible reality that lay beyond choice; and though this is an essay on food and eating, we cannot in justice pursue that topic unless we are aware of the harsh backdrop of famine or the threat of famine. It was the danger of famine that gave such urgency to agriculture and such joys to eating. The hardship can be traced through the litany of the phrase in the local gazetteers, "In this year people ate each other" (*hsiang shih*), even if this was meant as metaphor. It can also be traced through the diets of the starving as recorded painstakingly by Western observers: flour of ground leaves, sawdust, thistles, cotton seeds, peanut hulls, ground pumice (Peking United International Famine Relief Committee 1922, p. 13).

That said, we can turn to look at the staple foods that were generally available to the poor during the Ch'ing period. An impressive roster of these foods has been carefully marshalled in the great corpus of local gazetteers. This source of data is varied in scope and quality and awaits systematic analysis by nutritionists, economists, and social historians, but even a quick glance at a provincial gazetteer for a wealthy area, such as the *Chiang-nan t'ung-chih* (gazetteer of the present provinces of Anhwei and Kiangsu) compiled in 1737, during the major era of Ch'ing tranquillity and prosperity, shows the richness of the resources (see chap. 86). Listed in their original order are wheat, rice, pulse, millet, and hemp, and their glutinous, upland, or late ripening varieties, and the different strains within each variety. Also in the introductory section, dealing with the entire province, are numerous entries under the conventional categories into which food was subdivided at this time: vegetables, fruits, bamboos, grasses, flowering plants, and medicinal plants, as well as animal products, under the categories of feathered or quadruped, followed by fish, crustaceans, and insects. This section is followed by thirty-three pages in which the specialties of every prefecture and county are listed.

My special thanks to Andrew Hsieh for much help with this essay.—*J. S.*

Prefectural gazetteers give equally rich information. Thus in the gazetteer for Yunnan-fu compiled in 1696, there are similar general classifications to those for Chiang-nan, but these are then subdivided according to the eleven counties and *chou* in the Yunnan prefectural districts, making it easy to follow a specific product in a given area. We learn that K'un-ming county was apparently the most prosperous, with tea, textile, and mineral productions, but that each of the smaller areas had its special features: grass paper in Fu-ming, hemp in Lo-tz'u, noodles in Ch'eng-kung, honey and winter squash in K'un-yang, and vinegar in Lu-feng. All these Yunnan communities have one negative factor in common–not one of them lists any of the tailed animals, be it even sheep, cattle, dogs, or hogs, as being present with any abundance (*Yunnan fu-chih*, 2:1–7).

For the sake of contrast at the prefectural level, one can take the Fu-chou-fu gazetteer of 1754. Here, in rich detail but without separate regional classifications, we find that the ten categories have become twenty, filling forty-nine pages (*Fu-chou fu-chih*, chaps. 25, 26). The extra categories come from a much more specialized classification than those found in the Yunnan gazetteer, and the specialization tells us much about local eating habits: plant fruits (*lo*), such as melons, cucumbers, gourds, and taros, have a complete section, as do bamboos and creepers. Fish are distinguished from other scaled creatures, and both shrubs (*chih*) and grasses are sorted out from the broader range of plants and trees. Under *shrubs*, for instance, can be found both tea and tobacco. The latter, a note explains, came to China in the Wan-li period, under the name *tan-pa-ku*, and now grows around Fu-chou (ibid., 25:24). This sudden insertion of the name of a foreign plant into the list of Chinese names can be seen again in the vegetable section, where the sweet potato (*fan-shu*) receives a page of commentary to itself (ibid., 25:4). This commentary states that the sweet potato was made widely known in Fukien during the famine year of 1594 by the governor, Chin Hsueh-tseng. Chin's purpose was to teach the locals to grow a crop that would feed them even if the regular grains failed in times of drought, but his action had consequences far beyond localized famine relief. For, as the commentary points out, not only was this a multifaceted plant that could be boiled or ground or fermented and could be fed to old and young as well as to chickens and dogs, but also it was a plant that would grow in sandy, mountainous, and salty soils, where the regular grains could not take root.

Even the smallest county gazetteers can yield dietary information, either directly or in comparison with others. In the 1673 gazetteer for the poor southern Shantung county of T'an-ch'eng, there are only two pages on local produce (*T'an-ch'eng hsien-chih* 1673, 3:33–34), and there is no discussion of variant strains and nothing on food processing. Yet two things are especially suggestive in this source: first, that no draft or domestic animals are listed, and that the only quadrupeds mentioned are rabbits, two kinds of deer, foxes, and wolves; secondly, that much the largest section is on medicinal plants, thirty-six kinds being listed in all. The same county's gazetteer for the year 1764 has no more space for food than its predecessor (*T'an-ch'eng hsien-chih* 1764, 5:33–36); but the deer, wolves, and foxes are gone, and in their place are sheep and cattle, mules, horses, and hogs. The medicinal plants listed have been cut back to nineteen, and even if we have no firm evidence that this was because the early Ch'ing days of epidemics and warfare had spawned a desperate hunt for cures that was now less urgently felt, the change in the edible animal population does suggest a radical change in life-style.[1]

Though the history of the new Western crops in China starts in the late Ming dynasty, it is in the Ch'ing that their revolutionary effects are felt. The crucial importance of the new plants was not that they provided variety for either the poor or the rich (though they did that), but that they allowed a population that had reached the limits of its traditional resources to expand anew. The Ch'ing population explosion—a rise from approximately one hundred fifty million persons in the early 1700s to about four hundred fifty million by the mid-nineteenth century—was so striking that it must have affected every facet of local life, even though to date scholars have not been able to reconstruct all the elements of that experience. In the course of his studies on the population of China, Ho Ping-ti has come up with some major findings on the effect of these new crops (1959, pp. 183–95). He has demonstrated how maize, sweet potatoes, Irish potatoes, and peanuts all became basic crops in China during the Ch'ing, and how the story of their dissemination is enmeshed with the drama of China's internal colonization.

The sweet potato had become a staple food for the poor in the coastal southeastern provinces by the early eighteenth century; imperial edicts exhorted the people to grow more, and the plant spread west and north. By the end of the eighteenth century, in Ho Ping-ti's estimation, "along the rocky Shantung coast sweet potatoes often accounted for nearly half a year's food for the poor" (ibid., p. 187). Maize transformed agricultural life in Yunnan, Kweichow, and Szechwan during the early Ch'ing and was a key factor in enabling migrants from the overpopulated Yangtze delta region to farm the hills in the inland Yangtze provinces as well as the high ground in the Han River drainage areas of Shensi and Hupei. In these same areas, by the middle of the Ch'ing, the Irish potato made it possible for still other farmers to find a livelihood in lands that were too poor for maize (ibid., p. 188). The changes brought by the peanut were less dramatic, but Ho Ping-ti still found them extensive: "Throughout the last three centuries peanuts have gradually brought about a revolution in the utilization of sandy soils along the lower Yangtze, the lower Yellow River, the southeast coast, particularly Fukien and Kwangtung, and numerous inland rivers and streams. Even within the crowded cropping system of some rice districts, they usually have a place in the rotation because farmers, without knowing the function of the nitrogen-fixing nodules at the roots of the peanut plant, have learned empirically that it helps to preserve soil fertility" (ibid., p. 185). Though accurate figures are impossible to obtain, it is Ho Ping-ti's estimate that the percentage of rice in the national food output may have dropped by about one half in the period between the late Ming and the 1930s, from about 70 percent down to 36 percent. There were also major declines in barley, millet, and sorghum (ibid., pp. 189, 192).

It is not easy to reconstruct local eating habits among the poor either from gazetteers or from specialized population studies, and detailed sources are rare. Fortunately there were some observers like the magistrate Li Hua-nan, who served in Chekiang (in Hsiu-shui Hsien and Yü-yao Hsien) during the 1750s. Li was interested in the local diet, and as he traveled around on business he used to question the locals and jot down his findings.[2] Li did not group the foods in the order customarily followed in the local histories, though he does start his notes with the basic grains and beans. Thereafter he looks at, in turn, pork products, fowl, game, fish, eggs, milk and cheeses, sweet dishes and dumplings, sweet potatoes, mushrooms and squash, ginger, preserved plums, and a variety of vegetables such as garlic and radishes, peanuts, greens, and dates. There is no central theme in this profusion, but certainly Li was deeply interested in the preservation of food rather than in problems of flavor or variety, and we may hazard that this interest was dictated by local realities. When food was rigidly seasonal and in short supply, correct treatment and preparation for storage was essential. The section on flavored sauces made from beans or grains, for instance, has careful instructions on the use of mustard or pepper to keep out insects, the need for cleanliness on the part of the preparer, the cleanliness of the water used, and the rhythms to be followed in opening or closing the storage pots on sunny or humid days (H. N. Li 1968 ed., pp. 76–78).[3] Similar care is taken with the storage of eggs: they should be placed in a crock, big ends up, each covered in a paste composed of 60 to 70 percent reed or charcoal ash, and 30 to 40 percent earth, with wine and salt added. Water should not be added to the paste, or the whites would get too tough. These directions are followed by simple recipes: for boiled eggs and egg rolls, for eggs with milk, for eggs with grated almond and sugar, and for preparing eggs (chicken, duck, or goose) overnight in a scoured pig's bladder (ibid., pp. 31–32b).

This last recipe is a good example of Li's meticulousness in listing all the ways that the pig can be used in cooking, and again it would seem to be an obvious reflection of local preoccupations, since pigs were expensive when one earned perhaps one hundred cash a day, and a pound of pork cost half that (Macartney 1962, p. 162, pp. 244, 254). The farmers had methods for pressing salted pork in a barrel (turning it every five days for a month) before drying it in the wind, and methods for pressing strips of pork; the pork fat could be extracted in boiling water and then preserved with bean sauce; balls were made of pork fat and rolled in egg; pigs' trotters could be stewed with mushrooms; pigs' intestines were used in various recipes, and old pigs' meat was softened up enough to make it edible by repeated boilings followed by soaks in cold water. Li observed other methods for preserving pork leftovers (which could be used with chicken as well): the meat was cut in strips, the strips were notched and salted, crushed garlic was pressed into the meat, which was soaked in wine vinegar. The meat was then smoked over bamboo strips (or supported on metal wires if the peasants had them) and sealed in a clean jar (H. N. Li 1968 ed., pp. 17–21). Li also described newer crops like sweet potatoes and peanuts, though he did not single them out for special attention: he mentions that the sweet potato was peeled, steamed, and pressed through a rice strainer to remove the fibers, before being rolled into strips or dried in cake form (ibid., p. 40); peanuts were boiled, reboiled in salted water, then stored in the water they had been boiled in, or they were drained and stored in pickle juice (ibid., p. 44).

Even with such detailed local descriptions, it is still hard to make any interconnections between the availability of food and the eating of that food. The two variables that remain are the cost of separate items of food and the amount of money available to the purchaser; and there are naturally so many regional differences and price fluctuations that any kind of generalization is immensely difficult. We are fortunate, however, to have for the early Ch'ing period at least one detailed source that gives us prices for a large number of foods—namely the "expenses" (*chih-yung*) section of the Imperial Banqueting Court (the *Kuang-lu Ssu*). These prices were fixed in the early eighteenth century and represent a revision down from earlier figures, which had presumably become inflated because of careless spending habits or because of scarcities in the late Ming and early Ch'ing period. The prices apply to Peking and presumably also represent prices for high-quality goods; but at the very least they give us a comparative base between types of staple food costs, which is essential to any informed survey of Ch'ing food (*Kuang-lu ssu tse-li* 1839, 59:1–12). (See table 1.)

This run of figures can be supported by the comments of a late eighteenth-

Table 1

Grain	Price in copper cash*	Unit
rice	1300	per *shih* (picul; 133 lbs.)
millet	1050	per *shih*
wheat	1200	per *shih*
white beans	1100	per *shih*
red beans	800	per *shih*
Meat, poultry, fish		
pig	2500	each
sheep	1430	each
goose	520	each
duck	360	each
chicken	120	each
small water duck	60	each
quail	25	each
chicken egg	3.5	each
pork	50	per *chin* (catty; 1.33 lbs.)
mutton	60	per *chin*
dried fish	300	per *chin*
venison strips	120	per *chin*
pigs' trotters	28	per *chin*
pigs' liver	27	per *chin*
pigs' bladder	19	each
pigs' intestines	6	each
Fruit		
orange	50	each
apple	30	each
peach	20	each
pear	15	each
persimmon	8	each
betel nut	5	each
walnut	1	each
apricot	3	each
plum	3	each
litchi	100	per *chin*
raisins	80	per *chin*
fresh grapes	60	per *chin*
cherries	60	per *chin*
fresh lotus roots	20	per *chin*
watermelon seeds	40	per *chin*
Dairy		
cow's milk	50	per *chin*
butter	180	per *chin*
Vegetable products		
white honey	150	per *chin*

Vegetable products	Price in copper cash*	Unit
white sugar	100	per *chin*
edible seaweed	100	per *chin*
red honey	80	per *chin*
pickled ginger	70	per *chin*
fresh ginger	46	per *chin*
pickled vegetables	30	per *chin*
pickled cucumbers	25	per *chin*
bean meal	25	per *chin*
millet spirits	21	per *chin*
rock soda	20	per *chin*
soy	12	per *chin*
vinegar	8	per *chin*
bean curd	6	per *chin*

* Assuming 1000 *li* (cash) to the *liang* (tael)

century visitor. In the notes to his journal concerning his 1793 embassy to China, Lord Macartney gave these prices in copper cash for various articles of food: one pound of mutton or pork, 50; a goose, 500; a fowl, 100; a pound of salt, 35; a pound of rice, 24 (Macartney 1962, p. 244). On the basis of his observations, he estimated that a Chinese peasant could live on 50 cash a day; the boatmen who conducted Macartney were paid 80 cash a day; a Chinese foot soldier received 1,600 cash a month, and ten measures of rice (each equivalent to about 130 cash), and his wages accordingly were in the area of 100 cash a day (ibid., pp. 224, 254). Robert Fortune, checking the wages of local tea pickers in the China of the 1850s, found that they received about 150 cash a day, of which about one third was in cash and two thirds in food; he felt that, although their food was simple, "the poorest classes in China seem to understand the art of preparing their food much better than the same classes at home." He contrasted their diet favorably with those of his native Scotland, where "the harvest labourer's breakfast consisted of porridge and milk, his dinner of bread and beer, and porridge and milk again for supper" (Fortune 1857, pp. 42–43).

Even if the diet of the poor was adequate, the question of variety is still unanswered. J. MacGowan, late in the Ch'ing period, found that the coolies in north China ate sweet potatoes three times a day, every day, all through the year, and that the only variations came from small amounts of salted turnip, bean curd, and pickled beans (MacGowan 1907, p. 9). A much more sophisticated analysis, by T. P. Meng and Sidney Gamble, taken from the food sellers' account books of the late Ch'ing, also found comparatively little variety in diet, but they were able to give some precise price fluctuations for a number of the staple items of working-class diet in Peking. (See tables

2, 3, and 4. Prices in tables were computed in dollars at a rate of one dollar to 0.72 taels.) Other calculations show comparative increases between the late Ch'ing and the early warlord period (see table 5).

Table 2

Flour and Grain

Annual Average Prices—Dollars per 100 Catties

Year	Wheat Flour	Wheat Wholesale	Hsiao Mi Mien	Lao Mi	Bean Flour	Millet Retail	Millet Wholesale	Corn Flour
1900	6.41	——	3.90	6.32	5.55	4.45	——	3.06
1901	5.76	3.71	3.29	4.27	5.26	3.62	2.70	2.14
1902	5.52	3.75	3.84	5.37	5.17	4.00	3.40	2.92
1903	5.77	3.87	4.36	6.01	5.38	4.56	3.74	3.48
1904	5.29	3.33	3.90	5.52	5.08	4.35	3.39	3.11
1905	4.88	3.39	3.80	5.35	4.84	4.25	——	2.87
1906	5.71	3.90	4.08	5.80	5.05	4.50	3.47	3.24
1907	6.32	4.50	4.25	6.25	4.95	4.90	——	3.13
1908	5.75	3.91	4.36	6.11	5.07	5.01	3.57	3.65
1909	5.85	3.98	4.32	6.08	5.29	4.98	3.35	3.25
1910	5.94	4.21	4.26	6.53	5.58	5.01	3.73	3.48
1911	6.77	4.88	4.90	7.33	5.97	5.56	4.34	3.74
1912	6.10	4.37	5.10	7.40	6.60	5.91	4.66	3.97

Source: Meng and Gamble 1926, p. 28.

Table 3

Pork and Mutton

Dollars Per 100 Catties

Year	Pork Average	Maximum	Mutton Minimum	Average
1900	9.45	16.20	11.10	14.00
1901	8.75	18.40	12.30	15.30
1902	10.10	13.80	8.70	10.00
1903	10.40	15.60	8.90	11.30
1904	10.80	——	——	——
1905	10.70	16.00	12.80	14.60
1906	10.70	15.90	11.60	13.80
1907	11.40	18.10	9.80	14.80
1908	11.40	14.10	11.10	12.50
1909	10.80	13.10	8.50	10.50
1910	11.40	13.30	9.00	11.00
1911	11.40	19.40	10.80	14.63
1912	11.20	19.50	9.80	13.10

Source: Meng and Gamble 1926, pp. 38–39.

Table 4

Oils, Salt, Salt Vegetable

Annual Average Prices—Dollars Per 100 Catties

Year	Sweet Oil	Peanut Oil	Salt	Salt Turnip
1902	16.00	13.20	2.98	1.11
1903	16.70	13.30	2.98	1.25
1904	16.40	13.60	2.98	1.11
1905	17.40	13.85	2.98	1.25
1906	16.95	13.20	3.62	1.11
1907	18.09	13.85	3.62	1.25
1908	17.50	13.60	3.62	1.25
1909	17.22	13.30	4.45	1.39
1910	18.09	13.60	4.45	1.25
1911	18.75	13.85	4.45	1.39
1912	18.09	15.25	4.17	2.08

Source : Meng and Gamble 1926, p. 57

Table 5

Percentage Increases

	1900–1924	1913–1924
Wheat Flour	42	49
Bean and Millet Flour	87	11
Corn Flour	102	59
Rice	14	53
Millet	58	17
Black Beans	150[b]	47
Green Beans	122[a]	44
Bean Flour	40[a]	17
Pork	101	62
Mutton	14	3
Sweet Oil	44[c]	18
Peanut Oil	44[c]	37
Salt	56[c]	7
Salt Turnip	109[c]	4
Wine	31[c]	31
Chiang Yu	40[c]	44
Bean Sauce	37[c]	24
Vinegar	150[c]	118
Cloth	160	51
Coal	16	37
Index Number	80	44
Copper Exchange	264	106
Copper Wages		
Skilled	258[a]	80
Unskilled	232[a]	100

Percentage Increases

	1900–1924	1913–1924
Silver Wages		
Skilled	61	48
Unskilled	27	34
Real Wages		
Skilled	–2	12
Unskilled	–17	8

Source: Meng and Gamble 1926, p. 71.

[a] 1900 to middle of 1924
[b] 1901–1924
[c] 1902–1924
– = Decrease

One of the other findings of the same investigators was that the monthly fluctuations could be extreme in times of political unrest. White flour, for example, was $5.84 per 100 catties in January 1900; in May it was $5.15; by September it was $8.33; in December $6.94, and back to $5.53 in July 1901 (Meng and Gamble 1926, pp. 11–12). Such figures still do not give exact prices for individual worker's diets during the Ch'ing—the nearest we can get to these is through the study made by L. K. Tao of the poor families in Peking, most of whom were ricksha men with wives who supplemented the tiny family income with sewing or the making of artificial flowers. The list of foods consumed by these families in the 1920s may well still reflect the Ch'ing conditions. Tao found that the foods purchased by every family were, among the grains, millet, millet flour, hand-milled wheat flour, and coarse corn flour. Other staples were cabbage, sesame oil, salt, soy paste, and vinegar. The only meat bought by all was mutton. The foods bought in some quantity by over 90 percent of the families were rice, buckwheat flour, salted *ke-te*, sweet potatoes, yellow bean sprouts, garlic, *Allium odorum*, sesame paste, and shrimp. Peanuts were bought by 89.6 percent (L. K. Tao 1928, table 14, pp. 78–79). Expressed in percentages by category, 80 percent of the workers' food expenditures went to cereals, 9.1 percent to vegetables, 6.7 percent to condiments, 3.2 percent to meats, and only 1 percent to all refreshments, including fruit (ibid., table 16, p. 96). There was more variety, however, among mill workers in Shanghai during the same period. They spent only 53.2 percent of their income on cereals, 18.5 percent on legume and vegetable products, 7 percent on meats, 4.4 percent on fish and seafoods, and 1.9 percent on fruit (S. Yang and Tao 1931, table 26, p. 51). But even if this was a survival diet, it left little leeway for the other expenses of life. The 230 Shanghai families surveyed spent 0.3 percent on toilet accessories,

0.3 percent on amusements, and 0.2 percent on education (ibid., table 38, p. 68). It is possible that standards were often higher in the Ch'ing country-side, and also that the rosters of local religious festivals provided both entertainment and dietary variety on a seasonal basis,[4] but there is probably little reason to challenge the assertion made by John Barrow during his visit to China in the Chia-ch'ing reign: that in the assortments of food there was a wider disparity in China between rich and poor than in any other country of the world (cited in Williams 1883, 1:772).

The Gourmets

Clearly, the many rebellions that occurred during the Ch'ing sprang from a base of rural misery and hunger that was exacerbated by a soaring population living on marginal lands as well as by the serious disruptions of Western imperialism. At the same time, among the gentry there was a sense of cultural pride—of having inherited the accumulated richness of a long and varied past. Here, the culinary arts were treated as a serious matter, as a part of the life of the mind. There was a Tao of food, just as there was a Tao of conduct and one of literary creation. Food, in some form, was taken as a subject by many Ch'ing writers. Often they merely reproduced, or commented briefly on, various older recipe collections; but some, such as Li Yü, Chang Ying, Yü Huai, Wu Ching-tzu, Shen Fu, and Yüan Mei—all significant figures in the history of Ch'ing culture—had strong views which they expressed forcefully.

An entrance into this world of gourmet sensibilities is provided by Wu Ching-tzu in *The Scholars* (*Ju-lin wai-shih*), written during the Ch'ien-lung reign. In this novel, the characters are not defined merely in terms of their appetites and their approach to food, they are presented as being what they eat. The characters of Chou Chin and Wang Hui, for instance, are perfectly caught in this brief paragraph:

> As they were chatting, lights were brought in, and the servants spread the desk with wine, rice, chicken, fish, duck and pork. Wang Hui fell to, without inviting Chou Chin to join him; and when Wang Hui had finished, the monk sent up the teacher's rice with one dish of cabbage and a jug of hot water. When Chou Chin had eaten, they both went to bed. The next day the weather cleared. Wang Hui got up, washed and dressed, bade Chou Chin a casual goodbye and went away in his boat, leaving the schoolroom floor so littered with chicken, duck and fish bones, and melon-seed shells, that it took Chou Chin a whole morning to clear them all away, and the sweeping made him dizzy. [C. T. Wu 1957, p. 59]

Such a simple contrast, between rectitude and greed, could be carried further into pure parody when discussing the salt merchants—often a butt of the literati—with their solemn talk of trying to find some "hibernating toad" to round off the perfect meal (ibid., p. 325). The wedding feast given by the pretentious Lu family is another illustration. In this remarkable scene, first a rat falls from the rafters into the bird's-nest soup, and then, as the cook kicks at a dog, one of his shoes flies off and lands squarely upon a dish of pork dumplings and dumplings stuffed with goose fat and sugar (ibid., pp. 168–69). The meal is well and truly ruined, and a social point is firmly made.

This literary representation was one aspect of the intelligentsia's culture tightly enmeshed with gourmet living. Of the many Ch'ing scholars interested in food and its principles, Yüan Mei was probably the most vociferous and the most persuasive. He prefaced his recipe book, *Shih-tan*, with a dozen pages of exhortations and warnings to his contemporaries, phrased as basic premises (*hsü-chih*) of cookery which could not be ignored if the execution was to be successful—the message seems to be directed both to the cook and to the reader as a sensitive eater. The initial principle was to understand the natural properties (*hsien-t'ien*) of a given food (M. Yüan 1824 ed., p. 1). Thus the pork should be thin skinned and fragrant, the chicken in its prime, the carp white of stomach and slender in shape. The search for ideal ingredients meant that the credit for any fine banquet must be divided two ways, with 60 percent going to the cook and 40 percent going to the man supervising the marketing (*mai-pan*). The choice of the condiments was equally important: soys, oils, wines, and vinegars all have their own attributes and defects. Yüan does not retreat here into generalities but gives specific advice (presumably for products in the Nanking area where he was living in the mid-eighteenth century). Thus, for oil one should choose the best grade of the Su-chou "Ch'iu-yu"; with vinegar one should guard against those with fine coloration but a flavor not quite sharp enough to provide the true purpose (*pen-chih*) of vinegar. Chen-chiang vinegar suffered from this flaw; the vinegar from Pan-p'u in Kiangsu was undoubtedly the best, with that from P'u-k'ou in Chekiang ranking second (ibid., p. 16). Washing and cleanliness of the food were also important: obviously, no trace of feather should adhere to the birds' nests, no mud should remain on the sea slugs, and no sand should be left with the sharks' fins; the meat must be without gristle, the venison without any rancid parts, and care must be taken to see that the fishes' gall has not been ruptured so that the flesh is bitter (ibid., pp. 1b–2).

Yüan then proceeded to consider fundamental questions of balance in a given meal. Flavoring must be discriminating and clear, closely allied to the food's nature: the use of wine and water, salt and sauces, separately or in combination, was one focus; the balance of foods in a dish, in terms of blandness, clarity, and richness, was another. It would be folly to put powdered crab (*hsieh-fen*) with the birds' nest, for example, or lilium japonicum (*pai-ho*) with chicken and pork. Good strong flavors, such as eel, turtle, crab, shad (*shih*), beef, and mutton, should all be left to stand on their own (*tu-shih*) (ibid., pp. 2–3).

These initial sections show the gourmet's approach to the overall strategy of a meal, and in his section on warnings (*chieh*), a few pages further on, Yüan Mei gives two amusing personal examples of what he considered disastrous meals:

A good cook cannot with the utmost application produce more than four successful dishes in one day, and even then it is hard for him to give proper attention to every detail; and he certainly won't get through unless everything is in its right place and he is on his feet the whole time. It is no use to give him a lot of assistants; each of them will have his own ideas, and there will be no proper discipline. The more help he gets, the worse the results will be. I once dined with a merchant. There were three successive sets of dishes and sixteen different sweets. Altogether, more than forty kinds of food were served. My host regarded the dinner as an enormous success. But when I got home I was so hungry that I ordered a bowl of plain rice-gruel. From this it may be imagined how little there was, despite this profusion of dishes, that was at all fit to eat.

I always say that chicken, pork, fish and duck are the original geniuses of the board, each with a flavour of its own, each with its distinctive style; whereas sea-slug and swallows-nest (despite their costliness) are commonplace fellows, with no character—in fact, mere hangers-on. I was once asked to a party given by a certain Governor, who gave us plain boiled swallows-nest, served in enormous vases, like flower-pots. It had no taste at all. The other guests were obsequious in their praise of it. But I said: "We are here to eat swallows-nest, not to take delivery of it wholesale." If our host's object was simply to impress, it would have been better to put a hundred pearls into each bowl. Then we should have known that the meal had cost him tens of thousands, without the unpleasantness of being expected to eat what was uneatable. [Ibid., pp. 8b–9; trans. Waley 1956, pp. 195–96]

A group of Yüan's exhortations are directed firmly to the cook, such as the heat of the fire that should be maintained, the type of utensils, and cleanliness while cooking. He divided fires into two basic categories, *wu-huo* ("military heat") for fast frying and *wen-huo* ("civil," or "literary," heat) for slower cooking. Clams, eggs, chicken, fish—each has the heat that is right for it; the cook must gauge this and not constantly peer into the pot to check the food's progress. If he does so, the water will bubble too much, and the flavor will be lost; the fish will become dead in taste. "Certainly to have a fresh fish and to cause it to become unfresh is a terrible act" (M. Yüan 1824 ed., p. 3; my translation). Also, strong flavored foods should each be cooked in a separate pot. Some people cook up chicken, duck, pork, and goose in a single pot, and the result is an indistinguishable mass—it's "like chewing wax. I fear that these chickens, pigs, geese, and ducks have souls and will lodge a formal complaint with the god of the underworld" (ibid., p. 4; my translation). The same principles applied to other utensils: you don't cut bamboo with a knife that has just cut scallions; you don't crush food with a pestle that has just been crushing pepper; nor do you use a dirty dish cloth or cutting board, the flavor of which can linger on the food. The good cook sharpens his knives, uses a clean towel, scrapes down the chopping-board, and washes his hands; he keeps tobacco ash, flies, ash from the fire, and his own sweat, all safely away from the food (M. Yüan 1824 ed., p. 6).

At one point in his cookbook, Yüan Mei criticized a recipe of the earlier Ch'ing writer Li Yü for being "profoundly artificial" (*chiao-jou tsao-tso*) (ibid., p. 9). This was not just a squabble between gourmets, since Li Yü (Li-weng, 1611–1680) had considerable fame and literary influence. What Yüan objected to in Li seems to have been a kind of overdeveloped rusticity combined with fancifulness, which led Li to tamper with decent materials, thus violating one of Yüan's basic canons. In his cookbook, Li had criticized meat eaters for being vulgar and wasteful, though he was not a vegetarian; and he recommended meats on the basis of the animal's nature (instead of on the actual flavor and texture of their flesh, as Yüan would have done). Li did not want to discuss eating cattle or dog, since they were friends to humans; chickens he valued because they awoke humans in the morning; geese could be readily eaten, since they were of no use to humans, and fish and shrimp could be eaten with a light heart since they laid so many eggs (Y. Li 1963 ed., pp. 264–69).[5] Li also rejected scallions and garlic, because of their "foulness" (*wei*) on the breath; he would eat only the tips of chives; and instead of any of these three, he recommended the tender flavor of the rarer, and more fragrant, juniper berry (ibid., pp. 258–59; Lin and Lin 1969, p. 43). Radishes he rejected because they caused hiccups and fouled the breath, though he accepted pepper because it would liven up a sleepy person and was like "meeting a virtuous man" (Y. Li 1963 ed., p. 259). To make the best rice, Li would send his maid to gather the dew from the flowers of the wild rose, the cassia, or the citron and would add this to the water at the last minute; dew from garden roses, however, was too strong in flavor, felt Li, and could not be recommended (ibid., p. 261; Lin and Lin 1969, p. 43). With noodles, too, Li sought an extreme purity of taste, though in his concentration on a few light, clear tastes in his noodle recipes he seems to have been nearer to Yüan than in some of his overrefined moments: his method depended on keeping a light broth, with only a touch of soy or vinegar in the water, which would then be poured over the noodles, which had been prepared with a touch of sesame and bamboo shoots, with a flavoring of mushroom or shrimp sauce (Y. Li 1963 ed., p. 263).

One modern culinary critic has felt that "there may have been something of the *poseur* in Li" (Lin and Lin 1969, p. 43). It certainly seems that he allowed his moral biases and his overrefinement to interfere with the pursuit of robust flavors. He also professed a liking for a type of culinary order— "five fragrances in my daily foods, eight flavors when I have guests" (Y. Li 1963 ed., p. 263)—which was just the kind of thing that irritated Yüan. It was Yüan's feeling that strict patterns in a dinner were only good in very rare circumstances, like the formal T'ang poetic modes; otherwise, the sixteen dishes, eight platters, four desserts, etc., of both the regulated Manchu and Chinese dinner parties became too constricting (M. Yüan 1824 ed., pp. 11b–12).

The manner of serving a meal was also of major importance to Yüan, as it was to his wealthy contemporaries. Invitations should be issued at least three days in advance, to allow the meal to be planned properly. If traveling, one must have along some special recipes for foods that could be cooked in a hurry if one had suddenly to give hospitality—fried chicken strips, bean curd and tiny shrimp, fish cured in grain spirit (*tsao-yü*), or fine ham. In serving up the food, one should keep away from overexpensive Ming porcelain, and build up the table simply with a variety of shapes from the finer Ch'ing potteries. Small bowls should be used for the cheaper dishes, fried food should be served on platters, and simmered food should be warmed only in pottery, not in metal (ibid., p. 46). It was important to use as many expensive ingredients as possible, and as few cheap ones, but it was also important not to cook too much in bulk: half a *chin* (about ten ounces) was the maximum amount of meat that would fry through properly in one pan, Yüan thought, and six ounces the maximum amount of chicken or fish. Other dishes, of course, had to be cooked in bulk if they were to have any real flavor: for broiled white pork you needed at least twenty chin (about 26 pounds), and for a thick conjee a peck of rice was ideal (ibid., p. 5b). Dishes must always be cooked and eaten one by one, not piled on the table in profusion, and the cook should utilize as many parts of a given fish or animal as possible (ibid., pp. 9b–10)—here Yüan shared some of the basic frugality of Li Hua-nan. The elegance that such serving could attain has been described by Yüan's contemporary Shen Fu, who talked of the economies worked out by his wife, Yuen:

> Poor scholars, who must of necessity be economical about such things as clothes and food, houses and furniture, can try, nevertheless, to see that their surroundings are clean and in good taste. In order to be economical, the proverb says "act in accordance with circumstances," or "cut one's coat according to one's cloth."
>
> I am very fond of a little wine with my meals but I do not like elaborate food, nor too many dishes at a time. Yuen made a plum flower tray, for which she used six deep white porcelain dishes, about two inches in diameter, arranging five of them about the centre dish in the manner of a five-pointed star. When the box had been painted a light grey, the whole thing looked like a plum blossom, the tray and its cover both having indented edges, and the cover having a handle like the stem of a flower. When it was placed on the table, the tray looked like a fallen plum blossom, and the lifted cover showed the vegetables served in the petals. One of these trays, with its six different dishes, contains enough for a pleasant meal for two or three close friends. If the dishes are emptied, they can always be refilled for second helpings.
>
> We also made another tray, a round one with a low border, which we found handy for holding our cups, chopsticks, wine pots and such things. These trays could be carried to any place one wished and were easy to remove again afterwards. This is an example of economy in the matter of food. [F. Shen 1960 ed., p. 70]

Shen Fu emphasized that friendly word games and steady drinking went hand in hand with gourmet eating of the highest order; and though fairly poor, he and his wife were usually able to sit down to perfect dishes of melon, shrimp, vegetables, and fish (ibid., p. 65). This combination of frugality and refinement was a part of the genre of elegant simplicity much appreciated in mid-Ch'ing China; thus we find Shen Fu, a paramount sensualist, describing the eating of fresh Canton litchis as one of the keenest pleasures of his whole life, and packing up his own stock of crabs steeped in wine, for the journey south that was to give him this pleasure (ibid., pp. 38, 52). And a novel like Ts'ao Hsüeh-ch'in's *Hung-lou meng* is dotted with references to special items of rare food (or perfect specimens of simple food) that brought unusual pleasure: goose foot preserves, for instance, or a soup with chicken skin; junket and mince; a particularly fragrant koumiss; or cypress-smoked, Siamese suckling pig (H. C. Ts'ao 1973 ed., pp. 192, 195, 370, 376, 519).

The eating habits of one group of Yüan's contemporaries and fellow provincials, the Chinese merchants of Kiangsu and Chekiang who were temporarily residing in Nagasaki, were studied with interest by a Tokugawa official, Nakagawa Shundai. He noted that the basic essentials of daily diet for the merchants were rice and tea, vinegar, soy, pickles, squash, and black beans; their average daily meal was only three or four dishes: for breakfast, some conjee and dried vegetables with pickled cucumber and radishes; and simple dishes of either meat or fish for the noon and evening meals (Nakagawa 1965, pp. 9, 31). But in their meals for guests, they followed a clear ritual of sixteen dishes, including bear's paw, deer tail, sharks' fins, birds' nests, and sea slugs; as well as fried lamb, pigs' trotters "in the Su Tung-p'o style" (a dish which Li Yü had found vulgarized), two kinds of chicken, duck, goose, steamed fish, crab sauce, dried mussels, and fish belly (ibid., pp. 19–24; Y. Li 1963 ed., p. 265). In the ten-dish meal, for second-class occasions, the dishes omitted were bear's paw, deer tail, wild chicken, goose, crab, and mussels. The sharks' fins and lamb were further omitted if the meal was a third-class one of eight dishes (Nakagawa 1965, p. 26).

The Chinese at Nagasaki also drank a good deal of wine, noted Nakagawa (ibid., p. 9), thus alerting us to another problem in trying to assess the general gourmet eating habits of the Ch'ing. Shen Fu, who was disarmingly frank about such matters, admitted that he got so drunk on his wedding night in 1780 that he passed out even before reaching the nuptial chamber (F. Shen 1960 ed., p. 7). Yüan Mei was quite certain that wine in excess would spoil one's appreciation of the food, but he also had a deep love of good wine and confessed to drinking sixteen cups of an irresistible dark wine made from millet in Li-shui, until his head reeled; on another occasion, a sweet and heavy Su-chou wine led him to take fourteen cups, despite his best intentions (M. Yüan 1824 ed., p. 78).[6] In a delightful passage, he likened wine to the bullies among the people, or the runners in the county yamen: the bullies prove their worth when they chase away more dangerous bandits, and the runners can be useful in getting rid of thieves; so wine is at its most useful when you have a cold or have overeaten. He thought that the wine made in Fen-chou fu, Shansi, was probably the best, with the kaoliang wine of Shantung second. Such wine could be stored for a decade, till it grew greenish and sweet—just like a bully who has been a bully so long that he's lost his temper and could now be a true friend of yours. Such wine was delicious with pig's head or lamb's tail. Su-chou wines were often inferior, and he thought Shao-hsing wine overrated. There was even a Yang-chou quince (*mu-kua*) wine which was considered so unworthy that one was vulgarized just by tasting it (*shang-k'ou pien-su*) (ibid., p. 78).

It is hard to distinguish the various social and personal functions of heavy drinking, but it was not just a mid-Ch'ing phenomenon. In the K'ang-hsi reign (1662–1722), Han T'an apparently drank himself to death while president of the Board of Rites. Also during this reign, the membership of one drinking club included such worthy scholars as T'ang Pin, Shen Ch'üan, and Chang Ying, and each member had his own special cup inscribed with his name (Liang 1969 b ed., 4:1–2). Earlier in the same reign, Yü Huai described drinking parties that went on in Nanking till all the guests vomited and fell asleep on the ground (Yü Huai 1966 ed., p. 95). This was in the brothel quarter, where drinking was naturally heavy, and where courtesans were prized for their abilities to direct, monitor, and participate in heavy drinking games (ibid., p. 74). But such drinking games were also common in polite society. Shen Fu's wife drank heavily with his new potential concubine (F. Shen 1960, pp. 55–56). P'u Sung-ling has a story of a remarkable drinking game that depended on one's luck in drawing various terms with food and drink radicals out of the text of the Rites of Chou (P'u 1969 ed., p. 70). There is enough evidence to suggest that, among the literati, wine and food were firmly intertwined as parts of the good life.

Food blurred with wine, and the wine itself blended into moments of sensual pleasure; and in this epicurean Ch'ing atmosphere, with money and women amply available to men of power and taste, it is not surprising that the vocabularies of food and lust should overlap and blend into a language of sensuality. Shen Fu saw the sixteen year old virgin Han-yuan—who became, briefly, the love of both his and his wife's life—as being "sweet and ripe as a melon ready for cutting" (F. Shen 1960 ed., p. 54). Such similes had been common in male poetry (though perhaps blossoms and flowers and leaves were seen as more appropriate) and had been strongly present in female poetry since at least the eighth century, as we can see from the evocative poems of the prostitute Chao Luan-luan, with her "fresh peeled spring onions," "small cherries," "white melon seeds," and "purple grapes" (Rexroth and Chung 1972, pp. 26–30); and we need not trouble to compile a list of these from the Ch'ing. But a few brief examples from the *Hung-lou meng* are a proper concern for a study of Ch'ing food and are relevant at this point, since the readers of the novel were presumably the same gourmets we have been discussing: the literate elites, the educated merchant families, and their women, who found satisfaction in taking elegant time off from the classics or their work. Certainly these readers would have found pleasure in Ts'ao Hsüeh-ch'in's imaginative plays upon conventional imagery: "blinds looped and fringed like a prawn's belly" (H. C. Ts'ao 1973 ed., p. 359); a little girl with "cheeks as white and fresh as a fresh lychee and a nose as white and shiny as soap made from the whitest goose-fat" (ibid., p. 89)—even if Ts'ao Hsüeh-ch'in was near self-parody here; and they would have appreciated the young girls of the novel being linked to Pao-yü, the lipstick eater, by images of redness and fruit, with their "apricot" and "peach" quilts and their "strawberry" dresses (ibid., pp. 392, 415, 469).

But the vocabulary of food was able to enrich the language all the more through the complex plot structure of the novel that developed in the Ch'ing. For here the form gave room to a new kind of leisurely exploration of metaphor and to the use of echoes, not of past works in a similar genre, but of past sections of the same work. One way Ts'ao Hsüeh-ch'in developed a subplot was to link it to food or drink. Thus, the moving scene in which Pao-yü realizes, for the first time, that his family cannot control everything and that his beloved maid and lover, Aroma, might actually buy her freedom out of bondage comes just after the koumiss he had saved for her has been drunk out of spite by Nanny Li. This episode, in turn, is prepared for by Pao-yü's sexual innuendo to Aroma in her own home, when (referring to the koumiss) he whispers, "I've got something nice waiting for you when you get back"; Aroma whispers, "Sh! Do you want them all to hear you?" As she says this, she reaches out and takes the Magic Jade from his neck (ibid., p. 381–82). David Hawkes, the translator of this novel, has pointed to the sexual role of the Jade in Pao-yü's life, while the koumiss itself was originally a gift from the Imperial Concubine (ibid., p. 32, n. 8; p. 376).

A similar type of echo is used to add poignancy to Ch'in Chung's death. In a scene of love and youthful sensuality, Ch'in Chung jokes with the pretty novice, and she ripostes, "I must have honey on my hands" (ibid., p. 296). And as Ch'in Chung dies, Pao-yü and his servants rush to the bedside "like swarming bees" to gaze at his "waxen" face (ibid., p. 321). These images of bees and honey are only one fragment of the intricate pattern of oral and anal imagery that Ts'ao Hsüeh-ch'in had woven around the two young boys: they get to know each other while eating (ibid., p. 179); Ch'in Chung is admitted to the clan school after the extraordinary scene in which an old family servant shouts of the family's filth and has his mouth stuffed with manure as a punishment (ibid., pp. 183–84); the two boys are mocked by schoolfellows with a suggestive jingle about "nice hot cakes" (*hao shao ping*) (ibid., p. 208);[7] Ch'in Chung's sexual initiation with the novice and with Pao-yü takes place in Wheatbread Priory ("so-called because of the excellent steamed wheatbread made in its kitchens") (ibid., pp. 294, 299–300); Ch'in Chung's exhaustion after these goings-on is expressed by "loss of appetite" (ibid., p. 302); and his brief respite from death is ended by choking (ibid., p. 323).

An equally complex series of ambiguities lies behind one of the few pastoral poems that appears in the *Hung-lou meng*. Nothing could seem much more conventional than this:

The Hopeful Sign

An inn-sign, through the orchards half-discerned,
Promises shelter and a drink well-earned.
Through water-weeds the pond's geese make their way;
Midst elms and mulberry-trees the swallows play.
The garden's chives are ready to prepare;
The scent of young rice perfumes all the air.
When want is banished, as in times like these,
The spinner and the ploughman take their ease.

[Ibid., p. 370]

But Ts'ao Hsüeh-ch'in does not let his Ch'ing readers rest in that bucolic vision. For, in arriving at the selection of this poem as the decoration for a certain spot in the Imperial Concubine's progress, Pao-yü had cited the lines, "A cottage by the water stands / Where sweet the young rice smells," as if to echo the musings of his father, who had just been moved enough by the sight of neat rows of vegetables to declaim that "it awakens the desire to get back to the land, to a life of rural simplicity" (ibid., pp. 334–35). The irony is intense, because Pao-yü is echoing his own earlier thought that came to him when, for the only time in his life, he actually visited a farm, talked to a farm girl, and saw the conditions of life there: only then, says Pao-yü, did he begin to understand the lines, "Each grain of rice we ever ate / Cost someone else a drop of sweat" (ibid., p. 292). Yet Pao-yü remained trapped in his upbringing, with the gourmet tastes he had acquired. For, in his only other visit to a poor family's home, after surveying the carefully arrayed dishes of cakes, dried fruits, and nuts, the best that they could offer to their young master, Pao-yü's maid realized sadly "that there was nothing there which Pao-yü could possibly be expected to eat" (ibid., p. 381).

The Imperial Level

At the level of the imperial court, food played many roles. One was the symbolic and sacrificial—the use of food as sacrifice to the gods, with the regulation of those offerings to the minutest detail of vessel and of placement (*Ch'in-ting Ta-Ch'ing hui-tien t'u*, pp. 1139–437). Here the Ch'ing followed precedent, and there do not seem to have been any significant innovations as far as the Chinese ceremonial usages were concerned. The Manchus did add their own new level of ancestral shamanistic religion; and, in their own temples, they added further sacrifices of pigs and grain to placate their own gods—even though the meanings or significance of these gods' names had already been forgotten as early as the Ch'ien-lung reign (*Ch'in-ting pa-ch'i t'ung-chih*, chaps. 89–93).

The maintenance of food production, of course, was at the center of the court's preoccupations, since it was the taxation on the peasants' surplus that sustained the entire apparatus of empire and bureaucracy; here again, the Ch'ing did not significantly modify earlier policies concerning dike construction and maintenance, emergency grain price stabilization, assessment and collection of taxes, or the shipping northward of the "grain tribute" from the south to feed the capital troops. The most significant shift was in the percentage of the total Ch'ing tax yields that the land tax represented; for, while the amount of land tax did steadily increase during the Ch'ing, the percentage of total revenue that this represented dropped from 73.5 percent during the Ch'ien-lung reign to 35.1 percent by the end of the dynasty—the massive new revenue sources being the Maritime customs and the *likin* (customs charges) (Wang Yeh-chien 1973, pp. 79–80).

Feeding the court was a massive enough problem, as it had been in all earlier dynasties. Here the Ch'ing slowly moved from reliance on the produce of their own estates and the collection of miscellaneous "tribute" items of local specialities, to a centralized purchasing system operated by the Accounts section of the Imperial Household. In the late Ch'ien-lung reign, this office annually purchased 750,000 piculs of cereals, 400,000 eggs and 1,000 catties of wine (Chang Te-ch'ang 1972, p. 254), though these enormous quantities only represent a small part of the overall administrative concerns with food. The Imperial Buttery (*ch'a shan fang*) section of the Imperial Household, as described in the Ch'ing Statutes, is a network of offices for meats, tea and milk, pastries, wines, pickles, and fresh vegetables. A huge staff of cooks and their assistants worked to prepare the daily specifications for persons of varying ranks in the Household, from the Emperor himself downwards in decreasing amounts through the hierarchy of consorts to the princes and princesses (*Ch'in-ting Ta-Ch'ing hui-tien shih-li*, chap. 1192).

There is evidence that, despite their general reputation for extravagance, many of the Ch'ing emperors had in fact quite simple tastes: K'ang-hsi liked fresh meats, simply cooked, fish, and fresh fruit (Spence 1974, chaps. 1, 4); Kuang-hsü would breakfast lightly on milk, rice gruel, and flat wheat cakes (Der Ling 1935, p. 73). A menu of one of Ch'ien-lung's meals in 1754 sounds delicious, but far from flamboyant (C. Su 1966, p. 16):

Main Course Dishes

A dish of fat chicken, pot-boiled duck, and bean curd, cooked by Chang Erh

A dish of swallows' nests and julienned smoked duck, cooked by Chang Erh

A bowl of clear soup, cooked by Jung Kui

A dish of julienned pot-boiled chicken, cooked by Jung Kui

A dish of smoked fat chicken and Chinese cabbage, cooked by Chang Erh

A dish of salted duck and pork, cooked by Jung Kui

A dish of court-style fried chicken

Pastries

A dish of bamboo-stuffed steamed dumplings

A dish of rice cakes

A dish of rice cakes with honey

Pickles

*Served in a ceramic container patterned
with hollyhock flowers*

Chinese cabbage pickled in brine

Cucumbers preserved in soy

Pickled eggplant

Rice

Boiled rice

But the personal tastes of the emperor had little to do with the scale of culinary operations or their costs. The regulations were firm about the exact content of all major meals, which were carefully graded in accordance with their level of ritual significance.

The records of the Imperial Banqueting Court (*Kuang-lu Ssu*) were published late in the Ch'ing, and from these we can note some of the variations. There seem to have been six basic grades of Manchu banquets (*Man-hsi*) and five of Chinese (*Han-hsi*), and a ranking of occupations and offices can be drawn up by observing who got what kind of meal. Senior Mongol princes (*beile*), for example, got served at the imperial level of Manchu feast, while the Khalka princes ate at the third Manchu level, and the envoys from the Dalai Lama ate at the fifth Manchu level (*Kuang-lu Ssu*,

24:1b, 3; 25:1). Foreign tributary missions, whether from Korea, the Ryukyu Islands, or Annam, got sixth-level Manchu food (fig. 27), and it is into this precise slot that we can see the first Western envoys being fitted as they entered China in the Shun-chih and K'ang-hsi reigns. Chinese banquets were similarly graded: first level for compilers of a completed block of the Veritable Records (*Shih-lu*), second level for chief examiners at the palace exams, third level for the guards' officers and physicians in attendance, fifth level for the top three students in the examinations.

The levels of food varied both by volume and by type of food provided, and perhaps also by the amount of people seated at a given table, since that is the only way that the quantities provided seem to make sense. Thus at the highest level of Manchu feast, each sitting (*mei-hsi*) had, among other things, 120 chin of white wheat flour, 8 chin of dried bean flour, 150 hen's eggs, 18 chin of white sugar, 4 chin of white honey, 6 chin of sesame, a variety of dried fruits, and a shifting menu of fresh fruits, according to season (ibid., 43:3–7).[8] For a sixth-level Manchu feast, the quantities were reduced to 20 chin of white flour, 2.8 chin of white sugar; eggs were dropped altogether, and variety was provided by offering a much wider range of dried fruits than at the upper level (*Kuang-lu Ssu*, 46:1–5). The Manchu meals listed in the Banqueting Court lists were vegetarian. However, more research is needed before we can decide precisely what Manchu meats were served at which meals, and to which envoys; for the Emperor K'ang-hsi declared in 1680 that henceforth the New Year's Feasts should be Han-hsi rather than Man-hsi, because of the large number of animals that had to be slaughtered for the latter (*Ta-ch'ing Sheng-tsu Jen Huang-ti Shih-lu*, p. 1513); and when John Bell visited Peking with the Russian embassy of 1721, he was served large portions of excellent stewed mutton and beef (Bell 1965, pp. 119, 136).

A complete range of meat and fish dishes appears only in the Chinese menus. The Chinese level one meal included pork and intestines, duck, goose, chicken, and fish, as well as a much wider variety of condiments (*Kuang-lu Ssu*, 47:3b–6); while the Chinese fifth level had pork (though no intestines) and some fish, but substituted mutton for fowl. A note at the end of the source states that chicken had been included in this meal until 1787, when it was dropped from the menu (ibid., 47:15–17). Of considerable interest to a history of Ch'ing cooking might be some of the appended lists in the same source, which give more precise contents for each bowl (*wan*) in the Chinese first-level meal. Each sitting (*hsi*) had thirty-four bowls of main dishes and four plates (*tieh*) of condiments and pickle. To give a few examples, one goose would be shared between three bowls, a whole chicken would be in one bowl, one and eight tenths chin of pork composed a separate dish, two ounces of edible seaweed and six ounces of pork were combined for one bowl, five hens' eggs were used in an egg dish, and *pao-tzu* came twelve to a bowl and each one was made with two ounces of white flour and half an ounce (five *ch'ien*) of pork (ibid., 48:1–3).

The logistic data behind each meal were, of course, equally precise: for an upper-level Manchu banquet, eighty chin of wood and fifty of charcoal; one set of stoves for each ten hsi (with special arrangements for over two hundred); the cooking for every ten hsi required four large bowls, a steamer, an open frying pan, metal ladles, a metal roasting pan, a red cloth cover to keep off the flies, and a red oiled cloth for the table. This was not to mention the carrying rods and food boxes, the chopping blocks and benches, the baskets, the strainers of different mesh, the brooms, the skimmers, the buckets, and the scoops (ibid., 43:2–3). Ivory chopsticks were specified for the Chinese meals but not for the Manchu (ibid., 47:3).

This incredible barrage of precise regulation leads us to the last area where food was truly important at the Ch'ing imperial level, namely in the field of compilation and codification. Just as the court collected and compiled its own history and imperial writings, so it had an official corpus of agricultural literature, of which food was an integral part. A basic and approved bibliography was provided in the Ch'ien-lung reign in the form of the commentaries to the immense collection of accepted literature known as the *Ssu-k'u ch'üan-shu*. The references to that work in *Tsung-mu t'i-yao* began, predictably enough, with the great sixth-century classic of animal husbandry, the *Ch'i-min yao-shu* (*Ssu-k'u ch'üan-shu tsung-mu t'i-yao*, p. 2074). Official data on food and food taxes were organized into the Three Imperial Encyclopedias (*Huang-ch'ao San-t'ung*), which were designed to be continuations of the great Sung encyclopedic works and were printed during the Ch'ien-lung reign. Virtually the entire history of Chinese food and its eating and production was assembled in the immense compendium the *Ku-chin t'u-shu chi-ch'eng*, which, after the disgrace of its main compiler, appeared in the Yung-cheng reign in type that had been set in the K'ang-hsi period. About fifty *chüan* ("volumes") of this work (the whole has been estimated to have a hundred million characters) are given over to the literature of food and wine, traced down to the early seventeenth century from the earliest references in the books of rituals. There are entire sections on vinegars, wines, honey and sugar, edible oils, meats, rice, poisonous foods, festival foods, and on the poetry across the ages that celebrated the joys of food (*Ku-chin t'u-shu chi-cheng*, chaps. 257–307). The arts of weaving and ploughing were celebrated in new imperial editions (by both K'ang-hsi and Ch'ien-lung) of the Sung *Keng-chih t'u*. Other great Ming works related to food, such as the pharmacopoeia *Pen-ts'ao kang-mu*, were expanded under private auspices during the Ch'ing; others, like the *T'ien-kung k'ai-wu*, which contains valuable data on technology related to food, were never reprinted during the Ch'ing, though a few parts were printed in the *Ku-chin t'u-shu chi-ch'eng*. It would seem that private readers shared with the imperial compilers a comfortable feeling that every-thing of importance dealing with food and its production had already been said. And the one careful work on agricultural technique that was sponsored and printed by the Ch'ing state, the *Shou-shih t'ung-k'ao*, under the nominal editorship of Ortai and Chang T'ing-yu (in 1742), has been described, by a recent Chinese scholar of agricultural history, as being merely in the class of "orthodox developments of the *Ch'i-min yao-shu* with extensions or annex-ations" (S. H. Shih 1958, pp. 102–03).

This state of affairs did not change in the nineteenth century. Though, after the suppression of the Taiping Rebellion, the emperors did respond to Western impetus in some ways—for instance, through the development of the Kiang-nan arsenal and of schools with some foreign components, like the T'ung-wen kuan—a desire to broaden or expand domestic agriculture does not seem to have figured high on the list of priorities. Guns and ma-chinery absorbed their attention along with the skills of engineering, physics, chemistry, and mathematics. Among the many books that John Fryer translated for the Kiang-nan arsenal, when he worked for this establishment, between the 1860s and the 1890s, there seem to have been only two related to agriculture: a bibliography of agricultural reference works and a book on agricultural chemistry (Bennett 1967, p. 96). Only at the very end of the century did a few Self-strengthening Reformers point to the importance of agriculture in strengthening the nation. In their joint memorial of 1901, Liu K'un-i and Chang Chih-tung noted how few Western works on agri-culture had been translated but observed that good, modern Japanese works existed in abundance and should be used by the Chinese (Teng and Fairbank 1954, p. 202). Sun Yat-sen urged attention to scientific agriculture in his manifesto of the *Hsing-chung-hui*, to improve plant and animal husbandry and to save human labor with farm machinery (ibid., p. 224). Chang Chih-tung probably went further in a practical direction than any other officials, by engaging two American specialists to investigate agricultural conditions in Hupei and by making experimental plantings of new seeds. In 1902 he developed an experimental farm of 2000 *mu* near Wu-ch'ang (Ayers 1971, p. 132), and he attempted to make his contemporaries aware that Western food yields per *mu* were substantially higher than Chinese yields (ibid., p. 167).

Such probes, however, were still ahead of their time, and Chinese comments on Western food remained vague or flamboyant.[9] Tucked into one of the lists of books that Fryer ordered from England for his own use in 1868 was a request for *Family Cookery* (Bennett 1967, p. 76). Whether he planned to introduce some elements of English cuisine to the Chinese, we do not know. Nor do we know if he would have recommended the diet common among treaty port Westerners in Shanghai at the time:

> Begin dinner with rich soup, and a glass of sherry; *then* one or two side dishes with champagne; *then* some beef, mutton, or fowls and bacon, with *more* champagne, or beer; *then* rice and curry and ham; *afterwards* game; *then* pudding, pastry, jelly, custard, or blancmange, and *more* champagne; *then* cheese and salad, and bread and butter, and a glass of port wine; *then* in many cases, oranges, figs, raisins, and walnuts. . . *with* two or three glasses of claret or some other wine. [J. K. Fairbank 1969, pp. 160–61]

There seems to have been little meeting of the culinary minds at this time despite the "opening" of China; and William Hunter's wry parody of the Chinese reaction to Western cooking may not have been too wide off the mark:

> Judge now what tastes people possess who sit at table and swallow bowls of a fluid, in their outlandish tongue called *Soo-pe*, and next devour the flesh of fish, served in a manner as near as may be to resemble the living fish itself. Dishes of half-raw meat are then placed at various angles of the table; these float in gravy, while from them pieces are cut with swordlike instruments and placed before the guests. . . . Thick pieces of meat being devoured, and the scraps thrown to a multitude of snappish dogs that are allowed to twist about amongst one's legs or lie under the table, while keeping up an incessant growling and fighting, there followed a dish that set fire to our throats, called in the barbarous language of one by my side *Kā-tē*, accompanied with rice which of itself was alone grateful to my taste. Then a green and white substance, the smell of which was overpowering. This I was informed was a compound of sour buffalo milk, baked in the sun, under whose influence it is allowed to remain until it becomes filled with insects, yet, the greener and more lively it is, with the more relish is it eaten. This is called *Che-Sze*, and is accompanied by the drinking of a muddy red fluid which foams up over the tops of the drinking cups, soils one's clothes, and is named *Pe-Urh*—think of that! But no more. [Hunter 1885, pp. 38–39]

Despite these varying levels of Western perception, for the young Emperor P'u-i, as the dynasty came to its end, nothing had ostensibly changed in the palace kitchens since the seventeenth century. And even as he lived in seclusion during the first years of the Republic, the old, wasteful rituals continued. Processions of eunuchs brought tables of lavish dishes to his presence on his command, each silver dish placed upon a porcelain dish of hot water to keep it warm; but these dishes were never eaten by P'u-i, since he could not bear these heavy meals that often had been cooked days in advance. The. "imperial" meals were returned untasted, to the kitchens, where they were presumably consumed by the palace staff. These procedures raised the emperor's alleged consumption of food to 810 catties of meat and 240 chickens and ducks, every month. In fact, he was eating small, delicious meals specially prepared for him in the imperial consorts' own kitchens. But whatever he ate, of whatever quality or quantity, the eunuchs would always report the emperor's food consumption in terms of that same rustic simplicity which might once have seemed like emulation of peasant virtues but now had become a cruel parody: "Your slave reports to his masters: the Lord of Ten Thousand Years consumed one bowl of old rice viands, one steamed breadroll and a bowl of congee. He consumed it with relish" (Aisin-Gioro 1964, pp. 43–44).

Service and Distribution

The subject of service and distribution related to food consumption is immense and diffuse, demanding a far-ranging knowledge of social and economic history which this author does not have. But certain aspects of food services during the Ch'ing seem worth considering.

The Ch'ing was a time of flourishing corporate organizations. At the lowest levels, these might consist of small groups of poor families who would pool scarce resources so as to club together for an occasional dinner—even beggars formed such associations to alleviate the regular misery of their existence (Simon 1868, pp. 12–13, 21). At a wealthier level, there were the powerful associations (*hui-kuan*) composed of merchants and officials from the same province who now found themselves living far from their native place. In their own meeting halls, they could dine on their own foods from common funds and preserve far-off patterns of eating and drinking (Morse 1932, and Ho Ping-ti 1966).

Merchant guild organizations frequently specialized in a given area of food production or sale and were in a position to control prices. In Ning-po, for example, Fukienese merchants specialized in dealing in salt, fish, and oranges and also maintained a special section for dealing with sugar products, which could provide seventy days free storage facilities to guild merchants (MacGowan 1886, pp. 138, 142, 146). Shantung merchants in Ning-po were able, for a time, to successfully defend their right to monopolize carriage of pulse and bean cake, even against Western merchants (ibid., pp. 149–50); they gave credit to their members to the tune of forty days on grain sales and fifty days on oils and bean cake—we find the Amoy guild in the same city giving ten days credit on breadstuffs sales (ibid., pp. 147, 150). Wen-chou millers, with a fixed leading group of sixteen mill owners, could fix prices for a full month ahead (ibid., p. 175), while the Ning-po fishmonger's association, with a reserve fund of over $700,000, were able to control virtually every aspect of the fishing business: the boats, weights, quality, and retail outlets (ibid., p. 171; Jametel 1886, part 4). Such fishing operations were aided, in turn, by carefully coordinated groups of ice makers who preserved their catches in the summer (Ku Lu, 6:4, on ice; Jametel 1886, p. 195, on Ning-po).

Surviving inscriptions from various Ch'ing commercial groups give us valuable glimpses further into these mutually protective associations—and into the abuses which they either perpetuated or tried to protect themselves against. A number of texts from the city of Su-chou show how the dealers in pork products built their own hall, agreed on fair prices, arranged to prevent the pig slaughterers from taking part of their pay in pork instead of in cash, and finally so abused their power that they had to be publicly reprimanded by the financial commissioner of Kiangsu (Chiang-su po-wu-kuan 1959, pp. 203–05). Other incidents involved dried seafood dealers organizing against dishonest brokers; bakeries and tea shops seeking official protection against thugs who took their food; and date merchants getting a guarantee that accurate weights should be used (ibid., pp. 186–89). At least two other associations, that of the soy and bean curd dealers and that of the wine distillers, seem to have successfully defended their claims to have unlicensed competition suppressed or discouraged (ibid., pp. 194–96).

Distribution and carriage of food was of course an immense business, involving vast numbers of people. Through surviving merchants' handbooks, it is possible to chart many of the trade routes followed and the important junctions on the way (Wilkinson 1973). Also, at least for the later part of the Ch'ing, the meticulous work of the clerical staff in the Imperial Maritime Customs allows us to chart at least three different movements of food. A first would be the comparative levels of imports, by product, into a given province: Anhwei, for example, drawing massive amounts of brown sugar from Wu-hu, along with sizable purchases of mushrooms, pepper, and edible seaweed (China Imperial Maritime Customs 1885, p. 135). A second would be the different levels of goods purchased by different provinces, forwarded under transit passes to the interior: Nan-yang in Honan providing the largest market for brown sugar, Hsiang-yang in Hupei for nutmeg and sugar candy, Chungking, Szechwan, for seaweed, pepper, and cuttlefish, and Ch'ang-sha in Hunan for dried clams (ibid., pp. 91–99). A third would be the exports of foods from China—major sellers, besides tea, being sugar, vermicelli, beans and bean cake, fruit, medicines, preserved vegetables, and rhubarb (ibid., p. 10). One side of this new entrance into the international food market that must be considered is the fact that Chinese farmers now became dependent on fluctuations of world trade prices. For example, as we can see from a report from Swatow in 1884, the increased beet production by European growers had an almost immediate impact on local Chinese prices (ibid., p. 313).

Among the many areas of retail and distribution that can be observed in the Ch'ing dynasty through surviving sources, we might note at least three major areas: restaurants, itinerant vendors, and cooks. Restaurants and inns, of course, existed at every level of expensiveness and taste in Ch'ing China. Those of eighteenth century Yang-chou have remained famous and attractive through Li Tou's engaging work *Yang-chou hua-fang lu*. Here are: the tourists crowding into the tea shops, famous for their snacks (T. Li 1795, 1:24b–25); a restaurant that cooks lamb so well that people start queuing at dawn to get a serving (ibid., 9:10b–11); the mansion of a former merchant now made over into a restaurant, famous for its snacks and the beauty of the owner's daughter (ibid., 9:12b); the restaurant where the former pig seller "big-foot Chou" waits on tables, where you could get a fine meal and enough wine to make you drunk for two ch'ien and four fen, and where you can also watch cricket fights and fighting birds (ibid., 9:25). There were bars that stocked wine from all over the country and had special wines for every season (ibid., 13:1–2); there were restaurants famous for frogs' legs or for duck or for pigs' trotters in vinegar (ibid., 9:11); and there were others famous simply for good food, served in a beautiful setting by beautiful girls, where scholars could settle for an evening and write poems while they ate and drank (ibid., 15:3a). Famous in Yang-chou, also, were the floating boats that had given Li Tou's collection its name. Those desiring a special dinner could order in advance at a number of restaurants, and once the food had been prepared, it was transferred to one of the floating boats; there the host, with his guests and servants, could eat and relax, while ordering whatever wines they needed from the wine boats that floated nearby in attendance (ibid., 11:3, 16b–17). Many such boats were clearly exceptionally fine restaurants, though others served as meeting places for dallying, or literally as brothels, like those visited by Shen Fu in late eighteenth-century Canton, which specialized in girls from various provinces (F. Shen 1960 ed., pp. 42–45). The latter boats were elaborately furnished with mirrors, beds, curtains, and lamps; at least by the late Ch'ien-lung reign, opium was served with the meals in such floating restaurants (ibid., p. 44), and by the late nineteenth century, opium smoking was common in Canton and had also spread to major restaurants in Peking (Jametel 1886, pp. 231–32; 1887, p. 251).

In any small town, the inns and restaurants were the centers for social contact and gossip, as can be seen repeatedly in fiction like P'u Sung-ling's short story collection, *Liao-chai chih-i*, or Wu Ching-tzu's novel, *Ju-lin wai-shih*. Buddhist temples also had their great temple kitchens, where people came to eat at festivals (T. Li 1795, 4:24b–25). According to one account, such temple kitchens vied for customers and, to enhance the flavor of their vegetarian meals, were not above cooking their noodles in a little chicken broth or having a cloth soaked in chicken fat, with which to touch up a bamboo shoot and mushroom broth (*Ch'ing-pai lei-ch'ao*, vol. 24, no. 56: 47–48). At the level of the rural poor, restaurants and inns were natural social centers but could also be centers of elaborate frauds, as the magistrate Huang Liu-hung noted in the southern Shantung town of T'an-ch'eng; for there peasants coming into town to attend legal proceedings were forced to stay in special inns where their food bills were inflated by handouts to the yamen runners and other attendants. The result could be personal bankruptcy for the unwary (L. H. Huang 1973 ed., p. 127). For other poor people, the network of inns provided meeting places away from the watchful eyes of the state, where uprisings could be planned, and weapons and money exchanged (Naquin 1974). Perhaps for this reason, the Ch'ing had, at least on the statute books, elaborate systems of registration for all those staying at inns, and these registers were meant to be turned over at regular intervals to the magistrate's yamen (L. H. Huang 1973 ed., pp. 214, 247).

A number of account books kept by travelers in Ch'ing China have recently been found and published by Fang Hao, and they enable us to get some detailed views of Ch'ing food costs. For example, restaurant receipts for the year 1747 in Hsiu-ning show that a sitting (*hsi*) with nine standard dishes cost 9 ch'ien (0.9 taels); the price for a sitting with nine large dishes was 1.08 taels (Fang Hao 1972a, p. 58); soup for the whole table was 5 ch'ien extra. Possibly there were reductions for bulk orders, since an apparently similar dinner of nine standard dishes cost only 7.2 ch'ien when an order was placed for eleven sittings at one time. Such restaurants handled large orders, and a receipt has survived from the one referred to above (the Wang Wan-ch'eng kuan on Wan-an Street), showing an order placed for 156 bowls of noodles at 1.2 fen a bowl, for a total cost of 1.872 taels. From a surviving menu of the same restaurant, we know that an eleven-dish meal consisted of mixed cut meats, trotters, venison and dumplings, mussels, sharks' fins and fresh fish dishes, fresh chicken, and preserved eggs (ibid., p. 59).

For many travelers, however, such prices were prohibitive, and other account books show the care with which prices were compared and coppers doled out along the road: in November 1790, winter bamboo shoots, 30 cash per chin in Hang-chou, were up to 32 cash in Su-chou; pork was 80 cash per chin, beef 38 cash, mixed meats 72 cash, fish 50 cash, and chickens 115 cash each. In terms of general purchasing power, these foods can be compared with a chin of candles, costing 212 cash; a haircut, costing between 30 and 40 cash, depending on the location; or a chin of Shao-hsing or Su-chou wine, both priced at 28 cash per chin (Fang Hao 1971, p. 369). The accounts of six examination students, traveling as a group to Nanking in 1875, enable us to compare some purchases across the span of a century and see that, despite the ravages of the Taiping Rebellion, many prices were remarkably close. Rice, which had cost the 1790 travelers 2.1 taels per picul (shih), had risen to 3.2 taels a picul by 1875; and pork fat, which had been 72 cash per chin was up to 128; but plain pork was only up from 80 cash to 96 in Nanking, and it was still around 80 or as low as 75 in the countryside (Fang Hao 1972b, pp. 289–90).

At the poorer levels, the restaurant network blended into the world of itinerant vendors and peddlers. The restaurants often had little sheds nearby, where a simple meal could be bought or taken home, or a concoction of leftovers from the restaurant's richer customers could be bought for a few cash (*Ch'ing-pai lei-ch'ao*, vol, 47, no. 92:12); there were stalls for coolies and for women who came to the coolies' place of work to sell their salted vegetables and rice (ibid., vol. 47, no. 92:1). Even on tiny salaries, one could get something from such vendors: little candies of peanut and sugar or of spun sugar and molasses for one cash (MacGowan 1907, p. 300); pastries for five cash, a slice of dried pork for seven, a bowl of conjee for ten, a full bowl of rice for twenty cash, and one of salt meat for forty (*Ch'ing-pai lei-ch'ao*, vol. 47, no. 92:12). For those without any stoves or fuel, there were hot water vendors who enabled a family to cook its own hot meal at the lowest possible cost (S. Yang and Tao 1931, p. 75).

Paintings and woodblocks give a better sense of the variety than do words: early Ch'ing genre paintings show us a mother and her children buying soft drinks and a scholar tasting one of a large variety of teas. Other woodblock illustrations from downtown Peking in 1717 show an endless variety of stalls and booths and sheds, where the hungry and thirsty could rest a moment and refresh themselves (fig. 32). Many of these vendors had elaborate apparatuses for serving hot food or drinks and functioned as mobile restaurants; they too, like the innkeepers, served as centers for exchange of news and gossip and also as the potential carriers of the messages or weapons of revolt. They were also a prominent part of the festival life of the great cities. From Ku Lu's study of Su-chou festivals during the Ch'ing, we can see how vendors responded to the religious and seasonal cycle, and together with other retailers combined to enrich the diet of the urban dwellers: announced by written signs or vendors' cries were the spring cakes of the first month, the green dumplings (with lotus root) of the third month, the summer wines, sea scallops, mustard greens, and salt eggs to celebrate summer's coming, the special, heavy, round dumplings for the dragon-boat festival in the fifth month, the watermelon at the autumn solstice, the delicate, coiled cakes of sugar and flour sold at the autumn festival of the weaver and the cowherd (Ku Lu).[10] As the year ran towards its end, there were the glutinous rice dumplings with red bean stuffing for the kitchen god's festival (these dumplings were also believed to soften the feet, so on this day little girls' feet customarily received their first binding), the lake crabs of the early winter (when the roe was at its most delicate), as well as the many special delicacies prepared for the New Year festivities (ibid., 8:4; 10:3; chap. 12, passim).

But perhaps it is with the cooks that we should leave the last word. They are not a widely known group, but they could become so abusive, if attached to official households, that special proclamations had to be issued to control their behavior around Su-chou (Chiang-su po-wu-kuan 1959, pp. 210–11). In Yang-chou their names were remembered with some of the dishes that made them famous (T. Li 1795, 11:3). In Peking a cook, after serving his apprenticeship in Canton, could rise to own his own restaurant, employing a dozen porters to handle take-out orders, with an extra four chefs on his own staff just to rent to wealthy families (Jametel 1887, pp. 269–72). Cooks from Shantung who had dominated the Ming imperial kitchens with their incomparable skill had yielded to Manchu cooks, to cooks from Chekiang, and to some from Su-chou, after Ch'ien-lung had been charmed by central Chinese cooking, and all these cooks attached their names to their dishes (C. Su 1966, pp. 18–19). In his general cookbook, Yüan Mei had been rather hard on cooks: they were usually rather petty people (*hsiao-jen*), he wrote, who had to be rewarded and punished if they were to be kept up to the mark (M. Yüan 1824 ed., p. 13b). But in his literary collection, *Hsiao-ts'ang-shan fang wen chi*, Yüan Mei included a biography of his own cook Wang Hsiao-yü which is affectionate and informative. According to Yüan Mei, Wang had decided to stay on in the Yüan household, despite its comparative poverty, because he had a demanding and critically acute master who really cared about food (Waley 1956, p. 53). There may be a touch of literary embellishment in Yüan's analysis here and in the summary he gave of Wang's belief that cooking was like medicine—you had to apply your whole heart to the problem of diagnosis, so as to attain the perfect blending and balance (M. Yüan 1933 ed., 7:7).[11] But in his discussion of Wang at work, Yüan gave a fitting epitaph for some of the tastes and joys of Ch'ing cuisine:

When he first came and asked what was to be the menu for the day, I feared that he had grand ideas, and I explained to him that I came of a family that was far from rich and that we were not in the habit of spending a fortune on every meal. "Very good," he said, laughing, and presently produced a plain vegetable soup which was so good that one went on and on taking it till one really felt one needed nothing more. ... He insisted on doing all the marketing himself, saying, "I must see things in their natural state before I can decide whether I can apply my art to them." He never made more than six or seven dishes, and if more were asked for, he would not cook them. At the stove, he capered like a sparrow, but never took his eyes off it for a moment, and if when anything was coming to a boil someone called out to him, he took not the slightest notice, and did not even seem to hear. ... When he said, "The soup is done," the kitchen-boy would rush up the tureen and take it, and if by any chance the boy was slow, Wang would fly into a terrible rage and curse him roundly. ... I once said to him, "If it were a question of your producing your results when provided with rare and costly ingredients, I could understand your achievements. What astonishes me is that, out of a couple of eggs, you can make a dish that no one else could have made." "The cook who can work only on a large scale must lack daintiness," he replied, "just as one who can handle common ingredients but fails with rare and costly ones can only be reckoned as a feeble practitioner. Good cooking, however, does not depend on whether the dish is large or small, expensive or economical. If one has the art, then a piece of celery or salted cabbage can be made into a marvellous delicacy; whereas if one has not the art, not all the greatest delicacies and rarities of land, sea or sky are of any avail" [trans. Waley 1956, pp. 52–53].

NOTES

1. The population figures for the *hsien* (county) show an increase of about 40 percent for the period between the printing of the two gazetteers (*T'an-cheng hsien-chih* 1764, 5:19; working from *ting* equivalents).

2. His son later had these notes printed just as they had been written; they fill fifty-one printed pages (H. N. Li 1968 ed., preface).

3. For the crops available in this area, see *Hsiu-shui hsien-chih* 1596.

4. Festival foods can be seen in any of the above gazetteers. See also Ku Lu's work cited below and the study of Ch'ing festivals in Peking by Fuca Tun-ch'ung, *Yen-ching Sui-shih chi*.

5. Li Yü felt that geese who had had their feet tenderized by being placed in hot oil while they were still alive should not be eaten—the practice was too cruel (1963 ed., p. 267).

6. One incident is translated in Waley 1956, p. 197.

7. Hawkes makes the innuendo more direct in his translation.

8. Place settings for Mongol envoys in the Pao-ho tien can be seen in *Todo Meisho Zue*, 1:27.

9. See the passages on Western food in *Ch'ing-pai lei-ch'ao*, vol. 24, no. 56:49, 56; vol. 47, no. 92:2, 7, 8.

10. Each month has a chüan in *Ch'ing-chia lu*; the various references are 1:12; 3:2b; 4:1; 5:3; 7:2.

11. This brief section of the biography is not translated by Waley.

7: MODERN CHINA: NORTH

VERA Y. N. HSU AND FRANCIS L. K. HSU

Ask any Chinese born and raised in China what he liked best in the days of his childhood and "Chinese New Year" is the most likely reply. That reply certainly agrees with our experiences. We were not, therefore, surprised to read in the autobiographies of some well-known Chinese of the Republican period that they, too, found Chinese New Year most memorable (see Ts'ao 1966).

Among the great classical operas of China is one entitled *P'ing Kui Hui Yao.*[1] It features a poor but talented man who, by a fluke, married the daughter of a rich high official in government. Her father was totally opposed to the union and disowned his beautiful daughter when she persisted. The couple had to keep house in an abandoned old kiln. Her mother, taking pity on the newlyweds, discreetly made them a substantial gift of money, with which the husband set out to make good in the wider world. It was not until eighteen years later that he returned to their love nest, in worldly glory. Popular legend in most northern Chinese villages in the 1930s claims that, upon his triumphant return, the husband asked his wife, who had waited for him in poverty and misery for eighteen years, to name her heart's desire, and she asked for New Year festivities. So he ordered one New Year celebration to be held every day. After eighteen such celebrations, she took ill and passed away.

Why? The old ladies who used to recount this story to one of the authors as a child explained, "Because the Ruler of Heaven was to have rewarded her with eighteen years of luxurious life for her eighteen years of misery. But since she had had eighteen New Year celebrations, she had used up those eighteen years, and therefore she died."

The Chinese New Year Celebrations

Why do so many Chinese regard New Year celebrations with such delight? We think it is due to a combination of circumstances, among which food is very important. Besides good food there are many other ingredients: (1) a real sense of family togetherness and of the good life, (2) holidays (plenty of rest and fun), (3) new clothes, (4) ritual fanfare to ancestral spirits, and (5) general festivity.

During this celebration, food is not important for the living alone: a large part of the ritual fanfare to ancestral spirits consists of fancy food and drink (tea and alcohol) offerings.[2] Another custom at this time is that, just after midnight on New Year's Eve, junior members of the family pay ceremonial respects to those senior to them, and the latter show their benevolence to the former through small monetary gifts. This is called *ya sui ch'ien* ("anchor the year money"). Consequently, this is one time in the year when all the youngsters have lots of coins in their little pockets, to be freely spent on their hearts' desires. Also, in many houses, children, teen-agers, and adults pass several days gambling.

Today, under the new government, although the household rites to ancestral spirits are either absent or abbreviated and gambling with money is no longer permitted, the lunar New Year remains more important than any other festive occasion. For example, of the seven regular public holidays each year, only the lunar New Year occupies three days.

For this chapter, food and drink and their consumption are our main concern, and in the lunar New Year we see this aspect of Chinese life at its best. For weeks before the New Year, women in every northern Chinese home are busy making meat dumplings called *chiao tzu*. These consist of a filling of chopped pork and cabbage, salt, ginger, scallions, and ground white and black pepper, wrapped in a thin skin of dough. In a large household the number of dumplings may run into the thousands.

If they have no powered means of refrigeration, the northern Chinese make use of the cold of their winter. Neatly arranged on separate, large trays, the dumplings are put in an unheated, empty room, or on tables in the open air. They are promptly frozen. Then, instead of busying themselves with cooking for the holiday meals, the women simply toss the needed number of frozen dumplings into boiling water for some ten minutes, and a delicious hot lunch or dinner is had by all. The dumplings are eaten after being dipped in a little dish of vinegar and sesame oil. Soy sauce is also poured into the same dish if a more salty taste is desired. A meal made up of these dumplings usually is augmented by a few side dishes: several kinds of pickles, sliced salted eggs, sliced fermented eggs (commonly but erroneously referred to in the United States as "thousand-year-old eggs"), roasted peanuts, and the like.

But pork and cabbage dumplings, though ubiquitous at all income levels, are only part of the New Year fare. Many northern Chinese households make wine, bean curd, and sausages and slaughter a pig or two for home consumption. This even in towns and cities, despite the fact that meat and other foods can be bought at permanent stores not too far away. For days before New Year's Eve, regular stores in towns and cities are supplemented by temporary markets with hundreds of trading stands. Streets are always crowded at this time of the year with *nien huo* ("New Year goods") purchasers. When all the shopping is done, the celebration begins with New Year's Eve dinner.

This dinner begins in late afternoon (five o'clock) and is usually sumptuous. Even among the relatively poor, it would include four to six big bowls (*ssu ta wan* or *liu ta wan*) featuring vegetables (chiefly cabbage, turnips, and dried mushrooms), chicken, fish, mussels, and especially pork. For the better-off families, there would definitely be eight big bowls (*pa ta wan*), preceded by four or six cold plates and followed by one or two "big items" (*ta chien*). In the cold plates are pickles, sliced cold meat, pigs'-feet jelly, roasted peanuts, thin-sliced jellyfish skin in vinegar and soy sauce, sugar-preserved green apricots or kumquats, or salted dried shrimp with peas, and so on. In the eight big bowls are, besides the foods mentioned above, also such delicacies as sea cucumbers, sharks' fins, birds' nests, pork sausages, ham, giant pork meatballs euphemistically termed "lions' heads," with cabbage, and fresh and dried shrimp. One of the big items usually is "eight precious rice," a sweet production of sticky rice mixed with eight other ingredients including lotus seeds, almond seeds, sliced red dates, several kinds of candied fruits, sweet bean paste, and brown-sugar syrup. In addition, there is usually a fancy, sweet soup, such as that made with white tree ears (a kind of edible fungus) and crystal sugar, which comes after the other dishes. White rice and wine or spirits are served with the entire meal. On this special occasion even children of eight or ten are allowed to taste a little of the alcohol if so inclined.

This feast is the opener. Beginning with New Year's Day, quite a few other sumptuous meals for members of each household and for visiting relatives and friends follow. Snacks in the form of watermelon seeds, sesame candy and other sweets, roasted peanuts, fruits such as pears and oranges, and cakes are available at all times. Visitors are served tea, watermelon seeds, and sweets on a tray as soon as they sit down, before going on to heavier things. In some families, this license with food lasts till the third of the First Moon. For others, it continues more or less to the fifteenth of the month, which is the traditional Lantern Festival.

At this time, besides another round of festivities, each child, up to the age of fifteen, is given a candle in the shape of his or her birth animal made of mung-bean dough filled with candle wax and a wick. (Each Chinese year is represented by one of twelve animals, all of which are real except for the dragon. The twelve proceed cyclically, the first animal being the mouse and the last being the pig, after which the cycle starts once more with the mouse. Everyone, therefore, depending on his or her year of birth, has a particular astrological animal for life.) During the Lantern Festival, in the evening, the children hold these lighted candles to show off their animals and to guess who is older or younger than whom and by how many years. They have their lighted animal candles by their sides even when they play other games. It is a beautiful sight.

The Staples

In speaking of food in China, one fundamental clarification must be made. When we go to a Chinese restaurant in the United States, we order some dishes such as egg foo yong or pepper steak and then some bowls of rice. To Americans, the term *rice* means only one thing—white grains (*Oryza sativa*) cooked to a fluffy consistency. But many Chinese in China, especially in northern China, do not eat that kind of rice. Instead they eat corn, millet, and glutinous millet. All these, when cooked, are called *fan*, which term has also commonly but mistakenly been equated with rice in English.

The Chinese make a basic distinction between *fan*, which includes all food made of grains and served in a separate bowl to each diner, and *ts'ai*, which includes all meats and vegetables cooked and placed in the center of the table in big bowls or dishes for all diners to share.

Throughout this chapter, we shall use the terms *fan* and *ts'ai* as defined here. Fan is further differentiated into *kan fan*, or grains cooked to a fluffy consistency (as most Americans know it in Chinese restaurants), and *hsi fan*, or grains served in the form of porridge, usually for breakfast and for late evening snacks (which most Americans have not tasted). When the Chinese speak of fan cooked with rice, they call it *pai mi fan*, or "white rice" fan, as distinguished from *kaoliang mi fan* or "sorghum" fan, and *hsiao mi fan* or "millet" fan. Wheat is eaten in the form of bread (*man-t'ou*); noodles of various shapes (round, flat, square, fine or thick); the skin of dumplings; flat pancakes with onion, lard and salt; sesame cakes; twisted pretzel-like items called *ma hua*; and *yu tiao*, a sort of Chinese doughnut.

It has been said many times that rice is common in southern China, and wheat in northern China. That is generally true. But the northern Chinese consume quite a few other staples besides wheat. Two of these staples found in most of Manchuria and in many parts of Shantung, Hopei, and Honan provinces are sorghum (*kaoliang*) and soybean. Sorghum is prepared and eaten exactly like rice, but is cheaper than rice. It was more easily grown in the climate and soil of Manchuria before the large-scale irrigation, begun in 1949, made rice cultivation possible. Thus, it was *the* food of a majority of the people. The poor ate rice only during New Year celebrations and at weddings, funerals, and birthdays. This was so characteristic of the Chinese that they spoke of eating kaoliang as a mark of differentiation between themselves and the Japanese. Before 1945 the Japanese were very much in evidence in Manchuria. They were in control of the South Manchurian Railway, Port Arthur, Dairen, concessions in all the cities as far north as Mukden and Ch'ang-ch'un, and enjoyed the privileged position of colonialists and traders with extraterritoriality. They ate only white rice.

So when one Chinese spoke to another about a situation of desperation from which there was no pleasant way out, he would say: "That's like a Japanese eating kaoliang."

How scarce and precious rice was can be seen by the following episode witnessed by one of the authors during his adolescence in Chin-chou: A child of four or five was playing in the yard of his grandmother. Pointing to a pot, the elder called him and asked if he would like to have a little food. It was rice, but the grandmother had mixed some red beans with it. Consequently, the color of the cooked rice was not white but purple. The little boy gave one look and said no, he did not want any, because he thought it was kaoliang, which he had as daily fare. But his grandmother called on him to examine the shape of the grains—they were long and not round, although the color was like that of kaoliang. The boy at once decided to eat a bowl, even without the aid of ts'ai.

Soybean grows easily as a companion crop with kaoliang or corn. It is consumed all over China as bean curd, as soybean milk, and as bean brain (*tou fu nao*; slightly coagulated bean milk, hence softer than bean curd). *Tou cha*, the finer remains of the soybean from which the bean milk has been extracted, is usually used to feed pigs, but can be a poor man's ts'ai dish. Also, young soybeans in pods, freshly plucked from the field, are cooked in water or baked on the fire and consumed as snacks. These are served with soy sauce and sesame oil and eaten by using the teeth to scrape the beans into one's mouth. There are a variety of other soybean products: bean sprouts, fermented bean curd (*fu ju*), molded bean curd (*ch'ou tou fu*), dried bean curd (*tou fu kan*), and so forth. For example, bean sprouts can be eaten either cooked with oil and shredded meat or, after submersion in boiling water for one or two minutes, treated like salad.

As we move from Manchuria and the few provinces named before to other parts of north China, we find the picture described above changes slightly. Wheat becomes more common, but the very poor still eat a lot of cornmeal bread and millet porridge. In addition, the sweet potato becomes common. In a survey of Ting Hsien in Hopei province in the twenties, Sidney Gamble and co-workers found the sweet potato to be the major food consumed by families of all income levels—more than millet, the second staple, and all other grains combined (1954, p. 112). The importance of the sweet potato and millet as staples is also reported for Shantung province by Martin C. Yang (1945, pp. 32–34).

A large survey under J. L. Buck of Nanking University in the early twenties, involving 1,070 farm households in four provinces (Anhwei, Chihli [Hopei], Honan, and Kiangsu) resulted in similar findings. In the more southern of these provinces, Anhwei and Kiangsu, wheat and rice are the more important staples, but in the two more northern ones (Honan and Hopei) sorghum and millet and corn prevail. In fact in Hopei, the most northern of the four provinces, wheat constitutes less than 5 percent of the grain consumed. It was also commonly known that even if people grew some wheat or rice, they often sold it for cash while consuming the cheaper foods such as sorghum, millet, or sweet potatoes (Buck 1930, pp. 366–71).

Baked sweet potato is also served as a snack in cities. During the winter months, the streets of Peking and Tientsin used to be frequented by numerous hawkers of baked sweet potatoes who sold their wares by the ounce and the catty. These hawkers carried a portable oven at one end of a pole and the raw sweet potatoes in a basket at the other end. Charcoal fire burned brilliantly at the bottom of the oven, over which sweet potatoes hung from hooks on all sides in several layers. Children as well as adults were good customers of such hawkers.

Animal Products and Vegetables

The meat most in demand in China was and is pork, except among the Moslems who, like the Jews, do not eat pork, but beef and mutton. In China the Moslems alone customarily consume milk and butter. The rest of the Chinese do not: the milk for babies is either from their mothers' breasts or powdered or canned. The Moslems maintain their food customs today under communism. In 1972 we saw a number of Moslem restaurants in Peking, including one in the Summer Palace. Non-Moslem Chinese can patronize them, but Moslems will not eat at other restaurants. Before 1949 one of the best, and best known, Moslem restaurants in Peking was Tung Lai Shun, which specialized in mutton.

Taking the Chinese population as a whole, the consumption of meats was strikingly low before 1949. According to J. L. Buck's survey, Chinese farmers received 89.8 percent of their food energy from grains and their products (contrasted with 38.7 percent for the average American family), 8.5 percent from roots, mostly sweet potatoes, and only 1 percent from animal products (contrasted with 39.2 percent for the average American family). Vegetables, sugar, and fruit together gave 0.7 percent of the food energy (contrasted to 13.1 percent in sugar and fruit alone for the average American family) (Buck 1930, pp. 363–64).[3] From what we actually experienced and saw, this picture is generally correct, except possibly that farmers in the richer south ate more meat and meat products than their counterparts in the poorer north. The farm population ate meat and other animal products mainly during festivals, including the New Year, and on special occasions such as weddings, birthdays, and funerals. For the day-to-day meal most Chinese eat pickles and a variety of vegetables in quantity, but sometimes get a little salted pork, or salted fish, or vegetables cooked in lard. The common non-animal oils are those extracted from peanuts, cotton seeds, sesame seeds, and vegetable seeds.

The Chinese philosophy of food is that cooked vegetables, meat, and meat products (i.e., ts'ai), are for the purpose of *hsia fan*, to assist the intake of bowls of fan (rice, sorghum, millet, or whatever), in sharp contrast to the American philosophy of food in which the order is reversed. This philosophy is so important that all meals are also termed *fan*. *"Ch'ih fan la mei yu?"* ("Have you eaten?"), and *"Mei yu fan ch'ih,"* ("no food to eat" or "no job"), are among the common Chinese expressions. Children are taught this philosophy very early in life. A child who can eat a lot of fan and very little ts'ai is an object of praise. Many times, the after-school meal of one of the authors was one salted duck's egg to assist in the eating of two bowls of fan.

Some Chinese were not without envy toward others who could eat better. Martin Yang reports that poor villagers in Shantung spoke of "a Christian preacher, a school teacher, or a businessman from the market town [by saying], 'He is a man who eats wheat flour every day, why should he not have a smooth face!'" And, "When a person has a run of good luck, his fellow villagers might say: 'Just as meat is always served with wheat-flour rolls.'" (M. C. Yang 1930, p. 34).

As the above quotations indicate, wheat flour is identified with the diet of the well-to-do and the city people. Meat and other animal products are even more so. The old and the sick are given more of the latter two, especially chicken and eggs. If at all financially possible, the eldest male and his spouse usually include in their breakfast one or two poached eggs. For younger women, the customary confinement period is one month after the birth of the child. During that time the mother has at least one poached egg a day, and some chicken or chicken soup with her other meals. Also, pig's-stomach soup is considered the best for mother's milk. A variety of other inside parts of animals, such as liver, kidney, brain, stomach, and intestines are valued and desirable foods. After the birth of a child, especially a son, the mother's family sends over gifts of foods such as wheat flour, or wheat-flour noodles, a couple of chickens, and especially a basket of eggs. These are primarily intended for the new mother. The new father's family makes a lot of red-dyed eggs and distributes them to relatives and neighbors very much in the same way that proud new parents in the United States give away cigars.

Meals and Meal Times

In north China, the village people tended to have three meals during the busy season, when the days were long—late spring, summer, and early fall—and two meals in the slack season, when the days were short. But even during the latter period, late evening snacks of a substantial nature were common in most, if not all, households. In the cities and towns, people generally ate three meals a day.

If there were two meals, one took place about 8:00 A.M. and the other about 4:00 or 5:00 P.M. The snacks occurred at 8:00 or 9:00 P.M. before going to bed. If there were three meals, the first one occurred very early, about daybreak, after which the men went to the fields. The midday meal, at about 12:30, was usually bifurcated. Women or children sent the food in containers to the men in the fields, while they themselves ate at home. The evening meal occurred at about 7:00 when all workers returned from the field.

In the villages, men and women ate at separate tables. Children below five or six of both sexes ate with their mothers, but, as they got older, males joined their fathers and older brothers. The one exception was that the wife of the senior-most male, the head of the household, sometimes ate at the men's table. Cooking for the household was done by younger women— usually daughters-in-law. If there was more than one daughter-in-law, they took turns at it—usually ten days at a time. Naturally, servants instead of daughters-in-law did such work in well-to-do families. Hired farmhands generally ate with the men.

In towns and cities, men and women ate separately in some households and together in others, while servants ate after their employers at a table of their own.

The typical Chinese dining table is round or square. The ts'ai dishes are laid in the center, and each participant in the meal is equipped with a bowl for fan, a pair of chopsticks, a saucer, and a spoon. All at the table take from the ts'ai dishes as they proceed with the meal.

Good eating manners require that each participant take equally from the different ts'ai dishes, so that all will have an equal chance at all the dishes. One very common point of instruction from parents to children is that the best-mannered person does not allow co-diners to be aware of what his or her favorite dishes are by his or her eating pattern. On the other hand, good eating manners do not preclude resting a piece of meat (or other items) in one's bowl between bites. However, multiple bites are less necessary in Chinese food than in American food since all ingredients are diced, chopped, minced, or otherwise cut or sliced into bite-sized pieces.

There are several other points of good food manners. If there are diners of different seniority at the same table, the junior ones must wait to eat until the senior ones have begun to do so. In eating fan, the bowl must be raised to one's lips with the left hand while using chopsticks in the right hand to shove the food into one's mouth. The diner who lets his fan bowl stay on the table and eats by picking up lumps of fan from the bowl is expressing disinterest in or dissatisfaction with the food. If he or she is a guest in someone's house, that is seen as an open insult to the host.

As children we were always taught to leave not a single grain of fan in our bowl when we finished. Our elders strongly impressed upon us that each single grain of rice or corn was obtained through the drops of sweat of the tillers of the soil. Finally, children are told to listen to the conversation of adults while dining but not to speak unless asked.

Dining Out

The usual Chinese village had hardly any permanent stores and practically never a restaurant. It relied mainly on periodic markets, held once in three or six days (or at longer intervals), to which farmers from many villages came to sell and to buy. Cooked-food hawkers and open-air food stands abounded in such markets. It was in towns and cities that one found most of the restaurants, the butcher shops, the grocery and grain stores, and the manufacturers of cakes, biscuits, bean- and wheat-flour noodles, and many other kinds of prepared food.

A ubiquitous sight in Chinese towns and cities was the street hawkers. They went from street to street like the Good Humor man in the United States, except that the variety of goods and services they provided was enormous. Besides those who sold kerosene by the ounce, the repairmen who could fix to perfection any broken porcelain or pottery, and those who offered hundreds of women's items, from cosmetics to needles and thread, many hawkers came with portable food stands.

The simplest of these sold noodles by the bowl or hot biscuits (*shao ping*) and Chinese doughnuts (*yu t'iao*), or watermelons, or, in the thirties, sherbet of some kind. The customers for noodles or doughnuts might eat their purchases on the spot, after which they returned the bowl and the chopsticks to the peddler for washing and reuse.

The most artful peddlers were the men who sold *t'ang jen*, or "sugar figures," as they made them. They were always surrounded by many children and even adults who were fascinated by their skill. They carried a portable charcoal stove and a supply of molds in the shapes of boys, girls, theatrical characters, animals, fish, insects, and so forth. They plucked a small lump from a big puttylike candy mass softened by fire and put it at the end of a blowing tube. Before blowing they put the soft candy in a particular mold. Taking the shape of the mold, the formless lump became a beautiful rooster, cow, angel, or whatever had been ordered. For additional effect, they colored the finished piece or added bits of other colored candies here and there to make it lifelike. After playing with it for a while the child ate it.

More stationary than the hawkers were the food stands on the sidewalks, during morning markets and at temple fairs. These served the customers in the same way the food hawkers did except that the menu was slightly more elaborate. Instead of single-item foods, such as roasted sweet potatoes or noodles, they served a more complete meal with fan and ts'ai or some variety of chiao tzu. Also, they sometimes provided a few tables and benches for the comfort of the diners.

The restaurants were great in variety. In Peking they ranged from one- or two-room affairs found in the Ch'ien Men district to palatial establishments such as Tung Hsing Lou and Tung Lai Shun. The modest ones were enlarged editions of the food stands described before, with a somewhat more expanded menu. The palatial ones had really impressive and sizeable menus. But whether modest or palatial, several features were common to them all.

The kitchen, or a main part of it, was generally situated at the main entrance to the restaurant, so that customers could see how the dishes were prepared and the great skill the chef or chefs could exhibit. For example, in many northern dishes the principal cooking process is sautéing. This involves putting the ingredients into a hot, greased saucepan for just the right amount of time (a few minutes). We have seen many a chef flipping the contents of his saucepan over a flaming fire with even greater skill than American flippers of pancakes. The chef also announced by loud yells the arrival of customers.

Another feature common to all Chinese restaurants was that many of the customers ate in private rooms. Some of these were separated from others by actual walls and doors. Others were separated by screens.[4] In a large restaurant there was usually a sizeable hall on the ground floor where many customers dined. There was no absolute rule governing who dined where. Generally parties of four or more were assigned the private rooms while those of fewer persons or singles ate in the common hall. But here we come to another common feature of northern Chinese restaurants, that is, the mixing of clients of different spending levels.

In the West it is customary for people to decide in advance to dine out at an elegant restaurant or a cheap joint. At the former everything is expensive, while at the latter everything costs less. In north China very palatial restaurants would cater to different purses. (Most Chinese restaurants in the United States still retain this characteristic.) Tung Lai Shun of Peking is a good example. This was a Moslem restaurant best known for its thin-sliced mutton cooked at the table in a "fire pot" by the diners as they ate. This restaurant had some fifty private rooms in addition to a common dining hall on the ground floor. It served those who wanted pa ta wan feasts (eight-course dinners), but it also satisfied day laborers and ricksha coolies who could afford no more than twenty boiled mutton and cabbage dumplings for lunch or supper. The pa ta wan feasters would of course be assigned one of the larger private rooms, while the twenty-dumpling customer would eat in the ground-floor common hall. However, if the dumpling customer came, not alone, but with several friends, they too might be assigned a private room. There was no segregation of the customers by class.

Before 1949 the custom of tipping in restaurants was common in China as elsewhere. Since then, however, no tipping is the rule everywhere in China.

Earlier we mentioned the Chinese philosophy of food, which is that dishes of ts'ai are secondary while bowls of fan are primary. Ts'ai assists the diner to eat fan. That philosophy is generally reversed in most restaurants and in feasts connected with funerals and with weddings, New Year's, and other festive occasions. Here most of the attention is devoted to the quality of the ts'ai dishes, and not to that of the fan, which in north China is always augmented and often replaced by wheat-flour bread, round, square, or pretzel-like in shape.

Furthermore, during festivals and especially when acting as hosts, all Chinese seem to ignore their sense of frugality and indulge in extravagance. Ts'ai dishes are served in abundance. The host or hostess will heap the guests' saucers with piece after piece of meat, fish, chicken, and so on, in spite of repeated excuses or even protests on the guests' part. When fan is finally served, most around the table are full and can at best nibble a few grains.

Tea, Wine, and Spirits

The Chinese do not drink water with their meals. Hot tea is usually available. Orange and other sodas came into vogue among students in the 1930s. Alcohol or wine is warmed up and served with the meal in small cups on festive occasions or when guests are present. The usual meal ends with a big bowl of hot soup in the center of the table from which everyone takes.

Tea is universal in China and is served at most meals and at other times.

Tea drinking in north China is less sophisticated than in the south, although there is no tea ceremony as such in any part of China. There are many kinds of tea, each with a fancy name and often associated with a particular locality. To name a few: Dragon's Well (Lung Ching) is associated with Chekiang, as is Fragrant Flakes, or Hsiang P'ien; Black Dragon (Wu Lung) is associated with Kiangsi, and Brick Tea comes from Yunnan. A tea called Ta Hung P'ao or Big Red Robe is supposed to come only from three old trees in Hangchow and, in the thirties, cost something like five United States dollars an ounce. Most of these fancy names are from the south, not the north.

The Chinese way to make tea is to pour boiling water into a pot containing some tea leaves and let the tea steep for ten minutes or so. It is then ready to be served in cups. A few tea leaves will drift into the drinking cups with the tea, but that is part of the Chinese cup of tea. No external strainer is used. The only straining effect is achieved by the several small holes, instead of one big opening, separating the teapot from its spout.

The Chinese do not distinguish between *wine*, in which the alcoholic content is low, and *spirits*, in which it is high. One term, *chiu*, covers them both.[5] Different kinds of wines and spirits have been known to the Chinese for centuries. *Mao t'ai* is from Kueichou province, *Fen chiu* is from Fen Chou in Shansi province, and *Shao chiu* is from Shao Hsing in Chekiang province. In alcoholic content Mao t'ai and Fen chiu are very high, while Shao chiu is rather low. But they are all known as *chiu*. Except for Fen chiu, north China does not seem to have produced other famous alcoholic drinks. The two most common ones are *Pai kan* ("white dry"), or *Pai chiu* ("white wine"), and *Huang chiu* ("yellow wine"). The former is about 100 proof while the latter is equal to the usual American sherry.

In contrast to their sophisticated approach to food and the high development of their culinary art, the Chinese, even those who drink heavily, are remarkably unparticular about alcohol. Traditional Chinese novels often make references to solitary drinkers who drown their sorrows in wine shops, or to the lone "Robin Hood" who takes alcohol generously before assaulting a corrupt official, but the most common Chinese way of drinking is with meals, especially on festive occasions and banquets. They do not drink cocktails before meals as Americans do, and no mixed drinks of any kind are served. We have been to many such Chinese occasions and have never heard the prospective consumers being asked what they individually preferred. Instead the host has one kind of chiu served, and the guests simply enjoy it. Everyone at the same table partakes of the same drink, if he or she drinks at all.

The Chinese custom is for drinking to be interspersed with ts'ai dishes: one new dish served, one new round of cup-filling. The Chinese custom is also for the host to press more cups on the guests, the guests on the host and on each other. One game played during drinking is called *hua ch'üan,* or "guessing fingers." This was especially popular in north China, including Manchuria, but was also known in the south. Any two drinkers could decide to play. Each player would stick out zero to five fingers at the other while loudly yelling a number from one to ten. The player who yelled the number that equaled the sum of the fingers extended by both players was the winner. The loser had to drink a fresh cup bottom up. This could go on indefinitely till one or both players gave up. It made some Chinese banquets extremely noisy, especially since several pairs could play simultaneously.

Regional Variation

Because of a lack of refrigeration and nationwide food processors and manufacturers in China, Chinese foods tend to exhibit regional peculiarities. One large regional difference—rice for the south, wheat and other grains for the north, and kaoliang, corn, and soybean for the northeast—has already been discussed. The variety of ts'ai dishes is much greater in the south than in the north. And there are many more nationally known fancy dishes identified with some areas of the south than with those of the north.

The northern Chinese often comment on the wealth and good life of the "southerners"—the inhabitants south of the Yangtze River, or "South of the River People" (Chiang Nan Jen). They wear more silk and satin and eat rice all the time and delicacies often, the northerners believe. The northerners also comment on the comparative "bitterness" of their own life and promote frugality and industriousness as a way of dealing with their lot.

We examined a recent book entitled *Chung kuo ming ts'ai ta ch'üan* (Encyclopedia of famous *ts'ai* in China) published in Taiwan (comp. Yeh Hua 1967), and found that its contents were in line with this popular impression. The book contains 614 entries. These are Canton, 67; Ch'ao-chou (Swatow), 58; Tung-chiang (of Kwangtung province), 60; Fukien, 67; Shanghai, 66; Huai-yang (of Kiangsu province), 124; Szechwan, 76; and Peking, 96. In other words, a mere 15 percent of the ts'ai the compiler could find are identified with Peking, the only northern city on the entire list. And Peking, it should be remembered, was for centuries the place where reigning aristocracy, bureaucrats, and office seekers from all over the country congregated.

What are the qualitative differences between northern and southern cuisine? The compiler of the same book gives some highly suggestive ideas:

For example, Cantonese ts'ai, its variety is great, it has mild and strong tastes, it uses really novel and unusual ingredients; Fukienese ts'ai is

strong in its use of seafood, it is especially known for its soup and its
sautéed dishes; Swatow ts'ai is also long on seafood, especially famous
for those in which the ingredients float in soups; Tung-chiang ts'ai is
heavy with fat, strong taste; Peking roast duck is well known all over
the world; Huai-yang ts'ai is special for its fine cuts and delicate taste,
it particularly excels in sweet and salty pastry. [Yeh Hua 1967, p. i; our
translation]

These ideas generally agree with our personal experiences and observations.
Take pastry for example: Moon cakes are special to the Moon Festival in
autumn everywhere in China, but the moon cakes in the north have only
two kinds of filling—white sugar paste or brown date paste. The moon
cakes in the south, on the other hand, have fillings that are made of a large
variety of ingredients from ham, dates, or preserved apricots to walnuts,
lard, and watermelon seeds. Fish is eaten in the north also, but since fresh
fish is not common, most of it is salted.

Peking duck is not the only northern speciality. "Fire pot" is enjoyed in
all northern homes and many restaurants, especially during the long winter
months. This involves a round, charcoal-burning stove wedged into the
center of a ring-shaped pot in which clear chicken soup is boiling. Each
diner helps himself from large plates of well-sliced raw food at the table—
chicken, beef, vegetables, bean curd, and other edibles—and cooks his or
her own food in the pot of boiling soup.

Another favorite northern type of food is Mongolian beef. The reader
who has eaten Mongolian beef in a Japanese restaurant will not recognize
this. In Japan what is called Mongolian beef is consumed raw. The typical
Mongolian-beef restaurant in Peking serves medium-sized slices of raw beef
on a plate. Each diner, using chopsticks some two feet long, cooks his own
meat on a grill over a large charcoal burner which is set on the table. When
the meat gets to a condition of his liking, each diner dips it into the concoction in his own bowl made up of raw egg, soy sauce, chopped ginger,
and scallion before eating it. The best spot for this dinner is on a roof garden
when the temperature is about fifty degrees Fahrenheit.

The most unusual feature about this food is the manner in which the
diners conduct themselves at the table. Instead of sitting on the benches
around the table, the diners stand behind them and step on them with one
foot. As far as we know, the Mongols eat on the floor in their tents. Since
the Chinese prefer tables and chairs, this stand-up-with-one-foot-on-the-
bench way of dining is probably a compromise.

Of course there are variations of cooking within the north. Shansi province,
for example, is famous for its vinegar. When one of the authors visited

T'ai-yüan, its capital, he found that a Shansi chef could not even poach eggs without putting in a lot of vinegar. The author's reaction to this profusion of vinegar in Shansi cooking was not unlike that of the Shanghai people to the liberal use of hot peppers in the cuisine of Hunan or Szechwan. Liang-hsing district in Hopei province is famous for chestnuts. They are sold as far south as Shanghai and Japan. The streets of Kobe and Osaka are dotted with Liang-hsiang chestnut stands in the winter months.

While chestnuts and dried fruits can travel considerable distances without refrigeration, fresh fruits are confined to a small radius around their natural habitats and are available in season only. Thus the long watermelons of Te-chou, in northern Shantung province, are most in evidence in the district itself and in nearby areas. In the thirties we used to feast on them when our train passed through Te-chou station, between Tientsin and Pukow.

One emperor of the T'ang dynasty (618–907) used to order litchis to be sent from Kwangtung province to Changan, the capital, for his favorite concubine, who loved the fruit. The distance of nearly a thousand *li* was covered by relays of galloping horses. Such feats were obviously not for the majority. Consequently, not only had northerners never eaten litchis but also they rarely saw bananas. A well-known story in the thirties runs as follows: Wu Chün-sheng, the reigning warlord of Heilungkiang in northern Manchuria, was being royally entertained one day in Peking at a giant feast, at the end of which a big bowl of fresh fruit was placed at the center of the table. Never having seen or tasted a banana, the warlord took one and ate it, peel and all. The host, wishing to help his honored guest but not wanting to embarrass him, merely took a banana in hand and conspicuously peeled it before biting. Realizing his mistake but not willing to admit that he was a country bumpkin, the visiting warlord grabbed another banana and said, "I always eat these things with the peel on." Thereupon he ate the second banana the same way he had the first.

Food and Drink in New China

Throughout the foregoing pages, we have used the present tense except where it is obviously inapplicable. There have been many changes in the life of the Chinese since 1949, but without systematic inquiry it is, of course, hard to determine their extent. From our nine-week visit to the People's Republic of China in the summer of 1972 (see Hsu-Balzer et. al. 1974), and from recent written reports, we can offer some brief thoughts.

All China, both cities and villages, is now organized into communes. There is no privately owned agricultural land except for a small plot amounting to no more than 0.16 of a *mu*[6] surrounding the four sides of each privately owned home in every commune. In this plot, the owner can grow vegetables, raise a couple of chickens or even a pig for private consumption. In case of surplus, he or she can even sell it for cash.

Throughout China, the area of agricultural land is being expanded through massive efforts at reclamation and irrigation. The total area of China's land under cultivation is now surely somewhat more than the 11 percent often quoted in geography books, although we do not know exactly how much more. In Huang T'u Kang Commune some distance from Peking, for example, the head man showed us that the cultivated area had been expanded several-fold since its beginning. A small enclosure displaying the bare, yellow earth before the reclamation efforts serves as a monument to remind present and future members of the commune of the progress they have made.

In spite of these efforts, China has imported many millions of tons of wheat from Australia and Canada during the last ten to fifteen years. Just how much of this imported wheat is needed for immediate consumption is unknown. We surmise that at least part of it is for the purpose of reserve. A ubiquitous slogan seen in China is "Pei chan, pei huang, wei jen min" (Prepare for War, Prepare for Famine, Serve the People).

A scrupulous system of rationing of certain foods is being enforced throughout the country. The rationed items are rice, wheat flour, meat (mainly pork), and, unexpectedly to us, bean curd in some places.

Due to irrigation projects and soil improvement, wheat and rice are grown in areas where formerly only sorghum, millet, and other grains could be grown. For example, in the August First Commune, some forty miles out of Shen-yang in Liaoning province of Manchuria, irrigated rice is now a principal crop on land where formerly only corn and soybeans prevailed.

Finally, the age-old custom of extravagant feasting on the part of the rich at all times and on the part of the not-so-well-off during funerals, weddings, birthdays, visits from honored guests, and so on, has been drastically reduced or at least altered. Even the quantity (and quality) of food and drink during the important New Year's celebrations has been curtailed, though it is still considerable.

In view of these developments, we can say that most northern Chinese now consume rice, wheat, and soybeans as their staples, relegating sorghum, millet, and sweet potatoes to minor roles. With the rationing of meat, all get a fair share of the supply of animal protein, and this means the majority now consumes more meat and animal products than before. The meat consumption level is probably still a fraction of that of most Americans, but it is obviously no longer as minuscule as shown in J. L. Buck's survey, quoted above. All recent visitors to the People's Republic have reported seeing a healthy and vigorous population with no signs of malnutrition, chronic illness, or epidemics.

The street stands of food and fruit are less in evidence than before. Except for occasional popsicle or newspaper vendors, such stands are outlets for public enterprises. All restaurants, except for those in hotels for foreign visitors and overseas Chinese, provide less elegant but more inexpensive ts'ai dishes than before. They do a thriving business as more Chinese can now afford to go to restaurants than at any time in the past in their long history.

In the hotels for foreigners and overseas Chinese, the elegant and variegated pre-1949 cuisine is commonplace. Whether it was in the Ch'ien Men Hotel or the Hsin Ch'iao Hotel in Peking, the Hua Ch'iao Ta Hsia (Overseas Chinese Hotel) in Canton, the Chiang Han Hotel in Wuhan, or the Tientsin Hotel in Tientsin, the exquisite food clearly indicated that politics has made no difference in China's culinary skills. At a reception in our honor at Peking's Tung Hsing Lou, we were treated to a complete Peking-duck banquet. The chef not only gave us the best Peking duck we had ever tasted but served us separate little dishes of sautéed duck's kidneys, sautéed duck's liver and intestines, deep-fried duck's tongue, salt-fried duck's pancreas, smoked duck's brain, and eggs steamed with duck fat.

In alcoholic beverages, a Chinese-manufactured beer has been added since the revolution. Otherwise there is no indication that alcoholic consumption has increased in quantity and variety. The finger guessing game during banquets is no longer in vogue. In one Chung Kuo Kuo Huo Kung Ssu (Emporium of Chinese Goods) in Hong Kong, operated by the government of the People's Republic, we counted some fifty different kinds of chiu on display, with fancy names, such as Dragon Flea Tonic chiu, Shansi Bamboo Leaf Pure chiu, Ch'angch'un Medicated chiu (Ch'angch'un is a provincial capital city in Manchuria), Chinese White Grape chiu, Chiu Chiang Double Evaporated chiu, Fen chiu, Chrysanthemum Bubble chiu, Ginseng brandy, Crab Apple Bubble chiu, and Five Dragons and Two Tigers chiu. Some of these names, such as Fen chiu and Dragon Flea Tonic chiu, are traditional, but many others are new. However, most of these varieties of chiu appear to have been created for sale abroad.

Nutrition

When one talks about food, one cannot ignore its nutritional aspect. From the foregoing description and analysis, the reader will have gathered that the daily diet of a majority of the Chinese primarily consists of grains, legumes, and other vegetables. The question is, Is this kind of diet adequate and healthful?

The answer is yes. Take proteins for example. According to the Food and Agricultural Organization (FAO), the protein content of isocaloric portions of foods is as in the table below.

A brief examination of this table will convince the reader that protein is substantial in the Chinese diet. Pork, the preferred meat of the Chinese, shows up poorly in comparison with beef, as does the sweet potato, which

Protein Content of Isocaloric Portions of Food

Food	Proteins per 100 calories grams
Beef (thin)	9.6
Pork	2.6
Fish, fresh, fatty	11.4
Fish, dried	15.3
Milk, whole, fluid, 3.5% fat	5.4
Milk, skim, dried	10.0
Wheat flour, medium extraction	3.3
Millet (Eleusine coracana)	2.0
Millet (Setaria italica)	2.9
Millet (Pennisetum glaucum)	3.4
Sorghum (Sorghum vulgare)	2.9
Maize, whole meal	2.6
Rice, home pounded	2.0
Rice, milled white	1.7
Cassava, manioc (Manihot utioissima)	
fresh	0.8
meal and flour	0.4
Yams (Dioscorea sp.)	2.3
Taro (Colocasia esculentum)	1.7
Sweet potatoes	1.1
Plantains, fresh	1.0
Beans and Peas, different species	6.4
Soybeans, whole seeds, dry	11.3
Voandzou, bambarra nuts (Voandzeia subterranea)	5.7
Groundnuts	4.7

Source: J. F. Brock and M. Autret, *Kwashiorkor in Africa*, FAO Nutritional Studies No. 8 (Rome: Food and Agriculture Organization of the United Nations, 1952), p. 49. See also R. F. A. Dean, "Use of Processed Plant Proteins as Human Food," in A. M. Altschul (ed.), *Processed Plant Foodstuffs* (New York, Academic Press, 1958), p. 221.

many northern Chinese consume in quantity rather than milk or skimmed milk. But soybeans, beans and peas, and peanuts (groundnuts), which form an important part of the diet of the Chinese in both the north and the south, are rich in proteins, soybeans spectacularly so. Salted and dried fish, which most Chinese consume in moderate amounts, are the best protein of all— better than thin beef, fresh fish, and skimmed milk. As for grains, there is not much difference between rice and wheat on the one hand, and millet, sorghum, and corn on the other.

More intensive and localized studies of the Chinese diet confirm this. For example, according to Guy and Yeh, even in the thirties the diets of the rich and that of the poor in Peking were both "completely adequate." The diet of the rich consisted of milled cereal-meat while that of the poor was of whole cereal-legume. The latter was made up of "mixed flours of maize and soybean, and millet and soybean, plus vegetables, sesame oil, and salted turnip" (Guy and Yeh 1938, p. 201). This diet was the same as that of a majority of northern Chinese at that time. Its only fault was monotony.

Guy and Yeh did not mention the additional fact that the diet of the poor in the thirties, in Peking and elsewhere, was enriched by rice or wheat and meat on special occasions and by salted fish much of the time. J. L. Buck's survey of farm families covering 1922–25 confirms the adequacy of the proteins and offers substantial data on the daily consumption of calories as well (Buck 1930, pp. 372–81). According to that survey, the average number of calories consumed daily per adult male Chinese farmer was 3,461, as compared with "the Western requirement of 3,400 calories for a man doing moderate manual work" (ibid., p. 373).

The primary source of malnutrition before 1949 lay in the inequality in distribution of the whole-cereal–legume diet of the poor, not in its quality. Many used to go to bed hungry. Since the revolution, the new government has taken a number of measures well known to the world: increased food production at home and wheat purchases abroad, combined with an equitable and efficient system of rationing, as well as some attention to vitamins. There is little doubt in the authors' minds that, although food and drink for the majority are still not luxurious, they are decidedly adequate and healthful.

Concluding Remarks

Revolution or not, food will always have a special significance for the Chinese. No celebration is complete without feasting. Where Western hosts would devote their attention to silverware, tablecloths, candles, and center-pieces to underline the formality or importance of a dinner, the Chinese would escalate the quantity and variety and quality of the contents in the plates and bowls for the same purpose. A Chinese tablecloth, if one is used, is never meant to be immaculate afterward, and many an exquisite feast is had on tables with only lacquered tops.

The revolution has, as we noted before, reduced the former extravagance on the part of the well-to-do at all times and of the rest on special occasions, but it has increased the alimentary adequacy and pleasure of the majority. In the early days after the revolution, guests to weddings reportedly shared no more than a few sticks of candy. But this certainly is no longer the case. There are still no Chinese social gatherings where drinks are served with no more than pretzels.

North and south, the main Chinese concerns in their cuisine are color, flavor, and taste (respectively *se*, *hsiang*, and *wei*). For example, Peking duck must look golden brown, steamed fish must be prepared in sesame oil and fresh ginger root and scallion to achieve its delicate flavor, while sweet and sour pork must contain the right balance between its sweet and sour components to give the delicious taste to the tongue. As long as the Chinese survive as a people, they are not likely to give up their distinct food culture —the art of its preparation and the way of its enjoyment.

NOTES

1. "P'ing Kui Returns to His Humble Home."

2. One other occasion on which important food and drink offerings to ancestral spirits are made is during Ch'ing Ming, the Chinese counterpart of Easter, when the living visit the graveyards of their dead. One story has it that, on their way home, some members of one family heard one spirit asking another about the quality of his alimentary enjoyment that day. The second spirit replied, "Good *chiu* (alcohol) and good *ts'ai* (dishes), only the *popo* (bread) is not so clean." The members of the family who allegedly heard this knew at once that the "not so clean" comment referred to their offerings. When they had been leaving the house with the many food offerings for the graveyard, they could not find the proper container for the bread. In a hurry they wrapped the loaves with a piece of cloth with which they had planned to make a pair of trousers.

3. The American consumption of animal products is, of course, much higher now than in the 1930s when Buck's survey was made.

4. This pattern is not restricted to north China. It prevails even in Hong Kong today.

5. One of the authors, on his way from Paris to London, where he was pursuing graduate studies, brought back a bottle of brandy, intending to give it to a friend. After he verbally declared one bottle of wine, the customs official to whom he made the declaration rebuked him severely when he saw the bottle. The official asked angrily: "You call this wine?" The truth is, up to that time, the author never knew the difference.

6. One *mu* is equal to 0.164 acre.

8: MODERN CHINA: SOUTH

E. N. ANDERSON, JR., AND MARJA L. ANDERSON

The food of contemporary southern China is, in the opinion of many, the finest in the world. It combines quality, variety, and a nutritional effectiveness that allows it to sustain more people per acre than any other diet on earth except modern laboratory creations that demand a major industrial input. This presents a fascinating problem: how did this mountainous and often infertile corner of the earth produce so effective an ecological adjustment? Traditionally, outsiders have ascribed the success of the Chinese to their adjustment to the pressure of "teeming millions." However, both history and logic lead us to believe that the "foodways" came first, permitting the teeming millions to follow. Until about a thousand years ago, south China was lightly populated. Rapid population increase, here as elsewhere in China, has involved adoption of New World crops and expansion of land cultivation, but little technological advance or actual devolution (Perkins 1969; Elvin 1973). We have begun to analyze the dynamics of the system elsewhere (Anderson and Anderson 1973a). Here we will confine ourselves to describing the current state of the art—the foodways of south China.

We take as our unit of analysis the "rice region" of John L. Buck (1937). Buck's classification is well established in the literature, basically accurate, and useful to us because Buck's indefatigable helpers collected food-consumption statistics sorted by region (Maynard and Swen in Buck 1937), thus giving us a good baseline of data on actual consumption in a period still largely traditional. In using the rice region as our unit, we include as "south Chinese" the food of such areas as Szechwan and Shanghai, food that is always called "north Chinese" in the restaurant trade. To the restaurateur, south Chinese food means Cantonese food, and anything north of Kwangtung is north Chinese. However, the diets of the rice region are variations on a theme. Rice is the staple; served with it, as topping, is a piquant and sauce-rich dish or series of dishes, including many vegetables (several of them from the New World) and, if the eater is wealthy enough, pork, fowl, or aquatic animals. North China eats very differently. Food in the wheat region consists of wheat bread (usually leavened and steamed, but not always), grain porridge, or noodles; with it go fewer vegetables, most of them native (only rarely of New World origin). The rich man is much more likely to have lamb and somewhat less likely to have aquatic foods than his southern counterpart. Only soybeans and other legumes and a few other vegetables are equally important in both regions. According to Maynard and Swen's figures (in Buck 1937, p. 413), the average citizen of the most rice-eating part of the wheat region (the winter wheat—millet area) gets only 1 percent of his calories from rice; in the least "oryzivorous" (rice-eating) area, southward, the figure shoots up to 56.9 percent in the Szechwan rice area along the upper Yangtze, and it rises to a high peak in the double-cropping rice area, China's southeastern corner, at 76.9 percent. These figures are, of course, not 100 percent accurate, but they are unquestionably close enough to show that there is a quite spectacular difference in staple food that sets off our southern China from the areas north. The line, of course, is set by the northward limit of profitable, large-scale rice cultivation.[1]

Within the broad limits of this area, we will try to touch on food behavior among both the rich (who could afford variety) and the poor (who lived on grain staples for the most part). We will confine our attention primarily to the Chinese, with only the briefest of notes about the many minority groups in the area, since information on the latter is fragmentary. As a matter of fact, information on the Chinese groups is neither extensive nor comprehensive. Buck's figures give the broad view for a period just before the great upheavals that have transformed China in the last forty years. We know of nothing comparable for more recent times. We have been unable to cover the literature fully; library resources available to us at the time of writing have forced us to limit ourselves primarily to English-language sources, and to the most widely available and easily found of those. (We hope we can remedy this limitation in the near future.) We have relied heavily on our own field work, supplementing it with other ethnographies and, to some extent, with early travel accounts. More general information on Chinese food comes from two sources: cookbooks and works on agriculture (it is presumed that people did indeed eat what they raised for local consumption!). Food has all too often been considered a subject too earthy and gross for scholarly attention—a puritanical Western attitude that would seem to have spread to China. We have failed to find any modern Chinese gourmet-writers who equal, say, Yüan Mei—though Kenneth Lo (1972) and F. T. Cheng (1962) have made a good start. Chinese cookbooks proliferate, but the vast majority of them are subtitled or advertised with the deadly line "Adapted to Western Kitchens," or some equally sad phrase, and are useless for our purposes. Many others are brief or merely repeat well-known recipes with no new information. For what it is worth, we have relied most on the cookbooks of B. Y. Chao (1963; but much of it is north Chinese cooking), Fu (1969), Handy (1960), K. Lo (1971, 1972), Miller (1967), and Sis and Kalvodova (1966). These and others are by no means perfect. They mix different schools, differ on what is a school and what isn't, reflect primarily the tastes of the urban rich, occasionally introduce modifications of dishes, or otherwise transgress against scholarship—or else they are all too brief. There is nothing in the literature on China even remotely comparable to Root's great books *The Food of France* (1958) and *The Food of Italy* (1971).

On the agricultural side, fortunately, we are much better served—the world of international scholarship holding that, while consumption of food is unworthy of attention, production of food makes money and is therefore a serious business. We have consulted only the standard references here, leaving less well-known references, especially the non-English literature, for another occasion. The classic works of King (1911) and Buck have been supplemented by a host of excellent books, not only in agriculture itself (e. g., Herklots 1972; C. C. Hu 1966; P. P. Li 1963), but also in geography (e. g., Buchanan 1970—perhaps the most useful book for our purposes that deals with modern mainland China) and history (e. g., Laufer 1919), and about individual crops, such as the soybean (Piper and Morse 1923; Smith and Circle 1972). There are also the fascinating works of Hommel (1937) and Mallory (1926), dealing respectively with folk crafts (including the food industry) and famines.

Lastly we have relied for reference (scientific names, nutritional analyses of foods, and the like) on such standard works as Uphof's *Dictionary of Economic Plants* and the food tables of Bowes and Church (Church and Church 1970) and Watt and Merrill (1963).

In view of the importance and fame of Chinese food, we were surprised to find how poorly described it is in the travel accounts, modern literature, and other general works by Chinese or about China. Chinese novels of dynastic times are excellent sources of information about food, but—from our limited search—it seems that European models stimulated a turning away from such discourse. The heroes of our times all too often have no food, and when they can find a bit to eat, it is a cup of tea and a bowl of noodles, or at best a well-known and briefly noted dish whose mention adds little to our knowledge. May we hope that this book will stimulate greater interest in describing Chinese food—perhaps even give rise to a new literature.

The Ingredients: Foodstuffs of South China

South China may well cultivate more crops, at least on a commercial scale, than any other comparable region. Certainly it is well endowed with native (or long-cultivated) crops and has also been quick to add new importations to its roster; to pick a recent example, Taiwan has taken up cultivation of asparagus (*Asparagus officinalis*) and European mushrooms (*Agaricus bisporus*). In addition to cultivated plants and animals—from microscopic yeasts to giant palms, and from carp to water buffalo—wild plants (especially herbs) and wild animal life (especially aquatic, but also including game) contributed much to the diet. South China, specifically southwestern China, has the most diverse flora of any region outside the wet tropics. A complexly faulted and folded landscape blessed with abundant rain and warmth encouraged tremendous diversity, and the human inhabitants of the region were not slow to make use of this. Indeed, they increased it, by borrowing every easily adaptable crop from every major region on earth. Only such crops as figs and true dates, accustomed to totally different climatic regimes and not of prime world importance anyway, remained of little account. With animals, the borrowing was less extensive, but even so a large number of domesticated strains is found (Epstein 1969).

Under these circumstances, it is logical that the staple foods are those which are exceptionally productive and nutritious. Rice (*Oryza sativa*) produces more calories per acre than any other crop of much nutritional value. (Manioc and the starchier white potatoes, as well as sugar cane and sugar beets, produce more calories per acre, but almost exclusively in the form of carbohydrates.) Rice, when not polished, has a substantial amount of protein and B vitamins, as well as other nutrients. We will leave nutrition for a later section, but here we must emphasize the importance of a staple crop that actually feeds people. Manioc cannot sustain dense populations, in spite of its yield; rice can. In addition, it is easy to process, easy to digest, and can be either tasty or a near tasteless absorbing medium, depending on the cooking process. No wonder that it is the favored food as well as the most abundant. Rice is somewhat loosely classified as variety *indica* (the long-grained, starchy rice favored in China), *japonica* (short-grained, adapted to longer days and shorter growing seasons, favored more in Japan than China though it is more productive and nutritious than *indica*), and the various glutinous rices, including the red and black rices. Many intermediates and hybrids of indicas and japonicas are found in northern south China; the famous "miracle" rices developed by the International Rice Research Institute (IRRI) in the Philippines were based on peasant-created hybrids —local miracle rices—in Taiwan, where both japonicas and indicas have long been important. As a matter of fact, the world of rice is far more complicated than the above picture suggests (see Grist 1965). There are literally thousands of varieties of each of the main divisions. In a southern Chinese peasant plot, before the days of miracle grains, chance pollination and natural selection for diversity probably guaranteed that no two plants were genetically identical, or at least that a field would be a marvelous genetic mosaic— allowing resistant strains to develop naturally, heterosis to occur, and microhabitat differences to encourage microdifferentiation in rices. Lower-yield but higher-protein rices occurred in dry cultivation and no doubt elsewhere; there were salt-tolerant rices for tidal marshes, flood-tolerant rices, and so on without end. The coming of standardized modern seed strains will no doubt lower diversity and perhaps also nutritional quality, since the new rices tend to be starchy, though the IRRI is aware of the problem and is trying to maintain good protein content in the varieties it distributes, and presumably the mainland Chinese breeding stations are doing likewise. A connoisseurship of rice developed in traditional China; the longer-grained and starchier indicas were the choicest. Interestingly enough, the many varieties of rice are far more similar to each other than are the widely diverse varieties of maize developed by the American Indians. This is, no doubt, partly a function of the fact that rice is used basically as a substratum— a neutral substance to be topped with *sung*, as the Cantonese call the many dishes that give flavor to a meal—whereas the Indians of the Americas grew corn for many different uses. (This, of course, begs the question of why the south Asians did not grow rice for more diverse uses.)

Rice dominated wherever the soil and water conditions were right. As it became marginal in a given area, or at a given season, other staples encroached, eventually becoming dominant as one proceeded out of areas where rice could grow. As one went north, winters became colder and wheat replaced rice as the rotation crop for the cool season. (Even in southernmost China, winters at their height are often cold enough to discourage rice growing, but a catch-crop of quick-growing vegetables is found there between the double crops of rice.) As one went up the mountains, cold increased again, but this time the cold was year round—during short-day and long-day seasons both—and was less subject to intense fluctuations. Here rice gave way to barley and, especially on poor soil, to buckwheat. Areas that were warm enough but too steep and infertile for rice had once depended on millets and sorghums, but by our period they were dominated by the New World crop maize (*Zea mays*). Also, the moist mountains of the interior had come to depend on Irish, or white, potatoes (*Solanum tuberosum*), popularized by French missionaries during the late Ch'ing period. Lastly, sweet potatoes dominated in warm sandy soils.

Here we may introduce the tables given by Maynard and Swen (in Buck 1937, p. 413). Compiled during a period of relative peace and security, and taking little account of the Chinese tendency to show a visitor the best of a region and give him the best possible statistics, these tables unquestionably overestimate the amount of rice and underestimate the amounts of other grains, especially in such areas as the far west and the mountainous center of south China (Kueichou and area), where, especially among the non-Han minorities, rice was often virtually unknown. (Buck's figures have often been criticized as overoptimistic; see, for example, Fei 1939. No accounts of south Chinese rural areas by actual on-spot observers fail to stress the importance of these secondary staples, or the frequent lack of rice—and even of the secondaries). However, these are the only figures we

Animal Food Calorie Intake

17,351 persons, 2,727 families, 136 localities, 131 hsien, 21 provinces, China, 1929–1933

Regions and areas	Number of localities	Daily intake of calories supplied by animal foods per adult-male unit	Percentage of animal calorie intake supplied by different animal foods										
			Pork	Lard	Mutton	Eggs (chicken)	Beef	Chicken	Fish	Duck	Eggs (duck)	Shrimp, dried	Meat, salted
China	136	76	54	18	8	8	4	2	2	1	1	*	*
Wheat Region	67	32	59	7	17	10	6	*	1	—	*	—	—
Rice Region	69	122	51	31	*	5	3	3	4	1	1	1	*
Wheat Region Areas:													
Spring Wheat	13	35	51	5	36	2	6	*	*	—	—	—	—
Winter Wheat–Millet	21	17	63	5	23	7	2	*	—	—	—	—	—
Winter Wheat–Kaoliang	33	40	59	8	5	16	8	1	3	—	*	—	—
Rice Region Areas:													
Yangtze Rice-wheat	22	98	58	24	1	8	2	2	3	*	1	—	1
Rice–Tea	19	106	54	31	*	5	1	3	4	1	1	—	—
Szechwan Rice	6	165	48	37	2	3	7	1	1	—	1	—	—
Double Cropping Rice	11	102	42	22	*	3	7	6	8	6	2	4	—
Southwestern Rice	11	196	46	44	*	2	4	2	*	1	1	—	—

Percentage of Calories Supplied by Different Important Staple Crops

17,351 persons, 2,727 families, 136 localities, 131 hsien, 21 provinces, China, 1929–1933

Regions and areas	Number of localities	Rice	Wheat	Millet	Kaoliang	Corn	Millet, proso	Potatoes, sweet	Barley	Soybeans	Green beans	Oats	Potatoes, Irish	Field peas	Rice, glutinous	Broad beans	Soybeans black	Other grains	Other legumes
China	136	35.0	14.4	10.4	7.5	7.5	2.8	2.6	2.0	2.0	1.2	1.2	0.9	0.8	0.7	0.6	0.6	0.2	1.3
Wheat Region	67	0.6	23.5	19.9	14.6	11.9	5.8	2.5	1.3	3.2	2.0	2.2	1.7	1.3	—	0.2	1.2	2.3	1.4
Rice Region	69	68.4	5.6	1.2	0.6	3.2	—	2.8	2.7	0.9	0.4	0.1	0.1	0.3	1.5	1.1	*	1.3	1.3
Wheat Region Areas																			
Spring Wheat	13	*	15.3	20.0	4.5	*	21.7	—	1.3	0.4	0.4	10.9	7.3	3.2	—	1.0	0.7	8.6	0.8
Winter Wheat–Millet	21	1.0	26.7	23.2	11.5	17.4	4.1	0.3	0.8	2.2	1.4	0.3	0.8	1.5	—	—	0.9	1.4	1.9
Winter Wheat–Kaoliang	33	0.6	24.7	17.9	20.5	13.0	0.5	4.9	1.7	4.9	3.0	—	*	0.5	—	—	1.6	0.5	1.2
Rice Region Areas:																			
Yangtze Rice-wheat	22	57.8	12.8	1.2	1.6	2.1	—	1.8	7.4	0.7	1.2	—	—	0.2	1.3	1.5	—	1.9	1.1
Rice–Tea	19	75.8	3.1	0.4	0.1	2.1	—	2.0	0.3	0.8	*	*	0.1	0.1	1.8	0.5	0.1	1.7	1.5
Szechwan Rice	6	56.9	5.3	—	0.1	14.0	—	3.1	0.3	1.9	0.3	1.5	0.1	2.2	0.8	1.2	—	0.7	1.2
Double Cropping Rice	11	76.9	0.5	0.1	—	—	—	8.2	1.2	0.6	0.1	—	—	*	0.6	0.1	—	0.1	1.5
Southwestern Rice	11	74.7	1.0	*	—	4.8	—	0.5	0.3	1.4	*	—	0.3	0.1	2.4	2.1	—	1.3	1.1

have that cover the whole region, and they are a great deal better than nothing. So, for what they are worth, above are the tables on food consumption—grain and other—in south China, with the northern Chinese figures left in for comparison (since there seems no point in leaving out information so neatly and economically tabulated).

It will be noted that the other category of foods that is important enough to be rated on these tables is the category of protein foods: animal products and leguminous plants. Soybeans—fifth of the classic Five Staples (or Five Grains)—are usually the most important, though other legumes make a surprisingly good showing in south China, no doubt because soybeans grow better in the north. The soybean (*Glycine max*) produces more protein per acre and per pound than any other common humanly edible crop, plant, or animal. This has caused them to become more important than any animal food as a protein provider in China. The Chinese have long recognized their similarity to animal products and, indeed, have built up a huge cluster of imitation-meat foods (probably developed originally by, and certainly now associated with, vegetarian Buddhists). The Chinese lack of interest in dairy products is almost certainly, in part, a result of the fact that the soybean provides the same sorts of nutrition more economically—though a desire to differentiate themselves from the border nomads and to be independent of them in food economy must also be taken seriously as an explanation. (It is the classic Chinese explanation of the phenomenon but has been dismissed by those moderns who believe that all traditional explanations must necessarily be wrong.) Further discourse on the soybean belongs properly to the following section on food processing, for the soybean is used neither in its raw state nor, usually, in a simple boiled or roasted form. There are good reasons for this. The soybean, being so nutritious and succulent, has been faced with intense natural selection pressure by seed-eating insects and other animals; surviving soybean strains contain whole galleries of poisons and other unfortunate chemicals, which protect the seeds against destruction but make them dangerous food in the uncooked and unprocessed state (Committee on Food Protection 1973). Simply prepared soybeans are not very digestible, since heat bonds some of the nutrients into hard-to-digest form in the intact bean. Thus almost all soybeans consumed in China are fermented, ground into flour, and then processed, sprouted, or otherwise milled.

Other legumes are surprisingly important in south China. The soybean is so famous that one is surprised to discover from Buck that the broad bean outranks it in some parts of south China. The broad, or fava, bean (*Vicia faba*) is a Near Eastern/Mediterranean crop, usually associated with cool rainy winters and dry summers. In genetically susceptible individuals, it

produces favism, a condition characterized by acute anemia and other unpleasant symptoms. It is not at all comparable with the soybean in nutritional
value or productivity. Could Buck's investigators have been mistaken about
its value? It is known, however, to be cultivated widely in China and must
dominate among beans locally where soybeans cannot grow well. An assortment of other legume crops grows in China: besides the field pea (*Pisum
arvensis*, presumably) and black soybean (a variety of soybean) mentioned
by Buck, we must stress the importance of the mung bean (*Phaseolus aureus*).[2]
While the mung bean is not by percentage a large part of Chinese diets,
it provides the pea-starch noodles and many of the bean sprouts (more
accurately, it provides the *ya ts'ai*, or "pea sprouts," as opposed to the *tou
ya* from the soybean, but the two are mixed in everyday usage). All these
make a significant contribution to the protein in the diet, at least locally.

Bean sprouts bridge the gap between grains and *ts'ai* "vegetables," since
they are considered *ts'ai* but are made from grains (beans). (Beans eaten in
the immature pod state, as snap beans, are in a similar situation.) In addition
to these, a vast number of green vegetables are found cultivated in south
China. Preeminent, though not so totally dominant in the vegetable scene as
they are in the north, are the members of the cabbage family, and specifically
those of the genus *Brassica*. The species in question are not the ones known
in the rest of the world (except as spread from China), but are native Chinese
cultigens. Their classification in botany is controversial and difficult to work
out. Herklots (1972, pp. 190–93) gives a good up-to-date summary and
balanced taxonomy of some of them. The dominant ones are *Brassica
pekinensis* (*Pai ts'ai* of many forms, Chinese cabbage, and a host of local
names in various languages), the long cylindrical-headed forms; *Brassica
chinensis* (*ch'ing ts'ai* in Mandarin books but the *pak choi* of Cantonese),
the non-headed, white-petioled forms and their close relatives: and *Brassica
juncea* (*chieh ts'ai* in Mandarin, *kaai choi* in Cantonese—same characters),
which, though its Mandarin name is a metaphor for pettiness and unimpor-
tance, is vitally important in southern China. In addition to these there are
Brassica alboglabra (the *kaai laan* of the Cantonese—if anyone else grows
it we do not know of them), very similar to collards; *Brassica campestris*
(the Chinese rapeseed that is a major oil crop), whose leaves are occasionally
used; and various minor crops, including *Brassica oleracea*, European
cabbage, a recently introduced crop from the West. The Cantonese *choi sam*
("vegetable heart"), so vital to southern Chinese cooking, is a form of *B.
chinensis*, or at least it is believed to be and is usually so listed, though quite
distinct in appearance. Herklots (1973, p. 208) lists it as var. *parachinensis*,
citing other names used. Related to the Brassicas quite closely is the radish,
Raphanus sativus, whose enormous-rooted varieties are native to China and

abound under the general name *luo-po* (Mandarin; Cantonese *lo pak*). These crops—the cabbages, mustards, and radishes—are by far the most important "minor" crops of China, the cabbages and mustards being the principal leaf crops. With rice and soybeans, they are the ordinary person's food. A huge bowl of rice, a good mass of bean curd, and a dish of cabbages—fresh in season, otherwise pickled—is the classic fare of the everyday south Chinese world. A little chili or preserved soybean for flavor, some *B. campestris* oil to stir-fry the greens, and a perfectly adequate, nutritionally excellent meal results, without the use of animal products or of any plant that takes much land or effort. The cabbage-family vegetables yield enormous harvests and are available the year round in southern China, where *pekinensis* grows in the cold season, *alboglabra* in the hot season, and *chinensis*, in some form or other, all the time. Hong Kong vegetable growers sometimes get a crop of *choi sam* in every month—twelve harvests in the year—all copious and nourishing. The plant grows extremely vigorously and responds well to fertilizing.

Next in importance are the plants of the genus *Allium*—onions, garlic, and chives. In addition to common onion *A. cepa* and garlic *A. sativum*, there is the famous *ts'ung*, or green onion, *A. fistulosum* (the "bunching," or "Welsh," onion of the West); *A. chinense* (*ch'iao ts'ai* in Mandarin, *k'iu ch'oi* in Cantonese), a small pleasant-flavored onion much used for pickling; and *Allium tuberosum*, Chinese, or garlic, chives. The last named are an immensely popular flavoring herb—one of the few in common use. Among other values, they have given China the charming phrase "chive-cutting mentality," immortalized in William Hinton's *Fanshen* (1966), meaning the mentality of those who feared, in the early Communist days, that whenever they got any wealth or produced anything of value it would immediately be expropriated and redistributed, just as any chive leaf that sticks up is picked for cutting.

The New World vegetables stand out as a special class because of their common and recent origin in China and their extreme importance. The white and sweet potatoes have become staples, as has corn. In addition to these, the peanut (*Arachis hypogaea*) has become the most important oilseed through much of south China, as well as a much-used food. Squashes of the *Cucurbita* group and New World beans (*Phaseolus* spp.) have remained minor due to competition with well-established Chinese equivalents, but two other New World crops have transformed southern Chinese (and, indeed, most Old World) cooking: the tomato (*Lycopersicon esculentum*), only adopted in the last hundred years or so, and the pepper (*Capsicum annuum* and the far hotter *C. frutescens*). Of the latter, *annuum* is far more important than *frutescens*, and the hotter forms of *annuum*, the chili peppers, are more important and longer established than the sweet (bell) forms. Tomatoes and chilis not only transformed the taste of southern Chinese cooking, they also provided new and very rich sources of vitamins A and C and certain minerals, thus improving the diet of the south Chinese considerably. Easy to grow, highly productive, and bearing virtually year round in the subtropical climate, these plants eliminated the seasonal bottlenecks on vitamin availability caused by the lack of good productive vegetables in such seasons as spring. They thus contributed largely to the rise of China's population and wealth over the last few hundred years, as we will discuss more fully below. Chilis, of course, were most widely adopted in Szechwan and Hunan, where they fitted into a cuisine already spicy due to use of brown pepper (fagara) and probably also to contact with India.

In addition to these, south China has and utilizes a vast collection of vegetables that do not give themselves easily to classification. None is strikingly important; all are used. From among a host, we may arbitrarily select for special discussion, or at least listing, those that are both common and interesting. Among these the largest (as good a place to start as any) is the *Benincasa hispida* (winter melon, wax gourd, hair gourd, etc.). While not nearly as diverse in its forms and qualities as the New World's *Cucurbita pepo*, the wax gourd has a striking number of forms, so different that few would imagine them to be conspecific. The winter melons are huge, dark-skinned, hard-rinded, and used most characteristically as soup kettles: filled with various ingredients and sometimes carved on the outside into lovely designs, they are steamed, adding to the finished soup their faintly spicy flavor and their tendency to absorb overgreasy or overspicy tastes. The young Benincasas of other varieties are used as summer squash: sliced and eaten boiled or stir-fried, slightly waxy and bristly, these tongue-shaped fruits are usually known as *mao kua*, "hair gourds." A wide variety of other cucurbits are grown, from the worldwide cucumbers and melons (*Cucumis melo*) to the long, serpentine, bizarre snake gourd (*Trichosanthes cucumerina*) and the angled and smooth luffas (*Luffa acutangula* and *L. cylindrica*). Most interesting of these minor cucurbits is the *Momordica charantia* (bitter melon, bitter gourd, balsam pear, or karela—the last is an Indian vernacular name). Light green and warty, with red-peeled seeds when ripening, this fruit is used in unripe stage, cut up and stir-fried with meat slices or shrimps or both; it brings out their flavors, while they seem to neutralize, partially, the fruit's bitterness. Bitter melon is an acquired taste, and one well worth the trouble of acquiring.

A whole range of root crops has declined to minor importance due to the spread of the New World potatoes and of the European carrot, *Daucus carota* (*hung lo pak* in Cantonese; believed to have great medicinal value, perhaps due to its superior carotene content that would cure the mild avitaminosis-A that must have been common in certain times and places in old China). Most of these root crops, indeed all of them known to us, deserved their fate; they were very much less nutritious, less productive, and more coarse, fibrous, hard to prepare, and hard to use than the supplanters. The best of them, and the only one to retain much importance, is taro *Colocasia antiquorum*, the grayish or purplish potato-like stem of an aroid. It is perhaps most familiar from its use in one of the very few Chinese dishes we really dislike: slices of taro bedded between fat bacon slices and then steamed, thus producing a starchy, greasy, bland, drippy dish worthy of a stereotypical British boardinghouse.

Actually, of course, taro is a stem, not a root, and so are several other aquatic crops. South China is a world of water; at least the densely inhabited parts are, with their paddies and flooded fishponds. Where the water is too deep (or apt to flood too deep) for rice but too shallow for fish, a unique world of crops is found. A stem like taro (but spared the misnomer of "root" crop) is the water chestnut (*Eleocharis*, or *Scirpus*, *tuberosa*, or *E. dulcis*), the corm of a tule or other bulrush. Totally different in every way, but confusingly also called "water chestnut" in English, is the fruit of *Trapa bicornis*, a broad-leaved, floating aquatic plant. The *Eleocharis* chestnut is the Chinese *ma t'ai* ("horse hoof"), the round, crisp, sweet water chestnut used with meat. *Trapa* is the *ling kuo* (Cantonese *leng kok*), the two-horned nut that is often poisonous raw. It is cooked for a snack or sweetmeat, and its flour is a standard thickener and binder, now mostly replaced by cornstarch. It is often called "water caltrop" to distinguish it from *Eleocharis*—the "true" water chestnut—but actually the ling kuo probably has a better claim on the name, for its close relative *T. natans* of Europe is really the original water chestnut, a frequent though minor European food. *Scirpus* stems similar to *Eleocharis* were widely eaten by primitive peoples of the New and Old Worlds under the name of "tule roots" or "bulrush roots." Should the Chinese system of names be rectified? Probably not; there is no hope of ending the confusion in English; scholars should cleave to the Chinese and scientific names.

Another aquatic non-root is the lotus root—a rhizome (horizontal, bottom-growing stem) of *Nelumbo nucifera*, whose seeds are also important. Lotus rhizomes make a fine flour. Sticky within, they are eaten at weddings: the rhizome is broken and the halves pulled apart, but threads of sticky gum bind them together, thus symbolizing that nothing can pull the happy couple apart. Other important aquatic crops include *weng ts'ai*, or water spinach, *Ipomoea aquatica* (well described in Edie and Ho 1969) and watercress, *Nasturtium officinale*. The former may be grown in summer, the latter in winter, in the same fields. Both are notably "cooling" in folk medicine. Water spinach shares with *Trapa* the dubious distinction of being a lurking ground for parasites and so should be well cooked before eating. It is a close relative of the sweet potato but cultivated for its leaves and native to the region. It is the most important (at least in Hong Kong) of several minor leaf crops that supplement the cabbages (especially in hot weather) but are less productive or nourishing. These grade off into wild herbs, and we have no space to list them; their contribution to diet is minor.

Last, among vegetables, we may note eggplant (*Solanum melongenum* and okra (*Hibiscus esculentus*), two fruits from India and Africa respectively that reached the region, probably, via southeast Asia; sweet corn, eaten on the cob, especially in mountain districts; and the strange wild "rice" (*Zizania aquatica*), not eaten as a grain like its American counterpart, but grown because a fungal infection of the stem makes the shoots swell and become tender. It is, in this state, a delicacy vaguely similar to asparagus.

We turn now to plants used in small quantities only, and thus deserving to be called herbs and spices rather than vegetables, though the dividing line is notably vague. China has many fewer herbs (i.e., plants whose green parts, in small amounts, are used for flavoring) than does southern Europe (the world center of herb use), and many fewer spices (i.e., plants whose non-green parts are the flavoring substances) than southern and Southeast Asia. Of course, medicinal herbs are a separate category; we are concerned here only with plants whose chief value is as food, not as medicine. One plant illustrates difficulties in classification: the day lily (*Hemerocallis* sp., or spp. with hybrids), whose roots and buds are a medicine, herb/spice, or vegetable, as one chooses. Its buds are the "golden needles"—*chin chen* (*hua*)—of Chinese cuisine and medicine. More clearly herbs are chives, already noted, and coriander greens (*Coriandrum sativum*; *yüan sui*; Cantonese *iun sai*), the Mexican cilantro—frequently miscalled "Chinese parsley," but actually a Near Eastern spice that evidently spread through central Asia. It is still most important in northwestern Chinese cuisine but is widely used everywhere. Its strong flavor is usually either loved or hated (we love it) and is definitely an acquired taste—like bitter melon, one well worth acquiring. Among spices, most important is ginger—if fresh ginger root is a spice; it is used enough to be a vegetable (*Zingiber officinale*). "Heating," good for fertility and sex life in traditional belief, it enters into almost any meat dish (at least it does when some cooks are at work; others avoid it). The other distinctive southern Chinese spice is much more rare and local: *Xanthoxylum piperitum*, the brown, or Szechwan, pepper or fagara (no English name is well agreed on), the original Chinese *chiao*, now *hua chiao* or *huang chiao*. A native of western China and used primarily in Szechwan-

Hunan cuisine, it bears fruits that look like brown peppercorns twinned on a short stem. The whole looks like a tiny set of human male genitalia, providing the Chinese language with a simile that dates back to the *Book of Songs* and has been amply and lasciviously used from then to the present. In addition to these, "extra" flavor in Chinese cooking comes largely from the myriad of preserved soybean preparations that develop distinctive and spicy flavors. More accessible than spices, these have largely taken their place. Curry powder and other non-Chinese spices have, of course, come into Chinese cuisine in the last few decades or even centuries, but they remain very much an alien phenomenon, and Chinese cooks are not comfortable or skilled with them. In Southeast Asia this generalization is not so; contact and fusion with Thai, Malay, and other cuisines has led to the development of superb and distinctive cuisines, such as the "Nonya" cooking of Malaysia and Singapore (*nonya* is Malay for a Chinese lady of means). These local tradi- tional hybrids must be left outside this discussion, however, since they would require as much space again as we have allotted to us.

In another category of plants used in cooking are those whose main function is to add less flavor than the spices and herbs, less bulk than the real vegetables, and to absorb differentially the flavors of a made dish, in order to bring out, by subtle chemistry, the highest and most delicate tastes. This class of foods is essentially coterminous with the category Fungi. Dominant among these, and central to many dishes (especially vegetarian ones) while playing an assisting role in many more, is the *tung ku* (*Lentinus edodes*), a mushroom that grows on fallen trees and is cultivated in Japan (where it is called *shiitake*). The padi-straw mushroom (*Volvariella volvacea*) is also found, but we have not heard a Chinese name for it. Both these two are almost certainly cultivated in south China—as, today, in Taiwan at least, is the European mushroom *Agaricus bisporus*. (See Singer 1961). Very characteristic of south Chinese cooking are the earlike wood fungi, known as *mu erh* ("wood ears") or *yün erh* ("cloud ears"), species of *Auricularia* or *Tremella* or both. Like truffles in French cuisine, these add little of their own but somehow bring out the finest flavors of the dishes to which they are added, as well as providing a distinctive and pleasant texture that con- trasts with the other ingredients.

At a higher level of contrast with *ts'ai* vegetables are the *kuo*, "fruits and nuts." South China is a world center of these: southern Taiwan and the facing coast, particularly the Ch'aochou (Teochiu) region, are especially famous for subtropical fruit (see descriptions of fruit-raising villages by Kulp, 1925, and Ch'en, 1939). Szechwan is so for various fruits and nuts, and other areas are renowned for their regional specialties. All accounts of south- ern Chinese villages mention a variety of fruit trees. Even so, fruits and nuts were not a major part of the southern Chinese scene, except in the specialized parts of Ch'aochou. They demanded too much work and took up too much space for too many years of nonbearing growth and too little product. They tended to be relegated to corners and to odd bits of land and were skimped in regard to care, except where they were a major commercial crop. The Chinese as a whole had perhaps the least sweet tooth of any people on earth, until quite recently, when the blandishments of soft-drink and candy hucksters ruined their resistance and, consequently, their teeth. Fruit was a light snack, not made into fancy desserts, and was liked in a fairly sour state; many Europeans who comment much on food in early accounts of modern China complain of being given green fruit. The fact is that the fruit was preferred a bit unripe or naturally sour or pithy. It was often picked green and salted. Very sweet fruits preserved in honey were often eaten in the north (but even there as minor snacks), but less so in most of the south. Sugarcane was grown in the south, but on a small scale, to a great extent for children to nibble on the raw, unprocessed cane, which is pretty low in sugar per foot. How many were like Ku Kai-chih, who started eating cane from the least sweet end so that he might "gradually enter the region of bliss"? Nuts were used more, in cooking especially, but cannot be said to have a major part in the southern Chinese diet. In tree-rich Szechwan, the walnut *Juglans regia* was important in both meat dishes and desserts, including a walnut cream similar, and perhaps related, to a nut halvah. Nuts were frequently eaten as snacks, though the seeds of watermelons, *Citrullus vulgaris* (from specially selected strains with thousands of seeds and little pulp), were more favored. Even lotus seeds were used more than true nuts, at least until the coming of the peanut from South America.

Many Chinese fruits have spread to the rest of the world and need little comment here: orange, oriental persimmon (*Diospyros kaki*, the oriental replacement species of the original persimmon, *D. virginiana*, of the eastern United States), peach, plum, tangerine. Others are less well known: the pomelo (*Citrus mitis*), like a large woody grapefruit; the King orange, *kan* (Cantonese *kam*; *Citrus nobilis*), an ancient and long-established hybrid of orange and tangerine, now known in a wonderful variety of forms and colors all over the Far East; the citrus-like *huang p'i* or "wampee" (*Clausena lansium*); the grape-flavored litchi (*Nephelium litchi*); the kumquat (*Fortunella* spp.), like tiny sweet-skinned tangerines; and many more. Most widespread and well known is the *mei* (Cantonese *mui*; *Prunus mume*). Almost always called "plum" in English and thus confused with the totally dissimilar, though related, *li* (*Prunus salicina*), the mei is a distinct species, much closer to apricot than to plum, and more correctly translated as "oriental flowering apricot." Even this is unsatisfactory, as the tree is not very similar to the common apricot (*Prunus armeniaca*; the Chinese *hsing* or *heng*, Cantonese *hang*). It is the mei that is so famous in art and poetry, and so rich a source of images, from the sublime to the degrading (cf. the "mei disease," syphilis). It deserves to be called mei in Western languages; it can stand on its own. In any case, it is the source of the salted, pickled (*suan mei*), or soured fruits that are universal snacks or accompaniments to meat in China. The fruits are small and sour, of apricot appearance and flavor, and barely edible without processing. Another important Chinese fruit little known and usually misnamed in the West is the *tsao* (Cantonese *tsou*, *Zizyphus vulgaris*, syn. *Z. jujuba*), the jujube, or "Chinese date." The fruit does look like a date, though usually red instead of brown, and even tastes somewhat datelike and has a long hard datelike stone, but it is not related to the date; it is borne on a small thorny tree that suckers profusely and is closely related to the original "lotos" of the West (nothing like the lotus). The jujube thrives in dry country and is thus a marginal cultigen in rain-soaked southern China, but many are imported from the north, where they are the most important fruit except possibly for the oriental persimmon.

A vast assortment of tropical fruits and nuts—from coconut and areca nut (the palm fruit used in the betel quid, once very popular in south China) to star-fruit and mangoes—are or have been grown in the extreme south of China. They are marginal to the region and insignificant in the overall food picture but have some local importance and a potential for development.

Last of all, it is worth noting, as a curiosity, that bamboos almost never fruit; but when they do, all the bamboos of a region will fruit together and then die, or at least take long in recovering. The fruit is reportedly edible. Mass fruitings of this kind are the basis of many local legends, all with the following plot: the bamboos never fruited; then came a famine; devout people prayed to the gods; the gods answered by making the bamboos fruit, and the people were saved. More cynical phrase-makers will say "when the bamboo fruits" to mean something very close to "never." Bamboo shoots are more properly a vegetable but might better be considered here as a tree crop—one cultivated tree that is indeed common and widespread. Many species of bamboo, especially of the genus *Phyllostachys* but also of the giant-sized genus *Sinocalamus* and others, produce this well-known vegetable. Since some of the giant bamboos grow more than a foot a day in the tropics, the supply can be large. The outer leaves are husked off, and the core—the future woody "trunk" of these large grasses—is eaten.

We now turn, with a slight sigh of relief, to domestic animals. Here the story is much shorter. One main source of animal protein in the southern Chinese diet is fish. Most of the fish are caught wild, and there are hundreds or thousands of species of fish and shellfish used. Some fish, however, are pond-reared.[3] Those that have been effectively domesticated are carps. These have several advantages: they produce vast amounts of protein per acre; they do not have to be specially fed since they eat algae and weedy grass and small animals of the ponds and pond fringes; they can live in foul water, and thus in stagnant ponds and in market fish barrels; they are efficient converters, putting a large percentage of their feed into growth; and relative to other fish, they are easy to breed in captivity. The first fish farmed in the world were probably the Chinese carps. At a guess, they were domesticated first in south China, perhaps the Yangtze basin, before the Chinese moved in, by people speaking Thai or some other language. In any event, the most widespread—disseminated over the world in historic time—is the omnivorous *Cyprinus carpio*, the common carp. Others occur in complementary feeding niches in the ponds: *Carassius auratus* (crucian carp, goldfish) living in small ponds and streamlets; *Ctenopharyngodon idella* (grass carp) feeding on grasses near or at the surface; *Mylopharyngodon pictus* (black carp) feeding on small animal life; *Hypophthalmichthys molitrix* (silver carp) feeding on plankton at mid levels; *Aristichthys nobilis* (big-head carp) feeding on even smaller game; *Cirrhina molitorella* (mud carp) living in the mud at the pond bottom. All these species, along with the common carp (which then grubs in the mud for worms and other larger pond-bottom game), are stocked together in ponds, and between them they utilize everything available at the lower trophic levels. Fish that feed higher on the food chain—a variety of mullets, eels, catfish, snakeheads (*Ophicephalus argus*), and so on—enter the ponds and are caught; the eels and mullets are often caught as fry and introduced for rearing in the ponds. Prawns and other shellfish (shrimps, crayfish) also abound in fresh and brackish ponds and are much used. Thus a fish-based protein supply is available wherever water is abundant in all of south China. Even on the high plateau of Yünnan, the lakes support a large fishery—for wild fish to be sure—with boat people living in a way similar to the boat people of Hong Kong (Osgood 1963). The freshwater fish, at least the pond-reared ones, are sold alive whenever possible and fresh at almost all times. Sea fish and oversupplies of freshwater fish are often or usually dried or salted or both for transport. The cheap grades of salt fish—where just enough salt is used to keep deterioration from becoming total while the fish is drying—are the poor man's protein luxury in southern China. These develop nitrosamines, due to bacterial breakdown of nitrates during the curing process; these chemicals are carcinogenic and may possibly relate to the high incidence of certain cancers in the area (Fong and Chan 1973). Shellfish are often dried also; oysters are boiled down, in what amount to giant vats of oyster soup, until the remaining liquid is thick and heavy flavored; this oyster sauce is used in cooking meat. Dried shrimp, oysters, and squid are staples. On the coast, shrimp paste is made by putting tiny shrimp in huge jars with enough salt to keep them from spoiling; the shrimp digest themselves, their digestive enzymes lysing the body proteins. The resulting purplish solid paste is used as a flavoring agent and is one of the richest sources of protein and calcium known. It is not significantly different from the *belachan* of Malay use and other shrimp pastes of Southeast Asia. Occasionally the same is done with small fish, producing pastes or oils of the class known as *nuoc man* in Vietnam, *bagung* and *patis* in the Philippines. These preparations are by no means as popular as they are in Southeast Asia; they are peripheral extensions of the Southeast Asian technology.

Working up the vertebrate order, we pass briefly over the reptiles. Snakes are eaten mostly as medicine and occasionally as an oddity, especially in the dish (more talked about than eaten) "Dragon, Phoenix and Tiger," that is, snake, chicken and cat combined. Poultry is far more important. The chicken was domesticated in Southeast Asia, the common domestic duck (*Anas platyrhynchos*, the mallard) and Oriental tame goose, or swan-goose (*Anser cygnoides*), in China itself; all are used, the goose much less than the others, and the eggs are a staple. Duck eggs are often preserved various ways: the yolks removed and dried and salted; the whole egg salted; and, of course, the famous hundred-year-old eggs or even thousand-year-old eggs. These are a typical bit of hyperbole; they are cured for two to four months, depending somewhat on season and on market, by being placed in limy mud or in a mixture of lime, fine ash, and salt, sometimes with tea. The chemicals osmose through the eggshell and both preserve and flavor the egg. Duck eggs spoil much faster than chicken eggs, and this presumably explains the greater use of preserving technology for them. Also, ducks are more localized than chickens (being restricted to areas with a decent amount of water), and thus the question of transporting the eggs is more pressing; furthermore, the duck eggs are firmer, or stiffer, and better for such preserving while less satisfactory as a whipped-in or stirred binder for other foods.

Mammal meat is more important than that of birds. Beef, from cows and water buffaloes, and mutton, from sheep or goats indifferently, are not too common. (Westerners sometimes protest at the equation of sheep and goats in many Far Eastern languages. Young goat is tenderer, more delicate flavored, and less greasy than lamb, and goats are better adapted to south Asian conditions.) The important meat—which, as the Maynard and Swen table in Buck (1937) shows, is more important than all other animal foods combined in south China—is pork. (Actually, fish clearly outranks it in importance near any large body of water. Away from water, though, pork is clearly *the* flesh food.) Pork consumption in south China is quite respectable by world standards. With the increased raising of pigs and good egalitarian distribution of food under the present mainland government of China, protein is evidently more than ample when one takes into account the legumes as well as the meat. In many areas, especially the far west and the Fukien coast, pigs are as important for lard as for meat and are bred for both maximal fat content and maximal separation of fat and lean meat (the opposite of the "marbling" so coveted, to their ill health, by Americans). In these areas, lard is the preferred, or at least *a* preferred, cooking oil, instead of the clear light-flavored vegetable oils liked elsewhere. Since the latter are polyunsaturated, their users are presumably less prone to circulatory diseases—a hypothesis worth checking.

Food Processing

The purpose of this section is to get the food from the field to the store; the section on food preparation will take it up from the time it is sold to the final consumer.

Rice, the staple food, is of course milled and then eaten as it is. Today, it is polished—tragically, since polishing removes the nutrients, or most of them, except for bulk starch. Rice is also floured, but for cosmetics as much as for food.

Wheat, on the other hand, is always used in the flour form. For some obscure reason, the use of whole or coarsely broken (bulgur) wheat never expanded much beyond the range of wild native wheats in the Near East and the Balkans, and everywhere else in the world wheat is almost invariably milled to flour. In China, the flour is made into solid, heavy steamed buns —usually unleavened in the south—or noodles. These are not ordinarily homemade in the south; restaurants and tea shops make the various buns and breadstuffs, while special small-scale noodle factories make the longer goods and, often, the thin wrappings for small dumplings. The noodles are usually nothing but flour and water, but the Cantonese and sometimes other groups are also fond of egg noodles. As low-extraction bleached flour becomes more widespread, the taste and nutritional quality of the flour-and-water noodles are declining steadily. Noodles are collectively known as *mien*, Cantonese *min*, Hokkien *mi* or *bi*, depending on dialect. In areas known to us, the Hokkien speakers are the chief users and have more specific categories: *mi* is reserved for spaghettilike noodles; thinner ones (thin vermicelli) are *mi sua*; wide flat ones are *kue thiau*; and there are others. A very thin clear noodle is made from mung-bean flour, and occasionally rice, buckwheat, and other flours are used. Closely related to noodles in technology, and made from the same base, are the skins used for *hun-t'un* and *chiao-tzu*.

There is much question as to the origin of these noodles. The old legend that Marco Polo brought pasta from China (including spaghetti derived from mien and ravioli from chiao-tzu) is probably wrong (Root 1971); at least some sorts of pasta were clearly known well before that. Egg noodles seem definitely Chinese, and the rest may well be, but there is little evidence. Small, thin-skinned, meat-filled dumplings virtually identical to *hun-t'un* and *chiao-tzu* are found widely in Asia: Russian pelemeni, Jewish kreplachs, and Tibetan *mo-mo*, with especially important and elaborate versions in Afghanistan and neighboring areas. China might have got them, and Italy too (indirectly), from central Asia. They grade into the fried, thicker-skinned *samusa* of India and the Near East. About all we can say is that other foods with similar patterns of distribution mostly have Persian or central Asian origins.

To turn to other grains: corn, buckwheat, and occasionally other minor grains are made into thick, large, flat, dry cakes like large, mealy pancakes. The millets and sorghums are usually eaten as porridge—as all the other grains except wheat often are also. The flat-cake method of cooking is centered among the highlands of western China and the Tibetan borderland and appears to be the originally favored method of preparing barley and buckwheat among the Tibeto-Burman peoples of that area; it has spread to Chinese and other grains as these moved into the region.

The grain technology of south China is fairly simple, because of the dominance of the very simply prepared staple rice. Soybean technology moves us immediately to the other extreme. There is no space in this chapter (or in this whole book) to discuss that subject, which in any case has not been studied by food scientists as much as it might be. Information is reviewed in Piper and Morse (1923) and Hesseltine and Wang (in Smith and Circle 1972); Hommel (1937, pp. 105–09) discusses bean-curd production. Soybeans are almost always processed, since the beans are rather indigestible if simply cooked. They are either ground to flour or fermented or both. The most common process is the manufacture of *tou-fu* (Cantonese *tau-fu*, Hokkien *tau-hu*), bean curd. This involves wet-grinding the beans into a slurry, straining this, coagulating the mass with gypsum or any of a large number of other coagulants that cause the proteins to precipitate, and then straining and pressing this product to eliminate excess fluid. The resulting solids are bean curd; the fluids are used in various ways. The most common bean curd is very watery, but drier forms are prepared by pressing harder, and even drier ones are made by drying the result slightly. The Hokkien cooks in particular relish drier, firmer bean curd. Bean curd is often sold fried. Boiling the slurry is usually a step in the manufacture, and the resulting skin (similar to the skin on boiling milk) is skimmed off, dried, and widely used. Other closely related processes produce the range of imitation meats developed by vegetarians, specifically Mahayana Buddhists. Credible imitations (very good tasting, if not always tasting quite like the originals) are made for chicken, abalone, and other white meats, and even beef and pork. The West has picked up the idea and developed it much further, climaxing in the production of textured vegetable protein (TVP), but has—characteristically!—ignored the problem of making the result taste good. The ideal in the West seems to be to make it tasteless. (Cynical Chinese readers will not be surprised at this redefinition of goals!) Local variations in all the above processes are essentially infinite; modernization and change are guaranteeing that the set of processes remains open ended.

The most common ferment product is soy sauce (Mandarin *chiang yu* or *shih yu*, Cantonese *si yau*). Here again an infinite number of variations is possible, but the general process is to ferment a mix of soy flour or beans and lightly ground grain (wheat, barley, etc.) with *Aspergillus oryzae* and *A. soyae* (fungi) and whatever other *Aspergillus* or similar microorganisms happen to be in that particular producer's starter. The result is then brined and refermented with *Lactobacillus* spp. (bacteria related to those that produce yogurt and supply the sourness of sourdough bread and summer sausages) and yeasts—the mix and any further microorganisms again depending on the producer's starter. The liquor resulting from this is strained off and bottled. The process takes time, for the various steps and for aging. *Aspergillus* spp. growing in wet peanuts and such substrates produce aflatoxins, highly poisonous and the most powerful carcinogens known, but so far as we are aware, no cancer or serious aflatoxin problem has been reliably traced to soy ferments.

Other ferments include yellow and red soybean pastes, black beans (*tou shih, tau si*), pickled bean curd (*su fu* and other forms), and the like. Little research has been done on traditional methods of making these. The varicolored pastes and cheeselike substances, bean jams, and the like, are probably made by soaking and cooking the beans, then fermenting them with *Aspergillus*, yeasts, *Rhizopus* spp., and bacteria—some or all of these. They differ in whether the beans are mashed or not, mixed with other ingredients, and so forth, as well as in the mixes of microorganisms used. Black beans are heavily salted and are evidently at base a *Lactobacillus* ferment. (Not much besides *Lactobacillus* bacteria could survive the salt or produce the characteristic taste.) Prebrining treatment with other ferments is not ruled out. *Su fu* is dryish bean curd fermented with the fungi *Mucor* spp. and *Actinomucor* spp. (the species, again, depending on whatever happens to be in the producer's starter culture). The firmer soybean cheeses and pickled bean curds are all of this class. The fermented curd is usually pickled, with "wine," red peppers, brine, and even rose essence (Hesseltine and Wang, in Smith and Circle 1972 p. 412). Other ferment products will doubtless turn up as they are sought. In Indonesia, the Chinese immigrants have encountered and come to use the various soy and other ferments in which a cooked cake or mass is fermented with *Rhizopus* spp. (and whatever else is around); the soy form of this is *tempe* in Malay. Perhaps similar cakes are prepared in China.

It should be emphasized that these fermentation processes make the protein in soybeans much more digestible and add the various vitamins and other nutrients manufactured by the microorganisms—a very substantial amount.

The technology of soybean fermentation continues to grow and progress. Soybean milk—the imitation milk made more or less simply from soy meal in water—has been cultured with the standard yogurt starter *Lactobacillus bulgaricus* in Japan, producing an imitation yogurt that is reportedly good to taste and higher in protein than the original (ibid., p. 415). Who knows what wonders lie ahead?

Treatment of other foods for sale is an anticlimax after the soybean. Drying and salting are the common processes and are, in a phrase, applied to everything possible—vegetables, fish, meat, and so on. Vegetables, especially the cabbages and, to a lesser extent, white radish and others, are pickled. They are brined heavily, such that *Lactobacillus* bacteria grow and flourish, producing the characteristic pickle tastes, but other contaminants are kept out. This process is basically the same as that used to make sauerkraut in Europe, dill pickles in America, kim chi in Korea, pickled vegetables of all sorts in Japan, and the like, but the Chinese process is simpler and produces less marked flavors. It is possible, indeed probable, that some Chinese sausages (Cantonese *laap ch'eung*) also undergo some *Lactobacillus* fermentation, as summer sausages such as salami do in the West. Otherwise, pork is usually treated simply by salting and drying—often hung up in the wind. In the far west on the Tibetan frontier, whole pigs are boned and the meat also removed, leaving a carcass that is mostly fat and which is sewed up and put in a more or less cool place to cure and keep indefinitely. Superior hams are made not far away. The famous Yünnan hams are rather similar to salt-cured Virginia hams and are presumably made by a similar process (the process is a trade secret). Ducks are flattened and cured, or otherwise preserved. The treatment of fish and eggs has been discussed already.

Dairy products are not usually used by Chinese, as everyone knows, but fewer persons know that the Yünnan Chinese produce and use both cheese, especially goat cheese (Osgood 1963) and yogurt (or at least a milk product described by the traveler William Gill, an excellent observer of foods, as "like Devonshire cream"—i.e., sour cream—and apparently made in typical yogurt fashion). This dairy-product technology is probably derived from the Mongols and their followers and concentrated among Yünnan Muslims, who trace their origin as a community from troops brought in with Kublai Khan's army in the thirteenth century (Paul Buell, personal communication), but it may be derived from, or at least encouraged by, the nearby emphasis on dairy foods among the Tibetans. (See Wheatley, 1965, for general discussion of dairy-food use in eastern Asia.) The Mongol/Muslim hypothesis is supported by the fact that it is cheese and yogurt that are produced; the Tibetans would surely have emphasized butter and soured butter. But Tibetans did once range more easterly than they do now. Other non-Han minorities of south China, except for those who are culturally very close to the Tibetans, apparently all share the Chinese avoidance of dairy products. The east Asian avoidance of dairy products is probably due primarily to the fact that bean and pig products are equivalent and more economical. Most Asians cannot digest raw milk except when they are children, because the enzyme lactase (which breaks down lactose, a milk sugar that otherwise causes digestive upsets or worse) stops being produced in the gut at about six years of age. However, this does not stop the Indians and central Asians from being the world's most dairy-dependent peoples; they simply treat the milk with bacteria such as *Lactobacillus* that break down the lactose. This technology was too thoroughly identified with the central Asian "barbarians" to spread much in China. (On lactase and lactose, see McCracken 1971.) In addition, there was probably a feeling that reliance on dairy foods would mean reliance on trade with the barbarians, already all too well established in trade as a result of their predominance in, among other things, horse breeding, and this would have finally tipped the balance of trade too far in the Central Asians' and Mongols' favor. There is certainly no religious taboo or even much disgust relating to milk drinking, and milk has been quickly and easily adopted all over the Far East today—perhaps too easily, given the digestive upsets and the tendency to consume the heavily sugared, condensed canned milks. There is still some resistance to rank cheese, which we love, and we were amused to find it considered by our informants as the putrefied mucous discharge of an animal's guts. But, after all, many Westerners resist strong cheese too.

Drinks

Beverages follow naturally as an appendage of food processing. Hot water is a common drink that involves little processing, but other drinks are more complex. The standard beverage, green tea, can be simply the dried leaves of the tea plant, but minimally involves preliminary careful choice and plucking of the outermost leaves of the tea plant (the tea quality depends on their stage of growth, as well as as on place of origin and variety of tea), preliminary drying, rolling of the leaves to bruise them gently, such that flavoring chemicals are released, and final thorough drying (Schery, 1972, pp. 591–92). Semifermented teas, such as Oolong (*wu lung*, "black dragon"), are often more highly regarded; they are allowed to cure for a while in a moist atmosphere for fermentation. Strongly fermented and heat-dried black teas are not favored and are produced almost entirely for export. These *hung ch'a*, "red teas" (from the color of the infusion; the color of the dried leaf is black), are the subjects of an origin myth told by Chinese: the foreigners wanted tea; the tea producers took the coarsest leaves and sticks and shovelled them into boat holds, where they rotted on the long voyage home. It is true that black teas are often made from the coarser leaves and, of course, are fermented. Most Western words for tea are derived from *ch'a*, often via Mongol *chai* (*ch'a* plus grammatical suffix); *te*, the Hokkien pronunciation of the same character (and derived from the same root), supplied the word in westernmost Europe. Tea continues to hold its own and increase in use, but in Malaysia, Singapore, Indonesia, and increasingly in the United States and elsewhere, immigrant Chinese have shifted to coffee. Soft drinks and fruit squashes are so widely used and so popular among all Chinese everywhere that they must be considered an integral part of the diet and a common substitute for tea, though they are a Western innovation of very recent spread. Soybean milk, always used some, has spread along with the soft drinks and has become widely popular.

Alcoholic drinks, *chiu* (Cantonese *chau*), are usually called "wines," but they are not wines in the correct use of the word—that is, alcoholic drinks made from fruit. Of course real grape wine is made in China, but by central Asian peoples outside our area of discourse. In south China, all alcoholic drinks are correctly either beers (undistilled drinks from grain) or vodkas (distilled, unaged alcoholic drinks made from starch bases—not usually potatoes, despite the common myth). A few may be aged long enough to qualify as whiskeys, but we have encountered none that seemed aged long or well enough. Some of the vodkas are distilled twelve times over and are exceedingly strong, running far over 100 proof (roughly, 50% alcohol is 100 proof). Even the beers are usually stronger than occidental beers, except, of course, for those made by the occidental lagering process in modern breweries on strictly Western lines (all Far Eastern countries now have these, apparently). Chiu are often used to infuse medicines, to produce tinctures of herbs and even tinctures of five snakes and similar dubious cure-alls. Thus ginseng wine, produced in the north or in Korea but widely drunk in the south, is simply ginseng root soaked in ferociously strong vodka. A more bizarre drink, outside our area but of interest to show how medicinal wines are made, is mutton wine, in which a two-year-old castrated ram is soaked in distilled fermented milk, fresh skimmed milk soured, and sweet things including raisins to nourish the yeasts. It is not strongly alcoholic—only 9.14 percent (Tannahill 1968, p. 107). The many herbal chiu are used for any and all ills and show a tendency (similar to, but not as pronounced as, that found in the West with vermouth and liqueurs) to move from the category of medicines to the category of indulgences. The root of all these chiu, ultimately, is grain—soaked, sprouted to develop the malt (which may be separated out as malt syrup, a popular sweetener of some theoretical medicinal value, instead of driven on to alcohol), then inoculated with yeasts that ferment the malt sugar, maltose, to alcohol.

In connection with chiu, it is worth noting that the Chinese phrase "to get red faced," meaning slightly under the influence, has a basis in fact. East Asians have an inherited tendency to flush very easily (more so than people of other parts of the world) after drinking even very small quantities of alcohol. This has been scientifically demonstrated (Wolff 1972).

Sugar, Oil, and Salt

In addition to honey and the maltose syrup mentioned above (a molasseslike substance), sugar is made by pressing sugarcane and boiling down the juice, then refining the result as much as wanted (or not at all) by filtering the juice through clay before it is boiled down to a solid. Salt is similarly boiled out of brine obtained from wells or made by seawater dehydration. Chinese in the interior were aware that differences in goiter incidence were correlated with differences in salt source, and in areas of high incidence, they explained their goiter by saying there was something wrong with the salt (Hosie 1897; Hosie dismisses this as just another silly Chinese belief—but like so many Chinese folk beliefs, it is quite correct).

Oil in the Chinese diet is often lard, especially in the far southwest (Yünnan's plateaus) and among the Hokkien. But vegetable oil is more common. The traditional source, especially in the Yangtze area, was rapeseed —not from the European *Brassica rapa*, but from the native Chinese *Brassica juncea* (and some other Brassicas, in some areas). The seeds were crushed and the oil pressed out. Today, peanuts have become more important in areas where they grow better than rapeseed.

Hommel (1937) gives full details on the manufacture of sugar, salt, and oil. There is less information on use. Oil of some sort is basic and necessary, in fairly substantial amounts, in all Chinese cooking except the very simplest preparation of staples. Contrary to popular belief, deep-frying is quite common in south China, and stir-frying—while using less oil—is so universal a cooking method that it leads to substantial oil use. Sugar is far less used, and very sweet foods were not liked in traditional southern China. Recently this has changed, and sugar consumption is increasing with explosive rapidity— soft drinks pioneering the way, candy and cookies following, then other sweet foods. We will have more to say about this in the next section; here we need only say that, before this recent development, the south Chinese used very little sugar. Salt tended to enter the diet in soy sauce, salted soybeans, pickled vegetables, and salted fish; families observed by us used little or no free salt, especially the Cantonese, who added black beans (very salty fermented soybeans) if they wanted to make a dish salty. Otherwise, soy sauce and pickled vegetables were used enough to provide all necessary salt.

Nutrition and Nutritional Values in South China

It is hard to find a dish in the Middle Kingdom that is not based upon the recipe of some sage who lived centuries ago and who had a hygienic principle in mind when he designed it. [E. Nichols 1902, p. 26]

Nichols overstates the case, but the nutritional virtues of Chinese cooking are well known (see B. Y. Chao 1963). The accumulated experience of the Chinese people, over the millennia, has done better than Nichols' delightful but imaginary sages ever could have done. Not only does ordinary Chinese cooking provide an adequate diet, but more to the point, the southern Chinese diet permits a higher population density than any other diet. It is, as we have shown elsewhere (Anderson and Anderson 1973a), a minimax game: maximize the number of people supported, minimize the amount of land (including energy and nutrients) used. Agriculture involves clever trapping and recycling of nutrients and careful, conservative inputs of energy, so that nothing is wasted that can possibly be retained (see, e. g., King 1911, and Anderson and Anderson 1973a). More striking, though, are the choices of crops—that is, of foods. These turn out to be those crops that yield the most nutritional value for the least land. They are often labor-intensive; the evolution of Chinese agriculture has been toward ever more lavish uses of labor (with actual devolution in technology) to sustain ever higher populations. In our opinion, the agricultural refinements preceded and made possible the population expansion, though they did not cause it directly and did not follow as an effect of higher population density, a point that must be stressed (Elvin 1973; Anderson and Anderson 1973a). But at its best, the southern Chinese system of food procurement is the best in the world, with many lessons to teach the West, whose fantastically wasteful use of energy and nutrients in agriculture cannot continue much longer. (For statistics on energy in the American food system, see Steinhart and Steinhart 1974.)

Carbohydrates being the chemicals produced in the most quantity by plants (because they are the direct products of photosynthesis and the main food of plants) and being also necessary to human diets, most human societies get the majority of their calories from them. Thus most agricultural systems are based on a carbohydrate-rich staple crop, and successful systems include back up crops to ensure against crop failure. The most successful systems are those that are based on a staple that not only has a high yield of carbohydrates but also yields many other nutrients, thus making efficient use of land and of people's time. ("Success" here is defined simply as "ability to feed more people over more time than other systems.") The best such staple is rice. Producing more calories per acre than any other grain—at least when it is wet-grown—it also produces high amounts of plant protein, for a grain, and is very rich in B vitamins (Schery 1972, and other sources). Polishing eliminates these side benefits and reduces the grain to virtually pure starch, but high polishing did not become a factor until the coming of modern machinery in the late nineteenth century. Ordinary old-style millings does eliminate some nutritional values, but much remains, and the lightly milled white rice is more versatile, easier to cook, easier to store, and easier to digest than brown rice. (White rice, like white flour, is associated with status, but storability is an important element, indeed, the connection with status arose partly because higher milling was more expensive but also because the product was usually fresher and less bug ridden. Of course, the storability is to a great extent due to the reduction in nutritional value—the more milled a grain is, the fewer bugs can live on it!) Actually, reasonably lightly milled rice is not strikingly worse than brown rice, except in the famous matter of thiamine and in a few less well-known vitamins of the B complex. Brown rice is notably rich in B vitamins, but most of them are in the seed coats that are milled off. In fact, the discovery of vitamins dates back to the realization that polished rice was associated with beriberi, but the polishings could cure that condition. Beriberi was later discovered to be the result of thiamine deficiency. However, even ordinary polishing does not destroy all the vitamin or protein value of the grain.

Wheat, the other important grain in wide use, is notably richer in protein and B vitamins than rice but is less productive per acre, so that under Chinese conditions it probably produced less of these nutrients per acre. (The new high-yield, high-protein wheat strains, known in China as "Albanian" and in the rest of the world as "Mexican" from the respective areas where they were bred, have apparently changed this.) The highly milled, bleached white flour, now all too popular with Chinese communities, is far worse in relation to its original than polished rice is. In fact, it is not much more than starch with some grain protein. However, enrichment (replacing some of the more obvious B vitamins, basically) is usual. "Minor" but vital B vitamins and trace minerals are not replaced, unfortunately.

The back up staples of south China are less nutritious, usually, and certainly less productive of nutrients per acre, with a few fascinating exceptions. Corn yields more calories per acre than any other grain except paddy rice but is notoriously poor in protein and vitamins—though strains differ, and higher-value ones are found in China, while new ones with better nutrient content are being introduced. Corn also has chemicals that make protein and calcium less available in digestion, and China apparently never acquired the long-established New World technology of cooking or treating corn with lye and lime, thus neutralizing the chemicals and supplementing the calcium in corn. White potatoes have more vitamin C than grains, by far, but the C is in the peels and is usually boiled out or peeled away or both. The sorghums, millets, barley, and buckwheat of China have been little investigated, but their low yield and relatively low nutrient value in other areas makes one suspect that they are not great sources of nutrition—though strains differ spectacularly in such matters as protein content. Lastly, the sweet potato is exceedingly low in everything except vitamin A, in which it is very high. Actually, it contains no vitamin A, but does contain carotenes, which, especially beta-carotene, the body converts into vitamin A. The carotenes are a brilliant scarlet orange, and the vitamin A value of a sweet potato can be judged by the intensity of this color. Strains vary enormously but most are high. Some Chinese sweet potatoes may have respectable amounts of protein; ordinary sweet potatoes do not, but New Guinea highland strains probably do (Karl Heider, personal communication) and are presumably descended from South American strains not too distant from those that might have come to China. Analysis of local peasant strains of Chinese vegetables is eagerly awaited.

In summary, the south Chinese and other inhabitants of the area get plenty of carbohydrates from their staples; they can also get much of their protein from them and probably do (Buck 1937); they can get B vitamins and various minerals from them if they are not too highly milled; and they can get carotene from sweet potatoes. The grains, however, provide too little protein to sustain health (in most cases) and provide virtually no vitamin C; they are also generally inadequate as sources of iron, calcium, vitamin A (sweet potatoes not being a grain), and, in many cases, riboflavin and niacin. If milled highly they are inadequate sources of literally everything except starch, unless artificial enrichment is carried out.

Most of the above deficiencies are made up by that miracle, that noblest of crops, that wondrous plant, the soybean. A pound of ordinary dry soybeans has twice the protein of a pound of beefsteak and is the richest in protein—pound for pound—of all foods. Admittedly the beef is ahead if one counts only lean meat and compares calorie for calorie instead of pound for pound (dry soybeans have more than twice as many calories as meat), but the beef recedes into insignificance on per-acre production comparisons: soybeans produce ten or twenty or more times as much protein per acre as cows do (unless the cows are supplemented in feed). It is sometimes said that plant proteins are not "complete," meaning that they lack essential amino acids, but this is untrue; they merely have relatively less of certain ones than meat does. Most grain proteins, corn in particular, are low in lysine; soybeans are much better in this regard. All plant proteins, including soybean protein, are relatively low in methionine; a pound of soybeans has only an equal amount of methionine as a pound of beef. However, that is still a respectable amount, and clearly soybeans are a superb protein source. Moreover, conversion of them to bean curd (tofu) improves the situation; the protein, with the oil, precipitates and coagulates, while much of the carbohydrate is left behind in the remaining liquid. Thus the protein-per-calorie ratio is improved.

But protein is not the only virtue of the soybean. A pound of dry soybeans has more iron than beef liver, three times the thiamine and six times the riboflavin of *brown* rice, and appreciable amounts of vitamin A, calcium, and many other nutrients. Conversion into tofu eliminates much of the thiamine, riboflavin, and other B vitamins, which are water soluble, but concentrates the iron and calcium (often adding more of the latter from the chemicals used in precipitation). The less fortunate aspects of soybeans must be noted as well. They are apt to contain chemicals that form relatively indigestible compounds with iodine, their protein is unavailable or hard to digest in some situations, and they have a range of toxins. Heating and processing destroy these problems.

Broad beans and peanuts are less nutritious than soybeans, but not strikingly less so, and can supplement the diet very well. Other vegetables that are most used are those that are both highly productive per acre under peasant farming conditions and rich in precisely those nutrients that are apt to be scarce in the rest of the diet—especially iron and vitamins A and C. The cabbages, commonest of vegetables, are high in these last two. Chili peppers are among the richest sources of all three and are very high in other minerals as well. Tomatoes and carrots are also high in A, tomatoes in C, and most of the southern Chinese fruits are high in one or the other or both of these. To be specific, fresh chili pods are the richest common source of C; carrots, sweet potatoes, and chilis vie for the honors of the richest vegetables in carotene, precursor of A; soybeans and chilis are about the richest common vegetable sources of iron, a mineral deficient in many American diets as well as in those of less well-nourished parts of the world. (For nutritional value of foods just described, see Church and Church 1970, table 30, pp. 98–135).

In regard to animal foods, eggs are noted because their protein (specifically from the white) is remarkably well balanced in amino acid content and thus is useful to compare with the amino acid balance of soybeans and other foods. Pork is a particularly valuable meat because of its very high riboflavin content—most other foods, including meats, are much lower—and because pork liver has a strikingly high amount of iron, more than twice that in most livers. Other vitamins and minerals are also well represented in this meat. It will be seen that pork is not only valuable because it can be raised on little feed, and that of the worst kind, but also because of its high nutritional value. Fish and poultry are distinguished by having less fat and very high amounts of the scarcer amino acids (methionine, the greatest lack in vegetable protein, being common in these). Lard is, of course, a saturated fat, but peanut and rapeseed oils are polyunsaturated and contain plenty of linoleic acid, a dietary requirement.

In regard to other nutrients not yet mentioned, vitamin D is usually manufactured in the skin, under the influence of sunlight; in dark urban conditions it is often inadequate. It is found most richly in liver, but also in seed kernels. Other vitamins needed in small quantities (E, K, folic acid, etc.) are, similarly, most richly present in organ meats, wheat, and other seeds (specifically the germ, and hence lost in milling) and exist in lesser but adequate amounts in fresh vegetables and fruits, or in yeasts, where many of them are found in considerable amounts (relative to the human body's needs). While there are no figures available to us on either the incidence of these vitamins in Chinese foods or on their adequacy in Chinese diets, we assume they are adequate in otherwise adequate or near-adequate diets, since this is the usual finding. (Vitamin E deficiency has never been demonstrated in humans outside of institutional situations where a controlled, artificial-type diet was being given. But not much search has been made in the Orient for this deficiency.) The wide use of soybean ferments, in which both the soybeans and the yeasts and other microorganisms are particularly rich in most of these nutrients, is especially important in this regard; even small amounts of such ferments should provide adequate nutrition. Yeasts are often high in the better-known B vitamins, also. Soybean ferments should be studied in detail; the microorganisms unquestionably serve both to add their own nutritional values and to make those of the soybeans more available.

Cooking methods protect the vitamins and minerals in the food, and in one case, actually improve nutritional value: use of cast-iron woks increases available iron in the food, because cooking at high temperatures causes some of the iron from the wok to be incorporated into the food. A good, old, well-used wok has no doubt kept many a family from anemia. Chinese food is, as everyone knows, cooked for a relatively short time and is often or usually stir-fried; if it is boiled, the water is used as soup and rarely discarded; deep-frying in which the oil is discarded is even rarer. Thus there is minimal chance for vitamins to be oxidized or dissolved and thrown away. This aspect of Chinese food has been exaggerated in the popular press—after all, many Chinese dishes are simmered for a long time, and much water, oil, and other dissolving agents are lost as dish waste, plate waste, and so on. The comparative nutritional value of Chinese food, in this regard, is perhaps most apparent when compared with those Western cuisines (such as the British) that boil vegetables for very long periods, sometimes in two or three changes of water, and discard all the water.

Chinese food is also reputed to be low in cholesterol—an equivocal virtue, since a high-cholesterol diet is not always associated with heightened risk of circulatory diseases and is certainly not *the* cause of them. In any case, Chinese food has been greatly overrated on this matter. While the ordinary individual ate a low-cholesterol diet by sheer necessity, the minute he got a decent living he began to invest it in plenty of eggs (the yolk of which is one of the richest sources of cholesterol) and pork—nice fat pork, with the organ meats favored (brain is liked and is the highest in cholesterol content of any food). In areas where polyunsaturated vegetable oils are used, such as the Cantonese area, the situation is enormously better than in places such as Yünnan, where lard is the common, or at least one common, cooking oil.

In one way, the south Chinese are certainly among the healthiest people in the world—or, rather, once were: they consume so few sweets. Sugar consumption is a major contributor to tooth decay, and sugar is nutritionally worthless except for calories, driving more nourishing foods out of the diet; it is also possibly associated with heart disease and certainly associated with diabetes incidence (Yudkin 1972). The Hong Kong surgeon Li Shu-fan reports: "In the whole of my practice, I had only encountered two patients of the poor class suffering from diabetes. They were men who worked as cooks of western food for European families. On inquiry, I found they were in the habit of eating the left-overs of their masters" (S. F. Li 1964, p. 65). The only conceivable difference that could be relevant here is sugar.

The southern Chinese diet is not perfect. Use of dairy foods could well be increased (indeed, it is increasing). The current trend toward more and more processed foods and more and more sugar could and should be reversed. The hillsides, now often deforested wasteland, could produce such vitamin-rich fruits as mangos. Spices could be used much more; we have noted that the chili pepper is a fantastically rich source of vitamin A and very good for

many other nutrients, and most of the other curry spices of southern Asia—
turmeric, cumin, coriander seed, and others—are also rich in many nutrients.
These, like the fruits, could be raised easily in areas now wasteland. However,
all this is a counsel of perfection. The high population densities and surprising
lack of famines unassociated with social breakdown in south China prove
what the figures confirm: the southern Chinese diet feeds more people,
better, on less land, than any other diet on earth.

Change in Nutritional Levels During the Twentieth Century

Our charge is to cover modern China—roughly the twentieth century.
During this period, the quality of nutrition in south China has changed
more than at any other time in its history. Clearly we cannot ignore this
phenomenon. However, the few and scattered figures given are so inadequate that they are not worth citing, except for those in Buck (1937) noted
earlier in this chapter. Synthesizing information from travel accounts, agricultural reports, a few surveys and studies, ethnographies, and our own
observations, we can produce a hypothetical account.

The disastrous social events of the nineteenth century—the Taiping Rebellion, the Hakka-Cantonese wars, the Yünnan Muslim rebellion, and
others—reduced the population drastically in most of south China and thus
increased the amount of cultivated land per capita. Thus the inhabitants of
south China could, theoretically, have been better fed than before. Such
was apparently not the case. Travelers through the affected areas—the most
perceptive and agriculturally aware of these travelers was Alexander Hosie
(1897, 1914)—reported them to be worse off than regions more densely
populated and less stressed by rebellion. The reason, evidently, is that
southern Chinese agriculture is labor intensive and trade dependent; reducing
the labor supply drastically and ruining the trade networks did more harm
than the thinning of population per acre could offset, at least in many areas.

The late Ch'ing period in south China was stagnant and by no means
wealthy, but it was a time of relative peace and security, except in the bandit-
infested wilder mountains. Most of the citizenry were rather poorly fed,
partly due to the enormous use of opium—consumers' dollars and producers' croplands went to the drug. On the other hand, the fact that a huge
percentage of China's cropland, especially in the southwest (Hosie 1914),
could be diverted from food production to opium production without
causing mass starvation indicates that there was considerable leeway in the
food procurement system. During this period, the peasants lived on grain
staples primarily, eked out their diet with soybeans, cabbage, and white
radish, and, in the southwest, with animal products. The rich ate the great

range of dishes appropriate to their station. The troubled times during and after the fall of Ch'ing in 1911 were characterized by enough unrest and disruption to guarantee hunger and hardship in many areas.

A return to stability occurred during the 1920s. Buck's surveys in the late twenties and early thirties were done in a period of relative peace and sufficiency. The depression of the thirties seems to have brought less hardship than it might have, since most of the southern Chinese were true peasants, raising much of their own food; their trade was hurt but their rice paddies yielded none the less. Marginal areas and landlord-ridden areas had serious problems (see H. S. Ch'en 1936, 1949). Village studies of the 1920s and 1930s generally describe a situation in which the poor were hungry much of the time and not well nourished, but the ordinary villager clearly did all right, and anyone with more than a tiny plot or more than a very marginal job had a varied and good diet (e.g., Kulp 1925; Fei 1939—and Fei was not one to overlook problems; Fitzgerald 1941). While there were unquestionably local famines, and the ethnographers can be expected to have done work in villages where they could eat, the situation is clearly a world away from the chronic hunger and frequent famine of the dry north (see Nichols 1902; Mallory 1926; MacNair 1939; Hinton 1966; Crook and Crook 1966), except in the lower Yangtze River provinces where famines were frequent (MacNair 1939, esp. table between pp. 13, 14) but usually localized. In the warm and rainy climate, there was not the seasonal no-growth period, when people had to stop moving around to conserve the few calories they had, as Hinton reports in northern China before the revolution of 1949 (Hinton 1966); in the wondrous plant diversity of the south, there was not the need to restrict diet to millet.

The Japanese invasion, even before it reached the south, changed all this. Poor areas were ruined, rich areas impoverished. Our informants in Hong Kong remembered the period as one of living on sweet potato vines, wild herbs, and worse; virtually every family had lost members to starvation. The hunger grew worse throughout the war. The number of people who died will never be known; it was far in the millions. War's end meant recovery, but continuing civil strife prevented full recovery. The Communist victory in 1949 (the more remote parts of the south not consolidated until later than that) brought peace and equity at last. Within a few years, starvation had probably been eliminated. Production rose, distribution was equalized, and —an often overlooked but critically important point—food quality and rapid, easy distribution of food became goals. Great progress was made and continues to be made. Stores well stocked with safe, uniform, good-quality canned and preserved and dried goods are now the rule, and localized famine is a virtual impossibility today. The real hunger of the poor was eliminated, and usually the ordinary person could get a varied and adequate diet. There was a sharp setback in 1960–61 and perhaps for a while thereafter, due to the overeager policies and poor weather of the Great Leap Forward (see Perkins 1968, Vogel 1969, and other standard sources). For some this may have meant real hardship. Informants in Hong Kong told us that while the rations available were perfectly adequate for the ordinary person, they were not so for fishermen doing hard work. A southern Chinese fisherman during a fish run on a winter sea will use over five thousand calories a day (our findings), and food distributors had not taken enough account of this admittedly very high figure. But the fishermen could, and did, work somewhat less and eat their trash-fish catch; they were far from starving. (There was real malnutrition among fisherman refugees in Hong Kong in 1965. How much was acquired in Hong Kong we do not know; these were refugees who could no longer fish and were not eating adequate diets in the Colony.)

In any case, the situation has improved steadily since 1961, and all accounts, photographs, and so forth, now go to prove that want has been eliminated in south (and north) China, a victory that appears to be beyond the capability of the rich nations of the world to emulate. Moreover, it is evident that this has been done without sacrificing the quality, variety, and virtuosity of Chinese cuisine. Indeed, the ordinary person can now enjoy these delights, and the cuisine has thus spread itself widely among the populace. How laughable now are the cold-war strictures of the Time-Life Series book *The Cooking of China*, with its talk about "standarized lists of commune food" and "only the plainest meals" (Hahn 1968, p. 186). The cold warriors, here as always, reckoned without the Chinese. Far more Chinese, far more Maoist, and far, far more believable (being an eyewitness account) is the story related by David and Isabel Crook (1966, pp. 151–56)—admittedly from northern China, but too good to miss: One commune did indeed socialize cooking, and some bad cooks tried to turn out institutional fare. The villagers, being Chinese and sensible, quickly rose in a body and convinced the cooks that cooking was an honorable occupation, that bad food was un-Communist and, indeed, anti-Communist (it caused dissension and lowered production), and that the clear, pressing duty of a Communist cook was to turn out the best food possible. The commune kitchens forthwith vied to produce the best. The commune also discovered that their local brand of "white lightning", distilled from millet, would sterilize medical instruments, a worthy reason to keep producing it. Surely, similar cases occurred in the south.

Outside China, the nutritional status of the people of southern Chinese origin has also steadily improved, and malnutrition is not common now in places like Singapore and Hong Kong. However, the picture is not one of pure bliss. At an equal pace with improvement in quality and availability of food has been a pernicious sort of Westernization, involving low-extraction flour, highly polished rice, and above all white sugar in all its forms. This is perhaps most serious in Malaysia, where we have studied it (Anderson and Anderson 1973b). Here the Chinese acculturation to British ways began with British colonialization and has continued to intensify since the British left. However, they no longer borrow from the extremely nutritious and high-quality cooking of the Malays, as they once did to produce the marvelous hybrid known as Nonya food. The tendency now is to eat less fruit and vegetables, more fat and flour and sugar. Soft drinks, candy, cookies, factory-made cakes (essentially unenriched flour, white sugar, and cheap cooking oil), and the like, have come to constitute a major part of diet. Children studied by us were getting up to 25–30 percent of their calories from white sugar, almost all the rest from refined flour, polished rice, and refined oil. Their nutritional status was poor, and their teeth were decaying as fast as they grew in. The excellent and nutritious local fruit was shunned, because it was grown by peasant Malays, despised by the Chinese; cheap sugar candy was consumed instead, because it was identified with the prestigious and modern West. The universal soft drinks, whose advertising is very careful to stress their nature as the leading edge of the Modern World, have become established even in China itself. Even in Hong Kong, that bastion of Chinese epicurism, soft drinks are universal, and sugar snacks are spreading fast. Bean curd and pickled vegetables, always identified with the poor, are probably declining in consumption (based on preliminary observations).

Preparation and Uses of Food

Unity and Diversity in South Chinese Cuisine

South Chinese food is so diverse that we must begin by describing some of the diversity and then proceed to an attempt to pick out what is shared. Southern Chinese cuisine—the actual lore of cooking, the strategies and rules, not the list of ingredients and nutritive values—is, however, a unity. It is admittedly poorly defined; it grades into north Chinese, Vietnamese, and other cuisines; the minority peoples of south China have variants of it that become more and more distinct until we must speak of really different culinary cultures. But the core is a distinctive one, shared by all southern Chinese cooks, and fading away as one leaves the region and its centers.

What strikes the outsider first is the diversity, though, and we will begin there. Chinese cuisine is traditionally divided into five regional cuisines, or at least five "principal" or "great" ones: those of Szechwan, Canton, Fukien, Shantung, and Honan (Miller 1967; Howe 1969; Hughes 1972). These are supposedly characterized by flavors: Szechwanese or Hunan-Szechwan food is hot with chilis; Cantonese runs to sweet and sweet-sour dishes; Fukien is most distinctively characterized by its soups; Shantung is the home of sea foods, garlic, and the most venerable skills; Honan is famous for sweet-sour freshwater fish.

This classification is an interesting demonstration of the Chinese obsession with grouping everything by fives, but it is little more than that. It can be criticized on the basis both of selection (why those five?) and characterization. Leaving the northern Chinese cuisines of Shantung and Honan as being outside our scope, we will turn to the southern three. Here we would respectfully add at least three more schools of cooking that we have appreciated, as worthy of equal rank: Yünnanese, lower Yangtze (including the cuisines of Yangchow, Hangchow, the Huai area, and more recently the eclectic cooking of Shanghai), and Hakka. Richard Hughes quotes James Wei as saying that a school should be recognized by the fact that its restaurants can "offer . . . patrons on demand on any night more than one hundred different courses prepared from local products" (1972, p. 27). We are in a position to guarantee that the Hakka and lower Yangtze cuisines can do that, and we feel fairly sure about Yünnan. These three cuisines have been heretofore ignored because Yünnanese is enough of an offshoot of Szechwanese that its distinctiveness has been underestimated; lower Yangtze is apparently lumped with Shantung or even Fukien by many; and the Hakka are regarded as simple mountain folk who do not cook much—a most mistaken belief. Also, we have heard rumors of distinctive cuisines in the other southern provinces, notably Kueichou. The cuisines of the non-Han population probably do not meet Wei's criterion and are not strictly "Chinese" in the sense intended by classifiers of cooking schools. They are also very little known; but they should not be ignored either.

We would distinguish the schools as follows, specifying what we hope are enough distinctive marks to identify the better-known schools, and at least listing distinctive local dishes for the others.

Szechwan-Hunan: Distinguished by intensive use of fagara, chilis, and garlic; wide and complex use of nuts and poultry; pungent flavors of all sorts harmoniously blended. Especially characteristic dishes—both for their fame and for proving what has just been said—include hot and sour soup, camphor and tea smoked duck, beef with dried tangerine peels, and an oily walnut-paste-and-sugar dessert that seems related to the walnut creams eastward but also to the nut halvahs of central Asia.

Yünnan: Close to Szechwanese and possibly derived from it, but now distinct. Its use of dairy products—yogurt, fried milk curd, cheese—is particularly striking. Flavors are hot and spicy, but with less of the variety of pungent flavors and more use of focused sharpness to bring out the subtle flavors of the main ingredients. There is an enormous use of pork in all forms, including the best hams and headcheese or otherwise cured or prepared pig heads in China. Mountain products, such as game and fungi, are found. An account of typical dishes is found in Neill (1973), but little is known to the world at large about this cuisine, and recipes are almost undiscoverable.

Cantonese: To non-Cantonese or, perhaps better, to non-initiates into this style of cooking, Cantonese food means chop suey and sweet-sour pork. Chop suey is not a typical Cantonese dish, as everyone knows who has much sophistication in Chinese food, but less well known is the fact that true Cantonese food goes very lightly on sugar; sweet-sour dishes are rare and not much favored except for sweet-sour pork (and even that is often avoided) and sweet-sour yellow croaker (a seasonal fish). Using fruit in the meat dishes is a Cantonese trait but exaggerated greatly in less good Cantonese restaurants abroad. (The northern Chinese stereotype that Cantonese cooks try to conceal incompetence with sugar is very true of a certain class of Cantonese cook, but not a class that could make a living in Canton or Hong Kong.) Much more characteristic of Cantonese cooking are stir-fried dishes often flavored with black beans (salted, strongly fermented soybeans); seafood, both fresh and dried or salted; the use of both seafood and meat in the same dish; preference for vegetable oil instead of lard in cooking; variety of fine-cut vegetables, including semitropical ones. Distinctive dishes that come to mind as representing the best in Cantonese cooking are the simpler seafood and fish dishes: steamed prawns with chili sauce to dip them in, and steamed crabs with good vinegar; steamed mullet with slivers of ginger, bunching onion, tangerine peel; fish with black beans; and a host of others. The Cantonese are the past masters at the simple snack foods: wonton soup, noodles (especially the Cantonese egg noodles with fresh mustard greens, and noodles with *ch'a siu,* the Cantonese red roasted pork), and the infinite kinds of *tim sam* ("dot hearts") that are part of the rite of drinking tea (*iam ch'a*). (Cantonese rarely specify the snacks, and the term *tim sam* is a bit bookish; *heui iam ch'a,* "going to drink tea," implies the snacks as surely as it implies the relaxed socializing and more intensive politicking that are the breath of life in a tea shop.)

Like all Chinese cuisines, Cantonese is subject to many regional variations. A distinctive one is that of Toisan, the area south of Canton from which about half of all American Chinese trace their ancestry. Its main claim to fame is that it gave the world chop suey (Cantonese *tsap sui,* "miscellaneous things" or, at worst, "miscellaneous slops"). Typically a sort of hash of leftovers warmed up with bean sprouts, a very folklike dish, this food now has a widely known origin myth: one night, after hours, a Cantonese restaurateur in San Francisco was importuned, by persons he could not refuse (drunken miners in one version, Li Hung-chang or other famed Chinese visitors in others), to serve food. However, he had no food left. So he stir-fried the day's slops and thus created the dish. Its origin in old Toisan was traced down by the indefatigable hunter (of big game and food) Li Shu-fan (1964). Toisan food has many far better dishes to offer, most of them broadly similar to other Cantonese dishes but with less ingredients mixed in the same dish.

Hakka: This style of cooking is characterized by a particularly sensitive way of combining the freshest of crisp vegetables, cut and mixed in many ways, and cooking them lightly to bring out the most delicate flavors. There is no heavy use of garlic, spices, or strong oils. Every part of the animals used is introduced into some dish; we have had a most excellent dish of the spinal nerve cord of a calf, delicately stir-fried with the usual delightful vegetables. Another characteristic Hakka dish is salt-baked chicken, which is simply chicken rubbed with salt and baked—a description as accurate and revealing as saying that Chateau Latour 1964 is fermented grape juice. Also found are many vegetables stuffed with minced fish—chili peppers so stuffed are our favorites, followed by bitter melon—and the famous *jang tou fu*, which is firm bean curd cut into pockets and stuffed with the same mince. The stuffed bean curd and vegetables have been widely borrowed by other Chinese groups in Singapore.

Fukien: The school considered here is identified with the Min languages more than with the province of Fukien per se. Thus the people of Teochiu and Swatow in Kwangtung have preserved a variant of it, with Cantonese influences but with the basic nature recognizable. The Hainanese, long separate from their Min relatives but still discernibly close linguistically to the Hokkien (Southern Min), retain some of the cooking distinctions. The famous emphasis on soups is true enough; stews and rich meaty stocks are also common, and all manner of conjees. ("Conjee" is derived from a south Indian, Dravidian, word; the Mandarin is *chou*, Cantonese *tsuk*.) Many of these liquids are drunk boiling hot, a possible cause of the high rate of esophageal cancer among Southern Min-speaking people. Fish balls, turtle meat, fungi, and small clams are among the more interesting and characteristic ingredients or bases of soup. Another trait, perhaps more distinctive if less well known, of the Fukien school is the use of pig's blood and poultry blood, coagulated by a method borrowed from soybeans (i.e., gypsum, alum, and so on, are used). The pig's blood is usually cut in squares like bean curd and stir-fried with green bunching onions. The poultry blood is sliced thin and served with various dip sauces, usually along with other parts of the bird; thus the Teochiu cuisine features steamed goose, goose liver, and goose blood with garlic-vinegar dip sauce. The Hainanese (traditionally restaurateurs and coffee-shop owners) are famous throughout the Southeast Asian Chinese world for chicken rice (Mandarin *chi ping*; Hokkien *ke png*, *kue pui*; or other dialect variants). This dish involves boiling chickens, preferably very young ones raised by the family on a diet of sesame seeds, using the stock as soup base and also to boil the rice. The blood, intestines, and all giblets are served with the chicken. Thus one has various dishes plus soup and excellent rice from the one bird.

Hokkien cooking uses much lard, and at its worst can be a mess of unrelated vegetables and odder parts of beasts, simmered in lard until all is a greasy mash. Teochiu cooking has absorbed more variety and more emphasis on quick cooking, from the Cantonese one assumes.

Lower Yangtze: Under this label we lump a vast range of local cuisines from the lower Yangtze and Huai valleys; they relate northward to Shantung and should presumably be placed there if one insists on the five-school classification, but they are much more varied. Aside from a good deal of oil in the dishes—usually vegetable oil—the main characteristic of the whole region is that it is so diverse and varied. If the tyro finds himself with an obviously complicated and sophisticated dish that is not clearly from one of the other cuisines, he can safely assign it here, particularly if it is cooked a little longer with a bit more oil and features a notable variety of seawater and freshwater products, or one particularly unusual and interesting one. Here we also reach the area of red-cooked meats (stewed with soy sauce) and diverse cold appetizers, and of wheat as a truly significant staple (wheat is actually much used in Hokkien cooking also, but in the form of noodles). In the north, this world of aquatic foods and endless variety grades into several northern schools as well as Shantung's. There is much need for a culinary cartographer or "foodlorist" to draw boundaries and divisions in this region. Mrs. Chao (1963) speaks as if her home area in Anhwei had its own special cuisine; no doubt it does; no doubt all the other regions down the Yangtze and Huai do too. We need to know more about them.

As if the regional diversity were not enough, we must briefly touch on the different processes used. No two authorities agree on what methods of cooking are to be recognized. The authorities also fail to agree on the extent to which combining two processes during different stages of cooking an item (a standard practice in every cuisine in the world) creates a new process. They also do not list distinct areas where specific methods dominate. Synthesizing this is impossible without further research, so we will content ourselves with broad observations. For more useful directions (if one is a cook) and more culturally relevant categories (if one is an ethnoscientist), see Miller 1967; K. Lo 1972; and above all B. Y. Chao 1963, where the best explanations and translations of Chinese terms are found. Better yet, see a good cookbook in Chinese.

The broadest division in methods is between cooking with water and cooking with oil. To begin with water: one can boil food or steam it. Whatever the books say, boiling is the most important process in the Chinese kitchen. This is primarily because the staple foods—rice and noodles—are boiled. (In areas where rice is rare, dumplings are often boiled, or flour of, for example, buckwheat or corn is made into mush and cooked dry as cakes, like American corn bread.) But soups are also boiled, and soups and stews form an important part of the day's food for virtually everyone. Slow simmering of pot dishes, notably the "sand pots," and rapid boiling of foods for subsequent further cooking or marinating are merely variants of boiling. So are the self-help dishes, for which the eaters are provided with boiling water or stock and finely sliced or otherwise prepared raw ingredients which they cook on their own. Plunging and rinsing are words often used for this. The most common dishes of this sort are the fire pots (*huo kuo* in Mandarin; Cantonese *ta pin lou*, which means approximately "action-on-the-sides stove"; often called Mongolian chafing dishes in English). But other dishes occur, including what in Singapore is known as "Teochiu saté"—clams and quail eggs and other good things impaled on tiny wooden skewers (used by the Malays for making saté, grilled meat strips) and then placed in the boiling water to cook.

Steaming is usually used for snacks (most of the *tien-hsin*) and aquatic foods—fish, crabs, and the like. Anything is good steamed and is sometimes so prepared, but many people believe Chinese food is mostly steamed, which it is not. Even boiled rice is often called, and believed to be, "steamed" rice when it reaches foreign shores. Steaming usually involves putting foods on slatted wooden or bamboo trays over boiling water and covering the whole tightly. Sometimes the steaming is done in a deep dish rather than on a tray, in which case the water may collect there as it recondenses, providing a distilled broth for the food, a recondite delight of Yünnan (K. Lo 1971, p. 123).

Cooking in oil usually means stir-frying (*ch'ao* in both Mandarin and Cantonese). However, deep-frying is more common than often alleged. Some deep-fried things are sold ready-cooked in markets, notably fried bean curd. Stir-frying grades into deep-frying via the following steps: the "stirred" part is the Cantonese method of heating the oil till it smokes, then tossing thinsliced vegetables and meat into it and stirring very quickly for a few seconds while the food sears. This preserves maximum flavor, freshness, vitamins, and crispness. Larger pieces, such as fish and egg fu yung, are cooked longer with more oil and less stirring. Often the sound of the crackling oil tells whether they are done enough; the cooks cook by ear more than by eye. (Some even tell if steamed foods are ready by the sound of the hiss of steam.) Deep-frying often involves plunging items rapidly into boiling, or at least hot, oil, again searing them, but in a thicker, crisper, oilier coat. At the "fried" end, comes the folk Hokkien method of putting mixed vegetables and meat (often chunks of organ meat) into melted, lukewarm lard and slowly simmering them, producing an exceedingly mushy, greasy dish that is the very antithesis of the popular conception of Chinese cooking. This is a standard, almost *the* standard, way of cooking such dishes among the Malaysian Hokkien but may represent something of a degeneration from ancestral ways. (The popularity of soggy *yu-t'iao* and similar goods in Taiwan is perhaps indicative of the contrary—Taiwan having surely not degenerated one whit in these things.)

Cooking in heat without water, oil, or anything, is not a common Chinese practice. Roasting is done by specialty merchants to produce Cantonese *ch'a siu* and other local specialties. The smoking of Szechwanese camphor-and-tea-smoked duck is done by roasting, but only for a short time, and the duck is really cooked by frying. Baking has become common now as a Western borrowing—cakes, tartlets, and even *pao* (filled buns) are baked. Pao were classically steamed, but baked ones are widespread and surprisingly good. How traditional this is we do not know, but clearly it is primarily a modern invention. The main baked good of traditional China—northern, but penetrating far south—is the *shao-ping*, the wheat-flour and sesame-seed buns that are baked by sticking them to the sides of a large pot or pot-shaped oven. This is a standard Near Eastern way of cooking—developed in northwest India, Pakistan, and Persia into the incomparable *tandur* method—and it no doubt spread to China in the not too distant past, as indeed did the sesame-roll concept. Classic spit-roasting and ash-roasting are virtually unknown, except that ducks and sometimes other meats are marinated and spit-roasted by Cantonese specialists and some others. Ch'a siu is made by a related roast form.

Cooking the same item by sequential methods is a refinement often found. A food may be smoked (roasted over smoking items), then boiled, then fried; or boiled and stir-fried; or partly boiled, set aside till needed, than shoveled into the eater's hot soup to finish boiling there as he eats it—for example Yünnanese "across-the-bridge" noodles. (The name refers to their being poured out of the cooking dish into the eater's bowl, for final cooking.)

Last of all, leaving food uncooked is not at all common. Fruit is eaten plain. Not much else is. The many cold plates and cold dishes almost invariably have been cooked and then cooled. "Noncooking" is mostly confined to making dips (chili in soy sauce, garlic crushed in vinegar, plum sauce, etc.), and even here much of the material is subjected to heat somewhere in its manufacture. Millennia of experience have taught the eaters that anything like American salads (America's most involved contribution to world gastronomy, we should think) or Japan's sashimi is too dangerous under Chinese conditions. Raw fish was once much eaten in China but now is found only very rarely—for example, in Cantonese raw-fish conjee, a dish most Cantonese know is often infested with parasites, and so to be avoided. Even salted and fermented foods, which are usually safe because the curing process kills bacteria and parasites, are usually cooked. This is not to say that Chinese food is safe; contaminated dishes and water often intervene, and, more important, stir-fried foods are not cooked long enough to kill such things as amoeba cysts and parasitic worm eggs and cysts. One takes chances in the name of good food. The alternative is longer frying or half an hour of boiling—enough to do more damage to nutritional values and fuel supplies and food quality than one gains in safety from parasites.

The foregoing, including the sections on ingredients as well as those on regional styles and diverse methods, does not begin to exhaust the subject of culinary diversity in south China. What, then, gives unity to southern Chinese cooking?

We have already considered the most basic element of unity, the ingredients: rice, fish, pork, vegetables, with less of the wheat, soybeans, and mutton of the north. In combining them, still other dimensions of unity are added. South Chinese food can be distinguished from Vietnamese, from Non-Han south Chinese (usually), and even more or less from north Chinese by the following characterization, ignoring regional variations.

1.   Foods are either snacks, rice with meat/vegetable topping (the main dishes), or soups. In feasts, the rice is more or less ignored and the toppings (*sung* in Cantonese) take over as the main dishes.

2.   A very wide variety of vegetables is used, as fresh as possible in this land of ten- and twelve-month growing seasons. Most dishes mix them with meats.

3.   Tastes are piquant and pungent, with fermented soybean products typical, often combined with vinegar, chili, and other similar ingredients. Vinegar, sugar, and peanut or rape oil are common. By contrast, south of China the true spices, the curry spices, are found, and in north China there is less vinegar and sugar and fewer vegetables, and the food is flavored

more with sesame oil, star anise, garlic, onions, and soybean jams (but not the black beans of the south).

4. Food tends to be cooked fast. Curries to the south, pot dishes, red-cooked dishes, and simmered dishes to the north are slow-cooked. This speediness reaches its apogee in the lightninglike stir-frying and quick-boiling of the Cantonese, but the Hakka and Szechwanese are not far behind, and other groups can work as fast on occasion.

Other distinguishing features could be listed, but these are enough to identify the basic principles of south Chinese cooking. Many of the principles are shared widely in eastern Asia, some are specific to the south, but the total pattern they produce is what is distinctively south Chinese.

The minimax game played in the nutritional aspects of diet is also played in cooking: Minimal input for maximal output, except, as in the case of agriculture, for labor time. Specifically, fuel use, kitchenware use, and use of food ingredients, especially the expensive ones, is minimized, for a maximum output. This is not always done, but it is done regularly enough to be characteristic of the whole cuisine. Cooking the shortest possible time saves fuel, even if one must turn up the heat to do it; using a lot of fuel thoroughly in a short time is more efficient than slow simmering. Food is cut very thin and with maximal surface area exposed, so it cooks as quickly as possible; it is best when still "raw" enough to be crisp (vegetables) or tender (meats). As noted, this is most true in the Cantonese area, with its smoking-hot oil, but it is relatively important everywhere, compared to the world's other cuisines. Oil and expensive spices are economized—the oil by stir-frying, as is well known. Use of a few slices of meats in a big dish of vegetables gives maximal meat taste and visibility for minimal use of meat. The affection for fresh produce, young and tender items, and seasonal foodstuffs means minimal waste (no tough parts to discard), minimal cost (out-of-season items are not bought), and minimal loss to rot. Cantonese housewives and househusbands in rural Hong Kong, during our research there (1965–66), insisted on knowing that the vegetables they bought had been gathered no more than an hour or two before, the pork butchered no less recently, and the fish caught within a day. Urbanization was making this impossible, but insofar as it remained possible it was done. Live fish commanded prices up to ten times that of dead fish of the same kind; and the water used to keep them alive was evaluated—the cleaner the water, the better the fish. In addition to improving taste quality, this saved the eaters from spoilage or contamination. Lastly, preparing and mixing many foods in one dish means that fewer dishes need be used and washed up.

Flavors should be mixed, piquant, strongly marked without being over-

powering. Only rarely are foods eaten plain and unadorned; almost everything is mixed and seasoned. Seasoning, however, is neither the diversely
fiery sort found to the south, nor the simple and direct garlic-chili combination of Korea and parts of north China. Ideally, the flavors of vegetables,
and sometimes fruits or fungi, blend with meats, and the whole is brought
out and heightened by slight to moderate amounts of chili, garlic, ginger,
vinegar, soybean ferments, and so on, and occasionally by such stronger
spices as star anise and brown pepper (fagara). Even the Hunan-Szechwan
cuisine is handled so. Once one is used to the chili, one finds that its rather
mild taste (note: taste, not physical impact!) is used with strong flavors of
other sorts, so it never becomes overpowering, as it does in some other
cuisines of the world. Of course, the above is not true of minor snacks, but
the gourmet eats them with more interesting fare, as counterpoint.

The food is designed to be cooked or eaten with absorbers—substances
that add little taste, but whose real function is to absorb all or some of the
gravy and flavors, emphasizing them, uniting them, and adding texture.
Rice is the original and principal one, of course, but the cuisine has added
more and fancier ones: cloud-ear fungus and birds' nests, for example.
They are not mere substrates; they give body to the food and absorb some
flavors more than others, making each bite a distinct experience.

The line between cook and diner is blurred, partly as a corollary of the
above. Miller (1967) rightly points out that the diner does not "season"
his food (in the sense of salting and peppering it), because seasoning is an
integral part of the cooking and cannot reasonably be done later; salt, for
instance, is added in the form of salted black beans in much of Cantonese
cooking, no free salt being used. The black beans have to be cooked. However,
most meals would include a sauce, if only soy sauce, as a dip or for dripping
on certain items. Fancier food than ordinary often involves complex dips.
The French habit of serving everything drowned in sauces would repel a
Chinese gourmet; he prefers to dip the food in sauce at will, thus keeping
it crisp and controlling the amount of sauce per bite. Sweet-sour dishes are
often served with the sweet-sour sauce on the side, and among sophisticated
Cantonese this is especially typical; the method of drowning the meat in
the sauce, by Chinese restaurants outside the country, is a concession to
undiscriminating tastes. Many dishes have their "official" dip sauce; in
Cantonese food, examples would be chili-and-soy sauce for boiled prawns
and vinegar for fresh crab; in Teochiu food, vinegar with freshly crushed
garlic for steamed goose, and a strange, fascinating sauce with a malt syrup
base for certain types of fish balls. Other examples abound. The glorious
culmination of dishes regulated by the diner is, of course, the fire-pot, where
the diner does the cooking, to his taste. But even the ordinary routine of

mixing sung dishes on top of rice is part of the same phenomenon; the diner controls the ways in which flavors mix and combine. No two bites are the same; each is a separately managed event.

Diversity is consciously and continually sought. There is no rule about what must be eaten at a certain time, except for the classes of festival foods that are part and parcel of a specific day, and they merely prove the point, for festivals are used as an excuse to bring in classes of foods that would otherwise be missed because of the trouble and expense of producing them. Of this more, presently.

Food taboos are foreign to south China. Famines have long ago eliminated those. True, dairy products were not much used except in Yünnan, but that has changed a fair amount. Blood is not much used outside the Hokkien world, but there is no religious rule (as in Judaism and Islam) or unwritten cultural taboo (as in the United States) against it. Similarly, there is little commitment to a certain diet. The cultural superfood, rice, is bland and goes with anything. South Chinese are usually quick to experiment with new and different foods—they show some resistance, as does everyone confronted with a strange diet, but they adjust much faster and more easily than do people from most other cultures. (In our experience, but this is only a guess, it seems that the more varied and good one's diet is, the more easily one adjusts to different diets, and vice versa.)

There is continual concern with the quality of food. Surely no culture on earth, not even the French, is so concerned with gastronomy as the Chinese. This point is too well known to need elaboration, but too important to disregard. Everyone from the lowest beggar (looking for scraps) to the highest official knows where to find the best. There was, and at last report (1971) still is, a wonton shop in Yün Long, in the New Territories of Hong Kong, that was famous throughout the western New Territories; everyone yearned to eat there. It was a perfectly ordinary, working-class neighborhood wonton and noodle place, a small bare room with a few tables and chairs, not a fancy restaurant; yet people from all walks of life flocked to it. Western gourmets tend to require an elegant ambience as part of a meal. The Chinese are concerned with the food.

Dimensions of quality are many and impossible to analyze, but some have been noted before: harmonious blend of flavors, including piquant ones, and some absorbers; freshness, the more complete the better; texture, with crispness retained, and contrasts developed; appropriateness to the season, time and occasion; markedness and subtlety of flavors. The rules of quality are observed, theoretically at least, in every cooking transaction. Of course there are exceptions. China has its share of bad cooks. Moreover, in overseas communities, isolated from the main tradition and often victims of prejudice and discrimination, standards often fall. Among poorer Malaysian Chinese, for instance, specifically those whose economic and political position is worsening, concern with food has given way to despair; standards are not maintained and concern with quality is a vanishing remnant of an idea (Anderson and Anderson 1973b). Chinese traditions are being abandoned, and the worst and most nutritionally disastrous traditions of the West are becoming more and more dominant. Even here, though, much is retained, and economic upturn would be followed by a return to involvement with good food. Such is occurring in areas of progress.

The aim of the foregoing is to allow the reader to cook Chinese food without recipes. One last note is needed: some guide to Chinese kitchenware. There seems no need to list it here, since any good cookbook does that, but we will include some discussion of its relation to the general minimax model. In the case of cookingware, the game is to minimize the amount of utensils you have to buy for maximal usefulness in cooking. Thus there are few items, and all of them—particularly those used most often—are durable. A good tool should last lifetimes and be made of cheap materials so it is also easily replaceable. It should be useful in the production of anything and everything.

The ultimate in this regard is, of course, the wok (Mandarin *hu* or *huo* or other names; Cantonese *uok*, now thoroughly established in English as a loanword). It is the standard curve-bottomed cooking pan, ideal for stir-frying and deep-frying both. A small amount of oil makes a pool in the bottom and goes a long way, while food can be moved up the sides to drain. For boiling it is likewise good. Placing steamer racks in it, with a cover over the whole, converts it to a steamer. With the wok goes a flat-bladed metal spoon to stir with and a bamboo-handled wire-net spoon to scoop things out of liquid. With these, the bamboo slat-bottomed steamers and the cover, and a chopping block and knife, the kitchen is equipped with the basics. The knife will be the large familiar cleaver—useful for splitting firewood, gutting and scaling fish, slicing vegetables, mincing meat, crushing garlic (with the dull side of the blade), cutting one's nails, sharpening pencils, whittling new chopsticks, killing pigs, shaving (it is kept sharp enough, or supposedly is), and settling old and new scores with one's enemies. Not even the machete is more versatile.

The perfect kitchen will also have some small saucepans and a sand-pot and, if possible, another taller, egg-shaped sand-pot. These are named for their very sandy, coarse earthenware construction; the earthenware absorbs grease and allows some evaporation of water through it, thus holding flavors in (flavors absorbed to the inner sand of the wall season the pot through the years) and allowing excess moisture to diffuse out slowly when the pot is sealed. They also allow slow transmission of heat. They are the ideal stewpans, and that is their function—the wok gets too hot and cools too suddenly for good simmering. Rice may be boiled in a sand-pot glazed inside, but in modern times a metal pot is used. A number of ancillary tools, such as twisted bamboo to pick up large pieces from liquid and long chopsticks for manipulating, can be improvised when needed or acquired very cheaply. Not much involves special expense. A major exception to this rule is the class of moulds: carved wooden ones for glutinous small cakes or for cookies, waffle-ironlike ones for thin cakes, special moulds for moon cakes. These must be bought and are neither cheap (by Chinese standards) nor easy to make. The tea services, including kettle and pot, are also a more important order of purchase; beautiful, well made, serviceable ones are desired and are apt to be far and away the most expensive items in the kitchen.

The stoves in a kitchen are of two classes: the small, mobile ones and the huge one built up from the floor, which looks like an altar and is one (the kitchen god resides in it or regards it as his special center of interest, even though he has a small altar for incense, and so forth, on the wall behind). The small ones are often electric hotplates or kerosene stoves today, but the traditional charcoal-burner is still seen: a bucket is coated inside with clay; when the clay has set, it is removed and its bottom carved with air inlets; a perforated clay grate is put in, and the whole is then fired (see Hommel 1937 for more detailed descriptions of stoves). Charcoal is the best medium for cooking Chinese food; it gives the right amount of heat, cools at the right speed or can be fanned to incredibly high temperatures, is controllable, and flavors the food as much as one desires. But the hotter-burning gas fuels, such as propane, are good substitutes.

Eating utensils are another feature that provide unity in the southern Chinese culinary world, and reveal the same emphasis on durability, quality, and economy (the first two being aspects of the last). Aside from chopsticks, porcelain rice bowls, main-dish platters, and tiny sauce-and-dip dishes, there is little. The ordinary family will have their individual bowls, a few of the ancillary dishes, and will use the cooking pots for serving the main dishes, though they will have fancy platters for special occasions. The most common rice bowls are porcelain, most often blue and white (in forms and with patterns not much changed in five hundred years), and they hold about twelve fluid ounces. After a feast they are often used to hold wine. They are the traditional wine cups of poorer people. More recently, Western-style glasses have become usual, in addition to the more traditional teacups. Teacups usually hold about five or six fluid ounces, but among tea connoisseurs of the Hokkien area (and no doubt at least some other main tea-producing areas) tiny cups holding about one fluid ounce are preferred. In addition to these various basics, there are soup bowls and conjee bowls, various types of sauce dishes, pottery soupspoons, small dishes for tien-hsin, and a host of other forms. These do not differ significantly from those found in northern China and from those of earlier eras, except those that are recent borrowings from the West, and other chapters in this book describe them well. The important point to make here is that they are of clay and bamboo— common, easy-to-work, cheap materials—and are made (from the choosing of the material to the final glazing or carving) to last and to be decorative. Again, maximal utility for minimal input is approximated. (By contrast, Western-style utensils are complex and consume too much energy and raw material in, for example, metal and plastic; conversely, the simple arrangement found in India, of a banana leaf for a dish and fingers for eating tools, would be considered by the Chinese too spartan for utility.)

Non-subsistence Aspects of Food

Madeleine Leininger has pointed out that every society uses food in many ways, including all of the following: (1) for nutrition; (2) to "initiate and maintain interpersonal relationships" (3) "to determine the nature and extent of interpersonal distance between people"; (4) for "expression of socioreligious ideas"; (5) for "social status, social prestige, and for special individual and group achievements"; (6) to "help cope with man's psychological needs and stresses"; (7) to "reward, punish, or influence the behavior of others"; (8) "to influence the political and economic status of a group"; and (9) to "detect, treat, and prevent social, physical and cultural behavior deviations and illness manifestations" (Leininger 1970, pp. 153–79). This may not be the definitive list, but it covers the ground. All these uses are well represented in southern Chinese foodways. The basic concept is that food is the great social facilitator. It is needed every day; it is highly divisible and quantifiable; it is usually prepared and consumed socially, and almost all eating is a social event. Thus sharing food is a great social bond, and the foods shared communicate the forms and contents of social interactions. In fact, second only to its nutritional value is its communication value. Often a message will be communicated by food when words are forced to serve ritual formulas of politeness. Many a non-Chinese has come away from a meal cursing the "inscrutable" Chinese for saying nothing but bland, polite phrases, when the meal itself was the message, one perfectly clear to a Chinese. In short, food management is critical to all harmony—in one's own body, in one's social life, and in one's interaction with the world.

Maintenance of harmony is a basic goal of much southern Chinese behavior. We propose, on much evidence, that there is a basic congruence between maintaining bodily harmony, social harmony, and cosmological harmony, and that these are main goals of the medical, social, and religious behavioral systems. Food relates to them as follows: In folk belief even more than in classical medical tradition, the proper choice food is *the* way of maintaining bodily harmony—specifically, balancing *jeh ch'i*, "spiritual heat," and *liang ch'i*, "spiritual coolness," by appropriate manipulation of "hot" or "cold" foods. Meals, from snacks with friends to formal banquets, are the most important concrete expressions of social bonds, actually creating and maintaining them. Food sacrifice is obligatory in all major rituals and serves as a key way of communicating to the gods. The equation between human feasting and sacrificing to the gods is perfectly explicit in Chinese folk belief; informants have told us "we sacrifice in order that the gods will be content (*shu-fu*) with us," and even, at a sacrifice to the ghosts and the King of the Underworld, "we are getting the gods drunk so they will be happy and let our ancestors out of hell." Equations about specific foods are found. The equation between cosmological harmony and bodily harmony is also perfectly explicit: *yang* and *yin* must balance in the cosmos and also in the human body (the jeh/liang distinction being one manifestation of this). As the body maintains its health by eating the proper proportions of the proper foods and cures itself by consuming foods and herbs appropriate to the disease (often prescribed by spirit-medium healers and blessed or accompanied by charms), so the social and religious congregations maintain stability and balance with the appropriate foods. There is a certain complementarity: the body is the nexus point of many different foods; a meal is the nexus point for many different people or for people and gods. The basic belief is that the world is a harmonious place, in which harmony must be maintained by these realistic and down-to-earth measures. There is little of the Indian attitude that all food transactions are sacred and even the humblest meal is like a divine sacrifice. The Chinese belief is the other way round: a sacrifice to the gods is a projection or type of a meal, a subset of ordinary meals in which gods and spirits, rather than visible, tangible humans, are the fellow diners.

In these realms of food, the minimax game no longer counts. If anything, the reverse is true. A festive occasion—secular feast or religious sacrifice—is marked by a graduated series of luxuries, involving the most expensive goods. A major rite, such as the ones repeated only every several years in Taiwan, requires sacrificial foods of the most expensive kind, taking years to accumulate.

In what follows, we will discuss, in greater detail, three major non-subsistence aspects of food: the personal aspect, the social aspect, and the cosmological aspect.

The Personal Aspect.   Folk medication in south China is largely by oral prescription. Acupuncture, surgery, and the like, are matters for the elite, too expensive and recondite for the ordinary person. Dietetics and herbal medication are the main curative methods and are of constant use. We have recently reviewed this subject at length elsewhere (Anderson and Anderson 1974) and will merely summarize it schematically here.

The category of food grades into that of herbs; such foods as day lily are more or less intermediate (see above under Ingredients). Foods can be almost exclusively medicinal, or often so, or eaten as food only, but with health aspects well known; herbs can be a substantial part of diet. Watercress and carrots are probably eaten almost as often for more or less medical reasons as they are for food; both are highly "cooling," at least in Cantonese folk medicine. Herbal and dietary medicine can involve either secular self-medication or sacred curing in which a medium contacts gods or ancestors and receives prescriptions from them. Many cases in which the healer-medium treats disease involve administering something orally to the ailing person—most often a charm written by the medium with his own blood, then burned, and the ash drunk in tea. The tea is often one made from medicinal herbs. Frequently the god or spirit tells the patient (via the medium) to correct or change dietary patterns—eat more strengthening foods or more cooling foods or, perhaps, some specific item or items.

The general belief is that food is necessary, and important, to health. The major concern is with foods that are jeh ("hot, heating") or liang ("cold, cooling"). There is a continuum; in the middle are foods that are balanced, of which rice is the prime example. (Among our Cantonese informants, ordinary boiled white rice was balanced and conjee was cooling because of all the water used. Among Malaysian Hokkien, the continuum was shifted toward the hot end; conjee was balanced, boiled rice heating. Other foods were correspondingly shifted. This seems to go with the greater insecurity and fear of the future among the Hokkien, who were less knowledgeable about the system but more afraid of getting too little heat, and thus wasting away; they felt they needed a heating staple to sustain them.) Cooling foods are bland, low in calories, vegetal; watercress and day lily are extremely cold, as are many herbs. Heating foods are stronger, richer, spicier; strong alcoholic drinks and spicy, fatty feast foods (the association with feasts and other *yang* occasions is specific and deliberate) are the hottest. Certain processes make foods colder or hotter, from cold-water infusing (coldest) through boiling (cool), to stir-frying (heating, but not very), to roasting, baking, and especially deep-frying (very heating). The longer the process goes on, the more heating the food becomes, so long-baked foods are especial concerns. A balance of hot and cold must be maintained; men should be slightly toward the hot side, being more *yang*, but correspondingly have a greater risk of overheating; women, more *yin*, should stay cooler but risk getting too cool.

Crosscutting the hot/cold dichotomy is the rarely invoked *kan/shih*, "dry/wet," dichotomy. Few if any foods are dry, or cold and wet, but catfish and some shellfish are hot and wet. They are usually poisonous (*tu*) as well. Venereal disease, a hot, wet disease associated with poisons, is associated with these; if a man avoids shellfish at a dinner, he is in for good-natured teasing. Otherwise, the dry/wet dichotomy has little meaning to the southern Chinese we know but may well have great importance elsewhere.

Variation is typical in such systems everywhere, and southern China is no exception (Anderson and Anderson 1974). This "humoral" medical system, which extends all over the Old World and to many New World areas influenced by the Old World, is subject to person-to-person and village-to-village modification. It is hard, if not impossible, to elicit the same lists of hot and cold foods from two consecutive informants, in China or elsewhere, though the general trend of the system is obvious, with very rich foods always considered hot, and very thin, bland, low-calorie ones usually deemed cold.

Related but somewhat distinct is the class of strengthening foods, foods that build *ch'i*. These aid, in various ways, the vital functions of the body. General systemic tonics like ginseng and ginger belong here (their widely known aphrodisiac or fertility-increasing qualities are strictly apocryphal and follow from the belief that they are general stimulants and tonics). Chicken boiled in broth is also valuable (chicken soup is the most universal cure-all in the world) and is given to women recovering from childbirth. Many local beliefs also occur; among Cantonese fishermen there is a belief that all the ch'i of the powerful giant grouper goes into any gill parasites it may have when it dies, and thus these are the most concentrated source of *ch'i* or, at least, of stimulants to one's own ch'i. Far more study of these local beliefs and variations is needed: virtually nothing is known about them.

In general, the sick are treated by feeding them with slightly heating foods for diseases believed to be cooling or associated with too much cold, and conversely for opposite problems. The healthy must try to maintain a balance in all things, occasionally taking some ginseng, ginger, or the like for good measure, but in practice, unless a person is ill, only those tending toward hypochondria worry very much about the balance. However, since such things as stomach upsets and hangovers are "hot" diseases, self-doctoring is frequent. Since feast foods and alcoholic drinks are generally hot, literally and figuratively (though the tradition of warming the wine is far less important in hot southern China than in the wintry north), and since it is possible to take countermeasures, self-medication works much of the time, thus greatly strengthening belief in the system.

Appropriate foods for children are the balanced ones (children can become unbalanced in heat and cold more easily than adults) and especially bland starchy foods; rice conjee is perhaps the epitome. In Malaysia, among poorer Hokkien Chinese, the diet of children was almost exclusively rice, noodles in thin soup, and sweets—a diet producing exceedingly poor nutrition and high levels of tooth decay (Anderson and Anderson 1973b, 1974). Children are introduced fairly early to vegetables and bits of fish and other protein-rich, low-fat foods, however. Among most groups these soon become a main part of the diet, but among Malaysian Hokkien and several other groups, the diet is mostly starch and sugar for quite a while, especially when the adult food is very spicy, as it often is in Malaysia.

Other aspects of folk dietetics and medicine, such as the beliefs relating to poisons (tu) and foods that carry them or flush them out of the system, are important but little known; their principles and variations are not known in sufficient detail for discussion here. The whole question of folk medicine and diet needs further research. Here we will leave it and return to themes more central to this work.

The Social Aspect. In traditional south China, virtually every eating transaction is social. The balance is not worthy of mention: individuals might snack or drink a little tea, but this is not true "drinking tea" (*he ch'a, iam ch'a*). An individual living alone and in abject poverty would be almost the only person who would eat alone much of the time. Others eat with the family or, if lacking family, in tea shops, with friends, at work, or in some other social situation. Even if all members of the family come home at different times and eat as they come in, there is a definite bond, a feeling of sharing rice and eating together; after all, the food was cooked by the family's women at the family center, the stove, and a late and lone eater is usually sociably talked to and often is joined, in a token manner, by other family members. Ordinary meals—the unqualified *ch'ih fan* ("eating rice"), a substrate of rice or other staple topped with sung of any available kind—are eaten in the family or as noted above. Other eating transactions usually take place outside the home. These are discussed, in the following, in ascending order of their importance and formality.

Minor snacks, such as bowls of noodles, can be bought from street vendors. Small groups of people will frequently resort to this universal pastime. Mobile noodle vendors provide the "catering service" at schools and work places.

Drinking tea or, more recently, coffee, soda, beer, and other foreign importations is a more serious affair. It can mean a social occasion of a casual and friendly sort but often means something more formal and specific. Adult men are expected to be found in local tea shops or the local equivalent (e.g., coffee shops, in Malaysia, Singapore, and Indonesia) at specific or, at least, approximately known times, to meet people and keep up on local affairs and to transact any business afoot. Boys are initiated slowly into the rite, first by stopping for an occasional soda, then by sitting with their fathers, next by gradually frequenting the shops by themselves, but at less regular times and sitting in less prominent places than their fathers. Finally, when they become heads of households, they become regulars. Local leaders—the informal experts at dispute settling and face-to-face politics—are particularly careful to have daily "office hours" at a specific time, at a specific shop (see Anderson 1970a, for Hong Kong; unpublished data for Southeast Asia). This is evidently a pan-Chinese phenomenon but is far too rarely discussed in the anthropological literature.

A more formal subset of the above involves specific, arranged meetings to drink tea, eat snacks such as tien-hsin or noodles, or even drink some chiu at small shops of the sort noted. This is done when a specific but not very important matter is to be discussed, when people meet after some fairly long separation, and sometimes when they meet for the first time.

Another related behavior is a visit to a home for tea and snacks, in which case the fare is about the same but the setting different. Usually, this is the female equivalent of the men's visit to the tea shop; the latter is very definitely a male preserve. Sometimes whole families visit for tea. But if only males are involved, they will adjourn to the shop, in most regions, and not invade the domestic hearth.

Still higher up on the formality scale is a meal in a restaurant. Business deals and other important and specific affairs are discussed and finalized in this context. Families may go out for very special occasions, such as reunions. Any and all important matters involving the head of the family and equals from outside the family must at some time be discussed over food. The more important the event and the more important the diners, the finer the food must be. Quality is even more important than price.

A truly major event, such as a wedding, sixtieth birthday, visit from a close, long-absent relative of some importance, and the like, demands a formal feast, arranged in advance, with many main dishes served sequentially (eight is about minimal, more depending on the importance of the occasion and the resources of the hosts), much wine, much meat and little rice or other mere starch, and lasting four to six hours or more. The most formal of these occasions involve such token dishes as shark fins, whose sole function is to show that the feast is more than the ordinary, and they often include a band and other entertainment. Chefs are urged to create the best and most characteristic local dishes. The number of guests at a feast is more than at an ordinary meal, there being eight or ten or more, depending, again, on the occasion and the resources and local importance of the host.

Just as the local informal leader—and official persons of all kinds, too—must appear in his local tea shop on regular occasions, so must he give feasts. The more official and important the person, the more frequent and splendid his feasts must be. Since guests of similar importance must reciprocate, the time one spends eating away from home is a moderately good measure of one's importance. The pattern is quite a drain on the resources of a poor but upwardly mobile person. As such, it has been downplayed in China proper, but it is very far from being abolished there.

Degree of formality—number and precision of etiquette rules observed—increases with the importance of the occasion and the social class of the group involved. A banquet among Hong Kong's boat people or Malaysia's poor rural Chinese fishermen (rather, less-than-poor; the poor ones cannot afford banquets) is a reasonably informal occasion, marked by relaxed and heavy eating, with drinking of strong liquids beginning fairly early and intensifying after the food. The boat people of Hong Kong are by nature of their occupation heavy eaters and drinkers, since fishing is one of the most physically demanding of all jobs. Among middle- and upper-class Chinese, even a meal at home has a set of rules, and banquets can be quite formal, though rarely approaching the formality of the Western world in seriousness and detail. (After all, it is impossible to use the wrong fork.) The basic rules are fairly straightforward, though the specific application of them is touchy in the extreme in high-status situations. Detailed and excellent descriptions of eating codes are found in Pillsbury and Wang (1972) and B. Y. Chao (1963) and need not be given here. Following are the main ones that apply in all situations except ordinary at-home family meals.

Most basic, there is a sort of role overkill. The host should exaggerate his interest in getting the guests to eat and drink; the guests should exaggerate their unwillingness to put the host to so much trouble. Thus the host invites very enthusiastically, continually urges the guests to eat, puts food on their plates, keeps their glasses filled, and circulates with encouragements of all sorts. The guests refuse everything two times or more (the seriousness of the tone of the second or third refusal being the actual cue as to whether they will accept or are really declining), try to eat and drink moderately in spite of the urging, and are profuse with thanks and above all with apologies for putting the host to so much trouble and with denials of their own deservingness. The host urges them not to stand on ceremony, not to be polite, and not to apologize; they respond that they are not just being polite, they really mean it. People are expected to compliment the host on the quality of the food, and usually there is no need to be hypocritical in bestowing superlatives here. As noted before, the host tries to arrange the best in quality. Sentiments of a similar order are probably worldwide; the Chinese merely repeat them more often than some others. Men are expected to drink moderately, women still less. However, the definition of "moderate" varies with occasion and social group. Many middle-class Hokkien women do not drink at all at feasts; on the other hand, at a wedding among the boat people, the male leaders of the community are expected to get in serious drinking contests with each other and with their clientele among the fishermen, and they typically consume incredible quantities of liquor—enough to kill any untrained drinker. [4]

As mentioned briefly, earlier, certain foods are specific markers of prestigious situations. The best-known and most universally high-status or high-value food is shark fins (made into thick soup); local specialties often figure—in Hong Kong these include live fish and the fancy grades of dried and salted sea foods. In Penang, Malaysia, the great status food was the pomfret, and some other seafoods, notably crabs, were not far behind. In other areas, birds' nests, bears' paws, and the like, have been used. Many of the famous oddities of Chinese cuisine, like those just named, were used, not for their taste or their curiosity value, but for their status-marking and occasion-marking functions. Because they are rare and expensive and conspicuous, they carry the message: This is not just an ordinary feast; we have done something truly special. Of course, the higher the status of the host and the more special the occasion, the higher the rank of the foods served; rank is pretty well determined by price. Rarity in part determines price, but sometimes a quite common, and apparently quite undistinguished, article of food is the telling status food. Thus the fish of high status in Penang are not any rarer, better tasting, fresher, or more exotic than many other fish. (Actually they are rarer now, since the fisheries targeted them and have overfished them seriously.) They are perhaps a tiny bit more like the ideal southern Chinese fish (juicy, of delicate flavor, with white flesh) than other fish, and this no doubt gave them their start as a status food, but now their value is inflated far beyond any such difference and is assigned by purely social factors. (More recently, their rarity is having some effect.) By contrast, of course, other foods are so ordinary, everyday, and cheap that they are identified with poverty, and thus they rarely appear at feasts even if they are extremely good and well liked. Salted vegetables and some of the secondary staples are examples. There is some tendency, for special occasions, to seek out foods one does not ordinarily eat; thus the Hong Kong Cantonese made forays to obtain many rare and fine seafoods, while the Cantonese fishermen sought out meat to vary their usual diet of fish. Rice, the great staple, is too ordinary to be prominent, too vital and basic to meals to be ignored. It is served late in the proceedings at the fanciest feasts, as boiled or fried rice or both, and only the most hungry (or tactless) consume much of it. At regular special lunches and dinners, it continues to serve as the great substrate.

Status emulation is apparent in food choice. Traditionally, people tried to emulate the Imperial court, or whatever local representative of the Imperial government was available. Today, the emulated high-status group tends to be the Western world. Even when considerations of status are not the case, other considerations—for example, need to produce for export, resulting local familiarity with "international"-style goods, desire to try new and different things that succeed elsewhere, and interest in variety—make people adopt foreign foods. The needs of the economy and the blandishments of advertisers and other interested parties may influence choices. Canned and powdered milk initially caught on due to their use in giving children good nutrition, and now they proliferate beyond real need in many communities (see Berg 1973). Least affected by Western foods is China itself, where national pride and economic independence have led to a brilliantly successful canning, preserving, bottling, and exporting industry that has adopted many Western techniques (such as canning) for preserving and distributing Chinese foods. Safety and standardization were achieved early; quality continues to improve in the products. Most interesting is that the Chinese have met the West on its own ground, exporting food abroad, primarily for Chinese markets to be sure (e.g., in Singapore and Hong Kong) but more recently with appeal to wider groups. Near us, the outlets for Chinese foods in Los Angeles are in the city's Chinatown, but their customers are by no means all of Chinese background. In foreign communities such as those mentioned, these diverse and high-quality products have acquired prestige comparable to that of Western-style items, and a swing back to them is discernible among groups that formerly were acquiring Western tastes in food. However, the Chinese products include some imitation Western goods, notably liquors and soft drinks, and secondarily candy, cookies, and the like.

At the other extreme from China, the weaker and smaller overseas communities are Westernizing at increasingly rapid rates. This is hardly surprising in California, but in Malaysia emulation of Western eating habits is striking. The reason, briefly, is that the tension since independence between Chinese and Malays has led to Chinese refusal to adopt or continue to adopt

Malay ways; lack of pride in their own traditions is causing younger Chinese to turn away from Chinese ways; and the new "international" culture of the world business and government community lures them. We have discussed this trend at length above and elsewhere (Anderson and Anderson 1973b). By contrast, in Thailand and Indonesia, there seems to be more tendency to assimilate local (i.e., Thai and Indonesian, respectively) foodways as well as Western ones.

There is no question, however, of Chinese food disappearing—even in these Chinese communities abroad. Milk and ice cream, candy and bread may add themselves to the diet, just as Chinese restaurants have added themselves to the occidental food scene, but the Chinese retain far too much pride in and awareness of their food tradition to lose it. This may be contrasted with the fate of traditional clothing and architecture, and even of much music, folk theatre, and other arts, all of which are being replaced in most areas by Western forms. But, if anything, the world dietary prognosis may well be the other way; as the world food problem intensifies, other nations may adopt the food that combines quality and diversity with extreme efficiency in land and capital utilization. After all, private individuals throughout the world, as well as restaurants, are cooking more and more Chinese food of more and more different styles.

Finally, a word on ethnic characterization by food may be added. Food distinguishes ethnic groups—non-Han or Han (or T'ang, if one prefers—the southern Chinese call themselves "men of T'ang," not "men of Han" as the northerners do, thus implying specific periods of unification and sinicization in the two areas). The non-Han minorities of south China are little studied in this regard, but presumably they have special dishes that mark them. Chinese everywhere retain certain foods and cooking styles as conscious reaffirmations of ethnicity. Within the Chinese communities, local origin is expressed in foods, and certain foods become widely accepted and recognized markers, such as sweet-sour dishes for Cantonese and stuffed bean curd for Hakka. In areas where many Chinese groups are living together, such as Singapore and Malaysia, there is much borrowing and learning of each other's styles, and the styles tend to blur, especially since some members of some groups have assimilated in varying degrees into other groups, to say nothing of the Chinese whose native language is Malay or English. In Taiwan, however, groups from different parts of the mainland have not merged to any great extent, and still less have they merged with the Taiwanese. Here cooking styles are still of great importance as origin markers and affirmations of identity—and also as commercial advantages, since purveying traditional styles to eager buyers (of all origins) is a favorite business in Taiwan.

In short, food is communication. No conclusive or important business can be transacted, no firm contacts made, no importance marked or asserted, without the sharing of food. The expense, status value, quality, and setting of the food communicated more about the critical social dynamics of the situation than language can; much that is hard to verbalize, and more that would be impolite to verbalize, is communicated by this channel. Such use of food is worldwide, as every anthropologist knows; but no culture has developed it more than the Chinese.

The Cosmological Aspect.   We have seen that food is communicative. Like language, it combines phonemic units (ingredients) according to rules (cooking methods and, at a deeper level, principles of social interaction and of world view) to communicate messages about society, the individual, and so on. Unlike language, it has the pragmatic and positive value of nourishing the body in the process.

It is natural, indeed inevitable, that food should be used as a critical part of the most demanding and difficult communication of all—communication with the invisible portion of the world. In the folk religion of south China, there is no firm distinction between sacred and secular, or between this world and the other world; there is simply one universe, but one in which certain realms and certain classes of beings can only be reached by worship and sacrificial rites (*pai* in Mandarin, *paai* in Cantonese). In ordinary folk religion, which is *not* a hybrid of Confucianism, Taoism, and Buddhism but is a separate and pre-existing if unnamed entity (Anderson 1970a), the nearest thing to a general term for religion, worship, and the practice of the religion's teachings is *pai shen*, or *paai san* ("worshiping divinities"). The religious system has been described elsewhere many times and need not be detailed here. (See references cited in following discussion.) We are concerned here with the use of food in religious practice.

Southern Chinese folk religion postulates a similarity between the invisible and visible sectors of the world, in that the strategies, structures, and systems of the visible part are basically the same as they are in the other. If something is efficient, successful, useful, or desirable here, it is assumed to be so there. There is also a complementarity. It is assumed, logically enough, that things we cannot control (specifically health and luck) are under the control of the beings in the other realm, while things we can control (specifically material possessions, including food) are the specialty of "our side" and are not so controllable by the *shen*. Thus we depend on them for a good deal of our health and fortune, and they depend on us for a good deal of their clothing, money, and food. Burning paper representations of money, clothing, and goods (even houses and cars) is central to sacrificial rites; the representations, when burned with appropriate ceremony, become the real thing in the invisible realm. Food is offered; the shen consume the spiritual essence of the food, or some aspect thereof, while the gross material remainder is consumed by the worshipers. As the other papers in this volume show, the real material food (and other goods) was once buried with the dead; the economical modern belief has saved a lot of food but has deprived archaeologists of a rich source of information. Economizing has not ceased. Not only has the folk religion been essentially abolished in China proper, but it is fading very fast among all Chinese. Today, such dubious reverences as renting a roast pig to offer the ancestors are practiced, for example, in Malaysia. Since the same pig may be offered to twenty sets of ancestors during a Ch'ing Ming festival, one wonders if the pig's essence is renewed every time, or if each set of ancestors gets only 1/20 of a pig. Our informants did not know, and what is more, they did not care. Thus the decline of faith in our secularizing age.

Since the invisible realm is part of the total world, food serves the same functions in religion that it does in society. The religious uses are definitely extensions of the social ones. There is none of the reverse tendency, so pronounced in Hinduism, to base social usages on strictly theological or ritual considerations. Food serves to mark the importance of an occasion, with foods being ranked hierarchically in this regard. Food also marks the spatial and temporal location of a rite. In practice, this means that the more important the occasion, the bigger the sacrifice; specific occasions have specific ritual foods; and foods are sacrificed in specific locations at specific times. There is a general code of sacrificing, but some shen have distinctive foods, and each major festal day has its own traditional dishes.[5]

The lowest-ranking pai rite consists simply of the burning of three sticks of incense, without food. Anything higher involves offering food. Tea and fruit is the lowest level here; the fruit and, usually, the tea are found at all rites or nearly all, since subsequent levels build from this base rather than substituting. The canonical fruits are red or orange, scarlet gold being the religious color, the color associated with good fortune, auspicious events, and religion in general. Thus the usual fruits are jujubes, oranges, and tangerines. Pomelos are also used and believed to have magical qualities; water in which pomelo skins are soaked is a ritual wash, keeping away ghosts and ritually purifying the worshiper. Is it the fact that pomelos are citrus, like the scarlet fruit, or is it some ancient and deeper belief that makes them important? Other fruits, neither red nor citrus, are often sacrificed, but they have less magical association; bananas and apples are the most common of these. Sugarcane has a number of religious uses and associations, all of uncertain origin and poorly described in most of the literature. It is used in many rites, usually as a marker of an auspicious occasion of some importance, such as the opening of a temple. Fruit in general has enormous significance in Chinese religion; peaches, though not sacrificed, are extremely important in magic and religious art (de Groot 1892–1910), and Ahern has described a bizarre and unique equation of women and fruit trees in a Taiwanese village (1973).

A more important sacrificial rite will involve some wine as well as some tea, and a bowl of noodles or other minor staple food as well as the fruit. Here, if not earlier in the sequence, a pattern of threes is characteristic. Just as the least possible sacrifice is three small incense sticks, so three plates of fruit, three cups of wine, three cups of tea, and so on, are characteristic. Sacrifices are usually either ones or threes. Fours are found also; there are often four oranges or tangerines on a plate. Twos are conspicuously uncommon; no doubt this is related to the fact that twos are correct offerings in the visible world (one brings as presents two bottles of wine, two baskets of fruit, etc.). But sometimes twos are found.

The next level above this last is one in which more or less ordinary dishes are offered. These virtually always involve a whole chicken or duck as one of the dishes (sometimes the only one). Larger versions of this will include more birds or dishes made with pork (pork and vegetables, pork and noodles, roast pork) or both.

The fourth and highest sacrifice class involves offering a whole pig or something close to one. In Cantonese worship this will almost always be a *chin chu* (*kam tsü*), "golden pig"—one roasted whole with a sugar glaze that makes it the scarlet gold color associated with religion. Like the jujube and the tangerine, it must be the auspicious color. In Hokkien worship, the golden pig is not found as a key concept in offering, and there is a complex alternation or patterning of raw and cooked foods—raw being needed in some rites, cooked in others, raw food cooked during the ceremony in others. This varies from community to community. (Ahern, 1973 and personal communication; Gary Seaman, personal communication. We have observed but not studied this patterning in Malaysia and Singapore.) In many rites, especially those in which major favors of fortune are requested of the gods, steamed wheat buns, similar to pao but unstuffed, are colored scarlet and offered in large, sometimes enormous, quantities. Red-colored eggs are also found in such situations, especially if the fortune requested is birth of a son, in which case it is the woman who offers the eggs. Undyed eggs are seen at more routine ceremonies. Huge numbers of red buns are often seen at annual festivals of favor-granting deities. In Hong Kong they are so prominent at one Buddhist festival, celebrated primarily on Cheung Chau Island, that the festival is popularly known as the "bun festival"; three huge towers are made, once entirely of buns, now of bamboo and paper thinly stuck with buns on the outside to make the buns go as far as possible.

While almost any food may be offered as a treat to the shen, it is significant that the most important canonical offerings are pigs and fowl. Chickens are of religious significance—cock's blood drives away ghosts, for example —but ducks and geese are also much used in sacrifice. This religious significance of pigs and fowl is apparently a Southeast Asian pattern of great spread and age, now submerged in many areas because of recent religious conversion (e.g., to Islam) but persisting among practitioners of traditional religions. Like much else in southern Chinese religion, especially local cults and foodways, it was possibly taken over by the Chinese when they spread south and assimilated non-Chinese groups.

Food is offered directly in front of the image or shrine of the shen. Fruit is arranged left and right of the main offering, tea and wine in front of it, other dishes around it. This may vary according to rite or locality but is generally the rule. Temples have offering tables, typically with a scene, on the side facing the worshiper, of soul judging or, at least, of the soul-judging court in the invisible realm. The offering is arranged here, flanked by burning incense offerings. Often when many people must offer at the same image, there will be a steady circulation of people, each bearing their offering, depositing them briefly on the table, then carrying them out again. Fruit and buns and the drinks may be left, but the meat and main dishes are always carried away to be eaten. If a voluntary association has clubbed together to provide the offering, the meat is shared according to lot or to prearranged formula, in a more or less equable manner, depending on the amount of shares held by members. Sometimes food used in rites acquires magical properties. Ginger hung on huge paper constructions offered to the deity acquires vastly heightened powers of increasing fertility and may be auctioned off at the voluntary-association feast and food-dividing session. The buyer will have a son within the year, if he observes proper behavior rules. At least this belief flourishes in Hong Kong; we have not encountered it elsewhere.

Temporal patterning involves time of day, time of month, time of year, and even longer cycles up to sixty years. At dawn and evening, incense is offered, and sometimes food also, to any and all household guardians and other shen of the domestic world. The annual round of major festivals means that the canonical sacrifice—fruit, main dishes, pork, and so forth—is being offered by someone, somewhere, at almost any given time. Each family will offer it two or three times a year: on New Year, to ancestors or any powerful shen; to ancestors on Ch'ing Ming; and to their community's patron and guardian shen on his or her annual day. Thus T'ien Hou, otherwise known as Ma Tsu, patroness of many fishing and sea-oriented communities as well as of some land communities near the southern Chinese coast, is worshiped with major rites on the twenty-third day of the third lunar month. But in fishing villages that happen to have other patrons, she does not get the big sacrifice; the local patron does. There seems to be some tendency for neighboring villages to have different patrons, thus allowing villagers to visit each other's festivals, just as they have different (secular) fair days, if they are large enough to have special fairs.

In addition to the canonical sacrifices, special foods are eaten on certain occasions. A complete list of these is neither necessary nor useful here, nor is anything like a complete list available for anywhere in south China. (See Tun 1965, for Peking.) The best-known and most widespread special foods are the moon cakes of the mid-autumn moon festival, the sweetish glutinous-rice dumplings wrapped in leaves on Dragon Boat Day, and the fruits and seeds eaten at New Year. These last each have their own mythology, but it is interesting that all of them are fruits and seeds; there is clearly a general fertility-ensuring aspect to this, as there is for many of the specific seeds—for instance, lotus seeds have a well-known similarity in name, *lien tzu*, to a phrase meaning "many sons," The folklore behind these foods is interesting but fairly well known (see Eberhard 1958). In general, special festive-day foods are either small, sweet snacks—cakes, cookies, and the like—or fruits and seeds. These are economical, distinctive, infinitely modifiable, and special in that they are not the usual foods. The sweets especially are a class of food very rare in the traditional diet. Small sweets are always a cheap and easy way to make an occasion special. Since they are always highly popular with children, they are a potent agent in all higher cultures and many primitive ones for marking a special day and making it memorable and eagerly awaited by the young. Thus sweets may be essential in acculturating people to a festive round.

More generally, southern Chinese festivals involve much feasting, drinking and celebratory behavior. They are deliberately made as sensational and exciting as possible—relief in a drab world. The blazing color, the ear-splitting din, and the strong-flavored, superb, long-awaited feast foods, to say nothing of smells and sensations generally, mark the festival and indeed serve to make it the most emotionally and physically intense experience available. This not only makes the day important, it also creates a mood in which ecstatic, supernormal religious experiences are easily and frequently aroused. It is a vital part of maintaining an intense religious tradition.

Conclusion

In this chapter we have progressed from showing that Chinese food makes maximally efficient use of resources to describing lavish feasts and sacrifices. We have established that Chinese food tends toward maximization of dietary adequacy for minimum input of land and capital—that is, it usually uses the most productive sources of nutrients in the most efficient ways. Can this be reconciled with the splendid festival meals? We believe so. Authorities on cultural ecology have cautioned the world that seemingly wasteful customs often have very pragmatic functions, even in "otherworldly" India (Beals 1974; Harris 1966, 1968), let alone in "practical" China. In a negative sense, it is easy to show that Chinese feasting does not cost much ultimately, since all the food is consumed except for a few fruits and buns, and since it is the ordinary, everyday food. As we have seen, pigs and chickens are maximally efficient converters of waste products into high-quality protein. The exigencies of festivals and of sacrifices allow people to get high-quality protein and varied and diverse vegetable foods. Feasts may be an economic drain, but they are ecologically useful, causing people to grow and eat highly nutritious products that they might otherwise feel unable to afford—at a cost to their health in the long run and, consequently, at a cost to the functioning of the ecosystem.

But what about the positive sense? Do feasts, per se, with all their expense, with all their status bias (such that the least needy get the most food), actually improve the system, rather than merely stabilizing and aiding it? Here again we believe so, and as evidence we may point out that even the intensely practical and economics-minded government of modern China has not abolished good eating. However, we do not think that the benefits of feasts are only or even primarily in the realm of nutrition, of ecology in the narrow sense. "Man does not live by bread alone" nor by nutrients; and food is neither bread nor nutrients alone. If food is universally used throughout the world to maintain and create interpersonal bonds (and it is), if food sharing is the universal method of making humans true companions (com-panions are "sharers of bread"), it is logical and indeed inevitable that the Chinese should use it in a particularly sophisticated way as a marker and communicator in social transactions. Moreover, of all the enjoyable things of this world, food and drink are the easiest to manipulate and the easiest to manage in public occasions. They can be used to heighten or relax a group's emotions, to communicate trivial or vital messages. Everyone eats and eats fairly often, everyone can learn to enjoy good food, and in a natural environment where diversity is favored, there is every reason to strive for diversity and quality in diet. The food system is the most natural one to draw on for concrete expressions and tangible symbols of shared community realities. Constant and careful attention to quality in diet is the surest and best guard against eating poorly or eating foods detrimental to health. Moreover, it is more than a mere guarantee of survival. It is the most constant, the most reliable, and the cheapest of all ways to enjoy life.

NOTES

1. Recently, rice has been grown on a large scale well north of Buck's line, due to modern developments in agricultural technology and organization; we have no data on accompanying diet shifts, unfortunately. Also, there is no doubt a zone of intergradation where rice is one of many grains; but we have only scattered evidence for such a zone.

2. Note that the scientific name of the mung bean is not *Phaseolus mungo*. The Indian vernacular name of *aureus* was Latinized for the wrong bean, the Indian black gram, due to botanical confusion in the eighteenth century.

3. See Anderson 1972 for accounts of the principal fish and shellfish found around Hong Kong. Most of them are also dominant up and down the coast. For references to fish ponds, see Anderson and Anderson 1973a.

4. The boat people are always heavy drinkers at feasts and frequently consume a fair amount in ordinary life, but alcoholism is virtually unknown among them. According to our observations, its occurrence is even less among them than among Chinese in general, who are famous for their lack of it. The expense of alcohol and the social rules about consuming it explain part of this, but the highly supportive and mutually interlinked nature of Chinese society is also of critical importance.

5. Sadly, none of the religious foodways of south China are very well described, especially for the contemporary period. There are no modern compilations remotely comparable to those of de Groot (1892–1910) and Doré (1914–38) for an earlier day. There is nothing known to us for southern China that corresponds to Tun's excellent account of festivals and festival foods in Peking (1965). Many accounts of religion in southern Chinese communities ignore food almost completely. The best recent account for our purposes is that of Emily Ahern (1973), but it is not comprehensive. Other useful accounts covering local communities are those of Jordan (1972 and personal communication), Gary Seaman (personal communication, including film footage of major sacrifice rites), Baker (1968, especially the photographs, which include some of the best and most revealing photographs of sacrifices to ancestors), and others. We have described Cantonese and Malaysian Hokkien religious foodways in some detail elsewhere (Anderson 1970a, 1973; Anderson and Anderson 1973a, 1973b). There is need for serious work on this topic comparable to that of Geertz (1960) and Lévi-Strauss (1964–71). Use has been made of the techniques of ethnoscience (see especially the influence of Frake, 1964) but not enough speculation along the lines of Lévi-Strauss, Douglas (1970, 1971), Lehrer (1969), and others. We say this in hopes that it will stimulate ethnographers to pay as much attention to food as the Chinese themselves do. Apparently due to the Anglo-American bias against indulgently belly-pleasing food, ethnographers have ignored this vitally important domain, except for ethnographers from less puritan cultures. It is not surprising that the French have led in this field (notably Lévi-Strauss) and that other continental ethnographers, such as the Swedish group around Nils-Arvid Bringeus (Bringeus and Wegelmann, eds., 1971), have also taken more initiative than the Anglo-American ones. Southern China has had the misfortune to be studied by British and American ethnographers and Chinese trained in England or America.

GLOSSARY OF CHINESE CHARACTERS

a-la-chi 阿剌吉
ai 艾
an 案
an-mo-le 菴摩勒
ao 熬
a-yüeh-hun tzu 阿月渾子
beile 貝勒
bi 麫
bi hun 米粉
cha 炸
cha 鮓
ch'a 茶
ch'a shan fang 茶膳房
ch'a-shao 插燒
ch'a-siu 插燒
cha-tzu 樝子
ch'ai 豺
chan 鱣
Chan-tao 占稻
ch'ang 鬯
ch'ang 鯧
ch'ao 炒
che 蔗
che-ku 鷓鴣
chen-wu 珍物
cheng 蒸
ch'eng 橙
cheng tien 正店
ch'eng weng 棖甕
chen shih 榛實
chi 鯽
chi 稷
chi 棘
ch'i 氣
ch'i 芑
ch'i fen pao 七分飽
chi-mi-fan 穄米飯
chi-li 吉禮
chi ping 鷄餅
chi-shê-hsiang 雞舌香
ch'i-tzu 棋子
chi-yü 鯽魚
chia 假
chia-li 嘉禮
chia-tzu 甲子
Chia-yu 嘉祐
chiang 醬
chiang 薑
chiang 漿
Chiang Nan Jen 江南人
chiang yu 醬油
chiao 椒
chiao 鮫
Chiao-fang Ssu 敎坊司
chiao-jou tsao-tso 矯揉造作
chiao-ku 嚼穀

ch'iao-mai 蕎麥

chiao-pai 茭白

chiao-sun 膠笋

ch'iao-ts'ai 蕎菜

chiao-tzu 餃子

chia-yü 嘉魚

chieh 桔

chieh 戒

ch'ieh 茄

chieh ts'ai 芥菜

chien 煎

ch'ien 簽

ch'ien 錢

chien hsin 薦新

ch'ien-shih 芡實

ch'ien-ts'eng-kao 千層糕

chih 雉

chih 觶

chih 炙

chih 植

chih 枳

chih-ch'i 枳棋

ch'ih-fan 吃飯

ch'ih-fan la mei-yu？吃飯了沒有

chih-yung 支用

chin 斤

chin 董

ch'in 芹

chin-chen-hua 金針花

ch'in-chiao 秦椒

chin-chieh 金桔

chin-chu 金豚

chin-chü 金橘

chin-fa 金花

Chin-hua 金華

chin-shih 進士

ch'ing-chiu 清酒

ch'ing-ts'ai 青菜

ch'ing-yü 青魚

chiu 韭

chiu 炙

chiu 酒

ch'iu 鰍

ch'iu 糗

chiu-ch'i 酒旗

chiu huang 救荒

chiu-huang 韭黃

chiu-lou 酒樓

chiu-mu 酒母

chiu-ssu 酒肆

chiu-tien 酒店

chiu-ts'ai 韭菜

ch'iung 檁

ch'iung-ch'iung 芎藭

cho-chiu 濁酒

choi sam 菜心

chou 州

chou 皺

chou 粥

ch'ou tou fu 臭豆腐

chu 煮

chü 橘

ch'ü 麴

chu men chiu jou ch'ou lu yu tung ssu ku
    朱門酒肉臭路有凍死骨

ch'u i 厨役

chü-chiang 蒟醬

chü-jen 舉人

chu-liu 竹餾

chu-shih 煮食

chu-shih 主食

chu-sun 竹筍

chu-tzu 櫧子

chu-ya 竹芽

chü-yuan 枸櫞

chüan 卷

chüeh 玦

chüeh 蕨

chüeh-ch'i 脚氣

ch'un 蕈

ch'un-chüan 春捲

chün-li 軍禮

chün-tzu 君子
chung 鍾
chung-tsun 中尊
Ch'ung-yang 重陽
fa-chiao 花椒
fa feng tung ch'i 發風動氣
fa-sheng 花生
fan 飯
fan 燔
fan 繁
fan-ch'ieh 番茄
fan-kuo 飯鍋
fan-shu 番薯
fang 舫
fang ts'ao 芳草
fang-chih 方志
fei-shih 榧實
fen 分
feng 葑
feng ch'i li 鳳棲梨
Fen chiu 汾酒
fen shih 粉食
Feng Hsien Tien 奉先殿
Feng T'ien Tien 奉天殿
fou i 浮蟻
fu 釜
fu 賦
fu 簠
fu-ju 腐乳
fu-ling 茯苓
fu-shih 副食
ha la chi 哈剌吉
hai 醢
hai-hung 海紅
hai-t'ang 海棠
hai-wei 海味
Han-hsi 漢席
hang 杏
hao shao ping 好燒餅
he ch'a 喝茶
heng 杏

heui iam ch'a 去飲茶
ho 禾
ho 荷
ho-chi 鷚鷄
ho-chieh 蛤蚧
ho lan shu 荷蘭薯
ho-li-le 訶黎勒
ho-t'ao 核桃
ho-t'un 河豚
hou 鱟
hou 餱
hsi 席
hsia fan 下飯
hsiang 香
hsiang 饗
hsiang 享
hsiang-keng 香粳
hsiang-p'ien 香片
hsiang-shih 相食
hsiang-ts'ai 香菜
hsiao 殽
hsiao-jen 小人
hsiao-mi 小米
hsiao-mi-fan 小米飯
hsiao-mo 小麥
hsiao-ts'ung 小葱
hsiao-tsun 小尊
hsieh 薤
hsieh-fen 蟹粉
hsien 籼
hsien 縣
hsien 餡
hsien 䰞
hsien-ping 餡餅
hsien-t'ien 先天
hsien-ts'ai 莧菜
hsi-fan 稀飯
hsi-kua 西瓜
hsi-yang-ts'ai 西洋菜
Hsin-li mei chiu 新豊美酒
hsing 杏

hsing 腥
hsiu 脩
hsiung-li 凶禮
hsü 盨
hsü-chih 須知
hsüan-jou wei lin 縣肉爲林
hsün 鱘
hu 瓠
hu 斛
hu 鑊
hu 胡
hu-chen-tzu 胡榛子
Hu chi 胡姬
hu-chiao 胡椒
hu fan 胡飯
hu-kua 胡瓜
hu-luo-po 胡蘿蔔
hu-ma 胡麻
hu-ma-ping 胡蔴餅
hu-ping 胡餅
hu-sui 胡荽
hu-t'ao 胡桃
hu-tou 胡豆
hua-chiao 花椒
hua-ch'üan 划拳
huai 檜
huan 鯇
huang-cheng 黃烝
huang-ch'eng 皇城
huang-chiao 黃椒
huang-chiu 黃酒
huang-kua 黃瓜
huang-mi 黃米
huang-p'i 黃皮
huang-su 黃粟
huang-ya-chiu 黃芽韭
hui 膾
hui-hsiang 茴香
hui-kuan 會館
hun-tim 餛飩
hun-t'un 餛飩

hung-cha 紅茶
hung-ling-chiao 紅菱角
hung-lo-pak 紅蘿蔔
huo 鍋
huo cheng 火證
huo-chiu 火酒
huo-kuo 火鍋
i 飴
i 匜
i-chih-tzu 益智子
i-i 薏苡
iam-ch'a 飲茶
iong 陽
iun sai 芫荽
jang-ho 蘘荷
jang tou fu 釀豆腐
jê 熱
jê-ch'i 熱氣
jê-lo-ho 熱洛河
jen-shen 人參
jou-lin 肉林
jou-tou-k'ou 肉豆蔲
ju 濡
ju-chiu 乳酒
ju-fu 乳腐
ju-lao 乳酪
ju-i 儒醫
kaai choi 芥菜
kaai laan 芥藍
kam 柑
kan 乾
kan/shih 乾濕
kan-chiao 甘蕉
kan-fan 乾飯
kan-lan 橄欖
kan-t'ang 甘棠
kan-ts'ao 甘草
k'ang 糠
kao 蒿
kao-liang 高粱
kao-liang-chiang 高良薑

kao-liang-mi fan 高粱米飯

kao-mi 膏糜

k'ao-yang-rou 烤羊肉

ke-te 飲饉

keng 羹

keng 粳

keng-mi 粳米

k'iu-choi 蕎菜

ko p'eng 割烹

ko-ta 飲饉

kou-pi 鼀鼈、蚼蠑

ku 穀

k'u-kua 苦瓜

k'u-mai-ts'ai 苦賈菜

kua 瓜

kuai 膾

k'uai 塊

kuan 官

kuan 館

kuan 罐

kuang-lang 桄榔

Kuang-lu Ssu 光祿寺

kui 桂

kui 殴

k'ui 葵

kui hsin 桂心

kui tzu 桂子

K'un-lun tzu-kua 崑崙紫瓜

K'un-ning Kung 坤寧宮

k'un-pu 昆布

kung-nü 宮女

kuo 果

kuo 鍋

kuo-chi jih 國忌日

la-chiao 辣椒

la-pa-chou 臘八粥

laap ch'eung 臘腸

lai 萊

lai-fu 萊菔

lao 酪

lao 醪

lao mi 老米

lao su 酪酥

leng kok 菱角

li 李

li 栗

li 醴

li 貍

li 鯉

li 鱧

li 鬲

li 蠡

li 里

li-chih 荔枝

li-huo 藜藿

li-huo chih keng 藜藿之羹

liang 涼

liang 粱

liang 量

liang ch'i 涼氣

Liang-hsiang 良鄉

liao 蓼

lien 奩

lien 蓮

lien chiang 廉薑

lin-ch'in 林檎

lien-tzu 蓮子

ling 苓

ling chüeh 菱角

ling kuo 菱角

Ling-ling hsiang 零陵香

liu 醹

liu ta wan 六大碗

lo 酪

lo 落

lo 蓏

lo pak 蘿蔔

long-an 龍眼

lou 蔞

lu 壚

lu 鱸

lü-tien 旅店

lü-tou 綠豆
luo-po 蘿蔔
ma 麻
ma-hua 蔴花
ma-ju 馬乳
ma-ling-shu 馬鈴薯
ma-lo 馬酪
ma-t'ai 馬蹄
ma-tao 馬刀
ma-t'i 馬蹄
ma-t'ung 馬桐、馬湩
maer hua 蔴花
mai 麥
mai-pan 買辦
man-ch'ing 蔓青
Man-hsi 滿席
man-li yü 鰻鱺魚
man-t'ou 饅頭
man-ts'ao 蔓草
mao 卯
Mao-kua 毛瓜
Mao-t'ai 茅台
mei 梅
mei-hsi 每席
mei jen chiao 美人蕉
mei yu fan ch'ih 沒有飯吃
mi 米
mi 糜
mi 麪
mi hun 米粉
mi lu 麋鹿
mi sua 麪線
mi-ying 蜜櫻
mien 麪
mien shih tien 麪食店
min 麪
mo ch'a 末茶
mou 牟
mou 畝
mu 畝
mu 木

mu-erh 木耳
mu-kua 木瓜
ni 臲
ni tsao 泥竈
nien huo 年貨
niu pai keng 牛白羹
no 糯
nü 女
pa-chiao 芭蕉
pa-chüeh 八角
pa-hsien cho 八仙桌
pa ta wan 八大碗
pai 拜
pai chiu 白酒
pai-ho 百合
pai-huo 敗火
pai-kan 白乾
pai-mao 白茅
pai mi fan 白米飯
pai-pai 拜拜
pai shen 拜神
pai-ts'ai 白菜
pak choi 白菜
pao 包
p'ao 炰
pao-tzu 包子
pei 柸
pei 糒
p'ei 醅
Pei chan pei huang, wei jen min
        備戰、備荒、爲人民
pen-chih 本旨
p'eng 烹
p'eng 蓬
pi 碧
pi 椑
p'i 皮
pi-ch'eng-ch'ieh 畢澄茄
p'i-li-le 毗黎勒
pi-lo 餑饠
p'i-p'a 枇杷

pi-po 蓽茇
pi-tou 蓽豆
pieh 鱉
pien 邊
p'ien t'ao jen 偏桃人
pin-lang 檳榔
pin-li 賓禮
pin-t'ieh 賓鐵
ping 餅
ping ch'a 餅茶
P'ing Kui hui yao 平貴回窯
p'ing p'eng ts'ao 萍蓬草
ping shih 氷室
p'ing-t'o 平脫
po-chieh 白芥
po-shih 柏實
Po-ssu tsao 波斯棗
po-tou 白豆
po-ts'ai 白菜
po-ts'ai 菠菜
po-yü 白魚
pou-t'ou 麹麩
p'u 蒲
p'u 脯
p'u-k'ui 蒲葵
p'u-t'ao 浦陶
Sai-pei 塞北
sai yeung ch'oi 西洋菜
san 籔
san 糝
san hsien mien 三鮮麵
sang 桑
sang-lo chiu 桑落酒
se 色
sha mu 莎木
sha t'ang 沙糖
sha yü 沙魚
shan 鱓
shan 膳
shan cha 山楂
shan chiang 山薑

shan-hsiu 膳羞
shan ts'ao 山草
shan-yao 山藥
shang huo 上火
shang-k'ou pien-su 上口便俗
Shang-shan Chien 尚膳監
Shang-shih Chü 尚食局
shang-tsun 上尊
shao 燒
shao 杓、勺
shao-chiu 燒酒
Shao chiu 紹酒
shao-ch'un 燒春
shao-mai 燒賣
shao-ping 燒餅
shao-tzu 韶子
shao-wei 燒尾
she 畬
shen 申
shen 神
shen nü kuan 神女館
sheng 升
shih 豉
shih 食
shih 柿
shih 石
shih 鰣
Shih-ching 食經
shih chu-yü 食茱萸
shiu ch'un 石蓴
shih huo 食貨
shih i 食醫
shih-lo 蒔蘿
shih-lu 實錄
shih mi 石蜜
shih pi yü 石鮅魚
shih ts'ao 隰草
shih yu 豉油
shiitake 椎茸
shou 莏
shou-pei 守備

shu 黍
shu 菽
Shu chiao 蜀椒
Shu chieh 蜀芥
shu-fu 舒服
shu-yü 薯蕷
shuan-yang-jou 涮羊肉
shui 水
shui-kua 水瓜
shui-ma 水馬
shui-sheng-ts'ai 水生菜
shui-ts'ai 睡菜
shui-ts'ao 水草
si yau 豉油
ssu 巳
ssu 肆
Ssu Chu Chien 司竹監
ssu-kua 絲瓜
Ssu-li Chien 司禮監
ssu ta wan 四大碗
ssu yüan 司苑
su 酥
su 粟
su fu 宿腐
Su kao 蘇糕
su mai 粟麥
su yu 酥油
suan 蒜
suan-mei 酸梅
suan-t'ou 蒜頭
sui chin 歲進
sung 菘
sung 艇
sung shih 松實
sung tzu 松子
t'a 榻
ta chien 大件
ta-hsiang 大饗
ta-huang 大黃
Ta Hung P'ao 大紅袍
ta-keng 大羹

ta lu mien 大滷麵
ta-mo 大麥
ta-pin-lou 打邊爐
ta p'o le fan wan 打破了飯碗
ta-tou 大豆
ta-ts'ung 大葱
Ta-yen-hsiang 大宴饗
T'ai-ch'ang Ssu 太常寺
T'ai Miao 太廟
tan-lo 擔羅
tan-ts'ai 淡菜
tang 鐺
t'ang-hsieh 糖蟹
t'ang jen 糖人
tang-lu 當壚
t'ang-ping 湯餅
Tang-shan 碭山
t'ang-shuang 糖霜
t'ang-ti 唐棣
t'ao 桃
tao 稻
tao-nieh tzu 倒捻子
tau-fu 豆腐
tau-hu 豆腐
tau si 豆豉
t'i-hu 醍醐
ti-huang 地黃
t'iao 銚
t'ieh 帖
tien-hsin 點心
t'ien-men-tung 天門冬
t'ien-ts'ai 甜菜
tim sam 點心
ting 鼎
ting 丁
ting-hsiang 丁香
t'ing-li 葶藶
ting-t'ieh 定鐵
t'o-pa 駝骰
tou 豆
tou cha 豆渣

tou-chiang 豆漿

tou-fu 豆腐

tou-fu kan 豆腐乾

tou-fu nao 豆腐腦

t'ou-keng 頭羹

tou-k'ou 豆蔻

tou-shih 豆豉

tou-ya 豆芽

ts'a 鰪

ts'ai 菜

ts'ai kuo 菜鍋

ts'an-tou 蠶豆

tsao 棗

tsao 灶

tsao 糟

ts'ao 草

tsao-k'ang 糟糠

tsao-tzu 棗子, 早子

tsao-yü 糟魚

tsap sui 雜碎

tseng 甑

ts'o 醝

tsou 棗

tsu 俎

tsu 葅

tsuk 粥

tsun 尊

tsung 糉

ts'ung 葱

tsung-lü 棕櫚

ts'ung-shih 從食

tsung-tzu 棕子

t'u 茶

t'u-fu-ling 土茯苓

tu-nien tzu 都念子

t'u pu yü 土步魚

tu-shih 獨食

tui 敦

tui 餛

tung-ku 冬菇

tung-kua 冬瓜

t'ung-ts'ao 通草

T'ung-wen Kuan 同文館

tzu 葴

tzu 鯔

Tz'u en ssu 慈恩寺

tz'u-hua 辞話

tzu-kan-su 紫桿粟

tz'u-mi 刺蜜

tzu-ts'ai 紫菜

wan 碗

wan-tou 豌豆

wei 味

wei 薇

wei 蔚

wen-huo 文火

wen-ko 文蛤

weng-ts'ai 甕菜

Woo Lung 烏龍

wu 午

Wu chi 吳姬

wu-ching 蕪菁

wu chu-yü 吳茱萸

wu-hsing 五行

wu-hun 五葷

wu-huo 武火

wu-lung 烏龍

ya sui ch'ien 壓歲錢

ya-ts'ai 芽菜

yang 陽

yang-chiu 羊酒

yang-mei 楊梅

yang t'ou ch'ien 羊頭簽

yang-tz'u 羊刺

yeh 椰

yeh-chi 野鷄

yeh-tzu 椰子

yen 鷃

yen-fu-tzu 鹽麩子

yen mei 鹽梅

yin 飲

yin-shih 飲食

yin-yang 陰陽

yin yen 印鹽

ying-yü 蘡薁

yu 柚

yü 芋

yü 鱮

yu hua shih tsang 油畫食藏

yü-keng 酪羹

yü kui 玉桂

yu mou 蝤蛑

yu-ping 油餅

yu-shih yüeh 佑食樂

yu-t'iao 油條

yü-t'ou 芋頭

yüan 杬

yüan 黿

yüan-hsiao 元宵

yüan-sui 芫荽

yüeh-kua 越瓜

yün-erh 雲耳

yün-t'ai 蕓薹

yung-ts'ai 蕹菜

BIBLIOGRAPHY

All bibliographical entries are listed below in alphabetical order by the last names of the authors and compilers. For historical works, except for standard texts with numerous editions, which are listed separately at the beginning of the following list, the years under which they are listed are either the years of their first editions or the years of the particular editions that the writers of this volume consulted. In the latter case, the abbreviation "ed." has been added to the year, e.g., 1939ed., referring to the 1939 edition of an ancient text.

At times the writers of the various chapters in this volume consulted and cited different editions of the same book. All such editions are included in the bibliography. Certain well-known classical works which are cited in the text are not listed, since there are too many editions for such a listing to be helpful to the reader.

In the text of the book, references are cited in parentheses and include the last name of the author or compiler (or the last name and initials to distinguish among different authors with the same surname), the year of the publication (e.g., 1939 for a modern work or 1939 ed. for a modern reprint of an ancient work), and the pagination. For standard historical annals, collections, anthologies, governmental archives, and classical texts, the titles in full or shortened form are given in the parentheses. These titles are listed immediately below.

Chiu T'ang shu 1.   Liu Hsü. Ssu Pu Pei Yao ed. Shanghai: Chung Hua shu chü, 1936 ed.

Chiu T'ang shu 2.   Liu Hsü. As quoted in T'ai p'ing yü lan (vol. 857, p. 2) Shanghai, 1892 ed.

Chou li Cheng chu.   Cheng Hsüan's annotations of *Chou li*. Ssu Pu Pei Yao ed. Shanghai: Chung Hua shu chü, 1936 ed.

Ch'üan T'ang shih.   Taipei: Fu Hsing shu chü, 1967 ed.

Ch'üan T'ang wen.   Taipei: Wen Yu shu chü, 1972 ed.

Han shu.   Pan Ku. Po-na ed. Shanghai: Commercial Press, 1932 ed.

Hou Han shu 1.   Fan Yeh. Shanghai: K'ai Ming shu chü, 1935 ed.

Hou Han shu 2.   Fan Yeh. Po-na ed. Shanghai: Commercial Press, 1932 ed.

Hsin T'ang shu.   Ou-yang Hsiu. Ssu Pu Pei Yao ed. Shanghai: Chung Hua shu chü, 1936 ed.

Hsin Yüan shih.   K'o Shao-min. Tientsin: T'ui Keng T'ang, 1922 ed.

I li (*I li cheng i*).   Hu P'ei-hui, commentator. Wan Yu Wen K'u ed. Shanghai: Com-
    merical Press, 1933 ed.

Ku chin t'u shu chi ch'eng.   Ch'en Meng-lei and Chiang T'ing-hsi, compilers. Shang-
    hai: Chung Hua shu chü, 1934.

Ku-pen (*Ku-pen Yüan Ming tsa-chü*).   144 dramas from Yüan and Ming times, 32
    vols. Han Fen Lou ed. Shanghai, 1941. Reprint, Peking, 1957.

Kuang-lu Ssu (*Kuang-lu Ssu tse-li*).   Peking: Imperial Publications, 1839.

Li chi.   Ssu Pu Pei Yao ed. Shanghai: Chung Hua shu chü, 1936 ed.

Li-tai chih-kuan piao.   Shanghai: Chung Hua shu chü, 1936 ed.

Ming T'ai-tsu shih-lu.   Taipei: Academia Sinica, 1963 ed.

San kuo chih.   Ch'en Shou, Po-na ed. Shanghai: Commercial Press, 1932 ed.

San-shih chung (*Chiao-ting Yuan-k'an tsa-chü san-shih chung*).   Cheng Ch'ien, editor.
    Taipei: Shih Chieh shu chü, 1962.

Shih chi 1.   Ssu-ma Ch'ien. Peking: Chung Hua shu chü, 1959 ed.

Shih chi 2.   Ssu-ma Ch'ien. Po-na ed. Shanghai: Commercial Press, 1936 ed.

Sung shih.   T'o T'o et al. Shanghai: K'ai-ming.

Ta Ming hui-tien.   228 vols. Wan Yu Wen K'u ed. Shanghai, 1929.

Ta T'ang liu tien.   Hsüan Tsung. Kyoto: University of Kyoto, 1935 ed.

T'ai p'ing kuang chi.   San Jang Mu Chi, publisher, 1846 ed.

T'ai p'ing yü lan.   From Mr. Pao's collection. Shanghai, 1892 ed.

T'ang tai ts'ung shu.   Taipei: Hsin Hsing shu chü, 1968 ed.

Ts'e fu yüan kui.   Wang Ch'in-jo. Wu-hsiu T'ang, 1642 ed.

Tso chuan (*Tso chuan chu shu*).   K'ung Ying-ta. Ssu Pu Pei Yao ed. Shanghai:
    Chung Hua shu chü.

Tzu chih t'ung chien.   Ssu-ma Kuang. Hōbunkan ed. Tokyo, 1892.

Wen hsüan.   Chao Ming T'ai Tzu, compiler. Taipei: Wen hua t'u shu, 1971 ed.

Ahern, Emily. 1973. *The Cult of the Dead in a Chinese Village.* Stanford: Stanford
    Univ. Press.

Aisin-Gioro Pu Yi. 1964. *From Emperor to Citizen—the Autobiography of Aisin-Gioro
    Pu Yi.* Translated by W. T. F. Jennes. Vol. 1. Peking: Foreign Language Press.

Altschul, Aaron M. 1965. *Proteins, their Chemistry and Politics.* London: Chapman
    and Hall.

Amano, Motonosuke. 1965. "Yüan Ssu-nung Ssu chuan *Nung-sang chi-yao* ni tsuite."
    Tōhōgaku, 30:7.

An, Chih-min. 1972. "Lüeh shuo wo-kuo hsin-shih-ch'i shih-tai ti nien-tai wen-t'i."
    K'ao Ku 1972, no. 6: 35–44, 47.

An, Chih-min, et al. 1959. *Miao-ti-kou yü San-li-ch'iao.* Peking: Science Press.

An, Chin-huai, and Wang, Yu-kang. 1972. "Mi Hsien Ta-hu-t'ing Han-tai hua-hsiang
    shih-mu ho pi-hua-mu." *Wen Wu* 1972, no. 10: 49–62.

Anderson, E. N., Jr., 1970a. *The Floating World of Castle Peak Bay.* Anthropological
    Studies no. 3. Washington, D.C.: American Anthropological Association.

———. 1970b. "Réflexions sur la cuisine." *L'Homme* 10, no. 2: 122–24.

————. 1972. *Essays on South China's Boat People*. Taipei: Orient Cultural Service.

————. 1973. "Oh Lovely Appearance of Death: The Deformations of Religion in an Overseas Chinese Community." Paper read at the annual meeting of the American Anthropological Association at New Orleans, Louisiana.

Anderson, E. N., Jr., and Anderson, Marja L. 1973a. *Mountains and Water: The Cultural Ecology of South Coastal China*. Taipei: Orient Cultural Service.

————. 1973b. "Penang Hokkien Ethnohoptology." *Ethnos* 1972: 134–47.

————. 1974. "Folk dietetics in two Chinese communities, and its implications for the study of Chinese medicine." Paper read at the Conference on Chinese Medicine, February 1974, at the University of Washington, School of Medicine.

Anonymous. 1885. *China, Imperial Maritime Customs, Returns of Trade at the Treaty Ports for the Year 1884*. Shanghai.

————. 1936ed. *Pen-hsin chai shu-shih p'u*. Written by a follower of Ch'en Ta-sou. Ts'ung-shu chi-ch'eng ed. Shanghai.

————. 1966ed. *Nung-sang chi-yao*. 1314, preface date 1273. Officially compiled by the Ssu-nung Ssu (Office of Agricultural Affairs) of the Yüan dynasty government. Reprint of Chü-chen-pan ed., 1774, 2 vols. Taipei.

————. 1973. *The Genius of China*. An exhibition of archaeological finds of the People's Republic of China, held at the Royal Academy, London, from 29 September 1973 to 23 January 1974. Sponsored by the *Times* and *Sunday Times* in association with the Royal Academy and the Great Britian/China Committee; Westerham, Kent: Westerham Press.

————. 1974. *Han T'ang pi hua*. Peking: Foreign Language Press.

Ayers, William, 1971. *Chang Chih-tung and Educational Reform in China*. Cambridge, Mass.: Harvard Univ. Press.

Baker, Hugh. 1968. *A Chinese Lineage Village*. Stanford: Stanford Univ. Press.

Beals, Alan R. 1974. *Village Life in South India*. Chicago: Aldine.

Bell, John. 1965. *A Journey from St. Petersburg to Pekin, 1719–1722*. Edited by J. L. Stevenson. Edinburgh: Edinburgh Univ. Press.

Bennett, Adrian. 1967. *John Fryer, the Introduction of Western Science and Technology into Nineteenth Century China*. East Asia Monographs. Cambridge, Mass.: Harvard Univ. Press.

Berg, Alan D. 1973. *The Nutrition Factor*. Washington, D. C.: Brookings Institute.

Bishop, Carl W. 1933. "The Neolithic Age in Northern China," *Antiquity* 7: 389–404.

Boodberg, Peter A. 1935. "Kumiss or Arrack." *Sino-Ataica* 4, no. 2. Berkeley.

Bringeus, Nils-Arvid, and Wegelmann, Gunter, eds. 1971. *Ethnological Food Research in Europe and USA*. Göttingen: Otto Schwartz.

Brock, J. F., and Autret, M. 1952. *Kwashiorkor in Africa*. FAO Nutritional Studies, no. 8. Rome: Food and Agriculture Organization of the United Nations.

Brothwell, Don, and Brothwell, Patricia. 1969. *Food in Antiquity*. New York: Praeger.

Buchanan, Keith. 1970. *The Transformation of the Chinese Earth*. London: G. Bell and Sons.

Buck, John Lossing. 1930. *Chinese Farm Economy*. Chicago: Univ. of Chicago Press. Chicago Press.

————. 1937. *Land Utilization in China*. Nanking: Univ. of Nanking.

Chaney, R. W. 1935. "The Food of Peking Man." *News Service Bulletin*, Carnegie Institute, vol. 3, no. 25: 199–202. Washington.

Chang, Kwang-chih. 1964. "Some dualistic phenomena in Shang society." *Journal of Asian Studies* 24: 45–61.

————. 1968. *The Archaeology of Ancient China*. 2d ed., rev. New Haven: Yale Univ. Press.

————. 1972. "Preliminary remarks on a comprehensive study of form, decoration and inscription of Shang and Chou bronzes." *Bulletin of the Institute of Ethnology*, Academia Sinica, no. 30: 239–315.

————. 1973a. "Food and food vessels in ancient China." *Transactions of the New York Academy of Sciences*, 2d ser. 35: 495–520.

————. 1973b. "Radiocarbon dates from China: Some initial interpretations." *Current Anthropology* 14: 525–28.

Chang, Lu. 1966–67ed. *Huang Ming chih-shu*. 2 vols. Tokyo: Koten Kenkyūkai.

Chang, Ping-ch'üan. 1970. "Yin tai ti nung-yeh yü ch'i-hsiang" *Bulletin of the Institute of History and Philology*, Academia Sinica, no. 42: 267–336. Taipei.

Chang, Shih-cheng. N.d. "Chüan yu tsa lu." In *Wu ch'ao hsiao shuo*. Hangchou: Yüan Wei Shan T'ang. Early 17th century.

Chang, Shou-chung. 1960. "1959-nien Hou-ma Niu-ts'un ku ch'eng nan Tung Chou i-chih fa-chüeh chien pao." *Wen Wu* 1960, no. 8/9:11–14.

Chang, Te-ch'ang. 1972. "The economic role of the Imperial household in the Ch'ing dynasty." *Journal of Asian Studies* 31: 243–73.

Chang, T'ung-chih. 1947. "Pai-men shih-p'u." *Nan-ching wen-hsien*, no. 2, 12 pages.

Ch'ang-chiang liu-yü ti-erh-ch'i wen-wu k'ao-ku kung-tso jen-yüan hsün-lien-pan. 1974. "Hupei Chiang-ling Feng-huang Shan Hsi-Han-mu fa-chüeh chien-pao." *Wen Wu* 1974, no. 6: 41–54.

Chao, Buwei Yang. 1963. *How to Cook and Eat in Chinese*. New York: John Day.

————. 1972. *How to Cook and Eat in Chinese*. New York: Vintage Books.

Chao, Hung, ed. 1936ed. *Meng Ta pei-lu*. Vol. 25. Kuo-hsüeh wen-k'u ed.

Chao, Y. R. 1953. "Popular Chinese plant words; a descriptive lexico-grammatical study." *Language* 29: 379–414.

Chekiang Sheng wen-wu kuan-li wei-yüan-hui. 1957. "Shao-hsing Li-chu ti Han-mu." *K'ao-ku Hsüeh-pao* 1957, no. 1:133–40.

————. 1960. "Wu-hsing Ch'ien-shan-yang i-chih ti i erh ts'e fa-chüeh pao-kao." *K'ao-ku Hsüeh-pao* 1960, no. 2:73–91.

Ch'en, Ch'i-yu, ed. 1974. *Han Fei Tzu chi-shih*. Hong Kong: Chung Hua shu chü.

Ch'en, Han-seng. 1936. *Agrarian Problems in Southernmost China*. Shanghai: Kelly and Walsh.

————. 1949. *Frontier Land Systems in Southernmost China*. New York: Institute of Pacific Relations.

Ch'en, Ta. 1939. *Emigrant Communities in South China*. New York: Institute of Pacific Relations.

Cheng, Ch'ien, 1962. *Chiao-ting Yuan-k'an tsa-chü san-shih-chung*. Taipei: Shih chieh shu chü.

Cheng, F. T. 1962. *Musings of a Chinese Gourmet*. 2d ed. London: Hutchinson.

Ch'i, Ssu-ho. 1949. *"Mao Shih* ku ming k'ao." *Yenching Journal of Chinese Studies* 36: 263–311.

Chia, Ming. 1968ed. *Yin-shih hsü-chih*. In *Yin-chuan p'u-lu*, compiled by Yang Chia-lo. Taipei.

Chia, I. 1937ed. *Hsin shu*. Shanghai: Commercial Press.

Chia-yü Kuan Shih wen-wu ch'ing-li hsiao-tsu. 1972. "Chia-yü Kuan Han hua-hsiang chuan mu." *Wen Wu* 1972, no. 12: 24–41.

Chiang, Ming-ch'uan. 1956. *Chung-kuo ti Chiu-ts'ai*. Peking: Ts'ai cheng ching chi.

Chiang-su po-wu-kuan. 1959. *Chiang-su sheng Ming-Ch'ing i-lai pei-k'o tzu-liao hsüan-chi*. Peking: Wen Wu Press.

Ch'ien, Mu. 1956. "Chung-kuo ku tai pei fang nung-tso-wu k'ao." *New Asia Journal* 1, no. 2: 1–27.

Ch'in, Kuang-hsien, et al. 1962. "Chiang-hsi Hsiu-shui shan pei ti-ch'ü k'ao-ku tiao-ch'a yü shih chüeh." *K'ao Ku* 1962, no. 3: 353–67.

Chin, Shan-pao. 1962. "Huai pei p'ing-yüan ti hsin-shih-ch'i shih-tai hsiao-mai." *Tso Wu Hsüeh Pao* 1962, no. 1: 67–72.

Chinan Shih po-wu-kuan. 1972. "Shih-t'an Chinan Wu-ying Shan ch'u-t'u ti Hsi-Han yüeh-wu tsa-chi yen-yin t'ao-yung," *Wen Wu* 1972, no. 5: 19–23.

Chou, Mi 1957ed. *Wu-lin chiu-shih*. Shanghai: Ku tien wen hsüeh ch'u pan shê.

———. 1959ed. *Ch'i-tung Yeh-yü*. Ts'ung-shu chi-ch'eng ed. Shanghai: Commercial Press.

Ch'ü, Hsüan-ying. 1937. *Chung-kuo she-hui shih-liao ts'ung ch'ao*. Shanghai: Commercial Press.

Chu, Hung. 1927ed. *Pei-shan chiu-ching*. Shuo-fu ed.

Chu, Kuo-chen. 1959ed. *Yung-ch'uang hsiao-p'in*. 2 vols. Peking.

Chu, Yü. 1939ed. *P'ing-chou k'o-t'an*. Ts'ung-shu chi-ch'eng ed. Ch'angsha.

———. 1957ed. *Chien-teng hsin-hua*. Shanghai.

Ch'üan, Han-sheng. 1948. "Nan-Sung tao-mi ti sheng-ch'an yü yün-hsiao." *Bulletin of the Institute of History and Philology,* Academia Sinica, no. 10: 403–32. (Summarized in de Francis and Sun, *Chinese Social History,* 1956, under title "Production and distribution of rice in southern Sung".)

Ch'üan, Heng. 1963ed. *Das Keng-shen wai-shih: Eine Quelle zur späten Mongolenzeit*. Translated by H. Schulte-Uffelage. Berlin: Akademie-Verlag.

Chuang, Chi-yü. 1936ed. *Chi-le pien*. Ts'ung-shu chi-ch'eng ed. Shanghai.

Ch'ung-ch'ing Shih po-wu-kuan. 1957. *Ssu-ch'uan Han-mu hua-hsiang chuan hsüan-chi*. Peking: Wen Wu Press.

Chung-kuo k'o-hsüeh yüan k'ao-ku yen-chiu-so. 1958. *K'ao-ku Hsüeh Chi-ch'u*. Peking: Science Press.

———. 1959. *Lo-yang Chung-chou Lu*. Peking: Science Press.

———. 1962. *Feng Hsi fa-chüeh pao-kao*. Peking: Wen Wu Press.

Chung-kuo k'o-hsüeh yüan k'ao-ku yen-chiu-so Man-ch'eng fa-chüeh tui. 1972. "Man-ch'eng Han mu fa-chüeh chi-yao." *K'ao Ku* 1972, no. 1: 8–18.

Chung-kuo k'o-hsüeh yüan k'ao-ku yen-chiu so, and Hunan Sheng po-wu-kuan. 1975. "Ma-wang-tui erh-san hao Han mu fa-chüeh ti chu-yao shou-huo." *K'ao Ku* 1975, no. 1: 47–61.

Church, Charles F., and Church, Helen N. 1970. *Food Values of Portions Commonly Used: Bowes and Church.* 11th ed. Philadelphia: Lippincott.

Clair, Colin. 1964. *Kitchen and Table.* New York and London: Abelard-Schuman.

Committee on Food Protection, Food and Nutrition Board. 1973. *Toxicants Occurring Naturally in Foods.* 2d ed. Washington, D. C.: National Research Council.

Cooper, William C., and Sivin, Nathan. 1973. "Man as a medicine: pharmacological and ritual aspects of traditional therapy using drugs derived from the human body." In *Chinese Science,* edited by Nayakama and Sivin, pp. 203–12. Cambridge, Mass: MIT Press.

Creel, H. G. 1937. *The Birth of China.* New York: Ungar.

Crook, David, and Crook, Isabel. 1966. *The First Years of Yangyi Commune.* London: Routledge, Kegan Paul.

Dardess, John W. 1974. "The Cheng Communal Family: Social Organization and Neo-Confucianism in Yüan and Early Ming China." *Harvard Journal of Asiatic Studies* 34: 7–52.

Dean, R. F. A. 1958. "Use of processed plant proteins as human food." In *Processed Plant Foodstuffs,* edited by A. M. Altschul. New York: Academic Press.

Der Ling, Princess. 1935. *Son of Heaven.* New York: Appleton.

Doré, Henri. 1914–38. *Researches into Chinese Superstitions.* 31 vols. Shanghai: T'usewei.

Douglas, Mary. 1970. *Natural Symbols.* London: Barrie and Rockliff.

———. 1971. "Deciphering a Meal." *Daedalus,* Winter 1971. pp. 61–81.

Eberhard, Wolfram. 1958. *Chinese Festivals.* New York: Abelard-Schuman.

Edie, Harry H., and Ho, B. W. C. 1959. "*Ipomoea aquatica* as a vegetable crop in Hong Kong." *Economic Botany* 23, no. 1: 32–36.

Egerton, Clement, trans 1939. *The Golden Lotus* [*Chin-p'ing-mei*]. 4 vols. London; Routledge & Sons. 1939.

Elvin, Mark. 1973. *The Pattern of the Chinese Past.* Stanford: Stanford Univ. Press.

Epstein, H. 1969. *Domestic Animals of China.* Farnham Royal, England: Commonwealth Agricultural Bureaux.

Fairbank, John King. 1969. *Trade and Diplomacy on the China Coast: the Opening of the Treaty Ports, 1842–54.* Stanford: Stanford Univ. Press.

Fairbank, Wilma. 1972. *Adventures in Retrieval.* Harvard-Yenching Institute Series, no. 28, Cambridge, Mass.: Harvard Univ. Press.

Fang, Ch'ien-li. 1846ed. *T'ou huang tsa lu.* T'ai p'ing kuang chi ed. San Jang Mu Chi.

Fang, Hao. 1971. "Ch'ien-lung wu-shih-wu nien tzu Hsiu-ning chih Pei-ching lü-hsing yung-chang." *Shih-huo* 1, no. 7: 366–70.

———. 1972a. "Ch'ien-lung shih-i nien chih shih-pa nien tsa-chang chi chia-chih-chang." *Shih-huo* 2, no. 1: 57–60.

———. 1972b. "Kuang-hsü yüan-nien tzu Hsiu-ch'eng chih Chin-ling hsiang-shih chang." *Shih-huo* 2, no. 5: 288–90.

Fang, Yang. 1964. "Wo kuo niang chiu tang shih yü Lung-shan wen-hua." *K'ao Ku* 1964, no. 2:94–97.

Fei, Hsiao-tung. 1939. *Peasant Life in China*. London: Routledge, Kegan Paul.

Fei, Hsiao-tung, and Chang, Chih-i. 1948. *Earthbound China*. London: Routledge, Kegan Paul.

Feng, Chih. 1939ed. *Yün hsien tsa chi*. Ts'ung-shu chi-ch'eng ed. Shanghai: Commercial Press.

Feng, Han-chi. 1961. "Ssu-ch'uan ti hua-hsiang chuan mu chi hua-hsiang chuan." *Wen Wu* 1961, no. 11:35–45.

Feng, Meng-lung. 1947ed. *Ku-chin hsiao-shuo*. Shanghai (Taipei, 1958).

———. 1958. *Ching-shih T'ung-yen*. Edited by T. Y. Li. 2 vols. Taipei (Peking, 1957).

———. 1959. *Hsing-shih Heng-yen*. Edited by T. Y. Li. 2 vols. Taipei (Peking, 1956).

Firth, Raymond. 1939. *Primitive Polynesian Economy*. London: Routledge and Sons.

Fitzgerald, C. P. 1941. *The Tower of Five Glories*. London: Cresset Press.

Fong, Y. Y., and Chan, W. C. 1973. "Bacterial production of di-methyl nitrosamine in salted fish." *Nature* 243:421.

Fortune, Robert. 1857. *A Resident Among the Chinese: Inland, On the Coast, and at Sea*. London: John Murray.

Frake, Charles. 1961. "The diagnosis of disease among the Subanun of Mindanao." *American Anthropologist* 63:113–32.

———. 1964. "A structural description of Subanun Religious Behavior." In *Explorations in Cultural Anthropology: Essays in honor of George Peter Murdock*, edited by W. H. Goodenough, pp. 111–29. New York: McGraw-Hill.

Franke, H. 1970. "Additional notes on non-Chinese terms in the Yüan Imperial Dietary Compendium *Yin shan cheng-yao*." *Zentralasiatische Studien* 4:7–16.

———. 1975. "Chinese texts on the Jurchen: a translation of the Jurchen monographs in the *San-ch'ao pei-meng hui-pien*." *Zentralasiatische Studien* 9:172–77.

Franke, W. 1968. *An Introduction to the Sources of Ming History*. Kuala Lumpur: Univ. of Malaya Press.

Fu, Pei-mei. 1969. *Pei-Mei's Chinese Cook Book*. Taipei: Chinese Cooking Class.

Fuca, Tun-ch'ung. 1969ed. *Yen-ching sui-shih chi*. Taipei: Kuang-wen shu chü.

Gamble, Sidney. 1954. *Ting Hsien, a North China Rural Community*. New York: Institute of Pacific Relations.

Geertz, Clifford. 1960. *The Religion of Java*. Glencoe, Ill.: Free Press.

Gernet, Jacques. 1962. *Daily Life in China on the Eve of the Mongol Invasion 1250–76*. Stanford: Stanford Univ. Press.

Goodrich, L. C. 1940. "Brief communication." *Journal of the American Oriental Society* 60:258–60.

Grist, F. 1965. *Rice*. 4th ed. London: Longmans.

Groot, J. J. M. de. 1892–1910. *The Religious System of China*. 6 vols. Leiden, Netherlands: Brill.

Gulik, Robert van. 1951. *Erotic Color Prints of the Ming Period*. 3 vols. Privately printed. Tokyo.

Guy, R. A., and Yeh, K. S. 1938. "Peking diets." *Chinese Medical Journal* 54:201.

Hagerty, Michael J. 1940. "Comments on Writings Concerning Chinese Sorghums." *Harvard Journal of Asiatic Studies* 5:234–63.

Hahn, Emily, and the Editors of Time-Life Books. 1968. *The Cooking of China*. New York: Time-Life Books.

Han, Yen-chih. 1936ed. *Chü-lu*. Ts'ung-shu chi-ch'eng ed. Shanghai.

Hanan, Patrick. 1961. "A landmark of the Chinese novel." In *The Far East: China and Japan*, edited by Douglas Grant and Millar McClure. Toronto: Univ. of Toronto Press.

———. 1962. "The text of the *Chin P'ing Mei*." *Asia Major*, n.s. 9, no. 1:1–57.

———. 1963. "Sources of the *Chin P'ing Mei*." *Asia Major*, n.s. 10, no. 1:23–67.

———. 1973. *The Chinese Short Story: Studies in Dating, Authorship, and Composition*. Cambridge.

Handy, Ellice. 1960. *My Favorite Recipes*, 2d ed. Singapore: M. P. H.

Harlan, Jack R., and de Wet, J. M. 1973. "On the quality of evidence for origin and disposal of cultivated plants." *Current Anthropology* 14:51–62.

Harris, Marvin. 1966. "The cultural ecology of India's sacred cattle." *Current Anthropology* 7, no. 1:51–66.

———. 1968. *The Rise of Anthropological Theory*. New York: Crowell.

Hawkes, David. 1959. *Ch'u Tz'u, The Songs of the South*. Oxford: Clarendon Press.

Hayashi, Minao. 1961–62. "Sengoku-jidai no gazōmon." *Kokogaku Zasshi* 47: 190–212; 264–92; 48:1–22.

———. 1964. "Inshū seidō iki no meishō to yōto." *Tōhōgakuhō* 34:199–297. Kyoto.

———. 1975. "Kandai no inshoku." *Tōhōgakuhō* 48:1–98.

Herklots, G. A. C. 1972. *Vegetables in South-East Asia*. London: Allen and Unwin.

Hinton, William. 1966. *Fanshen*. New York: Monthly Review Press.

Ho, Hao-t'ien. 1958. *Han-hua yü Han-tai she-hui sheng-huo*. Taipei: Chung Hua ts'ung shu.

Ho, Ping-ti. 1955. "The introduction of American food plants into China." *American Anthropologist* 57:191–201.

———. 1956. "Early-ripening Rice in Chinese History." *Economic Historical Review*, 2d ser., 9:200–18.

———. 1959. *Studies on the Population of China, 1368–1953*. Cambridge, Mass.: Harvard Univ. Press.

———. 1966. *Chung-kuo hui-kuan shih lun*. Taipei: Hsüeh-sheng shu chü.

———. 1969a. *Huang-t'u yü Chung-kuo nung-yeh ti ch'i-yüan*. Hong Kong: Chinese Univ. of Hong Kong Press.

———. 1969b. "The loess and the origin of Chinese agriculture." *American Historical Review* 75:1–36.

Hommel, Rudolf P. 1937. *China at Work*. New York: John Day.

Honan sheng po-wu-kuan. 1973. "Chi-yüan Ssu-chien san-tso Han-mu ti fa-chüeh." *Wen Wu* 1973, no. 2:46–53.

Honan sheng wen-hua-chü wen-wu kung-tso-tui. 1959. *Cheng-chou Erh-li-kang*. Peking: Science Press.

———. 1964. "Lo-yang Hsi-Han pi-hua-mu fa-chüeh pao-kao." *K'ao-ku Hsüeh-pao*

1964, no. 2:103–49.

Hopei sheng wen-hua-chü wen-wu kung-tso-tui. 1959. *Wang-tu erh-hao Han-mu.* Peking: Wen Wu Press.

Hosie, A. 1897. *Three Years in Western China.* New York: Dodd, Mead.

———. 1914. *On the Trail of the Opium Poppy.* London: George Philip and Son.

Howe, Robin. 1969. *Far Eastern Cookery.* New York: Drake.

Hsi Hu Lao Jen [pseud]. 1957ed. *Hsi Hu Lao Jen Chi Sheng Lu.* Shanghai: Ku tien wen hsüeh ch'u pan shê.

Hsia, C. T. 1968. *The Classic Chinese Novel, a Critical Introduction.* New York: Columbia Univ. Press.

Hsia, Tsi-an. 1968. *The Gate of Darkness: Studies on the Leftist Literary Movement in China.* Seattle: Univ. of Washington Press.

Hsiang, Ta. 1957. *T'ang-tai Ch'ang-an yü Hsi-yü wen-ming.* Peking: Hsi Yü.

Hsieh, Chao-che. 1959ed. *Wu Tsa-tsu.* 2 vols. Shanghai: Chung-hua shu-chü.

Hsü, Cho-yün. 1971. "Liang Chou nung-tso chi-shu." *Bulletin of the Institute of History and Philology,* Academia Sinica, no. 42:803–27.

Hsu, F. L. K. 1967. *Under the Ancestor's Shadow.* 2d ed. Garden City, N.Y.: Doubleday and American Museum of Natural History.

Hsü, K'o, ed. 1918. *Ch'ing pai lei-ch'ao.* Shanghai.

Hsü, Shen. 1969ed. *Shuo Wen chieh-tzu.* Hong Kong: T'ai P'ing shu chü.

Hsü, Sung, ed. 1957ed. *Sung hui-yao chi-kao.* Facsimile of 1809ed. Peking: Chung Hua shu chü.

Hsu-Balzer, Eileen; Balzer, Richard; and Hsu, Francis L. K. 1974. *China Day by Day.* New Haven: Yale Univ. Press.

Hu, Ch'ang-chih. 1966. *Shu ts'ai hsüeh ke lun.* Taipei: Chung Hua shu chü.

Hu, Hou-hsüan. 1945. "P'u ts'e chung so chien chih Yin tai nung-yeh." In *Chia-ku-hsüeh Shang Shih Lun Ts'ung.* Vol. 2. Ch'eng-tu: Ch'i Lu Univ.

Hu, Ssu-hui. 1938ed. *Yin-shan cheng-yao.* Ssu-pu ts'ung-k'an hsü-pien ed. Shanghai: Commercial Press.

Hu, Tao-ching. 1963. "Shih shu p'ien." In *Chung-hua wen shih lun ts'ung.* Vol. 3:111–19, Shanghai: Chung Hua shu chü.

Hua-tung wen-wu kung-tso-tui Shantung tsu. 1954. "Shantung I-nan Han hua hsiang shih mu." *Wen-wu Ts'an-k'ao Tzu-liao* 1954, no. 8:35–68.

Huan, K'uan. 1974ed. *Yen t'ieh lun.* Shanghai: Jen Min Ch'u Pan Shê.

Huang, Chang-chien. 1961. "*Lun huan Ming tsu-hsün-lu* so chi Ming-ch'u huan-kuan chih-tu." *Bulletin of the Institute of History and Philology,* Academia Sinica, no. 33: 77–98. Taipei.

Huang, Liu-hung. 1973ed. *Fu-hui ch'üan-shu.* Edited by Yamane Yukro. Tokyo.

Huang, Sheng-chang. 1974. "Chiang-ling Feng-huang-shan Han-mu chien-tu chi ch'i tsai li-shih ti-li yen-chiu shang ti chia-chih." *Wen Wu* 1974, no. 6:66–77.

Huang, Shih-pin. 1958. "Lo-yang Chin-ku-yüan Ts'un Han-mu chung ch'u-t'u yu tzu ti t'ao-ch'i." *K'ao-ku T'ung-hsün* 1958, no. 1:36–41.

Huang, Tzu-ch'ing, and Chao, Yün-ts'ung. 1945. "The preparation of ferments and wines by Chia Ssu-hsieh of the later Wei." *Harvard Journal of Asiatic Studies* 9:24–44.

Hucker, C. O. 1958. "Governmental organization of the Ming dynasty." *Harvard Journal of Asiatic Studies* 21:21.

———. 1961. *The Traditional Chinese State in Ming Times, 1368–1644.* Tucson: Univ. of Arizona Press.

Hughes, Richard. 1972. "A toast to Monkey Head." *Far Eastern Economic Review* (April 29), pp. 27–28.

Huizinga, J. 1949. *Homo Ludens; A Study of the Play-element in Culture.* London: Routledge, Kegan Paul.

Hummel, Arthur, ed. 1943. *Eminent Chinese of the Ch'ing Period, 1644–1912.* 2 vols. Washington, D.C.: U.S. Government Printing Office.

Hunan Sheng po-wu-kuan. 1973. *Ch'ang-sha Ma-want-tui i-hao Han-mu.* Peking: Wen Wu Press.

———. 1974. "Ch'ang-sha Ma-wang-tui erh san-hao Han-mu fa-chüeh chien-pao." *Wen Wu* 1974, no. 7:39–48.

Hunan Sheng po-wu-kuan; Chung-kuo k'o-hsüeh-yüan k'ao-ku yen-chiu-so; Wen Wu pien-chi wei yüan-hui. 1972. *Ch'ang-sha Ma-wang-tui i-hao Han-mu fa-chüeh chien-pao.* Peking: Wen Wu Press.

Hung, Mai. 1941ed. *I Chien Chih.* Ch'angsha: Commercial Press.

Hung, William. 1952. *Tu Fu, China's Greatest Poet.* Cambridge, Mass.: Harvard Univ. Press.

Hunter, William C. 1885. *Bits of Old China.* London: Kegan Paul.

Hutchinson, J. G. 1973. "Slash and burn in the tropical forests." *National Parks and Conservation Magazine* (March), pp. 9–13.

Hymowitz, T. 1970. "On the domestication of the soybean." *Economic Botany* 24:408–44.

Ishida, Mikinosuke. 1948. *Tō-shi sōshō.* Tokyo: Yōshohō.

Ishida, Mosaku, and Wada, Gunichi. 1954, *The Shōsōin: An Eighth-Century Treasure House.* Tokyo: Mainichi shimbunsha.

Jametel, Maurice. 1886. *La Chine inconnue.* Paris: J. Rouam.

———. 1887. *Pékin, Souvenirs de l'Empire du Milieu.* Paris: Plon.

Jordan, David. 1972. *Gods, Ghosts and Ancestors.* Berkeley and Los Angeles: Univ. of California Press.

Juan, Yüeh. 1922ed. *Shih hua tsung kui.* Ssu pu ts'ung k'an ed. Shanghai: Commercial Press.

Kao, Ch'eng. 1969ed., *Shih Wu Chi Yüan Chi Lei.* Taipei: Hsin hsing shu chü.

Kao, Hung. 1974. "Ch'ün-chung yin-shih huo-tung ti shê-hui i-i." *P'an Ku* 71:11–13. Hong Kong.

K'ao Ku pien-chi-pu. 1972. "Kuan-yü Ch'ang-sha Ma-wang-tui i-hao Han-mu ti tso-t'an chi-yao." *K'ao Ku* 1972, no. 5:37–42.

Kao, Ming. 1963. *Li chi hsin t'an.* Hong Kong: Chinese Univ. and Union College.

Kao, Ssu-sun. 1927ed. *Chieh-lüeh.* Shuo-fu ed.

Kao, Yao-t'ing. 1973. "Ma-wang-tui i-hao Han-mu sui-tsang p'in chung kung shih yung ti shou-lei." *Wen Wu* 1973, no. 9:76–80.

Kates, George N. 1967. *The Years That Were Fat: The Last Years of Old China.* Cambridge: MIT Press.

Keng, I-li, ed. 1959. *Chung-kuo Chu-yao Chih-wu T'u-shuo Ho-pen-k'o*. Peking: Science Press.

King, F. H. 1911. *Farmers of Forty Centuries*. New York: Mrs. F. H. King.

Kitamura, Jirō. 1963. "*Yū-yō zasso* no shokubutsu kiji." In *Chūgoku chusei kagaku gijutsu-shi no kenkyū*, Tokyo.

Ko, Hung. 1937ed. *Hsi Ching Tsa-chi*. Han wei ts'ung-shu ed.

K'ou, Tsung-ch'ou. 1930 ed. *Pen Ts'ao Yen I*. Quoted in *Pen ts'ao kang-mu*, compiled by S. C. Li. Shanghai: Shang wu yin shu kuan.

Krapovickas, A. 1969. "The origin, variability, and spread of the groundnut (*Arachis hypogaea*)." In *The Domestication of Plants and Animals*, edited by P. J. Ucko and W. Dimbleby, pp. 427–41. London: Duckworth.

Ku, Ch'i-yuan. 1618 *K'e-tso chui-yü*. Peking Rare Books on Microfilm, Library of Congress. (Reprinted in *Chin-ling ts'ung-k'e*.)

Ku, Lu. n.d. *Ch'ing Chia Lu*. Ch'ing tai pi chi ts'ung k'an ed. Shanghai.

Ku, Yen-wu. 1929ed. *Jih Chih Lu*. Wan-yu Wen-k'u ed. Shanghai: Commercial Press.

Kuan P'u Nai Te Weng [pseud.]. 1957ed. *Tu Ch'eng Chi Sheng*. Shanghai: Ku tien wen hsüeh ch'u pan shê.

Kuang-chou Shih wen-wu kuan-li wei-yüan-hui. 1957. "Kuang-chou Shih wen-kuan-hui 1955 nien ch'ing-li ku-mu tsang kung-tso chien-pao." *Wen-wu Ts'an-K'ao Tzu-liao* 1957, no. 1:71–76.

Kueichou Sheng po-wu-kuan. 1972. "Kueichou Ch'ien-hsi Hsien Han-mu fa-chüeh chien-pao." *Wen Wu* 1972, no. 11:42–47.

Kulp, Daniel Harrison, II. 1925. *Country Life in South China*. New York: Columbia Univ. Press.

Kuo, Mao-ch'ien, ed. 1955ed. *Yüeh-fu Shih-chi*. Peking: Wen hsüeh ku chi.

Kuo, Mo-jo. 1964. "Lo-yang Han-mu pi-hua shih-t'an." *K'ao-ku Hsüeh-pao* 1964, no. 2:1–7.

Kuwabara, Jitsuzō. 1935. *Chang Ch'ien Hsi-cheng K'ao*. Translated by Yang Lien. 2d ed. Shanghai: Commercial Press.

Kuwayama, Ryūhei. 1961. "*Chin P'ing Mei* inshoku-kō," part 2, "Gyokai." *Tenri Daigaku Gakuhō* 35, July 1961, pp. 41–48.

Lang, Ying. 1959ed. *Ch'i-hsiu lei-kao*. 51 *chüan*, 2 vols. Peking.

Langlois, John D. 1973. "Chin-hua Confucianism Under the Mongols 1279–1368." Ph.D. dissertation, Princeton.

Lao, Kan. 1939. "Lun Lu Hsi hua-hsiang san shih." *Bulletin of the Institute of History and Philology*, Academia Sinica, vol. 8, no. 1:93–127.

———. 1960. *Chü-yen Han-chien k'ao-shih*. Taipei: Institute of History and Philology, Academia Sinica.

Lao, Yan-shuan. 1969. "Notes on non-Chinese terms in the Yüan Imperial Dietary Compendium *Yin-shan cheng-yao*." *Bulletin of the Institute of History and Philology*, Academia Sinica, no. 39:399–416. Taipei.

Lau, D. C., trans. 1970. *Mencius*. Harmondworth, Middlesex, England: Penguin Books.

Laufer, Berthold. 1909. *Chinese Pottery of the Han Dynasty*. Leiden, Netherlands.

―――. 1919. *Sino-Iranica; Chinese contributions to the history of civilization in ancient Iran; with special reference to the history of cultivated plants and products.* Field Museum of Natural History, Anthropological Series, vol. 15, no. 3. Chicago.

Legge, James, trans. 1872. *The Ch'un Ts'ew, with the Tso Chuen. The Chinese Classics,* vol. 5. Oxford: Clarendon Press.

―――. 1885. *The Li Ki* [trans. of the *Li Chi*]. *The Sacred Books of the East,* edited by F. Max Müller, vols. 27, 28. Oxford: Clarendon Press.

―――. 1893. *Confucian Analects* [trans. of *Lun Yü*]. *The Chinese Classics,* vol. 1. Oxford: Clarendon Press.

―――. 1895. *The Works of Mencius* [trans. of *Meng Tzu*]. *The Chinese Classics,* 2d ed., vol. 2. London: Henry Frowde.

―――. 1967. *Li Chi: Book of Rites.* New York: University Books.

Lehrer, Adrienne. 1969. "Semantic cuisine." *Journal of Linquistics* 5, no. 1:39–56.

Lei, Chin. 1969ed. *Ch'ing-jen shuo-k'ui.* Taipei: Kuang wen shu chü.

Leininger, Madeleine. 1970. "Some cross-cultural universal and non-universal functions, beliefs and practices of food." In *Dimensions of Nutrition,* edited by J. Dupont, pp. 153–79. Denver: Colorado Associated Universities Press.

Leppik, E. E. 1971. "Assumed gene centers of peanuts and soybeans." *Economic Botany* 25:188–94.

Lévi-Strauss, Claude. 1964–71. *Mythologiques.* 4 vols. Paris: Plon.

―――. 1965. "Le triangle culinaire." *L'Arc (Aix-en-Provence),* no. 26: 19–29. (English translation in *New Society,* December 22, 1966, pp. 937–40. London.)

Li, Ch'iao-p'ing. 1955. *Chung-kuo Hua-hsüeh Shih.* 2d ed. Taipei: Commercial Press.

Li, Chin. 1961. "Kuang-chou ti Liang-Han mu-tsang." *Wen Wu* 1961, no. 2:47–53.

Li, Chin-hua. 1932. *Ming-tai ch'ih-chuan shu-k'ao.* Pei-p'ing.

Li, Chün. 1968ed. *Chih i chi.* T'ang tai ts'ung shu ed. Taipei: Hsin hsing shu chü.

Li, Han-san. 1967. *Hsien Ch'in Liang Han chih yin-yang wu-hsing hsüeh-shuo.* Taipei: Chung Ting.

Li, Hua-nan. 1968ed. *Hsing-yüan lu.* In *Han-hai,* compiled by Li T'iao-yuan. Taipei: I-wen.

Li, Hui-lin. 1959. *The Garden Flowers of China.* New York: Ronald Press.

―――. 1969. "The vegetables of ancient China." *Economic Botany* 23:253–60.

―――. 1970. "The origin of cultivated plants in Southeast Asia." *Economic Botany* 24:3–19.

Li, P'o-pien. 1963. *Shu ts'ai fen lei hsüeh.* Taipei: Chung Hua shu chü.

Li, Shih-chen, comp. 1930ed. *Pen ts'ao kang mu.* Shanghai: Commercial Press.

―――. 1957ed. *Pen ts'ao kang mu.* Reprint of 1885ed. Peking.

―――. 1965ed. *Pen ts'ao kang mu.* Hong Kong: Commercial Press.

This book incorporates the following works on plants by earlier authors, now largely unpreserved, which have been cited by Schafer extensively in his chapter:

Chen, Ch'üan. *Yao hsing pen ts'ao.*
Ch'en, Ts'ang-ch'i. *Pen ts'ao shih i.*
Hsiao, Ping. *Ssu sheng pen ts'ao.*
Li, Hsün. *Hai yao pen ts'ao.*

Meng, Shen. *Shih liao pen ts'ao.*
Su, Kung. *T'ang pen ts'ao chu.*
Sun, Ssu-mo. *Ch'ien chin shih chih.*

Li, Shu-fan. 1964. *Hong Kong Surgeon.* New York: Dutton.

Li, Tou. 1795. *Yang-chou hua-fang lu.* 18 chüan. Tzu Jan An.

Li, Wen-hsin. 1955. "Liao-yang fa-hsien ti san-tso pi-hua ku-mu." *Wen-wu Ts'an-k'ao Tzu-liao* 1955, no. 5:15–42.

Li, Yang-sung. 1962. "Tui wo-kuo niang-chiu ch'i-yüan ti t'an-t'ao." *K'ao Ku* 1962, no. 1:41–44.

Li, Yü [Li Li-weng]. 1730. "Li-weng Ou Chi." In *Li-weng I-chia-yen Ch'üan-chi.* Chieh-tzu-yüan ed.

———. 1936ed. *Hsien-ch'ing ou-chi.* Shanghai: Chung kuo wen hsüeh chen pen ts'ung shu.

Liang, Chang-chü. 1969a ed. *Kui-t'ien so-chi.* Taipei: Kuang wen shu chü.

1969b ed. *Lang-chi hsü-t'an.* Taipei: Kuang wen shu chü.

Lin, Hsiang Ju, and Lin, Tsuifeng. 1969. *Chinese Gastronomy.* New York: Hastings House.

Lin, Nai-hsin. 1957. "Chung-kuo ku-tai ti p'eng-t'iao yü yin-shih." *Pei-ching Ta-hsüeh Hsüeh Pao (Jen Wen K'o Hsüeh)* 1957, no. 2:59–144.

Lin, Yutang. 1935. *My Country and My People.* New York: John Day.

Ling, Meng-ch'u. 1957ed. *Erh-k'e p'ai-an ching-ch'i.* Wang Ku-lu ed. Shanghai.

———. 1967ed. *Ch'u-k'e p'ai-an ching-ch'i.* T. L. Li ed. Hong Kong. (Wang Ku-lu ed. Shanghai, 1957.)

Ling, Shun-sheng. 1957. "Chung-kuo yü Tung Ya ti chiao chiu wen-hua." *Bulletin of the Institute of Ethnology,* Academia Sinica, no, 4:1–30.

———. 1958. "Chung-kuo chiu chih ch'i-yüan." *Bulletin of the Institute of History and Philology,* Academia Sinica, no. 29:883–907.

———. 1961. "Pi chang yü li ssu k'ao." *Bulletin of the Institute of Ethnology,* Academia Sinica, no. 12:179–216.

Liu, Chih-wan. 1974. *Chung-kuo Min-chien Hsin-yang Lun Chi.* Institute of Ethnology, Academia Sinica, Monograph Series, no. 22. Taipei.

Liu, Hsi, ed. 1939ed. *Shih Ming.* Shanghai: Commercial Press.

Liu, Hsiang. 1967ed. *Shuo Yüan.* Han Wei ts'ung shu ed. Taipei: I Wen yin shu kuan.

Liu, Hsien-t'ing. 1957ed. *Kuang-yang tsa-chi.* Peking: Chung Hua shu chü.

Liu, Hsün. 1892ed. *Ling piao lu i.* Quoted in T'ai p'ing yü lan. Shanghai.

———. 1913ed. *Ling piao lu i.* Jung yuan ts'ung shu ed. Kuang-ling mo hsiang wu.

Liu, I-cheng; Wang, Huan-piao; et al., compilers. 1935. *Shou-tu Chih.* Compiled under direction of Yeh Ch'u-ts'ang. 2 vols. Nanking.

Liu, Meng. 1934ed. *Chü P'u.* Ku Chin T'u Shu Chi Ch'eng ed. Vol. 96:57. Shanghai: Chung Hua shu chü.

Liu, Pin-hsiung. 1965. "An interpretation on the kinship system of the royal house of the Shang dynasty." *Bulletin of the Institute of Ethnology,* Academia Sinica, no. 19: 89–114.

Liu, T'ung. 1957ed. *Ti-ching ching-wu lüeh.* Peking.

Liu, Wen-tien, annotator. 1974. *Huai-nan Hung-lieh chi-chieh.* Taipei: Commercial Press.

Lo, Fu-i. 1956. "Nei Meng-ku Tzu-chih-ch'ü T'o-k'o-t'o Hsien hsin fa-hsien ti Han-mu pi-hua." *Wen-wu Ts'an-k'ao Tzu-liao* 1956, no. 9:41–43.

Lo, Kenneth. 1971. *Peking Cooking.* New York: Pantheon.

———. 1972. *Chinese Food.* Harmondsworth, Middlesex, England: Penguin Books.

Lo-yang Ch'ü k'ao-ku fa chüeh-tui. 1959. *Lo-yang Shao-kou Han-mu.* Peking: Science Press.

Lu, Gwei-djen, and Needham, Joseph. 1951. "A contribution to the history of Chinese dietetics." *Isis* 42:13–20.

Lü, Ssu-mien. 1941. *Hsien Ch'in Shih.* Shanghai: Commercial Press.

———. 1947. *Ch'in Han Shih.* Shanghai: Commercial Press.

———. 1948. *Liang Chin Nan-pai Ch'ao Shih.* Shanghai: Commercial Press.

Lu, Wen-yü. 1957. *Shih ts'ao mu chin shih.* Tientsin: Jen Min ch'u pan shê.

Lu, Yu. 1922ed. *Ju-shu chi.* Ssu-pu ts'ung-k'an ed. Shanghai.

———. 1930ed. *Lao Hsüeh An Pi Chi.* Sung Jen Hsiao Shuo ed.

Lu, Yü. 1968ed. *Ch'a ching.* T'ang tai ts'ung shu ed. Taipei: Hsin Hsing shu chü.

Ma, Ch'eng-yüan. 1961. "Man t'an Chan-kuo ch'ing-t'ung-ch'i shang ti hua hsiang." *Wen Wu* 1961, no. 10:26–29.

Macartney, Lord George. 1962. *An Embassy to China, being the Journal kept by Lord Macartney during his embassy to the Emperor Ch'ien-lung 1793–94.* Edited by J. L. Cranmer Byng. London: Longman's Green.

MacGowan, D. J. 1886. "Chinese Guilds or Chambers of Commerce and Trade Unions." *Journal of the North China Branch of the Royal Asiatic Society,* n.s., 21: 133–92.

———. 1907. *Sidelights on Chinese Life.* London: Kegan Paul.

MacNair, Harley Farnsworth. 1939. *With the White Cross in China.* Peking: Henry Vetch.

Mai, Ying-hao. 1958. "Kuang-chou Hua-ch'iao Hsin-ts'un Hsi-Han mu." *K'ao-ku Hsüeh-pao* 1958, no. 2:39–75.

Mallory, Walter H. 1926. *China: Land of Famine.* American Geographical Society, Special Publication, no. 6. New York.

Mao, Tse-tung. 1927. "A report of the investigation of the peasant movement in Hunan." In *Selected Works of Mao Tse-tung,* vol. 1. Peking, 1968.

Marugame, Kinsaku. 1957. "Tōdai no sake no sembai." *Tōyō gakuhō* 40, no. 3:66–332.

McCracken, Robert D. 1971. "Lactase deficiency: an example of dietary evolution." *Current Anthropology* 12, nos. 4–5:479–517.

Mei, Yi-pao. 1929. *The Ethical and Political Works of Motse.* London: Probsthain.

Mendoza, Juan Gonzalez de. 1853. *The History of the Great and Mighty Kingdom of China.* Edited by George Staunton. London: Hakluyt Society.

Meng, T'ien-p'ei, and Gamble, Sidney. 1926. *Prices, Wages and the Standard of Living in Peking, 1900–24. The Chinese Social and Political Science Review,* Special Supplement, July 1926.

Meng, Yüan-lao. 1957ed. *Meng-hua lu.* Shanghai: Ku tien wen hsüeh ch'u pan shê.

Miller, Gloria Bley. 1967. *The Thousand Recipe Chinese Cookbook.* New York: Atheneum.

Morse, Hosea Ballou. 1932. *The Gilds of China.* New York: Longman's.

Mote, F. W. 1974. "Introductory Note." In *A Catalogue of the Chinese Rare Books in the Gest Collection of the Princeton University Library,* compiled by Ch'ü Wan-li. Taipei.

Moule, A. C., and Pelliot, Paul, trans. 1938. *Marco Polo: The Description of the World.* 2 vols. London.

Movius, H. L., Jr. 1949. "Lower Palaeolithic cultures of Southern and Eastern Asia." *Transactions of the American Philosophical Society,* n.s., 38:330–420.

Museum of Fine Arts, North Kyūshū. 1974. *Chung-hua Jen-min Kung-ho Kuo Han-T'ang pi-hua chan.* Tokyo.

Nakagawa, Shundai. 1965. *Shinzoku Kibun.* Tokyo: Tokyo Bunko.

Nakao, Sasuke. 1957. "Honan Sheng Lo-yang Han-mu ch'u-t'u ti tao-mi." *K'ao-ku Hsüeh-pao* 1957, no. 4:79–82.

Nakayama, Shigeru, and Sivin, Nathan, eds. 1973. *Chinese Science: Explorations of an Ancient Tradition.* Cambridge, Mass.: MIT Press.

Naquin, Susan. 1974. "The Eight Trigram Rising of 1813." Ph.D. dissertation, Yale University.

Needham, Joseph. 1970. *Clerks and Craftsmen in China and the West.* Cambridge.

Nei Meng-ku wen-wu kung-tso-tui, and Nei Meng-ku po-wu-kuan. 1974. "Ho-lin-ko-erh fa-hsien i-tso chung-yao ti Tung-Han pi-hua mu." *Wen Wu* 1974, no. 1:8–23.

Neill, Peter. 1973. "Crossing the bridge to Yunnan." *Echo* 13, no. 5:20. Taipei.

Nichols, Francis H. 1902. *Through Hidden Shensi.* New York: Scribner's.

Nunome, Chōfū. 1962. "Tōdai ni okeru sadō no seiritsu." *Ritsumeikan bungaku* 200: 161–187.

Odoric of Pordenone. 1913ed. *The Travels of Friar Odoric of Pordenone, 1316–30.* Translated by Henry Yule. *Cathay and the Way Thither.* New ed., revised by Henri Cordier, vol. 2, London: Hakluyt Society.

Okazaki, Tsutsumi. 1955. "Chūgoku kodai no okeru kamado ni tsuite—fu-sō-keishiki yori ka-keishiki e no hensen wo chūshin to shite." *Toyoshi kenkyū* 14, no. 1/2:103–22.

Osgood, Cornelius. 1963. *Village Life in Old China.* New York: Ronald Press.

Ou-yang, Hsiu. 1967ed. *Ou-yang Wen-chung Kung chi.* Kuo-hsüeh chi-pen ts'ung shu ed. Taipei.

Peiching li-shih po-wu-kuan, and Hopei Sheng wen-wu kuan-li wei-yüan-hui. 1955. *Wang-tu Han-mu pi-hua.* Peking: Chung-kuo Ku-tien I-shu ch'u pan shê.

Peking United International Famine Relief Committee. 1922. *The North China Famine of 1920–21, with special reference to the West Chihli area.* Peking.

Pelliot, P. 1920. "A propos des Comans." *Journal Asiatique,* 11th ser., 15:125–203.

Perkins, Dwight, assisted by Wang, Yeh-chien, et al. 1969. *Agricultural Development in China, 1368–1968.* Chicago: Aldine.

Pillsbury, Barbara. 1974. "No Pigs for the Ancestors: the Chinese Muslims." Paper read at the Conference on Chinese Religion, at the University of California, Riverside.

Pillsbury, Barbara, and Wang, Ding-ho. 1972. *West Meets East: Life Among Chinese.* Taipei: Caves Books.

Piper, Charles V., and Morse, William J. 1923. *The Soybean.* New York: McGraw-Hill.

Potter, Jack M. 1968. *Capitalism and the Chinese Peasant.* Berkeley and Los Angeles: Univ. of California Press.

P'u, Sung-ling. 1969ed. *Contes extraordinaires du pavillon du loisir.* Translated by Yves Hervouet et al. UNESCO, Chinese Series. Paris: Gallimard.

Pulleyblank, E. G. 1963. "The consonantal system of Old Chinese" (part 2). *Asia Major* 9:205–65.

Pyke, Magnus. 1970. *Man and Food.* New York: McGraw-Hill.

Rawski, Evelyn Sakakida. 1972. *Agricultural Change and the Peasant Economy of South China.* Cambridge, Mass.: Harvard Univ. Press.

Renfrew, Jane M. 1973. *Paleoethnobotany: The Prehistoric Food Plants of the Near East and Europe.* New York: Columbia Univ. Press.

Rexroth, Kenneth, and Chung, Ling. 1972. *The Orchid Boat: Women Poets of China.* New York: McGraw-Hill.

Rockhill, W. W. 1900. *The Journey of William of Rubruck to the Eastern Parts of the World, 1235–55.* London: Hakluyt Society.

Roi, Jacques. 1955. *Traité des plantes médicinales chinoises. Encyclopédie biologique,* vol. 47. Paris.

Root, Waverly. 1958. *The Food of France.* New York: Random House.

———. 1971. *The Food of Italy.* New York: Atheneum.

Schafer, E. H. 1950. "The camel in China down to the Mongol dynasty." *Sinologica* 2:165.

———. 1954. *The Empire of Min.* Tokyo: C. E. Tuttle.

———. 1956. "Cultural history of the Elaphure." *Sinologica* 4:250–74.

———. 1959a. "Falconry in T'ang times." *T'oung Pao* 46:293–338.

———. 1959b. "Parrots in Medieval China." In *Studia Serica Bernhard Karlgren Dedicate,* edited by S. Egerod, pp. 271–82. Copenhagen: E. Munskgaard.

———. 1962. "Eating turtles in ancient China." *Journal of the American Oriental Society* 82:73–74.

———. 1963. *The Golden Peaches of Samarkand; a Study of T'ang Exotics.* Berkeley and Los Angeles: Univ. of California Press.

———. 1965. "Notes on T'ang culture, II; Bacchanals." *Monumenta Serica* 24:130–34.

———. 1967. *The Vermilion Bird; T'ang Images of the South.* Berkeley and Los Angeles: Univ. of California Press.

———. 1970. *Shore of Pearls; Hainan Island in Early Times.* Berkeley and Los Angeles: Univ. of California Press.

Schafer, E. H., and Wallacker, Benjamin. 1958. "Local tribute products of the T'ang dynasty." *Journal of Oriental Studies* 4:213–48.

Schery, Robert W. 1972. *Plants for Man.* Englewood Cliffs, N.J.: Prentice-Hall.

Shang, Ping-ho. 1938. *Li tai shê-hui feng-su shih-wu k'ao.* Shanghai: Commercial Press.

Shantung Sheng wen-wu kuan-li wei-yüan-hui. 1955. "Yü-ch'eng Han-mu ch'ing-li chien-pao." *Wen-wu Ts'an-k'ao Tzu-liao* 1955, no. 6:77–89.

Shen, Fu. 1960ed. *Chapters From a Floating Life; the Autobiography of a Chinese Artist*. Translated by Shirley M. Black. London: Oxford Univ. Press.

Shen, Pang. 1961ed. *Wan-shu tsa-chi*. Peking.

Shen, Yüan. 1962. "Chi-chiu P'ien yen-chiu." *Li-shih Yen-chiu* 1962, no. 3:61–87.

Shiba, Yoshinobu. 1968. *Sōdai shōgyō-shi kenkyū*. Tokyo. (Partially translated by Mark Elvin as *Commerce and Society in Sung China*, Michigan Abstracts of Chinese and Japanese Works on Chinese History, no. 2, 1970.)

Shih, Chang-ju. 1950. "Ts'ung *pien tou* k'an T'ai-wan yü ta-lu ti kuan hsi." *Ta Lu Tsa Chih* 1, no. 4:16–17. Taipei.

———. 1953. "Ho-nan An-yang Hsiao-t'un ts'un Yin mu chung ti tung-wu ku hsieh." *Bulletin of the College of Arts*, National Taiwan University, no. 5:1–14.

———. 1969. "Yin tai ti tou." *Bulletin of the Institute of History and Philology*, Academia Sinica, no. 39:51–82.

Shih, Chung-wen. 1973. *Injustice to Tou O: A Study and Translation*. Cambridge.

———. 1976. *The Golden Age of Chinese Drama: Yuan Tsa-ch'ü*. Princeton: Princeton Univ. Press.

Shih, Hsing-pang, et al. 1963. *Hsi-an Pan-p'o*. Peking: Science Press.

Shih, Sheng-han, annotator. 1957. *Ts'ung "Ch'i-min Yao-shu" k'an Chung-kuo ku-tai ti nung-yeh k'o hsüeh chih shih*. Peking: Science Press.

———. 1958. *Ch'i-min Yao-shu chin-shih*. Peking: Science Press.

———. 1959a. *On "Fan Sheng-chih Shu": an Agriculturalist's Book of China Written by Fan Sheng-chih in the First Century B.C.* Peking: Science Press.

———. 1959b. *Ch'i Min Yao Shu Kai Lun*. Peking: Science Press.

———. 1962. *Ch'i Min Yao Shu Kai Lun*. 2d ed. Peking: Science Press.

Shinoda, Ōsamu. 1955. "Mindai no shoko seikatsu." In *Tenkō Kaibutsu no kenkyū*, edited by K. Yabuuchi, pp. 74–92. Tokyo.

———. 1959. "Kodai-Shina ni okeru kappō." *Tōhōgakuhō* 30:253–74. Kyoto.

———. 1963a. "Chusei no sake." In *Chūgoku chūsei kagaku gijutsu-shi no kenkyū*. Tokyo: Kadokawa Book Co.

———. 1963b. "Shokkyō kō." In *Chūgoku chūsei kagaku gijutsu-shi no kenkyū*. Tokyo: Kadokawa Book Co.

———. 1963c. "Tō-shi shokubutsu-shaku." In *Chūgoku chūsei kagaku gijutsu-shi no kenkyū*. Tokyo: Kadokawa Book Co.

———. 1967. "So-en shuzō shi." In *So-en jidai no kagaku gijitsu-shi*, edited by Yabuuchi Kiyoshi. Kyoto.

———. 1974. *Chugoku Tabemono shi*. Tokyo: Shibata shoten.

Shinoda, Osamu, and Tanaka, Seiichi. 1970. *Chūgoku Shokkei Sōsho*. 2 vols. Tokyo.

Simon, G. E. 1868. "Note sur les petites sociétés d'argent en Chine." *Journal of the North China Branch of the Royal Asiatic Society*, n.s., 5:1–23.

Singer, Rolf. 1961. *Mushrooms and Truffles*. New York: Wiley-Interscience.

Sis, V., and Kalvodova, Dana. 1966. *Chinese Food and Fables*. Prague: Artia.

Smith, Allen K., and Circle, Sidney J. 1972. *Soybeans: Chemistry and Technology*. Westport, Conn.: Avi.

Spuler, Bertold. 1972. *History of the Mongols, Based on Eastern and Western Accounts of the Thirteenth and Fourteenth Centuries*. Translated by Helga and Stuart Drummond. Berkeley and Los Angeles: Univ. of California Press.

Steele, John. 1917. *The I Li, or Book of Etiquette and Ceremonial*. London: Probsthain.

Steinhart, John S., and Steinhart, Carol E. 1974. "Energy use in the U.S. food system." *Science* 184, no. 4134:307–16.

Stobart, Tom. 1970. *Herbs, Spices and Flavorings*. London: David and Charles.

Stuart, G. A. 1911. *Chinese Materia Medica; Vegetable Kingdom*. Shanghai: American Presbyterian Mission Press.

Su, Chung [Lucille Davis]. 1966. *Court Dishes of China: the Cuisine of the Ch'ing Dynasty*. Rutland and Tokyo: Tuttle.

Su, Shih. 1970ed. *Tung-po ch'i-chi*. Reprint of original Sung ed. Taipei.

Su, Shih, and Shen, Kua [attributed to]. 1939 ed. *Su Shen liang-fang*. Ts'ung-shu chi-ch'eng ed. Ch'angsha.

Su, Sung. 1930ed. *T'u Ching pen ts'ao*. In Pen ts'ao kang mu, compiled by S. C. Li, vol. 44:120. Shanghai: Shang Wu yin shu kuan.

Sun, Ch'eng-tse. 1881 ed. *Ch'un Ming meng-yü-lu*.

———. 1968ed. *T'ien-fu kuang-chi*. 1704ed. Re-edited Peking, 1962. Reprinted Hong Kong.

Sun, Mien. 1935ed. "T'ang yün." In *Jung chai hsü pi*. Kuo-hsüeh Chi-pen ts'ung shu ed. Shanghai: Commercial Press.

Sun, Tso-yun. 1959. "Han-tai she-hui shih-liao ti pao-k'u." *Shih-hsüeh Yüeh-k'an* 7:30–32.

Sung, Ying-hsing. 1966ed. *T'ien-kung k'ai-wu*. Translated and annotated by E-tu Zen Sun and Shiou-chuan Sun. University Park, Penn.

Swann, Nancy, trans. and annotator. 1950. *Food and Money in Ancient China: the Earliest Economic History of China to A.D. 25*. Princeton: Princeton Univ. Press.

Takakusu, J. 1896. *A Record of the Buddhist Religion as Practised in India and the Malay Archipelago (A.D. 671–95) by I-Tsing*. Oxford: Clarendon Press.

Tamba, Yasuyori. 1935. *I hsin hō*. Nihon koten zenshū, compiled by Masamune Atsuo et al. Tokyo: Nihon Koten Zenshū Kankōkai.

Tannahill, Reay. 1968. *The Fine Art of Food*. London: Folio Society.

———. 1973. *Food in History*. New York: Stein and Day.

T'ao Ku. 1920ed. *Ch'ing-i lu*. Liu Heng-mao.

Tao, L. K. 1928. *Livelihood in Peking, an Analysis of the Budgets of Sixty Families*. Peking: Social Research Dept.

T'ao, Tsung-i. 1939ed. *Cho Keng Lu*. Ts'ung-shu chi-ch'eng ed. Shanghai.

Tao-shih. 1922ed. *Fa yuan chu lin*. Ssu pu ts'ung k'an ed. Shanghai: Commercial Press.

Teilhard de Chardin, P., and Young, C. C. 1936. *On the mammalian remains from the archaeological site of Anyang. Palaeontologia Sinica*, C ser., vol. 12, no. 1.

Teng, Ssu yü, and Fairbank, John K. 1954. *China's Response to the West; a Documentary Survey 1839–1923*. Cambridge, Mass.: Harvard Univ. Press.

Treudley, Mary B. 1971. *The Men and Women of Chung Ho Ch'ang*. Taipei: Orient Cultural Service.

Trubner, Henry. 1957. The Arts of the T'ang Dynasty. A loan exhibition organized by the Los Angeles County Museum from collections in America, the Orient, and Europe, January 8–February 17, 1957. Los Angeles: Los Angeles Museum.

Ts'ai, Hsiang. 1936a ed. *Ch'a-lu.* Pai-ch'uan hsueh-hai ed.

———. 1936b ed. *Li-chih p'u.* Ts'ung-shu chi-ch'eng ed. Shanghai.

Ts'ao, Hsüeh-ch'in. 1973ed. *The Story of the Stone. The Golden Days,* translated by David Hawkes, vol. 1. Harmondsworth, Middlesex, England: Penguin Books.

T'sao, Ju-lin. 1966. *I sheng chih ching yen.* Hong Kong: Ch'un ch'iu tsa chih shê.

Tseng, Chao-yü; Chiang, Pao-keng; and Li, Chung-i. 1956. *I-nan ku-hua-hsiang shih-mu fa-chüeh pao-kao.* Peking: Wen-hua-pu wen-wu kuan-li-chü.

Ts'ui, Shih. 1965ed. *Ssu-min Yüeh-ling.* Peking: Chung Hua shu chü.

Tuan, Ch'eng-shih. 1937ed. *Yu yang tsa tsu.* Ts'ung-shu chi-ch'eng ed. Shanghai: Commercial Press.

Tuan, Kung-lu. 1968ed. *Pei hu lu.* T'ang tai ts'ung shu ed. Taipei: Hsin Hsing shu chü.

Tuan, Yü-ts'ai, commentator. 1955ed. *Shuo-wen Chieh-tzu chu.* Taipei: I-wen yin-shu kuan.

Tun, Li-ch'en. 1965. *Annual Customs and Festivals in Peking.* Translated by Derke Bodde. Hong Kong: Hong Kong Univ. Press.

Tung, Ku. 1937ed. "Pi-li tsa-ts'un." In *Yen-i chih-lin,* chaps. 28–29. Facsimile of 1623 ed. Shanghai.

Tung-pei po-wu-kuan. 1955. "Liao-yang San-tao-hao liang-tso pi-hua-mu ti ch'ing-li chien-pao." *Wen-wu Ts'an-k'ao Tzu-liao* 1955, no. 12:49–58.

Uphof, J. C. T. 1968. *Dictionary of Economic Plants.* Würzburg: Cramer.

Vavilov, N. I. 1949/50. *The origin, variation, immunity and breeding of cultivated plants. Chronica Botanica* 13, no. 1/6.

Verdier, Yvonne. 1969. "Pour une ethnologie culinaire," *L'Homme* 9, no. 1:49–57.

Vogel, Ezra. 1969. *Canton under Communism.* Cambridge, Mass.: Harvard Univ. Press.

Wada, Sei. 1957. *Minshi Shokkashi yakuchū.* 2 vols. Tokyo.

Waley, Arthur. 1956. *Yuan Mei, Eighteenth Century Chinese Poet.* London: Allen and Unwin.

———. 1960. *The Book of Songs* [trans. of *Shih Ching,* the Book of Poetry]. New York: Grove, Evergreen Books.

Wang, Chen. 1956ed. *Nung Shu.* Peking.

Wang, Chen-to. 1963. "Tsai lun Han-tai chiu-tsun," *Wen Wu* 1963, no. 11:13–15.

———. 1964. "Lun Han-tai yin-shih-ch'i chung ti chih ho k'ui." *Wen Wu* 1964, no. 4:1–12.

Wang, Ch'ung. 1937ed. *Lun Heng.* Kuo-hsüeh chi-pen ts'ung shu ed. Shanghai: Commercial Press.

———. 1974ed. *Lun Heng.* Shanghai: Jen min ch'u pan shê.

Wang, Chung-shu. 1956. "Han-tai wu-chih wen-hua lüeh-shuo." *K'ao-ku T'ung-hsün* 1956, no. 1:57–76.

Wang, Jen-yü. 1968ed. *K'ai-yüan T'ien-pao i shih.* T'ang tai ts'ung shu ed. Taipei: Hsin Hsing shu chü.

Wang, Kuo-wei, commentator. 1929ed. *Chiao Sung-chiang pen Chi-chiu P'ien.* Wang Chung-ch'üeh Kung i-shu ed.

Wang, Nien-sun, Commentator. 1939ed. *Kuang-ya shu-cheng.* Ts'ung-shu chi-ch'eng ed. Shanghai: Commercial Press.

Wang, P'ei-cheng, ed. 1958. *Yen-t'ieh lun cha-chi.* Peking: Commercial Press.

Wang, P'u 1935ed. *T'ang hui yao.* Kuo-hsüeh chi-pen ts'ung-shu ed. Shanghai: Commercial Press.

Wang, Shao. 1936ed. *T'ang-hsiang p'u.* Ts'ung-shu chi-ch'eng ed. Shanghai.

Wang, T'ao. 1969ed. *Weng-yu-yü-t'an.* Taipei: Kuang Wen shu chü.

Wang, Ting-pao. 1968ed. *Chih yen.* T'ang tai ts'ung shu ed. Taipei: Hsing Hsing shu chü.

Wang, Yeh-chien 1973. *Land Taxation in Imperial China, 1750–1911.* Cambridge, Mass. Harvard Univ. Press.

Wang Yü-ch'eng. 1922ed. *Hsiao hsü chi.* Ssu pu ts'ung k'an ed. Shanghai: Commercial Press.

Watson, Burton, trans. 1961. *Records of the Grand Historian of China* [trans. of *Shih Chi*]. New York: Columbia Univ. Press.

Watt, Bernice, and Merrill, Annabel. 1963. *Composition of Foods.* Rev. ed. U.S. Government, Agriculture Handbook no. 8. Washington, D.C.

Weber, Charles D. 1968. *Chinese Pictorial Bronze Vessels of the Late Chou Period.* Ascona, Switzerland: Artibus Asiae.

Wei, Chü-yüan. 1920ed. "Shih p'u." In *Ch'ing i lu.* Liu Heng-mao.

Wei, Po-yang. 1937ed. *Ts'an t'ung ch'i cheng wen.* Ts'ung shu chi ch'eng ed. Ch'ang-sha: Commercial Press.

Wen Wu pien-chi-pu. 1972. "Tso-t'an Ch'ang-sha Ma-wang-tui i-hao Han-mu." *Wen Wu* 1972, no. 9:52–73.

West, Stephen H. 1972. "Studies in Chin Dynasty (1115–1234) Literature." Ph. D. dissertation, Univ. of Michigan.

Wheatley, Paul. 1965. "A note on the extension of milking practices into Southeast Asia during the first millennium A.D." *Anthropos* 60:277–90.

Whyte, Robert O. 1973. "The gramineae, wild and cultivated. of monsoonal and equatorial Asia. (Section) I. Southeast Asia." *Asian Perspectives* 15, no. 2:127–51.

Wilbur, C. Martin. 1943. *Slavery in China during the Former Han Dynasty 206BC–AD25.* Reissued 1967. New York: Russell and Russell.

Wilkinson, Endymion. 1973. "Chinese merchant manuals and route books," *Ch'ing-shih wen t'i* 2, no. 9:8–34.

Williams, S. Wells. 1883. *The Middle Kingdom; a Survey of the Geography, Government, Literature, Social Life, Arts and History of the Chinese Empire and its Inhabitants.* rev. ed. 2 vols. New York: Scribner.

Wolff, Peter H. 1972. "Ethnic differences in alcohol sensitivity," *Science* 175, no. 4020: 449–50.

Wu, Ch'i-chün. 1936ed. *Chih wu ming shih t'u k'ao ch'ang pien.* Shanghai: Commercial Press.

Wu, Ching-tzu. 1957. *The Scholars.* Translated by Yang Hsien-yi and Gladys Young. Peking: Foreign Language Press.

Wu, Han. 1935. "Wan Ming shih-huan chieh-chi ti sheng-huo." *Ta Kung Pao* (Tientsin), History and Geography Weekly Supplement, April 19, 1935.

————. 1957. "*Chin-p'ing-mei* ti chu-tso shih-tai chi ch'i she-hui pei-ching." In *Tu-shu Cha-chi*. Peking: San lien shu tien.

————. 1960. *Teng-hsia Chi*. Peking.

Wu, Hsien. 1928. "Checklist of Chinese foods," *Chinese Journal of Physiology* 1:153–86.

Wu, Hsien-wen. 1949. "Yin Hsü ti yü ku." *Chinese Journal of Archaeology* 4:139–53.

Wu, Tzu-mu. 1957ed. *Meng-liang lu*. Shanghai: Ku tien wen hsüeh ch'u pan shê.

Yabuuchi, Kiyoshi, ed. 1955. *Tenkō Kaibutsu no kenkyū*. Tokyo.

————. 1967. *Sō-Gen jidai no kagaku gijutsu shi*. Tokyo.

Yabuuchi, Kiyoshi, and Yoshida, Mitsukuni, eds. 1970. *Min-Shin jidai no kagaku gijutsu shi*. Tokyo.

Yanai, Wataru. 1925. "Moko no saba-en to shison-en." In *Shiratori Hakushi kanreki kinen Tōyōshi ronso*. Tokyo. Reprinted in Yanai's *Mōkōshi kenkyū*. Tokyo, 1930.

Yang, C. K. 1965. *Chinese Communist Society: the Family and the Village*. Cambridge, Mass.: MIT Press.

Yang, Chien-fang. 1963. "An-hui Tiao-yü-t'ai ch'u-t'u hsiao-mai nien-tai ti shang-chüeh." *K'ao Ku* 1963, no. 11:630–31.

Yang, Fang. 1935ed. *Tzu-ch'i chi*. Ssu-k'u ch'üan-shu ed. Shanghai.

Yang, Hsien-yi, and Yang, Gladys, trans. 1974. *Records of the Historian* [trans. of *Shih Chi*]. Hong Kong: Commercial Press.

Yang, Lien-sheng. 1961. *Studies in Chinese Institutional History*. Harvard-Yenching Institute Studies, no. 20. Cambridge, Mass.: Harvard Univ. Press.

Yang, Martin C. 1945. *A Chinese Village*. New York: Columbia Univ. Press.

Yang, Simon, and Tao, L. K. 1931. *A Study of the Standard of Living of Working Families in Shanghai*. Peiping: Institute of Social Research.

Yao, Shih-lin 1937ed. "Chien-chih pien." In *Yen-i chih-lin*, chap. 53–55. Facsimile of 1623ed. Shanghai.

Yeh, Hua, comp. 1967. *Chung kuo ming ts'ai ta ch'üan*. Taipei: Hung Yeh Book Store.

Yeh, Shao-weng. 1774. *Ssu Ch'ao Wen Chien Lu*. Chih Pu Tsu Chai Ts'ung Shu ed.

Yeh, Tzu-ch'i. 1959. *Ts'ao-mu Tzu*. Peking.

Yen, K'o-chün, comp. 1958ed. *Ch'üan Shang-ku San-tai Ch'in Han San-kuo Liu-ch'ao wen*. Peking: Chung Hua shu chü.

Yin, Chung-jung. 1958. *Lü Shih Ch'un-ch'iu Chiao Shih*. Taipei: Chung Hua wen hua ch'u pan shih yeh wei yüan huei.

Ying, Shao. 1937ed. *Feng-su T'ung-i*. Han Wei Ts'ung-shu ed. Shanghai: Commercial Press.

————. 1962ed. "Han Kuan-i." In *Han Kuan Ch'i-chung*, compiled by Sun Hsing-yen. Taipei: Chung Hua shu chü.

Young, C. C., and Teilhard de Chardin, P. 1949. "Supplementary materials on the mammalian remains from the archaeological site at An-yang." *Chung Kuo K'ao Ku Hsüeh Pao*, no. 4:145–52.

Yü, Ching-jang. 1956. "Shu chi su liang yü kao-liang." *Ta-lu Tsa-chih* 13:67–76, 115–20.

Yü, Hsing-wu. 1957. "Shang tai ti ku lei tso-wu." *Tung Pei Ta Hsüeh Jen Wen Hsüeh Pao*, no. 1:81–107.

Yü, Huai, 1966ed. *A Feast of Mist and Flowers: the Gay Quarters of Nanking at the*

End of the Ming. Translated by Howard Levy. Mimeographed edition. Yokohama.

Yü, Ying-shih. 1967. *Trade and Expansion in Han China.* Berkeley and Los Angeles: Univ. of California Press.

Yüan, Kuo-fan. 1967. "Shih-san shih-chi Meng-ku jen yin-chiu chih hsi-su i-li chi ch'i yu-kuan wen-t'i." *Ta-lu Tsa-chih* 34, no. 5:14–15.

Yüan, Mei. 1824ed. *Sui-yüan Shih-tan.* Hsiao-ts'ang shan-fang ed.

———. 1933ed. *Hsiao-ts'ang shan fang wen chi.* Shanghai: Chung Hua shu chü.

Yuan, Tsing. 1969. *Aspects of the Economic History of the Kiangnan Region During the Late Ming Period, ca. 1520–1620.* Ann Arbor, Mich.: University Microfilms.

Yudkin, John. 1972. *Sweet and Dangerous.* New York: Wyden.

INDEX